THE

DOCTRINE OF HOLY SCRIPTURE

RESPECTING

THE ATONEMENT

THE

DOCTRINE OF HOLY SCRIPTURE

RESPECTING

THE ATONEMENT

BY

THOMAS J. CRAWFORD, D.D., F.R.S.E.

PROFESSOR OF DIVINITY IN THE UNIVERSITY OF EDINBURGH
AUTHOR OF THE 'FATHERHOOD OF GOD,' 'THE
MYSTERIES OF CHRISTIANITY,' ETC.

FOURTH EDITION

Wipf and Stock Publishers
EUGENE, OREGON

Wipf and Stock Publishers
199 West 8th Avenue, Suite 3
Eugene, Oregon 97401

The Doctrine of Holy Scripture Respecting the Atonement
By Crawford, Thomas J.
ISBN: 1-59244-211-0
Publication date: April, 2003
Previously published by Scribner, Welford, & Armstrong, January, 1875.

PREFACE TO THE FIRST EDITION.

THE Atonement is a pure matter of revelation. Whether as regards the truths which it embodies, the principles on which it rests, or the ends to which it is conducive, we have no reliable means of information beyond what God has given us in His Word. In approaching such a subject our question ought ever to be, "What is written in the Scriptures? How readest thou?" Nor can we be too careful lest we advance any position but such as, on full and fair inquiry, has been found to be either expressly set down in the Holy Scriptures, or by good and necessary consequence deducible from them.

Accordingly, I have chosen the *inductive* in preference to the ordinary *dogmatic* method of discussing this subject, believing the former to be not only the more satisfactory to an intelligent inquirer, but at the same time the more consistent with that reverence which is due to the oracles of God.

It did not fall within the scope of this treatise to enter particularly into the controversy respecting the *extent* or *destination* of the Atonement. Some allusion, however, to this question, was unavoidable,

vi   PREFACE.

in so far as it is necessarily connected with the *completeness* and *efficacy* of the mediatorial work of Christ.

It will be observed that in Part III. of this volume I have availed myself of the substance of several lectures which I published some years ago. Should any apology be deemed necessary for so doing, I may state that I have been repeatedly urged to publish these lectures in a separate form—apart from that controversy respecting "the Fatherhood of God" with which they were originally connected.

UNIVERSITY OF EDINBURGH,
   24th *March* 1871.

PREFACE TO THE SECOND EDITION.

IN publishing a Second Edition of this work, I have endeavoured, by some additions and amendments, and by a careful revision of the whole volume, to render it more worthy of that highly favourable and gratifying reception which it has already met with. The chief additional matters are indicated by an asterisk in the Table of Contents.

UNIVERSITY OF EDINBURGH,
   10th *November* 1874.

CONTENTS.

	PAGE
Order of discussion proposed,	1
Divinity and incarnation of Christ assumed,	2
*Authority of Scripture in matters of doctrine assumed,	2

PART I.—DOCTRINE OF NEW TESTAMENT RESPECTING THE ATONE-
MENT, ... 3
Inductive preferred to the dogmatic method of discussion, . . 3
* Objections to inductive method obviated, ... 4
§ I. General considerations, ... 6
II. Passages which speak of Christ (1) as "*dying for sinners,*" . 19
" " " (2) as "*dying for our sins,*" . 26
III. Passages which speak of Christ (3) as "*bearing our sins,*" . 33
" " " (4) as "*made sin,*" and "*made a curse for us,*" . 42
IV. Passages which ascribe to Christ (5) "*remission of sins,*" and "*deliverance from wrath,*" . 46
V. Passages which ascribe to the death of Christ (6) "*justification,*" . 56
" " " (7) "*redemption,*" . 60
VI. Passages which speak of the death of Christ as (8) "*reconciling us to God,*" . 65
" " (9) a "*propitiation for sin,*" . 77
VII. Passages which speak of Christ (10) as a "*priest,*" . 84
" " " (11) as a *representative,* . 91
VIII. Passages which represent the sufferings of Christ (12) as *sacrificial,* . . 96
IX. Passages which (13) connect the sufferings of Christ with His *intercession,* . 114
" " (14) represent His mediation as *procuring the Holy Spirit,* . 117
X. Passages which speak of Christ (15) as delivering us from the dominion of Satan, . . 123
" " " (16) as obtaining for us *eternal life,* 127

• The chief matters added in this Edition are marked with an asterisk.

CONTENTS.

XI. Passages which indicate (17) the state of the Saviour's mind in the prospect and endurance of His sufferings . 130

XII. Passages which speak of the mediation of Christ in relation (18) to the free calls and offers of the Gospel, . . 140

" " " (19) to the necessity of faith in Him, 143

XIII. Passages which speak of the mediatorial work and sufferings of Christ in relation (20) to His covenant with the Father, 148

" " ' (21) to His union with believers, 151

XIV. Passages which speak of the death of Christ as (22) a manifestation of the love of God, . . . 158

" " " (23) an example of patience and resignation, . . 161

" " " (24) designed to promote our sanctification, . . . 165

XV. Result of the foregoing induction of Scriptural testimonies, . 171
    1. Christ is a Saviour, ... 175
    2. The sufferings of Christ were *sacrificial*, . . . 176
    3. " " *vicarious*, . . . 177
    4. Christ, by His obedience unto death, *reconciles us to God*, . 179
    5. Christ is our *Redeemer*, and His death our *ransom*, . . 180
    6. The death of Christ is a *satisfaction to divine justice*, . 181

XVI. Result of the foregoing induction of Scriptural testimonies—*continued*.
    7. Our sins were imputed to Christ, ... 188
    8. The sufferings of Christ were penal in their character, . 190
    9. The Atonement originated in the love of God, . 192
    10. The Atonement secures sanctification as well as pardon, . 194
    11. The mediatorial work of Christ is *complete*, and of unfailing efficiency, ... 196
    12. The benefits of the Atonement are freely offered to all who will receive them, ... 200

PART II.—CONFIRMATORY EVIDENCE OF OLD TESTAMENT RESPECTING THE ATONEMENT, ... 203

§ I. Prophecies of the Old Testament respecting the sufferings of Christ, 205

II. The Levitical sacrifices, (1) their divine institution, . . 217

" " (2) their piacular character, . 220

III. The Levitical sacrifices, their piacular character—*continued*.
Review of non-expiatory theories regarding them—
    Theory of Bähr. 234
    Theory of Hofmann, ... 238
    Theory of Keil, ... 241
    Theory of Young, ... 243

CONTENTS.

IV. The Levitical sacrifices—*continued*.

        (3) The extent of their atoning efficacy, . 246

        (4) Their typical reference to Christ, . 254

V. The Patriarchal sacrifices, ... 265

PART III.—REVIEW OF VARIOUS THEORIES RESPECTING THE SUF-
FERINGS OF CHRIST WHICH HAVE BEEN PROPOSED AS SUB-
STITUTES FOR THE CATHOLIC DOCTRINE OF THE ATONE-
MENT, ... 285

§ I. Theories of   (1) Martyrdom, ... 287

"   (2) Subserviency to the resurrection of Christ, 289

"   (3) Example, ... 291

"   (4) Manifestation of the divine character, . 292

"   (5) Manifestation of the love of God, . 294

"   (6) Arian, or "Middle Theory," . . 299

II. Review of Theories
(*continued*),   (7) Realistic theory (1), as held by Maurice, 303

"   * (2), as held by Alford, . 311

III. Review of Theories
(*continued*),   (8) Theory of self-sacrifice, . . . 318

IV. Review of Theories
(*continued*),   (9) Theory of sympathy or identification, . 327

V. Review of Theories
(*continued*),   (10) Theory of Mr Robertson of Brighton, . 348

VI. Review of Theories
(*continued*),   (11) Theory of Dr Young, . . . 357

    (12) Theory of Dr Bushnell, . . . 371

VII. Review of Theories
(*continued*),   (13) Rectoral or governmental theory, . 380

* VIII. General Remarks on the Theories above reviewed, . . 395

PART IV.—REVIEW OF OBJECTIONS TO THE SCRIPTURAL DOCTRINE
OF THE ATONEMENT, ... 403

§ I. Alleged silence or reserve of Christ Himself respecting the Atonement, ... 404

II. Allegation that the Atonement is unnecessary, . . 421

III. Allegation that the Atonement derogates from the perfections of
God, ... 440

IV. Allegation that the Atonement is incredible because mysterious, . 456

V. Allegation that the Atonement is injurious in its practical tendency, 473

———

APPENDIX.

NOTE A. Import of the preposition ὑπέρ, as used by Classics, . . 493

NOTE B. Tischendorf and Baur on the use of ὑπέρ, as indicating substitution, ... * . 495

CONTENTS.

* Note C. Mr Goodsir on the author's view of Justification, . . 497
* Note D. Trench and Bloomfield on καταλλαγή and καταλλάσσεσθαι, . 499
  Note E. The Passover a sin-offering, ... 500
  Note F. The fiducial nature of Christian faith, . . . 501
  Note G. The invitations of the Gospel, ... 510
  Note H. God's remonstrance with Cain, ... 517
  Note I. Natural and moral laws, ... 517
  Note K. Progressiveness of Christ's teaching, ... 520
  Note L. Suitableness of the Atonement to human wants, . . 523
* Note M. *Supplementary* — Bushnell on 'Forgiveness and Propitiation without Expiation,' 526

THE

DOCTRINE OF HOLY SCRIPTURE

RESPECTING

THE ATONEMENT.

THE aim of this treatise is to ascertain and vindicate the doctrine of Holy Scripture with respect to the mediatorial work and sufferings of Jesus Christ, or as it may be summarily called, the Doctrine of the Atonement.

The subject is one of unquestionable importance, relating as it does to what is generally and justly esteemed the great central truth of the Christian revelation, and vitally affecting the faith and hope of all believers. In discussing it we shall observe the following order:— *Importance of the subject.*

In the first place, we shall endeavour to analyse and classify those passages of the New Testament which bear upon the subject, and to deduce from them such conclusions as a fair induction and interpretation of them may seem to warrant. *Order of discussion.*

Secondly, we shall consider how far the results of this inquiry into the doctrine of the New Testament are confirmed by a survey of the prophetic intimations and sacrificial institutions of the Old Testament.

Thirdly, we shall examine the various theories which have been proposed, with the view of accounting for the

2   SCRIPTURAL DOCTRINE OF THE ATONEMENT.

Saviour's work and sufferings in some other way than by
the Scriptural explanation of them.

And, *fourthly*, we shall endeavour to obviate those
objections with which the doctrine of Holy Scripture
respecting the Atonement has been ordinarily assailed.

Divinity and incarnation of Christ assumed. It is proper to state that, in the following investigation,
our Lord's divinity, united with humanity in the constitu-
tion of His adorable person, is assumed.   This is a subject
which, according to the usual and most approved order of
theological discussion, is fully investigated before entering
on the question of the Atonement.   The present treatise,
accordingly, is addressed to those who are already persuaded that the Lord Jesus Christ truly is the Son of God
incarnate in our human nature ; its sole object being to
ascertain, by a fair and full examination of the Scriptural
evidence, for what purpose the God-man " became obedient unto death."

Authority of Scripture in matters of doctrine assumed. It need only be added that, while ourselves maintaining
the *plenary* inspiration of the Scriptures, we deem it unne-
cessary for the purpose we have now in view, to make any
further assumption upon this subject than that of the
supreme authority of the Scriptures respecting those things
which they were principally designed to teach—namely,
" *what man is to believe concerning God, and what duty God
requires of man.*"   This is an assumption to which many
who might demur to a fuller recognition of the inspiring
influence, as extending to other matters which do not
directly bear on the faith and practice of religion, will
assent.   And though it appears to us to come short of
what is affirmed and claimed by the sacred writers, it still
furnishes a broad enough basis for our present inquiry.
For if there be any subject in regard to which the teaching
of prophets, evangelists, and apostles, is entitled to our
full and unqualified acquiescence, that subject must certainly be the doctrine which they set forth respecting the
mediatorial work and sufferings of the Son of God when
He came on His great errand of mercy to our fallen world.

PART I.

INQUIRY INTO THE DOCTRINE OF THE NEW TESTAMENT RESPECTING THE MEDIATORIAL WORK AND SUFFERINGS OF JESUS CHRIST.

———

IT is customary with writers on the subject of our present inquiry to treat it *dogmatically*,—laying down at the outset what they hold to be the doctrine of Scripture respecting the Atonement, together with a statement of those principles of the divine government which it embodies or assumes, and thereafter supporting the views thus enunciated by such positive proofs or defensive arguments as they are able to adduce. This method, however, though in some respects the more convenient, when we are stating the results of any process of investigation, and defending them against those by whom they are assailed, is neither so scientific in its nature, nor so satisfactory to an intelligent and inquiring mind, as the humbler and more cautious method of *induction*,—according to which we first of all address ourselves to the actual statements of Holy Scripture upon the subject—deferring in the meanwhile all theories and assumptions—and endeavour, by a fair examination and a careful comparison and classification of these statements, to arrive at such conclusions as are deducible from them.

There are some persons, indeed, who hold that the inductive method is not fairly applicable to any theologi-

PART
I.

Inductive
preferred
to the
dogmatic
method of
discussion.

4   STATEMENTS OF THE NEW TESTAMENT

PART I.

Objections to the inductive method obviated.

cal subject respecting which the person who so applies it already entertains a definite opinion or belief. The use of it by such a one appears to them to be no better than a transparent artifice, whereby a plausible semblance of Scriptural testimonies may be marshalled and arrayed so as to lead up to a foregone conclusion.

In this view of the matter we cannot acquiesce. Any one who considers how useful in times past hypotheses and theories have often proved to be in furthering the progress of various departments of physical science, will rather be disposed to come to an opposite judgment. A distinguished natural philosopher affirms, that " in physical inquiries the work of theory and observation must go hand in hand— more especially if the matter is very complicated, for then the clue of theory is necessary to direct the observer."

Playfair's Huttonian Theory of the Earth, p. 525-528.

" Theory and observation," he continues, " mutually assist one another ; and the spirit of system, against which there are so many and so just complaints, appears, nevertheless, as the animating spirit of inductive investigation. The business of sound philosophy is not to extinguish this spirit, but to restrain and direct its efforts. . . . It cannot be denied that the impartiality of an observer may often be affected by system ; but this is a misfortune against which the want of theory is not always a complete security. The partialities in favour of opinions are not more dangerous than the prejudices against them ; for such is the spirit of system, and so naturally do all men's notions tend to reduce themselves into some regular form, that the very belief that there is no theory becomes itself a theory, and may have no inconsiderable sway over the mind of an observer. Besides, one man may have as much delight in pulling down as another has in building up, and may choose to display his dexterity in the one occupation as well as in the other. The want of theory, then, does not secure the candour of an observer, and it may very much diminish his skill."

There is no reason why the remarks of this philosopher should not be applied to the investigations of theology as well as to the researches of physical science. Besides, if the holding of definite opinions disqualifies an author for treating theology *inductively*, it must equally disqualify him for treating it *dogmatically;* for there is, to say the least, an equal danger of his being unduly biassed in his judgment when using the latter method as when he employs the former. And may we not venture to suggest the possibility, that *persons whose theological opinions are* INDE-FINITE may, as well as others, be misled in their inquiries by the disinclination, so frequently avowed by them, to anything like exact definitions or determinate conclusions in matters of religious doctrine? Indeed, the authority before quoted has farther remarked, that " an opposition between the business of the theorist and that of the observer can only occur *when the speculations of the former are vague and indistinct,* and cannot be so embodied as to become visible to the latter."

Add to this, that if one who has definite views of Christian doctrine should be led by them to set forth an unfair or imperfect induction of Scriptural testimonies on the subject to which they relate, his readers are forewarned to which side his bias tends, so that they may forearm themselves against its influence. Nor are there wanting a sufficiency of other writers, holding opinions equally definite on the opposite side, who are sure to be on the watch for his halting, and ready to correct his prejudices and mistakes.

It does not appear, then, that there is any valid objection to the use of the inductive method in theology. Accordingly, we propose to follow this method in our present discussion. Instead of setting out with a definite statement of doctrine, as is usually done in our theological systems and symbolical books, and then adducing Scriptural testimonies and reasonable arguments with a view to its establishment, we shall take the opposite course of primarily investigating the import of those Scriptural statements which bear upon the matter in question, allowing such doctrinal principles as may seem to be either implied in them, or deducible from them, to evolve or develop themselves in the course of our inquiries.

6   STATEMENTS OF THE NEW TESTAMENT

SECTION I.

GENERAL CONSIDERATIONS.

PART
I.
SEC. I.
——
General
considera-
tions.

BEFORE entering on a full induction of those passages of Holy Scripture which bear on the important subject of our present inquiry, there are some general considerations, with reference to the mission and sufferings of Jesus Christ, with which we may be allowed to preface our investigations, as too plainly lying on the very surface of the New Testament, to need any formal array of evidence in confirmation of them.

Christ not
a mere
teacher,
but a
Saviour.

I. One of these is, that the office or work of Christ is that, not of a *mere teacher* sent to reveal the will of God, but of a divinely appointed *Saviour*. A great prophet, or teacher sent from God, He certainly was. But this is not the only character, nor is it even the most prominent character, in which He is presented to us. We are evidently taught in Scripture to regard Him as somehow the *procurer* of blessings, as well as the *proclaimer* of them. He came, not merely to instruct us by His doctrine, to reform us by His precepts, to guide us by His example, to cheer us with assurances of the divine mercy and placability, and to comfort us with the hope of immortal life beyond the grave ; but for the further purpose of delivering us from evils and miseries inseparable from our sinful state, and of securing for us spiritual privileges and benefits, which are only to be enjoyed as the fruit of His mediation. How else can we give any reasonable account of the manner in which He is so frequently and so emphatically spoken of in Scripture as " our Saviour;" " our Redeemer;"

Heb. v. 9.
John, iii.
17.

" the author of eternal salvation to them that obey Him ;" as " sent into the world, not to condemn it, but that the

RESPECTING THE ATONEMENT.   7

world through Him might be saved;" as "come to seek
and to save that which is lost;" as "called *Jesus*, because
He should save His people from their sins;" as "able to
save them to the uttermost who come unto God through
Him;" as bearing the "only name given under heaven
and among men whereby we must be saved"? These
and the like expressions manifestly point to Him, not
merely as *the revealer of certain truths*, which, had it not
been for His disclosure of them, would have remained unknown, but as *the author and source of certain blessings*, which,
apart from his interposition, would have been unattainable.
With no such point and emphasis are similar statements applied in Scripture to any divinely commissioned teacher—
however salutary, edifying, and precious may be the instructions he conveys—if we are no farther beholden to him for
mercies and deliverances, than as having been employed
and authorised to show us the way which God has appointed
for the attainment of them   And yet, if this were all that
such statements can be held to mean in their application
to Jesus Christ, there is no apparent reason why they might
not have been with equal force and frequency affirmed of
prophets and apostles, whose words are divinely inspired,
and "able to make us wise unto salvation."

> PART
> I.
> SEC. I.
> —
> Luke, xix.
> 10.
> Matt. i.
> 21.
> Heb. vii.
> 25.
> Acts, iv.
> 12.

II. Further, there is evidently *a prominence assigned, and
an importance attached, in the New Testament to the mission
of Christ*, above that of every other divine messenger, which
lead to the conclusion that some blessings of a very special
and altogether unparalleled nature have been secured by it.

> Promin-
> ence of
> Christ's
> mission
> above that
> of other
> prophets.

For example, the mission of Jesus Christ is represented
as "a performance of the mercy promised unto the
fathers;" as a "visiting and redeeming of God's people,
according to what He spake by the mouth of His holy
prophets, which have been since the world began;" as
providing for us a "salvation concerning which the prophets have inquired and searched diligently, when they
prophesied of the grace that should come unto us." And
numerous appeals are made to the predictions of the Old
Testament as having been fulfilled in the incidents of the

> Luke, i.
> 70, 72.
> 1 Pet. i.
> 10.

8 STATEMENTS OF THE NEW TESTAMENT

PART
I.
SEC. I.
———
Christ
alone pre-
dicted.

Saviour's life, and more particularly in His sufferings at the close of it. In this respect the Lord Jesus is broadly distinguished from all other bearers of a divine commission who have ever appeared. None of the other prophets, not even Moses himself, the great founder of the Jewish dispensation, was thus distinguished.* Why so? Why were not Moses, Samuel, Isaiah, Elijah, or Daniel predicted, as well as Christ, if *He* came, like them, for no higher purpose than simply to announce to men the mind and will of God? Why had He only His preparatory prophets and eager expectants, if there was nothing peculiarly exalted in the character He sustained, or peculiarly important in the work He undertook? The advent of Christ, if we suppose Him to have come into the world merely to instruct men in religious truth and moral duty, would, as we cannot help thinking, have been somewhat of a poor and disproportionate conclusion to that lengthened course of preparation which was made for it. On the other hand, if we believe Him to have been, in respect of personal dignity, incomparably superior to all those forerunners who, "at sundry times and in divers manners," paved the way for His approach,—and to have contemplated, as the purpose of His appearance, some transcendent work of deliverance for the human race, such as beseemed the more than prophetic character that belonged to Him,— there is then a proportion or harmony that may be traced between so wonderful a manifestation of heavenly grace, and the long train of prophecies which were preparatory and subservient to it. The vast extent and majestic character of the avenue which leads to the shrine of Christianity are then seen to be in full keeping with the grandeur and sanctity of the mysterious edifice itself.

Christ's
mission an
unequalled
display of
God's
love.

A like conclusion is warranted by the strong terms in which the sacred writers are wont to speak of our Lord's mission as an unparalleled display of the love and grace of God, and by the warmth of admiring transport and adoring gratitude with which they are frequently animated in the contemplation of it. "God so loved the

* The Baptist was predicted, but only in connection with Christ.

RESPECTING THE ATONEMENT. 9

world," they say, "that He gave His only-begotten Son, that whosoever believeth in Him should not perish, but have everlasting life;" "God commendeth His love toward us, in that, while we were yet sinners, Christ died for us;" "In this was manifested the love of God toward us, because God sent His only-begotten Son into the world, that we might live through Him;" "What shall we then say to these things? If God be for us, who can be against us? He that spared not his own Son, but delivered Him up for us all, how shall He not with Him also freely give us all things?" "For this cause I bow my knees unto the Father of our Lord Jesus Christ, of whom the whole family in heaven and earth is named: that He would grant you, according to the riches of His glory, to be strengthened with might by His Spirit in the inner man; that Christ may dwell in your hearts by faith; that ye, being rooted and grounded in love, may be able to comprehend with all saints what is the breadth, and length, and depth, and height; and to know the love of Christ, which passeth knowledge."

PART I. SEC. I.

John, iii. 16.

Rom. v. 8.

I John, iv 9.

Rom. viii 31, 32.

Eph. iii. 14-19.

Such is a specimen of the manner in which the inspired writers are wont to express themselves respecting the mission and work of Jesus Christ. And how is such language in any way to be interpreted, on the supposition that He came on no higher errand than that of a divinely appointed messenger from heaven? If we view Him merely as a teacher sent from God, like those inspired men who followed or preceded Him; if His life was only an example of what He taught, and His death a proof of His sincerity in teaching it; if His work was merely to announce blessings before unknown, and not to procure blessings otherwise unattainable;—where shall we then look for the unparalleled peculiarities of that love to which His mission is ascribed, or where discover the grounds of that unutterable admiration and gratitude with which it is regarded? How comes it to pass that the "giving" of Him is represented as specially "*commending*" and "*manifesting*" the love of God, above all other benefactions and loving-kindnesses, and is confidently appealed to as a

10   STATEMENTS OF THE NEW TESTAMENT

PART
I.
SEC. I.
——

pledge of every other blessing, so perfectly sure, and so wonderfully great, as to render it incredible that any good thing can possibly be withheld from those on whom this "unspeakable gift" has been conferred? And why should the love thus exhibited be spoken of as so immeasurable in its "height and depth, and length and breadth," that men must be inwardly "strengthened with might by the Spirit," in order that they may be "able to comprehend" it; and that even those who have the fullest appreciation of it should be obliged to own that it "passeth knowledge"? On the supposition of our Lord having been a mere prophet, sent to proclaim to us the mind and will of God, there is no satisfactory answer that can be given to these questions. Most certain it is, that to no prophet or apostle do we ever find language applied having the remotest analogy to that which is thus habitually used by the sacred writers with reference to the mission and work of the Lord Jesus Christ.

Prominence of *death* of Christ above other events in His history.

III. But yet, farther, on taking even the most general and cursory view of the doctrine of the New Testament, we can hardly fail to see that *the death of Jesus Christ* has so very marked a prominence assigned to it, above every other incident in His history, as to show that it must have had some special efficacy in securing the ends to be accomplished by His mission.

Spoken of as sum of the Gospel.

I Cor. ii. 2.
I Cor. xv. 3.
I Cor. i. 23.
Gal. vi. 14.
I Cor. i. 18.
Rom. vi. 3.
Philip. iii. 18.

Mark, for example, how frequently the death of Christ is spoken of by the Apostle Paul, *as comprehending the sum and substance of the Gospel.* "I determined," he says, "not to know anything among you save Jesus Christ and Him crucified;" "I delivered unto you first of all, that which I also received, that Christ died for our sins;" "We preach Christ crucified;" "God forbid that I should glory, save in the cross of our Lord Jesus Christ." In like manner, we find that the preaching of the Gospel is emphatically styled by him "the preaching of the cross;" the initiatory rite of Christian baptism, a "baptism unto the death of Christ;" the adversaries of the Gospel, "enemies of the cross of Christ;" and the fiery trials

RESPECTING THE ATONEMENT.

endured by the primitive Christians, a "persecution for the cross of Christ." From this it is quite evident that the crucifixion of our Lord was, in the estimation of the great apostle of the Gentiles, possessed of an interest exclusively its own ; and that it was habitually regarded by him, not only as a very memorable incident in the evangelical *history*, but as a most vital and essential article of the evangelical *doctrine*, insomuch that it might be singled out from all the others, as giving its peculiar and distinctive character to the Christian system.

Observe farther, that the death of Christ *has a place of special prominence assigned to it among the preordained purposes of His mission.* Thus we are told that "Christ died for our sins, *according to the Scriptures;*" that the Spirit, which was in the prophets, "testified beforehand the sufferings of Christ, and the glory that should follow;" that in what the Jewish rulers "did through ignorance," "God was fulfilling those things which He had before showed by the mouth of all His prophets, that Christ should suffer;" that Jesus "was delivered" into the hands of those that slew Him "by the determinate counsel and foreknowledge of God;" and that "they did to Him whatsoever things the hand and counsel of God had before determined to be done." It is abundantly clear, from these and the like statements, that the death of the Lord Jesus is to be regarded, not as a mere casualty incidental to His mission, but as an event which was specially contemplated in the counsels of heaven when that mission was devolved upon him, and which stood in a relation altogether essential to the purpose for which He was sent into the world.

Nor is it less clear from many of His own sayings, that His death was habitually thus regarded by our Lord Himself. Even in the earlier stages of His ministry, we find Him ever and anon making allusions to it, which show how constantly it was present to His mind; as when He declares that "the Son of man must be lifted up, as Moses lifted up the serpent in the wilderness, that whoso-

PART I.
Sec. I.

Gal. vi. 12

Prominence of Christ's death among the predicted purposes of His mission.

I Cor. xv. 3.

I Pet. i. 11.

Acts, iii. 17, 18.

Acts, ii. 23; iv. 28.

His death so regarded by Christ Himself.

John, iii 14, 15.

12 STATEMENTS OF THE NEW TESTAMENT

PART
I.
SEC. I.
——
John, vi.
51; x. 11.
Matt. xx.
28.
Luke ix.
31.
Luke, xii.
50.
Matt. xvi.
21.

ever believeth in Him should not perish, but have everlasting life;" and speaks of "giving His flesh for the life
of the world," "laying down His life for His sheep," and
"giving His life a ransom for many." When Moses and
Elias met with Him on the mount of transfiguration, the
subject of their conference was, "His decease, which He
should accomplish at Jerusalem." On other occasions
He speaks of Himself as "having a baptism to be baptised with, and being much straitened till it be accomplished;" and "shows His disciples how that He must go
unto Jerusalem, and suffer many things, and be killed."
When the period of His last sufferings was fast approaching, He utters these significant exclamations: "The hour
is come that the Son of man should be glorified: Verily,
verily, I say unto you, Except a corn of wheat fall into the
ground and die, it abideth alone; but if it die, it bringeth

John, xii.
23, 24, 27,
32.

forth much fruit;" "Now is my soul troubled, and what
shall I say? Father, save me from this hour; but for
this cause came I to this hour;" "And I, if I be lifted up
from the earth, will draw all men unto me." And after
His resurrection from the dead, He rebuked His disciples
for their "slowness of heart to believe all that the prophets

Luke, xxiv.
25, 26, 45,
46.

had spoken;" and "opening their understandings that
they might understand the Scriptures," He showed them
that "thus it behoved Christ to suffer," and that "Christ
ought to have suffered these things, and to enter into His
glory."

To die was
pre-emi-
nently
Christ's
work on
earth.

From all this it is apparent that the death of Jesus was,
from first to last, contemplated by Him as inseparably
bound up with the purpose of His mission. Never did
He cease to think of it as an integral and most essential part of the work assigned to Him. In this respect
He assuredly stands alone, of all the generations of men
that ever lived. For though it be "appointed unto all
men once to die," it cannot be said that dying is their
appointed work—still less that it is thus habitually regarded by them. They come into the world, not mainly
for the purpose of dying, but for the purpose of "doing
with all their might whatsoever their hand findeth," so

RESPECTING THE ATONEMENT.   13

long as life endures. And death is to them, not only the
termination, but often the utter subversion and frustration,
of all that throughout life they have been striving to
accomplish. Of the Lord Jesus, however, it may be truly
said, that He came into the world pre-eminently *in order
to die*, and that by His death the end of His life was fully
accomplished. Accordingly, when He bowed His head
upon the cross, He cried, "It is finished," proclaiming to
heaven and earth the consummation of that great work
which had been given Him to do.

PART
1.
SEC. I.

John, xix.
30.

Observe yet farther, that the death of Christ has been
singled out as the special subject of commemoration in
one of the most solemn ordinances of the Christian
Church. This is a remarkable fact. It is not usual among
men to celebrate the *deaths* of those whom they esteem
and venerate. The birthday of such persons we often keep
in remembrance, or the day on which they received some
distinguished honour, or performed some notable achieve-
ment. But we do not usually commemorate their *dying-
day ;* least of all if their death has been ignominious, however fully we may be persuaded of their innocence of the
alleged crime for which they were condemned. The ignominious death of one whom we greatly loved we should
naturally seek to bury in oblivion ; and even the most
distant allusion to it would be painful to us. How, then,
comes it to pass that Christians are enjoined in all ages
to celebrate the death of Jesus Christ? That death was
cruel and shameful in the highest degree. It was for
many years, moreover, one of the greatest obstacles with
which the preachers of the Gospel had to contend, being
"to the Jews a stumbling-block, and to the Greeks foolishness." And yet there is a pre-eminence assigned to it,
not only, as we have before seen, in the general strain of
the apostolic doctrine, but specially in the institution of
the Lord's Supper by Christ Himself, above every other
event in His history. The Lord Jesus has not required
us to keep any festival in memory of *His birth ;* although
since the fourth century the practice has widely prevailed

Death of
Christ
commemo-
rated in
Lord's
Supper.

1 Cor. i.
23.

Neander's
Church
History,
Period II
Sec. III.

14   STATEMENTS OF THE NEW TESTAMENT

PART I. SEC. I.

of setting apart a day in honour of His nativity. Neither has He told us to commemorate the splendours of His transfiguration, or the triumphs of His last entry into Jerusalem, or even the surpassing glories of His ascension. But the ignominy and anguish of His crucifixion He has commanded us to show forth until He come again. What reasonable account can we give of this procedure, so different from the usual customs of the world? Surely there must be something peculiar in the death of Christ, something that has a more important and essential bearing on the purposes of His mission for the benefit of mankind, than in those other incidents of His history to which, as a subject of commemoration, He has preferred it. That such is actually the case, indeed, we learn from the words employed by Him when instituting the Lord's Supper,

Matt. xxvi. 28.
1 Cor. xi. 24.

declaring, as these do, that " His body was broken for us," and that " His blood was shed for many for the remission of sins." But apart from all reference to these significant words, the simple fact of His death being selected by Him as the subject of a great commemorative ordinance, affords presumptive evidence that some special efficacy in furthering the ends of His beneficent mission must belong to it, and that on this account it has an especial claim to be held in perpetual remembrance by His disciples.

Sufferings of Christ exceptional and unique.

IV. There is one other general consideration respecting our Lord's sufferings to which we may advert, before investigating the statements of Holy Scripture with reference to the ends for which they were endured by Him. And it is this, that the sufferings of Christ are in themselves *so exceptional and unique,* so foreign to all actual or even conceivable human analogies, that we ought not to wonder if the Scriptures should attribute them to some extraordinary plan or purpose in the mind of God, the nature of which is but imperfectly comprehended by us.

The sufferer holy and divine.
2 Cor. v. 21.

The sufferer in this case was a Being of consummate excellence. He " knew no sin ;" " He went about doing good ;" " He was holy, harmless, undefiled, and separate from sinners : " the one solitary example of faultless inno-

RESPECTING THE ATONEMENT. 15

cence and perfect rectitude who ever has appeared among
the fallen sons of men. And He was a divine person,
the only-begotten Son of God, in whom dwelt all the
fulness of the Godhead. There is no apparent reason
why such a Being should have been subjected to sufferings
at all. Certainly His sufferings are not to be explained
on any assignable grounds of a personal nature. They
were neither merited by Him as a punishment, nor needed
as a purifying and corrective discipline, on His own account. Nor are they such as we should naturally have
expected to have come, by the determinate purpose and
counsel of God, on His own beloved Son, in whom He
was well pleased.

It is the fact, however, that this excellent and august
person was visited with sufferings more poignant and intense than are ordinarily endured by the vilest and worst
of sinners. Emphatically may He be styled "a man of
sorrows and acquainted with grief." His whole life on
earth was one unvarying scene of humiliation, contumely,
and affliction, terminating in a death of awful and mysterious anguish.

Nor can it be said that the sufferings He had to bear
were merely *incidental* to His heavenly mission. For they
were, as we have already seen, pre-eminently *essential* to
it. He did not merely encounter them *in the course* of
executing the work which His Father had assigned to
Him ; but the endurance of them was, in itself considered,
a necessary and most important part of His appointed
work. Nay, there were some of the most grievous of His
afflictions, with which it would seem as if His Father had
been concerned in the way, not only of appointing, but of
inflicting them ; so as to fulfil these memorable prophetic
words, " It pleased the Lord to bruise Him ; He hath put
Him to grief." No human agency was at work with Him
in that mysterious hour, when " His soul was exceeding
sorrowful even unto death," and when the prayer of agony
was wrung from Him, " O my Father, if it be possible, let
this cup pass from me." Nor was it so much the tortures
which men inflicted, as the hiding of His Father's coun-

PART
I.
Sec. 1.

Acts, x.
38.

Heb. vii.
29.

His suf-
ferings not
to be ex-
plained on
personal
grounds.

Isa. liii. 3.

Not inci-
dental
merely to
His mis-
sion.

Isa. liii. 10

Matt. xxvi
38, 39.

16   STATEMENTS OF THE NEW TESTAMENT

PART
I.
SEC. I.
——
Matt.
xxvii. 46.

tenance from Him, that prompted His cry of anguish on the cross, "My God, my God, why hast Thou forsaken me?" His case, then, is not one of undeserved suffering inflicted *by the hands of men* upon the subject of it, or coming upon Him in the way of natural consequence from the circumstances in which He is placed, with nothing more than the *permission* of Divine Providence.

God the chief agent in His afflictions.

No. God Himself is the prime origin and the chief agent in His afflictions. It is God's fixed plan, ordained and announced beforehand, that His beloved Son shall come into the world for the purpose of being subjected throughout His life to the endurance of unmerited ignominy and affliction, and of ultimately laying down His life upon the cross. It would have been nothing remarkable, comparatively, that the Saviour should have been persecuted by wicked men. For *this* we might find a sufficient explanation in the enmity of the carnal mind against God, and consequently against Him who was the "express image" of God. And the only cause of wonder would have been, that One so mighty should have yielded to their malice. But, that it should have "pleased the Lord to bruise Him, and to put Him to grief;" that He should have thrice besought His heavenly Father to remove, "if it were possible," the bitter cup which was mingled for Him ; that He should have uttered on the cross the plaintive cry,

Christ's sufferings a great mystery.

1 Pet. i. 12.

"My God, my God, why hast Thou forsaken me?"—*this*, truly, is a "mystery of godliness" which the mind of man cannot reflect upon without amazement, and which the angels may well "desire to look into." And without by any means anticipating the conclusions which may be deduced from express statements of Holy Scripture, respecting the true ends and reasons of our Lord's sufferings,

No wonder if some mysterious purpose should be assigned to them.

we venture to affirm that, considered in themselves, and in all their attendant circumstances, they are so remarkable, and, as compared with all other instances of human affliction, so unparalleled and unique, that we may be prepared to find reasons assigned for them, and purposes attributed to them in the Word of God, which are not in all respects level to our comprehension.

RESPECTING THE ATONEMENT.

Passing, however, from these general considerations respecting the divine mission and sufferings of Jesus Christ, the questions still remain to be investigated, What was the precise nature of His mediatorial work? and in what way was His life of humiliation and obedience, culminating in His death, conducive to the accomplishment of it?

Some writers, indeed, are very much inclined to denounce such inquiries as unprofitable and presumptuous. They tell us, that everything beyond the general fact, that Christ is *somehow* our Saviour or Redeemer, and that His sufferings are *in some way* instrumental in securing for us all needful spiritual blessings, lies quite away from the legitimate sphere of our intelligence; that this general truth, however vaguely apprehended, is all we need to know, or can know, upon the subject; and that any attempt on our part to obtain clearer views, or to form more definite conceptions in regard to it, is an irreverent intrusion into matters beyond our reach, and can lead only to vain speculations and fruitless controversies.

We hold that there is no real ground for such assertions. By turning our minds, in a spirit of devout reverence, but not the less of searching investigation, to the Holy Scriptures, much more may be ascertained than the general truth with which these writers would have us to be satisfied. And at all events they are not entitled *in limine* to shut out all farther inquiry into the subject, on the assumption that such inquiry must be idle and unprofitable. The soundness of this assumption must first of all be put to the test. And a very slight survey of the statements of the Word of God will suffice to show that it is altogether unjustifiable, and that much more complete and exact views are there given of the nature and objects of the Saviour's mediatorial work than those which it holds to be exclusively within our reach. It would, indeed, be vain and unbecoming, with respect to this or to any matter of revealed truth, to affect to be wise *above* that which is written. But no less so would it be, on the other hand, to refrain from seeking to be wise *up to*

PART
I.
SEC. 1.
——
Special
question
as to the
purpose of
Christ's
work and
sufferings.

This inquiry not vain or presumptuous.

18   STATEMENTS OF THE NEW TESTAMENT

PART
I.
SEC. I.

that which is written.   And in so far as concerns the charge of *irreverence*, we venture to say that it is more justly applicable to those who would wilfully exclude themselves or others from the knowledge of anything which God has thought fit to reveal, than to those who would eagerly and thankfully avail themselves of the full extent of information which He is pleased to impart.   In short, the question is altogether *a question of fact*, Whether or not the Bible has afforded us any farther instruction with reference to our Lord's sufferings, than that they are *somehow* conducive to our benefit ?   And this question is not to be summarily decided by vague assumptions or sweeping assertions, but by a fair and full investigation of those statements which the Bible itself has made to us on the subject.   We may be very sure that God intended us to know *as much* of the method of our salvation by the death of Christ *as His Word reveals*.   And without a just apprehension of the full import of what He has there condescended to disclose to us, it is not to be thought that we can adequately experience those salutary effects which the revealed doctrine is designed to produce.

SECTION II.

PASSAGES WHICH SPEAK OF CHRIST—(1) AS "DYING FOR SINNERS;" AND—(2) AS "DYING FOR OUR SINS."

I. IN searching the Scriptures with reference to the question before us, our attention may be, first of all, directed to that very numerous class of passages in which the Lord Jesus Christ is represented as having suffered and died "for us," or "for sinners."

Of these passages the following may be taken as a sufficient specimen :—

"The Son of Man came, not to be ministered unto, but to minister, and to give His life a ransom for many." "This is my body which is given for you;" "This cup is the new testament in my blood, which is shed for you." "The bread that I will give is my flesh, which I will give for the life of the world." "I am the good Shepherd; the good Shepherd giveth His life for the sheep." "I lay down my life for the sheep. . . . No man taketh it from me, but I lay it down of myself; I have power (authority) to lay it down, and I have power to take it again : this commandment have I received of my Father." "This is my commandment, that ye love one another, as I have loved you. Greater love hath no man than this, that a man lay down his life for his friends." "When we were yet without strength, in due time Christ died for the ungodly; for scarcely for a righteous man will one die; yet peradventure for a good man some would even dare to die; but God commendeth His love toward us, in that, while we were yet sinners, Christ died for us." "He that spared not His own Son, but delivered him up for

20 STATEMENTS OF THE NEW TESTAMENT

PART I.
SEC. 2.

2 Cor. v. 14, 15.

2 Cor. v. 21.

Gal. ii. 20.

Gal. iii. 13.

Ephes. v. 2, 25.

1 Thess. v. 9, 10.

1 Tim. ii. 5, 6.

Titus, ii. 14.

Heb. ii. 9.

1 Pet. iii. 18.

1 John, iii. 16.

us all, how shall He not with Him also freely give us all things?" "If one died for all, then all died; and He died for all, that they which live should not henceforth live unto themselves, but unto Him who died for them and rose again." "He hath made Him to be sin for us, who knew no sin, that we might be made the righteousness of God in Him." "I am crucified with Christ; nevertheless I live: yet not I, but Christ liveth in me; and the life which I now live in the flesh, I live by the faith of the Son of God, who loved me and gave Himself for me." "Christ hath redeemed us from the curse of the law, being made a curse for us." "Christ hath loved us, and hath given Himself for us, an offering and a sacrifice to God for a sweet-smelling savour." "Christ loved the Church, and gave Himself for it." "God hath not appointed us to wrath, but to obtain salvation by our Lord Jesus Christ, who died for us." "There is one God, and one Mediator between God and men, the man Christ Jesus, who gave Himself a ransom for all." "Our Saviour Jesus Christ gave Himself for us, that He might redeem us from all iniquity." "We see Jesus crowned with glory and honour, who was made a little lower than the angels for the suffering of death, that He by the grace of God should taste death for every man." "Christ also hath once suffered for sins, the just for the unjust, that He might bring us to God." "Hereby perceive we the love of God, because He laid down His life for us."

In some of these passages substitution clearly indicated by the preposition ἀντί.

Matt. xx. 28.

Mark, x. 45.

In some of these passages the *substitution of Christ* in the room of those for whom He died is clearly indicated. This is the case with that memorable saying of our Lord Himself—recorded by two of the evangelists,—" The Son of Man is come, not to be ministered unto, but to minister, and *to give His life a ransom for many.*" Here the English word "*for,*" which is somewhat indeterminate, answers to the Greek preposition ἀντί, which properly expresses *the setting of one thing over against another,* and is generally employed to signify *commutation* or *substitution.* Thus in the Septuagint Greek translation of the

RESPECTING THE ATONEMENT.   21

Old Testament, the word ἀντί is used to convey this meaning in the following as well as in numerous other passages; "God hath appointed me another seed *instead of* Abel;" "Wherefore have ye rewarded evil *for* (or in the place of) good?" "Joseph gave them bread *in exchange for* horses and flocks and cattle;" "Aaron died, and Eleazar his son ministered in the priest's office *in his stead.*"

In the same sense this preposition is employed in the New Testament, as in the following instances: "Archelaus reigned in Judea *in the room of* his father Herod;" "Ye have heard that it hath been said, An eye *for* an eye, and a tooth *for* a tooth;" "If he ask a fish, will he *for* a fish give him a serpent?" "Recompense to no man evil *for* evil." In all these cases the idea of *substitution* or *commutation* is sufficiently apparent. Nor is it less so, assuredly, in our Lord's statement, "The Son of Man is come to give His life a ransom for many," λύτρον ἀντὶ πολλῶν. Indeed, were there any room for doubt as to the proper import of the preposition in the present instance, the doubt would be at once removed by its connection with the word λύτρον, which indicates that the life of the Son of Man was "the *ransom* given for many," or the price paid to redeem their forfeited lives.

The same interpretation must be put upon another passage, in which it is written of Jesus Christ, the "Mediator between God and men," that "He gave Himself a ransom *for* all." Here, indeed, the preposition is not ἀντί, but ὑπέρ. But then, the word translated "ransom" is ἀντίλυτρον, a composite word, which, having ἀντί as its prefix, conveys more strongly the commutative sense than the simple word λύτρον, used in the former passage.

In all the remaining passages, however, the preposition employed is ὑπέρ, which does not necessarily indicate substitution. Its radical meaning is "over" or "above." It conveys the notion of "covering," so as to suggest either "the covering of a person from danger," or "the covering of a thing from sight." In its secondary sense, when construed with a genitive and applied to persons,

PART I. SEC. 2.

Gen. iv. 25.
Gen. xliv. 4.
Gen. xlvii. 17.
Deut. x. 6.
Matt. ii. 22.
Matt. v. 38.
Luke, xi. 11.
Rom. xii. 17.

1 Tim. ii. 6.

22 STATEMENTS OF THE NEW TESTAMENT

PART I.
SEC. 2.

it may signify either "for the benefit of any one," or "in the room of any one," according to the connection in which it occurs, or the nature of the subject to which it has a reference. The question therefore comes to be, in which of these two senses are we to understand it in the passages above adduced? Is it to be considered as indicating merely that Jesus Christ suffered "for our advantage," or as farther expressing that He suffered "in our stead"?

Substitution may also be indicated where ὑπέρ is used.

Some writers affirm that the preposition ὑπέρ cannot in any case admit of the latter meaning. In this, however, they are evidently mistaken. For numerous instances occur in the Greek classics, in which the phrase ἀποθνήσκειν ὑπέρ τινος is undeniably used to signify "dying instead of a person." * And there are similar instances to be met with in the New Testament in which ὑπέρ conveys the same idea of "substitution." Thus, in his Epistle to Philemon, St Paul uses these words with reference to Onesimus,

Phil. 13.

"Whom I would have retained with me, that *in thy stead* (ὑπέρ σοῦ) he might have ministered unto me." Here the preposition assuredly indicates "substitution," because it is evident that Onesimus was to minister to Paul, not *for the benefit of Philemon,* but in his stead. Paul, and not Philemon, was the person to be benefited by the

2 Cor. v. 20.

ministrations. Elsewhere the apostle says, "Now then we are ambassadors for Christ (ὑπέρ Χριστοῦ), as though God did beseech you by us : we pray you *in Christ's stead* (ὑπέρ Χριστοῦ), be ye reconciled to God." Here, in like manner, St Paul represents himself as acting *in the place of Christ,* like an ambassador for his sovereign. Yet

1 Cor. i. 13.

farther, when he asks, "Was Paul crucified for you?" (ὑπέρ ὑμῶν), he does not merely inquire, "Whether, if he had himself been crucified, it might not have been said that he was crucified for their advantage?" For he could not doubt that his death would be conducive to the fur-

Philip. i. 12 ; ii. 17, 18 ; 2 Cor. i. 6.

therance of the Gospel and the good of the Christian Church ; and in various passages he has expressly stated his conviction, that important benefits to the Church and

* See Appendix, Note A

RESPECTING THE ATONEMENT.   23

cause of Christ would accrue from his own personal
sufferings and tribulations. But his question amounts to
this, " Was Paul crucified *instead of you*, in the sense in
which Christ, and Christ alone, can be said to have been
so ? "

It cannot be denied, then, that the preposition $ὑπέρ$
may fitly enough convey the idea of *substitution*. And
though we can hardly venture to say, that taken by itself
it necessarily has this sense in *all* the passages in which
it is used with reference to the sufferings of our Lord, we
may safely affirm that, in *some* of these passages, the
nature of the case, and the tenor of the context, clearly
enough show that such is its signification.

Thus it is evident, from the nature of the transaction
referred to, that the apostle has in view a case of substitution when he says, " Scarcely for a righteous man will
one die, yet peradventure for a good man some would
even dare to die ; " and hence we must hold him to be
alluding to a similar case, when in the context he speaks
of Christ as having " died for the ungodly," and as having
" died for us while we were yet sinners."

Again, when we read, " The love of Christ constraineth
us ; because we thus judge, that if one died for all, then
all died " ($πάντες\ ἀπέθανον$), it is very clear that the idea
of commutation or substitution was present to the apostle's
mind.   For, if otherwise, he could not soundly have " thus
judged, that if one died for all, then all died."   For it is
not when a person does a thing merely *for the good of
others*, but when he does it *in their stead*, as their sponsor
or representative, that *they* can be considered as having
done it.   And hence it is necessary to the force of the
apostle's argument that Christ should be held to have
died *in the place* of those who, by reason of His having
done so, may be " judged " or reckoned to have themselves " died."   This view of the matter is confirmed by
the succeeding clause, " He died for all, that they who
live should not henceforth live unto themselves, but unto
Him who died for them and rose again."   For the meaning of this declaration seems to be, that those who may

PART
I.
SEC. 2.
——.

Substitu-
tion im-
plied in
Rom. v.
6-8.

Also in
2 Cor. **v.**
14, 15.

24   STATEMENTS OF THE NEW TESTAMENT

PART
I.
SEC. 2.
———

be judged to have died when Christ died for them, have henceforth *no life of their own which they are entitled to lead*, inasmuch as they live only because Christ has exempted them from the personal endurance of death, by dying *in their stead*.

Also in
Gal. iii.
13.

Again, when we are told that "Christ hath redeemed us from the curse of the law, being made a curse *for us:* for it is written, Cursed is every one that hangeth on a tree,"—it seems plain that ὑπέρ must be understood in the *substitutive*, and not merely in the beneficiary sense. For "the making of Christ a curse" is represented as the *ransom* by which our "redemption from the curse" has been obtained.   The curse was *removed from us* by being *transferred to Him*.

Also in
1 Pet. iii.
18.

Farther, when it is said that "Christ hath once suffered for sins, *the just for the unjust*, that He might bring us unto God," the substitutive sense of the preposition is very apparent.   For Christ is here said to have "suffered for, or on account of sins,"—that is to say, on account of the sins of those "unjust" persons, for whom He, being Himself "just," endured the sufferings.   And I know not how otherwise this statement can be understood than as signifying that, though Himself "just," He bore instead of the "unjust" those sufferings, to which they, on account of their sins, must else have been subjected.

Thus does it appear, that in at least *four* of the passages in which the preposition ὑπὲρ is employed, the Lord Jesus is represented as *dying in the room of sinners*, with scarcely less distinctness than in the three passages previously noticed, in which His substitution, as indicated by the preposition ἀντί and the words λύτρον or ἀντίλυτρον, is placed beyond the possibility of dispute.

The other
texts,
though not
necessarily
implying
substitu-
tion, do
not ex-
clude it.

As for the remaining passages of the same class, there is perhaps nothing, either in the texts themselves or in their context, that necessarily fastens on them any farther meaning than that the Lord Jesus suffered *for our advantage*.   At the same time, it must be observed that this sense is not by any means incompatible with the other.   On the contrary, it may be fairly held to be inclu-

RESPECTING THE ATONEMENT. 25

sive of it. For when, in so many texts of a strictly
analogous kind, the statement that "Christ died for us"
has been found to convey the idea of substitution, we are
warranted to conclude that in those less determinate passages, in which the like form of expression has been used,
the sacred writers meant to teach us that *the particular
way* in which the Lord Jesus *suffered for our benefit*, was
by suffering *in our room and stead*. It is probable, moreover, that the reason why ὑπέρ is so frequently employed
in preference to ἀντί is, that it serves to convey *both* of these
meanings, expressing at once the general fact that Christ
died "for our benefit," and the special mode in which He
did so, by dying "as our substitute."*

Indeed, if we do not put this construction on the statement, there is no way in which we can satisfactorily
account for the *frequency*, and at the same time the *exclusiveness*, of its application in Scripture to the sufferings
of Jesus Christ. If His sufferings are "for us" in no higher
or more special sense than that of "having been conducive
to our advantage," then might the same language have
been applied to many others with no less emphasis and
significancy than to Him. Many important benefits have
unquestionably resulted to the cause of truth and to the
interests of believers from the sufferings of the apostles
and other primitive martyrs, as well as from those of their
divine Master. If, indeed, we keep out of view the special
efficacy ascribed to His sufferings in securing our redemption, *their* sufferings were, in all other respects—as examples of patience, heroism, and devotedness, or as con-
firmations of their testimony in behalf of the Gospel—of
similar, if not of equal, advantage to the Christian Church.
That they were so is repeatedly and distinctly affirmed by
the Apostle Paul. "The things which happened unto
me," he says, "have fallen out rather to the furtherance of
the Gospel;" "Yea, and if I be offered upon the sacrifice
and service of your faith, I joy and rejoice with you all;
for the same cause also do ye joy and rejoice with me;"
"Whether we be afflicted, it is for your consolation;"

PART
I.
SEC. 2.

"He died
for us" is
frequently
and exclu-
sively said
of Christ.

Why so, if
He merely
suffered,
like many
others, for
our bene-
fit?

Philip. i.
12.

Philip. ii.
17, 18.

2 Cor. i. 6.

* See Appendix, Note B.

26　STATEMENTS OF THE NEW TESTAMENT

PART
I.
SEC. 2.
———
2 Tim. ii.
10.

"I endure all things for the elect's sake, that they also may obtain the salvation by Jesus Christ." And yet the same apostle emphatically disclaims the thought, that he himself or any of his brethren had suffered or died "for men," in any such special sense as that in which the Lord Jesus is declared to have done so. How else are we to understand his appeal to the Corinthians, already referred

1 Cor. i.
13.

to "*Was Paul crucified for you?*" Surely he could not have reproved them in this manner for saying, "I am of Paul, and I of Apollos, and I of Cephas, and I of Christ," had he believed that the crucifixion of Christ had no other relation to the salvation of Christians than that merely of being "conducive to their benefit,"—a point of view in which it unquestionably stands on the same footing with the sufferings of Paul himself, or of Apollos, or of Cephas, or of any other martyr in the cause of truth and righteousness. We hold, then, that the singular frequency and emphasis with which the phraseology in question is applied in Scripture to the sufferings of Jesus Christ, and the circumstance of its being applied *to Him alone*, can only be explained by supposing that *He* suffered "for us" in some sense that is altogether special and unique,—not merely as having suffered, like many others, *for our advantage*, but as having suffered, like none besides Him, *in our stead.*

Christ suf-
fered "for
sins."

II. The next class of passages to which we may advert, are those which specify the *cause* or *reason*, on account of which the sufferings of Christ "for sinners" were endured by Him. Thus, it is written :—

Rom. iv.
25 ; viii. 3.

"He was delivered *for our offences.*" "God, sending His own Son in the likeness of sinful flesh and *for sin*,

1 Cor. xv.
3.

condemned sin in the flesh." "I delivered unto you first of all, that which I also received, that Christ died *for our

Gal. i. 4.

sins*, according to the Scriptures." "Who gave Himself *for our sins*, that He might deliver us from this present

Heb. x.
12.

evil world." "This man, after He had offered one sacrifice *for sins*, for ever sat down on the right hand of God."

1 Pet. iii.
18.

"Christ also hath once suffered *for sins*, the just for the

RESPECTING THE ATONEMENT.

unjust." And to these may be added the following statements of Isaiah, in a passage expressly applied to Christ in the New Testament: "He was wounded *for our transgressions*, He was bruised *for our iniquities;*" "*For the transgression* of my people was He stricken."

1. In the first of these passages the preposition employed is διὰ, governing παραπτώματα in the accusative. When thus construed, διὰ usually indicates the *instrumental or efficient cause* by which any event is brought about, and is translated "because of," "on account of," or "in consequence of." It is used in this sense in the Septuagint version of the last two of the above passages, "He was wounded *for* our transgressions, He was bruised *for* our iniquities;" "*for* the transgression of my people was He stricken." And this is undoubtedly its meaning in Romans, iv. 25,—namely, that Christ "was delivered *on account of* our offences"—these offences being *the cause* which led to His death.

Hill, Alford, and others have noticed it as a remarkable instance of the use of the same preposition in different senses, that in the clause immediately following, διὰ is employed to indicate, not the *instrumental cause* of a thing, but the *final cause*, when the apostle adds, "and was raised again *for* our justification," διὰ τὴν δικαίωσιν ἡμῶν,— that is, as these writers hold, "*with a view to* our justification." It is not necessary, however, thus to interpret this latter clause. For, as Horsley well argues, the resurrection of Christ was the consequence of His death having proved efficacious in securing the justification of His people. Believers being freed by His great sacrifice from the bonds of guilt, it was meet that He, their substitute and representative, should be loosed from the bonds of death. Accordingly, the apostle here points to "our justification," not as the contemplated result, but as the *cause or reason* of Christ's resurrection; just as in the previous clause he had pointed to "our offences," not as the contemplated result, but as the *cause* or *reason* of Christ's death. "We had sinned—*therefore* the Saviour died; our justification was secured by His obedience unto death—

PART I. SEC. 2.

Isa. liii. 5, 8.

Christ delivered for our offences.

Horsley's Nine Sermons, p. 261.

28 STATEMENTS OF THE NEW TESTAMENT

PART I. SEC. 2.

I Cor. xv. 17.

therefore He was raised again from the dead." I may add, that this interpretation of the latter clause throws light on an otherwise obscure statement of the same apostle, I Cor. xv. 17, " If Christ be not raised, your faith is vain, ye are yet in your sins ; " that is to say, " If Christ be not raised, you have no ground for trusting that His death has been accepted as an effectual atonement for you."

2. In the third and fifth of the above passages, the pre-position employed is ὑπέρ, governing the genitive. We have already remarked that ὑπὲρ, when thus construed

I Cor. xv. 3 ; Heb. x. 12.

and applied to a person, signifies either " for his benefit," or " in his stead." It is evident, however, that in the ex-pression ὑπὲρ τῶν ἁμαρτιῶν ἡμῶν neither of these two senses is admissible. For it could not with any propriety be said that Christ died either " for the benefit of our sins," or " instead of our sins." Accordingly, the preposi-tion must here be understood in another sense, which not unfrequently belongs to it, as signifying " because of," or

Rom. xv. 9.

" on account of." Thus we find St Paul using these words, τὰ δὲ ἔθνη ὑπὲρ ἐλέους δοξάσαι τὸν Θεὸν, " that the Gentiles should glorify God *for* His mercy,"—that is,

I Cor. x. 30.

" *because of* His mercy." Again, the apostle asks, τί βλασφημοῦμαι ὑπὲρ οὗ ἐγὼ εὐχαριστῶ; " Why am I evil spoken of *on account of* that for which I give thanks ? " There can be no doubt that this is the sense in which the preposition must be taken in the passages before us.

I have yet to notice two things in regard to one of these passages : (1.) The death of Christ " for our sins " is here represented as *a matter of primary importance* in the sys-

I Cor. xv. 1, 3.

tem of Christian doctrine. For Paul, when " declaring to the Corinthians the Gospel which he preached, and by which, if they kept it in memory, they should be saved," says, " For I delivered unto you, *first of all,* that which I also received, that Christ died for our sins, according to the Scriptures." This is quite in harmony with the em-phatic manner in which he so often speaks of the cross of Christ, as if it were the very sum and substance of the Gospel. And it furnishes a strong confirmatory proof

RESPECTING THE ATONEMENT.

that there is some peculiar efficacy attributable to our
Lord's sufferings in securing our salvation. (2.) Farther,
the apostle represents "the death of Christ for our sins"
as a thing which he had "*received.*" And there is a manifest similarity between this statement and what he had
said in a previous chapter regarding the Lord's Supper,
"*I received of the Lord* that which also I delivered unto
you." Accordingly, the best commentators agree in
thinking, that in the passage before us the word "received" must be held as referring to a divine communication. Now, apart from the atoning efficacy of the death
of Christ, there was nothing about it, as a mere incident
of His history—exemplifying like other incidents His
devotedness to His Father's will, or illustrating the sincerity of His claims as a professed prophet—that could
have required any divine announcement to reveal it. And
hence we may reasonably presume, that what Paul "received" was something more than this ; that it was some
such highly important, and, at the same time, deeply
mysterious doctrine as the atonement—a doctrine not
ascertainable by the light of reason, and therefore an
appropriate subject of divine teaching.—We do not bring
forward these two circumstances as being, in themselves,
by any means conclusive proof. But certainly they furnish an adminicle of presumptive evidence, which ought
not in our induction of Scriptural statements to be disre-
garded, and which may justly be held as lending confirmation to the more direct evidence derivable from other
sources.

3. In the remaining passages of the class under consideration, the preposition employed is περὶ. "God
sending His own Son in the likeness of sinful flesh, and
for sin (περὶ ἁμαρτίας), condemned sin in the flesh ;"
"He gave Himself for our sins" (περὶ τῶν ἁμαρτιῶν
ἡμῶν); "Christ also hath once suffered for sins (περὶ
ἁμαρτιῶν), the just for the unjust."

This preposition also, when governing the genitive,
frequently indicates *the reason on account of which a
thing is done.* Thus the Jews said to our Lord, Περὶ

*PART
I.
SEC. 2.*

1 Cor. xi.
23.

Rom. viii.
3.

Gal. i. 4.
1 Pet. iii.
18.

30 STATEMENTS OF THE NEW TESTAMENT

PART
I.
SEC. 2.

John, x.
33.

Levit. iv.
3. 14, 35;
v. 6; xvi.
6; xix. 22.

Heb. x. 6,
8, 18.

καλοῦ ἔργου ὀυ λιθάζομεν σε, ἀλλὰ περὶ βλασφημίας —"For a good work we stone thee not, but for blasphemy." In the Septuagint Greek translation of the Old Testament, περὶ ἁμαρτιῶν is the expression usually employed when the Levitical sacrifices are said to have been "offered for sins." In like manner, we find the same expression used in the Epistle to the Hebrews, where it is twice said, "In burnt-offerings and sacrifices for sin Thou hast had no pleasure;" and again, when it is said, "Now where remission of these is, there is no more offering for sin."

Import of
Christ
"dying for
our sins."

Woods's
Lectures,
ii. 412.

All these texts, then, are to be considered as pointing out the reason on account of which, or the cause in consequence of which, the Lord Jesus was delivered up to sufferings and death. They teach us that He did not suffer for any transgressions of His own, but that our sins were the cause or reason of His sufferings. This surely implies, as Dr Woods has well observed, "that His sufferings had substantially the same relation to our sins as our own sufferings would have had if we ourselves had suffered for them. Now every one knows the relation between sin and suffering, where the sinner himself is the sufferer. And how, then, can we mistake the sense of those texts, which declared that Christ suffered for our sins? When God inflicts evil upon men for their own sins, He shows His righteous displeasure against them as transgressors. He expresses his disapprobation of them, and of their sins, and deals with them as personally criminal and ill-deserving. When, therefore, we are told that 'Christ died for our sins,' or that He 'suffered on account of sins, the just for the unjust,' we are led to regard His sufferings as a manifestation of the holy displeasure of God, not against Him, but against us. The very terms of such a proposition imply, that whatever excited the displeasure of God, and made the displeasure of God proper and necessary, was in us, and not in the Lord Jesus Himself." And what else does this amount to, but that He was our substitute, who bore in our stead the penal consequences of our sins?

RESPECTING THE ATONEMENT. 31

A roundabout method has indeed been taken, with the view of otherwise interpreting these passages. It has been alleged, that by " Christ dying for our sins," no more is meant than that " our sins were the occasion of that divine mission which He undertook on our behalf, and of which His death was an unavoidable incident; " or that " His death was necessary for the confirmation and establishment of the Gospel, in which we are at once assured of God's willingness to forgive our sins, and are effectually persuaded to renounce them."

No support is given to this interpretation by the statement in one of the passages referred to, that " Christ gave Himself for our sins, that He might deliver us from this present evil world." For the *telic* particle ὅπως (*in order that*), which introduces the latter clause of this verse, shows, that " our deliverance from this present evil world " is here referred to, not as *explanatory of the sense* in which " Christ gave Himself for our sins," but simply as *indicating one of the purposes for which He did so.* And no one is concerned to deny that " our deliverance from this evil world " is one of the great ends to which the atonement is conducive.

It will readily occur, moreover, to any reader of the passages, that the proposed interpretation is exceedingly forced and circuitous. It is not such as would have suggested itself to any one who had no wish to support or to controvert a particular theory. And besides this, it is liable to some other serious objections.

In the first place, the death of Christ, according to this view, stood in no other relation to " our sins " than that of any persecuted prophet or apostle who has laid down his life in attestation of revealed truth ; and hence there is no reason why the same Scriptural language should not have been applied to other martyrs as well as to Him. But where do we ever find it to be so? Where do we ever read that any one of the prophets or apostles " died for our sins, according to the Scriptures "? Where do we read that Isaiah or Jeremiah " was wounded for our transgressions and bruised for our iniquities "? that Paul was

Margin notes:
PART I.
SEC. 2.

Evasive interpretation of these texts.

Shown to be inadmissible. Gal. i. 4.

32 STATEMENTS OF THE NEW TESTAMENT

PART
I.
SEC. 2.

"delivered for our offences"? that Stephen "gave himself for our sins"? or that Peter "once suffered for sins, the just for the unjust"? It is only the death of Christ that is thus spoken of, although there are unquestionably many others, as well as He, who sealed with their blood the truth of that gracious message with which they were charged to our sinful and apostate race.

In the second place, if the passages be thus interpreted, it is unaccountable that *the death* of Christ should be singled out as the only incident or circumstance of His ministry to which any special relation to " our sins " is ever attributed. Why is He not said, with like frequency and emphasis, to have "preached for our sins," to have "prophesied for our sins," to have "wrought miracles for our sins," since His preaching, and prophesying, and working of miracles were, no less than His death, according to this view of it, incidental to the prosecution, and necessary for the confirmation, of that gracious mission to a sinful world which He undertook? No such statements as these are ever met with in the Scriptures; although, on the supposition we are combating, they ought to have occurred as frequently, and ought to appear as natural and appropriate, as those expressions the meaning of which we are now concerned to ascertain. And from the absence of them—not to speak of their manifest harshness, uncouthness, and contrariety to the ordinary strain of the sacred writers—we conclude that, when Christ is said to have " died for our sins," some further connection is indicated as subsisting between His death and the sins of mankind, than that which consists in the former being a necessary incident merely, or an important confirmation, of that divine mission, of which the sins of mankind were the occasion, and their pardon or purgation the contemplated result.

SECTION III.

PASSAGES WHICH SPEAK OF CHRIST—(3) AS BEARING OUR SINS; AND—(4) AS "MADE SIN," AND "MADE A CURSE FOR US."

III. SOMEWHAT akin to the passages we have last referred to, is another class, in which the Saviour is represented as "*bearing our sins.*" Thus it is written in the Epistle to the Hebrews, " Christ was once offered *to bear the sins of many.*" The Apostle Peter says of Him, in like manner, " Who His own self *bare our sins* in His own body on the tree." And in the fifty-third chapter of Isaiah—which may almost be regarded as a part of the New Testament, so frequently and expressly is it there applied to Jesus Christ—we find these statements : " The Lord *hath laid on Him* the iniquity of us all ;" " By His knowledge shall my righteous servant justify many, for *He shall bear their iniquities;* " " He was numbered with the transgressors, and *He bare the sins of many.*"

PART I.
SEC. 3.

Christ a sin-bearer.

Heb. ix. 28.
1 Pet. ii. 24.

Isa. liii. 6, 11, 12.

To " bear sin " is a form of expression frequently applied in Scripture to persons who are charged with the guilt, and subjected to the merited penalties, of their own transgressions. Thus it is written, " Every one that eateth it shall bear his iniquity, because he hath profaned the hallowed thing of the Lord, and that soul shall be cut off from among his people ;" " They shall keep mine ordinance, lest they bear sin for it, and die therefor, if they profane it ;" " Whosoever curseth his God shall bear his sin ; and he that blasphemeth the name of the Lord shall surely be put to death ;" " The man that forbeareth to keep the passover, even the same soul shall be cut off from among

Levit. xix. 8.

Levit. xxii. 9.

Levit. xxiv. 15, 16.

Num. ix. 13.

34   STATEMENTS OF THE NEW TESTAMENT

PART I. SEC. 3.

Num. xviii. 22.

his people; because he brought not the offering of the Lord in his appointed season, that man shall bear his sin;" "Neither must the children of Israel henceforth come nigh the tabernacle of the congregation, lest they bear sin and die." In these and many similar passages, in which men are spoken of as "bearing their own sins," the meaning evidently is that they are charged with the guilt, and visited with the punishment, of the sins which they have committed.

Num. xiv. 33, 34.

Not unfrequently, however, do we find this phrase applied to the case of those who are subjected to forfeitures or involved in sufferings in consequence of the sins of others. Thus Moses writes, "Your children shall wander in the wilderness forty years, and bear your whoredoms, until your carcases be wasted in the wilderness; after the number of the days that ye searched the land, even forty days, each day for a year, shall ye bear your iniquities." Again, Jeremiah represents the afflicted Israelites as saying, "Our fathers have sinned and are no more, and we have borne their iniquities." And again, Ezekiel declares, "The soul that sinneth, it shall die; the son shall not bear the iniquity of the father, neither shall the father bear the iniquity of the son; the righteousness of the righteous shall be upon him, and the wickedness of the wicked shall be upon him,"—that is to say, each shall be dealt with according to his own doings, and not according to those of any of his fellow-creatures, however closely and intimately connected with him.

Lam. v. 7.

Ezek. xviii. 20.

In what sense did Christ bear our sins?

How, then, is this expression to be understood when applied to Jesus Christ, of whom we are emphatically told, that He "was once offered to bear the sins of many," that "He bare our sins in his own body on the tree," and that "the Lord laid on Him the iniquity of us all"?

Not in the way of mere natural consequence.

These statements are held by some to have no further meaning than this, that "our sins were the occasion of Christ's sufferings," or that "He was involved in sufferings on account of them in the way of mere natural consequence," just as a person may be said to "bear the sins

RESPECTING THE ATONEMENT. 35

of his ancestors," when in the ordinary course of events he
is subjected to forfeitures or calamities which have come
upon him as the natural result of their transgressions.
This construction of the phrase, however, is objectionable
on various grounds. For (1) it cannot be said that the
connection between our sins and the sufferings of Christ
arises from the ordinary constitution and course of nature.
Rather are we taught in Scripture to regard it as a special
arrangement constituted by God, according to whose
appointment our iniquities "were laid upon Him," and
He was " once offered to bear the sins of many." Besides,
(2), *whose* sins is it that Christ is said to have borne? It
is not exclusively the sins of persons, who were by any
special social ties connected with Him, or of persons
whose sins were prior to His sufferings, so that He might
be reasonably held to be involved in the evil consequences
of their misconduct. But it is " our sins," or " the sins of
many ;" the sins of His apostles and of those to whom
they wrote their epistles ; the sins of all such as put their
trust in Him, many of whom did not exist until long after
He had lived and died ; so that *their* sins could not possibly entail upon Him any calamitous results in the way
of natural consequence. Moreover, (3), in one of the
passages, His " bearing our sins" is closely connected [Heb. ix. 28.]
with *our obtaining the remission of them*, as any one may
see by looking at the context. In another passage it is
no less closely connected with our being " *healed by His* [1 Pet. ii. 24.]
stripes." And in a third passage it is viewed as securing
the "*justification of many*." The case of our Lord, there- [Isa. liii. 11.]
fore, is not at all that of a person who is involved in
suffering by the misconduct of other men, without lightening in any degree *their* burden of accountableness for
it. Rather is it the case of one who bears the sins of
others, with the view and to the effect of *exempting* the
transgressors from those penal consequences to which
otherwise they would have been subjected.

It is urged, indeed, by many of those writers who con- [Not in the]
trovert the doctrine of the Atonement, that by " bearing [sense of merely]
our sins" we are simply to understand " removing them," [taking]

36 STATEMENTS OF THE NEW TESTAMENT

PART I.
SEC. 3.
———
them
away.

Magee on
Atone-
ment, note
xlii.

or "taking them away," without reference to any vicarious endurance of their penalties. This interpretation, how-ever, is inadmissible. For it has been conclusively shown by Dr Magee, that the Hebrew word *sabal*, in Isaiah, liii. 11, uniformly signifies "the bearing of a burden;" that the Hebrew word *nasa*, which is used synonymously with *sabal* in Isaiah, liii. 12, has the same meaning when applied to "sins" in all cases in which the sense of "for-giveness" is not admissible; and that the "bearing of sins," as indicated by either word, signifies "the suffering, or being liable to suffer, some infliction on account of sin, which, in the case of the offender himself, would be pro-perly called punishment." The same author has farther shown, with reference to the corresponding passages in the New Testament, that the Greek verb ἀναφέρω, if it convey any idea beyond that of simply "bearing a burden," must be held to indicate "the lifting of it up," as the ancient sacrifices were lifted up upon the altar; and that "the removal of sins," if included in it at all, must be such a removal of them as was effected in one particular way—namely, by "bearing" or carrying them.

Besides, in interpreting this expression, we must take it, not alone, but in its connection with other expressions in the context which guide us to its true meaning. Thus, in Isaiah, liii., the "bearing of our sins" by the predicted Saviour is explained by the adjoining and parallel state-ment of the prophet, that "the Lord *laid on Him* the iniquity of us all," or "the Lord caused all our iniquities to fall upon Him," which plainly indicates that He was personally *burdened with them.* In like manner, St Peter's statement, that Christ "*Himself* bare our sins *in His own body*," manifestly implies that "they were laid upon Him as a burden." And further, if He took them away *other-wise* than by "Himself bearing them," His doing so would not have served the purpose for which the apostle has in this passage referred to it, as an example of the meekness and patience which Christians ought to display, "when, though doing well, they suffer for it."—Again, when we read that "Christ was once offered to bear the sins of

1 Pet. ii.
20.

RESPECTING THE ATONEMENT. 37

many," we find the following words added immediately after, "And unto them that look for Him shall He appear the second time *without sin* unto salvation." Here the apostle indicates a contrast between the two "appearings" of our Lord. And the very point of the contrast is this, that at His first advent He was *a sin-bearer*—sinless Himself, but burdened with the sins of others; whereas at His second advent "He shall appear *without sin*"—that is to say, "without the vicarious burden which He had formerly borne." If by ἀνενεγκεῖν ἁμαρτίας we understand "to take away the sins of many *otherwise than by Himself bearing them*," the contrast, so evidently intended, would be destroyed. For, according to this view, our Lord was "without sin," either personal or imputed, at *both* of His "appearings."

PART I. SEC. 3.
Heb. ix. 28.

Farther, in whatever sense this phrase may be understood, it evidently denotes something which our Lord accomplished *by His death*. For we are expressly told by St Peter that Christ "bare our sins in His own body *on the tree*." And the statement of St Paul, that "Christ was *once* offered to bear the sins of many," has a no less obvious reference to His death, of which we read in the preceding context that "Christ did not offer Himself *often*, as the high priest entereth into the holy place every year with the blood of others; for then must He have *often suffered* since the foundation of the world." Now, if it be thus clear that the "bearing of our sins" was something which the Saviour did "once," when He died for us, what meaning can be attached to the expression by those who deny that His sufferings were vicarious? Their doctrine does not admit of the supposition that the death of Christ was intended *to procure forgiveness for us*. They hold that He can only be considered as "taking away our sins" in one or other of these two ways: either, on the one hand, by turning us from the practice of sin through the sanctifying power of His precepts and example; or, on the other hand, by lightening our fears and self-reproaches under a sense of sin through His cheering assurances of the divine mercy and placability. Now, as to the *first* of these—

"Bearing sin" is something that Christ did by *His death*.

Heb. ix. 25, 26.

38 STATEMENTS OF THE NEW TESTAMENT

PART I.
SEC. 3.

turning us from the practice of sin—Christ cannot be said to have done this directly, exclusively, and once for all, by His death; for, in fact, He is continually doing it by the lessons of His Word and the grace of His Holy Spirit. And as regards the *second*—assuring us of the divine mercy—it is equally clear that He cannot be said to have done this "once" when He suffered on the cross; for His preaching, and miracles, and prophecies, as we have before observed, were no less efficacious in this respect than His sufferings. Unless, therefore, the passages in question be understood as indicating the substitution of Christ in the room of sinners, to bear the penal consequences of their transgressions, there seems to be no other satisfactory meaning that can be given to them. And when so understood, we find in them not only a confirmation, but a somewhat fuller development, of the meaning of those other passages, already considered, in which Christ is said to have died "for us" and "for our sins."

Bushnell's interpretation of Isa. liii. 4.

Matt. viii. 17.

Bushnell on Vicarious Sacrifice, p. 8, 9.

Before leaving these passages, it is proper to advert to the confident assertion of Dr Bushnell regarding a quotation of Isaiah by one of the evangelists. The words of the prophet, " Surely He hath borne our griefs and carried our sorrows," are thus applied to the Lord Jesus by St Matthew, " They brought unto Him many that were possessed with devils ; and He cast out the spirits with His word, and healed all that were sick ; that it might be fulfilled which was spoken by Esaias the prophet, saying, ' Himself took our infirmities and bare our sicknesses.' " Now, says Dr Bushnell, " This one Scriptural citation gives, beyond question, the *usus loquendi* of all the vicarious and sacrificial language of the New Testament." " If we desire to know exactly what the substitution of Christ for sin was, and how far it went—in what sense, for example, ' He bare our sins '—we have only to revert to what is here said of His relation to sicknesses, and our question is resolved. What then does it mean, that ' Christ bare our sicknesses '? Does it mean that He literally had our sicknesses transferred to Him, and so taken off from

RESPECTING THE ATONEMENT. 39

us ? Does it mean that He became blind for the blind, lame for the lame, a leper for the lepers, suffering in Himself all the fevers and pains which He took away from others? No one had ever such a thought. The meaning is, that He took our sicknesses on His feeling, that He had His heart burdened by the sense of them, that He bore the disgusts of their loathsomeness, and felt their pains over again, in the tenderness of his more than human sensibility. Thus, manifestly, it was that He bare our sicknesses. His very love to us put Him so far in a vicarious relation to them, and made Him so far a partaker in them."

I need scarcely observe that the method here proposed of fixing "beyond question" the *usus loquendi* of the New Testament, in regard to a particular phrase, by one single instance of the use of it, is altogether unwarranted and indefensible. For what is the *usus loquendi* but the ordinary sense in which an expression is understood by certain writers, as ascertained by a careful examination, not of one passage only, but of all the passages in which that expression is employed by them? It is plainly unreasonable, therefore, in Dr Bushnell to single out any " one Scriptural citation," which has no particular claim, that we are able to see, above many others, to the distinction thus conferred upon it, and to apply this solitary citation as a rule by which a great variety of other texts, more or less similar in their phraseology, must be interpreted. All the more unwarranted is such procedure in the present instance, when it is considered that the citation thus applied is very far from being in close or exact analogy to those numerous instances of "vicarious and sacrificial language," the true meaning of which is held to be determined by it. It is not of " *sins*" that the prophet here speaks,* or the evangelist when quoting him, as borne by our Saviour, but of " *griefs* and *sorrows*," of " *infirmities* and *sicknesses*." Doubtless " our sins " were borne by Him as

PART.
I.
SEC. 3.

Reply to Bushnell.

.* The reading of the Septuagint, τὰς ἁμαρτίας ἡμῶν φέρει, has been shown by Magee and Kennicott to be a corruption which has crept into the later copies of that version. See Magee on the Atonement, note xlii.

40 STATEMENTS OF THE NEW TESTAMENT

PART
I.
SEC. 3.

Heb. iv.
15.

Alford on
Matt. viii.
17.

well as these, and are so represented in the succeeding verses of Isaiah's prophecy; but certainly they were not borne by Him in the same sense or in the same manner. Our "sorrows" and "sicknesses" He might make His own by loving sympathy, but He could not in this way be partaker in our "sins." In these, as a sinless man, He surely was incapable of taking part in the way of sympathising with them. For in Himself there was nothing in the least akin, but rather everything uncongenial and abhorrent, to them. Of this we are certified in that most precious text, in which we are taught to rely upon His sympathy, "We have not an high priest which cannot be touched with the feeling of our infirmities, but was in all points tempted like as we are, *yet without sin.*"

Moreover, it is not without much difficulty, if not distortion, that Matthew's citation can be made to convey the sense which Dr Bushnell has ascribed to it. For what was it, according to the evangelist, that our Saviour did, in order that the words of Isaiah might be verified? Was it that He grievously burdened and afflicted Himself in sympathy with those distressed persons who were brought to Him? He may have done so; but of this the evangelist tells us nothing. What we are here told of, as verifying the prophet's words, is not any mere sympathy with human woes which the Saviour felt, but an actual relief or removal of them which He administered. "He *cast out* the spirits with His word, and *healed* all that were sick." "The true relevancy of the prediction, when applied to our Lord's miracles, is probably to be sought by regarding these miracles as typical of the great work of a sin-bearer which He came to accomplish, just as the diseases themselves, which the miracles removed, were so many testimonies to the existence, and so many types of the misery, of sin." Matthew might thus see in the Saviour's miraculous cures the visible signs and sure earnests of the blessed result to which His predicted sufferings should be conducive, and might thus feel himself warranted in applying to the one a prophecy which finds its full accomplishment in the other.

RESPECTING THE ATONEMENT.   41

But, be this as it may, our Lord's tender compassion for PART
the sicknesses and infirmities of those whom He miracu- I.
lously healed, is not to be considered as furnishing any SEC. 3.
key to the import of "all the vicarious language" that is
applied to Him. We say so for this plain and altogether
conclusive reason, that this vicarious language for the
most part has a reference to no sympathetic woes which
He felt for the distresses of others, *but to actual and severe
sufferings with which He was Himself afflicted.* Thus,
when Isaiah represents him as " numbered with the transgressors, and bearing the sin of many," it is in close
connection with the statements—" He was wounded for Isa. liii.
our transgressions, He was bruised for our iniquities;" 5, 7, 12.
" He is brought as a lamb to the slaughter;" " He hath
poured out His soul unto death." When Paul tells us
that " Christ was once offered to bear the sins of many,"
the allusion evidently is to the *one offering of the cross*, as
contrasted in the context with the repeated sacrifices of
the Levitical priesthood. The Apostle Peter speaks of
Him, in like manner, as " bearing our sins in His own body
on the tree," instead of merely bearing them in His own
spirit by the force of sympathy. And the truth is, that
His sympathy with our miseries is only referred to in a
few incidental passages, as constituting one of the bitter
ingredients in His cup of anguish; whereas the passages
are numerous in which there is broad and explicit mention of His personal sufferings, and more particularly
of His ignominious death. So frequently, indeed, is He
spoken of in Scripture as "giving His life a ransom for
many," "justifying us by His blood," "reconciling us to
God by His death," "putting away sin by the sacrifice of
Himself," "bearing our sins in His own body on the tree,"
" once suffering for sins, the just for the unjust, that He
might bring us to God, being put to death in the flesh,
but quickened by the Spirit," and as "washing us from
our sins in His own blood," that a more hopeless attempt
could scarcely be imagined, than to resolve these, and
other expressions of like import, into mere intimations
of the closeness and intensity of feeling with which He

42 STATEMENTS OF THE NEW TESTAMENT

PART
I.
SEC. 3.

Christ
"made
sin" and
"made a
curse for
us."

2 Cor. v.
21.

Gal. iii.
13.

identified Himself with us in our fallen condition, and made our sins and sufferings His own "through the tenderness of His more than human sensibility."

IV. We must now briefly notice two remarkable texts, which are at once so peculiar and so closely parallel that they cannot be well considered apart from one another. The first is Paul's statement to the Corinthians, "He hath made Him to be sin for us who knew no sin, that we might be made the righteousness of God in Him." And the second is the analogous statement of the same apostle to the Galatians, "Christ hath redeemed us from the curse of the law, being made a curse for us"

In the former of these passages some critics propose to read, "He hath made him to be a *sin-offering* for us," as, in their opinion, a better translation of the words in the original. But, without questioning that ἁμαρτία is sometimes used to denote "a sin-offering," we cannot suppose that it is so used in the present instance. For in the clause immediately adjoining—μὴ γνόντα ἁμαρτίαν—it unquestionably denotes "sin." There is, moreover, in this passage, an evident contrast between what "Christ was made for us"—namely, "sin"—and what "we are to be made in Him"—namely, "the righteousness of God." And this contrast would be very much obscured, if not destroyed, by the proposed new translation, "made a sin-offering for us." Still, though on these grounds our common translation is to be preferred, there can be no doubt that the expression is *metonymical*, since it is impossible that Christ, or any person, could be literally made "SIN." The abstract word "sin" must necessarily be held to be here put for some concrete. And there is no concrete that we can think of as denoted by it, except either "a sinner," or "one who bears or suffers for sin." Now, that Christ "was made *a sinner* for us" is inconsistent, not only with the testimony which the Scriptures elsewhere bear to His immaculate holiness, but with the express statement in the adjoining clause, that "He knew no sin." Accordingly, we are shut up to the other interpretation, that Christ was

RESPECTING THE ATONEMENT. 43

"made sin for us" in the sense of being divinely appointed to *bear the burden* or to *suffer the penal consequences* of our transgressions.

PART I. SEC. 3.

In the other passage, the expression, "made a curse for us," must be interpreted according to the same principle. It is a strong metonymical expression, signifying that Christ was "made the bearer of a curse for us," or that He was subjected to the endurance of that condemnation by which God expresses His righteous displeasure against sin, when uttering these words, as quoted in the context, "Cursed is every one who continueth not in all things which are written in the book of the law to do them."

Gal. iii. 10.

The chief thing, however, to be noticed in these texts is, that they evidently represent our Lord's sufferings as *vicarious*. They imply *an interchange of parts* between Him and us—a laying of our burden upon Him, with the view and to the effect of securing our deliverance from it. (1.) He "who knew no sin was made sin," and He in whom the Father was well pleased was "made a curse." (2.) It was "for us"—that is, probably, "instead of us," certainly "on our behalf"—that He was made so. (3) We, who were unrighteous, are "made the righteousness of God in Him;" and we, who were under the curse of the law, are "redeemed from it." (4.) It is in consideration and in consequence of what Christ "was made for us" that we obtain these benefits. In all this we perceive an interchange of parts, which certainly amounts to substitution or vicariousness.

These texts show that Christ's sufferings were vicarious.

If it had been merely said in these texts that Christ "was made sin for us," or "was made a curse for us," we might perhaps have understood the words as signifying only "that He suffered in consequence of our sins," as one person, though innocent, may be involved in the evil consequences of another person's misdeeds. And this certainly could not be considered as substitution. The one party suffers indeed, in such a case, for the sins of the other, but the latter derives no benefit on that account. For though

44   STATEMENTS OF THE NEW TESTAMENT

PART
I.
SEC. 3.

it should so come to pass that he is exempted from the calamitous effects of his own evil doings, yet such exemption is not owing to the sufferings which his evil doings may have entailed on any of his fellow-creatures. And hence those sufferings, in which others are involved by him, are not to be viewed as substitutionary or vicarious. But if to the idea of *sufferings endured on the part of one by whom they were not deserved,* we add the farther idea of *His endurance of them being conducive to the deliverance from sufferings of those by whom they were deserved,* we then make a most important step towards establishing a case of substitution.

Even here, however, there lacks something yet of what is implied in substitutive or vicarious suffering. It not unfrequently happens that men are saved from the merited consequences of their own folly, extravagance, or wickedness, by the generous interposition of a friend, who may ruin his own property, or impair his own health, or lose his own life, in accomplishing their deliverance. The undeserved evils, however, endured by such a deliverer, when seeking to rescue others from the fatal results of their misconduct, may be *merely incidental* to his interposition in their behalf. His suffering these evils may not be in itself considered the *direct and designed* means of securing their exemption from them. But if to the other ideas we add this farther one, that the sufferings endured by him who did not deserve them are *the proper, direct, and purposely adopted* means of averting sufferings from those by whom they were deserved, I know not what else can be deemed necessary to constitute *vicariousness* in the fullest sense of the expression.

Now we have all the three requisites I have referred to most evidently supplied in the two passages under review: (1.) The Lord Jesus Christ, "who knew no sin," "was made sin," and "made a curse for us." Here was the subjection of an innocent person to sufferings, not on His own account, but on account of us sinners. (2.) We are "made the righteousness of God in Him," and are "redeemed by Him from the curse of the law." Here

RESPECTING THE ATONEMENT. 45

is our deliverance from merited sufferings by the interposition of one who endured sufferings which he did not merit. (3.) And then, farther, " *God hath made* Him, who knew no sin, to be sin for us, *that we might be made the righteousness of God in Him ;"* and Christ hath redeemed us from the curse of the law, *being made* a curse for us." Here, lastly, is a *direct and designed connection* stated *between what the Saviour endured and what we are exempted from,*—His sufferings being not merely incidental to His gracious interposition in our behalf, but *the very means* deliberately chosen, and purposely employed, for accomplishing our deliverance.*

---

* There are some judicious remarks on the two texts above discussed in Macdonnell's Donellan Lectures, p. 161-164. There is a defect, however, in the argument founded on them by that very able writer, inasmuch as he takes no account of the *third* particular, above noticed, as essential to vicariousness.

46   STATEMENTS OF THE NEW TESTAMENT

SECTION IV.

PASSAGES WHICH ASCRIBE (5) THE REMOVAL AND RE-
MISSION OF SINS, AND DELIVERANCE FROM THEIR
PENAL CONSEQUENCES, TO THE DEATH OF CHRIST.

PART
I.
SEC. 4.
———
Remission
of sins, and
deliver-
ance from
wrath, by
the death
of Christ.

John, i. 29.

"Lamb of
God" a
sacrificial
title.

V. OUR attention is now claimed by a *fifth* class of passages, in which the *removal* or *remission* of sins, and *deliverance from the wrath* or condemnation due to sin, are
ascribed to the sufferings and death of the Lord Jesus.

1. Thus the Saviour is hailed by John the Baptist in
these words, "Behold the Lamb of God which taketh
away the sin of the world."

Although we are not for the present called to insist on
the *sacrificial import* of the title by which our Lord is here
designated, we cannot refrain from stating three obvious
grounds on which it may be considered as having an
import. (1.) The supposed personal reference of the title
to the lamb-like meekness and innocence of the Saviour,
however suitable it may appear to us who have now the
whole of His history before us, could not have been so
appropriate, or even so intelligible, at the time when the
expression was employed. For Christ was then only
entering on His public ministry ; He had not as yet
openly exhibited any of those lamb-like features of His
character which His subsequent trials brought prominently
into view. And consequently there was as yet no particular reason for directing to Him, as one who was conspicuously marked by these qualities, the special regard
and admiration of all around Him. (2.) The Baptist and
his hearers were Jews, accustomed to the ordinances of

RESPECTING THE ATONEMENT.   47

the ceremonial law, and naturally disposed, when speaking
or hearing of "the Lamb of God," to connect the expression with those sacrificial lambs which were constantly
offered up on the altar to the God of Israel. Nor is it
reasonable to suppose that the crowd who encircled the
Baptist would ever think of attaching to his words a
different meaning. (3.) The latter part of the Baptist's
statement, when he speaks of "the Lamb of God" as
"taking away the sin of the world," evidently shows that
he was referring to the Lord Jesus, not merely as a distinguished pattern of innocence and gentleness, but as the
great propitiatory sacrifice for human guilt.

It is, however, with the import of this latter clause
that we are for the present more particularly concerned.
The full meaning of the expression, ὁ αἴρων, is scarcely
brought out in our authorised translation. The Greek
verb, αἴρω, like its Hebrew equivalent *nasa*, primarily
signifies "to lift up," and secondarily, "to carry away,"
as one lifts up a burden, and then removes it to another
place. No doubt it may be translated "to take away,"
but it strictly means to take away *in one particular manner*
—namely, *by bearing* or *carrying* the thing that is taken
away. And as used in this passage it is highly significant,
implying that Christ took upon Himself the burden of our
sin, and *in this way* removed it from us. The expression,
indeed, as thus applied, is figurative. But it is not on that
account to be stripped of its obvious meaning. We find
it applied to the scape-goat, as "bearing upon him all the
iniquities of Israel into a land not inhabited." And, as
Tittman has shown in his commentary on the passage
before us, it is never used in Scripture to signify "removing
sin by instruction, authority, or example;" but always to
denote "expiating sin" or "bearing its punishment." Besides, however true it may be "that Christ takes away the
sin of the world by His precepts, His example, and His
promises, as tending to aid and encourage men in a life of
holiness," this is not *the* truth which the passage before us
seems to declare. For, certainly, a "lamb" is not the
appropriate emblem of one who "takes away sin" in the

*PART
I.
SEC. 4.*

How does
He take
away sin?

Levit. xvi.
22.

48   STATEMENTS OF THE NEW TESTAMENT

PART
I.
SEC. 4.
——

manner thus alleged. Had the Baptist's words been,
"Behold the Light of the world," or "Behold the great
Prophet and Teacher of righteousness," or "Behold the
Holy One and the Just, who taketh away the sin of the
world," there might have been some greater plausibility
in the suggestion, that "the sin of the world" is here said
to be removed by Him through the influence of His instructions and promises and example. But when His
words are, "Behold the *Lamb of God* which taketh away
the sin of the world," we cannot reasonably suppose that
any other mode of removing sins is indicated, than that of
making expiation or atonement for them. And *in this*
conclusion we are all the more confirmed, when we find

1 Pet. i.
19.

an apostle reminding believers that they were "redeemed
with the precious blood of Christ, as of a lamb without
blemish and without spot," and the saints in heaven represented in the Apocalypse as ascribing praise and worship

Rev. v. 9.

to "the Lamb who was slain, and hath redeemed them to
God by His blood."

2. Again, it is written concerning the Lord Jesus, that,

Heb. ix.
26.

"Now once in the end of the world hath He appeared *to
put away sin by the sacrifice of Himself.*"

Christ
"putting
away sin."

With the sacrificial reference of this passage we are for
the present only concerned in so far as it may throw light
on the apostle's meaning, when he speaks of Christ as
"*putting away sin.*" The word, ἀθέτησις, is in itself
somewhat indefinite in its reference. Whether, as applied
to sin, it expresses the remission of its guilt or the removal
of its pollution, there is nothing in the word itself that
could enable us to determine. The connection, however,
in which it is here used, removes all doubt as to this matter.
For "the sacrifice of Himself," by which Christ "put away
sin," is evidently contrasted in the preceding part of the
chapter, and in the first part of the chapter immediately
following, with those Levitical offerings which were presented by the Jewish priesthood, in respect that *these*,
being incapable of purging the conscience from sin, required to be continually repeated ; whereas the sacrifice of

RESPECTING THE ATONEMENT. 49

Christ required no repetition, inasmuch as it was effectual in securing the remission of sins, "and where remission of these is, there is no more offering for sin." Hence it is plain, that by "putting away sin" we are here to understand *the remission of its guilt and penalty*, to the effect that the sinner, "once purged, shall have no more conscience of sins."

Besides, whatever the "putting away of sin" may mean, it is here expressly said to be something which Christ accomplished "*once by the sacrifice of Himself.*" Now "the sacrifice of Himself" assuredly means *His death*, in whatever sense His death may be called a sacrifice. How, then, can He be said to have "put away sin" *once for all by His death?* Not, surely, in the sense of *delivering men from the enslaving power and moral pollution of sin;* for *this* is a thing which He is *continually and progressively* doing by the preaching of His Word and the agency of His Holy Spirit. As little can He be said to have done so in the sense of *assuring us of God's willingness to forgive our sins;* for, as I formerly observed in reference to another passage, His preaching and miracles and prophecies were, in this respect, equally efficacious with His death;—so that the exclusive, or at least pre-eminent, efficacy attributed to the latter, as the means of removing sin, would, on this supposition, be altogether unaccountable. On these grounds we hold that Christ is here said to have "put away sin by the sacrifice of Himself," in the sense of having thereby secured our *deliverance from the guilt and condemnation* of our transgressions.

3. Another important passage, belonging to the same class, is the statement of our Lord when instituting the Lord's Supper—"This is my blood of the new testament, which is shed for many for the remission of sins."

In these words there is an evident allusion to the ratification of the Levitical covenant by sacrifice, when Moses, having spoken every precept of the law, took the blood of calves and of goats, and sprinkled therewith both the book and all the people, saying, "This is the blood of

PART I. SEC. 4.

He did so by His death

Christ's words at Lord's Supper.
Matt. xxvi. 28.
Sacrificial reference of these words.

50 STATEMENTS OF THE NEW TESTAMENT

PART
I.
SEC. 4.

Exod.
xxiv. 8 :
Heb. ix.
20.

Heb. ix.
22.

the testament which God hath enjoined unto you." The
mention which our Lord made on this occasion of "the
new testament or covenant," naturally and unavoidably
reminds us of that prior covenant which, by the introduction of the new, was dealt with as "old and ready to
vanish away." And when we consider that this old
covenant was inaugurated by the shedding of sacrificial
blood, and that under it "almost all things were purged
with blood, and without shedding of blood there was no
remission," we cannot otherwise understand our Lord's
statement, "This cup is my blood of the new testament,
which is shed for many for the remission of sins," than as
a deliberate and solemn declaration, that *the shedding of
His blood was an expiatory sacrifice*, analogous in nature,
though of far superior efficacy, to those offerings which
were enjoined under the Levitical system.

Christ's
blood
shed for
remission
of sins.

Apart, however, from the sacrificial import of this passage, there is contained in it a clear and emphatic assurance that the blood of Jesus "was shed for the remission
of sins "—an assurance which, when we take into account
the peculiar circumstances in which it was uttered,—on
the occasion of instituting a rite which was to form an
essential part of Christian worship until the end of time,
—must needs be received by us according to its plain
meaning, as intended to convey, in explicit and intelligible
language, a great truth of paramount interest and import-

Not to be
explained
away as a
rhetorical
figure.

ance. The theory of those who would fain account for all
the atoning efficacy attributed to the death of Christ by
a "*rhetorical use of figures* taken from the Levitical ordinances, by way of adapting the Gospel to Jewish customs
and modes of thought," is utterly inadmissible when
applied to such a passage as this. How little, indeed,
there is in our Lord's recorded dealings with any class of
the Jewish people that should lead us to expect of Him
a concession to their prejudices, or an accommodation of
His doctrine to their views and customs, we may safely
leave it to any candid reader of the evangelical narratives
to decide. But even if there were reasonable grounds for
expecting of Him any such thing under other circum-

RESPECTING THE ATONEMENT.

stances, there is assuredly no room for it in the present instance. For, as has been well observed by an able writer, "We have here no rhetorical speech before a multitude, no apology for Christianity addressed to unbelieving Jews, who might be soothed by hearing the obnoxious tenets of the new faith clothed in imagery borrowed from the ritual they so blindly reverenced. The solemnity of the occasion, the character of the audience, the brevity of the words—above all, the fact that our Lord was now dealing with no temporary emergency, but appointing an ordinance intended for all ages and nations —alike forbid the supposition that He could have used any figure borrowed from the Jewish ritual, *unless it were the very fittest that could be found to embody His real meaning.* The apostles, as we are constantly reminded by our figurative interpreters, were Jews, strongly wedded to sacrificial language and ceremonies. Doubtless they were. And for that very reason they could only have understood their Master's words in accordance with their previous education. And our Lord, for the same reason, must have used the words just because He knew that they would so understand them, and because He wished and intended them to do so. If He did not mean to say that His death was an expiatory sacrifice, and that it was intended to procure remission of sins, just as the Jews expected certain blessings from the sin-offerings prescribed by the law of Moses—then He was using language which, as He must have known, was sure to be misunderstood by those who heard Him, and through them to mislead every Christian Church which should afterwards receive the Gospel from their lips."

Margin: PART I. SEC. 4. Macdonnell's Donellan Lectures, p. 75, 76.

4. Another text which conveys substantially the same truth is that declaration of St John, that "the blood of Jesus Christ His Son cleanseth us from all sin."

Margin: 1 John, i. 7.

Alford, indeed, and some others, insist that the "cleansing from all sin" here referred to is not the remission of its guilt, but *purification from its moral pollution.* It can scarcely be doubted, however, that "the blood of Christ,"

Margin: Christ's blood cleanseth from all sin.

52 STATEMENTS OF THE NEW TESTAMENT

PART I. SEC. 4.

by which the "cleansing" is said to be accomplished, indicates here, as elsewhere, His blood *shed in sacrifice*, and consequently, that the forgiveness of sins is the benefit more immediately secured by it. Besides, it cannot be said of any believer, however far advanced in the Christian life, while he remains on earth, that he is "cleansed from *all* sin" in the sense of being perfectly sanctified. His justification is complete so soon as he truly believes in Christ · but his sanctification is gradual and progressive. Accordingly, notwithstanding the statement here made, that "the blood of Jesus cleanseth us from all sin," the apostle declares in the verse immediately following, that "if we say that we have no sin, we deceive ourselves, and the truth is not in us." Farther, that the "forgiveness of sin" was present to the apostle's mind when he spake of the cleansing efficacy of the blood of Christ, is

1 John, i. 9.

evident from what he goes on to say—that "if we confess our sins, He is faithful and just *to forgive us our sins*, and to cleanse us from all unrighteousness;" as well as from

1 John, ii. 1, 2.

what he adds a few verses thereafter, that "if any man sin, we have an advocate with the Father, Jesus Christ the righteous; and He is the propitiation for our sins, and not for ours only, but also for the sins of the whole world."

5. Of the many other texts which set forth the same doctrine, it may be sufficient to quote the following, without commenting on them: "It behoved Christ to suffer,

Luke, xxiv. 46, 47

and to rise from the dead the third day; and that repentance and *remission of sins* should be preached in His name

Acts, x. 43; xiii. 38, 39.

among all nations." "Through His name, whosoever believeth in Him shall receive *remission of sins*." "Through this Man is preached unto you the *forgiveness of sins ;* and by Him all that believe are justified from all things from which ye could not be justified by the law of Moses."

Eph. i. 6, 7.

"He hath made us accepted in the Beloved, in whom we have redemption through His blood, *the forgiveness of*

Col. i 13, 14.

sins, according to the riches of His grace." "Who hath delivered us from the power of darkness, and hath trans-

RESPECTING THE ATONEMENT. 53

lated us into the kingdom of His dear Son ; in whom we
have redemption through His blood, even *the forgiveness
of sins.*" "Unto Him that loved us, and washed us from
our sins in His own blood, and hath made us kings and
priests unto God and His Father ; to Him be glory and
dominion for ever and ever."

In all these passages, "forgiveness" or "remission of
sins" is ascribed to the mediation of Jesus Christ, and in
all but two of them it is specially ascribed to His "blood"
or death.

6. Closely akin to the texts above adduced are those in
which the mediatorial work of Christ, and in particular
His sufferings, are represented as securing our *deliverance
from the penal consequences of sin.*

One of the most notable of these is His own statement
to Nicodemus : "As Moses lifted up the serpent in the
wilderness, even so must the Son of Man be lifted up, that
whosoever believeth in Him should not perish, but have
eternal life. For God so loved the world, that He gave
His only-begotten Son, that whosoever believeth in Him
should not perish, but have everlasting life. For God sent
not His Son into the world to condemn the world, but
that the world through Him might be saved."

Without entering on other topics suggested by these
verses, it is sufficient for our present purpose to advert to
the great truth, too obviously affirmed in them to be overlooked, that the purpose of our Lord's divine mission into
the world was to save men from the "condemnation"
which they had merited, and to rescue them from the per-
dition which they had incurred. I may only farther
observe, that there seems to be here a reference to His
own endurance of sufferings and death upon the cross as
the means by which this deliverance was to be accomplished. For when He says that "the Son of Man must
be *lifted up,* that whosoever believeth in Him should not
perish," we can hardly fail to see in these words a counterpart to another of His memorable sayings—"I, if I be
lifted up from the earth, will draw all men unto me."—con-

*PART
I.
SEC. 4.*

Rev. i. 5,
6.

Christ
saves from
penalties
of sin.

Believers
in Christ
shall not
perish.

John, iii.
14-17.

John, xii.
32, 33.

54 STATEMENTS OF THE NEW TESTAMENT

PART
I.
SEC. 4.

No con-
demnation
to those
who are
in Christ.
Rom. viii.
1 3, 4

Redemp-
tion from
curse of
law.
Gal. iii. 13.

cerning which we are expressly told by the evangelist that "this He said, signifying what death He should die."

The same truth is taught in Paul's statement to the Romans, "There is now no condemnation to them that are in Christ Jesus," followed as it is in the context by these words : " For what the law could not do, in that it was weak through the flesh, God, sending His own Son in the likeness of sinful flesh, and for sin, condemned sin in the flesh ; that the righteousness of the law might be fulfilled in us, who walk not after the flesh, but after the Spirit." Here we are assured that " to them who are in Christ Jesus "—that is to say, who are united to Him by faith—"there is now no condemnation." And if it be asked how this should be the case—the answer suggested is, that *our sin has been condemned in Christ.* The law was "weak through the flesh "—in other words, it was impotent to deliver us either from the guilt or from the power of sin, by reason of the corruption of our nature, which rendered us incapable of satisfying its requirements. But having regard to this impotency of the law, " God sent His own Son in the likeness of sinful flesh," although Himself sin-less, and "*for sin* "—that is, for the expiation of sin. Thus did He " condemn sin in the flesh "—namely, in the flesh of His own incarnate Son. And sin was thus condemned in Him in order " that the righteousness of the law might be fulfilled in us ; " or that its righteous demands might be satisfied in our behalf, who show the reality of our union with the Saviour, and our consequent interest in His mediatorial work, by "walking not after the flesh, but after the Spirit." Accordingly, "there is to us no condemnation," inasmuch as Christ has paid the penalty which our sins had incurred.

Another text of the like import is Paul's statement to the Galatians, which has been already noticed in a former section, that "Christ hath redeemed us from the curse of the law, being made a curse for us." And two similar passages occur in the First Epistle of the same apostle to

RESPECTING THE ATONEMENT.   55

the Thessalonians, in one of which believers are described
as " waiting for the Son of God from heaven, whom He
raised from the dead, even Jesus, who *delivered us from
the wrath to come;* " while in the other we are told that
" God hath *not appointed us to wrath, but to obtain salvation* by our Lord Jesus Christ, who died for us." ‗ In both
of these texts the Lord Jesus Christ is represented as "our
deliverer from wrath "—that is to say, from the righteous
displeasure with which God regards sin, and by which He
is moved to inflict its threatened penalties.   And in the
latter text, " our appointment, not to wrath, but to obtain
salvation," is closely connected with the Saviour's "dying
for us."   This connection, though plainly enough stated
in our English translation, is still more explicitly brought
out in the original; for the form of expression there employed is, διὰ τοῦ κυρίου ἡμῶν Ἰησοῦ Χριστοῦ, τοῦ
ἀποθανόντος ὑπὲρ ἡμῶν, which has the force of the well-
known Latin phrase *quippe qui*, and indicates that we
" obtain salvation through Jesus Christ, *inasmuch as* He
died for us," or "*in respect that* He died for us."

PART
I.
SEC. 4.
———
1 Thess. i.
10; v. 9,
10.
Christ our
deliverer
from
wrath.

… 56 STATEMENTS OF THE NEW TESTAMENT

SECTION V.

PASSAGES WHICH ASCRIBE (6) JUSTIFICATION AND (7) REDEMPTION TO THE DEATH OF CHRIST.

PART I. SEC. 5.
Justification through Christ.

VI. THERE are some passages of Scripture, worthy of especial remark, in which the sufferings and death of Jesus Christ are evidently set forth *as a ground of justification.*

Thus, in the fifty-third chapter of Isaiah, which is frequently applied to our Lord in the New Testament, we

Isa. liii. 11. are told that " by His knowledge shall my righteous servant justify many, for He shall bear their iniquities." In

Rom. v. 8, 9. the Epistle to the Romans it is written : "God commendeth His love toward us, in that, while we were yet sinners, Christ died for us ; much more, then, being now justified by His blood, we shall be saved from wrath through Him." In another passage of the same Epistle we are said to be

Rom. iii. 24-26. " justified freely by the grace of God through the redemption that is in Christ Jesus, whom God hath set forth to be a propitiation through faith in His blood, to declare His righteousness, . . . that He might be just, and the justifier of Him who believeth in Jesus." And to the same

2 Cor. v. 21. effect St Paul declares to the Corinthians, that " God hath made Him to be sin for us, who knew no sin, that we might be made (or become, $\gamma\epsilon\nu\dot\omega\mu\epsilon\theta a$) the righteousness of God in Him."

It cannot be gainsaid that in these passages sinners are said to be "justified by the blood of Christ," or by the sufferings He endured on their behalf when He " bare their iniquities," or was " made to be sin for them ;" while in one of the passages it is expressly affirmed that " He was set forth to be a propitiation through faith in His blood,"

RESPECTING THE ATONEMENT. 57

for the purpose of "declaring the righteousness of God," PART or in order "that God might be the justifier of him that SEC. 5. believeth in Jesus," consistently with His being a "just" or righteous God.

What, then, is justification? In other words, what is it What is that God is to be considered as doing when He "justifies justifica-tion? us through the redemption that is in Christ"? Does He, as some affirm, "infuse righteousness into us," or "make us personally righteous" by a change of moral character? Or does He, as is maintained by others, "account us or receive us as righteous" to the effect of changing our legal condition in relation to Himself?

That the *latter* is the true meaning of the word as used in the New Testament, and especially in St Paul's writings, we hold to be sufficiently clear on the following grounds : (1.) Justification is opposed to *condemnation ;* as when it is A forensic written, "Therefore as by the offence of one judgment or judicial act. came upon all men to condemnation, even so by the Rom. v. righteousness of one the free gift came upon all men unto 18. justification of life ;" and again, "Who shall lay anything Rom. viii. to the charge of God's elect? It is God that justifieth ; 33, 34. who is he that condemneth?" (2.) Justification is spoken of as equivalent to the forgiveness of iniquities," and Rom. iv. "the imputation of righteousness without works." (3.) St 6, 7. Paul thinks it necessary to vindicate the doctrine of justi-fication by faith alone from the charge of " making void Rom. iii. the law," and encouraging men to "continue in sin ;" 31 ; vi. 1. whereas it is palpably evident that his doctrine could not for a moment be deemed liable to any such objection, if justification were a change of moral character by which sinful men are made personally righteous.

On these grounds we hold that the justification of a sinner is what has been called "a forensic or judicial act," by which he is " accounted or received as righteous in the sight of God." When so regarded, it undoubtedly includes *the pardon of sin* as one of its essential elements. But this is not all. Offenders may be pardoned, so as to be no longer liable to punishment, without being at the same time

58   STATEMENTS OF THE NEW TESTAMENT

PART
I.
SEC. 5.
——

received into favour, admitted to confidence and fellowship,
and placed in a position of honour and of privilege. Not
so is it, however, when believers are "justified through the
redemption that is in Christ Jesus." It is not merely
pardon which they obtain from "God who justifieth," but
favour and *acceptance* ; not only an exemption from the
penalties of sin, but a title to the rewards of righteousness.

John, v.
24.

Accordingly, it is written of believers that "they have
everlasting life, and shall not come into condemnation, but

Tit. iii. 7.

are passed from death unto life ;" that "being justified by
the grace of God, they are made heirs according to the

Rom. v.
1. 2.

hope of eternal life ;" and again, that "being justified by
faith, they have peace with God through our Lord Jesus
Christ ; by whom also they have access by faith into this
grace wherein they stand, and rejoice in hope of the glory
of God."

Such is the great Christian privilege of justification.
And, as we have seen, this privilege is expressly said, in
the class of passages now under consideration, to have

Justifica-
tion ascrib-
ed to obe-
dience of
Christ.

been procured for us by the sufferings and death of Christ.
It is true there are other passages in which the same
privilege is ascribed to the Saviour's "*righteousness*" or

Rom. v.
18, 19.

"*obedience*,"—as, for example, where it is thus written :
" Therefore as by the offence of one judgment came upon
all men to condemnation ; even so by the *righteousness* of
one the free gift came upon all men unto justification of
life : for as by one man's disobedience many were made
sinners, so *by the obedience of one* shall many be made
righteous." There is no real conflict, however, between
the two statements. For it must be remembered that *the*

Philip. ii.
8.

death of our Lord was the crowning act or *consummation*
of His obedience, when, as it is written, " He became *obedient*
unto death, even the death of the cross ; " and that, on the
other hand, *His perfect obedience to the divine will* must be
taken into account in any conception we can form of Him
as our substitute, suffering vicariously, " *the just for the*
unjust."

It has been customary with theologians to distinguish

RESPECTING THE ATONEMENT. 59

between the "active" and the "passive obedience" of our
Saviour, ascribing to the latter our exemption from the
penalties of sin, and to the former our attainment of the
rewards of righteousness. The distinction is not very
happily expressed, since much of what is called the "active
obedience" of Christ was *passive*, consisting of the endurance of unmerited affliction ; while His "passive obedience,"
as it is termed, was truly *active*, as being a voluntary fulfilment of His Father's will. At the same time, the distinction is intelligible, and may be serviceable in the way of
illustrating the relation which subsists between the constituent elements of Christ's righteousness and those of a
sinner's justification, as well as the relation which both of
these may be held to bear to the law of God at once in
its penal and in its perceptive requirements. It must ever
be remembered, however, that the two things, thus distinguishable in thought, are *in fact* inseparably connected,
and that they form together that *"one righteousness"* of
Christ which is no more capable of being divided than
Christ Himself, and which constitutes the ground of our
being freely pardoned, and accepted or accounted as
righteous in the sight of God.

Some writers, not content with drawing the above distinction, have raised and keenly agitated the question,
whether the *active* as well as the *passive* obedience of Christ
is embraced in the atonement ? This is very much a mere
verbal controversy. If the word "atonement" be taken
in the limited sense which in popular usage is commonly
attached to it, as signifying only that aspect or department
of our Lord's mediatorial work which has reference to our
deliverance from the penalties of sin, there is then considerable plausibility in the opinion that His sufferings alone
are properly comprehended in it. And yet, even in that
case, it ought not to be forgotten that, apart from His perfect obedience to His Father's will, the sufferings of Christ
would not have possessed the character—essential to their
expiatory virtue—of sufferings, wholly unmerited by Himself, endured by a perfectly pure and righteous substitute
in the room of sinners. But if, on the other hand, the word

*PART
I.
SEC. 5.*

Distinction
between
Christ's
active and
passive
obedience.

Rom. v. 18,
margin.

Is our
Lord's
active obe-
dience em-
braced in
the atone-
ment ?

60   STATEMENTS OF THE NEW TESTAMENT

PART
I.
SEC. .5.

"atonement" be understood as comprehending *the whole* of the Saviour's mediatorial work, in its reference alike to our deliverance from the merited wrath, and our restoration to the undeserved favour, of God, with all the privileges and blessings thence accruing to us—or even if we keep in view that the atonement was made by Him, not only for sins of trespass or transgression, but also for sins of shortcoming or omission—then, beyond all doubt, the "active obedience" of Christ, no less than His sufferings, ought to be included in it.   The truth seems to be, that what have been commonly called the "active" and the "passive obedience" of our Lord are jointly concurrent parts of one perfect and finished work, which, though in some respects capable of being distinguished, are neither in themselves, nor in respect of the benefits they secure, to be separated from one another.*

Redemption by the death of Christ.

VII. We must now advert to an important class of passages, in which the sufferings of Christ are represented under the figure of a *price* or *ransom,* and the beneficial result which they have secured, under the corresponding figure of a *purchase* or *redemption.*

Of these passages—some of which have already received a partial notice in connection with other topics—the following may be taken as a sufficient specimen :—

Matt. xx. 28.

"The Son of Man is come, not to be ministered unto but to minister, and to give His life a ransom for many."

Acts, xx. 28.

"Feed the Church of God" (or of the Lord) "which He hath purchased with His own blood."   "All have sinned and

Rom. iii. 23, 24.

come short of the glory of God, being justified freely by His grace through the redemption that is in Christ Jesus ; whom God hath set forth to be a propitiation through faith in His blood."   "Ye are not your own, for ye are bought

1 Cor. vi. 19.

with a price ; therefore glorify God in your body and in

Gal. iii. 13; iv. 4, 5.

your spirit, which are God's."   "Christ hath redeemed us from the curse of the law, being made a curse for us."

Eph. i. 7 ; Col. i. 14.

"God sent forth His Son, made of a woman, made under the law, to redeem them that were under the law."   "In

---

* See Appendix. Note C.

RESPECTING THE ATONEMENT. 61

whom we have redemption through His blood, the forgiveness of sins." "There is one God, and one Mediator
between God and men, the man Christ Jesus, who gave
Himself a ransom for all." "Who gave Himself for us,
that He might redeem us from all iniquity, and purify
unto Himself a peculiar people, zealous of good works."
"Neither by the blood of goats and calves, but by His
own blood He entered in once into the holy place, having
obtained eternal redemption for us." "Ye were not redeemed with corruptible things, as silver and gold, from
your vain conversation received by tradition from your
fathers; but with the precious blood of Christ, as of a
lamb, without blemish and without spot." "Thou wast
slain, and hast redeemed us to God by Thy blood out of
every kindred, and tongue, and people, and nation."

The language employed in these passages is figurative;
and, like all figurative language, it is not to be held as
indicating a strictly exact and circumstantial conformity
between the subject to which it is literally applicable, and
the analogous subject which it is used to illustrate. Moreover, it does not appear that the figure we are now concerned with is taken from *any one* of those processes of
"redemption" which are ordinarily to be met with in the
transactions of men, but from a *variety* of such processes,
differing from one another in their minute details, while
all of them present some great general features of analogy
to the mediatorial work of Jesus Christ. Sometimes the
allusion is to the *payment of a debt*, as in those passages
in which "redemption" is identified with the "remission
of sins." Sometimes the *liberation of a slave or captive* is
the thing referred to, as when Christ is said to have "given
Himself a *ransom* for all," or to have "given His life a
ransom for many." Sometimes the reference is, not to the
restored liberties and privileges of those who have been
redeemed, but to the *recovered right to the possession of
them* that has been acquired by the person redeeming
them, as when we are said to be "redeemed unto God,"
and to be "not our own, being bought with a price." But
amidst all this diversity of reference (which ought of itself

Side notes:
PART I.
SEC. 5.

1 Tim. ii. 5, 6.

Tit. ii. 14.

Heb. ix. 12.

1 Pet. i. 18, 19.

Rev. v. 9.

This language figurative.

It alludes to various human transactions.

62   STATEMENTS OF THE NEW TESTAMENT

PART I. SEC. 5.

to guard us against overstraining the figure) there is one thing that is constantly and prominently kept in view— and that is, *the payment* made for our redemption. The debt—when it is redemption from debt that is referred to—is not simply cancelled, but liquidated and fully discharged. The bondman—when it is redemption from bondage that is referred to—is not liberated, either by conquest or by a gratuitous act of manumission, but in consideration of a ransom given for Him. And the alienated possession is not freely restored, but is bought back by its original owner " with a price."

The payment of a price is the main point of the analogy.

This is undoubtedly the main point of analogy which the figurative expressions under review are meant to indicate. And farther than this we are not warranted to press their import, by attempting to trace in the work of Christ an exact conformity to everything that is done in human acts of redemption.

Overstraining of the figure by the Fathers.

Such an attempt was made by not a few of those ancient writers who are commonly called the "Fathers." Arbitrarily confining the reference of the figure to the single case of the liberation of a slave or captive, and straining this limited application of it to the uttermost, they held our "redemption" to imply, not only the payment of a price in order to our deliverance, but also *the reception of this price by some enemy or oppressor* by whom we were held in bondage. And inasmuch as Satan is the great enemy, from whose thraldom Christ has set us free, they did not shrink from affirming that the sacrifice of Christ was a ransom paid in our behalf to the Evil One! And in order to account for Satan's acceptance of this ransom, to the effect of overthrowing his own dominion, they held that an imposition was put upon him by means of our Lord's incarnation, which led him to suppose that Christ would remain in his power if once given up to him. Indeed it was a favourite saying with some of the Fathers, that " the human nature of Christ was the bait which allured the devil ; while the divine nature, concealed under it, was the hook by which he was caught!" The gross absurdity and impiety of such a notion may well be regarded by us as a warn-

Hagenbach's History of Doctrines, vol. i. § 68, and 134.

RESPECTING THE ATONEMENT.   63

ing against the too minute interpretation of Scriptural
metaphors.

It is not by any means clear, however, that the figure
in question, though fully carried out, must necessarily
lead to any such absurd consequence as the Fathers drew
from it.   For our enthralment under the bondage of Satan
is not parallel to the case of a captive taken in war, for
whose liberation the captor may demand a ransom.   Our
captivity to Satan is *judicial*, and is only a secondary consequence of our subjection to the wrath of God.   Our
enslaving foe is but, as it were, the subordinate instrument
or executioner of God's righteous judgment.   The grand
requisite to our deliverance from his thraldom is, that the
sovereign Judge should cancel or revoke our sentence.
And therefore it is to Him, and not to Satan, that the
ransom is due.

It is not necessary, however, nor is it expedient, to
deduce *more* from the figurative language under review
than the grand prominent truth which it was obviously
meant to convey, that our salvation is accomplished by
a *process of commutation* analogous to the payment of a
ransom.   But *less* than this truth it is impossible to deduce
from it, without utterly destroying the significancy of the
metaphor.

It has, indeed, been urged that the word " redemption "
is often used in a loose and general sense, to signify
" deliverance " without respect to any equivalent rendered
for it.   But this statement, though perfectly true, is quite
inapplicable to the case before us.   For *here* we have not
merely the use of the word " redemption," as descriptive
of our deliverance from the evils of our sinful condition,
but the most distinct and pointed reference, in almost all
the passages in which it is so employed, to " *a price* " by
which the redemption is secured.   And this reference to
" a price " we cannot possibly ignore, without setting ourselves in downright opposition to the plainly declared
meaning of the oracles of God.   " When a Greek author,
in narrating the release of a prisoner, speaks repeatedly of
λύτρα or ἄποινα, as Homer does in the First Book of the

PART
I.
SEC. 5.
——

The ele-
ment of *a
price* essen-
tial to our
redemp-
tion.

Hill's Lec-
tures in
Divinity,
ii. 483.

64   STATEMENTS OF THE NEW TESTAMENT

PART I. SEC. 5.

'Iliad,' it cannot be supposed that the redemption which he thus describes is a simple discharge without equivalent or compensation. Every one feels the effect of introducing the nouns λύτρον or ἀντίλυτρον, in connection with the verb λύω, when applied to the case of a discharged debtor or released captive, as making it perfectly clear that his redemption is not gratuitous, but that some consideration is given for the securing of it. Nor is the significancy of these nouns in the least diminished when it is from penal consequences of a judicial nature that a person is released. The λύτρον, indeed, in that case, is not a price from which the lawgiver is to receive any personal advantage. It is the satisfaction to public law and justice upon which he consents to remit the sentence. But still, the mention of it, in this case as well as in the others, is absolutely inconsistent with a gratuitous remission."

SECTION VI.

PASSAGES WHICH SPEAK (8) OF RECONCILIATION TO
GOD BY THE DEATH OF CHRIST, AND WHICH (9)
REPRESENT HIS DEATH AS A PROPITIATION FOR
SIN.

VIII. AN eighth class of passages worthy of especial notice, are those in which *reconciliation to God* is attributed to the sufferings of Jesus Christ.

"Reconciliation," in its fullest sense, is *mutual.* It implies a change from enmity to friendship *in both of the parties* between whom it is brought about. In particular instances of the use of the expression, however, there may be a more especial reference to one of the alienated parties rather than to the other. And hence the question arises, *Which of the two is more especially referred to as the party conciliated*, in those passages which speak of the reconciliation between God and man through the sufferings of Jesus Christ?

This question will be most satisfactorily answered by a careful examination of the passages themselves. But before proceeding to answer it in this manner, it is necessary to advert to some general arguments, by which it has been attempted to show, that "reconciliation to God," as ascribed in Scripture to our Lord's sufferings, *must*, in all cases, refer exclusively to *the removal of our enmity against God.*

(1.) It is urged, for example, that "there is nothing on the part of God, at all answering to enmity, that needs to be conciliated."

To this we may simply reply by appealing to those

[marginal notes:]
PART I.
SEC. 6.

Reconciliation through sufferings of Christ.

Is God or man the party conciliated?

This question must be determined by the texts which speak of the subject.

Allegation, that God does not need to be reconciled, disproved

66 STATEMENTS OF THE NEW TESTAMENT

PART I.
SEC. 6.
—
by Scripture.
Ps. vii. 11;
xxiv. 16.
Isa. lix. 2.
Rom. i. 18.
These texts though figurative, are clear and forcible notwithstanding.

passages of Scripture which tell us that "God is angry with the wicked every day"—that "the face of the Lord is against them that do evil"—that "our iniquities have separated between us and our God, and our sins have hid His face from us, that He will not hear"—and that "the wrath of God is revealed from heaven against all ungodliness and unrighteousness of men." It avails nothing to say that these are figurative modes of expression, applied to God after the manner of men. Allow that they are so, this does not destroy their meaning. Men do not employ figures to *obscure* or *weaken* the import of their statements; but, on the contrary, *to make it clearer and more forcible.* And hence, when the inspired writers denounce the "wrath," and "hatred," and "vengeance" of God against wickedness, their evident purpose is to make us see more clearly, and feel more deeply, that there is *somewhat on the part of God* opposing the reception of sinners into His favour, which may be most fitly depicted by comparing it to those dispositions and feelings of the human heart, under which in these figurative expressions it is represented. Most certainly, when God is said to be " angry with sinners," it would be a gross outrage on all reasonable principles of interpretation to affirm, that what is figuratively called "anger" in such a statement exists, *not at all on the part of God against sinners, but solely and entirely on the part of sinners against God;* or, in other words, that it is not He who is said (figuratively) to be angry with sinners, but sinners who are said to be angry with Him! In like manner, when Isaiah ·uses these

Isa. xii. 1. words, "O Lord, I will praise Thee; though Thou wast angry with me, Thine anger is turned away," no fair interpreter would understand the prophet as expressing thankfulness *that he himself had laid aside his disaffection toward God,* and not that God had mercifully turned away what is figuratively styled "His anger" from the prophet. Let every reasonable qualification be applied to such statements, on the score of their being conveyed in figurative language, it must still be allowed *that they have a definite meaning,* such as we are capable of apprehending

RESPECTING THE ATONEMENT.   67

and appreciating. And that meaning evidently must be
somewhat that pertains *to God*, some barrier on *His* part
that needs to be removed in order that sinners may be
reinstated in His favour. Now, if there be anything pertaining to God in relation to sinners that can, however
figuratively, be designated as " wrath " or " anger,"—anything, the removal of which can be, however figuratively,
expressed by " being pacified " or " having His anger
turned away,"—there must then be full scope and urgent
necessity, not only for sinners being, on their part, reconciled to God, but also for God being, on his part, reconciled to sinners.

(2.) Further, it has been argued, that the reconciliation
between God and man, which the Scriptures ascribe to
the sufferings of Jesus Christ, must have reference exclusively to the removal of *man's* enmity, inasmuch as *God
Himself is the author and promoter of it*, so that His wrath,
if He ever had any, must have been pacified, before He
could, by the gift of His own Son, have afforded us so
rich a token of His loving-kindness.

Allegation that God is not the party to be reconciled, as being Himself the author of the scheme of grace.

In meeting this plausible, but really superficial, objection, it is not necessary that we should ignore the precious
truth, so plainly set forth in the pages of the New Testament, that God is the prime mover in the scheme of reconciliation, and that the Savour's death, instead of being
the means of inducing an otherwise implacable God to
have compassion on us, is the brightest proof of God's
pre-existing compassion and love that could have been
displayed to us. It is only necessary that we keep in
view the obvious distinction between *personal resentment*
and *judicial condemnation*. Whatever obstacles there may
have been to reconciliation with sinners on the part of
God, it is certain that these obstacles cannot have consisted in any such thing as *implacability or vindictiveness,*
rendering Him personally unwilling to be at peace with
them. *This* would undoubtedly be incompatible with His
actual procedure, in having Himself devised the method
of reconciliation. Still there may surely have been obstacles of *another kind,* arising from a sense of what was

Obstacles to reconciliation on the part of God not personal but judicial.

PART
I.
SEC. 6.

68   STATEMENTS OF THE NEW TESTAMENT

PART
I.
SEC. 6.

indispensably due to the claims of His justice, the obligation of His law, the authority and majesty of His government.   However well disposed to be at peace with sinners,
there may have been wise and good reasons, on account
of which His friendship could be restored to them *only in
the particular way* which He has Himself been pleased to
appoint for that purpose.   We have a case in point at the

Job. xlii.
7, 8.

conclusion of the Book of Job, where " The Lord said to
Eliphaz, My wrath is kindled against thee, and against
thy two friends ; for ye have not spoken of me the thing
that is right, as my servant Job hath.   Therefore take unto
you now seven bullocks and seven rams, and go to my
servant Job, and offer up for yourselves a burnt-offering ;
and my servant Job shall pray for you, for him will I
accept ; lest I deal with you after your folly, in that ye
have not spoken of me the thing which is right."   In this
case it is evident that God needed to be reconciled to
Eliphaz and his two friends ; for He expressly says, that
" His wrath was kindled against them, " and that a certain
prescribed course must be followed by them, " lest He
should deal with them according to their folly. "   And yet
it is equally undeniable, on the other hand, that God was
willing and ready to be at peace with them, inasmuch as
He Himself prescribes, and urges them to adopt, the
means of reconciliation.   Even so is it with that great propitiation by which sinful men are restored to the divine
favour.   God is not the less to be considered as requiring
it, for the satisfaction of His justice and the honour of
His law, that He has, of His unspeakable goodness, been
pleased to provide it.

Turretine,
De' Satis-
factionis
Christi
veritate,
Part I.
sec. 50.

" To us, indeed, " as Turretine has well observed, " it
seems hard to conceive that the same person who is
offended with us should also love us ; because, when any
affection takes possession of us, we are apt to be wholly
engrossed with it.   Thus, if our anger is inflamed against
any one, there is usually no room in us for favour towards
him ; and, on the other hand, if we regard him with
favour, there is often along with it the most unrighteous
indulgence.   But if we could cast off the disorders of

RESPECTING THE ATONEMENT.

passion, and clothe ourselves in the garments of righteous-ness, we might easily harmonise these things with one another. A father, offended with the frowardness of his son, loves him as a son, but yet is angry with him as being froward. A judge, in like manner, may be angry and moved to punish, yet, not the less on that account, in-clined by love to pardon the offender, if only some one would stand forth and be security for him. Why then should not God, who is most righteous and excellent, at once, by reason of His justice, demand punishment, and, by reason of His mercy, provide satisfaction for us?"

(3.) Again, it is argued that the "reconciliation" which the Scriptures speak of must have reference exclusively to the removal of man's enmity, because *God* is nowhere said in Scripture to be "*reconciled to us* by the death of Christ," but everywhere *we* are said to be "*reconciled to God.*"

This argument will be most satisfactorily dealt with when we proceed to the consideration of those passages of Scripture which contain the expression under dispute. In the meanwhile it may be sufficient to observe, that there is nothing in the mere form of this expression, apart from the connection in which it is introduced, to determine whether it has a more especial reference to the removal of God's judicial displeasure with sinful men, or to the reclaiming of sinners from their enmity against God. No doubt, when we find one person spoken of as "reconciled to another person," it may seem the most natural con-struction of such a statement to regard the *former*, who is said to be "reconciled," as the party whose wrath is re-moved, and whose friendship is conciliated. But yet there are some striking instances that may be adduced, in which the circumstances of the case render it indispensable that such a statement should be taken in the very opposite sense—namely, as indicating that the person whose anger is removed is not he who is said to be reconciled, but the other person. Thus our Lord says, in His Sermon on the Mount, "If thou bring thy gift to the altar, and there re-memberest *that thy brother hath aught against thee*, leave

PART I. SEC. 6.

Objection, that God is not said "to be reconciled to us," but "we to Him"—answered.

Matt. v. 23, 24.

70   STATEMENTS OF THE NEW TESTAMENT

**PART
I.
SEC. 6.**

there thy gift before the altar and go thy way; first *be reconciled* to thy brother, and then come and offer thy gift." The case here supposed is not that of *our having some cause of complaint against our brother*, but the opposite case of *our brother having some cause of complaint against us*. And hence the exhortation, "Be reconciled to thy brother"—διαλλάγηθι τῷ ἀδελφῷ σου—must necessarily signify, "*conciliate or appease* thy brother," inasmuch as *he* is the aggrieved or offended party. It cannot possibly mean, "Lay aside thine enmity against thy brother." It must, on the contrary, mean, "Strive to persuade thy brother to lay aside his resentment against thee." Indeed it would not be necessary for us to "leave our gift before the altar, and to go our way," in order to lay aside *our own* anger. *This* might be done *at once*, without leaving the altar; and it could not be done too soon; whereas it *would* be requisite to go to our offended brother, with the view of endeavouring, by suitable apologies or explanations, to remove his cause of offence.

In like manner, in the Septuagint version of the Book of Samuel, we read that, when David had fled from the wrath of Saul and joined himself to the Philistines, the princes of that people said respecting him, "Let not David go down with us to battle, lest in the battle he be an adversary to us. For *wherewith should* he reconcile himself to his master? (ἐν τίνι διαλλαγήσεται τῷ κυρίῳ ἀυτου.) Should it not be with the heads of these men?" Here it is evident that Saul was the offended party whose displeasure was to be removed, and whose favour was to be conciliated by David, in the way suggested by the lords of the Philistines. Accordingly, the meaning of their question cannot be, "Wherewith shall David remove his own enmity against his master?" but "Wherewith shall David recover his master's favour, or remove his master's anger against himself?"

A similar instance occurs in Josephus, in which it is said of a certain Levite, who, by his quarrelsome disposition, had offended and disgusted his wife, and led her to depart from him, that, being much attached to her, and uneasy at

1 Sam.
xxix. 4.

RESPECTING THE ATONEMENT. 71

her departure, he went after her to the house of her parents, and having removed the offence, "he was reconciled to her"—διαλυσάμενος τὰς μέμψεις καταλλάττεται πρὸς αὐτήν. Here again, it is evident that his being "reconciled to her" means that "her favour or affection was recovered by him."

Various other instances of the same kind are given by Hammond, Rosenmüller, Schleusner, and other distinguished critics and lexicographers. But those which we have now adduced are sufficient to show that when one party is said "to be reconciled to another," or "to reconcile himself to another," *the latter*, and not the former, may be the party whose friendship and favour are conciliated. Such being the case, the circumstance that sinners are said in Scripture "to be reconciled to God," instead of God being said "to be reconciled to them," is no sufficient reason for concluding that such statements refer only to the removal of their enmity against God. Whether the "reconciliation" thus referred to consists in the removal of God's wrath or of man's enmity, is in each particular instance to be determined, not by the mere phraseology of the statements, but by the connection in which they occur.*

These remarks appear sufficient to repel the general arguments which have been urged to show that "reconciliation to God," as ascribed in Scripture to the sufferings of Christ, must in all cases refer exclusively to the removal of our enmity against Him. But, as before observed, the proper reference of the expression to one or other of the parties who are at variance, will best be ascertained, in every particular instance, by a careful consideration of the passages in which it occurs.

1. Look, for example, at St Paul's statement to the Romans,—"If, when we were enemies, we were reconciled to God by the death of His Son, much more, being reconciled, we shall be saved by His life." If this statement be taken in connection with the previous verse, it evidently points to God as the party who has been conciliated. For

* See Appendix, Note D.

PART I. SEC. 6.

Antiquities, Book V. c. II. sec. 8.

Rom. v. 10.

72 STATEMENTS OF THE NEW TESTAMENT

PART
I.
SEC. 6.
——
Rom. v. 9.

Supra,
sec. v.

Hodge's
Com-
mentary
on the
Epistle
to the
Romans.

there the apostle had said, "Much more, then, being
now justified by His blood, we shall be saved from wrath
through Him." The phrase "reconciled to God by the
death of His Son," in verse 10th, must be taken as equivalent to, or at least as including, what is meant in verse 9th
by our "being justified by His blood." Any other supposition would destroy the coherence of the apostle's
reasoning. Now, we have already seen that "being justified by the blood of Christ" signifies, not any personal
change of character or disposition towards God by which
we are reclaimed from our former hostility to Him, but
simply a change of our legal standing in relation to Him,
when, "through the redemption that is in Christ Jesus,"
He pardons and accepts us as righteous in His sight.
Accordingly, the parallel expression, "when we were enemies we were reconciled to God by the death of His Son,"
must in like manner be understood as referring, not to the
removal of our enmity against Him, but to our restoration
to His favour. Besides, it is the evident design of the
whole of this passage to show what blessings we may confidently expect to receive from God, in consideration, not
of any change in our disposition towards Him which might
render us more deserving of His favour, but of the great
things which He, of His free mercy, has already done for
us, though altogether undeserving. But, by understanding
the phrase "we were reconciled to God" as signifying that
"we have laid aside our enmity against Him," it would
then indicate, not any great and unmerited benefit which
God has conferred on us, but rather something which we
had done towards Him, and on which we might found a
personal claim to future benefits. Such a construction
would evidently be inconsistent with the whole scope and
spirit of the passage.

In support of the view we have taken of this text, Dr
Hodge has further urged, that "the reconciliation here
spoken of is ascribed by the apostle to *the death of Christ ;*
and that the *direct object* of the death of Christ, according
to the constant representations of Scripture, is to satisfy
divine justice or to propitiate the favour of God, while the

RESPECTING THE ATONEMENT. 73

sanctification of believers is only its more remote conse- PART
quence." He adds, that the most liberal commentators— I.
that is, those who are the least bound by any theological SEC. 6.
system—admit this to be the doctrine of Scripture and of
this passage in particular. Thus Meyer says, "The death
of Christ does not remove the enmity of men to God; but
as being that which secures the favour of God, it removes
His displeasure with men; whence the removal of our
enmity against Him follows as a consequence." So also
Rückert observes, "The reconciled party here can only be
God, whose wrath against sinners is propitiated by the
death of His Son. On man's part nothing has happened—
no internal change—no step towards God; all this follows
as the consequence of the reconciliation here spoken of."
In like manner De Wette says, "The reconciliation must
mean the removal of the wrath of God: it is that reconciliation of God to man, which not only here, but in
Romans, iii. 25, 2 Corinthians, v. 18, 19, Colossians, i. 21,
and Ephesians ii. 16, is referred to the atoning death of
Christ."

2. The conclusion we have thus drawn from the passage
above referred to, is further confirmed by the verse immediately following. "And not only so, but we also joy in Rom. v.
God through our Lord Jesus Christ, by whom we have now 11.
received the atonement." The word καταλλαγὴν, here
translated " atonement," properly signifies " reconciliation."
Now the " reconciliation " of which the apostle speaks is
here represented by him, not as a thing *to which we had
consented*, but as a thing " *received by us*." But how
could it be so if it consisted exclusively in *the laying aside
of our enmity against God, and the yielding to Him of our
confidence and affection?* In that case it would have been
more properly spoken of as something *which God has received from us*, than as something which we have received
from Him. When, therefore, we are said to "joy in God
through our Lord Jesus Christ, by whom we have now received the reconciliation," we must understand the statement as implying, not that we have conferred our friendship upon God, but that God has conferred His friendship

74 STATEMENTS OF THE NEW TESTAMENT

PART
I.
SEC. 6.
———

Rom. xi.
15.

2 Cor. v.
18, 19.

2 Cor. v.
20.

upon us, and that we have received the great benefit of His recovered favour.

The meaning of καταλλαγή in this passage may be well illustrated by the use of the same word in another part of this epistle, where it is written respecting the Jewish nation, that "If the casting away of them (ἀποβολή) be the reconciling (καταλλαγή) of the world, what shall the receiving of them be, but life from the dead?" Here καταλλαγή, "the reconciling of the Gentile world," being contrasted with ἀποβολή, "the casting off or rejection of the Jews," must evidently be understood as signifying *the extension of the favour of God* to the Gentiles.

3. We must put the same construction on another statement of the same apostle, in which he thus writes: "All things are of God, who hath *reconciled us to Himself* by Jesus Christ, and hath given to us the ministry of reconciliation; to wit, that God was in Christ *reconciling the world unto Himself, not imputing their trespasses unto them,* and hath committed unto us the word of reconciliation." Here it seems evident (1) that "the reconciling of us, or of the world, to Himself by Jesus Christ," originated with God, and *took place prior* to the issuing of "the word or ministry of reconciliation," by which sinners are "besought to be reconciled to God;" and (2) that the "reconciling of the world to Himself" consisted, not in *the removal of their enmity* against Him, but in *the removal from them of His merited wrath,* as implied in His "not imputing their trespasses unto them."

In the verse immediately following, the apostle thus proceeds: "Now then we are ambassadors for Christ, as though God did beseech you by us: we pray you in Christ's stead, *Be ye reconciled to God.*" Perhaps it may be thought that, in this latter exhortation, sinners are besought to lay aside their enmity. It is not necessary to our position that this view should be controverted. For we hold, as before remarked, that the reconciliation which the Gospel contemplates is not one-sided but *mutual,* extending to man as well as to God. At the same time, the apostle's entreaty, "Be ye reconciled to God," is strictly parallel

RESPECTING THE ATONEMENT.   75

to our Lord's admonition, "First be reconciled to thy brother;" the meaning of which unquestionably is, "Conciliate or appease thy brother." And therefore it may reasonably be understood as signifying, "Avail yourselves of the offered terms of reconciliation with God."

Alford observes respecting this verse, that "our English version, by inserting the word '*ye*,' gives the erroneous impression of there being an emphasis on that pronoun, as if the exhortation had been καταλλάγητε καὶ ὑμεῖς τῷ θεῷ, *Be you also on your part reconciled to God;* whereas the word καταλλάγητε is strictly passive. *God* was the reconciler; and the meaning is, '*Let this reconciliation have effect upon you : enter into it by faith.*'"

Let it be supposed, however, that the other meaning is that which ought to be given to this exhortation; even then it cannot be considered as detracting from the *Godward reference* of that "reconciliation" which is mentioned in the preceding verses. On the contrary, the circumstance that God is there spoken of as having "reconciled us to Himself by Jesus Christ" in the sense of "not imputing our trespasses unto us," is the very ground on which the embassy of peace is now sent to us, whereby we are entreated to "be reconciled to God." If reconciliation *on our part* be the only thing required of us by this embassy, it is so, not because God *never had* any cause of judicial displeasure with us which needed to be removed, but simply *because God has already fully provided through Jesus Christ for the removal of every such obstacle to reconciliation* on His own part. In so far as regards the propitiating of the wrath of God against sinners, nothing is *now* required in order to the accomplishment of it. God has Himself done all that was necessary to reconciliation on His own part through the mediatorial work and sufferings of our Redeemer. All that remains for us is simply to take advantage of this finished work, which needs not to be supplemented by laying down the arms of our rebellion, and heartily consenting to be at peace with God.

4. Another passage belonging to the same class occurs in the Epistle to the Ephesians, where Christ is spoken of

*PART
1.
SEC. 6.*

*Matt. v.
24.*

*Alford on
2 Cor. v.
20.*

76   STATEMENTS OF THE NEW TESTAMENT

PART
I.
SEC. 6.

Eph. ii.
16.

as "reconciling both" (*i.e.,* both Jews and Gentiles) "unto God in one body by the cross, having slain the enmity thereby." It seems clear from the context that in this passage the reference is not so much to the winning back of man's alienated affections to God, as to the restoration of God's forfeited favour to man. For the Ephesians, in their unreconciled state, are represented in the context as

Eph. ii.
12.

"aliens from the commonwealth of Israel, and strangers from the covenants of promise, having no hope, and without God in the world :" a description which obviously marks their destitution of such spiritual privileges as God afterwards conferred on them, when He "brought them nigh by

Eph. ii.
13, 19.

the blood of Christ," and made them "no more strangers and foreigners, but fellow-citizens with the saints, and of the household of God."

5. There is one other passage bearing on the subject of reconciliation between God and man which we have still to notice. It is found in the Epistle to the Colossians, where, after stating that it pleased the Father " to reconcile all things unto Himself by Jesus Christ," the apostle adds

Col. i.
21, 22.

these words : "And you, that were sometime alienated and enemies in your mind by wicked works, yet now hath He reconciled in the body of His flesh through death, to present you holy, and unblamable, and unreprovable in His sight."

There is here a pointed allusion to the *former alienation from Him* of those whom God "hath now reconciled," as well as to their ultimate *sanctification.* And hence there may seem to be some ground for holding that the "reconciliation" spoken of in this passage has respect more prominently to the change wrought in their personal character, when they cease to be God's "enemies in their mind by wicked works."

It is worthy of remark, however, that in the 20th verse of this chapter, where the subject of "reconciliation" is first introduced, there is an evident allusion to something which has been done to deliver sinful men from the judicial wrath of God, as the groundwork of that which God is pleased to do in the way of removing the enmity of their

RESPECTING THE ATONEMENT. 77

minds against Him. For in that verse we read that "it
pleased the Father, *having made peace through the blood of*
His cross, by Him" (that is, by Christ) "to reconcile all things
unto Himself." The "peace" thus "made" assuredly
cannot be *the pacification of sinners towards God,* because
it is represented as something which had been made *prior
to,* and *with the view of effecting,* such a pacification of
sinners. In this clause, at least, the "peace" must be
understood as *peace on the part of God towards men,* and not
on the part of men towards God. And the "making of it
through the blood of the cross," to the effect of removing
from sinners the wrath which they have justly incurred, is
here represented as opening the way for those gracious
overtures by which God pleads with them to be upon their
part *reconciled to Him.*

Even were we to admit, however, that in the whole
of this passage the allusion is to a change wrought in the
disposition of men towards God, this concession would not
in any degree invalidate the conclusions we have already
drawn from other passages. We are not concerned to
deny that "reconciliation" must be *mutual,* extending to
both of the parties who were at variance. And assuredly no
sinner is ever restored to the favour of God without being
led, by the grace thus conferred on him, to yield up to
God his full confidence and affection. Such being the
case, we have no reason to be surprised that in *one of five*
instances in which reconciliation between God and man is
spoken of in the New Testament, there should be, as in
this passage, a more prominent reference to the part which
man may be said to have in this matter. Nor is it in any
respect the less certain on this account, that *God* has a
part to bear in the matter as well as *man;* that on His
side, as well as on that of the sinner, there were obstacles
that stood in the way of their being at peace with one
another; and that the removal of these obstacles is
attributed in Scripture to the sufferings and death of
Christ.

IX. Nearly allied to the passages we have last consi-

78   STATEMENTS OF THE NEW TESTAMENT

PART
I.
SEC. 6.

dered is a *ninth class*, in which the Lord Jesus Christ is represented as a *propitiation for sin.*

Christ a propitiation for sin.

1 John, ii. 2.

1 John, iv. 10.

1 and 2. Thus it is written of Him : "And He is the *propitiation* for our sins ; and not for ours only, but also for the sins of the whole world." And again : " Herein is love, not that we loved God, but that He loved us, and sent His Son to be the *propitiation* for our sins."

Num. v. 8 ; Ezek. xliv. 27.

Luke, xviii. 13.

In these texts the word translated "propitiation" is ἱλασμός, a word applied in several passages of the Septuagint to those offerings for sin which were presented under the Jewish law. To *propitiate* a person is to avert his wrath, or to conciliate his favour. And "a propitiation" is something done or given to him, by which his displeasure may be removed and his favour regained. Accordingly, the Greek verb ἐξιλάομαι or ἐξιλάσκομαι, which is commonly translated to "propitiate," is used in the Septuagint version of Genesis, xxxii. 20, where Jacob says, " I will *appease* Esau with the present that goeth before me, and afterwards I will see his face ; peradventure he will accept of me." And it also occurs in the Septuagint version of Proverbs, xvi. 14, where it is written, " The wrath of a king is as messengers of death ; but a wise man will *pacify* it." Our Lord, too, in His parable of the Pharisee and the Publican, represents the latter as praying in the temple thus, " God be merciful to me a sinner ;" the words in the original which are translated, " Be merciful to me," being ἱλάσθητί μοι, " *Be propitiated towards me.*" And whether the Publican, when thus praying in the temple, is or is not to be considered as referring to the propitiatory sacrifices daily offered in that place as his ground of encouragement in presenting this petition, the purport of his prayer unquestionably is, that he may be delivered from the wrath and restored to the favour of God.

Now, when Christ is said in the above passages to be " a propitiation," it cannot be maintained that He is so *because He propitiates man towards God,* or induces *man* to lay aside his enmity against God ; for in the context of the

RESPECTING THE ATONEMENT. 79

first passage it has just been said, "If any man sin, we PART
have an *advocate with the Father*, Jesus Christ the right- SEC. 6
eous;" so that most evidently it is "*the Father*" who is ———
here referred to as requiring "an advocate" to plead with
Him in our behalf. And in both passages the "propitiation is said to be "*for our sins;*" which clearly shows that
the obstacle to friendship, which it was meant to remove,
was not merely our sinful enmity against God, but God's
most righteous displeasure with us because of sin. Besides,
it is impossible to overlook the sacrificial reference of the
expression, taken as it is from the phraseology of the
Levitical system, and suggesting as it does an analogy
between Jesus Christ and those Jewish sin-offerings which
were intended to propitiate, not the worshippers, but the
object of their worship.

3. A third passage in which we find, not indeed the Heb. ii.
noun ἱλασμός, but the verb ἱλάσκομαι, from which it is 17.
derived, is Hebrews, ii. 17, where Christ is said to be "a
merciful and faithful high priest in things pertaining to
God, to make *reconciliation*," or, more properly, *propitiation or expiation*, "for the sins of the people."

The words in the original are εἰς τὸ ἱλάσκεσθαι τὰς
ἁμαρτίας τοῦ λαοῦ. The common expression used in the
Septuagint, when God is said to be "propitiated," is
ἐξιλάσασθαι or ἐξιλάσκεσθαι with περί τινος or with
περὶ τῆς ἁμαρτίας τινος. There are not a few passages
of that version, however, in which we find ἐξιλάσασθαι
ἁμαρτίας, corresponding to the expression in the passage Dan. ix.
before us, employed to signify that "sin is expiated," or 24; Sirach
that "God is propitiated towards those who have com- xx. 28;
mitted it." We cannot suppose that εἰς τὸ ἱλάσκεσθαι xxxiv. 19.
τὰς ἁμαρτίας τοῦ λαοῦ refers to *the propitiating of the people
towards God*. The "propitiation" has respect to "*the
sins* of the people," and undoubtedly consists in securing
the forgiveness of them, or averting the divine wrath
from those who are chargeable with them. Besides, the
"propitiation" was accomplished by the Lord Jesus in
the capacity of "our merciful and faithful high priest,"

80 STATEMENTS OF THE NEW TESTAMENT

PART I.
SEC. 6.

and must therefore be regarded as analogous to those priestly offerings for sin which were presented under the Jewish law.

Rom. iii. 25.

4. There is yet a fourth passage belonging to this class, in which it is thus written : "Whom God hath set forth to *be a propitiation* through faith in His blood, to declare His righteousness for the remission of sins," &c.

The Greek word here translated "propitiation" is ἱλασ-τήριον. It is held by Grotius, Alford, and some others, to be a substantive, like χαριστήριον, καθάρσιον, σωτήρια. And one instance of the use of it as a substantive is cited by Stuart, from Dio Chrysostom, Orat. ii. 184, where the Greeks are said to have offered ἱλαστήριον τῇ 'Αθήνᾳ. Others regard this word as an adjective in the accusative *masculine*, agreeing with ὅν—i. e., Christ ; and translate the clause thus, "Whom God hath set forth as one possessing propitiatory virtues." The majority of critics, however, insist that the word is an adjective in the accusative *neuter*, used in an elliptical manner with a substantive understood. And if this view be adopted, the question occurs, What is the substantive ? Is it, as many suppose, θῦμα or ἱερεῖον, a *sacrificial victim ?* or is it, as others maintain, ἐπίθεμα, a *cover* or *lid*, the reference being to the mercy-seat in the Jewish tabernacle, which was the lid or cover of the ark ?

The latter opinion is adopted by some writers who affirm the propitiatory efficacy of the death of Christ, and is for the most part earnestly maintained by those who deny the doctrine of the Atonement. By them the apostle is here regarded as teaching that Christ is to us Christians just what the mercy-seat was to the Jews— namely, the proclaimer or manifester of God's mercy. In Him, as on the mercy-seat, God takes His position and declares His gracious purposes to mankind. And the function of Christ, according to this view, is that merely of a *medium of divine communication.* He is the messenger or herald of mercy, not the source or procurer of it. In support of the supposed reference of ἱλαστήριον to the mercy-

RESPECTING THE ATONEMENT. 81

seat some passages of the Septuagint are appealed to, in
which it is certainly used in this sense ; and one passage
in the New Testament, in which we read of " the cherubims
of glory overshadowing the mercy-seat, το ἱλαστήριον."
This interpretation, however, is liable to serious objections.
Jowett observes that " it is too obscure and peculiar for
the present passage ; that it would require the article το,
which is absent here, but is present in other places where
the mercy-seat is referred to ; and that it is inappropriate
to the occasion, because Paul is not here speaking of a
declaration of the *mercy* of God, but of a declaration of
God's *righteousness.*" Besides these objections of Jowett,
it is remarked by De Wette and others, that an allusion
here to the mercy-seat would be incongruous, inasmuch as
Christ would be then represented as a *mercy-seat sprinkled
with His own blood.* And a further objection may be
drawn from the word προέθετο, which, as here used in
connection with the phrases εἰς ἔνδειξιν and πρὸς τὴν
ἔνδειξιν, must mean *to expose* or *hold up to public view;* and
is therefore utterly inapplicable to the mercy-seat, which
was *hid from every eye* but that of the high priest, and
was only disclosed, even to him, once a-year, on the day
of atonement. On these grounds, if ἱλαστήριον be a neuter
adjective, the substantive to be understood ought to be, not
ἐπίθεμα, " the covering of the ark," but θῦμα or ἱερεῖον,
a " sacrificial victim." Of this use of the expression,
Schleusner and Stuart have adduced a variety of instances
from the Apocrypha, Josephus, and other Greek writings.
And it certainly comports better than the other interpretation with the allusion which the apostle makes to
" faith in His blood," when here representing Christ as
ἱλαστήριον.

But even if ἱλαστήριον were held to refer to the mercy-
seat, the inference thence drawn by those who deny the propitiatory efficacy of the death of Christ would be unwarrantable. For no proclamation of mercy ever issued from the
mercy-seat, except in connection with the sacrificial blood
that had been sprinkled on it. And there is an express
reference, as we have just noticed, to " the blood of Christ,"

PART
I.
SEC. 5.

Heb. ix. 5.

82   STATEMENTS OF THE NEW TESTAMENT

PART
I.
SEC. 6.
———

when He is said in this passage to have been "set forth as ἱλαστήριον." Besides, it is evident that something more than a simple *declaration of mercy* must be here intended. The design of setting forth Christ was, as the apostle assures us, "to declare the *righteousness* of God for the remission of sins;" "to declare His righteousness, that He might be *just*, and the justifier of him that believeth in Jesus." Now we can very well understand how *divine justice or righteousness* was displayed if Christ died for sin, bearing for us its penalties, so as to propitiate God's judicial displeasure against it. But how there could be any such thing as a declaring or manifesting of God's *justice* in a simple and unconditional proclamation of His mercy, without respect to any expiation of human guilt, it is certainly not very easy to imagine.

It is unnecessary to discuss the two other interpretations, which regard ἱλαστήριον either as a *substantive* signifying "a propitiatory sacrifice," or as a *masculine* adjective, agreeing with Christ, and attributing to Him propitiatory virtues. Because they lead to substantially the same result to which we are brought by taking the word as a *neuter* adjective, when θῦμα or ἱερεῖον is the substantive understood.

On the whole, then, we may conclude that the four passages above considered represent Christ as *propitiating God* towards those sinful creatures who had incurred His righteous displeasure. In this respect they are in full accordance with the class of passages previously considered, which set forth the sufferings and death of Jesus Christ as the ground of *reconciliation between God and man*, or as having removed those judicial obstacles (if we may be allowed so to call them) on the part of God, which stood in the way of our restoration to His favour. Happily, too, in regard to these four passages there is no room for even agitating the question, which it was necessary to discuss with reference to the other texts, "Whether God or man be the party who is conciliated?" For here it is too plain a point to be disputed, that the beneficial effect attributed

RESPECTING THE ATONEMENT.

to the death of Christ is not the removal of the sinner's enmity against God, but the removal of God's displeasure with the sinner. And even were our arguments ever so insufficient against the exclusively *manward* reference of καταλλάσσω, διαλλάσσω, ἀποκαταλλάσσω and καταλλαγή, yet with such other terms applied in Holy Scripture to the benefits accruing from our Lord's sufferings as ἱλασμός, ἱλάσκεσθαι, and ἱλαστήριον, we can have no hesitation in concluding, that God is on His part reconciled to us through Jesus Christ, His favour being restored to us, and His righteous anger turned away.

84   STATEMENTS OF THE NEW TESTAMENT

SECTION VII.

PASSAGES WHICH SPEAK OF CHRIST (10) AS A PRIEST, AND (11) AS A REPRESENTATIVE.

PART
I.
SEC. 7.
———
Christ a
priest.

X. A *tenth* assemblage of texts claiming our especial attention, are those in which Christ has the *priestly office* ascribed to Him.

Ps. cx. 1.
4.

1. Under this head we may first of all refer to the clear and decided manner in which both our Lord Himself and two of His apostles have applied to Him the 110th Psalm, which contains a solemn designation of the Messiah, whom it predicts, to the office of the priesthood. The psalm thus begins,—" The LORD said unto my Lord, Sit Thou at my right hand, until I make Thine enemies Thy footstool." And three verses after, the following words occur, which evidently refer to the same person,—" The LORD hath sworn, and will not repent, Thou art a priest for ever after the order of Melchisedec."

This psalm
applied to
Christ in
New Tes-
tament.

In the Epistle to the Hebrews both of these verses are applied to Christ; the former in chapters i. 13 and x. 12, 13—and the latter in chapter vii. 1-17. In 1 Corinthians, xv. 25, there is an incidental reference to the *first* verse of Psalm cx. in these words, " For He must reign till He hath put all enemies under His feet,"—a reference which evidently proceeds upon the assumption that the psalm in question is applicable to Christ. In Acts, ii. 34, 35, the Apostle Peter expressly applies to the ascended Jesus the opening words of Psalm cx. And in Matthew, xxii. 44, Mark, x. 36, and Luke, xx. 42, we find our Lord Himself putting this question to the Pharisees, when they

RESPECTING THE ATONEMENT.   85

spoke of their expected Messiah as the son of David,— PART
"How then doth David in the Spirit call Him Lord, I.
saying, the LORD said unto my Lord, Sit Thou at my SEC. 7.
right hand, until I make Thine enemies Thy footstool?"
In these words our Lord distinctly and emphatically declares, or rather assumes as being undeniable, that the
110th Psalm has reference to the promised Christ. And
though it is the first verse that the occasion leads Him
specially to quote, yet in so doing He evidently sanctions
the belief that the whole of this short psalm admits of the
same application, and in particular the *fourth verse*, which
bears the clearest internal evidence of being addressed to
the same person as the first verse.

We are warranted to say, therefore, that the application
to Jesus Christ of these solemn words, "The Lord hath
sworn, and will not repent, Thou art a priest for ever after
the order of Melchisedec," as expressly made in Hebrews,
vii. 1-17, is fully corroborated, not only by Paul in his
First Epistle to the Corinthians, and by Peter in his
address to the Jews on the day of Pentecost; but by the
authority of the Son of God Himself, as conveyed to us
by three of the evangelists.

2. It is, however, chiefly in the Epistle to the Hebrews
that our Lord's priesthood is fully and emphatically declared. Again and again do we there find Him designated as "the high priest of our profession, Christ Heb. iii.
Jesus,"—"a merciful and faithful high priest in things 1; ii. 17;
pertaining to God,"—a "high priest over the house of 14; vii.
God,"—"a great high priest, who is passed into the 26.
heavens, Jesus the Son of God,"—"such an high priest
as became us, who is holy, harmless, undefiled, separate
from sinners, and made higher than the heavens." And
a great part of the epistle is occupied with a minute
and careful comparison of Him in this capacity with
those who held a similar office in the ancient Church—a
comparison tending to show the superiority of His priesthood in respect of its dignity, its efficacy, its permanence,
and the surpassing greatness of the benefits procured by it.

86   STATEMENTS OF THE NEW TESTAMENT

PART I.
SEC. 7.

3. What, then, was the distinctive character of the priestly office? And what were the peculiar functions pertaining to it?

What is a priest?
Heb. v. 1.

A clear and succinct answer to these questions is thus given by an inspired writer : "Every high priest, taken from among men, is ordained for men in things pertaining to God, that he may offer both gifts and sacrifices for sins." Here we are told (1) that the high priest was "*ordained*," by which we are to understand "divinely appointed ;" for in succeeding verses it is stated by the

Heb. v. 4-6.

same writer, that "No man taketh this honour to himself, but he that is called of God, as was Aaron ; so also Christ glorified not Himself to be made an high priest, but He that said unto Him, Thou art my Son, to-day have I begotten Thee ; as He saith also in another place, Thou art a priest for ever after the order of Melchisedec." Again, (2) He was "ordained *for men ;*" that is, appointed to represent them and to transact for them, "in things pertaining to God." In this respect the priestly was distinguished from the prophetic office. The prophet had to treat with men on the part of God, making known to them His counsels and commands ; whereas the priest had to treat with God on the part of men, with a view to their

Exod. xxxix. 6, 14.
Levit. iv. 3-21.

restoration to His favour. The representative character of the Jewish high priest was plainly indicated by his bearing on his breastplate the names of all the tribes of Israel ; as well as by the circumstance that any sin committed by him was regarded as the sin of the whole people, and required the same public expiation to be made for it. Farther, (3) He was "ordained for men that he might offer both gifts and sacrifices for sin." The offering of sacrifice, and the making of intercession founded on sacrifice, for the sins of the people, were the main and most essential functions of the priesthood. A "priest" and a "sacrifice," indeed, are correlative terms, the one of which naturally and unavoidably suggests the other. As well might we speak of a king without a kingdom, or of a general without an army, as of a priest without a sacrifice. Accordingly, it is written, "Every high priest is ordained

RESPECTING THE ATONEMENT. 87

to offer gifts and sacrifices ; wherefore *it is of necessity* that this one have somewhat to offer,"—words which show that the writer was well aware of the *sacrificial reference* which he would be understood as having, when he ascribed the priestly office to Jesus Christ. And in the sequel of the epistle he expressly connects our Lord's priesthood with the presentation of that great sacrifice for sins which He offered when He laid down His life upon the cross.

PART I. SEC. 7.

Heb. viii. 3.

4. Some of the early followers of Socinus endeavoured to separate the priesthood of our Saviour from that expiatory sacrifice with which in Scripture it is associated, and ascribed the salvation of sinners exclusively to the former, without reference to any saving efficacy in the latter. Under the law, they said, it was not the slaying of the victim, but the oblation of it by the priest, that procured forgiveness. And in particular, on the day of atonement the most important part of the ceremony was the entering of the high priest into the holy place, and his appearing before the mercy-seat for the people. The superior excellence of Christ's priesthood they held to consist in *this*, that He went not into a holy place made with hands, but into heaven itself, to make intercession for us. And the benefits He thus obtains for us were ascribed by them, not to any expiatory virtue in His sufferings, but entirely to the influence and authority conferred on Him when, as the reward of His obedience unto death, He was exalted to the right hand of the Majesty on high.

Attempt to separate Christ's priesthood from His sacrifice.

It must be obvious, however, to any one who takes a comprehensive view of the whole subject, that this representation of it is seriously defective. It is true that under the law the priests made the expiation ; but they did so by the blood of the victims which had been slain. And more particularly on the day of atonement, when the high priest made his annual entrance into the holy place, it was with the blood of the bullock and the goat, both of which he had previously slain with his own hand. Indeed it is emphatically said, in Hebrews, ix. 7, that the

The attempt vain.

Heb. ix. 7.

88 STATEMENTS OF THE NEW TESTAMENT

PART I. SEC. 7.

Heb. ix. 12.

high priest on this occasion entered into the holy place "*not without blood,* which he offered for himself and for the errors of the people." And in the 12th verse of the same chapter it is said of Jesus Christ, our "High Priest," that "Neither by the blood of goats and calves, but by His own blood, He entered in once into the holy place, having obtained eternal redemption for us." He did not become a high priest *after* "He entered in," but "He entered in" *in the capacity of a high priest.* It is utterly vain, then, to attempt a separation of our Lord's sacrificial offering from His priestly office. It may be admitted, that had He not ascended into heaven, after having laid down His life upon the cross, He would not have completely discharged the functions of the priesthood, which included both the making of the sacrifice and the presentation of it at the mercy-seat within the veil. But still more imperfectly would these functions have been discharged by Him, had He gone up on high without having made any sacrifice, it being "*of necessity* that," as a priest "He should have somewhat to offer."

Besides, it is not unworthy of consideration, whether the prevailing opinion be well founded, that the "entering of Christ into the holy place," referred to in Hebrews, ix. 12, did not occur until the period of His ascension. Some theologians have maintained, with much plausibility, *that it took place immediately after His death,* when His disembodied spirit entered into heaven—that His resurrection, the great proof that His sacrifice had been accepted, corresponded to the return of the Jewish high priest from the inner sanctuary—that the whole typical import of the *Aaronic* priesthood was *then* completed by Him—and that His ascension and subsequent glorification pertain to His royal priesthood after the order of Melchisedec.* I need scarcely remark that, if this view be adopted, it serves, even more effectually than the common opinion, to refute the allegation of the Socinians, that Christ did not enter on His priestly office while He was on earth.

---

* Witsius, De Oeconomia Fœderum, lib. ii. cap. 6, sec. 9; J. Honert, Collect. Misc., S.; Albert Schultens' Dutch Commentary on Heidelberg Catechism.

RESPECTING THE ATONEMENT. 89

5. There are some important characteristics of our Lord's sufferings which may be inferred from their connection with His priesthood. One of these is, that His sufferings were *official ;* in other words, that He endured them in fulfilment of the duties of an office to which He had been ordained. His priesthood was not, as some have alleged, *figurative,* but a *real and veritable* priesthood—quite as much so as that which subsisted under the Levitical dispensation, and at the same time incomparably more excellent and important. Otherwise, indeed, there would be no force in those statements and arguments in the Epistle to the Hebrews, by which it is shown that the priesthood of Christ, instead of being a mere figure or shadow of the Levitical priesthood, was actually the substance of which the other was an inadequate type ; and, in particular, that Christ was more surely and solemnly set apart than the sons of Aaron to the priestly office, inasmuch as "those priests were made without an oath ; but this with an oath by Him that said unto Him, The Lord sware, and will not repent, Thou art a priest for ever after the order of Melchisedec." Now, as we have already seen, the function of a priest is " to offer gifts and sacrifices for sin ;" and "this," we are told, " Christ did once, when He offered up Himself," having now " appeared once in the end of the world to put away sin by the sacrifice of Himself." Hence we conclude that the sufferings of Christ were undergone by Him in the discharge of His official functions. They were not incidental merely to His heavenly mission, but essential to it. Nor are they to be explained on any such principle as martyrdom, example, self-sacrifice, moral influence, or the like—on which we might account for the sufferings of others who had no official call or designation to the endurance of them—but on the ground of their having been devolved upon Him, and undertaken by Him, in the capacity of " a high priest, ordained for men in things pertaining to God."

6. Another characteristic of our Lord's sufferings which may be inferred from their connection with His priesthood, is *the union of action with passion in the endurance of*

[marginal notes:]
PART I. SEC. 7.

Sufferings of Christ official.

Heb. vii. 21.

Heb. v. 1 ; vii. 27 ; ix. 26.

Union of *action* with passion in sufferings of Christ.

90 STATEMENTS OF THE NEW TESTAMENT

PART I.
SEC. 7.

them. The priest under the Levitical system was different from the sacrifice; but under the Gospel the priest and the sacrifice are the same. For Christ fulfilled His office, as one " ordained for men to offer gifts and sacrifices for sin," by " once offering up *Himself* upon the cross." And thus in His death there is agency as well as suffering; not the mere passive endurance of a helpless victim, but the willing and active obedience of the priest.

Theologians have been wont to distinguish our Lord's " active " from His " passive obedience," signifying by the former the actions of His holy life, and by the latter the sufferings of His atoning death. This distinction, however, as we have before observed, must not be too sharply drawn, or too strictly pressed. For there is truth in the old saying of St Bernard, that " Christ showed passive action in His life, and active passion in His death." Specially may we say that there was agency — official, priestly

Matt xx. 28.

agency—in His sufferings. For it is written that "the Son of Man came to *give* His life a ransom for many;"

Eph. v. 25.

" He loved the Church, and *gave* Himself for it;" " He

Philip. ii. 8.

became obedient unto death;" " He learned obedience by

Heb. v. 8.

the things which He suffered." And He has Himself said,

John x. 17, 18.

" I lay down my life, that I might take it again. No one taketh it from me; but *I lay it down of myself.* I have power to lay it down, and I have power to take it again."

We must not suppose, then (to quote the words of a recent author), " that the agency of Christ was overborne before He died, leaving Him a mere victim to causes and means of death aside from His own active will and power offering Himself to God. Christ acted in dying. There was priestly action in it. We sometimes speak of ' His doing and His dying.' But, in truth, His ' dying ' was His grandest ' doing.' No priest, ' daily ministering and offering oftentimes,' was ever more free from coercion in his office, or more gloriously active in discharging it, than ' this Man, when He offered one sacrifice for sins.' Nor did He thereafter ' sit down on the right hand of God ' a

RESPECTING THE ATONEMENT.   91

more free and powerful agent than when He offered that
sacrifice which earned Him the throne." *

PART
I.
SEC. 7.

XI. Somewhat akin to the last-mentioned class of texts
is another class, which indicates that the Lord Jesus sustained a *representative character* in relation to those sinners
for whom He interposed.

Christ a
representa-
tive.

We have already seen that Christ's priestly office implies
that He was the representative of His people, inasmuch as
"Every high priest, taken from among men, is ordained
for men in things pertaining to God." The same truth is
indicated by the character assigned to Him in the Epistle
to the Hebrews, as " *Surety* of the better covenant." For
in this capacity the Saviour must be regarded as pledging
Himself, or making Himself responsible, for the fulfilment
of all that this covenant requires on the part of those who
are to share in its provisions.

Implied in
priest-
hood.

Heb. vii.
22.

There are some notable passages, moreover, in St Paul's
writings, in which a parallel is drawn between Adam, the
original head and representative of all mankind, and Christ,
the spiritual head of redeemed and renewed humanity, of
whom Adam is declared to have been a " type" or " figure"
—while, at the same time, the respective consequences flowing from their agency are strikingly contrasted,—the one
having entailed upon us sin and condemnation, and the other
having secured for us righteousness and eternal life. " By
one man," we are told, "sin entered into the world, and
death by sin ; and so death passed upon all men, for that
all have sinned. . . . Therefore, as by the offence of one
judgment came upon all men to condemnation, even so by
the righteousness of one the free gift came upon all men
unto justification of life. For as by one man's disobedience many were made sinners, so by the obedience of one
shall many be made righteous." Again, it is written,
" Now is Christ risen from the dead, and become the
first-fruits of them that slept : for since by man came

Parallel
between
Adam and
Christ.

Rom. v.
12, 18, 19

1 Cor. xv.
20-22, 45-
49.

* See this subject strikingly illustrated in an admirable treatise by the Rev.
Hugh Martin, D.D., on ' The Atonement in its Relations to the Covenant,
the Priesthood, and the Intercession of our Lord,' chap. iv.

92   STATEMENTS OF THE NEW TESTAMENT

PART
I.
SEC. 7.

death, by man came also the resurrection of the dead ; for as in Adam all die, even so in Christ shall all be made alive. . . . The first man, Adam, was made a living soul; the last Adam was made a quickening spirit. . . . The first man is of the earth, earthy; the second man is the Lord from heaven. As is the earthy, such are they also that are earthy ; and as is the heavenly, such are they also that are heavenly. And as we have borne the image of the earthy, we shall also bear the image of the heavenly."

Without any minute analysis of these statements, it may suffice for our present purpose to observe, that they evidently trace a close analogy between Adam and Christ, and set forth, or assume, as the very ground of this analogy, that each of these persons sustained a representative character, to the effect of involving others in the penalties which the former incurred, and securing for others the blessings which the latter merited.

I need only add, that there are many passages in which

John, vi. 38, 39.

the Saviour speaks of His faithful people as "those whom His Father had given to Him," and in whose behalf " He had come down from heaven, not to do His own will, but the will of Him that sent Him;"—as those in regard to

John, x. 11-18, 27-29.

whom He had received a special charge to "bring them into His fold," to "keep them that they should never perish," to "lay down His life for them," and to "raise

John, xvii. 19.

them up at the last day ; "—as those "for whose sakes He sanctified" (or devoted) "Himself, that they also might be sanctified in truth." While there are other texts which teach us that believers are closely united or identified with the Saviour, as the wife with her husband, the vine branches with their stock, the members of the human body with

Eph. v. 23-30.
John, xv. 1-5.

their head ; insomuch that "they abide in Christ, and He in them,"—"they live no more themselves, but Christ liveth in them,"—they "are crucified with Christ,"—

Gal. ii. 20.

"quickened together with Him,"—"raised up with Him,

Eph. ii. 5, 6.

and made to sit together in heavenly places in Christ Jesus." Now surely, *whatever more* (to be noticed in future Sections) we may be warranted to conclude from these and the like statements, they cannot be considered

RESPECTING THE ATONEMENT. 93

as indicating *less* than this,—that Christ sustains in relation to His people the character of a Surety or Representative, transacting for them and identifying Himself with them in the work which His Father had given Him to accomplish.

PART I. SEC. 7.

Some writers hold that our Lord's representative character is inconsistent with His substitution in the room of sinners, and maintain the former to the exclusion of the latter. Christ, they are wont to say, is not to be regarded as standing apart from men, and doing vicariously for them a work which they ought themselves to do, but cannot accomplish; He is rather to be viewed as identifying Himself with them, assuming their nature, entering into their condition, and making common cause with them as sinners, though Himself sinless, so that by all He did and suffered in obedience to the divine will they are brought into a near relation to God, being reconciled to Him, not *through* Christ as their substitute, but rather *in* Christ, as their "second Adam," the source and head of a renovated humanity.

Alleged that representation is inconsistent with substitution.

I am at a loss to see any incongruity between the two things thus alleged to be at variance. There seems, on the contrary, to be the most perfect harmony between them; or rather, I ought to say, the one necessarily implies the other. The very notion of a person doing anything vicariously, or in the way of substitution for another person, is just that with reference to the action which he thus performs, that other person is represented by him, or identified with him. And, on the other hand, the very notion of a representative is just that of one who is appointed to act in the name and stead of another person, with reference to those matters in which he represents him, so that that other person is held as himself doing whatsoever is thus done for him by the representative. Certain it is that, in the particular case we are concerned with, the alleged incongruity has no real existence. For the substitution of Christ in the room of sinners, whether as set forth in Holy Scripture, or as maintained by any of its intelligent advocates, is not that of one who stands,

No incongruity between them.

94 STATEMENTS OF THE NEW TESTAMENT

PART I. SEC. 7.

Representation the ground of substitution.

as it were, *aside* from those for whom He endured the penalties and perfectly fulfilled the requirements of the law of God,—but of one who is personally related to them in the closest manner, and with whom they are intimately united or identified. Indeed, the relation which He personally bears to them, as their living Head, their Surety, their Representative, may be held to be the ground on which His obedience and sufferings are graciously reckoned to them, or accepted in their behalf.

Macdonnell's Donellan Lectures, p. 157, 167, 168.

"It is easy to see," observes an able writer, "how closely this idea of representation is allied to that of substitution. In both there is the common idea expressed by vicariousness,—namely, the taking the place and discharging the functions of another. The chief difference seems to consist in the more usual and proper ascription of substitution to *things* and representation to *persons*. . . . The language which speaks of Christ's vicarious functions—of His substitutionary sufferings and obedience—is really open to no fair objection, if we distinguish, as we do in our ordinary use of such words, between substitution as applied to *things* and to *personal acts*. In the case of *things*, the possibility of substitution or interchange depends on their own relative value. On this depends all commercial barter all money dealings between man and man. A certain sum of money is always a discharge for a debt to that amount, no matter by whom it may be paid ; and one coin is as good as another of the same denomination for the purposes of exchange. It is altogether a question of *things*. But when we talk of *acts*, the value of one act as a substitute for another depends on its being able to produce equivalent effects ; and consequently, on the power, position, and other circumstances, of the person who performs it. And in general, to make an act of one person a sufficient substitute for that of another or others, he must be their adequate representative, or stand in some relation to them equivalent to that of a representative. Thus, the signature of an ambassador to a treaty is a sufficient substitute for that of the prince or governors who have duly appointed him to represent them ; and the signature of the

RESPECTING THE ATONEMENT. 95

monarch himself is a substitute for the act of the whole
nation over which he rules, not in virtue of any formal
appointment, but in consequence of his relation to them
as king—a relation which makes him include in his own
person certain powers of the State, certain political privileges of his subjects. Many, not perceiving this distinction, have sought a reason for the sufficiency of Christ's
sufferings as a substitute for ours, in their exact equality to those which all mankind were doomed to suffer;
as though He endured pang for pang, just as in paying a
debt we must pay pound for pound. *This is to confound
the substitution of things with that of personal acts;* it is to
make Christ's sufferings not to be figuratively called a
ransom, but really in their essence to be a matter of barter
and exchange. But if it be asked, Were Christ's sufferings
and obedience coextensive in their effects with man's sin
and guilt, so that the one could counteract the other?
then we may answer boldly, with abundant support from
Scripture, that they were; and that this was part of the
very truth the apostle meant to assert, when he said that
Christ was 'made sin for us,' and 'made a curse for us.'
And does not this fairly deserve the name of substitution,
or vicariousness?"

PART
I.
SEC. 7.

96   STATEMENTS OF THE NEW TESTAMENT

SECTION VIII.

PASSAGES WHICH REPRESENT THE SUFFERINGS OF CHRIST (12) AS "SACRIFICIAL."

PART I.

SEC. 8.

Death of Christ a sacrifice.

XII. WE now proceed to *a twelfth* class of passages, which are especially worthy of consideration,—those, namely, in which the death of Jesus Christ is represented as a *sacrifice or sin-offering*.

Under this head it is unnecessary to reproduce some Scriptural testimonies which have already been considered ; such as, the exclamation of John the Baptist, " Behold the Lamb of God, that taketh away the sin of the world ;" our Lord's words on the occasion of instituting the Lord's Supper,—" This cup is the new testament in my blood, which is shed for many for the remission of sins ;" and the four passages in which Jesus Christ is declared to be " a propitiation for our sins."

Passing from these texts, there are a variety of others, not yet adduced, to which we must advert.

Christ our Passover.

1. For example, in 1 Corinthians, v. 7, are these words : " *Christ our Passover is sacrificed for us ;* therefore let us keep the feast," &c. Here, without insisting for the present that the Paschal sacrifice is represented as a type or prefigurative emblem of the death of Jesus Christ, it is evident that a close analogy is stated to subsist between them. Nothing could be more clearly expressive of such an analogy than to apply to Christ, as the apostle does, the significant title " our Passover." It is strange indeed that this statement of St Paul, that " Christ our Passover is *sacrificed* for us," has been actually appealed to by Dr Priestley as a convincing proof that *Christ was not sacrificed*

RESPECTING THE ATONEMENT. 97

at all! The ground on which he attempts to maintain
this appeal, in downright opposition to the very statement
on which he founds it, is the allegation that *the Passover
was not a sacrifice.* His attempt, however, is vain. The
Passover is *called* a sacrifice, three times in Exodus, and
four times in Deuteronomy. Like all other Levitical
sacrifices, it was required to be offered up in the tabernacle, and afterwards in the temple. And the blood of
the victim was poured out as an offering to God, and was
sprinkled by the priests upon the altar, in the same manner as the blood of other sacrifices. The original Passover,
indeed, was slain in Egypt, before as yet the Levitical
system had been established. But the blood, on that
occasion, was sprinkled on the lintels and door-posts of
every Israelitish dwelling, so as to stand between the first-
born of the families of Israel and the uplifted arm of the
angel of the Lord, when he went forth on his dread mission to slay the first-born of man and beast throughout
the land. We have no cause to doubt, then, that the Passover is to be regarded as truly and properly an expiatory
sacrifice; and hence we must necessarily ascribe the same
expiatory character to the sacrifice of Christ which the
apostle here compares to it.*

2. Another passage, belonging to this class, is Ephesians,
v. 2: " Walk in love, as Christ also hath loved us, and
hath given Himself for us, an *offering and sacrifice* to God
for a sweet-smelling savour." Here, the two words employed, προσφορὰν and θυσίαν, are undoubtedly sacrificial in their reference; the first being a general term
including all kinds of offerings which were solemnly presented on the altar of the God of Israel, while the second
denotes a bloody oblation, involving the death of the
victim, as an expiation of the sins of those for whom he
was slain. Accordingly Christ is represented in this passage as having so loved us that He gave Himself to be
slain and offered up to God as a propitiatory sacrifice in
our behalf. The closing words of the verse, ἐις ὀσμὴν
εὐωδίας, indicate the acceptableness and efficacy of His

PART
I.
SEC. 8.
——
The Pass-
over a
sacrifice.
Exod. xii.
27; xxiii.
18; xxxiv.
25.
Deut. xvi.
2, 4-6.

Eph. v. 2.

* See Appendix, Note E.

98   STATEMENTS OF THE NEW TESTAMENT

PART
I.
SEC. 8.
——

oblation; and probably convey an allusion to Genesis, viii. 21, where, after Noah had offered up a sacrifice of every clean beast and of every clean fowl, we are told that "The Lord smelled a sweet savour—ὀσμὴν εὐωδίας— and said in His heart, I will not again curse the ground any more for man's sake."

1 Pet. i.
18-21.

3. Again, St Peter says in one of his epistles, "Ye were not redeemed with corruptible things, as silver and gold, from your vain conversation received by tradition from your fathers; but *with the precious blood of Christ, as of a lamb without blemish and without spot;* who verily was foreordained before the foundation of the world, but was manifest in these last times for you," &c.   Here again the language is evidently sacrificial, suggested by the solemn ordinances of the Levitical worship.   Probably there is, as Hofmann supposes, a more especial reference

Hof-
mann's
Schriftb.,
ii. 1, 194.

to the Passover.   "Just as Israel's redemption from Egypt required the blood of the Paschal lamb, so the redemption of those brought out of heathendom required the blood of Christ, the predestination of whom from eternity is compared to the taking up of the lamb on the tenth day of the month."

This text
alleged as
showing
that re-
demption
does not
imply ex-
piation.

This passage has been sometimes quoted to show that redemption does not imply expiation, inasmuch as the deliverance to which it specially refers was not from the wrath of God which the heathens had incurred, but from their own vain and ungodly conversation.   A deeper consideration of the passage, however, will lead to a very different conclusion.   For, as an able anonymous writer

Answer to
this objec-
tion.

has remarked, "The only natural explanation which can be given of this remarkable phraseology is, that in Peter's judgment the Gentiles were delivered from their old heathen life by a sacrifice, which atoned for their old heathen sins.   The emphasis which is placed upon 'the blood of Christ,' and the comparison of Him to 'a lamb without blemish and without spot,' evidently came from a mind to which the expiatory conception of our Lord's death was always present.   Most men would have said— (assuredly any one who ignored or repudiated the idea of

RESPECTING THE ATONEMENT. 99

expiation would have been careful to say)—that the Gen- PART
tiles were delivered from heathenism by the discovery of I.
the folly of idolatry, and by the revelation of the true God SEC. 8.
which is made in the Gospel. But St Peter cannot speak —-
of the great moral transition through which the Gentile
converts had passed, without founding it on that *expiation* Brit. Quar.
which is the true ground of their new relations to God." Review,
Besides, we are not in any way concerned to dispute that xlvi. 476.
other benefits, as well as the forgiveness of sins, have been
secured for us by the sacrifice of Jesus Christ. For it is
written, that "we are complete in Him,"—"blessed with Col. ii. 10.
all spiritual blessings in heavenly places in Christ." His Eph. i. 3.
death, by reconciling us to God, has opened a way for
sanctifying grace, no less than pardoning mercy, being
extended to us. And surely it is the reverse of a disparagement of the expiatory virtues of this great propitiation,
that everything which God does *in us*, as well as *for us*, in order to our full and final redemption, should be ascribed to it.

4. I may farther refer to the following well-known and Rev. i. 5,
striking passages which occur in the Apocalypse : " Unto 6 ; v. 9,
Him that loved us, and washed us from our sins in His 14, 15.
own blood, and hath made us kings and priests unto God
and His Father ; to Him be glory and dominion for ever
and ever. Amen."—" Thou (the Lamb) wast slain, and hast
redeemed us to God by Thy blood, out of every kindred,
and tongue, and people, and nation, and hast made us
unto our God kings and priests."—" These are they who
came out of great tribulations, and have washed their
robes and made them white in the blood of the Lamb ;
therefore are they before the throne of God, and serve
Him day and night in His temple ; and He that sitteth on
the throne shall dwell among them."*
The sacrificial reference of these passages is very appar-

---

* To these may be added Rev. xxii. 14, if the reading preferred by Alford
and some other modern editors be adopted : " Blessed are they *that have
washed their robes*, that they may have right to the tree of life." The commonly received text is, μακάριοι οἱ ποιοῦντες τὰς ἐντολὰς αὐτοῦ, "Blessed are
they that do His commandments." But in the Alexandrine and Sinaitic MSS.
the reading is μακάριοι οἱ πλύνοντες τὰς στολὰς αὐτῶν. And this reading is
followed in the Latin Vulgate, with the addition " in sanguine Agni."

100 STATEMENTS OF THE NEW TESTAMENT

PART
I.
SEC. 8.
——

ent from the mention made in them of "the *blood* of Christ," and "the *blood of the Lamb*," as the purifying agency. Nor can it be said that the "washing" of which they speak denotes only the *moral purification* of the saints, to the exclusion of their deliverance from the guilt of sin and restoration to the favour and fellowship of God. For the language is evidently taken from the Levitical sacrifices, the primary object of which was, as we shall afterwards show, to restore or preserve to the Jewish worshippers those privileges, as members of the Church and commonwealth of Israel, which by their sins and shortcomings they had forfeited. Besides, there is an express allusion in all the passages, not only to the washing of believers from their sins, but also to the acceptance of their persons, and to the high dignity conferred upon them as a priesthood, standing before the throne of God, and enjoying the most intimate communion with Him.

Heb. vii.
26, 27.

5. Of the numerous passages belonging to this class which are to be found in the Epistle to the Hebrews, the following may be taken as a specimen :—

"Such an High Priest became us, who is holy, harmless, undefiled, separate from sinners, and made higher than the heavens ; who needeth not daily, as those high priests, to offer up sacrifices, first for his own sins, and then for the people's ; *for this He did once, when He offered up Him-*

Heb. ix.
12-14.

self." "Not by the blood of goats and calves, but *by His own blood*, He entered in once into the holy place, *having obtained eternal redemption for us.* For if the blood of bulls and of goats, and the ashes of an heifer sprinkling the unclean, sanctifieth to the purifying of the flesh ; *how much more shall the blood of Christ, who through the eternal Spirit offered Himself without spot to God, purge your con-*

Heb. ix.
22-28.

science from dead works to serve the living God ?" "Almost all things are by the law purged with blood ; and without shedding of blood there is no remission. It was therefore necessary that the patterns of things in the heavens should be purified with these, but the heavenly things themselves with better sacrifices than these. For Christ is not entered into the holy places made with hands, which are the

RESPECTING THE ATONEMENT. 101

figures of the true ; but into heaven itself, now to appear in the presence of God for us : nor yet that He should offer Himself often, as the high priest entereth into the holy place every year with the blood of others ; for then must He often have suffered since the foundation of the world : but now once, in the end of the world, hath He appeared, *to put away sin by the sacrifice* of Himself. And as it is appointed unto men once to die, but after this the judgment ; *so Christ was once offered to bear the sins of many ;* and to them that look for Him shall He appear the second time without sin unto salvation." "Every high priest standeth daily ministering, and offering oftentimes the same sacrifices, which can never take away sins ; but this man, after He *had offered one sacrifice for sin*, for ever sat down on the right hand of God, from henceforth expecting till His enemies be made His footstool : *for by one offering He hath* perfected for ever them that are sanctified."

PART I. SEC. 8.

Heb. x. 11-14.

The sacrificial import of these passages is so evident that no comment can be deemed necessary to elucidate it. They most unequivocally ascribe to the death of Jesus an efficacy the same in kind with that which was understood by Jewish worshippers to belong to the Levitical sacrifices, but infinitely superior in the wideness of its extent, the excellence of its results, and the permanence of its duration. They speak of His blood as the "one sacrifice for sin," of ever-enduring virtue, that needs not to be repeated, availing not only for the "purifying of the flesh, but for the inward purgation of the conscience," "putting away sin," "obtaining eternal redemption," and "perfecting for ever them that are sanctified."

In order to appreciate the full significancy, not only of these statements in the Epistle to the Hebrews, but of all the other passages belonging to the same class, it is necessary to remember that, both among Jews and Gentiles, it was a prevailing practice—no matter, in the meanwhile, to what origin, divine or human, the practice may be traced —to propitiate the objects of their worship with the blood

Sin-offerings prevalent among Jews and Gentiles.

102 STATEMENTS OF THE NEW TESTAMENT

PART
I.
SEC. 8.
———
Hence
sacrificial
expres-
sions in all
languages.

of animal victims. This practice was familiarly known and generally observed at the time when Christianity was promulgated. And in connection with it, there were in all ancient languages certain special modes of expression appropriated to the ideas involved in the observance, such as ἁγιάζω, καθαίρω, ἱλάσκομαι, among the Greeks, and *expio, lustro, placo,* among the Latins, all of which must be considered as *voces signatæ*—that is to say, words which have a marked reference to a particular idea, and which cannot be rightly applied or justly interpreted if that particular idea be lost sight of.

These free-
ly applied
in Scrip-
ture to
death of
Christ.

Such being the case, it is surely a significant circumstance that this phraseology should have been frequently, freely, and unreservedly applied by the writers of the New Testament to the death of Jesus Christ. And how else is it, as so applied, to be understood, except in accordance with what is known to have been its received sense in the age and country of the writers who have thus employed it? No intelligent writers, setting aside their inspiration, would have used such language in a different sense, without an express certification of its change of meaning, unless it had been their intention to mislead us. And no ordinary reader, whether Jew or Gentile, would ever have thought of attaching to it another meaning, as applied to our Lord's sufferings, than that which he uniformly and as a matter of course attached to it when applied to his own

The use
of such ex-
pressions
misleading
if not
meant to
teach that
Christ's
death is a
sacrifice.

customary rites of sacrificial worship. Supposing that the writers of the New Testament really intended to teach that the death of Christ is a true and proper expiation, it is certain that they could not have taught this doctrine more intelligibly than by the free use of those *voces signatæ* which were specially appropriated, both by Jews and Gentiles, to the expression of it. On the other hand, supposing it to have been their intention by no means to set forth any such doctrine, but rather, as some allege, to inculcate the very opposite doctrine; to teach that the prevailing notions of all their contemporaries respecting the necessity of atonement to restore sinners to the enjoyment of the divine favour were utterly groundless; to

RESPECTING THE ATONEMENT. 103

assure men that they have nothing whatever to fear from
the wrath of God, if their dark and distrustful minds could
only be brought to believe it; and that however grievously
they may have offended Him, He is ready to receive them,
when in penitence they return to Him, without any satisfaction for their sins;—had such been the intention of the
writers of the New Testament, we may be very sure that
they would, with the utmost care, have shunned the use
of every expression which could in the remotest way be
thought to countenance those sacrificial notions and practices which they repudiated, and the prevalent influence
of which it was their purpose to counteract. So far are
they, however, from having done so, that they have, without the least scruple or qualification, applied to the death
of Christ those definite forms of expression which were
uniformly recognised, in the age in which they lived, as
indicative of the removal of human guilt and the recovery
of the divine favour by vicarious and piacular sacrifice.

PART I. Sec. 8.

The Scriptural evidence by which we have endeavoured
to show that the death of Christ is an expiatory sacrifice
appears, on the grounds above stated, to be conclusive.
There are two allegations, however, which have been
advanced with the view of evading or neutralising the
force of it. One of these is, *That the Levitical sacrifices
were not piacular, and consequently that no inference can be
drawn from the application of terms derived from them to
the death of Christ, in proof of the atoning efficacy of HIS
sufferings.* And the other is, *That the sacrificial terms
applied to the death of Christ in the New Testament are not
to be strictly or literally interpreted, being mere rhetorical
allusions to Jewish customs, or figurative representations of
Christian truth in a form adapted to Jewish sentiments and
prepossessions.*

*Two ob-
jections to
be answer-
ed.*

*1. That
Levitical
sacrifices
not piacu-
lar.*

*2. That
sacrificial
language
applied to
Christ is
figurative.*

It is customary with those who deny the atoning efficacy
of the death of Christ to avail themselves of *both* of these
allegations, and to turn from the one to the other as they
find expedient in any argumentative exigency to which
they may be reduced. I hardly think, however, that this

*Adver-
saries of
Atonement
cannot
urge both
of these
objections*

104   STATEMENTS OF THE NEW TESTAMENT

PART I.
SEC. 8.
——
but must confine themselves to one of them.

is altogether a fair or legitimate mode of dealing with the question. They are quite entitled, indeed, to urge *one or other* of the allegations above stated in support of their position, provided they tell us which of the two they prefer, and thereafter steadily and consistently adhere to it. But surely they are not entitled to advance *both*, or to pass from the first to the second as they find it convenient. For it so happens that the two are incompatible with one another. If the sacrifices of the Levitical dispensation *were not piacular*, it is plain that the hypothesis of a *figurative allusion to them* will not account for the use in the New Testament of those terms which, if literally construed, ascribe a piacular efficacy to the death of Christ. And, conversely, if those expressions in the New Testament which represent the death of Christ as piacular are mere rhetorical allusions to the sacrifices of the Jewish ritual, it is equally plain that they must have been applicable, strictly and literally, to these Levitical sacrifices, though alleged to be applicable to the death of Christ only in a figurative sense; or, in other words, that the Levitical sacrifices must have been truly and properly piacular.

Passing from this, however, let us look at the statements themselves, and consider what weight can be reasonably attached to them.

The Levitical sacrifices were piacular.

I. The first statement we shall have occasion fully to discuss, when we treat, in a subsequent part of this volume, of the symbolical import and typical reference of the Old Testament sacrifices, as bearing on the mediatorial work of Jesus Christ. For the present, the following brief remarks may be sufficient.

1. It is admitted that the Levitical sin-offerings were limited in their efficacy. They were available only for ceremonial offences and for certain moral offences of a less aggravated kind ; and, even for these, to the effect only of procuring exemption from the forfeitures and penalties annexed to them by the ceremonial law. Thus much

RESPECTING THE ATONEMENT. 105

we are expressly told in the Epistle to the Hebrews, *PART I. Sec. 8.*
where it is written respecting these sacrifices that "they
could not make him that did the service perfect as per- *Heb. ix*
taining to the conscience;" that "they stood only in meats, *9, 10, 13.*
and drinks, and divers washings, and carnal ordinances;" *The effi-*
and that "they sanctified unto the purifying of the flesh." *cacy of*
But that the efficacy, however limited, which was thus *sacrifices*
possessed by the Levitical sin-offerings, belonged to them *to them as*
as properly *vicarious and piacular*, is sufficiently clear from *properly*
various considerations; such as—(1.) the reasons or occasions *and piacu-*
of presenting them, which were either the commission of *lar.*
some particular sin, or the habitual sins and shortcomings
of the offerers; (2.) the imposition of hands by the offerers,
or their representatives, on the victim's head, accompanied
by a confession of the sin or sins for which he was immolated; (3.) the slaying of the victim, and sprinkling of his
blood upon the altar; and (4.) the declared effect of the
offering, which is thus expressed,—"It shall be accepted *Levit. i. 4;*
for him to make atonement for him;" "the priest shall *iv. 20, 26,*
make an atonement for him, as concerning his sin, and it *vi. 7.*
shall be forgiven him;" "the priest shall make an atonement for him before the Lord, and it shall be forgiven
him for anything of all that he hath done in trespassing
therein."

2. Farther, those passages of the New Testament in *The pas-*
which our Lord's death is likened to the Levitical sacri- *sages of*
fices, afford of themselves sufficient evidence (if otherwise *tament*
there could be any doubt upon the subject) that the *latter* *which*
truly were piacular in their nature. Take, for example, *Christ's*
the following statements, already referred to: "Not by *Levitical*
the blood of goats and calves, but by His own blood, He *sacrifices,*
entered in once into the holy place, having obtained eternal *these were*
redemption for us. For if the blood of bulls and of goats, *piacular.*
and the ashes of an heifer sprinkling the unclean, sanctified
to the purifying of the flesh; how much more shall the
blood of Christ, who through the eternal Spirit offered
Himself without spot to God, purge your conscience from *Heb. ix.*
dead works to serve the living God?" "Almost all things *22-26.*

106 STATEMENTS OF THE NEW TESTAMENT

PART
I.
SEC. 8.
———

are by the law purged with blood; and without shedding of blood is no remission. It was therefore necessary that the patterns of things in the heavens should be purified with these; but the heavenly things themselves with better sacrifices than these. For Christ is not entered into the holy places made with hands, which are the figures of the true; but into heaven itself, now to appear in the presence of God for us: nor yet that He should offer Himself often, as the high priest entereth into the holy place every year with blood of others; for then must He often have suffered since the foundation of the world: but now once in the end of the world hath He appeared to put away sin by the sacrifice of Himself." We hold that the allusion made in these passages to the Levitical sacrifices *embodies and proceeds upon the assumption of their piacular nature.* And it is not necessary to go beyond the passages themselves in order to see that they ascribe propitiatory virtues at once to the Mosaic sin-offerings and to the death of Christ, although doubtless they give the preference to the latter in respect of the greater extent and permanence of its efficacy.

Sacrificial terms of *Gentile* derivation applied to Christ.

3. We must not omit to notice, before leaving this topic, that much of the sacrificial phraseology applied to the sufferings of Christ in the New Testament is *of Gentile*, and not of Jewish, derivation; and that much of it occurs in writings which were addressed to converts, not from Judaism only, but from heathenism.

This consideration is all the more important, because those modern assailants of the Atonement who most earnestly strive to eliminate from the Jewish sacrifices that expiatory or vicarious element to which they are opposed, have freely and fully admitted the existence of it as an

Young's Light and Life of Men, p. 252.
Bushnell on Vicarious Sacrifice, p. 426.

essential and characteristic element in the heathen sacrifices. Thus Dr Young says, "Undoubtedly the pagan sacrifices were held to be expiatory by those who offered them." Dr Bushnell observes: "Expiations are always conspicuous in their meaning. No man could ever raise a doubt of the expiatory object of the pagan sacrifices."

RESPECTING THE ATONEMENT. 107

And Mr Maurice admits that the expiatory sense of the words ἱλασμὸς and ἱλαστήριον "may be gathered from all the history of the heathen world." Indeed it is usual with writers of this school to speak reproachfully of vicarious expiation as altogether a *heathenish notion*, and to lay it down, as the grand distinction between the worship of the true God in all ages and that of polytheism, that the sacrifices of the former did not include this notion, whereas it was included and prominently exhibited in those of the latter.

It is well, therefore, to remind these writers and their followers, that the very words by which the sacrifice of Christ is described in the New Testament—as, for example, θυσία, προσφορὰ ἱλασμὸς, ἁγιάζω, καθαίρω, ἱλάσκομαι—are borrowed from the sacrificial ritual of *the Greeks;* and that these words are freely, familiarly, forcibly, and without the slightest qualification, applied to our Lord's sufferings in discourses and epistles addressed to Christian communities, of which a large proportion of the members were of *Gentile* extraction. Setting aside, then, the converts from Judaism altogether, it is not to be questioned that the converts from heathenism, and the surrounding heathens yet unconverted — in Rome, Corinth, Galatia, Ephesus, Philippi, Colosse, and other places to which the apostolic letters were addressed, and in which at a very early period the Gospel narratives were circulated—would be perfectly sure to attach to these expressions, unless expressly warned and certified to the contrary, those same notions of *expiation* and substitution which, in their own habitual use of them, the words were understood to convey. This indeed is fully admitted by Mr Maurice, who says, in the passage above referred to,—" So far am I from pleading that these words have not the sense which we should gather from the whole history of the heathen world that they must have had, or that this sense was not one which would naturally suggest itself to the readers of Paul's epistle, baptised men though they were, that I would earnestly press the reflection on you that any other view of the case is incredible." And then he adds, that "in applying such

PART
I.
SEC. 8.
—
Maurice
on Sacrifice, p. 154.

These terms freely applied to Christ's death in writings addressed to Gentiles.

108   STATEMENTS OF THE NEW TESTAMENT

PART
I.
SEC. 8.

———

expressions to a Christian use, *their heathen signification
must be, not modified, but inverted!"*

What, then, are we to think of the conduct of the
apostles in freely applying these words to the death of
Christ, if the meaning which thereby they intended to convey were such as it is "incredible" that the words should
naturally have suggested to their readers? If, as Mr
Maurice affirms, "*the heathen signification of the words
when they are applied to a Christian use, must be, not merely*

Jowett on
St Paul's
Epistles,
ii. 479.

modified, but INVERTED;" or if, as Mr Jowett maintains,
"*the heathen and Jewish sacrifices rather show us what the
sacrifice of Christ was not than what it was;"* how then are
we to account for the conduct of the apostles in applying
to the death of Christ, without scruple or reservation, and
without the least warning or indication of a change of
meaning, those very expressions which, above all others,
they ought to have avoided, as they would not be thought
to teach the exact opposite of what they meant to
teach—expressions which require to be absolutely "inverted," as regards their well-known and current signification, before they can become the vehicles of Christian

Such ap-
plication
of them
mislead-
ing, if the
writers did
not mean
to teach
that
Christ's
death is
expiatory.

truth—expressions which, if the views of Messrs Maurice
and Jowett be well founded, were sure to mislead those to
whom they were addressed, and actually have misled the
vast majority of Christians in all ages into errors of a most
serious kind respecting the fundamental doctrines of the
Gospel? Certainly the use of such language by the apostles
must, on the principles of these writers, be regarded as
inconsistent—I do not say with their *inspiration* merely,
but with their soundness of judgment and accuracy of
apprehension regarding the most vital matters of Christian
doctrine, and as utterly subversive of any confidence we
might have placed in them as authoritative teachers of the
truth as it is in Jesus.

It avails nothing to say, in explanation of this apostolic
usage, that the Greek sacrificial expressions thus employed
had been previously applied to the Jewish sacrifices in the
Septuagint; for this only shows that those learned men
who made this ancient translation of the Old Testament

RESPECTING THE ATONEMENT.   109

regarded the words in question as fair equivalents for the
corresponding words in the original Hebrew. And if in
this respect the Septuagint translators were mistaken, there
was so much the greater need that the apostles, when
quoting these misapplied phrases from the Septuagint, as
well as when themselves making a like inaccurate use of
them, should give warning, which assuredly they have
never done, that "the customary signification of the words
must be not only modified, but *inverted*," in order to guard
their readers, and especially their Gentile readers, against
an otherwise unavoidable misconception of one of the most
essential articles of the Christian faith.

II. We must now shortly consider the *second* allegation,
by which it has been attempted to evade or neutralise the
force of those texts which ascribe a sacrificial efficacy to
the death of Christ. It is that these texts are expressed
in figurative or rhetorical language, such as was naturally
employed by the apostles from their tendency to look at
Christianity through a Jewish medium, and to convey its
doctrines in a manner conformable to Jewish customs and
modes of thought. "Ideas," we are told, "must be given
through something, and those of a new religion ever clothe
themselves in the language of the old. The apostles,
being Jews, could not lay aside those Jewish modes of expression to which they had been accustomed. Sacrifice
and atonement were leading ideas of their former religion,
under which, without shedding of blood, there was no
remission. Hence it was natural for them to speak of
Christ as a sacrifice and atonement for sin. But to build
on their use of such expressions a doctrinal system, is the
error of turning rhetoric into logic."

1. To this we reply, *first*, that it matters little to the
question before us whether the sacrificial phraseology
applied in the New Testament to the death of Christ be
figurative, and whether it was suggested by Jewish customs
and modes of thought. Another and much more important
question lies behind. *What is it that the use of such*

Margin notes:

PART
I.
SEC. 8.
——

Sacrificial
terms
alleged to
be figura-
tive as
applied to
Christ.

Jowett on
St Paul's
Epistles,
ii. 475.

The ques-
tion is not,
whether
the lan-
guage be
figurative,
but what
does it
mean?

110 STATEMENTS OF THE NEW TESTAMENT

PART I.
SEC. 8.

phraseology was meant to denote? Figurative language has a meaning as well as other language. And no writer of ordinary intelligence and integrity would describe a subject, respecting which he professes to give important information, in figurative expressions borrowed from another subject with which both he and his readers are already familiar, *unless there were some real analogy between the two subjects* to warrant the figurative transference to the one of phrases that are literally applicable to the other. It is therefore an idle expenditure of labour on the part of the opponents of the catholic doctrine of the Atonement to

Objectors must show that the use of such figures is inappropriate.

show that the expressions " sacrifice," " sin-offering," " propitiation," and the like, are applied to our Lord's death in a figurative manner, and in the way of allusion to Levitical ordinances, unless they can farther show *that such an application of them is altogether inappropriate and unwarrantable* in respect of there being no atoning efficacy in the death of Christ analogous to that of the Levitical sacrifices, which

If it be so, we can have no confidence in Scripture.

are thus employed as materials for its illustration. And we need scarcely say that if any such impropriety and inapplicability could be justly ascribed to these expressions, it would not only weaken our faith in the Atonement, but would undermine our confidence in the writers of the New Testament as competent and trustworthy expounders of revealed truth.

How came the Jewish mind to be so wedded to sacrificial language?

2. Farther, the question occurs, How came the Jewish mind to be so wedded to sacrificial modes of thought and forms of expression, that the writers of the New Testament unavoidably had recourse to them when alluding to the sufferings and death of Jesus Christ? It was, as Mr Jowett observes, because " sacrifice and atonement were leading ideas of the Jewish dispensation, under which without shedding of blood there was no remission." But what

Were the leading ideas of Mosaic religion unfounded and delusive?

then? Were these " leading ideas of the Jewish dispensation " unfounded and delusive? And were they so alien to the true spirit of the Gospel, that the application of terms suggested by them to our Lord's sufferings has led to the wide and continued prevalence of grievous

RESPECTING THE ATONEMENT.   111

errors with reference to a most vital article of the Christian faith? If so, we are necessarily brought to the conclusion that the Old Testament has no real affinity to the New— that Christianity, instead of being benefited, has, on the contrary, been seriously prejudiced and perverted by its supposed connection with Judaism as preparatory and subservient to it—in short, that the Mosaic and Christian dispensations are so radically different in their essential features and "leading ideas," that they cannot have proceeded from the same divine Author. I need scarcely say, however, that *this* is a conclusion in which it is impossible for any one to rest who bows to the authority of our Lord and His apostles. For *by them* the divine origin of the Mosaic institutions is so fully recognised, or rather so distinctly affirmed, that it cannot be repudiated without fatal injury to the claims and interests of Christianity itself.

PART I. SEC. 8.

Divine authority of Mosaic system recognised in New Testament.

3. There is another consideration, which serves to remove any plausibility which might otherwise have seemed to belong to the allegation against which we are now contending. It is *this*,—that the writers of the New Testament have not only applied sacrificial expressions to the death of Christ, but have at the same time *expressly told us why they did so*, by indicating the points of resemblance, and sometimes also the points of difference, between the sacrifice of the cross and the sacrifices of the ancient Church.

Apostles not only apply to Christ sacrificial expressions, but tell us why they do so.

Had they not done so,—had they merely applied the term "sacrifice" in a vague and indefinite manner to our Saviour—or had they, when so applying it, confined its reference to such merely superficial points of similarity between Him and the Levitical victims as the sufferings and death to which they were alike subjected,—we might not have been warranted to conclude that this expression was more truly applicable to the death of Christ than to that of Stephen, or of James, or of any other self-devoted martyr in the cause of truth and righteousness. The case, however, as it actually stands, is widely different. For we

They allege a correspondence between Christ and Mosaic sacrifices, not in mere accessaries, but in essentials.

112   STATEMENTS OF THE NEW TESTAMENT

PART I.
SEC. 8.

——

John, i. 29.

Matt. xxvi. 28.

Rom. iii. 25, 26.

1 John, ii. 1, 2.

Heb. ix. 26, 28 ; vii. 27.

Heb. ix. 9, 13, 14 ; x. 14.

find that, wherever the death of our Lord is thus compared in the New Testament to the Levitical sacrifices, *express reference is made, as the ground of such comparison, to those expiatory virtues which were common to them both ;* and that in some cases *these virtues are attributed in a higher degree to our Lord's sacrifice than to the sin-offerings of the ceremonial law.* Thus, when the Baptist calls us to "behold the Saviour under the sacrificial character of "the Lamb of God," he clearly indicates his reason for so designating Him by adding these words, " *who taketh away the sin of the world.*" When Christ Himself calls His blood "the blood of the new covenant," in evident allusion to that sacrificial blood by the shedding and sprinkling of which the old covenant had been inaugurated, He expressly tells us that this "blood of the new covenant" is "*shed for many for the remission of sins.*" When Paul affirms that Christ has been "set forth to be a propitiation through faith in His blood," he adds that this was done "*to declare God's righteousness for the remission of sins,* that God might be just, and the justifier of him that believeth in Jesus." When John ascribes to Christ the same character of a "propitiation," he does so in no less evident connection with the forgiveness of sin, for which, through the mediatorial work of Christ, we are taught to look, saying, " If any man sin, we have an advocate with the Father, Jesus Christ the righteous ; and He is the propitiation for our sins ; and not for ours only, but also for the sins of the whole world." And in the Epistle to the Hebrews we are told *in what respects* the death of Christ is termed a "sacrifice" in almost every case in which the designation is applied· to it. For we there read that "once in the end of the world hath He appeared *to put away sin* by the sacrifice of Himself ;" that "Christ was once offered to *bear the sins of many ;*" that " He needed not, like the Jewish priests, daily to offer sacrifices *for sin, for this He did once* when He offered up Himself ;" and that, whereas the Levitical sacrifices availed only to the "purifying of the flesh," or the removal of ceremonial penalties and defilements, and " could not make him that offered them perfect as pertain-

RESPECTING THE ATONEMENT.   113

ing to the conscience,"—the sacrifice of Christ, on the other hand, *was* available to the "*purging of the conscience*" and "the *perfecting for ever* of them that are sanctified."

Thus does it appear that sacrificial phraseology is applied in the New Testament to the death of Christ, not on account of its similarity to the Jewish sacrifices in points of a merely superficial or accessary character, but on account of the resemblance which it bears to them in points that are evidently *fundamental and essential.* And hence, in interpreting the phraseology as thus applied, we cannot be allowed to strip it of its full significancy. Nay, rather, we must give to it a fuller and higher import when used to delineate the sacrifice of Christ, than it originally bore in its reference to the Mosaic ordinances. For while both possessed an expiatory character, they did so *in a degree, and to an effect, that were widely different:* the one exempting from ceremonial forfeitures and restoring the outward rights of citizenship in Israel ; while the other cancels all the penalties of sin, restores the sinner to the favour and fellowship of God, and reinstates him in the spiritual privileges of membership in the true Israel, and citizenship in the heavenly Jerusalem. The death of Christ, therefore, instead of having less about it to warrant the use of sacrificial language with respect to it than the Levitical sacrifices, had, on the contrary, *much more* pertaining to it, by which the use of such language could be justified. *It was expiatory or propitiatory in a higher sense and in a greater degree.* And hence the assertion that it is only called a sacrifice in the way of figurative allusion to the Mosaic rites, is as nearly as possible *the opposite of the truth.* *They* were the figures, while *it* is the reality. *They,* as Paul declares to the Colossians (ii. 17), were "a shadow of things to come," while "Christ is the body or substance."

114   STATEMENTS OF THE NEW TESTAMENT

SECTION IX.

PASSAGES WHICH (13) CLOSELY CONNECT OUR LORD'S
SUFFERINGS WITH HIS INTERCESSION; AND WHICH
(14) REPRESENT HIS MEDIATION AS PROCURING THE
GRACE OF THE HOLY SPIRIT, WITH ALL THE SPIR-
ITUAL BLESSINGS IMPARTED BY IT.

PART
I.
SEC. 9.
——
Our Lord's
sufferings
connected
with His
interces-
sion.

XIII. IN farther prosecution of our inquiries, we must now
advert to those passages of the New Testament in which
the sufferings which Christ endured on earth are closely con-
nected with the intercession which He makes in heaven, as
paving the way for it, or constituting the ground of it.

This connection is clearly indicated by St Paul when,
having told us that "there is one Mediator between God
and men, the man Christ Jesus," he adds immediately
afterwards these words, "*who gave Himself a ransom for*
all." Nor is it less clearly indicated by St John, when,
after assuring us that "if any man sin, we have an advocate with the Father, Jesus Christ the righteous," he makes
this farther statement, as if setting forth the ground of our
advocate's efficacious pleading on our behalf, "*and He is*
the propitiation for our sins; and not for ours only, but
also for the sins of the whole world."

In like manner we find in the visions of the Apocalypse
a representation of the glorified Mediator, as standing in
the midst of the heavenly throne and the surrounding
worshippers, in the character of "*a Lamb as it had been*
slain," so as to remind us of the intimate relation between
His expiatory death and that state of pre-eminent dignity
in which He now makes continual intercession for us.

1 Tim. ii.
5, 6.

1 John, ii.
1, 2.

Rev. v. 6.

RESPECTING THE ATONEMENT. 115

Again, we are told in the Epistle to the Philippians that PART
our Lord's humiliation, when "He became obedient unto I. SEC. 9.
death," is the ground or reason of His subsequent exaltation. And in the description there given of His glorified
state there is a manifest reference to His intercession for
us, as one of the chief purposes for which He has been
thus exalted. For the apostle's words are these : " *Where-* Philip. ii.
fore God also hath highly exalted Him, and hath given 9, 10.
Him a name which is above every name ; *that in the name
of Jesus every knee should bow;*" not "*at* the name of
Jesus,"—as if merely in the way of rendering bodily
obeisance when that name is uttered,—but "*in* the name
of Jesus" (ἐν τῷ ὀνόματι Ἰησοῦ), as being that of our
only prevailing Intercessor, in whose name all prayer and
supplication must be offered up.

Still more evidently, however, does it appear that the Christ's
intercession of Christ is founded on His sacrifice, from a intercession is
consideration of the *character or capacity* in which He is priestly
represented as interceding. For His intercession is not in its char acter.
personal, but *official.* It is not the mere *exercise of
influence acquired by Him* as a friend who is warmly
interested in our welfare, whereby He secures from the
Father, with whom He pleads, whatever is needful or
serviceable for our advantage. No. It is *the discharge
of an official function devolved upon Him, as a priest*
"ordained for men in things pertaining unto God," with
the view of obtaining for us such blessings as He Himself is not more willing to plead for in our behalf than
is His Father, who ordained Him to the priestly office for
the very purpose of so pleading, to bestow them on us.
That such is the case we have the clearest Scriptural
evidence. For we are encouraged to "come boldly unto Heb. iv.
the throne of grace" by the consideration that "we have 14-16.
a great high priest who is passed into the heavens, Jesus
the Son of God ;" and that this high priest, exalted though
He be, is not one "who cannot be touched with the feeling
of our infirmities." And again, when we are told that Heb. vii.
Christ "has an unchangeable priesthood," it is added 24, 25.

116 STATEMENTS OF THE NEW TESTAMENT

PART I. SEC. 9.

immediately after, " *Wherefore* He is able to save them to the uttermost that come unto God by Him, seeing He ever liveth to make intercession for them."

As being priestly, it is founded on His sacrifice.

The intercession of Christ being thus evidently *sacerdotal,* or made for us by a priest in the discharge of his official functions, we are unavoidably led to the conclusion that it is connected with and founded on His sacrifice. For all intercession made officially by a priest, of which we have any information in the Scriptures, proceeds and rests on a sacrifice presented by him. And this was eminently the case with the intercession of *the Levitical priests,* with which, in the Epistle to the Hebrews, the intercession of Christ is specially compared. The sweet incense offered by the priests upon the golden altar was kindled from the fire on the altar of burnt-offerings ; and the high priest entered into the inner sanctuary on the day of atonement with sacrificial blood, which he sprinkled on the mercy-seat.

Connection of intercession with sacrifice expressly affirmed in Scripture.

We are not left, however, in regard to this matter, to *mere inference* from the analogy of our Lord's priesthood to that which was held by Aaron and his descendants. The connection between the intercession and the sacrifice is *one of those points with reference to which the analogy between the two priesthoods is expressly maintained and insisted on by the inspired writer.* For while, on the one

Heb. ix. 7, 11, 12.

hand, we are reminded by him that the Jewish " high priest went alone into the second tabernacle once a-year *not without blood,"* we are told, on the other hand, that " Christ being come an high priest of better things to come, by a greater and more perfect tabernacle, not made with hands, that is to say, not of this building ; neither by the blood of goats and calves, *but by His own blood* He entered in once into the holy place, having obtained eternal redemption for us." Again, after a statement that " the heavenly things themselves required to be purified with better sacrifices" than those which were

Heb. ix. 23-26.

needful to purify their Levitical " patterns," it is added that " Christ is not entered into the holy places made with hands, which are the figures of the true, but into heaven

RESPECTING THE ATONEMENT. 117

itself, *now to appear in the presence of God for us: nor yet that He should offer Himself often, as the high priest entereth into the holy place every year with the blood of others;* but now once in the end of the world hath He appeared to put away sin *by the sacrifice of Himself."*

PART I. SEC. 9.

On these Scriptural grounds we are warranted to hold that the intercession of Christ is founded on His sacrifice. And if so, then how clearly are we thus taught *the unfailing virtue and efficacy of this sacrifice,* as being the ultimate ground on which, through His prevailing advocacy, "all spiritual and heavenly blessings" are secured for us! Whatever He has encouraged us to ask of the Father in His name, and confidently to expect in answer to our supplications—whatever is necessary to render us "complete in Him," and to perfect His good work, when once He has begun it in us, until He has actually "saved us to the uttermost"—whatever fulness of grace here and of glory hereafter we are privileged to look for, through the pleading of our glorified Intercessor before the throne,—must be ultimately traced to that meritorious work of obedience and suffering which He perfected upon the cross. Yes. The attempt is vain to separate between the earthly and the heavenly part of the Saviour's mediation. The one is but the appropriate sequel of the other, indissolubly connected with it, and in the economy of grace dependent on it.

Hence we learn the unfailing efficacy of the sacrifice of Christ.

XIV. The texts we have now been considering may be appropriately followed by some Scriptural testimonies of a no less important class, in which the mediation of Christ is represented as *procuring the gracious influence of the Holy Spirit,* together with all the spiritual blessings imparted by it.

The mediation of Christ procures the grace of the Holy Spirit.

1. Thus we have the memorable testimony of the Baptist: "I indeed baptise you with water unto repentance; but He that cometh after me is mightier than I, whose shoes I am not worthy to bear; He shall baptise you with the Holy Ghost." Here it is plainly announced that the

Christ was to baptise with the Holy Ghost.

Matt. iii. 11.

118   STATEMENTS OF THE NEW TESTAMENT

PART
I.
SEC. 9.
———

communication of the Holy Spirit was to be one of the distinguishing characteristics of the Saviour's ministry, in respect of which He would prove to be much greater and mightier than the herald who was sent before Him to prepare His way.

The Spirit not yet given, because Jesus was not yet glorified. John, vii. 39.

2. To the like effect is that statement of the evangelist, when, commenting on one of our Lord's sayings, he tells us that "Jesus spake this of the Spirit, which they that believe on Him should receive ;" and adds, "for the Holy Ghost was not yet given, because that Jesus was not yet glorified." The words in the original, οὔπω γὰρ ἦν Πνεῦμα Ἅγιον, literally signifying " for the Holy Spirit was not yet," cannot of course be understood of the Holy Spirit *personally*, inasmuch as we have clear Scriptural proof of His eternal existence, but of His *influence, gifts,* or *operations*. Nor can it be understood even of these without restriction, for the agency of the Holy Spirit had undoubtedly been already exerted, not only in the inspiration of prophets, but in the conversion and sanctification of believers under the Old Testament. The statement specially refers to *that remarkable kind and measure* of

2 Cor. iii. 8.

spiritual influence "which they that believe on Jesus were to receive," and by reason of which the evangelical dispensation is emphatically termed "the ministration of the Spirit." In this sense St John tells us that "the Holy Spirit was not yet given, because that Jesus was not yet glorified." The word "glorified" doubtless refers more immediately to the Saviour's exaltation at the right hand of the Divine Majesty ; not, however, to His exaltation irrespective of His atoning death, but rather with an implied reference to His whole mediatorial work, and in particular to the completion of it on the cross, of which

John, xiii. 31, 32; xvii. 4, 5.

His exaltation was the recompense. For Christ Himself, on several occasions, uses the same expression when His last sufferings are specially and immediately in His view, so as to make it apparent that He has a reference, not only to His ascension into heaven, but to His cross and passion, as the necessary and appointed way by which

RESPECTING THE ATONEMENT. 119

alone His heavenly glory can be attained. And, indeed, the doctrine of Scripture is too clear to be overlooked, that the "glorification" of our Lord, and whatever blessings may accrue from it, must ultimately be ascribed to His "obedience unto death," on account of which we are expressly told that "God hath highly exalted Him."

PART I. SEC. 9.

Philip. ii. 9.

3. Farther, in the consolatory discourse of our Lord to His disciples on the eve of His crucifixion, we find Him using these remarkable words: "It is expedient for you that I go away, for if I go not away, the Comforter will not come unto you; but if I depart, I will send Him unto you." And in other passages of the same discourse He says to them, "I will pray the Father, and He will give you another Comforter, that He may abide with you for ever, even the Spirit of truth;" and speaks of this "Spirit of truth" as "the Comforter whom I will send unto you from the Father," and as "the Holy Ghost whom the Father will send in my name." In these words it is scarcely necessary to remark, that the mission of the Holy Spirit is expressly and inseparably connected with the mediatorial work of Christ, and more especially with that prevalent intercession which, on the ground of His finished work on earth, He should ever make as our high priest in heaven. And when our Lord speaks of *His own departure* as indispensably necessary to the coming of the Holy Spirit, we must hold Him as referring, not merely to His return to heaven, but to *the particular way* by which He was to return thither—namely, by the completion of that work of suffering obedience, as a recompense for which, "when He ascended up on high, He received gifts for men," and had "all power given to Him in heaven and in earth."

Christ had to go away in order that the Comforter might come.

John, xvi. 7.

John, xiv. 16-26; xv. 26.

Ps. lxviii. 18.

Eph. iv. 8.

Matt. xxviii. 18.

4. To the same effect is the explanation which St Peter gives of the great outpouring of the Holy Spirit on the day of Pentecost, when, after referring to the death and resurrection of Jesus Christ, he adds these words: "Therefore, being by the right hand of God exalted, and having

Spirit at Pentecost shed forth by Christ

Acts, ii. 33.

120   STATEMENTS OF THE NEW TESTAMENT

PART
I.
SEC. 9.
——

received of the Father the gift of the Holy Ghost, He hath shed forth this which ye now see and hear." And it must be remembered that this statement has a reference not only to the miraculous gifts of the Holy Spirit, but also to His converting and sanctifying grace, by which on that occasion no less a number than three thousand souls were added to the Church.

Christ hath redeemed us from the curse of the law, that we might receive the promise of the Spirit. Gal. iii. 13, 14.

5. In like manner St Paul declares to the Galatians, that " Christ hath redeemed us from the curse of the law, being made a curse for us (for it is written, Cursed is every one that hangeth on a tree) : that the blessing of Abraham might come on the Gentiles through Jesus Christ ; *that we might receive the promise of the Spirit through faith.*" In these words, our " receiving the promise of the Spirit " is evidently ascribed to the mediation of Christ, and in a more especial manner to His sufferings on the cross, whereby He " redeemed us from the curse of the law " by bearing it for us.

The Holy Ghost shed on us through Christ. Titus, iii. 5, 6.

6. Again, the same apostle states, in his Epistle to Titus, that " not by works of righteousness which we have done, but according to His mercy, God saved us by the washing of regeneration and renewing of *the Holy Ghost, which He shed on us abundantly through Jesus Christ our Saviour.*" In this statement it is much too obvious to be controverted that the grace of the Holy Spirit is represented as flowing to us through the mediation of our Redeemer.

All Christian graces which are fruits of the Spirit, conferred through Christ. John, i. 16; xv. 4, 5.

7. I need only add that there are many passages of the New Testament in which those Christian graces and virtues which spring from the operation of the Holy Spirit are said to be received by us or conferred on us through Jesus Christ. Of these the following may be taken as a specimen : " Of His fulness have all we received, and grace for grace." " Abide in me, and I in you. As the branch cannot bear fruit of itself, except it abide in the vine, no more can ye, except ye abide in me. I am the vine, ye are the branches : he that abideth in me,

RESPECTING THE ATONEMENT. 121

and I in him, the same bringeth forth much fruit: for
without me ye can do nothing." "I thank my God always
on your behalf, for the grace of God which is given you
by Jesus Christ; that in everything ye are enriched by
Him, in all utterance, and in all knowledge; even as the
testimony of Christ was confirmed in you: so that ye come
behind in no gift." "Of Him are ye in Christ Jesus, who
of God is made unto us wisdom, and righteousness, and
sanctification, and redemption." "Blessed be the God
and Father of our Lord Jesus Christ, who hath blessed us
with all spiritual blessings in heavenly places in Christ:
according as He hath chosen us in Him before the foundation of the world, that we should be holy and without
blame before Him in love." "We are His workmanship,
created in Christ Jesus unto good works." "Unto every
one of us is given grace according to the measure of the
gift of Christ." "In Him dwelleth all the fulness of the
Godhead bodily. And ye are complete in Him."

PART
I.
Sec. 9.
——
1 Cor. i.
4-7.

1 Cor. i.
30.

Eph. i. 3,
4.

Eph. ii. 10;
iv. 7.

Col. ii. 9,
10.

In these passages, not to mention others, we are taught
that all the graces of the Christian character, and all the
virtues of the Christian life, which are wrought in us by
the agency of the Holy Spirit—knowledge, wisdom, fruitfulness, good works—all enriching gifts, all spiritual and
heavenly blessings—are imparted through Christ and received out of His fulness. So plainly is this lesson taught
us in the Scriptures, that there seems to be scarcely a
possibility of misconceiving it. And I am very sure that
no humble and earnest believer, who carefully ponders
what is written in the oracles of God respecting the gifts
and graces of the Christian character with which by the
agency of the Spirit he is adorned, will for a moment think
of separating them from the mediation and atonement of
the Saviour, to which, as a redeemed and regenerated soul,
he is indebted for all that he is, and has, and hopes for.

If these things be so, the unfailing efficacy and full perfection of the Saviour's work are clearly apparent. For
while it provides a suitable and sufficient remedy for all the
evils and miseries of our sinful state, it also obtains that

Hence we
learn the
efficiency
and per-
fection of

122 STATEMENTS OF THE NEW TESTAMENT

*PART I.
SEC. 9.
———
the Saviour's work.*

grace of the Holy Spirit by which this remedy is effectually applied to those who are made partakers of its benefits. Thus does it not only *put them in a salvable position,* or place salvation, as it were, within their reach, but it secures salvation for them, and *actually " saves them to the uttermost."*

There are some who speak of "the *application* of redemption" as irrespective and independent of the *purchase* of it. But this it cannot be ; because we have now seen that the very grace of the Holy Spirit, by which the atonement is applied, is included among the benefits purchased by the atonement.

SECTION X.

PASSAGES WHICH SPEAK OF THE MEDIATION OF CHRIST
AS (15) DELIVERING US FROM THE DOMINION OF
SATAN ; AND (16) OBTAINING FOR US ETERNAL LIFE.

XV. THERE are some passages of the New Testament PART claiming our attention, in which *the deliverance of sinners* SEC. 10. *from the power of Satan*, and *the subversion of Satan's* ——— *dominion in the world*, are ascribed to the mediatorial Subversion work and sufferings of Jesus Christ. dominion through Christ.

Thus we have the general statement made by the beloved apostle, that " for this purpose was the Son of 1 John, iii. God manifested, that He might destroy the works of the 8. devil ;" from which we may understand that our Lord's mission was intended to frustrate the devices by which that arch-enemy had striven, but too successfully, to accomplish the ruin and depravation of our first parents and of their posterity.

Again, we have the declaration of our Lord Himself, uttered, as one of the evangelists has told us, not only in the immediate prospect of His last sufferings, but with a special reference to His death : " Now is the judgment of John, xii. this world : now shall the prince of this world be cast out. 31, 32. And I, if I be lifted up from the earth, will draw all men unto me." " The prince of this world " is an expression which our Lord has used on two other occasions, saying, at one time, " the prince of this world cometh, and hath John, xiv. nothing in me ;" and again, " the prince of this world is 30 ; xvi. 11. judged." We cannot doubt that the person thus desig-

124 STATEMENTS OF THE NEW TESTAMENT

PART
I.
SEC. 10.
———
2. Cor. iv.
4.
Eph. ii. 2.

Eph. vi.
12.

nated is no other than Satan, the inveterate adversary of
God and man, of whom St Paul speaks as "the *god of
this world*, who hath blinded the minds of them that
believe not;" and again, as "the prince of the power of
the air, the spirit that now worketh in the children of disobedience;" and whose emissaries are referred to by the
same apostle when he says, "We wrestle not against flesh
and blood, but against principalities, against powers,
against *the rulers of the darkness of this world*, against
spiritual wickedness in high places." This is the person
of whom our Lord declares, "Now is the judgment of this
world; now shall the prince of this world be cast out."
By twice emphatically repeating the word "*now*," He
plainly alludes to the nearness of His atoning death, by
which the great issue would finally be determined, whether
the world should be adjudged to Christ or to Satan. He
expresses at the same time His full confidence in the
approaching decision. From that time forward Satan,
who had hitherto been "the prince of this world," should
be ejected from his dominion; for the Saviour, when He
should be "lifted up from the earth" (a phrase by which
He "signified what death He should die"), would "draw
all men unto Him;" and the "prince of this world" would
have no power to detain his bondsmen when the greater
power, emanating from the cross, should withdraw them
from him. It is true the *actual* ejection of Satan is a
gradual process; for he still strives and struggles to
regain his lost ascendancy. But his ultimate overthrow
and expulsion are already secured. The Saviour is even
now the rightful sovereign among the nations; and in
due time His actual sovereignty shall be fully established,

Rev. xi.
15.

when at length "the great voices in heaven shall be heard,
saying, The kingdoms of this world are become the kingdoms of our Lord and of His Christ; and He shall reign
for ever and ever."

Heb. ii.
14, 15.

Again, we are told respecting the Son of God, that " He
took part of flesh and blood, that through death He might
destroy him that had the power of death, that is, the

RESPECTING THE ATONEMENT. 125

devil; and deliver them who through fear of death were all their lifetime subject to bondage." The " power of death," which the devil is here said to have had, is held by some critics to be equivalent to " deadly or destructive power." But this interpretation is unsuitable to the context. The mention of "death" in the clause immediately preceding and of the " fear of death" in the succeeding clause, leads us to conclude that the intervening expression, τὸν τὸ κράτος ἔχοντα τοῦ θανάτου, must here be translated " him that had the power of death." Nor is there any serious difficulty in apprehending the sense in which this " power " is attributed to the devil; for he may be held to have had " the power of death " as having been its prime author or originator, when his temptations led to the fall of that " one man, by whom sin entered into the world, and death by sin, and so death passed upon all men, for that all sinned." Besides, he may be said to have given death its terrific power, as being the continual promoter of "sin," which is the "sting of death." Now we are here told that one of the great ends of our Lord's incarnation was " to destroy him that had the power of death," or rather, as the word καταργήσῃ properly signifies, to " bring him to nought, or render his power of none effect." And this the Saviour accomplished " through death." He overcame the adversary with his own weapon. By the atoning sacrifice which He offered on the cross, He has changed entirely the aspect of death to all believers—making it to be no longer the penalty of sin and the gate of hell, but the safe entrance to everlasting blessedness in His heavenly kingdom. And thus has he " delivered those who through fear of death were all their lifetime subject to bondage," turning for His redeemed ones the curse into a blessing, and giving them cause to say with His apostle, " O death, where is thy sting? O grave, where is thy victory ? The sting of death is sin ; and the strength of sin is the law. But thanks be to God, who giveth us the victory through our Lord Jesus Christ."

The only other text of this class which I would advert

126   STATEMENTS OF THE NEW TESTAMENT

PART
I.
SEC. 10.
——

to is that notable passage in the Epistle to the Colossians, in which, after speaking of "the forgiveness of all our trespasses," and of the "blotting out the handwriting of ordinances that was against us, and taking it out of the way, and nailing it to His cross," the apostle adds these

Col. ii. 14.
15.

words, "And having spoiled principalities and powers, He made a show of them openly, triumphing over them in it."

Dean Alford insists that the word ἀπεκδυσάμενος, being a participle in the middle voice, cannot signify "having spoiled," but must be translated "*having put off*," or "*having divested Himself.*" And hence he infers that the "principalities and powers" must be understood as signifying, not "the infernal potentates whom the Saviour spoiled and triumphed over in His crucifixion," but "the angels by whom the law was ordained, and whom God *put off*, so that henceforth He should be manifested without a veil in the exalted person of Jesus," inasmuch as "the law was accomplished by the sacrifice of the cross, and Christ had all powers and principalities subjected to Him, and was made to be the only head of His people."

This interpretation is far from satisfactory. For in whatever sense the statements may be understood that

Acts, vii.
53; Gal.
iii. 19.

"the law was received by the disposition of angels," and "was ordained by angels in the hand of a mediator," it cannot be said that, by reason of any concern which the angels may thus have had in the giving of the law, they were " openly made a show of" and "triumphed over" by the sacrifice of Christ. I should rather say that they were *honoured* and *exalted*, inasmuch as the law, in whatever way they were connected with it, was so far from being in

Isa. xlii.
21.

any respect disparaged, that on the contrary it was "magnified and made honourable" by a sacrifice which maintained its unchangeable authority in the very redemption of those by whom it had been violated. Besides, even admitting the truth of Alford's statement, that ἀπεκδυσά-μενος cannot be understood in the active sense of "having spoiled," but must be taken in the middle sense of "having put off or divested Himself," there is no reason why it may not be applied to those *powers of evil* who had striven

RESPECTING THE ATONEMENT. 127

to counteract the merciful schemes of God for the benefit of mankind, and of whom the Redeemer may be said to have thoroughly divested or *rid Himself* when He vanquished and "openly made a show of them" on His cross.

Adhering on these grounds to the more obvious view of the passage, which almost all commentators have adopted, how striking a description does it give us of the glorious and triumphant issue of the Saviour's work! How clearly may we read in it the fulfilment of the ancient promise, that "the seed of the woman should bruise the head of the serpent, while the serpent should bruise His heel!" And how confidently may we be persuaded in contemplation of it, that "neither death, nor life, nor angels, nor principalities, nor powers, nor things present, nor things to come, nor height, nor depth, nor any other creature, shall be able to separate us from the love of God, which is in Christ Jesus our Lord"! "Our redemption," as has been well observed, "is a work at once of price and of power—of expiation and of conquest. On the cross was the purchase made, and on the cross was the victory gained. The blood which wipes out the sentence against us was there shed, and the death which was the death-blow of Satan's kingdom was there endured. Those nails which pierced Christ pierced also the sentence of doom,—gave egress to the blood that cancelled it, and inflicted at the same time a mortal wound on the hosts of darkness. That power which Satan had exercised was so prostrated, that every one believing in Christ is freed from his vassalage. The combatant died; but in dying He conquered. Hell might be congratulating itself that it had gained the mastery, and wondering what might be the most fitting commemoration and trophy; when lo! He who died arose the victor—no enemy again daring to dispute His power or challenge His right —and then God exhibited His foes in open triumph."

XVI. The next class of passages to which we must advert are those in which the blessings and glories of eternal life are connected with the mediatorial work and sufferings of Jesus Christ.

[Margin: PART I. SEC. 10.]

[Margin: Gen. iii. 15.]

[Margin: Rom. viii. 38, 39.]

[Margin: Eadie's Commentary on Colossians, p. 174.]

[Margin: Mediation of Christ obtains eternal life.]

128 STATEMENTS OF THE NEW TESTAMENT

PART I.
SEC. 10.

John, iii. 14-16.

John, v. 24.

John, vi. 40, 47, 51.

John, x. 27, 28.

John, xiv. 2, 3.

John, xvii. 1. 2.

Rom. v. 20, 21; vi. 23.

2 Tim. ii. 10.

Heb. v. 9; ix. 15.

Of these, which are very numerous, the following are a sufficient specimen :—

"The Son of Man must be lifted up, that whosoever believeth in Him should not perish, but have eternal life. For God so loved the world, that He gave His only begotten Son, that whosoever believeth in Him should not perish, but have everlasting life." "Verily, verily, I say unto you, He that heareth my word, and believeth on Him that sent me, hath everlasting life, and shall not come into condemnation ; but is passed from death unto life." "This is the will of Him that sent me, that every one who seeth the Son, and believeth on Him, may have everlasting life ; and I will raise Him up at the last day." "Verily, verily, I say unto you, He that believeth on me hath everlasting life." "I am the living bread that came down from heaven : if any man eat of this bread, he shall live for ever : and the bread which I shall give is my flesh, which I will give for the life of the world." "My sheep hear my voice, and I know them, and they follow me : and I give unto them eternal life ; and they shall never perish, neither shall any pluck them out of my hand." "In my Father's house are many mansions : if it were not so, I would have told you. I go to prepare a place for you. And if I go and prepare a place for you, I will come again, and receive you unto myself ; that where I am, there ye may be also." "Father, the hour is come ; glorify Thy Son, that Thy Son also may glorify Thee : as Thou hast given Him power over all flesh, that He should give eternal life to as many as Thou hast given Him." "Where sin abounded, grace did much more abound : that as sin hath reigned unto death, even so might grace reign through righteousness unto eternal life through Jesus Christ our Lord." "For the wages of sin is death ; but the gift of God is eternal life through Jesus Christ our Lord." "I endure all things for the elect's sake, that they may also obtain the salvation which is in Christ Jesus with eternal glory." "Being made perfect, He became the author of eternal salvation unto all them that obey Him." "He is the mediator of the new testament, that by means

RESPECTING THE ATONEMENT. 129

of death, for the redemption of the transgressions that were under the old testament, they which are called might receive the promise of eternal inheritance." "The God of all grace hath called us unto His eternal glory by Christ Jesus." "This is the record, that God hath given to us eternal life, and this life is in His Son." "Keep yourselves in the love of God, looking for the mercy of our Lord Jesus Christ unto eternal life."

PART I.
SEC. 10.
———
1 Pet. v. 10.
1 John, v. 11,
Jude, 21.

The import of these passages, in so far as regards the sole point for the establishment of which they are now referred to, is too plain to require any comment or illustration. Without the slightest ambiguity do they assure us that "eternal life is the gift of God through Jesus Christ;" that the "power which the Father hath given Him" to confer it, belongs to Him as "the mediator of the new covenant, who endured death for the redemption of transgressions under the old covenant," and "gave His flesh for the life of the world;" and that this power is exercised in behalf of "all who believe on Him," respecting whom we are expressly told that "they shall not perish, but shall have eternal life"—nay, that already "they have everlasting life, and shall not come into condemnation, but are passed from death unto life."

It need scarcely be remarked, that by the expression "eternal life," according to the usage of the New Testament, we must understand not that mere *eternity of existence* which is common alike to believers and to unbelievers, but that *eternity of happy and glorious existence* of which the faithful in Christ Jesus are alone partakers,—that state of everlasting union and communion with the source of all goodness and the centre of all excellence—of conformity to His holiness, of obedience to His will, of fellowship in His blessedness,—which constitutes the true life of an immortal creature, formed after the image of God, and destined, as his chief end, to glorify God and to enjoy Him for ever.

SECTION XI.

PASSAGES WHICH INDICATE (17) THE STATE OF THE
SAVIOUR'S MIND IN THE PROSPECT AND IN THE
ENDURANCE OF HIS SUFFERINGS.

PART
I.
SEC. II.
——
State of
our Lord's
mind when
anticipat-
ing and
enduring
His suffer-
ings.

Christ a
willing
sufferer.

John, 10,
17, 18.
Rom. i. 4.

Matt. xvi.
23.

Luke, iv.
51.

XVII. ANOTHER class of Scriptural testimonies which must not, in connection with our present inquiry, be overlooked, are those which indicate the state of the Saviour's mind in the anticipation and endurance of His sufferings.

1. That He was a *willing* sufferer is established by the fullest evidence. "I lay down my life," He says, "that I might take it again. No man taketh it from me, but I lay it down of myself. I have power to lay it down, and I have power to take it again." In these words the surrender of His life is represented as no less His own spontaneous act than was the resumption of it when He "was declared to be the Son of God with power by His resurrection from the dead." On another occasion He sternly rebuked Peter for deprecating the course of suffering that awaited Him, exclaiming, "Get thee behind me, Satan : thou art an offence unto me." He felt as if Peter, in urging Him to spare Himself, were casting a grievous stumbling-block in His way. And the vain attempt to turn Him from the cross excited in Him a feeling of resentment such as He did not cherish against His very crucifiers, for whose forgiveness indeed He prayed with His latest breath. Again, when the time of His crucifixion was drawing nigh, we are told that "He steadfastly set His face to go to Jerusalem." Instead of shunning or shrinking from a journey the bitter end of which was

RESPECTING THE ATONEMENT.   131

clearly in His view, He pressed onwards on His way with PART
earnest resolution, and suffered no obstacles or dangers to SEC. II.
withdraw Him from it. And yet again, when one of the
disciples sought to smite the band that came to drag Him
before His persecutors, our Saviour checked him with the
calm but firm remonstrance, " Put up thy sword into the John, xviii.
sheath: the cup which my Father hath given me, shall I 11.
not drink it?"

From all this we see how erroneous a conception those
persons have formed of the sufferings of our Lord who
speak of Him as forcibly constrained or even as pas-
sively submitting to the endurance of them. And no less
erroneous is it to regard Him as one who, by the assumption of our nature, had brought Himself within the operation of " laws or principles of evil," as they are called, from
the fatal influence of which it was impossible for Him, any
more than ordinary men, to be exempted. In all His
sorrows and agonies we must think of Him not as a
reluctant victim, but as a spontaneous sufferer ; for we
cannot doubt that, had He so willed it, He might by the
exercise of His great power have been delivered from
them. Even His cruel death, though inflicted by violent
men, was yet on His own part a voluntary act of self-
sacrifice. He was bound by no constraint to the endurance of it, unless it were that constraint which redeeming
love imposed upon Him. " I lay down my life," He says,
" of myself." And no man could have taken it from Him,
if it had not been for the great love wherewith He loved us.

2. It must not be thought, however, that He was the Christ's
less sensible of the poignancy of the sufferings awaiting deep sense
Him, for all His firmness and willingness in encountering sufferings
them. On one occasion we find Him thus expressing the awaiting
mingled feelings with which they were regarded by Him: Him.
" I have a baptism to be baptised with ; and how am I Luke, xii.
straitened till it be accomplished !" These words are 50.
strongly descriptive of that inward struggle with which we
might naturally look forward to some dreadful trial, from
the thought of which we are instinctively disposed to

132 STATEMENTS OF THE NEW TESTAMENT

PART I.
SEC. 11.

shrink, but which, with a view to great benefits to be secured by it, we are notwithstanding resolved to undergo —so firmly resolved that we cannot be at rest, but are "straitened" and ill at ease until we have endured it. Accordingly we have, in this utterance of the Saviour, what Stier has well termed His "*passio inchoata*"—the first indication of that "travail of the soul" which afterwards broke forth in tones of deeper wailing, but which was ever combined with earnest and devoted zeal for the great work He had undertaken to accomplish.

On another occasion, when His last sufferings were drawing nigh, He thus gave vent to the anguish of His spirit : "Now is my soul troubled ; and what shall I say ? Father, save me from this hour : but for this cause came I to this hour." There are two lights in which this saying has been regarded. Some writers consider the clause "What shall I say ?" as indicating a process of deliberation in our Lord's mind as to what course He should follow in His present deep affliction. The succeeding clause also is read by them interrogatively, as if He had asked Himself, "Shall I say *this*, Father, save me from this hour ?" And then He is supposed to have thus answered His own question, "But for this cause came I to this hour;" and thereafter to have substituted for the petition which had first occurred to Him that other petition which He prefers in the succeeding verse, "Father, glorify Thy name." To this view of the matter it has, I think, been justly objected that it ascribes to the Saviour on this occasion a train of self-reflection which does not well comport with that vehement emotion with which "His soul was troubled." Besides, there is much force in Bengel's shrewd remark, that our Lord's words are " *Quid dicam*," and not " *Quid eligam*." He does not say, like Paul, "What I shall choose I wot not ; for I am in a strait betwixt two things." He rather indicates that His sorrows are unutterable—so great that no language can adequately describe them, or that His human soul is so overwhelmed by them that He can find no words wherewith to give expression to them. According to this latter view, the

John, xii. 27.

Philip. i. 22, 23.

RESPECTING THE ATONEMENT.   133

succeeding clause is a veritable prayer, in which the PART
deep longings, which even His perfect humanity could not SEC. II.
but feel for deliverance, are expressed—accompanied, however, with entire submission to His Father's will, and with
earnest zeal for the purposes of His heavenly mission.
And in this respect His words are closely akin to those
which He soon after uttered in His agony : " O my Father,
if it be possible, let this cup pass from me : nevertheless
not as I will, but as Thou wilt."

In either view, our Saviour's language on this occasion
is evidently expressive of deep mental anguish—of a
"travail of His soul" unfathomable and unutterable—such
as it seems impossible to reconcile with the perfection of
His character and the divinity of His person by any mere
reference to the bodily sufferings that were awaiting Him,
apart from His vicarious position as the sin-bearer, " on
whom the Lord had laid the iniquity of us all."

3. A still more touching indication of the feelings with The agony
which the Saviour's sufferings were regarded by Him is in Geth-
given in the narrative of His agony, which is thus recorded semane.
by one of the evangelists : " Then Jesus cometh with them Matt. xxvi.
unto a place called Gethsemane, and saith unto the dis- 36-44.
ciples, Sit ye here, while I go and pray yonder.   And He
took with Him Peter and the two sons of Zebedee, and
began to be sorrowful and very heavy.   Then saith He unto
them, *My soul is exceeding sorrowful, even unto death :* tarry
ye here, and watch with me.   And He went a little farther,
and fell on His face, and prayed, saying, *O my Father, if
it be possible, let this cup pass from me : nevertheless not as
I will, but as Thou wilt.*   And He cometh unto the disciples, and findeth them asleep, and saith unto Peter,
What, could ye not watch with me one hour ?   Watch
and pray, that ye enter not into temptation : the spirit
indeed is willing, but the flesh is weak.   He went away
again the second time, and prayed, saying, *O my Father,
if this cup may not pass from me, except I drink it, Thy will
be done.*   And He came and found them asleep again ; for
their eyes were heavy.   And He left them, and went away

134   STATEMENTS OF THE NEW TESTAMENT

PART
I.
SEC. II.
———
Mark, xiv.
33.
Luke, xxii.
44.

again, and prayed the third time, saying the same words."
Two other evangelists give substantially the same account,
with these additional circumstances, that Jesus was " sore
amazed," and that, "being in an agony He prayed more
earnestly: and His sweat was as it were great drops of
blood falling down to the ground."

There is something deeply mysterious in this passage
of our Lord's history.   It seems scarcely a fit or becoming
thing to pry into it.   Nor can we speak of it without feeling that we speak inadequately, and fearing that we may
speak amiss.   Thus much, however, we may venture to

Not to be
explained
by His
mere
bodily
sufferings

affirm, that the agony of soul which He endured on this
occasion, His " sore amazement " and " exceeding sorrowfulness," and His " earnest " and thrice-repeated " prayer "
that " if it were possible the cup might pass from Him,"
cannot be ascribed to His mere anticipation of the outward
and bodily afflictions which were awaiting Him.   Apart
from the consideration of His divinity, such a supposition
would cast a foul disparagement on the excellence and
perfection of His humanity.   It would, moreover, be altogether inconsistent with the undaunted firmness and
dignified composure maintained by Him in the actual
endurance of these afflictions.   Nor must it be forgotten
that many a Christian martyr has submitted to outward
and bodily afflictions no less excruciating than those which
Christ endured without displaying aught of that depression
and perturbation of spirit with which, in this dark hour,
the Saviour was agonised.   And surely we cannot think
that these disciples were above their Master, or that these
servants were greater than their Lord.

Supposed
tempta-
tions of
Satan.

Some have supposed that our Saviour on this occasion
was more than ordinarily assailed with the temptations of
the devil.   It may have been so.   But we have no hint of
any such thing in the narratives of the evangelists.   And
when St Luke expressly mentions " the appearance to

Luke, xxii.
43.

Him of an angel from heaven strengthening Him," it
seems unaccountable that this evangelist should not have
noticed our Lord's severe conflict with another emissary

RESPECTING THE ATONEMENT.   135

from the world of spirits, if His agony had been truly or PART I.
mainly attributable to such a cause. SEC. II,

Others have thought, with much greater probability,
that the deep anguish which our Saviour experienced on Supposed
this occasion arose from some mysterious agency on the direct agency of
part of God. The words of Isaiah were receiving their God.
accomplishment—" It pleased the Lord to bruise Him, and
to put Him to grief." Whether by withdrawing from Him Isa. liii. 10.
for a season the sensible joys and comforts of the divine
fellowship, or by visiting Him with some positive inflic-
tions of the divine chastening, His heavenly Father was
causing Him to feel how bitter a thing it was to be " made
sin for us, that we might be made the righteousness of 2 Cor. v.
God in Him." 21.

Perhaps it may not be necessary to have recourse to
either of these suppositions in order to account for the
" exceeding sorrow" of Gethsemane, if only we keep in
view those Scriptural testimonies, the import of which we
have already endeavoured to ascertain, respecting the
mediatorial office and work of Jesus Christ. For it would
seem as if the very position in which He stood, as the con- His posi-
scious sin-bearer burdened with our iniquities, when closely tion as sin-
and vividly brought before His mind by the fast approach- source of
ing hour in which His great sacrifice should be consum- agony.
mated, might of itself be sufficient to explain the anguish
and heaviness of spirit with which He was afflicted. For
we may well conceive that to a perfectly pure and holy
Being it could not be other than a source of grievous
agony to have all the iniquities of a sinful world laid upon
Him, and that accursed thing imputed to Himself which
He cannot look upon in others without abhorrence. From
so bitter a cup as *this*, we can hardly wonder that all the
sensibilities of His perfect and sinless humanity should
have been ready instinctively to recoil, and that they
should have sought utterance in the prayer, expressive at
once of intense suffering and of meek submission, " O my
Father, if it be possible, let this cup pass from me : nevertheless not as I will, but as Thou wilt."

136   STATEMENTS OF THE NEW TESTAMENT

PART I.
SEC. II.

Cry of desertion on the cross.

Matt. xxvii. 46.

4. The agony of the garden finds its echo in the plaintive cry of desertion on the cross; when, amidst the ominous darkness with which for three hours the face of nature was overspread, the Saviour, after an interval of silent suffering, uttered with a loud voice these words of awful import, "My God, my God, why hast Thou forsaken me?"

Reference to His bodily sufferings not excluded.

This exclamation has commonly been held to refer exclusively to that mysterious anguish with which the soul of the Redeemer was afflicted, and not in any respect or in any degree to His bodily sufferings. It is questionable, however, whether by thus viewing it, its true meaning be not unwarrantably restricted. For we must remember that the words are a quotation of the 1st verse of the 22d Psalm, in which there is a notable prediction of the Messiah's agonies. And in that Psalm the words here quoted are followed by allusions, not merely to sorrows of a spiritual nature, but also to the "disjointing of His bones;" "the drying up of His strength like a potsherd;" the "cleaving of His tongue to His jaws;" the "melting of His heart like wax;" the "piercing of His hands and feet;" the "compassing of Him by assemblies of wicked men," who "shook their heads at Him, and laughed Him to scorn." And hence we have no sufficient reason for supposing that any of His manifold afflictions were excluded by Him, when quoting a verse which, as uttered by the prophetic Psalmist, was thus plainly applicable to all of them without exception.

Ps. xxii. 7, 12, 14, 15, 16.

All His sufferings traced to the will of His Father.

One thing is clear, however, that in using this language, the complicated woes with which He was afflicted are traced to the will and appointment of His Father in heaven. The human agents who occasioned them are overlooked, or viewed as mere subordinate instruments in the hand of God, doing to Him no other things than those which the purpose and counsel of heaven had ordained, as things to which it behoved Him to be subjected. And thus regarding all the sufferings that were laid upon Him as a punitive dispensation of divine justice, with which as the substitute of sinners He was visited, He might justly

RESPECTING THE ATONEMENT. 137

speak of Himself with respect to them as one who had been forsaken by the Lord.

In saying so, however, we are far from disallowing that there is in these words a more especial reference to those spiritual agonies which seem to have been endured by Him in the innermost recesses of His heart. In order to give its just meaning to His language, we can hardly suppose less than that, amidst His other sufferings, the sensible joys and consolations of His Father's fellowship and countenance were withheld from Him. Nor is it any very difficult matter to conceive that even in the case of the beloved Son of God some such spiritual privation may have been endured. For it is not beyond the bounds of human experience that the favour and love of God should actually be possessed, while no felt support and encouragement are derived from them. Although it be an unquestionable truth that "the Lord will never leave nor forsake His people," and that "nothing can ever separate them from His love," yet are there times in the history of His most devoted servants, in which we find them bitterly deploring that the light of His gracious countenance is hidden from them, and that they derive no conscious satisfaction from the joys of His favour and the comforts of His fellowship. May we not say, then, that this was the main source of the Saviour's lamentation on the cross? It certainly appears to be the kind of affliction which His words most naturally and obviously suggest. And I may add, that we should seem to be detracting in no small degree from His fortitude and devotedness were we to suppose that any affliction short of this, any accumulation of mere bodily tortures, apart from the overclouding of His Father's face, could have extorted from Him the loud and grievous cry, "My God, my God, why hast Thou forsaken me?"

Doubtless He was now as much as ever—we may almost say, more than ever—the object of His Father's love. But He was bereft of those tokens or expressions of it which heretofore had comforted and cheered Him. No approving smile, no commending voice, nc inward

PART I. SEC. II.

A special reference to His spiritual afflictions.

The Saviour bereft of sensible tokens of His Father's love.

138 STATEMENTS OF THE NEW TESTAMENT

PART
I.
SEC. II.
———

John, xvi.
32.

His an-
guish real.

Only to be
explained
by His sub-
stitution
for sinners.

manifestation of the divine favour, is given to support the "Man of sorrows" in His extremity. On a former occasion, when speaking of the hour in which all His disciples should be scattered and should leave Him alone, He had added, "And yet I am not alone, because the Father is with me." But now this, His chief solace, seems to have been withdrawn, or the light and peace which it had been wont to give are hidden from Him. For though He still clings to God, and claims Him as *His own,* He evidently expresses a sense of being forsaken by Him. We can put no other construction upon His words. As little can we doubt that He felt what His language expresses. It is not for a moment to be supposed that He was merely *personating* the case of a deserted soul, or speaking *like one* whose comfortable sense of the favour and fellowship of God had been obscured, while yet He was actually enjoying them as much as ever. No, surely. If there be any passage in the Saviour's history which may be said to be *intensely real,* it is this. He who had hitherto borne without a murmur the stripes, the wounds, the bruises, and the bitter taunts, would not, we may be sure, have uttered such a cry as that which proceeded from Him on the cross, for any inward grief in which there was no reality. But if so, how is His desertion to be accounted for? On what principle can it be explained, if His sufferings were private or personal, and not vicarious? Surely it is not in any way to be reconciled with the sinlessness of His character, the divinity of His person, the great love with which He was ever regarded by His heavenly Father— above all, with the fact that at the very moment of His endurance of it He was finishing the work which His Father had assigned to Him — unless there had been something in the nature of His work which required Him to be not only "persecuted" but "forsaken," in order that the full "chastisement of our peace should be laid upon Him," while " His soul was made an offering for sin."

Thus does it appear that the state of the Saviour's

RESPECTING THE ATONEMENT. 139

mind, in the anticipation and endurance of His sufferings, affords a most important confirmation of those testimonies of Scripture in which we are informed of the purpose for which these sufferings were appointed. For it perfectly accords with the Scriptural representations of Him, as " wounded for our transgressions, and bruised for our iniquities,"—" bearing our sins in His own body on the tree,"—" suffering for sins, the just for the unjust,"—" and " made sin for us, while He knew no sin, that we might be made the righteousness of God in Him."

PART
I.
SEC. 11.

SECTION XII.

PASSAGES WHICH SPEAK OF THE MEDIATION OF CHRIST
IN RELATION (18) TO THE FREE CALLS AND OFFERS
OF THE GOSPEL; AND (19) TO THE NECESSITY OF
FAITH IN ORDER TO OBTAIN THE BLESSINGS OF THE
GOSPEL.

PART
I.
SEC. 12.
———
Mediation
of Christ
in relation
to offers of
the Gospel.

XVIII. THE next class of passages to which we may advert are those which speak of the mediation of Christ, and of the inestimable benefits procured by it, in relation to the free calls and offers of the Gospel.

Salvation
offered
through
Christ
alone.
John, xiv.
6.
1 Cor. iii.
11.
1 Tim. ii.
5.
Acts, iv.
12.

In one respect the invitations of the Gospel are *exclusive.* They are so as offering salvation to sinners through Christ *alone.* Thus our Lord Himself has expressly declared, " I am the way, the truth, and the life ; no man cometh unto the Father but by me." St Paul also affirms that " other foundation can no man lay than that is laid, which is Jesus Christ ;" and that " there is one God, and one mediator between God and men, the man Christ Jesus." And to the same effect St Peter has assured us, that " Neither is there salvation in any other ; for there is none other name under heaven given among men whereby we must be saved."

The invita-
tions free.

But in another respect the invitations of the Gospel are in the highest degree *liberal and gracious.* They are held out to men of every clime, of every race, of every class, of every character, without distinction. So wide and indiscriminate are the calls which they address to all sinners— even to the chief of sinners ; so perfectly free and unfettered by limitations are the terms of access to the Saviour

RESPECTING THE ATONEMENT.   141

which they propose; so urgent the entreaties, so peremp- PART
tory the commands, so earnest the expostulations with SEC. 12.
which they are enforced; and so unqualified the assurances they give us that all who comply with them shall
attain the needful blessings;—that it is difficult to see
what larger or clearer warrant than that which they afford
us to receive the offered grace could reasonably be desired,
or, I may even say, imagined.

Take as a specimen the following statements, which
must be familiar to every reader of the Scriptures:—

"God so loved the world, that He gave His only-be- John, iii.
gotten Son, that whosoever believeth in Him should not 16, 17.
perish, but have everlasting life." " Come unto me, all ye Matt. xi.
that labour and are heavy laden, and I will give you rest." 28.
" Him that cometh to me I will in no wise cast out." "If John, vi.
any man thirst, let him come unto me, and drink." "Ye 37; vii. 37;
will not come to me, that ye might have life." "How Matt. xxiii.
often would I have gathered thy children together, even 37.
as a hen gathereth her chickens under her wings, and ye
would not!" "Go ye into all the world, and preach the Mark, xvi.
Gospel to every creature." "Believe on the Lord Jesus Acts, xvi.
Christ, and thou shalt be saved." "Now then we are 31.
ambassadors for Christ, as though God did beseech you 20; vi. 1.
by us; we pray you in Christ's stead, be ye reconciled to
God." " We then, as workers together with Him, beseech
you also, that ye receive not the grace of God in vain."
" How shall we escape, if we neglect so great salvation?" Heb. ii. 3.
"This is His commandment, that we should believe on the 1 John, iii.
name of His Son Jesus Christ." " I will give to him that 23.
is athirst of the fountain of the water of life freely;" "The 6; xxii. 17.
Spirit and the bride say, Come; and let him that heareth
say, Come; and let him that is athirst come; and whosoever will, let him take the water of life freely."

On reading these and suchlike passages, which are of
frequent occurrence in the Word of God, we may well ask,
What more can be required—what more can be wished
for—in the way of encouragement to embrace the Gospel,
than they supply? What further overtures of divine
mercy can be needed to disarm the most alienated mind

142   STATEMENTS OF THE NEW TESTAMENT

PART I.
SEC. 12.

of its suspicions, or relieve the most trembling spirit of its fears ? Suppose the most hardened sinner who has ever seemed to weary out the patience of Heaven by his provocations, or the most desponding sinner who imagines that he has sunk beyond the reach of mercy, were allowed to draw up, in words of his own selection, a series of invitations, entreaties, and commands, which should be sufficient to dispel his every doubt respecting his warrant to receive the Saviour's blessings, he could not have done so more effectually than the Spirit of God in these passages has done it for him.   So far is it, indeed, from being the case that any man is not fully warranted to embrace the Gospel, that on the contrary no man living is warranted in refusing or hesitating to embrace the Gospel.   If men would but seriously consider how the matter stands, they could hardly fail to see the folly of supposing that they are not entitled to do a thing which God has not only invited but enjoined them to do—that they dare not presume so far as to comply with His urgent entreaties and tender remonstrances—and that from their dread of offending Him by an unwarranted compliance, they have no alternative but to cast aside His offers, to resist His importunities, and to defy His express commandments!

Special invitations to those who feel their need, are not to be held as limiting the general invitations.

It is true that some of the invitations are specially given to those who "thirst," or to those who "labour and are heavy laden,"—descriptions which may be held to indicate a *felt need* of the offered mercies.   But this circumstance cannot be reasonably taken as any discouragement by such persons as fear that they are not sufficiently sensible of their spiritual wants.   For a *felt need* of the offered mercies is requisite, not in any respect as a *warrant to entitle us*, but simply as a *motive to prevail with us*, to come to the Saviour that our need may be supplied. Those who "thirst," or who "labour and are heavy laden," are specially invited to comply with the Saviour's call,— not because they are *more worthy* than others, but because they ought to be *more willing*—because they are more inexcusable if they withhold compliance—and be-

RESPECTING THE ATONEMENT. 143

cause, at the same time, they specially require encouragement, as being of all persons the most apt to be disquieted by doubts and fears about their warrant to embrace the Gospel.

PART I. SEC. 12.

It is also true that there are passages in Holy Scripture which speak of the Lord's redeemed people as those who have been "chosen in Him" or "given to Him." But neither can this consideration be regarded as a reasonable ground for declining the offered grace. Our conduct must be regulated—not by God's secret purpose, which for the present we have no means of ascertaining—but by His revealed will, which is clearly and fully declared to us in the invitations of His Word. No one to whom these invitations are addressed has any right or any reason to presume, before accepting of them, that he *is* among the number of those who have been "given to the Saviour;" and as little has he any right or any reason to be discouraged by the unwarranted assumption that he is *not* among their number. He knows not whether he has been "chosen in Christ;" but of *this* he is sure, that *he is invited to come to Christ.* And his ignorance respecting the purpose of election, which is hidden from him, is no ground for refusing the invitation, which is clearly announced to him and urgently pressed upon him. It is remarkable, indeed, that on one of those occasions on which our Lord was most distinctly alluding to those "whom the Father had given to Him," and declaring that "all such shall come to Him," He has effectually provided against any discouraging inference that might be drawn from such a declaration, by adding immediately afterwards the cheering assurance, "And him that cometh to me I will in no wise cast out."

That believers are said to have been "chosen in Christ" and "given to Him" is no ground for declining offered grace.

John, vi. 37.

XIX. Intimately connected with the texts above referred to is another and a very numerous class of passages, which indicate *faith in Christ* as the means by which we obtain the benefits of His mediation.

Of these it may suffice to quote the following :—

Faith in Christ the means of obtaining His benefits.

144   STATEMENTS OF THE NEW TESTAMENT

PART I.
SEC. 12.
———
John, i. 12.

John, iii. 18, 36.

John, vi. 35.

Acts, xiii. 38, 39; xvi. 31.

Rom. i. 16; iii. 28; v. 1.

Rom. x. 4.

Gal. v. 6.

Eph. ii. 8. 9.

"As many as received Him, to them gave He power to become the sons of God, even to them who believe on His name." "He that believeth on Him is not condemned ; but he that believeth not is condemned already, because he hath not believed in the name of the only-begotten Son of God." "He that believeth on the Son hath everlasting life ; and he that believeth not the Son shall not see life, but the wrath of God abideth on him." "Jesus said unto them, I am the bread of life; he that cometh to me shall never hunger ; and he that believeth on me shall never thirst." "Through this Man is preached unto you the forgiveness of sins ; and by Him all that believe are justified from all things, from which ye could not be justified by the law of Moses." "Believe on the Lord Jesus Christ, and thou shalt be saved." "I am not ashamed of the Gospel of Christ, for it is the power of God unto salvation to every one that believeth." "Therefore we conclude that a man is justified by faith without the deeds of the law." "Being justified by faith, we have peace with God through our Lord Jesus Christ ; by whom also we have access by faith into this grace wherein we stand, and rejoice in hope of the glory of God." "Christ is the end of the law for righteousness to every one that believeth." "In Christ Jesus neither circumcision availeth anything nor uncircumcision, but faith which worketh by love." "By grace are ye saved through faith ; and that not of yourselves, it is the gift of God : not of works, lest any man should boast."

Nature of faith.

Now, in regard to the *nature* of that "faith" which is so plainly set forth in these and other passages as the means of participating in the benefits of redemption, we hold that it cannot be rightly and fully defined as any *mere intellectual conviction* of certain revealed truths with reference to Jesus Christ, but that it includes also a *trustful reliance on Him*, and a *cordial reception of Him* for salvation, as He is offered to us in the Gospel. The Scriptural grounds on which this view of the nature of faith in the Saviour may be maintained we shall briefly state in the Appendix

RESPECTING THE ATONEMENT. 145

to this volume.* But for the present we may venture to assume it, and all the more so that even those who regard faith as being in itself considered a mere persuasion of the understanding, are ready to admit that wherever it is sincere and conducive to the spiritual good of those who have attained to it, a trustful reception of Christ, though not one of its essential elements, is certainly one of its most immediate and unfailing results.

PART I. SEC. 12.

Now, if it be so, that *a trustful receiving of Christ for salvation as He is offered in the Gospel* is essential to the nature, or, at all events, inseparable from the acting or exercise of faith in Christ, we can have no difficulty in apprehending *how it is* that this faith should be the means of salvation. It is so, not by any arbitrary appointment of God, who is, doubtless, entitled to dispense His offered mercies on any terms or conditions which He may be pleased to prescribe—still less by reason of any merit or intrinsic excellence in faith, by which it specially commends itself to the divine favour ; but on the obvious and perfectly intelligible principle that *invitations must be complied with, promises must be relied on, and proffered blessings must be received by us, in order that we may be personally benefited by them.* Food will not nourish us unless we partake of it ; a remedy will not cure us unless we consent to have it applied ; and no more will Christ, with all His fulness of spiritual blessings, be to us personally of any real advantage, unless we receive and rest upon Him for salvation. It is not God's method to save sinners against their will. He makes them a "willing people in the day of His power"—willing to come to the Saviour that they may have life.

How is it that we are saved by faith?

Ps. cx. 3.

I need scarcely observe that the passages above referred to afford a highly important corroboration to those other Scriptural testimonies before adduced, with reference to the benefits secured by the mediatorial work and sufferings of Jesus Christ. For if the remission of sins, justification, adoption, peace with God, salvation, eternal life,

This class of texts confirmatory of previous testimonies.

---

* See Appendix, Note F

146 STATEMENTS OF THE NEW TESTAMENT

PART I.
SEC. 12.
——

and, in short, all spiritual and heavenly blessings, are to be obtained by trustfully receiving and resting on the Saviour, it cannot be otherwise than that these blessings have been procured by Him, and are offered in His name to all who will put their trust in Him.

Completeness and efficacy of the work of Christ.

But this is not all. We may learn also from the above passages the *efficacy* and *completeness* of the mediatorial work of Christ.

Some persons affirm that the Atonement has no further effect than that of putting us into what they call "*a salvable position.*" It has removed obstacles, otherwise insurmountable, which stood in the way of our being saved; and has provided for us manifold and important facilities, by the due improvement of which our salvation may be accomplished. But while it has thus obtained for all sinners a *possibility of being saved*, it has not secured for any an *actual and complete salvation*. According to this view, something remains to be done, beyond what Christ has done, in order to turn the *possible* into the *actual*. And this something is done by the *faith* of the believer; which consequently falls to be regarded, not simply as the resting of the soul on a work already perfected, but as a supplement to that work which is necessary to the completion of it.

This opinion, however, is altogether inconsistent with sound Scriptural views of the nature and province of *faith*. It is essential to the exercise of faith to rely wholly on the doings or merits of its object, and utterly to disclaim all confidence in our own resources. And it is especially characteristic of the Christian's faith to rest with entire and unqualified trust on Christ alone. If faith, as conducive to salvation, were regarded as supplementing the Saviour's work, instead of simply resting on it, the broad distinction which the Apostle Paul has drawn between "faith" and "works" would be altogether obliterated, and his express declarations would be falsified, in which

Eph. ii. 8, 9.

Rom. iv. 16.

he has so unequivocally assured us that "by grace we are saved through faith, and not of works, lest any man should boast;" and that "it is of faith, that it might be by grace." Besides, the Scriptural representations given

RESPECTING THE ATONEMENT. 147

us of the exercise of faith with reference to the Saviour,— as "coming to Christ," "receiving Him," "trusting in Him," "committing ourselves to Him," " fleeing for refuge to lay hold" upon Him, "eating of the bread of life," "taking of the water of life,"—are evidently significant, not of anything done by believers to supplement the Saviour's work, but of a trustful application to Him, and dependence on Him, for those spiritual blessings which He has fully secured, and is ready to impart to all who truly seek them.

PART I.
SEC. 12.
——
John, vi. 35; i. 12.
Eph. i. 12.
2 Tim. i. 12.
Heb. vi. 18.
John, vi. 51.
Rev. xxii.

If such be the nature and such the functions of Christian faith, as simply "receiving and resting upon Christ for salvation, as He is offered to us in the Gospel," we are shut up to the conclusion that Christ's is a finished work, requiring and admitting of nothing on our part to supplement it. Whatever Christ is to those who by faith receive Him, *that* He must previously have been as offered to them ; for faith does not add anything to the properties of its object—it simply "receives and rests" on that object, *such as it is.* Accordingly, if Christ be to all believers an *actual* Saviour, and one who "is able to save them to the uttermost," it must be as a *complete and actual Saviour* that He was offered to them. For if we suppose Him to have been *less than this*, as offered to them, their mere acceptance of the offer could not have supplied the deficiency. If all that His work accomplished was *to put sinners into a salvable position,* our reliance on that work might give us the comfort of knowing that salvation is to us a *possible* attainment, but nothing more. Never in that case would we be warranted to say, in the words of Scripture, "He that believeth on the Son *hath* everlasting life;" "By Him all that believe *are* justified from all things;" "Being justified by faith, we have peace with God through our Lord Jesus Christ;" "There is now no condemnation to them that are in Christ Jesus;" "In whom we have redemption through His blood, the forgiveness of sins, according to the riches of His grace;" "Of Him are ye in Christ Jesus, who of God is made unto us wisdom, and righteousness, and sanctification, and redemption."

17.

John, iii. 36.
Acts, xiii. 39.
Rom. v. 1; viii. 1.
Eph. i. 7.
1 Cor. i. 30.

SECTION XIII.

PASSAGES WHICH SPEAK OF THE MEDIATORIAL WORK
AND SUFFERINGS OF CHRIST IN RELATION (20)
TO HIS COVENANT WITH THE FATHER, AND (21)
TO HIS UNION WITH BELIEVERS.

PART I.
SEC. 13.
———
Sufferings of Christ in relation to the covenant of grace.

XX. ANOTHER class of passages claiming our attention are those which refer to what is ordinarily called " the covenant of grace," or which represent the Lord Jesus Christ, in all that He did and suffered for us, as fulfilling the terms of a gracious compact or arrangement, into which He had entered with His heavenly Father on our behalf.

John, vi. 38-40.

1. Thus our Lord declares, " I came down from heaven, not to do mine own will, but the will of Him that sent me. And this is the Father's will that sent me, that of all which He hath given me I should lose nothing, but should raise it up again at the last day. And this is the will of Him that sent me, that every one which seeth the Son and believeth on Him may have everlasting life."

Without for the present insisting on other points of Christian doctrine which are deducible from these statements, we evidently learn from them, that the Son of God received a certain *charge* or *commission* from His Father, which He solemnly engaged and undertook to execute; and further, that the end contemplated in this arrangement was, not merely the *announcement* of spiritual blessings, but the *attainment* of them, in behalf of all such as should eventually believe in Christ. Nor must we omit to notice that *our Lord's sufferings* were present to His mind on this occasion, or forming a prominent part of the gracious

RESPECTING THE ATONEMENT.   149

work devolved upon Him. For in the context, when He
goes on to speak of Himself as "the living bread which
came down from heaven, of which if any man eat he shall
live for ever," He adds, "And the bread which I will
give is,"—not my edifying doctrine—not my salutary
precepts—not my encouraging example—not my consolatory promises—but " MY FLESH, *which I will give for
the life of the world."*

PART
I.
SEC. 13.
——
John, vi.
51.

2. In like manner the Saviour speaks in another passage
of a special charge He had received, in behalf of " His
sheep whom His Father had given Him," in fulfilment of
which charge He " brings them into the fold,"—"lays
down His life for them,"—"gives them eternal life," and
securely provides that " they shall never perish."

John, x.
14-18;
27-29.

3. Again, in His intercessory prayer, which He offered
up on the eve of His last sufferings, we find Him so constantly and evidently proceeding on the ground of a compact He had made with His Father, in behalf of those
" whom the Father had given to Him,"—of a work which
in terms of this compact He had undertaken,—and of the
finishing of this work by His death which was fast approaching,—that we cannot understand His language on
any other supposition than that His entire course of obedience and of suffering was undergone in fulfilment of a
determinate plan, devised and arranged in concert with
His heavenly Father, for the spiritual good of those who
had been committed to Him.

John, xvii.

4. The same truth is no less strikingly set forth by the
Apostle Paul, when he speaks of all manner of " spiritual
blessings," such as " redemption," " forgiveness," " holiness," " acceptance," " adoption," and " a heavenly inheritance," as conferred upon believers,—declares expressly of
each and all of these blessings, that it is *" in Christ "* that
believers are partakers of them, and traces them all back
to their ultimate source in the everlasting counsels of the
Godhead, by which their recipients were " chosen in Christ
before the foundation of the world," and " predestinated
according to the purpose of Him who worketh all things
after the counsel of His own will."

Eph. i. 3-
11.

150 STATEMENTS OF THE NEW TESTAMENT

PART
I.
SEC. 13.

Rom. v.
12-19.

1 Cor. xv.
20-23; 45-
47.

5. Again, there are several passages of St Paul's writings in which a parallel is drawn between Adam and Christ, and Adam is described as a "figure" or "type" of Christ. And these passages are most satisfactorily interpreted on the principle, that Adam and Christ are the respective *federal heads* or *representatives* of those whom the one has involved in sin and condemnation, and for whom the other has secured righteousness and eternal life.

Heb. xii.
24; vii.
22; viii.
6; xiii. 20.

Jer. xxxi.
31-34

Heb. viii.
8-13.

6. Add to all this, that Christ is repeatedly called "the Mediator of the new covenant," and "the Mediator" and "Surety of a better covenant;" that His blood is termed "the blood of the everlasting covenant;" that the words of Jeremiah, when he speaks of a "new covenant," containing the sure promise of those very blessings which the death of Christ has purchased for believers, are expressly applied to the dispensation of the Gospel; and that Christ Himself, when instituting the Lord's Supper, said, "This cup is my blood of the new covenant, which is shed for many for the remission of sins."

On these grounds it seems evident that the doctrine of "the covenant of grace," as a mode of representing the scheme of human redemption, although it may have been carried too far by some of the great divines of the seventeenth century, is yet in its main features fully sanctioned by the Word of God. For there are clear enough traces to be there discovered of a certain *agreement or arrangement* as having been made in the everlasting counsels of the Godhead, with a view to the spiritual good of Christ's people, in consideration of what He should do and suffer on their behalf. And if such a transaction may not be styled a "covenant," I know not by what other analogical term, suggested by the ordinary dealings of men with one another, it could be more fitly and significantly represented.

Now, as to the bearing of this conclusion on the subject before us, there are some who hold that the doctrine of

RESPECTING THE ATONEMENT. 151

"the covenant of grace" supplies a full solution of all the mystery in which the substitution of Jesus Christ, "the just for the unjust," would otherwise be enveloped. I am not prepared to maintain the soundness of this opinion. It seems to me that by connecting our Lord's sufferings with a covenant, of which they were the necessary fulfilment, we render the appointment and acceptance of them, in lieu of the merited condemnation of transgressors, in no respect less mysterious than it was before. By so doing we merely shift the difficulty instead of solving it. For no sooner have we, by referring to the covenant of grace, disposed of the original question, Why were the sufferings and death of the holy Jesus requisite and available for the salvation of sinful men? than this other and equally arduous question presents itself, Why was such a method of salvation for sinners arranged and agreed upon in the counsels of the Godhead?

PART I. SEC. 13.

Doctrine of covenant of grace does not solve the mystery of the Atonement;

But then, while the doctrine of "the covenant of grace," confirmed as we have seen it to be in its main features by the testimony of Scripture, cannot be considered as solving the deep mysteries involved in the substitution of Christ for sinful men, it certainly does supply *a strong corroborative evidence of the reality of this substitution*, considered as *a matter of fact*. In this respect we can scarcely overrate its mighty importance. For it shows that the Person whose sufferings and death are elsewhere declared to have been vicarious in their character, was one who stood towards His people in the relation of a *federal head* or *divinely sanctioned representative*, and who, consequently, *was acting in full accordance with that relation*, in all that He did and in all that He endured, while carrying out on earth the purposes of His heavenly mission.

but strongly confirms the reality of it.

XXI. Another and no less interesting class of passages, bearing on the mediatorial work and sufferings of Jesus Christ, are those in which believers are represented as *intimately and vitally united to the Saviour*.

Work of Christ in relation to union of believers with Him.

This union is set forth in various Scriptural similitudes

152 STATEMENTS OF THE NEW TESTAMENT

PART I.
SEC. 13.
——
Eph. v. 25-32 ; John, xv. 1-8; Eph. iv. 15, 16; John, xvii. 21, 22.
John, xv. 4 ; Rom. vi. 5 ; 2 Cor. iv. 10.

which show it to be of the closest and most indissoluble kind. It is likened to the union between husband and wife ; to the union between the vine branches and their stock ; to the union between the members of the human body and the head; and in one passage it even seems to be compared to the union between Christ Himself and the eternal Father in the Godhead. And by virtue of this union, it is written of believers that " they abide in Christ, and He in them ; " that " they are planted together in the likeness of His death, and shall be also in the likeness of His resurrection ;" that " they are always bearing about with them in the body the dying of the Lord Jesus, that the life also of Jesus might be made manifest in their

Gal. ii. 20; Eph. ii. 5, 6 ; Philip. iii. 10; Col. ii. 12; iii. 1.

body; " that they are " crucified with Christ, and live no more themselves, but Christ liveth in them ; " that they are " quickened together with Christ, and made to sit together in heavenly places in Christ Jesus ; " that they " know the power of His resurrection, and the fellowship of His sufferings, being made conformable to His death ; " that they are buried " with Christ and risen with Him ; " and that " their life is hid with Christ in God."

This union is between *individual men* and Christ.

It will be observed that this union with the Saviour is, as regards the subjects of it, an individual or personal matter. The one party to it is the Lord Jesus Christ, who is admittedly a distinct personal being; and the other party is, neither manhood in the abstract, nor all men indiscriminately in the mass, but *certain individual men*, whom the Scriptures plainly distinguish as united to Christ, from others who have no connection with Him. It is true that the Son of God, when He became incarnate, assumed our common nature. It cannot be said, however, that this is of itself sufficient to constitute such a union as the Scriptures describe. Something more is needed, on the part of those who are united to Him, to give them, individually and personally, a connection with Him, which does not pertain to other men, of whose nature, as well as theirs, He partook by His incarnation. And this something is just that appropriating *faith* which is wrought in

RESPECTING THE ATONEMENT. 153

each of them by the grace of His Holy Spirit, and by PART I. SEC. 13. which they become (as it were) ingrafted into Christ, so as to be not only partakers of His benefits, but animated by His Spirit, conformed to His likeness, and closely identified with Him in all His interests and concernments.

What, then, is the bearing of this union on the question before us?

1. May we not venture to say that it supplies us with *one element that may contribute in some degree towards a solution of the great mystery of the Saviour's substitution for sinful men?* It warrants us at least to say *thus much*, that the Saviour was not substituted for persons who are in no other way connected with Him than by His assumption of their common human nature, but for persons who are emphatically *one with Him*, as branches with the tree, or members with the head—*one*, not indeed by any confusion of their personalities, but yet by an intimacy of fellowship and interest which the closest of earthly unions are inadequate to represent.

Does not this union contribute in some measure towards a solution of the mystery of Christ's substitution?

It may be said, indeed, that our Lord's union with believers, which is brought about by the agency of the Holy Spirit and through the instrumentality of their faith, *bears only on their participation in the benefits* which Christ by His substitution has procured, but affords *no ground or rationale for the substitution itself*, by which in the order of things it is preceded.

There would undoubtedly be much force in this consideration, if it were not for the clear evidence furnished in the Scriptures that the union between the Saviour and His people, though not actually consummated until they have believed, *was all along provided for and proceeded upon in the counsels of the Godhead.* We cannot ignore those express statements of the Word of God, in which believers are said to have been "chosen *in Christ* before the foundation of the world." Nor can we forget how Christ Himself speaks of them as having been "given to Him by His Father," so that "He knows them" and claims them as *His* sheep, *before as yet they have been*

Eph. i. 4. 12.

John, x. 27-29.

154 STATEMENTS OF THE NEW TESTAMENT

PART I.
SEC. 13.

John, x. 16.

Acts, xviii. 9, 10.

actually gathered to Him, saying on one occasion, " Other sheep I have, which are not of this fold ; them also I must bring, and they shall hear my voice;" and on another occasion encouraging His apostle still to continue his labours, where hitherto they had been without effect, by the confident assurance, " I have much people in this city." The limitations of time are of no account with One who sees the end from the beginning, and speaks of things that are not as though they already were. And hence we may say that the union of believers with Christ, though in actual subsistence posterior to His mediation, was present to His own mind and to His Father's mind in those ever-lasting arrangements of the covenant of grace in which that work of mediation was devolved upon Him. As-suredly we do great injustice to the scheme of redemption when its excellence or its worthiness of the divine char-acter is the matter in question, if we do not regard it in all its aspects and relations. Especial injustice do we render to this gracious work, if we keep out of sight that it was appointed and undertaken in full view of the pro-vision, which we actually know to have been contemplated in it, *that it should take beneficial effect in behalf of those, and those only,* who should be so united to Christ as to be able to say that in interest, aim, and disposition, they are one with Him,—that they are " members of His body, of His flesh, and of His bones,"—that " they dwell in Him, and He in them,"—that " they die in His death, and live in His life,"—that " they are crucified with Christ, and live no more themselves, but Christ liveth in them."

This union at least *confirms the fact* of our Lord's substitu-tion.

2. But even if the statements of Scripture with respect to the union between the Saviour and believers were of no avail as indicating a ground or *rationale* of His substitution in their behalf, they are still of much importance as *afford-ing confirmatory proof of the fact* of His substitution.

Thus much appears from *the very terms* in which the union of believers with Christ is ordinarily set forth by our Lord and His apostles. For these terms are not such

RESPECTING THE ATONEMENT. 155

as can be adequately explained as mere *metaphors* expressive of the moral influence exerted on the hearts of Christians by the love, the doctrine, and the virtues of their divine Master, or by anything short of that work of mediation which He graciously undertook and executed for their redemption. When we hear Christ Himself representing His true disciples as "ingrafted into Him," "abiding in Him," "living by Him," "dwelling in Him and He in them," and being "one with Him, as He and His Father are one ;" or when we find His apostles representing themselves and their fellow-Christians as "dying in Christ," as "quickened and rising with Him," as "living no more themselves, but having Christ living in them," as "crucified and buried with Christ," as "raised with Him to sit in heavenly places," as "rooted and grounded in Him," as "growing up in all things unto Him who is their Head," and as "members of His body, of His flesh, and of His bones," we may venture to say that this is not such language as any one, either in Scripture or elsewhere, has ever used, or such language as any sober-minded man would ever think of using, to indicate the mere relation of disciples to a Master to whom they were ever so warmly attached, or by whose instructions and example they were ever so strongly influenced.

But this is not all. For in many of the passages in which these strong expressions are employed to denote the union of believers with the Lord Jesus, there is in connection with them a clear and explicit reference,—not to the doctrine of Christ, not to His example, not to His mere friendship and intimacy with His disciples, not to the moral influence, however powerful, which He has exerted upon them—but to *His sufferings and death*, as the great connecting principle by which they are indissolubly bound to Him.

Thus, when our Lord so emphatically speaks, in John, xvii., not only of His original disciples, but of "all who should believe on Him through their word," as "given to Him," belonging to Him, and united to Him, it is too

PART
I.
SEC. 13.

This appears from the terms in which the union is described.

In connection with this union there are express references to our Lord's sufferings.

156 STATEMENTS OF THE NEW TESTAMENT

PART
I.
SEC. 13.
——

evident to be overlooked that He is speaking with immediate reference to "the finishing of the work" assigned
to Him on their behalf by the sufferings and death which
on the morrow were awaiting Him. In like manner, the
parable of the vine and its branches, by which the union
of believers with Christ is so strikingly illustrated, is
closely followed by an allusion to that manifestation of

John, xv.
13.

His love which He was about to give, in "laying down
His life for His friends." And again, when he speaks
of His people as "dwelling in Him and He in them,"
as "feeding upon Him," and "living by Him," He declares that "the bread which He will give them," for the

John, vi.
51.

maintenance of their vital union with Him, is no other
than "His flesh, which He will give for the life of the
world."

2 Cor. v.
14.

The same remark applies to the statements of the
apostles. Thus, when Paul says, "if one died for all,
then all died," it is plain that the "dying of all" is connected with the fact that "one," that is Christ, had "died
for them;" and this is farther indicated by the clause
immediately following,—"and He died for all, that they
who live should not henceforth live unto themselves,
but *unto Him that died for them and rose again.*" In

Gal. ii. 20.

like manner, when he says, "I am crucified with Christ,
nevertheless I live; yet not I, but Christ liveth in me,"
he connects this statement with a manifest allusion to
the vicarious death of his Redeemer, by adding these
words,—"and the life which I now live in the flesh I live
by the faith of the Son of God, *who loved me and gave
Himself for me.*" And again, when he declares that

Eph. v. 23,
30.

"Christ is the Head of the Church, as the husband is
head of the wife," and that believers are "members of
His body, flesh, and bones," he does so in immediate
connection with the precious assurance that "Christ
loved the Church, and *gave Himself for it.*"

But, indeed, without any reference to their context, the
statements themselves to which I have referred are so
expressed as to show, in almost every instance, that it is

RESPECTING THE ATONEMENT.   157

specially with *the death and resurrection* of Christ that
believers are represented as being identified. And this
circumstance is of itself a sufficient proof that the Scriptural
representations of the union of believers with Christ are
only to be interpreted and accounted for *on the principle
of His substitution in their behalf,* when " delivered for
their offences, and raised again for their justification."

158 STATEMENTS OF THE NEW TESTAMENT

SECTION XIV.

PASSAGES WHICH SPEAK OF THE DEATH OF CHRIST
(22) AS A MANIFESTATION OF THE LOVE OF GOD;
(23) AS FURNISHING AN EXAMPLE OF PATIENCE
AND RESIGNATION; AND (24) AS DESIGNED TO
PROMOTE OUR SANCTIFICATION.

PART
I.
SEC. 14.
——
Sufferings
of Christ
a manifes-
tation of
the love of
God.

John, iii.
16; Rom.
v. 8; viii.
32.

1 John, iv.
9, 10.

XXII. OUR attention is now claimed by an interesting
class of passages, in which the death of Christ is represented as *strongly commending or displaying to us the love
of God.* Of these it may be sufficient to adduce the
following :—

"God so loved the world that He gave His only-
begotten Son, that whosoever believeth in Him should
not perish, but have everlasting life." "God commendeth
His love towards us, in that, while we were yet sinners,
Christ died for us." "He that spared not His own Son,
but delivered Him up for us all, how shall He not with
Him also freely give us all things?" "In this was manifested the love of God towards us, because that God sent
His only-begotten Son into the world, that we might live
through Him. Herein is love, not that we loved God, but
that He loved us, and sent His Son to be the propitiation
for our sins."

The me-
diation of
Christ ori-
ginated in
the love of
God.

1. No comment is necessary to show that in these
passages the mediatorial work and sufferings of the Son
of God are traced to the love of His heavenly Father as
their prime origin. For it is most evident that they could
not have been appealed to as proofs and pledges of the
unspeakable love of God, if it had not been His love that
appointed and provided them. Accordingly, those persons

RESPECTING THE ATONEMENT.   159

are grievously in error who represent the Scriptures as
affirming that the mediation of Christ induces God to
regard sinners with a kindness and compassion which
would otherwise have been withheld from them. It is, on
the contrary, the clear doctrine of Holy Scripture that the
mediation of Christ *originated* in the love of God, and that
whatsoever Christ did and suffered was *the consequence,*
and *not the cause,* of God's willingness to save sinners.
Nothing, indeed, but the most intense desire to save sinners—nothing but a love to fallen men "that passeth
knowledge"—can possibly account for His having secured
redemption for them by so costly a sacrifice as that of His
only-begotten son.

2. It is equally clear, however, that in these passages
the mediatorial work and sufferings of the Lord Jesus are
not represented as manifesting the love of God *without
reference to any atonement they have made for us, or to* any
direct efficacy they have had in exempting us from the
forfeitures and penalties of transgression. There is, on
the contrary, a reference to these things, more or less
explicit, to be found in all the passages,—as when it is
stated that "while we were yet sinners, *Christ died for us,*"
that "God delivered Him up *for us all,*" that "God sent
Him *to be the propitiation for our sins,*" and that "God
gave His only-begotten Son, *that whosoever believeth in
Him should not perish, but have everlasting life.*" The
expiatory and redemptive purpose of our Lord's mission is
very distinctly indicated in these words. And hence we
cannot be allowed to leave it out of account when interpreting those texts in which it is thus referred to. We
must necessarily conclude that it is not *in themselves considered* that the humiliation and sufferings of the Son of
God are represented as pre-eminently "commending" and
"manifesting" His Father's love to sinful men, but rather
*in respect of the expiatory virtues belonging to them, and the
consequent spiritual and heavenly blessings accruing from
them.* I may add that this conclusion is no less agreeable
to the dictates of reason than to the testimony of Scripture. For the humiliation and sufferings of the Son of

PART
I.
SEC. 14.
———

Sufferings
of Christ
do not
manifest
the love of
God apart
from their
atoning
efficacy.

160   STATEMENTS OF THE NEW TESTAMENT

PART
I.
SEC. 14.
——

God can only be viewed as commending His Father's love to us in so far as they were meant to be pre-eminently for our advantage. Apart from any beneficial purpose to be accomplished by them, in delivering us from evils which could not otherwise have been averted, and securing for us blessings which could not otherwise have been obtained, there is no apparent ground on which they can be appealed to, as affording us an unparalleled demonstration of the love of God.

Salvation of sinners through an atonement not inconsistent with the utmost extent of divine mercy towards them.

3. I need only farther remark that, in the face of these passages, there cannot be thought to be any inconsistency between the salvation of sinners through an atonement, and the utmost extent of the divine mercy and compassion towards them. It would be strange indeed were there any such inconsistency, when we find that the exceeding costliness of our redemption, as obtained by the sacrifice of the only-begotten Son of God, is the very circumstance which the Scriptures have insisted on as most of all displaying the greatness of the Father's love. We may not be able fully to comprehend the grounds on which such a sacrifice was necessary. But it is no incredible thing that God may have had His own sufficient reasons for requiring it, in order to the extension of His mercy towards us in such a manner as should be consistent with the perfections of His character, the authority of His law, and the rectitude of His government. Thus much is certain, that His procedure in this matter cannot be held as detracting in any respect from the greatness of His love as displayed in our redemption. It might have been so held if sinners had been left to find for themselves the needful expiation ; or if any other than He by whom they are forgiven had furnished the ground on which pardon is conferred upon them. But inasmuch as God has Himself provided all that He exacts as necessary for our salvation, the costliness of our ransom is so far from diminishing, that, on the contrary, it mightily enhances and gloriously magnifies the riches of His grace ; for in this was manifested the love of God towards us—not that He thought so lightly of our transgressions as without any

RESPECTING THE ATONEMENT. 161

sacrifice freely to forgive them—but that, with all His deep hatred of our sins, He thought so mercifully of us who were chargeable with them, as not to withhold that inestimable sacrifice which divine justice required in order to their forgiveness.

PART I. SEC. 14.

XXIII. There are a few passages, not to be overlooked, in which our Lord's sufferings are represented as *exemplary.*

Thus, we are exhorted to "run with patience the race that is set before us, looking unto Jesus, . . . who endured the cross, despising the shame;" and to "consider Him that endured such contradiction of sinners against Himself, lest we be wearied and faint in our minds." We are urged to "take it patiently when we do well and suffer for it," by the consideration that "Christ also suffered for us, leaving us an example that we should follow His steps." And Jesus Himself admonishes His disciples that they must be prepared to follow Him in the path of suffering when He says, "If any man will come after me, let Him deny himself, and take up his cross daily, and follow me; for whosoever will save his life shall lose it, but whosoever will lose his life for my sake, the same shall save it."

Sufferings of Christ exemplary.

Heb. xii. 1-3.

1 Pet. ii. 20, 21.

Luke, ix. 23, 24.

It cannot be doubted that in these and a few similar passages the sufferings of Christ are held forth as a pattern of the trials which His people must expect to meet with in their Christian course, and of the patience, fortitude, and devotedness with which these trials ought to be endured by them. Nor are we in the least disposed to underrate the value of those moral lessons which the sufferings of our Lord, when viewed in this light, are fitted to inculcate.

1. It must be observed, however, that this aspect of our Lord's sufferings does not in any way disparage or conflict with the expiatory virtue which in other passages has been ascribed to them. On the contrary, it was absolutely necessary to their being possessed of this expiatory virtue that they should at the same time be exemplary in the highest degree, exhibiting in all respects a pattern of

Their being exemplary quite consistent with their being expiatory also.

162   STATEMENTS OF THE NEW TESTAMENT

PART
I.
SEC. 14.
——

suffering rectitude that was acceptable and well-pleasing in the sight of God. For if the Lord Jesus had not been such a one, in all that He did and in all that He endured, as to furnish a perfectly faultless example for our imitation, neither would He have been such a substitute as was requisite for us ; one who could "offer Himself without spot to God ;" "suffering for sins, the just for the unjust."

To furnish an example not their sole or main purpose.

2. It must be farther observed, that in those passages of Scripture which set forth the sufferings of Christ in their exemplary aspect, there is no indication given that this is the *chief* aspect, far less the *sole* aspect, in which they are to be regarded. We may rather say, that it is only in a secondary sense, and in an incidental manner, that they are thus exhibited. Certainly we nowhere find the inspired writers stating *that Christ died for the purpose of affording us a matchless pattern of suffering virtue*, with aught of the point, explicitness, and emphasis with which they have so frequently represented Him as "delivered for our offences ;" "giving His life a ransom for us ;" "reconciling us to God by His blood ;" and "taking away sin by the sacrifice of Himself."

Express reference to their atoning efficacy in texts which point to them as an example.

3. It is worthy of remark also, that in some of those texts in which our Lord's sufferings are strongly urged as an example, *there is express reference made to their atoning efficacy*, although such reference lies beyond the immediate purpose for which at the time His sufferings are appealed to. This is very remarkably the case with the words already quoted from 1 Peter, ii. 21. The apostle is there admonishing Christian servants to "be subject to their masters with all fear ; not only to the good and gentle, but also to the froward." "For what glory is it," he says, "if, when ye be buffeted for your faults, ye shall take it patiently ? But if, when ye do well and suffer for it, ye take it patiently, this is acceptable with God. For even hereunto were ye called ; because Christ also suffered FOR US, leaving us an example that ye should follow His steps ; who did no sin, neither was guile found in His

1 Pet. ii. 20-24.

RESPECTING THE ATONEMENT. 163

mouth : who, when He was reviled, reviled not again : when He suffered, He threatened not ; but committed Himself to Him that judgeth righteously : WHO HIS OWN SELF BARE OUR SINS IN HIS OWN BODY ON THE TREE, that we, being dead to sins, should live unto righteousness : BY WHOSE STRIPES YE WERE HEALED."

Here it is distinctly stated that "*Christ suffered for us;*" that "*He Himself bare our sins in His own body on the tree;*" and that "*by His stripes we are healed.*" These repeated references to the *vicarious and expiatory nature* of our Lord's sufferings were not necessary to the purpose of the apostle, when drawing from these sufferings an example to believers of the manner in which it becomes them to bear unmerited afflictions. But yet St Peter could not appeal to the sufferings of Christ as a pattern of submissive endurance without again and again presenting them in another aspect, with which his heart and mind appear to have been so fully possessed, that he could not refrain, in season or out of season, from adverting to it.

A similar instance occurs in the following chapter of the same epistle : "For it is better, if the will of God be so, that ye suffer for well-doing than for evil-doing. *For Christ also hath once suffered for sins, the just for the unjust, that He might bring us to God.*" Here, again, it was foreign to the immediate purpose of the apostle to speak of our Lord's death as vicarious and piacular. It would have sufficed for the object he had directly in view, to have simply adverted to the *rectitude of* the sufferer, without any special allusion to His having suffered *on account of sins,* and *on behalf of the unrighteous.* But this would not have sufficed to give expression to those thoughts of Christ as the great propitiation, with which the mind of the apostle was ever engrossed. So strong was his faith in the atoning death of Jesus, and so deep his sense of its surpassing interest and importance, that he could not do otherwise than prominently advert to it when called at any time to mention our Lord's sufferings, even though the purpose and occasion of so mentioning them might naturally have led him to regard them under another aspect.

PART I. SEC. 14.

1 Pet. iii. 17, 18.

164 STATEMENTS OF THE NEW TESTAMENT

PART I.
SEC. 14.
——
The expiatory nature of our Lord's sufferings must be kept in view in order to vindicate the perfection of His example.

4. Add to all this, that it is necessary to keep in view the vicarious and expiatory nature of our Lord's sufferings, and to give due prominence to "the travail of His soul" when bearing the load of human guilt that was imposed upon Him, in order to vindicate the perfection of that example of patient and steadfast endurance which He has set before us. For if we put the case that His sufferings were *merely* exemplary, and that there was nothing peculiar in their nature as distinguished from those with which good men are often visited, there seems to be no explanation that can be given, consistently with the matchless excellence of His character, of the peculiar distress and depression which they occasioned Him. How, upon this supposition, can we account for it, that He who of all persons that ever appeared on earth had the least cause to dread any afflictions that might be laid upon Him, and the greatest inherent capacity of sustaining them, should yet, when looking forward to them in the garden, and when actually bearing them upon the cross, have shown a depth of anxiety and dejection—an exceeding sorrowfulness—a depressing and distracting gloom— opposed as far as could be to that spirit of triumphant joy which human martyrs have frequently displayed, when called to submit to tortures the most excruciating? Often have Christians, though compassed with infirmities, and deeply sensible of their weakness and their guilt, engaged in the last struggle, not only with calmness of spirit, but with joy and exultation. Whence this difference between the servants and their Lord? How came it to pass that *He* in His last trials should have been so deeply cast down and disquieted, while *they* could exult in the course they had finished, the good fight they had fought, and the crown that was awaiting them? The difference, as we cannot help thinking, is to be ascribed to something peculiar in the character of a vicarious sin-bearer which Christ sustained, and in the kind and measure of those sufferings with which, in this capacity, it behoved Him to be afflicted. It has been the consolation of martyrs to reflect, even in the utmost extremities of their anguish,

2 Tim. iv. 7, 8.

RESPECTING THE ATONEMENT. 165

that "though persecuted" by men, they were "not forsaken" by the Lord. But Jesus, in His hour of darkness, was apparently bereft of this consolation. *He* spoke as if He were *both* persecuted and forsaken. And we cannot doubt that He felt what His language expresses. It was no mere scenic display of fictitious woe that was exhibited by Him, but a deep intensity of real anguish that was experienced. And that it should have been so is best explained,—may we not say, is *only* to be explained?—by supposing that to the outward and bodily woes endured by Him, there were superadded *inward afflictions of a spiritual nature*, arising from the unique position in which He stood as the *representative and substitute of sinners*. Such a supposition is certainly countenanced by some very striking expressions of the Word of God, which on any other ground it would be difficult to account for. Thus, we read of "the travail of His soul,"—of "His soul being troubled,"—of "His soul being exceeding sorrowful even unto death,"—of "His soul being made an offering for sin,"—of "the Lord being pleased to bruise Him and to put Him to grief," and of His being "made a curse for us;" all of which expressions, though to some extent involved in mystery which we shall in vain attempt to fathom, appear to be descriptive of sufferings of a spiritual kind, proceeding from some direct agency of the invisible God; and are most satisfactorily explained upon the principle, that the Saviour, though Himself sinless, was standing in the room of sinners, and bearing, in this peculiar position, a weight of woe such as has never been undergone by human martyrs, inasmuch as He bore the imputation to Himself of that accursed thing which He cannot look upon without abhorrence.

PART I. SEC. 14.

2 Cor. iv. 9.

XXIV. There is a class of passages still to be considered, which speak of our Saviour's death as intended to promote the *sanctification* of believers.

Some texts, indeed, have been thought to have this import, which may with more propriety be otherwise interpreted; such as our Lord's saying, "For their sakes

Sufferings of Christ conducive to our sanctification.

John, xvii. 19.

166 STATEMENTS OF THE NEW TESTAMENT

PART I. SEC. 14.

Heb. x. 10; xiii. 12.

I *sanctify* myself, that they also might be *sanctified* through the truth;" and those statements in the Epistle to the Hebrews, "By the which will we are *sanctified* through the offering of the body of Jesus Christ once for all;" and "Jesus, that He might *sanctify* the people with His own blood, suffered without the gate." In these passages the verb ἁγιάζω is to be understood in its primary sense, which it usually bears in the Septuagint version of the Old Testament, as meaning "*to set apart or consecrate*," rather than in its secondary sense of *moral purification*, with which, in our ordinary use of the word "sanctify," we are more familiar.

There is no lack of other passages, however, in which it is unequivocally affirmed that the death of Christ was intended to secure the purification and elevation of our moral nature, or to turn us from the love and practice of sin to the service of God. Thus it is written :—

2 Cor. v. 15.

Gal. i. 4.

Eph. v. 25-27.

Tit. ii. 14.

1 Pet. ii. 24.

"He died for all, that they which live should not henceforth live unto themselves, but unto Him who died for them and rose again." "Who gave Himself for our sins, that He might deliver us from this present evil world." "Christ loved the Church and gave Himself for it, that He might sanctify and cleanse it with the washing of water by the Word; and that He might present it to Himself a glorious Church, not having spot, or wrinkle, or any such thing, but that it should be holy and without blemish." "He gave Himself for us, that He might redeem us from all iniquity, and purify unto Himself a peculiar people, zealous of good works." "Who His own self bare our sins in His own body on the tree, that we, being dead to sins, might live unto righteousness."

No one who looks at these statements, however cursorily, can fail to see that the *sanctification* of believers is represented in them as one of the great ends to which our Lord's sufferings were meant to be conducive. Unquestionably we are here taught that the purpose of the Saviour, in all that He has done and suffered on our behalf, was not merely to deliver us from the penal consequences of our transgressions, but to cleanse us from the

RESPECTING THE ATONEMENT. 167

pollution of sin—to free us from its enslaving power—and thoroughly to reform and rectify our moral nature.

It is not to be thought, however, that the *sanctifying power* ascribed in this class of passages to our Lord's sufferings is in any respect inconsistent with their *atoning efficacy*, of which we have elsewhere found the most abundant proof. A purpose to secure forgiveness for sinners, and a purpose to promote their moral purification, are certainly quite compatible with one another. And hence there is no reason why *both* of these purposes may not have been contemplated by our Lord when " He loved us and gave Himself for us." Indeed His very excellence as a Saviour consists in this, that He secures for us deliverance from sin itself, as well as from the evils and miseries resulting from it, being " made of God unto us wisdom, and righteousness, and sanctification, and redemption."

PART I. SEC. 14.

Sanctifying power of Christ's sufferings quite consistent with their atoning efficacy.

1 Cor. i. 30.

But here we must shortly notice an erroneous opinion which some persons entertain with reference to this matter. They hold that the death of Christ has no proper atoning efficacy by which it can *directly* secure the remission of sins ; but that *it simply exerts upon us a moral influence, causing us to renounce sin, and thereby to obtain forgiveness.* In other words, they affirm that our own repentance and amendment are the real and immediate ground of our restoration to the favour of God : while the Saviour's death is no otherwise conducive to it than in an indirect or secondary manner, by supplying strong motives or inducements to a life of holiness.

Allegation that the sufferings of Christ only secure forgiveness of sin by leading us to forsake sin.

1. I may, first of all, remark, with reference to this opinion, that it is utterly opposed to the plain import of those classes of texts formerly considered, in which our Lord's death is set forth as a " ransom," a " propitiation," a " sacrifice for sin ;" and as securing for us " justification," " forgiveness," " reconciliation to God," and " redemption from the curse of the law." It cannot be reasonably questioned that in these passages a proper atoning efficacy is attributed to the death of Christ, and not a moral power conducive to our sanctification.

This opinion opposed to testimonies already adduced.

168   STATEMENTS OF THE NEW TESTAMENT

PART I. SEC. 14.

As little can it be questioned that the benefits by which this atoning efficacy is displayed are represented as flowing *primarily and directly* from the great sacrifice of the cross ; and not as its *secondary results*, arising more immediately from the moral effects produced in us by the contemplation of it.   For the passages expressly state that " we are justified *by the blood of Christ ;*" that " we have redemption *through His blood*, the forgiveness of sins ;" and that " Christ hath redeemed us from the curse of the law, *being made a curse for us ;* for it is written, Cursed is every one that hangeth on a tree."   Nor is there the least reference to our own repentance and amendment, or to any moral change which the sufferings of Christ have wrought in us, as giving to His death that expiatory, justifying, and redemptive power, which in these statements is ascribed to it.

This opinion derives no support from those texts which speak cf our Lord's death as promoting our sanctification.

2. I may farther observe that the opinion we are controverting derives no support from the class of passages now before us, which speak of the Saviour's death as intended to promote our sanctification.   For in not one of these passages are we taught " that the only direct purpose of our Lord's sufferings is to sanctify us, and that they are no otherwise conducive to the remission of sin than as leading us by their moral influence to forsake sin."   Rather may we say that the doctrine taught in these passages appears to be *the very opposite* — namely, *that the direct purpose of our Lord's sufferings was to expiate the guilt and save us from the penalties of sin, and that it is mainly, if not entirely, to their expiatory virtues that the moral influence they exert upon us must be traced.*   Thus much is certain, that *it is not in themselves considered, but in connection with their expiatory virtues,* that a sanctifying power is in these passages ascribed to them.   It is not by merely " suffering or dying" that Christ is there represented as purposing to further the sanctification of believers, but by " dying for all," " giving Himself for our sins," " giving Himself for the Church," " giving Himself for us," and " bearing our sins in His own body the tree."   In all these expressions we can hardly fail a

RESPECTING THE ATONEMENT. 169

reference, more or less distinct, to the sacrificial nature
and atoning efficacy of the Saviour's death. This reference, accordingly, must be taken into account in faithfully
interpreting those texts in which it occurs. And if so, it
will be at once apparent that these texts lend no support
to the opinion we are contending against. For they
evidently speak of our Lord's death as propitiatory, or as
primarily designed to secure for us the remission of sins,
while they point to our sanctification as an ulterior result,
to which, *not irrespectively of its piacular virtues, but rather
by reason of its piacular virtues*, it is intended to lead.

PART
I.
SEC. 14.

3. I need only farther remark that, while the opinion under
review is thus unsupported by the testimony of Scripture,
it seems, on reasonable grounds, to be equally indefensible.
For, apart from the propitiatory character of the death of
Christ, there is no apparent reason for ascribing to it any
such pre-eminent influence of a sanctifying nature as that
which it is alleged to possess. We have already seen that
it is necessary to keep in view the vicarious and expiatory
nature of our Lord's sufferings, in order to vindicate the
perfection of that example of patient and steadfast endurance which they set before us ; and that it is equally
necessary to take account of the eminently beneficial purposes accomplished by them, in delivering us from evils
not otherwise to be averted, and securing for us blessings
not otherwise to be obtained, before they can make any
sensible impression upon us as an unparalleled manifestation of the love of God. Hence we are at a loss to see
what sanctifying power, apart from their atoning efficacy,
can belong to them.

This opin-
ion unreas-
onable as
well as un-
scriptural.

Once let the death of Christ, however, be regarded as
the great propitiatory sacrifice for the sins of the world,
and then it is at once seen to be invested with a moral
power that is wellnigh irresistible. So bright and full is
the demonstration which it makes to us of the love of
God, the grace of Christ, the evil of sin, the worth of the
immortal soul—and so mighty are the obligations it imposes upon us to yield ourselves up to Him who has
redeemed us—that it is well fitted to melt the hardest

Sanctify-
ing power
of our
Lord's
death
when
viewed as
expiatory.

170 STATEMENTS OF THE NEW TESTAMENT

PART I.
SEC. 14.

heart, to turn the chief of sinners to repentance, and to animate the soul of the believer with the most ardent love and the most sincere devotedness. And thus may we confidently say that the cross of Christ is so far from being indebted to its sanctifying power for any influence that may be ascribed to it in securing for us the forgiveness and favour of God, that, on the contrary, it is indebted to its atoning virtues for the sanctifying power with which it is so richly fraught.

SECTION XV.

RESULT OF THE FOREGOING INDUCTION OF SCRIPTURAL TESTIMONIES.

HAVING now concluded our survey of the testimonies which are to be found in the Scriptures of the New Testament respecting the mediatorial work and sufferings of Jesus Christ, it still remains that we endeavour to gather up into one general and comprehensive statement the substance or amount of the information we have derived from them.

It will be remembered that we prefaced our inquiry by stating some considerations of a general nature, which lie too plainly on the surface of the sacred volume to need any formal array of evidence to establish them—namely, that the office ascribed to the Lord Jesus is that *not of a mere teacher* sent to reveal the will of God, but of a divinely appointed *Saviour*—the procurer of blessings as well as the proclaimer of them ; that *a pre-eminent importance is attached to the mission of Christ* above that of every other divine messenger, which leads to the conclusion that some benefits of a very special and altogether unparalleled nature have been secured by it ; that the *death of Jesus* has so very marked a prominence assigned to it among the incidents of His history, as to show that it must have had some direct and special efficacy in securing the ends to be accomplished by His mission ; and that the sufferings of Christ are, in themselves and in their circumstances, *so exceptional and unique,* so foreign to all actual or even conceivable human analogies, that we ought not to

172 STATEMENTS OF THE NEW TESTAMENT

PART I.
SEC. 15.

be surprised if the Scriptures should attribute them to some extraordinary plan or purpose in the mind of God, the nature of which is but imperfectly comprehended by us.

Premising these general considerations respecting the divine mission and sufferings of Jesus Christ, we then proceeded to inquire more particularly, What was the precise nature of the salvation which He has secured? and in what way was His death conducive to the attainment of it?

In the course of this inquiry we have found that the following positions may be fully established by the most explicit Scriptural statements :—

(1.) That the Lord Jesus suffered and died "for sinners;" that is to say, as many of the statements imply, "instead of sinners," and, as all of them indisputably affirm, "on behalf of sinners ;" while the frequency and emphasis and exclusiveness with which this form of expression is applied to the sufferings of Christ, can only be explained by supposing that *He* suffered "for us" in some sense that is altogether peculiar to Himself—not merely as having suffered, like many others, "for our advantage," but as having suffered, like none beside Him, *as our substitute.*

(2.) That the Lord Jesus suffered "for our sins ;" that is to say, "on account of them ;" our sins being the cause or reason of His being visited, although Himself perfectly sinless, with severe afflictions, and ultimately with an ignominious death.

(3.) That He "bore our sins," or had them "laid upon Him," not in the way of mere natural consequence—as when one person is involved in suffering by the misconduct of other men, without thereby lightening their burden in the smallest degree—but in the sense of *vicariously bearing them* on our behalf, being charged with those penal liabilities to which on account of our sins we should otherwise have been subjected.

(4.) That He was "made sin," and "made a curse for us," in order that we, as the consequence of His being so,

RESPECTING THE ATONEMENT. 173

might be " redeemed from the curse of the law," and " made
the righteousness of God in Him."

(5.) That He " takes away our sins," " puts them away,"
secures their " forgiveness," and saves us from their merited
" condemnation ; " and that He does this, not by the
excellence of His precepts, the purity of His example, and
the preciousness of His promises, as leading us to renounce
our sins, and thereby to obtain the pardon of them, but
by " the shedding of His blood," or " the sacrifice of Himself."

(6.) That the obedience and sufferings of our Lord are
the ground on which believers are " justified ; " that is to
say, forgiven and received as righteous in the sight of
God.

(7.) That Christ hath " redeemed us by His blood," or
hath " given His life a ransom for many," and that we
have " redemption through His blood, the forgiveness of
sins ; " by which we are to understand, not that He has
delivered us in some undefined manner from the evil consequences of transgression, but that He has done so by
the payment of a price or ransom, and that the price or
ransom expressly specified was " His blood " or " His
life."

(8.) That He has " reconciled us to God by His death,"
not merely in the sense of so assuring us of the divine
mercy as to induce us to lay aside our enmity against
God, but in the sense also of turning away God's righteous
displeasure from us, and restoring us to the enjoyment of
His favour.

(9.) That He is the " propitiation for our sins," and is
" set forth as a propitiation through faith in His blood,"—
so expiating the guilt of the sins we have committed, " that
God may be just, and the justifier of him who believeth in
Jesus."

(10.) That Christ sustains the office of a " priest," as
being " ordained for men in things pertaining to God, that
He may offer gifts and sacrifices for sins ; " and hence
that His sufferings were not personal merely, but *official*,
and combined with the passive endurance of the victim

PART
I.
SEC. 15.

174 STATEMENTS OF THE NEW TESTAMENT

PART I.
SEC. 15.

the active agency of the priest in fulfilment of his appointed functions.

(11.) That Christ sustained a *representative character* in
relation to those sinners for whom He interposed, placing
Himself in their position, acting on their behalf, and closely
identifying Himself with them in all their interests.

(12.) That the death of Christ was a " sacrifice for sin,"
not in figure, but in reality—a sacrifice once for all offered
on the cross, availing not only for the " purifying of the
flesh," but for the inward " purgation of the conscience,"
and obtaining for all who rely upon it " eternal redemption."

(13.) That the sufferings of Christ are the foundation of
that " intercession which He ever lives to make for us "
in heaven, and by which " He is able to save them to the
uttermost who come unto God through Him."

(14.) That the mediation of our Lord obtains for us the
gracious influence of the Holy Spirit, with all the spiritual
blessings imparted by it.

(15.) That the Son of God, who " was manifested that
He might destroy the works of the devil," has secured our
deliverance from the dominion of Satan, and has triumphed
over the powers of darkness on the cross.

(16.) That Christ has purchased an everlasting inheritance of blessedness and glory in the life to come for all
believers.

(17.) That the state of the Saviour's mind in the prospect and in the endurance of His sufferings was such as
cannot be satisfactorily accounted for, apart from the
position in which He stood as the conscious sin-bearer, on
whom there had been laid the accursed thing which He
cannot bear to look upon.

(18.) That in the invitations of the Gospel Christ is
exclusively set forth as the only Saviour, while through
Him salvation is offered freely and unreservedly to all
sinners.

(19.) That the blessings of the Gospel are obtained by
faith in Christ—that is to say, by a trustful reception of
Him ; and that this faith does nothing to supplement the

RESPECTING THE ATONEMENT. 175

Saviour's work, but simply relies on it, as a work already PART
finished, by which a full and complete redemption has SEC. 15.
been obtained.

(20.) That Christ, in all He did and suffered for us, was
fulfilling the terms of a gracious compact or arrangement,
such as in human speech may be fitly termed a "covenant," into which He had entered with His Father on our
behalf, and by which, in consideration of His sufferings
and obedience, inestimable privileges and benefits are
secured to us.

(21.) That all true believers are united to Christ by an
identity of interests and an intimacy of fellowship which
the closest of earthly ties are inadequate to represent;
and that this union, if it be not available for *explaining the
grounds*, assuredly serves to *corroborate the fact* of the
Saviour's vicarious sufferings and obedience, inasmuch as
it is spoken of in terms that are inexplicable on any other
principle than His substitution in the room of sinners.

We have yet farther ascertained that the sufferings of
our Lord are in various passages of Scripture represented
(22) as manifesting the greatness of God's love to sinners;
(23) as furnishing a bright example of meekness and submission in the endurance of affliction; and (24) as designed
to promote our sanctification; but at the same time, that
these latter representations are so far from either obscur-
ing or invalidating, that, on the contrary, they clearly illustrate and strongly confirm those other Scriptural views of
our Lord's sufferings, by which, in the order of our discussion, they were preceded.

Such are the conclusions to which we have been led by Points of
a full induction of the statements of the New Testament doctrine
established
respecting the sufferings and death of Jesus Christ. And by our in-
on taking a conjoint view of these conclusions, we are duction.
warranted to lay down the following propositions, as
embodying the revealed doctrine on this most important
subject.

I. *In the first place*, the Lord Jesus Christ is presented

176 STATEMENTS OF THE NEW TESTAMENT

PART
I.
SEC. 15.
——
Christ is
the divine-
ly ap-
pointed
Saviour.

to us in a character and office peculiar to Himself alone, as distinguished from all other messengers from heaven. Not only is He a divinely appointed Prophet, sent to proclaim with supreme authority the will of God, but He is the divinely appointed Saviour — the only Mediator between God and men—the consecrated High Priest of His Church—the Surety of an everlasting covenant fraught with the surest and most inestimable promises. As such He was charged with the execution of a scheme of un-paralleled grace for the benefit of His people. And He had respect to the office which He thus sustained, and to the work thus given Him to accomplish, in all that He did and suffered while on earth.

His death
a truly ex-
piatory
sacrifice.

II. *Secondly*, the sufferings of our Lord were *sacrificial.* And they were so not in a loose or general sense, as belonging to *any one or other* of the divers kinds of offer-ings which may be designated by the word " sacrifice," but definitely as an *expiatory sacrifice* for sinful men, with special reference to the condemnation they have incurred, and in order to exempt them from the penal consequences of their transgressions. With great frequency and em-phasis, and in the most unqualified manner, has this character of an expiatory sacrifice been ascribed to our Lord's sufferings in the oracles of divine truth. Nor are the statements of Scripture in this respect to be regarded as mere figurative allusions to the ordinances of Jewish worship. For, as we have seen, the writers of the New Testament have not only applied sacrificial expressions to the death of Christ, but have at the same time *expressly told us why they did so,* by indicating the points of resem-blance, and also the points of difference, between the sacrifice of the cross and the sacrifices of the ancient Church; and by teaching us that the former, instead of having less about it to warrant the use of sacrificial language than the latter, had, on the contrary, *much more* pertaining to it by which the use of such language could be justified, being expiatory or propitiatory in a higher sense and in a greater degree.

RESPECTING THE ATONEMENT. 177

III. *Thirdly*, the sufferings of our Lord were *vicarious*— that is to say, they were endured by Him *as our substitute.* This, indeed, is implied in their sacrificial character, inasmuch as the victim, in all cases of piacular sacrifice, was understood to stand in the place, and to bear the penalty, of those in whose behalf he was offered up. But it is capable of being established on other grounds. It is plainly taught, for example, in those passages which state that Christ " came to give His life a ransom for many," that He is " the one Mediator between God and man, who gave His life a ransom for all "—that " He bare our sins in His own body on the tree"—that " He suffered for sins, the just for the unjust "—that " Christ hath redeemed us from the curse of the law, being made a curse for us "— and that God " hath made Him to be sin for us, who knew no sin, that we might be made the righteousness of God in Him."

The vicarious nature of our Lord's sufferings is farther deducible from a conjoint view of those several classes of texts in which He is said (1) to have " suffered and died *for us*," (2) to have " suffered and died *for our sins*," and (3) to have obtained by His sufferings " *the forgiveness of our sins,*" provided always that we keep before us the great fact that His sufferings and death *were endured by divine appointment, and were not merely incidental but essential to the ends of His mission.*

Suppose it were, for the sake of argument, to be conceded that no one of these classes of passages is of itself sufficient to establish our proposition. According to this concession, the passages of the *first class* would not of themselves prove that Christ was substituted for us, but merely that His sufferings were designed in the purpose of God to be *somehow beneficial to us.* Those of the *second class*, taken by themselves, would not be sufficient to prove His substitution for us, but merely that *our sins had*, by the divine appointment, *been somehow the cause of involving Him in sufferings.* And those of the *third class* would not, in themselves considered, suffice to show that He was substituted in the room of sinners, but merely that His

PART I. SEC. 15.

His sufferings were vicarious.

This shown by combining three classes of texts.

178 STATEMENTS OF THE NEW TESTAMENT

PART I.
SEC. 15.

death has been *somehow instrumental*, according to the arrangements of divine wisdom, *in securing our exemption from the penalties to which, by reason of our transgressions, we were justly exposed.* But *put all the three classes of passages together,* and keep always in view along with them that the sufferings of Christ, with the reasons and purposes for which they were endured by Him, were expressly designed and determined in the counsels of God, and held an essential and prominent place in His divine mission—and *then* we have as satisfactory a proof of our Lord's vicarious death as could reasonably be demanded. For *then* it is at once apparent (1) that He "died for us," not merely in the general sense of *dying for our advantage,* but in the special sense of *being divinely appointed to "die for our sins," or to "suffer on account of them;"* farther (2), that He suffered "for our sins," not merely as one might do who was innocently involved in the consequences of our transgressions, but from whose sufferings no deliverance from the evils in which he was thus involved was meant to accrue to us, but as one whose subjection to the consequences of our sins *was designed to secure our exemption from the endurance of them;* and yet farther (3), that His sufferings have obtained for us "the remission of sins," not merely as having been, in some indirect, incidental, or undefined manner, conducive to our enjoyment of that benefit, but as having been laid upon Him by the appointment of God, "*on account of our sins,*" and *with a view to the forgiveness of them.* Now this assuredly amounts to *substitution.* We have here an innocent person divinely appointed to suffer *on behalf of the guilty* — to suffer *on account of their sins* — to suffer *with a view to their exemption from the penalties of sin.* This evidently implies that interchange of parts which the word "vicarious" is understood to signify. And if any who otherwise agree with us in our conclusions still object to the use of this confessedly unscriptural, but certainly most convenient and compendious word, in giving expression to them, we need not be much concerned to answer them in this matter. The mere use of the word

RESPECTING THE ATONEMENT.   179

"vicarious" is a small question to contend about, so long
as *the thing* which we denote by it is fully admitted.

PART I.
SEC. 15

IV. *Fourthly*, Christ, by His obedience unto death, has
secured our *reconciliation to God*. And in this respect His
death is our *atonement*, or that which brings God and
sinners to be *at one*. The original meaning of *atonement*,
or *at-one-ment*, is generally understood to have been *the
reconciliation of parties who were at variance.* The word is
so used in the only passage of our English version of the
New Testament in which it occurs, as the proper equivalent
of the Greek word καταλλαγὴν : " We joy in God through
our Lord Jesus Christ, by whom we have now received
the atonement." More commonly, however, it is now
employed to signify, not the reunion or reconciliation of
conflicting parties, but rather the *ground of it,* or *the
efficient cause of its accomplishment.* And in this sense the
word may with special fitness be applied to the mediatorial
work and sufferings of Jesus Christ as being the grand
means, ordained by infinite love, for rectifying the dis-
turbed or suspended relations between God and man, and
taking away the obstacles which sin had interposed to
their peace and concord, and fellowship with one another.

Reconci-
liation to
God by
death of
Christ.

Rom. v
11.

It must be remembered, however, that this reconciliation
is not *one-sided,* but *mutual.* God has a part in it, no less
than man. It is no mere pacifying of sinners towards
God, from whom they have been alienated by their own
evil and distrustful hearts ; but it is also a pacifying of
God towards sinners, through that precious sin-offering
which He hath Himself provided ; so that His great love,
consistently with His other attributes, may go forth upon
them in all the fulness of its benefactions. That such is
indeed the case, we learn, not only from almost all the
passages of Scripture which expressly speak of " reconciliation by the death of Christ," but also from those in
which He is represented as a " sacrifice for sin ; " a " Redeemer from the curse of the law ; " a " Saviour from
wrath ; " a " ransom for many ; " a " Mediator between God
and men ; " a " sufferer for sins, the just for the unjust ; " a

180   STATEMENTS OF THE NEW TESTAMENT

PART
I.
SEC. 15.

"propitiation to declare the righteousness of God, that God may be just, and the justifier of believers."

Redemption through the blood of Christ.

V. *Fifthly*, Christ is the *Redeemer* of His people ; their deliverance by Him, whether from the servitude of sin or from its penal consequences, is a *"redemption ;"* and His blood or life, which He generously surrendered for them, is the *"ransom"* by which this deliverance has been secured.   This language, although figurative, has undoubtedly *a meaning*, of which we must be careful not to deprive it ; while, at the same time, we decline to press upon it a further import than the nature of the case to which it is applied, as otherwise plainly ascertainable, will admit of. Now, without seeking to trace any farther conformity between "the redemption that is in Christ Jesus" and those various human transactions which may be likened to it—as, for example, the discharge of a debt, the release of a bondman, or the recovery of an alienated possession —there is one point of conformity between them which must not be overlooked, inasmuch as it is prominently set forth as often as the subject is alluded to in the New Testament, and that is, *the giving of a price* for the redemption.   The debt is not simply cancelled, but liquidated. The bondman is not manumitted, but ransomed.   The alienated possession is not gratuitously recovered, but bought back.

It is not necessary certainly, nor is it expedient, to deduce *more* from the figurative language now referred to than the great prominent truth which it was obviously meant to convey—namely, that our deliverance from the evils of our sinful state *is accomplished by a process of commutation* analogous to the payment of a price.   But *less* than this truth we cannot deduce from it without nullifying the significancy of the figure, and frustrating the manifest purpose for which it is employed.   For though it be true that the word "redemption" is often used in a loose and popular manner to signify " deliverance," without reference to a price, or to any specific means by which such deliverance may have been accom-

RESPECTING THE ATONEMENT. 181

plished, it certainly is not so used in the case before us. And therefore we needs must assign to it its stricter sense, in so far at least as to include in it a reference to somewhat that is properly answerable to a *price* or *ransom.* The sacred writers have provided for our doing so, and have taken especial care to prevent us from doing otherwise, by expressly and pointedly connecting this idea with it in almost every instance in which it is employed by them with reference to the mediatorial work of Jesus Christ.

PART I. SEC. 15

VI. *Sixthly,* the sufferings and death of Christ may be properly regarded as a *satisfaction for sin,* or a *satisfaction to divine justice.*

It is true this mode of designating them is not Scriptural. The word " satisfaction," as applied to our Lord's sufferings, nowhere occurs in the authorised English version of the New Testament.* But although the *word* is not there, we are warranted to affirm that the *thing* which it denotes is there. And it is not mere words but things that we are concerned with. The idea of *satisfaction* is involved in *atonement, redemption, propitiation, expiation,* and various other phrases which the Scriptures have employed. It is no less evidently implied in those numerous passages which speak of Christ as " dying for us " and " for our sins," as "bearing our sins," as "delivering us from the wrath to come," as " shedding His blood for the remission of our sins," as "giving His life a ransom for many," as " redeeming us from the curse of the law, by being made a curse for us," and as "set forth to be a propitiation through faith in His blood, to declare God's righteousness, that He might be just, and the justifier of him that believeth in Jesus." On the

Death of Christ a satisfaction for sin, or a satisfaction to divine justice. The word "satisfaction" not found in Scripture.

But the thing denoted by it is there.

---

* There is only one passage of our English Bible in which the word "*satisfaction*" is met with—namely, Numbers, xxxv. 31, 32, where it is twice used as an equivalent for the Hebrew word which is ordinarily translated "*atonement.*" The passage is as follows : " Ye shall take no satisfaction for the life of a murderer, who is guilty of death ; but he shall be surely put to death. And ye shall take no satisfaction for him that is fled to the city of his refuge, that he should come again to dwell in the land, until the death of the priest."

182 STATEMENTS OF THE NEW TESTAMENT

PART I. SEC. 15.

Its use, like that of the word Trinity, is justifiable.

same ground, therefore, on which we hold ourselves entitled to use the word *Trinity*, although it does not occur in Scripture, as a highly appropriate and significant designation of the great mystery of three divine persons in the one Godhead, we claim an equal warrant to speak of the *satisfaction* which Christ on behalf of sinners has rendered to divine justice as one of the most convenient and compendious phrases which we can employ to indicate the nature and purpose of His mediatorial work.

Meaning of the word.

Hill's Lectures in Divinity, book iv. chap. iii. § 1.

The term "satisfaction," which is borrowed from the Roman law, signifies anything which a person may accept of in discharge of a claim he may have against another person, although it be not the precise thing he was entitled to demand. "It denotes," says Dr Hill, "that method of fulfilling an obligation which may either be admitted or refused. When a person by the non-performance of a contract has incurred a penalty, he is entitled to a discharge of the contract if he pays the penalty; but if, instead of paying the penalty, he offers something else in place of it, the person who has a right to demand the penalty may grant a discharge or not, as he sees meet. If he is satisfied with that which is offered, he will grant the discharge; if he is not satisfied, he cannot be called unjust, and he may be acting wisely, in refusing it. According to this known meaning of the word, the sufferings of Christ for sin have received the name of a *satisfaction* to the justice of God, because they were not the very penalty that had been incurred, but were something accepted by the Lawgiver instead of it. . . . From this account of the matter it appears that a satisfaction for sin cannot procure the pardon of the sinner without the goodwill of the Lawgiver, because it offers something in place of that which He was entitled to demand; and for this reason the Catholic opinion concerning the nature of the remedy brought in by the Gospel, far from excluding, will be found, when rightly understood, to magnify the mercy of the Lawgiver. Those who know best how to defend it never speak of any contest between the justice and the mercy of God, because they believe that there is the most

RESPECTING THE ATONEMENT.   183

perfect harmony amongst all the divine perfections. They
never think so unworthily of God as to conceive that His
fury was appeased by the interposition of Jesus Christ;
but they uniformly represent the scheme of our redemption as originating in the love of God the Father, who
both provided and accepted that substitution by which
sinners are saved. And they hold that the forgiveness of
sins is free, because, although granted upon that consideration which the Lawgiver saw meet to exact, it was given
to those who had no right to expect it, and who could
have fulfilled their obligation to punishment only by their
destruction."

PART I. Sec. 15.

In speaking of the Atonement as "a satisfaction to the
justice of God," we are not to be held as ascribing to the
divine mind, when contemplating the sufferings of Jesus
Christ, anything akin to the "satisfaction" with which the
vindication of their invaded rights, or insulted honour, or
aggrieved feelings, may be regarded by men of an unyield-
ing, passionate, or revengeful spirit. A due consideration
of the very terms of our statement might, one should
think, suffice to guard it against so gross a perversion of
its meaning; for assuredly the phrase "*satisfaction to
divine justice*" must by every fair interpreter be understood as indicating, not that any feelings of resentment or
vindictiveness on the part of God were gratified by our
Lord's sufferings, but simply that these sufferings were
accepted by the supreme Lawgiver and righteous moral
Governor of the universe, as a ground on which He might
show mercy to His sinful creatures consistently with the
rectitude of His character and the authority of those laws
which, as a just God, He is concerned to uphold.

No affinity to the "sa-tisfaction" which a vindictive man may demand for an injury or indig-nity.

Nor are we to be held, when using this expression, as
making ourselves in any way accountable for all those
subtle speculations and deductions which have from time
to time been founded on the use of it. The schoolmen
in the middle ages, and some others in more recent
times, have not been content with speaking of the death
of Christ as "a satisfaction rendered to divine justice for
the sins of men," but have striven to explain *how or in*

Not to be made the ground of subtle in-ferences and specu-lations.

184 STATEMENTS OF THE NEW TESTAMENT

PART
I.
SEC. 15.

what respects it was so. And in their attempt to elucidate this matter, they have raised and professed to solve such questions as the following: " Whether what Christ paid when He became obedient unto death was exactly what sinners owed, or neither more nor less than an equivalent for it?" " Whether the sum of suffering was so nicely adjusted between our Saviour and the objects of His love, that if there had been more sinners than there are to be eventually saved, His sufferings would have been proportionally augmented?" " Whether the value of His sufferings was not so incalculably great that one drop of His blood would have been sufficient to wash away the transgressions of the whole universe?" " Whether our sins, as having been committed against the infinite majesty of heaven, did not deserve an infinite punishment, so that none but an infinite person could render a satisfaction for it?"

These and suchlike questions may be truly said to be neither very becoming the limited range of our faculties, nor in any material degree conducive to our edification. It ought to be remembered that the word " satisfaction," as applied to our Lord's sufferings, *not being a Scriptural expression*, we are not entitled to draw inferences from it, or to found dogmatical conclusions upon it *as if it were so ;* although we may be perfectly warranted to make use of it as fairly and substantially expressing our views of the doctrine of Scripture. Nay, even if it were a Scriptural expression, it is still, like the word " redemption," to be considered as *anthropomorphic* — that is to say, it is applied to God after the manner of men. It is taken from human transactions and applied to divine transactions, in respect of there being certain broad features of analogy between them. The analogy, however, must not be pressed farther than the nature of the case, as otherwise ascertainable, will admit of. And when men insist on importing from it into the Scriptural doctrine of the Atonement ideas suggested by all the *minutiæ* of an ordinary case of compensation between man and man, they have cause to beware lest in so doing they involve themselves

Like the Scriptural word " redemption," it is analogical.

The analogy must not be unduly pressed.

RESPECTING THE ATONEMENT. 185

in consequences equally profane and preposterous with those into which some of the "Fathers" were led by following a like course with the Scriptural figure of "*redemption.*" When the death of Christ is represented under the divers characters of a *sacrifice*, a *substitution*, a *price* or *ransom*, and a *satisfaction*, it seems evident that these several representations of the same object, in all those specific and circumstantial points in which they differ from one another, cannot be strictly and literally realised. Our safeguard against unduly construing any one of them arises, as has been well observed, from the very variety of such figures; for they serve to limit and modify one another—each supplying somewhat in which the others might be defective, or curtailing somewhat in which the others, if severally carried out to their full extent, would be redundant. And thus, like so many sketches of the same object taken from different points of view, they help us, with all their imperfections when viewed apart, to form from them, when combined and compared together, a just and accurate conception of the whole.

PART I. SEC. 15.

See Mac-donnell's Donellan Lectures, p. 152.

It has been truly said that "the death of Christ for our sins is an event so august and stupendous, so extraordinary and unique, that those human transactions which most closely resemble it, and even those religious institutions which were appointed by God Himself to prefigure it, afford only an inadequate parallel. It possesses, however, the essence and substance, if not the circumstantials and accompaniments, of these various objects. It may be affirmed to be a *sacrifice*, a *ransom*, a *propitiation*, an *atonement*, a *satisfaction*, in a higher sense than that in which these terms were ever applied to any human transactions. And the fact of its being exhibited under such a variety of aspects precludes the possibility of doubt or misconception in regard to the great truth, which they all combine to establish—namely, the vicarious character and atoning efficacy which it truly possesses."

Balmer's Lectures and Discourses, vol. i. p. 412.

Confining ourselves, then, to a broad and general view of the import of the word "satisfaction," there need be no hesitation in applying it to the mediatorial sufferings of

186   STATEMENTS OF THE NEW TESTAMENT

*PART
I.
SEC. 15.*

*God cer-
tainly was
satisfied in
respect of
His justice
with the
Atone-
ment.*

the Son of God. We may truly say that the death of
Christ "has satisfied the justice of God." Or, if any
object to this form of expression, as seeming to *personify*
the divine justice, or to speak of it as something separate
from God Himself, we may vary the form of the statement,
without in the least changing its substance, by putting it
thus, that " *the death of Christ for sinful men satisfied a
just God,"* or " *satisfied God in respect of His justice."* To
say that it did so is simply to state, in other words, what we
have found to be the clear doctrine of Holy Scripture—
*that the sufferings of Christ, although they were not the very
penalty which God was entitled to demand from the transgressors of His law, have yet been appointed and accepted by
Him in place of it.* That such is the fact, we hold to be
unquestionable. Why else did God send His Son into
the world to give His life a ransom for many, and to be
the propitiation for our sins? Why else did He raise
Christ from the dead, in token of His approbation of all
that the Saviour had done and suffered in order to carry
out the ends of His heavenly mission? Why else does
He offer salvation to sinners, and actually bestow it on
believers, on the ground of our Lord's mediation and
atonement? Why else does He expressly declare that
" He hath set forth His Son to be a propitiation through
faith in His blood ; *to declare His righteousness, that He
may be just, and the justifier of him that believeth in Jesus"* ?
All this is unaccountable if God be not " satisfied," in
respect of His justice as well as of His other attributes,
with the sufferings of Christ instead of the merited sufferings of those sinners who are willing to receive and rest
on Him as their Saviour. The *principle* or *rationale* of the
divine procedure in this matter we may not be able fully
to explain. Like the *permission* of sin by a just and holy
God, *the remedy He has provided for sin* may involve mysteries which we cannot fathom. But whatever may have
been His reasons for appointing and accepting of the sufferings of our Lord as a propitiation for the sins of believers,
the *fact that He has done so* is, if there be any force in the
foregoing statement of Scriptural testimonies, undeniable.

RESPECTING THE ATONEMENT. 187

Now, this *revealed fact*, that God has been pleased to appoint and to accept of the sufferings of Christ as a propitiation for the sins of all who trust in Him—or that He has deemed these sufferings a sufficient ground for exempting all such from the penalties they have justly incurred —is the very truth intended to be conveyed when we speak of our Lord's death as a "satisfaction to divine justice." And if any by whom this revealed fact is fully admitted should take exception to the phrase thus employed to give expression to it, we have no need (as I before observed with reference to another topic) to contend with them about the mere use of a form of words, so long as they are substantially at one with us respecting *the thing* which these words are meant to denote.

PART I.
SEC. 15

188   STATEMENTS OF THE NEW TESTAMENT

SECTION XVI.

RESULTS OF THE FOREGOING INDUCTION OF SCRIP-TURAL TESTIMONIES CONTINUED.

PART
I.
SEC. 16.
——

THERE are some other conclusions from our induction of Scriptural testimonies, besides those which have been stated in the preceding section, to which it is of importance that we now advert.

Our sins
imputed to
Christ.

VII. One of these conclusions is, *That our sins were imputed to Jesus Christ.*

It is true there is no passage to be found in Holy Scripture in which this doctrine is expressly affirmed; but there are many passages in which it seems to be necessarily implied. For, when we read of Christ as "bearing our sins," as having "our iniquities laid upon Him," as "made sin for us," and "made a curse for us," we can hardly fail to recognise in these expressions the substance of what is *really intended* by all intelligent advocates of the doctrine that "our sins were imputed to Jesus Christ."

Miscon-
ception as
to *imputa-
tion*.

A great deal of misconception, indeed, prevails regarding the true import of this doctrine. By its adversaries it has been almost uniformly represented as implying *that the moral turpitude of our sins was transferred to Christ*, to the effect of rendering Him personally sinful and ill-deserving. Nor is it to be denied that some Antinomian writers have broadly maintained this view of imputation, and that some others, not professedly Antinomian, have occasionally expressed themselves in unguarded and in-accurate language that seems to give it countenance.

RESPECTING THE ATONEMENT.   189

Such a view, however, is altogether erroneous. The imputation of our sins to Jesus Christ has reference exclusively to *their legal forfeitures and liabilities*. It implies no such thing as a transference to Him of their inherent sinfulness or moral turpitude. Indeed such a transference is impossible in the nature of things. Our sins, as regards their moral qualities, are our own, and cannot by imputation become another's. Their legal liabilities may be laid to the account of another party, who undertakes, with the sanction of the supreme Judge, to bear these legal liabilities in our stead. And this, by a *metonymy* of the cause for the effect, may be figuratively spoken of as a transference of the sins themselves. But there can be no *literal* transference of the sins, to the effect of making him who has not committed them a sinful person, and of rendering us, who have committed them, pure and sinless.

It must be remembered, then, that the imputation of our sins to Jesus Christ implies only that He was made liable to endure their penalties, without any transference to Him of their moral turpitude or culpability. And when so regarded, there are not wanting analogies in the dealings of men that may be used in illustration of it. Thus, the debts of a person for whom I have become security may be said to be reckoned or imputed to me. But how, or to what effect? Simply to the effect of making me *legally answerable for the payment of them*, but not at all to the effect of holding me *morally culpable* for the fraud, extravagance, or reckless speculation, with which the debtor may have been chargeable in contracting them. In like manner, when Paul wrote to Philemon concerning Onesimus, "If he hath wronged thee, or oweth thee ought, put that on mine account. I Paul have written it with mine own hand, I will repay it,"—we cannot suppose the apostle's meaning to have been that he was willing to be held chargeable, in the judgment of Philemon, with the moral turpitude of any fraud or breach of trust which Onesimus might have committed. All that he meant evidently was, that he was willing to take upon himself the *consequences*

PART I. SEC. 16.

Implies only liability to penalties of our sins, not transference of their moral turpitude.

Philemon, 18, 19.

190 STATEMENTS OF THE NEW TESTAMENT

PART I. SEC. 16.

or *liabilities* which rested on Onesimus on account of what had been done by him; to make reparation for any wrong he might have inflicted, or to pay any debt which he might have incurred; so that Onesimus might, in consideration of Paul becoming thus answerable, be freed from these liabilities. It is in this sense that we are to understand the imputation of our sins to Jesus Christ. The meaning of it is, not that the moral turpitude of our iniquities was transferred to Him, so as to make Him personally sinful and ill-deserving, but simply that having, with the sanction of God, the Judge of all, undertaken to be our substitute, and to become accountable for our sins, He was dealt with as if these sins had been His own, by undergoing forfeitures or penalties on account of them— just as a surety, without the least impeachment of his own personal integrity and rectitude, is held bound to discharge the unfulfilled obligations of the person for whom he has made himself responsible.

Imputation of our sins to Christ not "a legal fiction," but a reality.

Let it not be thought that "the imputation of sin to Christ," as thus interpreted, degenerates into a mere "*legal fiction*," a putative or ideal thing, without substance or reality. No one who looks to Gethsemane and Calvary can for a moment regard it in such a light. For it is there seen to have been *most intensely real.* Assuredly the burden of our sins was "laid upon Him," not in name only, but in deed and in truth. He not only undertook,

Isa. liii. 7. *Lowth's translation.*

but actually paid their penalty. "It was exacted, and He was made answerable."

Sufferings of Christ *penal* in their character.

VIII. Another conclusion, closely allied to that which we have last stated, is, that the sufferings of Christ were *penal* in their character, or, in other words, that they were *judicially inflicted* in the execution of a law which denounced punishment on the sins of men.

Dissertations on the Atonement, No. XLII.

Some of the ablest defenders of the doctrine of the Atonement have strong scruples as to this mode of characterising it. "I will not contend," says Archbishop Magee, when speaking of the suffering of the innocent for the guilty, "that this should be called suffering *punishment*.

RESPECTING THE ATONEMENT. 191

But it evidently is, notwithstanding, *a judicial infliction;* and it may perhaps be figuratively denominated *punishment,* if thereby be implied a reference to the actual transgressor, and if that suffering which was *due to the offender himself* be understood, and which, *if inflicted on him,* would then take the name of punishment. In no other sense can the suffering of one person on account of the transgressions of another be called punishment; and in this light the bearing the punishment of another's sins is to be understood as bearing that which, in relation to the sins and to the sinner, admits of the name of punishment; but with respect to the individual on whom it is actually inflicted, abstractedly considered, can be viewed but in the light of suffering. Thus the expression may fairly be explained. It is, however, upon the whole, to be wished that the word *punishment* had not been used. The meaning is substantially the same without it. And the adoption of it has furnished the principal ground of cavil to the adversaries of the doctrine of the Atonement, who affect to consider the word as applied in its strict signification, and consequently, as implying the transfer of actual guilt."

We cannot help thinking it a groundless scrupulosity which Dr Magee shows as to the use of the expression referred to; for in stating that our Lord's death *was evidently a judicial infliction,*" or " a bearing of that which, in relation to the sins and the sinners, may be called *punishment,*" he concedes all that those who adopt the expression are disposed to contend for. This plainly appears from the following remarks of Dr Cunningham: "If men begin with defining punishment to mean *the infliction of suffering upon an offender on account of his offence* — thus including the actual personal demerit of the sufferer in the idea which the word conveys — they settle the question of the penality of Christ's sufferings by their mere definition. In this sense, of course, Christ's sufferings were not penal. But the definition is purely arbitrary, and is not required by general usage, which warrants us to regard and describe as *penal*

PART I. SEC. 16

Scruples of Magee as to this point groundless

Historical Theology, vol. ii. p. 271.

192 STATEMENTS OF THE NEW TESTAMENT

PART I.
SEC. 16.

That sufferings of Christ were penal is implied in the doctrine of Scripture.

any suffering inflicted judicially, or in the execution of the provisions of law, on account of sin."

We cannot admit, however, the truth of Dr Magee's statement, that "the meaning is substantially the same," whether the sufferings of Christ be called penal or otherwise; for if they were not penal, it does not appear in what way we could possibly regard them as satisfying divine justice, vindicating the broken law, displaying the evil of sin, or as furnishing a true substitute for the merited penalty of our transgressions. Nor is it easy to see what adequate meaning we could assign to those passages of Holy Scripture in which we are told that "He bore our sins in His own body on the tree;" that "the Lord laid on Him the iniquity of us all;" that "He was made a curse for us;" and that "God, sending His own Son in the likeness of sinful flesh and for sin, *condemned sin* in the flesh."

At the same time, while maintaining that the sufferings of Christ for our sins were penal in their character, we have no need to involve ourselves in the controversies which have sometimes been keenly agitated among theologians, as to whether, with respect to the penalty which we had incurred, they were an *idem* or a *tantundem*—that is to say, whether they were the very penalty which our sins deserved, or an adequate equivalent for it? Such questions are neither necessary nor profitable. All that it very much concerns us to be assured of is, that the sufferings of Christ were deemed sufficient in the judgment of God to satisfy His justice, to expiate our guilt, and to obtain for us eternal redemption.

Atonement originated in the love of God.

IX. Another great truth, which is so clearly established by the testimonies we have adduced that "he may run who readeth it," is, that *the Atonement originated in the love of God.* It is the *consequence*, and not the *cause*, of God's willingness to save sinners.

This is clearly declared by Christ and

In this light the Saviour Himself is careful to present it. Instead of ascribing to His Father all the sternness and severity, and claiming as His own all the tenderness

RESPECTING THE ATONEMENT. 193

and compassion, He takes especial pains to impress us
with the assurance that the purpose of His mission was to
proclaim the loving message, and to execute the loving
will of His Father who is in heaven. And as for the
apostles, so far are they from representing the mediation
of Christ as inducing God to regard sinners with a love
and pity which He would not otherwise have felt towards
them, that, on the contrary, they point to the mediation of
Christ as the brightest display and most wonderful commendation of God's pre-existing love and pity for sinful
men that could have been afforded.

PART
I.
Sec. 16.
His apos-
tles.

We must be careful, then, to view the Atonement in
this light. Never let us think of Christ as prevailing with
God to grant us a salvation which He was unwilling to
bestow, but always as the substitute whom God Himself
was pleased to provide, because in His great mercy He
desired our salvation. We have, in the mediation of
Christ, not a way of escape from God, but a way of access
to God, which God Himself hath opened for us. It was
necessary, for reasons satisfactory to the divine wisdom
and goodness, that there should be an expiation offered
for our guilt. But then the same God who exacted the
atonement has also provided it. And therefore, however
much it may become us to magnify the love of Christ in
dying for us, we ought not the less to magnify the love of
the Father in giving up His Son to death on our behalf;
for "herein is love, not that we loved God, but that He
loved us, and sent His Son to be the propitiation for our
sins."

In this respect there is a mighty difference between the
sacrifice of Christ and all others that may be likened to it.
In other sacrifices the victim is provided by the offending
party, and not by the Deity, whose favour is to be conciliated; and is, moreover, some object that is precious to
the offerer, but no otherwise valuable to the Being to
whom it is offered than as indicating the worth at which
His favour is appraised. In the sacrifice of Christ the
case is entirely reversed. Here the victim is unutterably
dear and inestimably precious to the great God to whom

Christ's
sacrifice
differs from
other sacri-
fices in this
respect,
that the
victim is
provided,
not by the
sinners,
but by
God.

194 STATEMENTS OF THE NEW TESTAMENT

PART
I.
SEC. 16.
——

He offers Himself; while, in the eyes of those who are to be redeemed by Him, He is at the time of the offering of no repute—"despised and rejected of men," and "with no beauty that they should desire Him." Nor is He provided by those for whom He suffered, but most freely given to them and given for them by God Himself. For "all things are of God, who hath reconciled us to Himself by Jesus Christ." "God commendeth His love toward us, in that, while we were yet sinners, Christ died for us." "God so loved the world, that He gave His only-begotten Son, that whosoever believeth on Him should not perish, but have everlasting life."

Work and sufferings of Christ designed to promote our sanctification.

X. Another point of great importance must be mentioned, as fully established by the testimony of Holy Scripture, respecting the mediatorial work and sufferings of Jesus Christ—namely, that they were intended, not only to obtain for us redemption from the guilt and penal consequences of sin, *but also to secure our personal sanctification.*

This truth often overlooked.

This is a truth which has too frequently been overlooked. In speaking or thinking of the "salvation" which Christ has purchased, there are many who seem to attach to it no farther idea than that of mere *deliverance from condemnation.* They forget that *deliverance from sin*—the cause of condemnation—is a no less important blessing comprehended in it. Assuredly it is just as necessary for fallen creatures to be freed from the pollution and moral impotency which they have contracted, as it is to be exempted from the penalties which they have incurred; so that, when reinstated in the favour of God, they may at the same time be made capable of loving, serving, and enjoying Him for ever. And in this respect the remedy which the Gospel reveals is fully suited to the exigencies of our sinful state, providing for our complete redemption from sin itself, as well as from the penal liabilities it has brought upon us.

Nay, it would seem as if *the former* of these deliverances—that is to say, our deliverance from sin itself—were re-.

RESPECTING THE ATONEMENT. 195

presented in some passages of Scripture as the grand and ultimate consummation of redeeming grace, to which *the latter*, though in itself inestimably precious and important, is preparatory. Witness these plain and forcible declarations : " He died for all, *that they who live should not henceforth live unto themselves, but unto Him who died for them and rose again."* " Christ loved the Church, and gave Himself for it, *that He might sanctify and cleanse* it with the washing of water by the Word, and that He might present it to Himself a glorious Church, not having spot or wrinkle, or any such thing ; *but that it should be holy and without blemish."* " You, that were sometime alienated and enemies in your 'mind by wicked works, yet now hath He reconciled in the body of His flesh through death, *to present you holy and unblamable and unreprovable in His sight."* " He gave Himself for us, that He might redeem us from all iniquity, and purify unto Himself a peculiar people, zealous of good works." " The blood of Jesus, who through the eternal Spirit offered Himself without spot unto God, shall purge your conscience from dead works, *to serve the living God."* " Who His own self bare our sins in His own body on the tree, *that we, being dead to sins, might live unto righteousness."* These statements seem to indicate that our redemption from the guilt and penal consequences of sin was intended to be the means to an ulterior end—that end being our personal sanctification.

PART I. Sec. 16.

2 Cor. v. 15.

Eph. v. 25-27.

Col. i. 21, 22.

Tit. ii. 14.

Heb. ix. 14.

1 Pet. ii. 24.

Be this as it may, there can be no doubt that the two great blessings of justification and sanctification are represented in the Word of God as inseparable results of the Saviour's mediation. Nor should we have any difficulty in apprehending how the mediation of Christ, as obtaining for us the *former* blessing, should thereby secure our attainment of the *latter.* For, in the first place, our redemption by the blood of Christ binds us to His service as a purchased or " peculiar people," according to the unanswerable argument of His apostle, " Ye are not your own, for ye are bought with a price ; therefore glorify God in your body and in your spirit, which are God's." Far-

How does mediation of Christ secure our sanctification?

1 Cor. vi. 19, 20.

196 STATEMENTS OF THE NEW TESTAMENT

PART I. SEC. 16.

ther, it gives us so impressive a manifestation of the grace of God, the love of Christ, the authority of the law, and the evil of sin, as must, if anything can, prevail with us to yield ourselves up devotedly to the Lord's service, and to be holy in all manner of conversation. Above all, it procures for us the grace of the Holy Spirit, "which is shed on us abundantly through Jesus Christ our Saviour," and by which we are renewed in the whole man after the image of God, and are enabled more and more to die unto sin and to live unto righteousness.

This sanctifying power of "the redemption that is in Christ" is practically displayed by the character and conduct of true believers. Even in this life they are witnesses of its reality, according to the measure of their growth in grace. But much more conspicuously will they be so in the life to come, when all those infirmities and blemishes and besetting sins which now cleave to them shall be

Jude, 24.

removed, and their blessed Lord shall "present them faultless before the presence of His glory with exceeding joy."

Never, then, was there a more unfounded calumny than the assertion that personal holiness is disparaged or dispensed with in the scheme of our redemption. So far from being so, it is magnified and honoured. True, it is not the *foundation* on which we are called to build ; but it is a prominent part of the *stately edifice* for the erection of which that foundation has been laid. It is not our *remedy*, but it is the completion of *the actual cure* which that remedy is designed to accomplish. It is not in any respect or in any degree *the means of salvation*, but it is one of the most essential and most precious elements of *salvation itself.*

Efficacy and completeness of the Atonement.

XI.. Farther, we learn from the preceding Scriptural testimonies the *efficacy and completeness* of the mediatorial work of Christ.

There are some, as I have already had occasion to remark, who hold that the Atonement has not *actually*

RESPECTING THE ATONEMENT. 197

secured the salvation of sinners, but has only made it
possible, by removing obstacles to it which would otherwise have been insurmountable, and by furnishing manifold
facilities and aids by which, if duly improved, salvation
may be attained.

There are others, not entirely satisfied with this view,
who hold that while God has provided through the Atonement a possibility of salvation for all sinners, He has
done something more for those who are eventually saved.
For *them* He has farther provided, *irrespectively of the
Atonement*, that special grace of the Holy Spirit whereby
they are brought to receive Christ and to rest upon Him,
so as to be actual partakers of those blessings which
the mediation of Christ has purchased for all sinners,
subject to the condition of their having faith in Him.

Now I venture to say that neither of these opinions
accords with the revealed doctrine as we have endeavoured
to ascertain it. For,

(1.) In the first place, we nowhere find it written that
the object or result of our Lord's mediatorial work was
merely *to put men into a salvable position*. We read, on
the contrary, that "He came into the world *to save*
sinners"—that He received "the name Jesus because He
should save His people from their sins"—that "He gives
to His sheep eternal life, and they shall never perish,
neither shall any pluck them out of His hand"—that we
are "now justified by His blood," and "reconciled to God
by the death of His Son"—that "Christ hath redeemed
us from the curse of the law"—that "in Him we have
redemption through His blood, the forgiveness of sins,
according to the riches of His grace"—that He "hath
obtained eternal redemption for us," and hath "put away
sin by the sacrifice of Himself." These, and the like
statements, surely indicate something more than merely
removing obstacles that stood in the way of our being
saved, or making it a *possible thing* for salvation to be
attained by us.

(2.) Secondly, we have seen that the function or province
of *faith*, by which we come to an actual participation in

198   STATEMENTS OF THE NEW TESTAMENT

PART
I.
SEC. 16.
——

all the privileges and blessings of the Gospel, is, *not to add
anything* to the mediatorial work of Christ so as to render
it more complete or more efficacious than Christ Himself
has made it, but simply to *rely upon it as a work already
perfected*, and trustfully to receive or appropriate it for our
Eph. ii. 8.
Philip. i.
29.
own behoof.   Moreover, this faith is itself "the gift of
God," and is conferred, like all His other gifts to sinful
men, through the merits of the Saviour.

(3.) Thirdly, we have found that the intercession of
Christ is inseparably connected with and founded on His
sacrifice ; so that we must ultimately trace to this sacrifice
whatever we are encouraged prayerfully to ask and hope-
fully to expect through the pleading of our High Priest,
who "is able to save them to the uttermost who come
unto God by Him, seeing He ever liveth to make intercession for them."

(4.) Fourthly—and more particularly with reference to
the *second* of the two opinions above objected to—we have
found that the grace of the Holy Spirit, by which "the
redemption purchased by Christ is *applied*" to those who
eventually partake of it, is *not* provided for us *irrespectively
of the Atonement*.   It is, on the contrary, one of the most
precious of those benefits which Christ by His mediatorial
work and sufferings has procured.   Vain is the attempt,
therefore, to separate, as some would do, between what is
called the "impetration" or "meritorious purchase" of
redemption, and the "application" of it.   These two
things, though distinguishable, are inseparable.   The
Atonement is not indebted for its actual efficacy to anything unconnected with or independent of itself, inasmuch
as the very grace of the Holy Spirit, by which it is "effectually applied," is included among the benefits secured by
Tit. iii 6.
it, being "shed on us abundantly through Jesus Christ our
Saviour."

Why, indeed, should we think that it can be otherwise ?
If God does not grant *forgiveness* to sinful men apart
from the Atonement by which their guilt is expiated, how
can we suppose that without reference to the Atonement
He would grant them *the inestimable gift of His Holy*

RESPECTING THE ATONEMENT.   199

Spirit? There seems to be precisely the same necessity, when either the one or the other of these unmerited blessings is to be conferred, that "the righteousness of God," in thus mercifully dealing with His sinful creatures, should be "declared," so that He may be "a just God and a Saviour."

(5.) I need only add, that all those "things which accompany salvation," or are necessary to the attainment of it, are ascribed to the mediation of the Saviour.

Thus, it is written: "Of his fulness have all we received, and grace for grace." "Abide in me, and I in you; as the branch cannot bear fruit of itself, except it abide in the vine, no more can ye, except ye abide in me." "Him hath God exalted with His right hand to be a Prince and a Saviour, to give repentance unto Israel and forgiveness of sins." "He that spared not His own Son, but delivered Him up for us all, how shall He not with Him also freely give us all things?" "I thank my God always on your behalf, for the grace of God which is given you by Christ Jesus; that in everything ye are enriched by Him, . . . so that ye come behind in no gift." "Of Him are ye in Christ Jesus, who of God is made unto us wisdom, and righteousness, and sanctification, and redemption." "God hath blessed us with all spiritual blessings in heavenly places (or things) in Christ: according as He hath chosen us in Him before the foundation of the world, that we should be holy and without blame before Him in love." "We are His workmanship, created in Christ Jesus unto good works." "Unto every one of us is given grace according to the measure of the gift of Christ." "In Him dwelleth all the fulness of the Godhead bodily; and ye are complete in Him." "I can do all things through Christ who strengtheneth me." "My God shall supply all your need according to His riches in glory by Christ Jesus."

From these and other like testimonies it appears that whatsoever is necessary or expedient for the Christian life is represented in Scripture as conferred upon us, not irrespectively of the mediation of Jesus Christ, but *through*

PART
I.
Sec. 16.

———

Heb. vi. 9.

John, i. 16;
xv. 4.

Acts, v.
31.

Rom. viii.
32.

1 Cor. i.
4-7, 30.

Eph. i. 3,
4; ii. 10;
iv. 7.

Col. ii. 9,
10.

Philip. iv.
13, 19.

200 STATEMENTS OF THE NEW TESTAMENT

PART
I.
SEC. 16.

His mediation, as the appointed and only channel by which all spiritual and heavenly blessings are conveyed.

When these considerations are taken into account, there seems to be no possibility of questioning the perfect and unfailing efficacy of the Saviour's work. We cannot think of it as merely removing obstacles or affording facilities in the way of our being saved, or as making salvation attainable on certain conditions, without also providing that these conditions shall be fulfilled. Rather does it seem to be the doctrine of Holy Scripture that

Confession of Faith, chap. viii. § 8.

"to all those for whom Christ hath purchased redemption, He doth certainly and effectually apply and communicate the same;" so that His Atonement may be truly called "a finished work," securing not only a *possible* salvation, but an *actual* salvation—yea, "salvation to the uttermost."

The benefits of the Atonement freely offered to all.

XII. There is one other truth very clearly ascertained by the foregoing induction of Scriptural testimonies which we have yet to mention—namely, that the Saviour and the benefits of His Atonement are freely offered in the Gospel to all sinners.

Of this precious truth it seems scarcely possible for any careful reader of the New Testament to entertain a doubt. So plainly are we there taught to receive it as "a faithful saying, and worthy of all acceptation, that Christ Jesus came into the world to save sinners" —so urgently are all men invited without distinction to come to Him for the fulness of His mercies—so graciously are we assured for our encouragement that "him that cometh to Him He will in no wise cast out," and that "whosoever believeth in Him shall not perish, but have everlasting life"—and withal so solemnly are we admonished that "it is God's commandment that we should believe on the name of His Son Jesus Christ,"—that no man living, although he were "the chief of sinners," is warranted to hold himself excluded from the call of the Gospel, or in any wise excusable for the rejection of it.

RESPECTING THE ATONEMENT.   201

I have already adverted to the difficulty which some
persons feel in regard to this matter when viewed in connection with certain passages of Scripture which speak of
those for whom the Saviour interposed as having been
"chosen in Him" and "given to Him" by the Father.
Nor can we wonder that the everlasting counsels of God,
in their bearing on the Atonement, as on every other
subject with reference to which they may be brought into
discussion, should involve mysteries too deep for the intellect of man to fathom.   It ill becomes us, however, to
suffer any mysteries connected with matters so unsearchable as the purposes of God, to turn away our minds from
the free offers and precious promises He has made to
us in the Gospel.   Whatever the Scriptures may have
expressly affirmed respecting the fact *that God has such
purposes*, we are bound, in a humble and teachable spirit,
to believe.   But when we proceed to *draw inferences* from
such affirmations, to the effect of weakening our confidence
in other statements emanating from the same source and
equally explicit, with reference to things more level to our
comprehension, we are certainly going beyond our proper
province.   And therefore, convinced though we may be
on the authority of Scripture that the sacrifice of Christ
was offered with a special reference to those who shall
eventually be partakers of its benefits, we cannot, and
never will, thence deduce any conclusions tending to
obscure the brightness of that manifestation which God
has made of His love to a sinful world in the mediatorial
work and sufferings of His beloved Son, or to cast a
shadow of doubt on the earnestness of His desire, as
indicated in the calls and invitations of the Gospel, that
all sinners should come to the Saviour that they may
have life.

In fine, whatever be the destination of the Atonement
when viewed from the stand-point of THE OMNISCIENT
GOD, to whom alone all His works are known from the
beginning, we may venture to say, *that when viewed from*
MAN'S *stand-point* (the only point of view from which *we*
can regard it), it cannot be otherwise looked at or dealt

PART
I.
SEC. 16.
―――
Supra, p.
143.

202   STATEMENTS OF THE NEW TESTAMENT

PART
I.
SEC. 16.

1 John, ii.
2.

with than as "a propitiation for the sins of the whole world"—*sufficient for all, suitable for all,* and, beyond all controversy, *pressed on the acceptance of all.* Assuredly no man has any reason or any warrant to exclude himself or any of his brethren from its reference. God's *decretive will* is one of those "secret things which belong unto Himself," and which it is not for us to pry into. But God's *revealed will* "belongs to us and to our children for ever," that we may faithfully hear it and cheerfully comply with it. And what *is* His revealed will as bearing on the matter in question? We have it clearly announced in

John, xx.
31.

such testimonies as the following: "These are written, that ye might believe that Jesus is the Christ, the Son of God; and that believing ye might have life through His

1 John, iii.
23.
John, vi.
37.
1 Tim. ii.
3, 4.
Ezek.
xxxiii. 11.

name." "This is His commandment, That we should believe on the name of His Son Jesus Christ." "Him that cometh unto me I will in no wise cast out." "God, our Saviour, will have all men to be saved, and to come unto the knowledge of the truth." 'As I live, saith the Lord God, I have no pleasure in the death of the wicked; but that the wicked should turn from his way and live." *

* See Appendix, Note G.

PART II.

CONFIRMATORY EVIDENCE OF THE OLD TESTAMENT RESPECTING THE MEDIATORIAL WORK AND SUFFERINGS OF JESUS CHRIST.

IN the preceding part of this volume we have sought to ascertain the doctrine of the New Testament respecting the mediatorial work and sufferings of Jesus Christ. And we now proceed to consider how far the results of this inquiry may be confirmed by a survey of the prophetic intimations and sacrificial institutions of the Old Testament.

PART II.

Doctrine of the Old Testament respecting the Atonement.

With reference to this matter it is no uncertain sound to which our Lord and His apostles have given utterance. St Paul declares that "Christ died for our sins according to the Scriptures." St John speaks of Him as "the Lamb slain from the foundation of the world." St Peter, when alluding to "the salvation of our souls," uses these words: "Of which salvation the prophets have inquired and searched diligently, who prophesied of the grace that should come unto you : searching what, or v·hat manner of time the Spirit of Christ which was in them did signify, when it testified beforehand the sufferings of Christ, and the glory that should follow." Our Lord Himself also appeals to the ancient Scriptures as bearing witness to the sufferings to be endured by Him in the execution of His

1 Cor. xv. 3.
Rev. xiii. 8.

1 Pet. i. 10, 11.

204   DOCTRINE OF THE OLD TESTAMENT

PART II.

Luke, xxiv. 25-27, 44-47.

mediatorial work ; for we read that on one occasion He thus expressed Himself: "O fools, and slow of heart to believe all that the prophets have spoken : ought not Christ to have suffered these things, and to enter into His glory ? And beginning at Moses and all the prophets, He expounded to them in all the Scriptures the things concerning Himself." At another time He said to His disciples,—" These are the words which I spake unto you, while I was yet with you, that all things must be fulfilled, which were written in the law of Moses, and in the prophets, and in the Psalms, concerning me. Then opened He their understanding, that they might understand the Scriptures, and said unto them, Thus it is written, and thus it behoved Christ to suffer, and to rise from the dead the third day : and that repentance and remission of sins should be preached in His name among all nations, beginning at Jerusalem."

We cannot afford the space that would be necessary fully to vindicate the justice of these appeals, by attempting to illustrate the whole, or even any considerable portion, of the prophetic and typical evidences of the Atonement. We must be content with furnishing a brief specimen of the corroborative testimonies to this important doctrine which are to be found in the Scriptures of the Old Testament.

SECTION I.

PROPHECIES OF THE OLD TESTAMENT RESPECTING
THE SUFFERINGS OF CHRIST.

1. BEGINNING this branch of our inquiries with *the Pro-* phecies, it may be observed that the first promise of a Saviour, made to Adam and Eve immediately after the Fall, bears reference—though, it must be owned, in a somewhat indefinite manner—to the sufferings which the Redeemer of our fallen race was Himself to endure in the course of frustrating that malignant scheme which their spiritual adversary had laid for their destruction. When we read that "the seed of the woman should bruise the head of the serpent, while it should bruise His heel," we are warranted to conclude that the Saviour thus indicated, was in some way to be Himself a sufferer in the course of executing the work devolved upon Him, when He should be " manifested to destroy the works of the devil." And well does the promise accord in this respect with the apostle's statement, when he speaks of the Son of God as "taking part of flesh and blood, that through death He might destroy him that had the power of death, that is, the devil ; and deliver them who through fear of death were all their lifetime subject to bondage."

PART II. SEC. I.

The first promise of a Saviour.

Gen. iii. 15.

1 John, iii. 8.

Heb. ii. 14, 15.

2. From the utterance of this primitive oracle to the time of David, we have many prophetic announcements of the Saviour ; but in none of these is there any very distinct reference to the nature of those spiritual blessings which He was to bestow, or to the cost of personal suffering at which He was to purchase them—unless, indeed, we

Subsequent prophecies.

206 DOCTRINE OF THE OLD TESTAMENT

PART
II.
SEC. I.
——

look for such reference to the rite of *Sacrifice*, which was divinely instituted under the Mosaic law, or probably at a still earlier period, and to which, as a typical prefiguration of our Lord's Atonement, we shall have occasion to refer in a subsequent section.

Prophetic psalms.

3. In the Psalms, however, there are numerous and striking allusions to the sufferings of the Messiah, and the blessings that were to flow from them.

Ps. xxii.

Thus in the 22d Psalm, which the Saviour expressly applied to Himself at the time when He was suffering the agonies of crucifixion, we have a singularly accurate and minute detail of the ignominy and anguish to which He was to be subjected, We there read of "His strength dried up like a potsherd;" of "His tongue cleaving to His jaws;" of "all His bones out of joint," and projecting so that one might "tell them;" of the "piercing of His hands and feet;" of "the parting of His garments, and of the lots cast for His vesture;" of the scornful taunts and sarcasms of His adversaries, and of His plaintive cry, as of one who was not only persecuted by men, but apparently deserted by His heavenly Father, "My God, my God, why hast Thou forsaken me?" And scarcely less striking is the description given in this psalm of the glory to Himself, and the blessedness to His people, with which His endurance of these sufferings should be crowned, —when "a seed should serve Him, and should be accounted to Him for a generation," and "when all the ends of the world should remember and turn unto Him, and all the kindreds of the nations should worship before Him."

Ps. xl. 6-8.

4. Again, in the 40th Psalm we find these words: "Sacrifice and offering Thou didst not desire; mine ears hast Thou opened" (or, according to the Septuagint version, "a body hast Thou prepared me"); "burnt-offering and sin-offering hast Thou not required: Then said I, Lo, I come: in the volume of the Book it is written of me, I delight to do Thy will, O my God; yea, Thy law is within my heart."

RESPECTING THE ATONEMENT. 207

The application of this psalm as a whole to the Messiah, is, it must be acknowledged, attended with some difficulties, for the solution of which I must refer to the writings of Hengstenberg, Delitzsch, Stuart, and other critics, by whom they have been largely and elaborately discussed. The chief difficulty arises from what is stated in the 12th verse: "Innumerable evils have compassed me about: mine iniquities have taken hold upon me, so that I am not able to look up;" these words being apparently inapplicable to one who was perfectly immaculate in his holiness. This difficulty, however, may be obviated by considering that the word translated "iniquity" is often used to signify "trouble," "calamity," or "punishment." Besides, if there be truth in the conclusions already deduced from the Scriptures of the New Testament respecting the Atonement, the Messiah might properly speak of our iniquities as "His" in respect of their penal consequences which were devolved upon Him. Indeed there is no greater incongruity in the Psalmist's language, when applied to Him in this sense, than in St Paul's statement that "He was made sin for us, who knew no sin, that we might be made the righteousness of God in Him."

Stuart on the Hebrews: Excursus, xx.

2 Cor. v. 21.

Respecting the application of those verses with which we are more immediately concerned, there is no dubiety; for not only are they expressly declared in the Epistle to the Hebrews to be applicable to the Messiah, but no other reference of them seems to be admissible. Of none but the promised Saviour could it be truly said "to be written of Him in the Book," that without any of the sacrifices and offerings which that Book enjoined He should come with acceptance, "delighting to do the will of God;" nay, more, that He should come to do the will of God with a view to the accomplishment of purposes which the sacrifices prescribed in the Book were incapable of effecting. But of Christ these things might with strict propriety be affirmed: for, as we shall afterwards have occasion to show more particularly, the volume of the Mosaic law referred to Him in all its ordinances as one in whose "obedience unto death" these ordinances were in

Heb. x. 5-10.

208   DOCTRINE OF THE OLD TESTAMENT

PART
II.
SEC. 1.

due time to find their full significancy, and who, in thus fulfilling, should also abrogate and supersede them. It is to this substitution in the fulness of time of the Saviour's great work of Atonement in the room of the Levitical offerings that allusion is made in the verses under review. It is not, we must carefully remark, the mere *inferiority* of sacrificial observances to the doing of God's will that is here expressed, but the absolute *rejection of the former* in the case of the person referred to, in order that some special and signal act of obedience to the divine will on His part might be substituted for them. As Paul argues,

Heb. x. 9,
10.

"He taketh away the first, that He may establish the second." He makes "sacrifice" give place to "the doing of the will of God"—that is to say, to "the doing of the will of God" *not by others, but by Himself,* in the execution of the specific work assigned to Him,—"by the which will," as the apostle adds, "we are sanctified through the offering of the body of Jesus Christ once for all." We need scarcely observe that the Saviour's own words are in full accordance with this prophetic description when He

John, iv.
34; vi. 38;
xvii. 4.

says: "My meat is to do the will of Him that sent me, and to finish His work;" "I came down from heaven, not to do mine own will, but the will of Him that sent me;" "I have glorified Thee on the earth, I have finished the work which Thou gavest me to do."

Ps. cx.

5. Again, in the 110th Psalm we have a clear testimony borne to the union of the priestly with the regal office in our Lord's person, which necessarily implies that the priestly functions of making atonement and intercession were assigned to Him. Perhaps there is no psalm of which the Messianic reference is more fully established both by external and by internal proofs. It is frequently

Matt. xxii.
41; Mark,
xii. 36;
Luke, xx.
42, 43;
Acts, ii. 34-
36; 1 Cor.
xv. 25;

quoted by the apostles, and by Christ Himself; and not only quoted, but reasoned from in a manner which plainly shows that they held it to have such a reference. The ancient Jewish interpreters viewed it in the same light, as sufficiently appears from the fact that when our Lord adduced it to prove that the Messiah was David's Lord as

RESPECTING THE ATONEMENT. 209

well as David's Son, the Pharisees, however desirous, were
unable to controvert Him. Besides, there is evidently
none else besides the Messiah to whom this psalm can
with any propriety be applied; for of Him only could
David affirm, as in the opening verses, " Jehovah said unto
my Lord, Sit Thou at my right hand, until I make Thine
enemies Thy footstool: Jehovah shall send the rod of Thy
strength out of Zion; rule Thou in the midst of Thine
enemies." And in Him only do we find that combination
of the sacerdotal with the kingly functions which is declared in a subsequent verse to have been solemnly and
unchangeably constituted by divine appointment. We confidently appeal, then, to this psalm as furnishing a strong
corroboration of the conclusions we have already arrived
at respecting the mediatorial work of Jesus Christ; for
it seems scarcely possible to set aside the plain import of
those words which, in the Epistle to the Hebrews, are so
largely commented on as illustrating the priesthood and
sacrifice of our Redeemer—" Jehovah hath sworn, and will
not repent, Thou art a priest for ever after the order of
Melchisedec."

PART
II.
SEC. I.
——
Heb.v. 10;
vi. 20; vii
1-25.

6. When from the Psalms we proceed onwards to the
books of the prophets, we find there such a profusion of
references to the promised Saviour and the salvation to be
wrought by Him, that a full discussion of them would far
exceed our limits. Our purpose, however, will be sufficiently served by a brief notice of some of those prophetic
passages, in which not only the fact of the Messiah's sufferings, but their reason and design, are stated with peculiar
clearness. And pre-eminent among these stands that
notable prediction which is contained in the 53d chapter
of Isaiah.

Sayings of
the pro-
phets.

Isa. liii.

That this passage was truly written by the great prophet
in the record of whose predictions it is contained, we are
not concerned for the present to establish;* for it is unquestionable that, by whomsoever written, it was extant

---

* A triumphant vindication of the genuineness of this chapter, and of all
Isaiah's prophecies from chapter xl. to the end of the book, will be found in

210   DOCTRINE OF THE OLD TESTAMENT

PART
II.
SEC. I.
———
Applied to
Christ in
New Tes-
tament.

in the canonical Scriptures of the Old Testament several hundreds of years before our Lord's advent. Its reference to Christ we hope to make sufficiently clear from the allusions which it contains to His expiatory sufferings. But as to this point the evidence of the New Testament ought in the judgment of all Christians to be decisive. In Matthew, viii. 17, the *fourth* verse of this chapter is said to have been fulfilled in Christ. In Mark, xv. 28, and Luke, xxii. 37, a like application is made of the *twelfth* verse. In John, xii. 38, the unbelief of the people, notwithstanding our Lord's miracles, is said to have been in fulfilment of the *first* verse. Philip, in discoursing to the Ethiopian treasurer, in Acts, viii. 30-35, took as his text the *seventh* and *eighth* verses, and "began at the same Scripture, and preached unto him Jesus." And Peter, in the second chapter of his First Epistle, quotes from the *fifth, sixth, ninth,* and *eleventh* verses, and applies them to Christ, when thus speaking of the Saviour, "Who did no sin, neither was guile found in His mouth;" "who His own self bare our sins in His own body on the tree;" "by whose stripes ye were healed; for ye were as sheep going astray, but are now returned unto the Shepherd and Bishop of your souls." These testimonies must be amply sufficient to convince all who regard our Lord and His apostles as trustworthy interpreters of the Old Testament, that this prediction of Isaiah truly refers to Jesus Christ. And then as to the import of it, as setting forth the nature of that mediatorial work which the Messiah was to execute, there seems scarcely to be a possibility of mistaking it.

Bears wit-
ness to the
Atone-
ment.

The ignominy and anguish to which He was to be subjected are here described in the most affecting manner. He is spoken of as "despised and rejected of men, a Man of sorrows and acquainted with grief"—as "wounded," "bruised," "stricken," "afflicted"—"led as a lamb to the slaughter"—"numbered with transgressors"—enduring an inward "travail of His soul"—as "cut off out

the Boyle Lectures for 1868, entitled "The Witness of the Old Testament to Christ," by the Rev. Stanley Leathes, M.A.

RESPECTING THE ATONEMENT. 211

of the land of the living," and "pouring out His soul unto death."

His perfect innocence, too, is forcibly contrasted with the severe and undeserved afflictions which were laid upon Him ; for He is emphatically called the Lord's "righteous servant"; and an explicit testimony is borne concerning Him, that " He did no violence, neither was any deceit in His mouth."

The concern which God had in His sufferings is clearly announced ; for we are told that " it pleased the Lord to bruise Him, He hath put Him to grief;" and that "the Lord laid on Him the iniquity of us all; *it was exacted, and He was made answerable.*" *

The beneficial results, also, of His sufferings are strongly indicated in the assurance given us, that "by His stripes we are healed "—that " He shall justify many by bearing their iniquities"—that He shall "make intercession for transgressors"—that "He shall see His seed, and shall prolong His days, and the pleasure of the Lord shall prosper in His hand."

But above all, the substitutionary or vicarious character of His afflictions is again and again affirmed in the most decided terms; as when He is said to have been "wounded for our transgressions and bruised for our iniquities"—to have had " the chastisement of our peace upon Him "—to have "borne the sin of many"—to have been "stricken for the transgressions of the people "—to have had " the iniquity of us all laid upon Him "—and to have had " His soul made an offering for sin."

It has been objected by some who deny the Atonement that Matthew has applied the *fourth* verse of this chapter to those miraculous cures of bodily maladies which the Saviour wrought, representing these miracles as done by Him, "that it might be fulfilled which was spoken by Esaias the prophet, saying, *Himself took our infirmities and bare our sicknesses.*" It appears, however, from the

PART II. SEC. I.

Matt. viii. 17.

---

* The first clause of verse 7th is thus translated by Bishop Lowth. Pye Smith translates the clause, "It is exacted, and He answereth to it;" and Seiler translates it, " Of Him it was exacted."

212 DOCTRINE OF THE OLD TESTAMENT

PART II. SEC. I. —— Magee on the Atonement, vol. i. p. 265-280.

comments on this passage by Gesenius, Rosenmuller, and Hengstenberg, as well as from the elaborate and able note of Archbishop Magee, that the words in the original, instead of being translated "Surely He hath borne our griefs and carried our sorrows," would be more appropriately rendered in such terms as exactly to agree with the quotation of them by the evangelist. And surely the circumstance that *one verse* of this prophetic chapter refers to our Saviour's miracles of healing does not in the least conflict with the reference of the adjoining verses to other incidents in His history, and in particular to His vicarious sufferings. The bearing of iniquities, indeed, and the healing of diseases, might very naturally be thus associated with one another, inasmuch as our Lord's miraculous cures might be regarded as visible types and sure pledges of His saving grace; just as the maladies healed by Him were proofs and consequences of that sinful state from which it is the great end of His mission to deliver us.

We confidently appeal, then, to this remarkable passage in confirmation of what we have found to be the doctrine of the New Testament respecting the Atonement; for if expressions so plain and so significant as those which are here employed by the prophet do not convey the idea of piacular sufferings, inflicted by divine appointment, and endured by an innocent person in the room of the guilty, we may well doubt the possibility of ever conveying this idea by any combination of terms which language can supply. Certainly there is no creed or confession of faith that can be referred to in which this idea is more distinctly set forth. And it is remarkable how frequently the writers of the New Testament betake themselves to the words of this prophecy, with the view not so much of *proving* the doctrine of the Atonement as of appropriately and forcibly *expressing* it.

Daniel's prophecy of the seventy weeks.

7. Another prophetic passage worthy of remark in connection with the subject of our present discussion is the well-known prediction of the *seventy weeks* contained in the 9th chapter of Daniel.

RESPECTING THE ATONEMENT. 213

Assuming the application of this passage to the Messiah, which is broadly affirmed in the very terms of the prediction itself, it seems scarcely possible to evade the testimony which it bears to His sacrificial death as an atonement for the sins of His people; for we read in the 26th verse that after the seven weeks and threescore and two weeks "the Messiah shall be cut off, but not for Himself." It would indeed be injudicious to attach much weight to the last clause of this verse, because the words rendered "but not for Himself" may admit of being otherwise translated "no one will be for Him"—that is to say, either "no one will take part with Him," or "no one will acknowledge Him to be truly the Messiah." But the word translated "cut off" implies a painful, violent, untimely death, and is interpreted by the Jewish Rabbis as signifying "a death inflicted by a judicial sentence," which sense they confirm by appealing to a variety of other passages of the Old Testament. Farther, that His death was a true and proper sin-offering is indicated in the immediately succeeding verse by the statement that He should "cause the sacrifice and the oblation to cease," which seems to mark Him out as the great propitiatory sacrifice, the offering up of which would necessarily put an end to all those preparatory and symbolical ordinances which had preceded it. But above all, we find it written in the 24th verse that the grand object of His mission into the world was "to finish the transgression, to make an end of sins, to make reconciliation for iniquity, and to bring in everlasting righteousness." These words have most evidently a sacrificial import. And when taken in connection with the circumstance already referred to, that the Messiah, when "cut off," was to "cause the sacrifice and the oblation to cease," we can hardly fail to see in them a declaration—in the very spirit of what is taught us in the Epistle to the Hebrews—that the Messiah was to make that all-sufficient atonement for the sins of the world which would dispense with the necessity of any other, and would "perfect for ever them that are sanctified."

PART
II.
SEC. 1.

Dan. ix.
20-27.

See Lowth
on Daniel
and the
Minor
Prophets,
vol. i. p.
105.

214   DOCTRINE OF THE OLD TESTAMENT

PART II. SEC. I.

Prophecy of the smitten Shepherd, Zech. xiii. 7.

8. There is one other prophecy to which we may shortly advert before closing this department of our inquiries, and that is the remarkable prediction of Zechariah: "Awake, O sword, against my Shepherd, and against the man that is my fellow, saith the Lord of hosts: smite the Shepherd, and the sheep shall be scattered; and I will turn mine hand upon the little ones."

We are not left in any doubt as to the questions, By whom were these words spoken? and, To whom do they refer? The prophet Zechariah, by whom they are re-corded, declares that they were spoken by "the Lord of hosts." And our Lord Jesus Christ has applied them to Himself, and has clearly indicated their reference to His last sufferings; for it was when He had gone out from the chamber of communion to the Mount of Olives, and was about to be betrayed into the hands of His enemies,

Matt. xxvi. 31; Mark, xiv. 27.

that He said to His disciples, "All ye shall be offended because of me this night; for it is written, I will smite the Shepherd, and the sheep shall be scattered." The words, then, are undoubtedly to be considered as spoken by God the Father concerning His Son Jesus Christ. And they give utterance to an awful and mysterious man-date, that sufferings and death should be inflicted on a Person who stood in a position of the closest equality and of the most intimate fellowship with Himself—a Person, too, who, instead of having done anything to incur or merit on His own account such afflictions, was actually employed, at the very moment when He was visited with them, in executing a work entirely agreeable to His Father's will—nay, a work which His Father had given Him to do, as the divinely-commissioned Shepherd of the flock intrusted to Him. Allusion is indeed made to the more immediate effect with which this "smiting of the Shepherd" should be attended, in the temporary disper-sion of His sheep. But this is immediately followed by the promise, "I will turn or bring back my hand upon the little ones,"—indicating the Lord's tender compassion for their deplorable condition, and His merciful purpose to recover and restore them. And this promise is after-

RESPECTING THE ATONEMENT.   215

wards followed by the assurance, "They shall call on my
name, and I will hear them: I will say, It is my people;
and they shall say, The Lord is my God."

PART II.
SEC. I.

Zech. xiii. 9.

Here, then, we have unmerited and severe sufferings
inflicted by the appointment of the Lord of hosts on One
who not only did not deserve them, but was, by reason of
the dignity of His person and the exceeding intimacy of
His relation to the Ordainer of them, of all beings the
most unlikely to be visited with them. And these sufferings are connected with the intimation of a merciful design
for the benefit of those sheep who were the objects of love
and care to the great Sufferer. In what other light, then,
are His afflictions to be regarded, than as a provision expressly made by the Lord of hosts for the deliverance
and restoration of perishing sinners? Or how can we fail
to see in this announcement of them a foreshadowing of
what the Saviour Himself declared when He thus spake,
"I am the good Shepherd; the good Shepherd giveth His
life for the sheep." "As the Father knoweth me, even so
know I the Father, and I lay down my life for the sheep."
"Therefore doth my Father love me because I lay down
my life." "I know my sheep, and am known of mine;"
"and I give unto them eternal life; and they shall never
perish, neither shall any pluck them out of my hands."

John, x. 11, 14, 15, 17, 28.

I need only farther observe that this prophecy is connected with another, contained in the close of the preceding chapter, and also applied to the Lord Jesus by an
evangelist, in which it is foretold that the penitent Israelites should "look on Him whom they have pierced;" and
that between these two Messianic prophecies (both of
which are appropriated in the New Testament to our
Saviour) there occurs a promise—evidently pointing to
that cleansing of the soul which is accomplished by His
great sacrifice—that "a fountain shall be opened to the
house of David and to the inhabitants of Jerusalem for sin
and for uncleanness."

Zech. xii. 10; John, xix. 37.

Zech. xiii. 1.

The instances above given may be taken as a sufficient
specimen of those inspired testimonies with reference to

216   DOCTRINE OF THE OLD TESTAMENT

PART
II.
SEC. I.
———

this subject which are to be found in the prophecies of the Old Testament. We are far from holding that they would be of themselves sufficient to establish the great truth in behalf of which they have been adduced. But certainly they lend a most important confirmation to the clear and distinct statements of it by the apostles and evangelists. And they fully bear out the affirmation of

1 Cor. xv. 3.

St Paul, when he says, "I delivered unto you first of all that which I also received, that Christ died for our sins *according* to the Scriptures;" and the still more explicit

Luke, xxiv. 46, 47.

statement of the Saviour Himself, that "thus it was written, and thus it behoved Christ to suffer, and to rise from the dead the third day, and that repentance and remission of sins should be preached in His name among all nations."

SECTION II.

THE LEVITICAL SACRIFICES—THEIR DIVINE INSTITUTION AND PIACULAR CHARACTER.

NEXT to the prophetic intimations of the Old Testament, we must turn our attention to its *sacrificial rites*, as serving still farther to illustrate and confirm the conclusions derived from the teaching of the New Testament respecting the great Christian doctrine of the Atonement. To these rites, indeed, we have already had occasion to refer, with the view of explaining the sacrificial expressions applied to our Lord's death by the apostles and evangelists. The subject, however, is so interesting and so important, as to merit a much fuller discussion than it has yet received. Confining ourselves for the present to the *Levitical sacrifices*, as being those in regard to which we possess the fullest means of information, we shall endeavour to arrange our remarks upon them under the *four* following heads: 1st, their divine institution; 2dly, their piacular character; 3dly, their beneficial efficacy; and 4thly, their typical reference to our Saviour.

PART II. SEC. 2.

Levitical sacrifices confirmatory of the Atonement.

I. The *divine institution* of the Levitical sacrifices cannot with any consistency be denied by those who believe in the divine mission of Jesus Christ. For by Him the authority of Moses as a lawgiver has been fully and unequivocally recognised. And no disparaging views which some may be disposed to take of the inspiration of the Mosaic *writings* can warrant them to question the authority of the Mosaic *ordinances*. These were undoubtedly divine, if there was anything divine in Judaism at all. For they are incorporated

Divine institution of Levitical sacrifices.

218   DOCTRINE OF THE OLD TESTAMENT

PART II.
SEC. 2.
——

with the very substance of that religion which Moses, in the name of Jehovah, prescribed to the children of Israel. And of the sacrifices, in particular, it is beyond dispute that every circumstance relating to the quality of the victims, or the time, place, and manner of their oblation, is professedly regulated by the express appointment of God.

Allegation that they were appointed to suit the heathenish customs which Israelites had acquired in Egypt.

It has, indeed, been alleged that these sacrifices were appointed simply in accommodation to the heathenish taste for such observances which the Israelites had acquired during their long sojourn in Egypt. And some countenance is held to be given to this allegation by the circumstance that the sacrificial precepts in the Book of Leviticus have reference, not to the institution of a new rite, but rather to the improvement or regulation of an old one,

Levit. i. 2, 10, 14; ii. 1, 4, 5, 7; iii. 1, 6, 12.

being thus expressed, " If any man of you bring an offering to the Lord, he shall offer it in this or in that manner."

This allegation refuted.

This mode of expression, however, may be satisfactorily explained, so as to give no manner of countenance to the allegation in support of which it is appealed to, by the fact that sacrifice was observed by the patriarchs, from whom the race of Israel were descended, as an acceptable method of worshipping the true God. Besides, it is worthy of remark that Moses, while yet in Egypt, demanded in the name of the Lord that Pharaoh would permit the Israelites " to go three days' journey into the wilderness to sacrifice unto the Lord their God ; " and that when Pharaoh told him that they might sacrifice to their God in Egypt, Moses

Exod. viii. 25-27.

rejoined, " It is not meet so to do, for we shall sacrifice the abomination of the Egyptians to the Lord our God, and

Compare 1 Kings, xi. 5, 7 ; 2 Kings, xxiii. 13.

will they not stone us ? " By " the abomination of the Egyptians " Moses does not mean " that which the Egyptians regarded as an abomination," but " that which was so regarded by himself," when made, as it was by the Egyptians, an object of idolatrous worship. He undoubtedly alludes to their grossly superstitious practice of giving divine honours to four-footed beasts. And his meaning is, that if the Israelites were to sacrifice to Jehovah those animals which were worshipped as gods in the land of Egypt, the Egyptians would assuredly stone them. Here,

RESPECTING THE ATONEMENT.   219

then, we have evidence of two things which are perfectly
conclusive against the assertion we are now combating.
One is, that the rite of sacrifice, as an approved and acceptable mode of worshipping the true God, was known
to the Israelites before the giving of the law at Mount
Sinai. And the other is, that this ordinance, as observed
among them, instead of being in accordance with the superstitions of the Egyptians, was, on the contrary, so utterly
opposed to them, that it could not be put in practice in
the land of Egypt without giving offence and incurring
persecution.

Besides, so far is it from being the case that God accommodated the institutes of the Mosaic ritual to the heathenish tastes which the Israelites had acquired in Egypt, that
He took especial means to prevent His own ordinances
from being in any way contaminated by an admixture of
heathen errors and superstitions. For forty years were
the Israelites led about in the wilderness, until the whole
generation who came out of Egypt, except only Joshua
and Caleb, had passed away, before they were permitted
to enter the promised land. And lest the new generation
who entered Canaan should be corrupted with any kind of
false worship, they were commanded utterly to destroy
those heathen tribes who had previously possessed the
land. Not only so, but the most solemn warning was
given them against conforming to the observances of any
heathen nation whatsoever, and in particular to those of
the Egyptians and Canaanites. " Speak unto the children
of Israel," said the Lord ; " after the doings of the land of
Egypt, wherein ye dwelt, shall ye not do ; and after the
doings of the land of Canaan, whither I bring you, shall
ye not do ; neither shall ye walk in their ordinances. Ye
shall do my judgments, and keep mine ordinances, to
walk therein." It cannot be thought, surely, that in spite
of the determination thus shown by the God of Israel to
prevent the most distant approximation on the part of His
chosen people to heathen superstitions, He would, after all,
assign a prominent place to the ordinance of sacrifice in
the ritual He prescribed to them, for no higher reason than

220 DOCTRINE OF THE OLD TESTAMENT

PART II. SEC. 2. to conciliate those prejudices and accommodate Himself to those habits which they had acquired in Egypt.

Levitical sacrifices were piacular. II. The divine institution of the Levitical sacrifices being thus evident, we proceed to show their *piacular character.* Some are inclined to think that such a character pertained more or less to all the Mosaic sacrifices. For our present purpose, however, it will suffice if we are able to prove that it truly belonged to the *animal oblations,* such as the sin-offerings, trespass-offerings, whole burnt-offerings, and peace-offerings, of which we are told in the Epistle to the Hebrews that "almost all things are by the law purged with blood, and without shedding of blood is no remission."

Heb. ix. 22.

The sin-offering. (I.) The *sin-offering* had special reference to the consciousness of sin and the need of an atonement on the part of the worshipper, and was indeed so identified with sin that the same Hebrew word was used to denote both. It was for the most part offered on special occasions, when some particular sin had been committed through ignorance, inadvertency, or error, against any of the commandments of the Lord, whether by a private individual, a ruler, a priest, or the whole people, as the case might be. The persons who brought the sacrifice—or if it was a public offering, the elders of the people as representing the community—were appointed to lay their hands upon the head of the victim, which was in all cases required to be without blemish, and thereafter to slay it and deliver it to the priest. The priest then sprinkled part of the blood upon the horns of the altar of burnt-offerings which stood before the entrance of the tabernacle, or, if the offering was made for himself or for the people, upon the altar of incense that stood within the tabernacle. He then poured out the remainder of the blood at the foot of the altar of burnt-offerings, and finally burned the kidneys and the fat of the animal upon that altar. Such were the prescribed ceremonies, by the due observance of which, as we are told in the Book of Leviticus, "the priest shall make an atonement for them, and it shall be forgiven them;" and again,

Levit. iv. 20, 31, 35; v. 10.

RESPECTING THE ATONEMENT. 221

"the priest shall make an atonement for his sin that he hath committed, and it shall be forgiven him."

In all cases in which a ruler or a private individual was the offerer, the flesh of the sin-offering, except what was burned on the altar, was eaten by the priests in the sanctuary, as being "most holy." But when the sacrifice was offered either for the priest himself or for the community, and its blood was carried within the vail of the tabernacle, no part of the flesh was allowed to be eaten; but the whole body of the victim was ordered to be carried forth and consumed with fire in a clean place without the camp.

(2.) The *trespass-offering* differs but little from the sin-offering; and the precise point of distinction between them has been much disputed. It seems now to be the prevailing opinion of the best critics that the trespass-offering had reference more especially to the *social evils* occasioned by any transgression, or to the violation of social rights involved in the commission of it; the primary aspect of sin, as committed against God, being not indeed overlooked, but somewhat less prominently exhibited. The ceremonial was the same as in the case of the sin-offering, except that the blood was only poured around the altar, instead of being sprinkled on the horns of it. And the like statements are made respecting the expiatory nature of this sacrifice—namely, "The priest shall make an atonement for him with the ram of the trespass-offering, and it shall be forgiven him;" and "the priest shall make an atonement for him before the Lord; and it shall be forgiven him for anything of all that he hath done in trespassing therein."

(3.) The whole *burnt-offering* was more general and comprehensive in its character than the other sacrifices. It undoubtedly included in it a reference to the expiation of sin; for the offerer was required to lay his hand on the head of the victim, and it was expressly said, like the sin-offering and trespass-offering, to be "accepted for him to make atonement for him." The guilt, however, which it was thus designed to expiate, was that not of any parti-

PART
II.
SEC. 2.
——

The trespass-offering.

Fairbairn's Typology, vol. ii. p. 343.

Levit. v. 16; vi. 7.

The whole burnt-offering.

Levit. i. 4.

222   DOCTRINE OF THE OLD TESTAMENT

PART II. SEC. 2.

cular acts of transgression, but rather of those continual shortcomings and imperfections which cleave to the most devout worshipper and taint his best services. And along with that sense of sin and desire of pardon which it thus expressed, there was combined a self-dedication of the offerer with all his powers and faculties to the service of God, as was symbolised by the distinguishing feature of the burnt-offering—namely, the consumption of the whole of the victim in the sacred fire, after its blood had been poured out around the altar.

This kind of sacrifice was frequently presented by private individuals as a "free-will offering,"—betokening their self-dedication to the Lord, following upon, and growing out of, pardon and acceptance with Him. It was also the kind of sacrifice offered for the nation at large, on the occasion of the new moons, the three great annual festivals, and in connection with the sin-offering on the day of atonement. Farther, it was presented every morning and every evening in behalf of the whole covenant people. And in the case of the evening sacrifice, provision was made that during the night, when the altar was not required for any other purpose, the burnt-offering should be so slowly consumed as to last until the morning. So that, as is observed by Dr Fairbairn, "it was the daily and nightly, and, in a sense, the perpetual sacrifice,—the symbolical expression of what Israel should have been ever receiving from the God of the covenant, and of what they, as children of the covenant, should ever have yielded to Him in return. And on account of its having such a position in the sacrificial institute, the altar of sacrifice came to be familiarly called *the altar of burnt-offering*."

Fairbairn's Typology, vol. ii. p. 345.

The peace-offering.

(4.) The *peace-offerings* were, for the most part, *sacrifices of praise and thanksgiving* for some remarkable tokens of the Lord's goodness, and sometimes *votive offerings*, in fulfilment of a vow which the worshipper had made, when either soliciting, or acknowledging that he had already experienced, some striking interposition of divine providence in his behalf. Their distinctive characteristic was the admission of the offerer to participate, along with his

RESPECTING THE ATONEMENT. 223

friends, in the flesh of the victim, as a token of his peace and fellowship with God. But not the less on this account did they involve a propitiatory element. For, like all the other offerings of blood, they were accompanied with the imposition of hands, and the sprinkling of the sacrificial blood round about the altar.

PART II. SEC. 2.

From this brief account of the several kinds of animal sacrifices, their piacular character is sufficiently apparent. We have noticed as one striking feature which belonged to them, that the offerer was required to lay his hands upon the head of the victim. This ceremony is expressly prescribed in the case of all the animal oblations, except that of the trespass-offering. We cannot doubt, however, that in this case also, as well as in the others, the ceremony was observed ; and that the express mention of it is omitted, merely because the trespass-offering bore so very close an affinity to the sin-offering, that the regulation was sure to be held as applying to both. In this, as well as in other respects, full force must be given to the statement in Leviticus, "*As the sin-offering is, so is the trespass-offering ; there is one law for them.*"

Their piacular character shown by the imposition of hands on the head of the victim.

Levit. vii. 7.

The laying-on of hands was a ceremony observed not only at the offering of sacrifice, but on various other occasions ; as, for example, the bestowal of blessing, the imparting of spiritual gifts, the conveyance of authority, and the designation to official functions. In all such cases it is evidently symbolical of the communication of something from the person who imposes the hands to him on whom they are imposed. And what less, in the case of the sin-offerings and burnt-offerings, can it be held to indicate as conveyed by the offerer to the animal which he was about to slay in sacrifice, than an appointment of him to be offered as his victim, and a consequent transference to him of his guilt ? The ceremony, even if taken by itself, imports, at the very least, a destination of the animal to that death to which he was immediately afterwards subjected, and to those sacrificial purposes which his death was intended to accomplish. But the ceremony

224   DOCTRINE OF THE OLD TESTAMENT

PART
II.
SEC. 2.

must not be taken by itself. It must be taken in connection with that reference to *the expiation of sin* which is so emphatically made in immediate proximity to it. And surely, when we read such a statement as the following,

Levit. i. 4.

"He shall put his hand upon the head of the burnt-offering, and it shall be accepted for him to make atonement for him," it is impossible to maintain that the two things, thus intimately connected, stood in no manner of relation to one another. We have it, moreover, on the authority of ancient Jewish Rabbis, quoted by Outram in his learned work on sacrifices, that the imposition of hands was always accompanied with confession of sins, and that the customary form of confession used by an individual

Outram,
De Sacri-
ficiis, lib. i.
cap. xv.
§ 8, 10, 11.

when presenting his own sacrifice, was in these words: "O God, I have sinned, I have done perversely, I have trespassed before Thee, and have done so and so; but lo! now I repent, and am truly sorry for my misdeeds; let, then, this victim be my expiation." Nor is it any valid objection against this mode of interpreting the symbolical action, to allege that the laying-on of hands was not confined to sin-offerings and burnt-offerings, but was used also in sacrifices of a votive and eucharistical character. For this circumstance only shows that votive offerings and thank-offerings, as well as the other sacrifices of the Levitical system, involved an acknowledgment of unworthiness on the part of the worshippers, and of their felt need of having their sins atoned for, in order that their offerings might be acceptable in the sight of God

Pouring of
the blood
upon the
altar.

A still more important and sacred part of the service, however, was the sprinkling or pouring of the blood upon the altar. This was the consummation of the sacrifice, betokening the divine acceptance of it on behalf of the worshipper; according to that solemn statement of the

Levlt. xvii.
11.

God of Israel, "The life of the flesh is in the blood; and I have given it to you upon the altar to make an atonement for your souls." What this atonement was, we learn from passages already referred to, in which it is written, that "the priest shall make an atonement for him concerning his sin, and *it shall be forgiven him.*" The atone-

RESPECTING THE ATONEMENT. 225

ment consisted in his exemption from the penalties of sin. And it was secured by the blood upon the altar, as that "in which the life was" of the victim which he had immolated. Life was given for life; the life of the victim for the life of the offerer.

PART II. SEC. 2.

The propitiatory nature of the Mosaic sacrifices may be well illustrated by a reference to those which were offered on the day of atonement. On this solemn anniversary the high priest was required, first of all, to slay a bullock as a sin-offering for himself and for the whole household of the priests, and to go with its blood into the most holy place—that sacred recess which none but he was permitted to enter, and even he only on this special occasion—and to sprinkle the blood seven times on and before the mercy-seat. When this act of expiation for the priesthood was completed, another for the sins of the whole people commenced. Two goats were presented at the door of the tabernacle, which yet are spoken of as constituting but one offering, each having his own part to bear in the solemnity, the one as exhibiting the means, and the other the results, of the atonement. Lots were then cast to determine which of the two should be slain. And the goat on which the Lord's lot fell was immediately put to death as a sin-offering for the people, and its blood carried, like that of the bullock, into the most holy place, and sprinkled, as before, on and beside the mercy-seat. When this was done, the high priest came out from the inner into the outer sanctuary, and sprinkled the altar of incense seven times with the blood both of the bullock and of the goat, "to cleanse and hallow it from the uncleanness of the children of Israel." Finally, he was required to lay both his hands upon the head of the surviving goat, which was still standing in front of the tabernacle, and to "confess over him all the iniquities of the children of Israel, and all their transgressions in all their sins, putting them upon the head of the goat," which was then "sent away by the hand of a fit person into the wilderness, bearing upon him all their iniquities unto a land not inhabited."

Sacrifices on the day of atonement were expiatory. Levit. xvi.

226 DOCTRINE OF THE OLD TESTAMENT

PART II. SEC. 2.

The symbolism thus employed was much fuller and more significant than that of the sin-offerings presented on ordinary occasions, two animals being used, one of which was sacrificed, while the other was sent away alive into the wilderness, so as to indicate the complete removal of the sins of the people which had been laid upon his head.

Kurtz's Sacrificial Worship, p. 130.

"Had it been possible," as Kurtz observes, "to recall the slain goat to life, and then to send him away alive with the sins atoned for, the same end would have been attained ; but since this could not be done, another goat, as it were an *alter ego*, in all respects identified with the first, performed this office."

The expiatory nature of the Mosaic sacrifices may be farther established by showing the insufficiency of the objections urged against it. To some of the more plausible of these objections we shall now advert.

Objection that words translated "to atone" do not convey the idea of *expiation.*

Bushnell on Vicarious Sacrifice, p. 427 ; Young's Light and Life of Men, p. 243.

1. It has been urged by Dr Bushnell and Dr Young that the original words in the Hebrew Scriptures and in the Greek Septuagint, which are translated to " atone " or to " make an atonement," do not convey the idea of expiation, and are employed in some passages where that idea is necessarily excluded. " The Hebrew word," says Bushnell, " simply speaks of " *covering* or *making cover* for sin ; and is sufficiently answered by anything which removes it, hides it from sight, or brings into a state of reconciliation where the impeachment of it is gone." " As the root of the word means simply *to cover*, we can see for ourselves that while it may be applied to denote a covering by expiation, it can certainly as well and as naturally be applied to anything which hides or takes away transgression."

Answer to this objection.

The question, however, is not, What meaning might this Hebrew word possibly bear or admit of *when applied to any subject?* but, What meaning does it bear or admit of, according to the usage of Scripture, *when applied to sin-offerings?* While truly stating that *to cover* is its radical sense, Bushnell admits that " covering *by expiation* " is one of the various modes of covering which it may be used to denote. Now, we venture to say that, when used in relation to *sin*, it always means *so to cover sin as to avert its penalties*. Assuredly, when used with reference to *sin-offerings*, it admits of no other than an expiatory sense, as we evidently see from the close connection, already noticed, between "making atonement" for the offerer, and securing for him "the forgiveness of his sin." Farther, we may safely challenge Dr Bushnell to produce a single instance in which the word *kaphar*, when used with reference either to "sins" or to "sin-offerings," can possibly bear the sense which his own theory of sacrifice requires—that, namely, of producing repentance or any other subjective effect in the mind of the sinner.

With respect, again, to the Greek verbs ἱλάσκομαι and ἐξιλάσκομαι, by which *kaphar* is usually translated in the Septuagint, Dr Young admits it to be "beyond all question that, according to ordinary Greek usage, they distinctly convey the idea of *propitiating* or *appeasing*, and are constantly employed by Greek writers to express the supposed effect of sacrifices in averting the anger of the gods." He insists, however, as does also Dr Bushnell, that the Septuagint translators could not have intended to use them in their heathenish or expiatory sense, "because they have employed them with reference to the tabernacle, the holy place, and the altar, which could commit no sin, and could awaken no divine anger which needed to be appeased."

To this the reply is obvious, that though these inanimate objects were necessarily incapable of sin, they yet needed cleansing or expiation in respect of that ceremonial defilement which they had contracted from the sins of the priests and people by whom they were used. Such is the explanation of the matter given in Leviticus, xvi. 16, where it is written, "He shall make an atonement for the holy place, *because of the uncleanness of the children of Israel, and because of their transgressions in all their sins;* and so shall he do for the tabernacle of the congregation, which remaineth among them *in the midst of their uncleanness.*"

228   DOCTRINE OF THE OLD TESTAMENT

PART
II.
SEC. 2.
———

Nor does it avail to say that the uncleanness thus spoken of was only of a *ceremonial* kind, and was consequently removed only in a ceremonial sense. For if, in the phraseology of Leviticus, the term "uncleanness" be applied, as it frequently is, to that which is only symbolical of moral impurity, we cannot wonder that the word "atone" in like manner should be used to denote a symbolical expiation. Nor are we entitled to conclude from such a use of it that its expiatory sense is wholly abandoned or ignored.

Objection that sacrifice is not used in some cases in which, if we might have expected it.

2. Again, it has been objected by the same writers that under the Jewish dispensation sacrifice is not resorted to in some remarkable instances of transgression, in which we might have expected it to be employed, if it really was possessed of any expiatory virtues. The instances to which they refer are—the apostasy of Israel when they worshipped the golden calf at Sinai ; the mutiny which followed the judgment of Korah and his accomplices ; and the grievous offence of David, under a sense of which he expressly said, " Thou desirest not sacrifice, else would I give it."

Reply to this objection.

It is not a little strange that the objectors should have forgotten that in all these instances the offences committed were of a kind for which no sacrificial expiation was provided. The veriest tyro in Biblical knowledge is well aware that such presumptuous sins as wilful apostasy, idolatry, adultery, and murder, were utterly excluded from the benefits of the Mosaic ritual. In one of the instances, indeed—that of the rebellion which broke out after the destruction of Korah—an atonement was offered, at the merciful suggestion of Moses, beyond what the law ordinarily allowed of, and proved successful. Dr Bushnell insists that this atonement was not sacrificial, inasmuch as it consisted of a mere offering of incense. But he overlooks the circumstance that the fire which burnt the incense *was taken from the altar of burnt-offerings*, so as directly to connect the incense with the ritual of sacrifice.

Num. xvi.
46.

Dr Young further urges, in support of this objection, that in Solomon's prayer at the consecration of the Temple,

RESPECTING THE ATONEMENT.   229

"there is not a single hint of sacrifice as the medium of pardon and reconciliation ; but the one method spoken of is confession, prayer, and trust in the revelation of free, forgiving mercy."

PART II. SEC. 2.

Young's Light and Life of Men, p. 275.

It is somewhat surprising that this passage of the sacred history should be pleaded as an instance of the disparagement of sacrifice. For it cannot be forgotten that Solomon, on the occasion referred to, was actually setting apart a gorgeous edifice, which he had reared at immense cost, for the purpose of sacrificial worship, and that the prayers and confessions of which he speaks were either to be offered up " in this house," or directed " towards this house," as the appointed place in which sin-offerings and burnt-offerings were continually to be presented on the altar of the God of Israel.

2 Chron. vi. 20-39.

3. It has been objected by Bähr, Hofmann, and others, that " if the Levitical sacrifices had been expiatory, the victim ought to have been slain by the priest, as representing God, and not by the offerer."

Objection that if sacrifices were expiatory, the priest and not the offerer ought to have slain the victim.

To this the reply of Kurtz is entirely satisfactory. " In sacrifice," he says, " God appears as the Merciful One, who desires not the death of the sinner, but his redemption (though doubtless in a manner accordant with justice) ; while the sinner, on the other hand, appears as one who has brought death and condemnation upon himself through sin, and is conscious of having done so. Hence it is peculiarly appropriate and significant that he should accuse himself, pronounce sentence of condemnation upon himself, and inflict it himself on his symbolical substitute."

Kurtz on Sacrificial Worship, p. 130.

We may add that this objection proceeds on an erroneous view of the priestly office. The priest was the representative, not of God, but of men. As we read in the Epistle to the Hebrews, " Every high priest, taken from among men, is ordained *for men* in things pertaining to God." Accordingly, when the priest committed any heinous sin, its penal liabilities were considered as falling upon the people. And the sacrifice prescribed for any sin with which he was chargeable was the same that was required for a sin committed by the whole community.

Heb. v. 1.

230   DOCTRINE OF THE OLD TESTAMENT

PART II. SEC. 2.

Such being the case, the argument that sin-offerings, if piacular, ought to have been slain by the priest as representing God, falls to the ground at once. For the priest represented, not God, but the people. Had *he* slain the victim, in the case of a private sin-offering, this would not have been symbolical of God inflicting punishment any more than the slaying of it by the offerer. It would, moreover, have confounded the distinction between the private and the public sin-offerings. For it would have indicated that the representative of the nation was charging himself with the guilt of one individual citizen.

Objection, that if the death of the victim was vicarious, he could only have been offered for sins punishable with death.

4. *Bähr* has revived an old objection, formerly urged by *Sykes* and *H. Taylor*, that " if the death of the victim was a vicarious endurance of the penalty of sin, then every sin for which a sacrifice was appointed must have been punishable with death; whereas, under the Levitical dispensation, none of those presumptuous and aggravated offences which were punishable with death had any sacrifice provided for them."

Answer to this objection.

This objection does not distinguish between the penalty of death denounced in the moral law against all sin, and the penalty of death as denounced against certain aggravated crimes by the statutes of the Jewish commonwealth. Although it be true that the offences for which sacrifice might be offered were not capital crimes according to the municipal code of Israel, this does not prove that in the judgment of God they were not liable to that death which is the common " wages of sin."

Besides, it is not necessarily implied in vicarious punishment that the suffering inflicted on the victim should be exactly the same with that which the offender had himself incurred. It rests with the Supreme Lawgiver and Judge to say what kind or measure of vicarious endurance, if any, He will accept of. And if this be the case where there is real vicarious punishment, much more may we hold it to be the case where the vicarious punishment is only typical or emblematical. It must not be forgotten that the Jewish sacrificial system was a mere " shadow of good things to come, and not the very image of the

RESPECTING THE ATONEMENT. 231

things." And being so, we have no cause to wonder that certain marks of imperfection should be discernible in it. It is little to say, then, that there is not an exact correspondence between the penalty which the victim endured and that which the offerer had merited, in respect that the offences of the latter were not punishable with death. The truth is, that if these offences *had been* so punishable, the want of correspondence would then have been still greater; for if the death of an irrational animal be no proper equivalent for those minor penalties which, under the Levitical dispensation, it atoned for, much less would it have been a proper equivalent for the penalty of death denounced against a reasonable and accountable agent.

5. There is another objection, urged long ago by *Sykes* and *Priestley*, of which Dr Bähr has not failed to take advantage—namely, that " the Levitical victims could not be vicarious sin-bearers, because in that case they would have been unclean ; whereas, on the contrary, they were evidently pure and holy, inasmuch as they were in some instances wholly offered on the altar of God, and in other instances were eaten by the priests, or shared between them and the offerers."

We cannot dispute the fact on which this objection proceeds, that the bodies of those animals which were slain in the Levitical sacrifices, instead of being unclean, were " most holy." We are expressly told that such was the case with those sin-offerings and trespass-offerings which were presented for the sins of private individuals ; for respecting the flesh of these it is expressly written,— " Every man among the priests shall eat thereof; it shall be eaten in the holy place ; it is most holy." It has often been supposed, indeed, that the case was different with those sin-offerings which were presented for the priests and for the whole nation of Israel, and particularly with those which were offered on the day of atonement, inasmuch as the bodies of the slain beasts in these instances were ordered to be " carried without the camp, and burned there." But without stopping to consider what may have been the ground on which the bodies of

Margin notes:

PART II. SEC. 2.

Objection, that victims, if offered for sin, would be unclean, and so could not be burnt on altar or eaten by priests.

Admitted that the flesh of the victims was not unclean.

Levit. vii. 6.

Fairbairn's Typology, ii. 338.

232   DOCTRINE OF THE OLD TESTAMENT

PART II.
SEC. 2.
——

these victims were thus disposed of, we may be very sure that that ground could not have been any uncleanness held to be attached to them. It is true that impure things were always " carried without the camp;" but it does not thence follow that everything which was " carried without the camp" was impure. And in the case of the victims referred to, it was expressly provided that the place in which they were to be burned should be " a clean place"—indicating that they were themselves "clean," and must be guarded from pollution; whereas unclean things,

Compare Levit. iv. 12; xiv. 40. 45.

such as the wood and stones of a leper's house, were ordered to be " cast into an unclean place without the city." Besides, we cannot suppose that the highest class of sin-offerings—those slain for the priests and for all Israel—were charged with pollution, when we find that the inferior class, slain for private individuals, are declared to be, not unclean, but " most holy."

Bähr's inference from this admitted fact is unwarranted.

While assenting, however, on these grounds, to Dr Bähr's statement, that the flesh of the Levitical sin-offerings was not unclean, we can see no warrant for the conclusion which he founds upon it; for, on the one hand, it does not necessarily follow that the victim must have become in itself unclean if its death were a substitute for the penalties incurred by him who offered it. Rather does it seem to be essential to the idea of a vicarious atonement, that the substitute should in himself be perfectly pure; and that he should be so regarded at the very time when he suffers and dies in the room of him by whom he is immolated. It is true the offerer, by placing his hand upon the victim's head, symbolically laid his sins upon him. But this imputation of sins must have had respect only to their *guilt* or liability to punishment, and not to their *moral culpability* or *impurity*, which, being a personal matter, is not transferable. Notwithstanding what was thus done to him, the victim continued to be in himself as pure and faultless as he was before; or else his immolation could not have been regarded as an unmerited endúrance of penalties by a substitute in the room of

RESPECTING THE ATONEMENT. 233

their infliction on the person by whom they were justly deserved.

But, on the other hand, even if the victim had been rendered unclean by having the sins of the offerer symbolically laid upon him, it must be remembered that he became *purged of this uncleanness* by having his blood shed and sprinkled on the altar, before his body was either devoted to God by fire, or eaten by the priest and the worshippers. The legal consequences of imputed guilt, whatever they were, terminated with the shedding and sprinkling of His blood. The sins laid upon him were thereby expiated. And thenceforward he might be considered as "most holy."

SECTION III.

THE LEVITICAL SACRIFICES—BRIEF NOTICE OF NON-EXPIATORY THEORIES IN REGARD TO THEM.

PART
II.
SEC. 3.

———

Non-expiatory
theories of
Levitical
sacrifices.

HAVING now endeavoured to show the expiatory nature of the Levitical sacrifices, and the insufficiency of the objections urged against it, it seems proper briefly to notice some of the most plausible attempts which have been made to explain the symbolism of these ordinances upon other principles than that of their vicarious and piacular nature.

Theory of
Bähr.

I. In doing so, we begin with the theory of Dr Bähr, as set forth in his learned, and in many respects valuable, treatise on the symbolism of the Mosaic worship.

Dr Bähr holds that sacrifice was intended to represent, not the forfeiture or penalty incurred by him who offered the victim, but that *surrender or sacrifice of himself*, that devotion of heart and life to the service of God, which the worshipper acknowledged to be his duty, and declared to be his sincere desire. Such an acknowledgment and desire might in certain cases be associated with penitential feelings on account of particular transgressions, and then the sacrifice was called a sin-offering or trespass-offering. In other cases it might be associated with feelings of gratitude for past mercies, or with special engagements of duty and devotion for the future, and then the sacrifice became a thank-offering or votive peace-offering. But in no case did it imply any reference to the worshipper's *liability to condemnation,* or any substitution of the sufferings of an innocent victim for that forfeiture or penalty which the

RESPECTING THE ATONEMENT. 235

worshipper had incurred. It symbolised, not the *taking away of life* in punishment, but the *giving up of life* to God in holy self-surrender.

In support of this theory, Dr Bähr appeals to the words of the Lord in Lev. xvii. 11 : " For the life of the flesh is in the blood ; and I have given it to you upon the altar to make an atonement for your souls ; for it is the blood which maketh an atonement for the soul." These words he considers as unfolding the true nature of the ordinance. It was not the *death* of the animal, he argues, but the sprinkling of the altar with his blood *as the emblem of life*, that held the central or prominent place in the symbolical transaction. The death was only inflicted as a means of obtaining the blood, by which, as representing the life, the atonement was made. Or if any symbolical meaning must be assigned to it, that meaning is held to be nothing more than the extinction of the selfish and carnal life of the worshipper as necessary to his consecration to the service of God.

Now the obvious, and, we think, conclusive, objection that may be urged against this view of the Levitical sacrifices is, that it implies a *palpable incongruity*, or rather *contrariety*, between the sign employed and the thing alleged to be denoted by it. The sign is *blood*, the blood of a *slain animal;* and the thing of which it is affirmed to be significant is not *life taken away* in penal forfeiture, but *life continued and consecrated to God in active service !* Now I venture to say that this is an interpretation of the symbol which never would have occurred to any unsophisticated mind. Blood may be appropriately held to represent *life*. But unquestionably blood *shed* represents life *ended*. When the " life of the flesh " is said to be " in the blood," this statement must be understood as applying to the blood while still running in the veins of the living animal. When the animal has been slain, the blood that is taken from it can only be held to denote life *forfeited* and *extinguished*.

An attempt is indeed made to overcome this objection, by suggesting that the death of the victim might be

PART II. SEC. 3.

Levit. xvii. 11.

Objection to this theory. Incongruity between the sign and the thing signified.

236   DOCTRINE OF THE OLD TESTAMENT

PART
II.
SEC. 3.
———

symbolical of *the extinction of the selfish and carnal life*, in order that the spiritual and godly life which the worshipper was thenceforward to lead might be substituted for it. But this suggestion, instead of removing the difficulty, is attended with other difficulties peculiar to itself.

In the first place, it does not in the least affect the incongruity of representing the blood of a *slain victim* as an emblem, not of *life extinguished*, which it well might be, but of *life continued* and *actively employed* in the service of God, which it could not, according to any natural or intelligible reading of the symbol, be supposed to be. Besides, this suggestion assigns to the blood a double function, as symbolical both of death and of life, which, instead of lessening, rather increases the incongruity.

No analogy between slaying a spotless animal and mortifying the carnal life of a sinner.

Further, the taking away of the life of an animal in sacrifice—more particularly of a pure and unblemished animal, perfect in its kind, as all victims were required to be—presents no analogy whatsoever to the mortifying of the selfish and carnal life of a sinful man ; for the natural life of such a creature is altogether innocent—in full conformity to the instinctive laws of its being, and to the purposes which its Maker designed it to serve ; whereas the natural life of a sinner is culpable and ungodly—opposed to the laws of his being, and to the will of his Creator. Here, therefore, instead of analogy we have contrast. That the ceasing of a life which is in perfect accordance with the will of God should symbolise the ceasing of a life of selfish opposition to the will of God on the part of him who puts to death the innocent victim, is altogether unnatural and anomalous.

Again, this supplementary adjunct of the theory in question derives no support from Lev. xvii. 11, on which the theory professes to be founded. When it is there said that "the *life* of the flesh is in the blood," the word "life" evidently signifies the mere *physical principle of vitality*, without reference to any *moral qualities* whatsoever. The "life" does not here mean "the conduct," or "the manner of living." There is no reference to the manner in which the life is spent, or the purposes to which it is made subser-

RESPECTING THE ATONEMENT. 237

vient, but simply to "the life" or animated condition of a living animal, as opposed to the inert and insensate condition of a mass of dead matter. And as for the alleged double function which, according to the hypothesis, "the blood" is held to discharge, as symbolising, first, *the cessation of a selfish and carnal mode of living*, and afterwards, *the commencement of a godly and spiritual mode of living*, there is not the least countenance given to it in the passage referred to. Nothing is there said of the symbolical transfiguration of a life distinguished by one kind of moral qualities into a life distinguished by an opposite kind of moral qualities. What the passage speaks of is something very different—namely, *the substitution of the life of one creature for the life of another creature.* "The life of the flesh," saith the Lord, "is in the blood ; and I have given it to you upon the altar to make an atonement *for your souls*," i.e., "*for your lives* "—for it is the same word, *nephesh*, that is here used both for "life" and for "soul."

This text, then, according to its plain and obvious import, teaches the *vicarious* nature of the rite of sacrifice. *Life was given for life*—the life of the victim for the life of the offerer. It was no mere *change of the moral characteristics of one and the same creature's mode of living* that was symbolised, but a *substitution of the life of one creature for the life of another creature*, instead of which it was immolated. And this substitution took place in order to "make atonement," or literally "covering," for the life of the offerer. Nor can it be said that this "covering" or "atonement" was altogether *subjective* in its nature, affecting only the worshipper's own character and disposition. On the contrary, it was primarily of an *objective* nature, affecting his standing and position towards the God of Israel. That it was so evidently appears from the passage itself. For God is there represented as saying, "I have given it (the blood) to you upon the altar, to make an atonement for your souls or lives." He does not say, "*You* are to give *me* the blood upon the altar as a symbol of the dedication of your lives to me ; " but "*I* have given *you* the blood upon the altar, to make an atonement for

PART II. SEC. 3.

Levit. xvii. 11 plainly indicates *life given for life*.

238   DOCTRINE OF THE OLD TESTAMENT

PART
II.
SEC. 3.

Levit. iv.
26, 35; v.
13, 18; vi.
7.

your lives." And the same conclusion may be drawn from the statements repeatedly made in the Book of Leviticus respecting the sin-offerings, that by means of these "an atonement shall be made for the offerer, *as concerning his sin, and it shall be forgiven him.*" These words plainly show that the atonement made by the sin-offerings was not merely to the effect of exercising a salutary influence on the minds of those by whom they were offered, but to the effect of substantially ameliorating their condition and standing in relation to the God of Israel, by securing the forgiveness of their sin, or their exemption from the forfeitures and penalties annexed to it.

Bähr's
theory
opposed
to views
alike of
Jews and
heathens.

It is no small confirmation of the justice of these remarks on the theory of Bähr as to the nature of sacrifice, that is furnished by the fact that this theory is utterly opposed to the sentiments entertained respecting that ordinance by uninspired Jewish writers of ancient times, and also by heathens of every age and of every nation. I cannot afford space for adducing the abundant testimonies by which this fact is incontrovertibly established. They will be found in Outram's elaborate 'Dissertation on Sacrifice,' and also in the Notes appended to Magee's 'Discourses on the Atonement.' But assuming it to be a fact—which few, if any, will venture to deny—it bears with crushing weight against a theory of sacrifice which is palpably at variance with the views of that ordinance entertained by all those who were habituated to the observance of it.

Theory of
Hofmann.

II. Another theory, which was not without its supporters in former times, has been recently revived in a somewhat modified form, and advocated with much ability by Hofmann. According to this theory, there was not in the Levitical sacrifices anything properly penal or vicarious. They were simply of the nature of *payments* rendered to God—in the case of the peace-offering, as an acknowledgment of His mercies ; and in the case of the sin-offering or burnt-offering, as a compensation for sins committed

RESPECTING THE ATONEMENT. 239

against Him. The imposition of hands signified nothing
more than that the offerer had power over the animal, and
purposed to avail himself of this power by putting it to
death. The slaying of the victim had no further object
than that of "obtaining its blood for the altar, and its
flesh for the fire-food of Jehovah." And the purpose of
sprinkling the blood upon the altar was "to bring to God
what had been the victim's life, as a payment rendered to
Him by its being shed." There was thus no substitution
of the victim for the offerer in the whole of the transaction,
but a mere payment by the latter, in discharge of his
liabilities, of a gift which God had empowered him to use
for that purpose, and had pledged Himself to accept of
when presented at the altar.

PART II. SEC. 3.
Hofmann's Schriftbe-weis, II. i. 191, 192.

Now we venture to say that this view of the Levitical sacrifices is not such as would have naturally suggested itself
to any ordinary mind in contemplation of them; and that
there are many, not of the mere accessories, but of the
most prominent and essential parts of their symbolism, of
which it affords no satisfactory account.

For example, (1.) if *the laying on of hands* was *only* a
symbolical indication that the animal was given up as an
offering to God, it would seem in that case to have been
altogether superfluous, inasmuch as a clear enough declaration to the same effect had been already made by bringing it to the altar and delivering it to the priest. (2.)
Again, if the true import of the whole observance had
been nothing more than a compensation to God in the
way of payment for the guilt of the worshippers, there
seems no assignable reason why such compensation should
have been almost uniformly rendered in the form of *animal
victims*. Even Bähr abandons any argument that might
be drawn from the permission, in certain exceptional cases,
to substitute offerings of flour for animal sacrifice. He
rightly reminds any who would lay stress on this circumstance, that this permission was granted only when the
offerer was so poor that he could not procure even a pair
of turtle-doves or two young pigeons; and that we must
not argue from the nature of an occasional and excep-

Objections to Hof-mann's theory.

Bähr's Symbolik, ii. 281.

240   DOCTRINE OF THE OLD TESTAMENT

PART
II.
SEC. 3.
———

tional substitute to that of the rite itself, in its normal and proper form. It seems, then, on Hofmann's hypothesis, unaccountable that the compensatory payment should not have been made from the fruits of the earth, or from any other species of property, in something like a fair proportion to the produce of the flocks and herds; whereas the rule unquestionably was, as Paul declares it, that "without shedding of blood there is no remission." (3.) Further, if the sacrifice was offered simply as a payment, there is no apparent reason for the immediate infliction of death upon the animal. The mere delivery of it might in that case have sufficed. And it might have been left to the disposal of the priesthood, in such ways and at such times as might be most conducive to pious uses; for the offerer had, according to this theory, no further concern in the matter than to bring his compensatory payment, and hand it over to the person who was duly authorised in the name of God to receive it from him. The function of the offerer, however, did not end with this. He was required, then and there, as an indispensable part of the service, to slay the animal with his own hand. And hence we conclude that it must have been presented by him, not merely as a valuable commodity to be surrendered, but as a living creature to be immediately deprived of life; in other words, not merely as a compensatory payment, but as an atoning victim. (4.) Equally unsatisfactory is the meaning assigned by Hofmann to the sprinkling of the blood upon the altar. "The essential purpose of it," he says, "must have been to bring to God what had been the life of the sacrificial animal as a payment rendered by its being shed." Here the peculiar significancy of the blood-offering, as distinguished from unbloody sacrifices, is entirely ignored. The blood is held to have been "brought to God as a payment,"—which it might have been equally well if it had been a libation of wine, or a cluster of fruits, or a sum of money. How differently does the Lord Himself speak of it! "The life of the flesh," He says, "is in the blood; and I have given it to you upon the altar to make an atonement for your souls." These words do not

Levit.
xvii. 11

RESPECTING THE ATONEMENT. 241

say "to make a compensatory payment," but to "make an atonement." And, as Delitzsch observes, "the Scriptural idea of *atoning*, or *covering*, can never be identified with *the covering of a debt by paying it*, which is a metaphor utterly foreign to the Hebrew language." Again, *how* is it that "the blood makes atonement"? Evidently in respect to the *nephesh*—that is to say, "*the soul or life* of the flesh"—being in the blood; otherwise there would be no coherence between the statements, 1st, that "the life of the flesh is in the blood,"—and 2dly, that "the blood is given to make atonement." * The blood, then, does not atone by virtue of aught that it has in common with other things which, considered merely *as gifts*, might equally well have been presented, but by virtue of *something which is peculiar to itself*. It is not a mere compensatory payment made for sin, but a vicarious substitution of *nephesh* for *nephesh*—of the life of the innocent victim for the life of the sinful offerer.

PART II. Sec. 3.

Delitzsch on Hebrews, p. 740.

Thus does it appear that the theory of Hofmann affords no satisfactory explanation of the symbolical import of the Mosaic sin-offerings. I may add that it does not seem entitled, *on reasonable grounds*, to any preference over the common view, which it is meant to supersede. For certainly it is more akin to the gross notions of the heathens, whose sacrificial rites in many cases assumed the form of trafficking with the gods or bribing them to secure their favour, than to the worship of the Holy One of Israel, who, when solemnly warning His judges to execute impartial judgment, reminds them that "with the Lord their God there is no iniquity, nor respect of persons, *nor taking of gifts.*"

2 Chron. xix. 7.

III. Another theory which may be briefly noticed is that

---

* This is more fully brought out in the last clause of the verse—" For it is the blood that maketh atonement *through* the soul "—that is to say, *through the soul which had been previously said to be in it.* It is as being the seat or principle of life that the blood atones. The translation of this last clause in our authorised English version, " For it is the blood that maketh atonement for the soul," is quite inadmissible. The translation "*through* the soul" is adopted by Bähr, Kurtz, Keil, Delitzsch, and Fairbairn.

242   DOCTRINE OF THE OLD TESTAMENT

PART II.
SEC. 3.
——
Theory of Keil.

Bib. Archäologie, §§ 43, 47.

of Keil. This writer holds that the slaying of the sacrificial victim had nothing in it of a *penal* or *judicial* character (though not very consistently admitting, at the same time, that the victim was laden with the sins of the offerer), but that his death represented " the transition of the soul from a state of alienation from God into a state of grace and vital fellowship with Him, or the door of entrance into the divine life out of the ungodly life of this world ;" and he considers the sprinkling of the blood upon the altar as symbolically denoting the reception of the person by whom the victim had been sacrificed into the divine fellowship.

Objections to this theory.

It will be observed that in this theory the sacrificial victim, though occasionally spoken of as " *substituted* " for the offerer, is in reality viewed rather as his *symbol* than as his *substitute;* for its death is held to represent the subjective change which takes place in the soul when it " passes from the ungodly into the divine life." According to this view the symbolism becomes incongruous. If all that it meant was to indicate the transition of the soul from a state of sinful separation from God into a state of holy fellowship with Him, there is no conceivable reason for the stringency of the provision that the victim should be absolutely faultless and without blemish ; whereas the grounds of such a provision are at once apparent if the death of the victim was significant of the sufferings of a perfectly pure and innocent substitute in the room of the guilty.

Further, the exhibition of *death*—which is associated in the ideas and feelings of men with sin, fear, suffering, and corruption—as the emblem of transition from a godless into a godly life, is much too abstruse and subtle for a symbolical rite addressing itself to the apprehension of the multitude, however much it may commend itself to speculative minds when seeking to devise all manner of ingenious theories. And though the figures of " dying to self," " dying to sin," or " being crucified to the world," as equivalent to the process of conversion and sanctification, be familiar enough to us from our acquaintance with the apostolic writings, we must not thence infer that it

RESPECTING THE ATONEMENT. 243

was equally familiar to the Israelites. Delitzsch has
justly remarked that there are no traces of any such
figure to be met with in the Old Testament. It seems to
have been utterly foreign to Jewish modes of thought.

With respect, again, to the alleged absence of any reference in the death of the victim to the penal consequences
of sin, I may simply quote the following judicious statements of Dr Fairbairn: " Appealing, as the rite did, to
popular apprehension, the slaying of the sinner's offering,
solemnly destined to death that its life might be accepted
in lieu of the sinner's, could not but wear the aspect of a
doom or judgment. It was a death not incidentally alone,
but formally associated with sin as its immediate cause ;
and whatever grace it might instrumentally be the channel
of conveying to the offerer, it manifestly fell with all the
severity of a curse on the victim. People were not in a
condition, at the sight of such a spectacle, to make nice
discriminations. Here, on the one hand, was the sin cry-
ing for condemnation ; and there, on the other hand, was
the victim slain that the cry might be silenced. Could
people look at this, or take part in it, and yet feel that
there was nothing of punishment ? We may judge of the
unlikelihood, when we find authors with fine-spun theories
to support, which would lead them to exclude the idea of
punishment, insensibly gliding into a mode of speech regarding it which ill accords with the demands of their
system. Thus Keil, when he comes to speak of the sin-
offering, says, that ' by being slain the animal is given to
death and suffers for the sinner *the death which is the
wages of sin.*' And of the trespass-offering he says, ' The
ram stood for the person of the guilty man, and *suffered
death in his stead as the punishment* of his guilt.' Such
language stands in irreconcilable opposition to the author's
own theory."

IV. There is one other view of the nature and design of
sacrifice, on which it may be proper to make a very few
remarks. Dr Young, while apparently adopting Bähr's
theory that the rite of sacrifice was a symbol of the

*PART
II.
SEC. 3.*

*Fairbairn's
Typology,
4th edi-
tion, ii.
532.*

*Young's
theory.*

244   DOCTRINE OF THE OLD TESTAMENT

PART II. SEC. 3.

Young's Light and Life of Men, p. 221.

worshipper's self-surrender and return to God, combines with it the further suggestion, that *sacrifice was connected with the divine permission to take away animal life* in order that animal substance might be used for food.   " Sacrifice," he says, " was first of all merely the divine provision for human sustenance ; but in connection with this, a manifest and merciful protection was thrown around the lower creation.   Animal life was exalted into a sacred thing, and the taking it away was hallowed as a solemn act of religion. From the first, God taught His rational offspring that a deed in itself strange and revolting must not be ventured heedlessly or wantonly—must be transacted under a distinct sense of His presence and His rights—and must, in fact, be nothing less than a surrender back to Him of that which was wholly His—a true act of worship."

Objections to Young's theory.

In regard to this opinion, it is enough to say, that anything more decidedly opposed to the well-known facts of the case which it professes to account for, could not easily be imagined.   For it is most certain that "the provision of food for human sustenance, combined with a merciful protection thrown around the lower creation," has no place assigned to it among the declared purposes for which the Levitical sacrifices were appointed.   It would be nearer the truth to say that these sacrifices were connected with *restrictions* on the use of animal food.   The blood and the fat were in all cases interdicted.   The sin-offerings and trespass-offerings were to be eaten by the priests only. The more solemn sin-offerings were not allowed to be partaken of even by the priesthood.   And the burnt-offerings, which were the most numerous of the Levitical sacrifices, were wholly consumed in the fire of the altar. The theory of Young, therefore, is not capable of furnishing any satisfactory explanation of these ordinances.   We find other purposes expressly assigned to them in the Word of God—namely, to make atonement for sin and to secure its forgiveness.   But no mention is made of any such purposes as " protecting animal life " and " providing for human sustenance."

RESPECTING THE ATONEMENT. 245

Thus have I endeavoured to show the insufficiency of some of the most plausible theories which have been devised, with the view of explaining the symbolism of the Levitical sacrifices upon other principles than that of their vicarious and piacular character. Of one and all of them we may venture to affirm, that they derive no countenance from the more obvious and prominent features of the Mosaic ritual, insomuch that they could not have naturally occurred—as we know that they never did occur—to those who lived under it. Of all things, a *symbol*, as Mr Rigg has well observed, "must be such as to strike the popular mind at once, and to speak out its meaning to the understanding of all who are concerned to know it. Symbols may become obscure by lapse of time, or loss of the history connected with them ; but it is inconceivable that their original significance should have been dark or subtle to those for whom they were appointed. The wider and more promiscuous the circle, too, in the midst of which the symbol was set up, so much the greater need is there of its being plain and obvious in its purport. A national symbol must either refer to some event of the national history known by all, or to some common feeling or idea of the nation. But most of all must a religious symbol, intended to represent the faith, not of one nation only, but of all mankind, be adapted to convey its meaning plainly and unmistakably to all men. Nothing could be more surprising than that such a symbol should be intended to be interpreted in a sense opposed to that which the feelings of mankind would naturally put upon it, and which, in fact, has been universally put upon it, except by a few subtle and mystical thinkers in modern times. Yet such would really be the case, if that interpretation were put upon the rite of sacrifice for which the new school of anti-evangelical interpreters contend."

PART
II.
SEC. 3.
———
All these
theories
untenable.

Modern
Anglican
Theology,
p. 371,
372.

246   DOCTRINE OF THE OLD TESTAMENT

SECTION IV.

THE LEVITICAL SACRIFICES—THEIR BENEFICIAL EFFI-
CACY, AND TYPICAL REFERENCE TO THE SACRIFICE
OF CHRIST.

PART
II.
SEC. 4.
———
Efficacy of
Levitical
sacrifices.

III. HAVING thus endeavoured to show that the Levitical
sacrifices were truly vicarious and expiatory in their character, we now proceed to consider, *in the third place,* the
extent of atoning efficacy that belonged to them.

Not con-
fined to
ceremonial
offences.

In doing so, it seems unnecessary to enter at any length
into the controversy respecting the *kind of sins* for which
they were available. Some writers have maintained that
these sacrifices were admissible only in such cases as
ceremonial uncleanness, or breaches of the positive institutions of the law, and sins committed through ignorance
or inadvertency, to which no moral criminality could be
attached. This opinion, however, cannot be reconciled
with any fair construction of the terms of the Mosaic
ritual. It is certain that the great public sin-offering, presented for the nation at large on the day of atonement,
was quite unqualified and unrestricted in its reference to

Levit. xvi.
21.

"all the iniquities of the children of Israel, and all their
transgressions in all their sins." In the case of the other
sin-offerings there is undoubtedly a limitation ;—not so
much, however, in regard to the kind of sins, as in regard
to the manner of their commission. The sins themselves

Levit. iv.
2.

are characterised thus generally : "If a soul shall sin
against any of the commandments of the Lord concerning
things which ought not to be done, and shall do against
any of them." And the qualification is, that the sin be

RESPECTING THE ATONEMENT. 247

committed "through ignorance," or, as some would trans- PART
late the word, "through error or inadvertency," as opposed SEC. 4.
to presumptuous sins, or "sins with a high hand," for
which no ordinary sin-offering was provided. With respect
again to the *trespass-offerings*, it is undeniable that these
were prescribed in the case of such offences as *fraud*, Levit. vi.
injustice, perjury, robbery, and *fornication committed with* 1-7; xix.
a bondwoman,—all of them gross violations of the moral 20-22.
law, and all of them indicative of a state of wilful depravity which could not be otherwise than highly criminal
in the sight of God. In the case of these offences, though
unquestionably neither ceremonial in their nature nor
inadvertent in their mode of commission, the offender was
required not only to make full restitution or reparation to
the injured party, but also to offer atonement by sacrifice
for his trespass as a sin committed against the Lord.

It is true there were certain moral offences of a pecu- No sacri-
liarly aggravated and presumptuous nature,—such as *idol-* fices for
atry, adultery, and *murder*,—which were wholly excluded tuous sins.
from the provisions of the sacrificial system. Some have
supposed the reason of this exclusion to be, that offences
of this description evinced such a spirit of obstinate rebellion against the theocratic constitution of Israel, that
those who were chargeable with them could not with propriety, or with safety to the public interests, be restored
—as they would have been by the acceptance of their
sacrifices—to the enjoyment of their forfeited privileges
as members of the Israelitish Church and commonwealth.
And an analogy has been drawn between these aggravated
crimes and certain sins involving a hardened rejection of
offered grace, for which, even under the Gospel, there
remaineth nothing but "a certain fearful looking for of Heb. x.
judgment and of fiery indignation which shall devour the 26, 27.
adversaries." Without disputing, however, the force of
this consideration, it must also be remembered that the
class of sins referred to were by the Jewish law visited
with the penalty of *death*, and hence that the necessity of
paying the statutory penalty—which was always enforced
before any sacrifice could be offered—precluded the offen-

248 DOCTRINE OF THE OLD TESTAMENT

PART II. SEC. 4.

ders, in the case of these capital crimes, from availing themselves of the ordinances of the tabernacle, and equally precluded them from the attainment of one of the chief ends for which the use of these ordinances was appointed —namely, the restoration of sinners to their forfeited position as citizens in Israel and members of the visible Church.

In what respects, or to what extent, were the Levitical sacrifices efficacious?

Without farther entering, however, into the question respecting the kind of sins for which they were available, there is another and much more important question on which it is necessary to make a few remarks—namely, *In what respects, or to what extent, were the Jewish sacrifices really efficacious in expiating those sins for which they were offered up?*

Various answers given to this question.

In regard to this question also there has been much controversy. Some appear to hold that the efficacy of these sacrifices extended to the full and perfect remission of sins, but that it depended on the faith and penitence of the offerers, and arose from no virtue in the sacrifices themselves, but wholly from the reference they bore to the great sacrifice of Christ, of which they were prefigurative.

Others maintain that the efficacy of the Levitical atonements extended merely to the remission of the temporal penalties of excision from the Church and commonwealth of Israel, which had been incurred by those who offered them ; that this efficacy was unfailingly exerted in every case in which the prescribed ceremonies were rigidly adhered to, irrespective of the inward disposition of the worshippers ; and farther, that it belonged by divine appointment to the sacrifices considered in themselves, without reference to any other and better sacrifice, of which they may now be regarded as emblematical.

There are others still who may be said to combine these two opinions with one another, affirming that the Levitical sacrifices were in themselves of sure efficacy, so far as to exempt the worshippers from the forfeiture of their civil and ecclesiastical privileges ; but that they possessed also, when offered with unfeigned penitence, and with humble

RESPECTING THE ATONEMENT.   249

reliance on the promised mercies of God, a farther efficacy
arising from their typical reference to our Lord's sacrifice,
in the way of securing the same spiritual and heavenly
blessings which true Christians now obtain through faith
in Jesus Christ.

Without attempting any discussion of the grounds on
which these several opinions have been advocated, which
would lead us too far away from our main purpose, we
must confine ourselves to a few general observations.

On the one hand, it seems very evident that the Mosaic
sacrifices have a certain *real efficacy* ascribed to them in
the Old Testament.   It is written again and again with
respect to them, in passages already quoted from the Book
of Leviticus, that when the prescribed victim has been
duly offered by the worshipper, " it shall be accepted for
him to make an atonement for him ; " or that " an atonement shall be made for him as concerning his sin, and it
shall be forgiven him."   And in particular the sacrifices
of the day of atonement were closed by a symbolical
action, very plainly significant of the expiation accomplished by them—the confessed " sins, iniquities, and transgressions of the people " being " all put by the high priest
upon the head of the scape-goat," that he might " carry
them away into a land not inhabited."   From this it seems
clear that a real atoning efficacy belonged by divine
appointment to the Mosaic sacrifices.   Nor is there a
word said to indicate that this efficacy depended either on
the inward dispositions of the worshippers, or on any prefigurative reference, whether understood or not, which
their offerings may have had to the great sacrifice of the
cross.   So far as we can learn from the terms of the
Mosaic statutes, the sacrifices seem to have been of unfailing benefit in all cases in which they were punctually
and exactly offered.   Their efficacy, such as it was, belonged to them *ex opere operato.*   The strict observance of
the prescribed form was sufficient to secure for any Israelite the acceptance of his sacrifice, to the effect of " making
an atonement for his sin that he had committed, so that it
should be forgiven him."

PART
II.
SEC. 4.
——

Old Tes-
tament
ascribes
to Leviti-
cal sacri-
fices a *real*
efficacy in
some re-
spects.

Levit. i. 4 ;
iv. 26-31,
35.

Levit. xvi.
20-22.

250 DOCTRINE OF THE OLD TESTAMENT

PART II. SEC. 4.

New Testament declares that they cannot take away sin. Heb. ix. 9, 13, 23; x. 1, 4, 11.

On the other hand, when we come to the New Testament, and especially to the Epistle to the Hebrews, we find there the most distinct and emphatic assurances that "the law, having a shadow of good things to come, but not the very image of the things, can never with those sacrifices, which they offer year by year continually, make the comers thereunto perfect;" that these sacrifices availed only "to the purifying of the flesh," but "could not make him that did the service perfect as pertaining to the conscience;" that "it was necessary that the patterns of things in heaven should be purified with these, but the heavenly things themselves with better sacrifices than these;" that the Jewish priests "offered oftentimes the same sacrifices which can never take away sins;" and that "it is not possible that the blood of bulls and of goats should take away sin."

How may these apparently opposite views be reconciled?

Here, then, we have two apparently very opposite views of the efficacy of the Levitical sacrifices presented to us. And how is the seeming contrariety between them to be reconciled? Simply, I apprehend, by adverting to the different aspects under which "sin" and the "remission of sin" are regarded by the Jewish lawgiver and by the Christian apostle respectively."

In *Leviticus,* sin is viewed as affecting the outward position and privileges of the sinner.

In the Book of Leviticus, "sin," of whatever description, whether consisting in a breach of ceremonial observances, or in a violation of moral precepts, is viewed merely *as affecting the position and privileges of the offending party as a member of the visible Church and commonwealth of Israel.* It is indeed regarded as committed against God, inasmuch as it was still requisite that He should be propitiated, even when other parties wronged by it had been compensated; against God, however, not as the great Judge of all the earth, to whom both Jews and Gentiles are alike accountable, but in His special relation to His ancient people, as the supreme Ruler and theocratic Head of the Jewish nation. "Remission of sins" is regarded in a similar aspect, as merely exempting the offender from those penalties of excision from the visible Church and kingdom of God which he had incurred, and

RESPECTING THE ATONEMENT.   251

restoring to him his forfeited privileges as a citizen and
worshipper in Israel.

In the New Testament, on the other hand, "sin" and
"remission of sin" are viewed in a very different light.
They are there viewed as affecting not merely our outward
standing and our temporal privileges, but as affecting our
spiritual condition with reference to God as His moral and
accountable creatures, our possession of His favour, our
interest in His promises, our enjoyment of His fellowship,
our adaptation for His service, not only in the life that
now is, but in that which is to come.

Keeping in view this wide difference of the aspects
under which "sin" and "remission of sin" are regarded
in the ceremonial law and in the Gospel, we find no difficulty in reconciling the apparent conflict between the
statements in Leviticus and those in the Epistle to the
Hebrews respecting the atoning efficacy of the Mosaic
sacrifices. These sacrifices, when offered in due form,
were really and unfailingly effectual in restoring the
offender to his forfeited position as a Jewish worshipper,
reconciling him to God as Head of the theocracy, and
saving him from the penalty of excision from the commonwealth of Israel. And this efficacy they possessed
without any reservation as to the inward purity or sincerity
of him who offered them, provided the required forms were
scrupulously and correctly observed. Just as in the exercise of discipline in the Christian Church, when the offender
makes a fair profession of his penitence, and otherwise con-
forms to all the requirements of the ecclesiastical court, he
is released from Church censure and restored to Church
privileges, so was an offending Israelite, when he offered
the prescribed sacrifice, exempted from the forfeitures and
penalties of the Levitical law, and restored to his position
and privileges under the Jewish polity. In the one case,
however, just as in the other, the recovery of outward
privileges did not necessarily carry with it the restoration
of inward and spiritual blessings. The Jewish priesthood,
when making atonement for sin, as affecting the outward
status of an Israelite, had no more power than has the

*PART
II.
SEC. 4.*

*In the
New Tes-
tament, sin
is viewed
as affecting
our spirit-
ual condi-
tion in the
sight of
God.*

*Sacrifices
of sure effi-
cacy in re-
storing to
outward
privileges
of the
Church
and com-
monwealth
of Israel;*

252   DOCTRINE OF THE OLD TESTAMENT

PART
II.
SEC. 4.
___
but did
not purify
the con-
science
or secure
spiritual
blessings.

court of a Christian Church, when absolving a scandalous member from ecclesiastical censure, to assure him at the same time of the remission of his guilt as affecting his inward and spiritual condition in the sight of God. And the Jewish sacrifices, with all the efficacy they undoubtedly possessed to "sanctify," as Paul expresses it, "unto the purifying of the flesh," could "never make him that did the service perfect as pertaining to the conscience," or secure for him the spiritual blessings of forgiveness and acceptance with God, as the Lord of conscience.

Had they
not a far-
ther effi-
cacy, when
offered in
faith, as
types of
the sacri-
fice of
Christ?

But here, it may be asked, was this the sole purpose to which the Levitical sacrifices were conducive? Besides being thus of sure efficacy, when duly offered, in the way of exempting the worshippers from temporal forfeitures and restoring to them the enjoyment of outward privileges as members of the Church and commonwealth of Israel, did they not possess also some farther efficacy, considered as types of the great sacrifice of the cross, in the way of sustaining the faith of God's people, enlivening their hope of better things to come, exciting penitential feelings and godly purposes, and thereby obtaining, for such as were "Israelites indeed," the same spiritual blessings which true Christians now receive through faith in the sufferings and merits of their Saviour?

There are good grounds for answering this question in the affirmative. We can hardly doubt that those sacrificial rites, which availed in all cases "for the purifying of the flesh," were fraught also with spiritual blessings to such faithful worshippers as were led by divine teaching to look beyond them to some better sacrifice, yet to be provided in the fulness of Messiah's time, whereby they might be "made perfect as pertaining to the conscience," and "purged from dead works to serve the living God."

Such far-
ther effi-
cacy did
not belong
to them as
sacrifices.

It must be observed, however, that any such ulterior efficacy which may be ascribed to these ceremonial ordinances *did not, properly speaking, belong to them as sacrifices*, but rather as symbols or prefigurations of the promised Saviour. They possessed it in common with

RESPECTING THE ATONEMENT. 253

other types which were not sacrificial in their character, and in common with the predictions of the ancient prophets. Allowing it to be the case that an intelligent Israelite, when finding provision so fully made in the Levitical offerings for restoring to him those outward privileges which his sins had forfeited, might be led to cherish the hope of some better provision, by which he might be fully reinstated in the divine favour and thoroughly cleansed from sin "as pertaining to the conscience;" it will readily be seen that the same effect might have been produced upon him by reading the 53d chapter of Isaiah, or some other clear prophetic announcement of the mercies of the Gospel. But any such secondary influence as the sin-offerings may thus have had, in the way of strengthening the faith of God's ancient people with reference to the promise of a coming Saviour, is not at all to be placed on the same footing with the *direct and clearly-defined* efficacy of these sacrifices in the way of securing exemption to the worshippers from those temporal forfeitures and penalties which they had incurred as subjects of the theocracy and members of the visible Church. This last was their *proper sacrificial efficacy;* whereas the other, as before observed, pertained to them, not in their sacrificial, but rather in their typical character, and was shared by them in common with the prophecies, and, I may add, in common with every other means by which their faith in a promised Saviour might be sustained and strengthened.

After all, however, it is immaterial to our present purpose whether any such ulterior efficacy, in obtaining spiritual and heavenly blessings, did or did not belong to the Levitical sacrifices; for, in whichever way this question may be decided, it is quite certain that they did possess a real, though a limited efficacy, by securing substantial benefits of an outward and temporal kind to all those by whom in due form they were offered up. And since, as we have already seen, these benefits were secured by them in the way of vicarious substitution and expiation, a strong corroborative argument may be thence derived

Margin notes:

PART
II.
Sec. 4.
They had
it in com-
mon with
all the
types and
prophecies
of Christ.

They cer-
tainly did
possess a
real efficacy
within cer-
tain limits.

And they
thus fur-
nish con-
firmatory
proof of
the Atone-
ment.

254   DOCTRINE OF THE OLD TESTAMENT

PART
II.
SEC. 4.
——

in proof of the great Christian doctrine of the Atonement. For even if we were not warranted to regard these ancient ordinances as types or designed prefigurations of the sacrifice of Christ, it cannot be denied that they bear a close analogy to it, and exemplify the same principles of the divine administration. And the confirmatory proof which they thus afford is the more valuable that it is derived from the analogy of institutions expressly and positively appointed by God Himself, as means by which the people of His covenant were for long ages to be kept in the continued enjoyment of manifold temporal privileges, if not also of spiritual blessings, flowing from the special relation in which He stood towards them.

Levitical
sacrifices
types of
the sacrifice of
Christ.

IV. The force of this argument, however, will be greatly increased if it can be shown that the sin-offerings of the Mosaic ritual not only bear a close analogy to our Lord's sacrifice, but that they were actually designed to *foreshadow it, as types or prefigurations of the death of Christ.*

Jowett's
objections
answered.

We proceed, therefore, to show the typical character of the Mosaic sacrifices. But in doing so, it is necessary to advert to some general arguments on the strength of which Mr Jowett has affirmed that such a character cannot be reasonably ascribed to them.

"Silence
of Old
Testament
on the
subject."
Essay on
Atonement
appended
to Jowett's
Exposition
of Paul's
Epistles.

(I.) One of these is, "the silence of the Old Testament itself upon the subject." "If the sacrifices of the Mosaic religion were really symbolical of the death of Christ, how can it be accounted for that no trace of this symbolism appears in the Books of Moses themselves?—that prophets and righteous men of old never gave this interpretation to them?—that it was reserved for those who lived after the event to which they referred had taken place to discover it?" "Such an afterthought may be natural to us, who are ever tracing a literary or mystical connection between the Old Testament and the New; it would have been very strange to us had we lived in the ages before the coming of Christ."

The plain answer to this objection is, that the Mosaic

RESPECTING THE ATONEMENT.

ordinances, in so far as they were of a prefigurative nature, were not intended to unfold their full import until the event should come to which they had an ultimate reference. We may say of them as St Peter says of the prophets, that "they ministered," not to those of their own day, "but *unto us*, the things that are now reported to us by them that preach the Gospel." It would be unreasonable to demand that a typical system should plainly point out its prefigurative import prior to its accomplishment. This, indeed, would be inconsistent with its very nature. A type, with its prophetic import clearly disclosed, would really amount to a full exposition, instead of a mere foreshadowing of its antitype. And Judaism, if the evangelical reference of its ordinances had been palpably exhibited, would have been, not a preparation for Christianity, but Christianity itself.

PART II. SEC. 4.

1 Pet. i. 12.

See Davison on Prophecy, p. 100.

(2.) But again, observes Mr Jowett, "It is incredible that God should have instituted rites and ceremonies, which were to be observed by a whole people throughout their history, in order to teach mankind 1500 years afterwards, uncertainly and in a figure, a lesson which Christ taught plainly and without a figure."

"God would not appoint rites to teach men long afterwards in a figurative manner what was then to be taught plainly and without a figure."

This objection proceeds on an unfair statement of the case. We do not maintain that the Mosaic rites were instituted *merely* with a view to the light they were eventually to cast, after the lapse of 1500 years, on the nature and divine origin of the Christian revelation. We only affirm that this is *one* end to which, while serving other important purposes, they have been made subservient. They were edifying and useful as symbolical acts of worship, and symbolical methods of religious teaching, apart from the prefigurative character which we assign to them. Nor must we allow ourselves to be biassed, in judging of their utility in this respect among those for whose observance they were instituted, by our own very different modes of communication. For the language of symbolism, however foreign to our habits, was in the most familiar use in ancient times and among Eastern nations. And we frequently find it employed in the Old Testa-

The rites served other purposes besides this.

256 DOCTRINE OF THE OLD TESTAMENT

PART II. SEC. 4.

ment, particularly by the prophets Jeremiah, Ezekiel, and Zechariah, as a lively and impressive mode of conveying religious truths. In this way, accordingly, the Mosaic ordinances might be of great advantage to many who observed them—apart from their prophetic reference to the Gospel—as serving to remind the Israelites of the claims of God and the duties of man, of the sins they had committed and the penalties they had incurred, of their constant need of pardon and purification, of the confidence which it became them to repose in the covenanted mercies of Jehovah, and of the devout consecration which they ought to make of all their powers and faculties to His service. And though it is not to be supposed that the mass of Jewish worshippers had any distinct conception of that great atonement to which their sacrifices were ultimately designed to point, we can hardly doubt that the more intelligent and reflecting among them, while

See Litton's Bampton Lectures, p. 83-86.

daily practising ceremonial rites which availed only "to the purifying of the flesh," would be led to cherish the hope of some better sacrifice, embodying the same principles with the Levitical offerings, but of superior efficacy, as destined to be made for them in those times of the Messiah, for which they were taught by their prophets habitually to look.

"No one would ascribe a spiritual meaning to the Homeric rites; why then to the Mosaic?"

(3.) Further, Mr Jowett affirms, "It would be ridiculous to assume a spiritual meaning in the Homeric rites and sacrifices; and although they may be different in other respects, have we any more reason for inferring such a meaning in the Mosaic?" "We do not imagine the Iliad and Odyssey to be a revelation of the Platonic or Socratic philosophy. The circumstance that these poems received this or some other allegorical explanation from a school of Alexandrian critics, does not incline us to believe that such an explanation is a part of their original meaning."

No parallel between the two cases.

To this argument, if so it can be gravely called, we need only reply, *first*, that there is no such correspondence discoverable between the Homeric rites and any system of Grecian philosophy, as that which may evidently be traced between the Mosaic rites and the Gospel plan of human

RESPECTING THE ATONEMENT. 257

redemption ; and *secondly*, that there is not the most remote analogy between the two cases,—of Homer, on the
one hand, incidentally referring to certain religious observances in the course of his narrative, without professing to
institute them by divine authority, or issuing any predictions of future events in connection with them—and
Moses, on the other hand, appointing a system of sacrificial ordinances for which he expressly claimed the divine
sanction, and accompanying these with prophetic notices
of a coming Deliverer, to whose advent the fond hopes of
the race of Israel were continually turned, and who, when
He at length came, declared Himself to be the expected
Messiah, to whom both the law and the prophets bore
witness.

PART II. SEC. 4.

Having thus endeavoured to obviate the objections
which have been urged against the typical reference of
the Levitical ordinances to our Lord's sacrifice, we now
proceed to notice some of the chief grounds on which this
typical reference may be ascribed to them.

Arguments for typical reference of Mosaic sacrifices.

1. First of all, we may observe that these ordinances
are not such as we should naturally have looked for in a
final and fully-developed system of revealed religion ; but
that, on the contrary, they bear all the marks of a rudi-
mentary and imperfect dispensation, intended to pave the
way for better things to come. On no other principle,
indeed, than that of their prefigurative character, does it
seem possible to vindicate them as altogether worthy of
that great God with whom they originated, or to show
their consistency with those pure and lofty views of
spiritual truth and moral duty with which we find them
so singularly associated. Let their typical reference to
the Gospel, however, be once admitted, and then we have
a clue to the chief difficulties connected with them. The
darkest and apparently weakest parts of the ancient economy may then be clearly explained and fully justified by
the dignity and excellency of the new covenant which has
succeeded it. And the cumbrous, burdensome, and we
may even say repulsive, ritual of sacrificial observances,

The Mosaic rites bear the marks not of a final but of a prepara-tory dis-pensation.

See Davi-son on Prophecy, p. 100-102.

258   DOCTRINE OF THE OLD TESTAMENT

PART
II.
SEC. 4.
——

They
strikingly
correspond
to the
sacrifice of
Christ.

which held so prominent a place in the religion of Israel, and seemed almost to obscure or set aside its weightier matters, "faith, justice, and mercy," receives its full significancy and its fit completion in the only real atonement of the cross.

2. Further, the striking correspondence that may be traced between the legal ordinances and the sacrifice of Jesus Christ, affords a strong corroborative evidence that the former were meant to be prefigurative of the latter. With regard to the Jewish sacrifices in general, there are many circumstances too palpable to be overlooked—such as the selection of the victim, the qualities which it was required to possess, its substitution in the room of the offerer, its death, the sprinkling of its blood upon the altar, and the exemption from theocratic penalties procured by it,—all of which are in remarkable accordance with the divine appointment, the unspotted purity, and the expiatory sufferings and death of the incarnate Saviour. And when we come to particular institutions, such as the ceremonies of the passover and the day of atonement, we find the points of coincidence to be still closer and more exact. It is scarcely possible, indeed, to take a minute survey of the complicated institutions of the Levitical system, and to mark the wonderful analogy which they present to the great spiritual truths and blessings of the Gospel, without being satisfied that the law of Moses truly is what Paul styles it, "a shadow of good things to come." The ritual offerings and purifications prescribed in it,—its priesthood—its tabernacle—its sacrifices—its festivals—inexplicable though they may have seemed to be, as divine institutions, if considered by themselves,— are no sooner broadly confronted with Christianity than they assume a significancy and a dignity before unknown. So plain and striking is the conformity of their leading features to the merciful provisions and arrangements of the new covenant, that any discerning mind can hardly fail to recognise them as prophetic emblems of that better dispensation of grace and truth by which they have been superseded.

RESPECTING THE ATONEMENT.   259

3. Add to this that the prophetic Scriptures of the Old
Testament contain many very significant intimations that
the Mosaic ritual was only for a season, and was destined
to give place to a higher and more spiritual system. They
speak of a time when " the ark of the covenant shall be
no more remembered nor visited,"—when " in every place
incense shall be offered and a pure offering, and the name
of the Lord shall be great among the Gentiles,"—when
God " shall take of all nations for priests and Levites,"
—when He " will make a new covenant with His people,
not according to that which He made with their fathers
when He brought them out of the land of Egypt,"—and
when " burnt-offering and sin-offering should not be required," at the coming of One of whom " it is written in the
volume of the Book, I delight to do Thy will, O my God."
It is remarkable, also, that the same prophets who foretell
the cessation of the Levitical ordinances, declare that the
Person at whose coming they were to cease, would sustain
an office and perform functions that were fitted to supply
their place. David, for example, speaks of Him as a priest ;
Isaiah tells us that He shall " make His soul an offering
for sin ; " and Daniel represents Him as " making an end
of sins, making reconciliation for iniquity, and bringing in
everlasting righteousness," at the time when He should
" cause the sacrifice and the oblation to cease," and
should " seal up the vision and the prophecy."

In this respect the providence of God has strikingly
confirmed the declarations of His Word ; for in a few
years after the death of Christ, the Temple at Jerusalem,
within which alone the Jewish sacrifices could be legitimately offered, was utterly and finally destroyed ; and
the Levitical genealogies were either entirely lost, or fell
into inextricable confusion, so that it became impossible
for any one to make good his claim to the office of the
priesthood. Thus has it been clearly indicated by divine
providence that the Mosaic institutions, having served
their purpose by foreshadowing the mercies of the Gospel,
may be now dispensed with.

4. But this is not all. We are not left to mere infer-

Margin notes:
PART
II.
SEC. 4.
———
The pro-
phets in-
timate that
the Mosaic
ritual is to
give place
to a more
perfect
system.
Jer. iii. 16.
Mal. i. 11.
Isa. lxvi.
21.
Jer. xxxi.
31, 32.
Ps. xl. 6-8.

Ps. cx. 4.
Isa. liii. 10
Dan. ix.
24, 27.

God's pro-
vidence in
this respect
confirms
His Word.

260   DOCTRINE OF THE OLD TESTAMENT

PART II. SEC. 4.

New Testament confirms the typical reference of the Mosaic ordinances.

ences, drawn from any such considerations as have been now mentioned, in regard to the typical reference of the Jewish ordinances to the sacrifice of Christ. We are able to appeal, in defence of our position, to the clear and authoritative statements of the New Testament.

When our Lord, for example, was referring on one occasion to the prophets as having spoken of His sufferings, we are told that, " *beginning at Moses*, He expounded to them in all the Scriptures the things concerning Himself." Again, when showing His disciples how " it behoved Christ to suffer, and that repentance and remission of sins should be preached in His name," He declared that " all things must be fulfilled which were written *in the law of Moses*, and in the prophets, and in the Psalms concerning Him." In like manner St Paul affirms that in his preaching " he witnessed none other things than those which the prophets and *Moses* did say should come, that Christ should suffer, and that He should be the first that should rise from the dead."

Luke, xxiv. 27, 44-47.

Acts, xxvi. 22, 23.

Now, where has " *Moses* " testified, in any such decisive manner as could be thus made the groundwork of an appeal to doubting or unbelieving men, respecting " the sufferings of Christ" and the "preaching in His name of repentance and remission of sins"? or what is there in " *the law of Moses* " to which Christ Himself and His apostles could thus point as bearing witness to His death and its beneficial results, unless we seek such testimony in the Levitical sacrifices? There is, indeed, in the first promise of " the seed of the woman who was to bruise the serpent's head, while the serpent should bruise His heel," a faint and distant allusion to some kind of suffering as awaiting Him who should come to destroy the works of the devil. But this allusion is much too vague and indistinct to be held as the sole ground of those broad and confident appeals which are made in the New Testament to " Moses " and to " the law of Moses," as bearing prophetic testimony to the Messiah's sufferings. Yet where are we to look for any other allusion to them ? Although the Books of Moses contain other predictions of Christ,

Gen. xxii. 18 ; xlix. 10.

RESPECTING THE ATONEMENT. 261

such as that "in Abraham's seed all the families of the FART
earth should be blessed;" that "the sceptre should not SEC. 4
depart from Judah, nor a lawgiver from between his ————
feet, until Shiloh should come, to whom the gathering of
the people should be;" that "a star should come out of Num.
Jacob, and a sceptre should rise out of Israel;" and that xxiv. 17.
"a prophet like unto Moses should the Lord God raise Deut.
up unto Israel,"—yet in not one of these predictions, nor xviii. 15.
in any others, from the time of the Fall to the death of
the Jewish lawgiver, is there any indication given that
the promised Saviour was to be a sufferer at all; much
less is there any allusion to the merciful purposes to
which His sufferings were to be conducive. We are
utterly at a loss to conceive how anything contained in the
Books of Moses or in the law of Moses could be appealed
to as predictive of the Messiah's sufferings, or as rendering it necessary that He should suffer in fulfilment of the
intimated purposes of Jehovah, unless it be the sacrificial
ordinances of the Levitical worship, as bearing typical
reference to that great propitiation which He offered on
the cross for the sins of a lost world.

But, farther, our Lord, when instituting the Lord's
Supper, indicated that His death stood in the same relation to the Gospel as that in which the sacrifices at the
giving of the law stood to that older dispensation which
they inaugurated. For in giving the cup, He said to His
disciples, "This is my blood of the new covenant, shed Matt. xxvi.
for many for the remission of sins." In like manner, 28.
John, having mentioned the circumstance that the soldiers
did not break the Saviour's legs, as they had done to the John, xix.
two malefactors who were crucified along with Him, refers 36.
to one of the directions given respecting the Paschal lamb,
that "a bone of Him should not be broken," as having thus
received its fulfilment; while Paul expressly speaks of the
Lord Jesus as "Christ our Passover, who is sacrificed for 1 Cor. v. 7
us;" and in many passages of the New Testament He is John, i. 29,
called "the Lamb of God," "the Lamb that was slain for 36.
us," "the Lamb without spot or blemish, by whose blood Rev. v. 9.
we are redeemed." We have seen also, in a former part 1 Pet. i. 19.

262   DOCTRINE OF THE OLD TESTAMENT

PART II. SEC. 4.

of this volume, that the death of Jesus is frequently referred to by the apostles and evangelists in language evidently taken from the Mosaic ordinances ; and that expiatory virtues, similar to those of the Jewish sacrifices, although of much higher efficacy, are ascribed to it. And though it may doubtless be said that this *directly* proves nothing more than an analogy or resemblance between the two things that are thus compared together : yet, if it be admitted that both were of divine appointment, we can hardly avoid the inference *that the correspondence between them was designed.* For how can we conceive of two dispensations of religion successively emanating from the same divine Author, and coinciding in all their essential principles and provisions, without concluding that the earlier and preparatory one was intended to prefigure the later and more perfect ?

But lest we should still hesitate to draw this conclusion, the most express Scriptural assurances have been given us that the correspondence between the Levitical sacrifices and the death of Jesus is not that of mere accidental similarity, but that of designed or intentional prefiguration. For Paul tells the Colossians that the ceremonies of the

Col. ii. 17.

Mosaic law were "a shadow of things to come," while "Christ is the body or substance." And the main object of one whole epistle—that to the Hebrews—is to show how thoroughly Christ has realised the true import and design of these provisional ordinances, to the effect of henceforth entirely abrogating and dispensing with them. In the view of the writer of this epistle, the work of Christ finds its counterpart in all the most significant parts of

Heb. ix. x.

the Jewish ritual. The inauguration of the Sinaitic covenant with the sprinkling of blood, both upon the book of the law and upon the people ; the ordinance of the red heifer, whose ashes, mixed with water, removed the pollution contracted by touching a dead body ; the imposing ceremonial of the day of atonement, on which alone the sacred recess of the inner sanctuary was entered by the high priest with the blood of bulls and goats, whereby the collective sins of Israel were expiated,—are held forth as

RESPECTING THE ATONEMENT.

presenting a vivid representation of the one great Atonement offered on the cross, and of the prevalent intercession of our High Priest in the heavenly sanctuary, with all the spiritual benefits procured by them. And not only so, but we are certified at the same time that "the law" was, in these respects, "a shadow of good things to come, but not the very image of them;" that the Jewish priests "served unto the example and shadow of heavenly things, as Moses was admonished by God when he made the tabernacle, to make all things according to the pattern shown him in the mount;" that by the vail which closed the entrance of the holy of holies from all but the high priest on the day of atonement, "the Holy Ghost signified this, that the way into the holiest of all was not yet made manifest;" and that "almost all things were by the law purged with blood," it being "needful that the patterns of heavenly things should be purified with these, but the heavenly things themselves with better sacrifices than these." Now from all this the conclusion seems to be unavoidable, that the relation between the law and the Gospel is, not merely that of *resemblance or analogy*, such as may be occasionally discovered between things that have no intentional bearing upon one another, but that of *designed correspondence or adaptation*—the ordinances of the law being so constructed and arranged as purposely to foreshadow the provisions of the Gospel.

PART II. SEC. 4.

Heb. x. 1.

Heb. viii. 5.

Heb. ix. 8, 22, 23.

Having thus endeavoured to establish our position that the sacrifice of Christ for the redemption of sinful men was prefigured by the ceremonial rites of the Old Testament, we deem it unnecessary to point out at any length the highly important inferences that may be drawn from it.

Inferences from the position thus established

In the first place, it effectually frustrates the attempt made by many objectors to the doctrine of the Atonement to resolve the sacrificial language applied in the New Testament to the death of Jesus Christ into mere *accommodation* to Jewish customs and opinions. For truly it warrants us to say that the "accommodation" was in

Sacrificial terms applied to Christ are not "accommodations to Jewish customs."

264   DOCTRINE OF THE OLD TESTAMENT

PART
II.
SEC. 4.
——

The Old
and the
New Tes-
tament are
in perfect
harmony
respecting
the Atone-
ment.

the *reverse order* to that which these objectors allege. Instead of the Gospel being accommodated, in the apostolic representations of it, to the Jewish ritual, we have full ground, on the contrary, for affirming that the Jewish ritual was originally framed and adjusted by its divine Author with a prospective adaptation and subserviency to the Gospel.

But, *in the second place*, the position we have sought to establish not only furnishes a defensive argument against objections with which the Atonement has been assailed, but supplies also a very strong positive confirmation of it. For it shows that, with reference to this vital article of faith, the Old and the New Testament are in perfect harmony with one another. It strikingly illustrates the unity of the divine counsels in those successive dispensations of religion which have been revealed to the fallen race of man ; and it greatly contributes to strengthen our confidence in the reality and efficacy of that method of redemption to which not only evangelists and apostles, but the law and the prophets and the Psalms, have borne witness. Most certain it is, that a denial of the Atonement would be utterly inconsistent with the conclusion we have arrived at ; for, apart from its vicarious nature and propitiatory virtues, there is really nothing in the death of Jesus Christ in which the provisional ordinances of the ancient Church can be said to have found their substance and fulfilment.

SECTION V.

THE PATRIARCHAL SACRIFICES CONFIRMATORY OF
THE ATONEMENT.

HAVING now seen that the conclusions drawn from the statements of the New Testament respecting our Lord's sufferings are strongly confirmed by the sacrifices of the Mosaic law, the question arises, Whether any similar confirmation be afforded by those of the patriarchal dispensation, by which the Mosaic or Levitical was preceded?

It is natural that such confirmation should be expected. For two or more dispensations of religion, successively established by divine wisdom, can hardly fail to be harmonious in their leading principles, however much they may differ in their minute details. If, therefore, the method of expiation for human guilt by the sacrifice of the Son of God be the grand and ultimate manifestation of redeeming grace which the typical ceremonies of Judaism foreshadowed, and which has now been fully unfolded in the Gospel, it may reasonably be presumed that a subject so important in its bearing alike on the plans of God and the destinies of man would not be altogether without its recognition in the sentiments and observances of the primitive fathers of our race. This natural presumption is greatly strengthened by the fact that, in so far as promises and predictions were concerned, it is certain that, long anterior to the Mosaic economy, and even so early as the period of the Fall, God did not "leave Himself without witness" respecting His merciful purposes for the redemption of sinners. And that hope of a Saviour, which held a prominent place even from the beginning in the communica-

PART
II.
SEC. 5.
——
Patriarchal
sacrifices.

Patriarchal, Levitical, and Christian dispensations may be expected to agree in their leading principles

266   DOCTRINE OF THE OLD TESTAMENT

PART II. SEC. 5.

tions of God with man, may not unnaturally be expected to have found for itself some expression in the worship rendered by man to God.

Argument for primitive institution of sacrifice from its universal prevalence.

It is no mean presumptive argument that may be drawn in favour of the primitive institution of sacrificial worship, from the universal prevalence of atoning sacrifices among the heathens. There seems, indeed, to be no other principle on which we can so satisfactorily explain the fact that in every nation, savage or civilised, before or since the promulgation of the law of Moses, we find in one form or in another the priest, the altar, and the victim. It will not be maintained that this fact is attributable to anything in the nature of the rite which strongly commends itself to the human understanding ; for there is no such obvious connection between the shedding of blood and the remission of sins—between the slaying of one of God's creatures and the receiving of pardon for the violation of God's laws—as should readily account for the universal adoption of such an expedient, with a view to such a result.

The sacrifices of the heathen were not mere thank-offerings rendered in return for the bounties of divine Providence ; for however justly this character may be ascribed to those offerings which consisted of the fruits of the earth, and which might naturally be viewed as expressions of dependence and tokens of gratitude, it is difficult to perceive on what principle the destruction of animal life could be regarded as an acceptable eucharistic offering to the Creator. The theory of some, that sacrifice had its origin in the grossly superstitious notion that the gods were invested with human passions and animal appetites, so that they might be conciliated by bribes, or gratified with the flesh of slain victims, is, as has been

Litton's Bampton Lectures, p. 320.

well remarked, " open to the objection that such extreme ignorance respecting the divine nature is hardly to be ascribed to the very early age in which the rite is found to have been prevalent, inasmuch as St Paul teaches, at the commencement of his Epistle to the Romans, that the grosser forms of idolatry were the result of a gradual process of deterioration," and a just retribution for the

RESPECTING THE ATONEMENT.

neglect of sinful men in failing to improve the measure of light vouchsafed to them. Equally unsatisfactory is the attempt to explain the origin and prevalence of sacrifices on the ground of their having been "federal rites," at which, after the manner of men, God feasted with His worshippers, as a symbol of continued or restored friendship between the two parties. For it so happens that in the earliest and most common species of sacrifice, that of the whole burnt-offering, no part was reserved for the use of the offerer, the entire victim being devoted to God and consumed upon the altar.

It is idle, however, to propose or refute theories which deal with the heathen sacrifices as other than what they professedly were ; for the fact is indubitable, and is indeed scarcely disputed, that these sacrifices were in most cases *vicarious* and *piacular* in the strict and proper sense of the expression, the victim slain being understood to bear the guilt and to suffer the due punishment of him by whom its blood was shed.* Nay, it is remarkable that those rationalistic writers who are most keenly opposed to the doctrine of the Atonement are wont to speak reproachfully of vicarious expiation as altogether a *heathenish notion*, and to lay it down as the grand distinction between the worship of the true God in all ages and that of polytheism, that the sacrifices of the former did not include this notion, whereas it was certainly included and prominently exhibited in the latter. Now, the notion of a *vicarious and piacular* sacrifice, in which there is made an actual substitution of an innocent victim in the room of the guilty worshipper, is not one that can be excogitated or reasoned out by any intellectual process with which we are acquainted. Accordingly, its universal prevalence among the heathens is best to be accounted for on one or other, or jointly on both of these two suppositions—1st, That it commends itself to some intuitive promptings or deep-seated yearnings of the fallen heart of man, which are too strong to be overborne by the calm conclusions of

Side notes: PART II. SEC. 5.

Heathen sacrifices were for the most part piacular.

How did they arise?

from instinctive promptings of a

---

* See Magee on Atonement, Note V. ; Pye Smith on Sacrifice, &c., of Christ, Note VI.

268 DOCTRINE OF THE OLD TESTAMENT

PART II.
SEC. 5.
——
sinful
heart ; or
by tradi-
tion from
some origi-
nal institu-
tion ?

his intellect ; or, 2dly, That it was derived by tradition from some common and authoritative source. Probably some influence ought to be attributed to *both* of these causes in accounting for its prevalence. On the one hand, we can hardly think that all religions would have uniformly adopted and steadfastly retained the principle of piacular sacrifice, if that principle had no stronger hold on the instincts and feelings of human nature beyond that of traditional custom. But, on the other hand, however much the yearnings of the human heart may cling to this notion when once it has been authoritatively suggested, it is not easy to see how the notion should have originated in every region of the world, and among every race of men, without being proposed to them by some common authority, or transmitted to them from some one venerated source ; for though the mere fancies or guesses of super-stition might possibly account for its existence among a few nations, these cannot so well explain its universal existence among all nations, however diversified in other respects as to characters, circumstances, habits, and dis-positions. The wonderful harmony observable as to this matter is best to be explained by supposing that the rite of sacrifice was communicated to the post-diluvian world by Noah, the second great progenitor of the human race, and was thereafter carried by his descendants to those various regions of the earth to which they emigrated ; although with this explanation, as has been already re-marked, there may be not unreasonably conjoined the further hypothesis, that there is somewhat in the very nature of the ordinance which commends itself, not indeed to the reasonable convictions, but to the instinctive long-ings of the human heart.

Scriptural
evidence
of the pre-
valence of
sacrifice
before the
time of
Moses.

It is not necessary, however, to insist on any merely pre-sumptive evidence of the ante-Mosaic institution of sacri-fice, such as may be derived from its general prevalence among all nations; for, happily, we are able to appeal to the much more direct and satisfactory evidence which is sup-plied by recorded facts and statements of Holy Scripture.

RESPECTING THE ATONEMENT. 269

1. For example, we may appeal to the history of Job, who is generally and on good grounds supposed to have lived at a period considerably before the time of Moses, and who was, moreover, not an Israelite, but a dweller in the land of Uz or Edom. We are told that this patriarch "offered every morning burnt-offerings according to the number of his sons; for he said, It may be they have sinned, and have cursed God in their hearts." It is evident from the terms in which Job himself speaks of the sacrifices thus presented by him that they were *sin-offerings*, intended to secure the remission of any sins which his children might have committed.

Again, we are told that "the Lord said to Eliphaz the Temanite, My wrath is kindled against thee, and against thy two friends; for ye have not spoken of me the thing that is right, as my servant Job hath. Therefore take unto you now seven bullocks and seven rams, and go to my servant Job, and offer up for yourselves a burnt-offering; and my servant Job shall pray for you, for him I will accept: lest I deal with you after your folly, in that ye have not spoken of me the thing which is right." Here we have an express command, issued by the Lord Himself, ordaining burnt - offerings to be presented for the remission of sins, to persons who were not placed under the law of Moses. It cannot be alleged that the sacrifices thus enjoined were mere *deprecatory gifts* offered to the Almighty, as one might offer bribes to a fellow-creature, with the view of purchasing exemption from his merited anger. For, however customary it might be with the idolatrous heathens to cherish the thought that their gods could be thus appeased, any such idea is altogether foreign to the worship of the only living and true God, and cannot be supposed to have been sanctioned by His authority. For of Him we are assured, that "with the Lord our God there is no iniquity, or respect of persons, or *taking of gifts*." Undoubtedly those sacrifices which He commanded Job's friends to offer, in consequence of their "not having spoken of Him the thing that was right," and in order that He might not "deal

270   DOCTRINE OF THE OLD TESTAMENT

PART II. SEC. 5.

Davison on Sacrifice.

with them after their folly," must have been of the same piacular kind with those which He afterwards appointed in the Mosaic ritual. Nor is there any force in the argument of Mr Davison, that the forgiveness of Eliphaz and his associates is here ascribed to the intercession of Job in their behalf, and not to the accompanying sacrifices. The sacrifices are expressly commanded because they had sinned, and lest God should deal with them as their sin had merited. Job, also, is told to pray for them, on the same account, doubtless, and for the same purpose. But surely we are not thence warranted to infer that of the two things thus enjoined with a view to their forgiveness, either the one or the other was exclusively necessary and efficacious. We ought rather to conclude that *both* had to be combined in order that the desired result might be secured. And whatever respect the Lord may have had to Job's intercession, when conjoined with and proceeding upon the accompanying expiation, we cannot doubt that if the required sacrifice had been withheld, the pleading of the patriarch would of itself have been without effect.

Sacrifices of Abraham, Isaac, and Jacob.

Gen. xii. 8; xiii. 4, 18; xxvi. 25; xxxiii. 20; xxxv. 1, 7.

Gen. xxii. 7.

2. We may further appeal to the histories of Abraham, Isaac, and Jacob, as furnishing evidence that the rite of sacrifice was familiar to these ancient patriarchs, as well as to the children of Israel who descended from them. For it is recorded that wherever they pitched their tents they "built an altar"—doubtless for sacrificial worship— "and called upon the name of the Lord." More especially in the case of the first two of these patriarchs,—the command given to Abraham to offer up his son Isaac, and the expression of surprise which the young lad uttered, when he found that his father was going to worship God without taking the customary victim along with him—"Father, behold the fire and the wood ; but where is the lamb for a burnt-offering?"—are clear proofs that the rite of animal sacrifice was in those days a perfectly familiar and approved method of religious worship. And that special interposition of divine Providence by which, while the human sacrifice was prevented, a ram was at the same

RESPECTING THE ATONEMENT. 271

time provided as a victim, amounts to an evident sanction
given by God Himself to the practice of seeking His favour
by the shedding of sacrificial blood.

PART II. SEC. 5.

3. In the history of Noah we find still earlier indications
of the prevalent and approved observance of the rite of
sacrifice. This patriarch was directed to take into the
ark "of every clean beast by sevens, the male and his
female, but of beasts that were not clean by two, the male
and his female." Here we have a distinction, recognised
by God, between animals that are "clean" and animals
that are "not clean." This distinction cannot be supposed
to have reference to the use of animals for food, for it was
not till after the Flood that this kind of food was permitted.
To what else, then, can it be thought to refer, except to
the use of animals for sacrifice? If so, we have then
evidence that, even at this early period, God had not
only sanctioned the rite of sacrifice, but had specified the
kind of victims that were proper to be offered on His altar.

Sacrifices of Noah.

Gen. vii. 2.

That this really was the reason of the above distinction
appears from a subsequent passage in the life of Noah,
which may be further adduced in confirmation of our
argument. No sooner had Noah come out of the ark
than "he built an altar, and took of every clean beast,
and of every clean fowl, and offered burnt-offerings upon
the altar." From this passage it is evident that Noah
was well aware of the sacrificial reference of the distinction above noticed. For his burnt-offerings consisted of
"clean beasts and clean fowls," as being the only ones
that could be fitly and acceptably used in the services of
religion. That the sacrifice which Noah presented on this
occasion was of an *expiatory* character, there are several
circumstances connected with it that tend to assure us.
With respect to the acceptance of it, we are told that
"the Lord smelled a sweet savour,"—according to the
marginal translation, "a savour of rest," or as the Syriac
version renders it, "an odour of placability,"—implying
that one who was previously offended has been appeased.
Aben-Ezra, cited by Buxtorf, explains it as "a resting of

Gen. viii. 20.

272   DOCTRINE OF THE OLD TESTAMENT

PART II.
SEC. 5.

Gen. viii. 21.

God from His anger or displeasure." And then, as regards the gracious answer which Noah received, " I will not again curse the ground any more for man's sake, though the imagination of man's heart is evil from his youth ; neither will I again smite any more everything living, as I have done ; " there is no other way in which this answer can be construed than as an intimation on the part of God that, pursuant to the design of the sacrifice, He would cease from His wrath, and would not again punish the wickedness of man, as He had recently done, by the waters of the Deluge. " From the drift of the answer," as Faber has well remarked, " we clearly learn the drift of the petition." We may reason back, from the reception which the sacrifice met with, to what must have been the intention of the sacrifice—namely, to propitiate the anger of a justly-offended God.

Faber on Sacrifice, p. 77.

Again, we are told that, shortly after the Deluge, the Lord was pleased to permit Noah and his descendants to use the flesh of animals for food, but, at the same time, strictly to prohibit the use of blood. " Every moving thing that liveth," saith the Lord, " shall be meat for you ; even as the green herb have I given you all things ; but flesh with the life thereof, which is the blood thereof, shall ye not eat." The reason of this prohibition is not expressly stated in the passage in which it is thus imposed. But there can be no reasonable doubt that it was the same reason which God afterwards gave for the same restriction in the Mosaic law, when he thus declared,—" I will set my face against that soul that eateth blood ; for the life of the flesh is in the blood ; and I have given it to you upon the altar to make an atonement for your souls ; for it is the blood that maketh an atonement for the soul." This, doubtless, was, in the time of Noah as in the time of Moses, the reason why the blood of animals must be abstained from. And if so, we must conclude that the shedding of sacrificial blood was the recognised and acceptable method of seeking the remission of sins, eight hundred years and more before the Jewish ritual was established.

Gen. ix. 3, 4.

Levit xvii. 10, 11.

RESPECTING THE ATONEMENT.

4. But this is not all. We are warranted to claim a much higher antiquity than the days of Noah for this observance. The first instance of worship subsequently to the Fall of which any Scriptural record has come down to us is thus described: "In process of time it came to pass that Cain brought of the fruit of the ground an offering unto the Lord; and Abel, he also brought of the firstlings of his flock and of the fat thereof. And the Lord had respect unto Abel and to his offering; but unto Cain and to his offering He had not respect." Here was a very notable distinction made between these primitive worshippers. And the question to be solved is, Whence did this distinction arise, or on what principle can we satisfactorily account for it?

It were vain to seek an answer to this question in any supposed difference in the value of the things presented. In the sight of that great Lord to whom they were devoted, neither of the gifts was possessed of any intrinsic value. To Him they could not in any respect be profitable. Nay, if there were any difference between them in the judgment of God, we might with some plausibility have supposed that, of the two offerings, Abel's would have been the less acceptable; inasmuch as there seems at first sight to be something unnatural and incongruous, or, we may even say, something hateful and revolting, in the very attempt to conciliate the great God, whose tender mercies are over all His works, by deliberately putting to death an unoffending animal. On the other hand, as regards the worshippers themselves, we have not the least reason to think that there was any difference in the estimate they formed of the worth of their respective offerings; for if it be alleged that Cain, as being a husbandman, brought what was cheapest and easiest for him, "the fruit of the ground," it might with equal justice be said of Abel that he also, as being a shepherd, brought what was to him the least costly offering when he sacrificed "the firstlings of his flock."

Equally vain were it to seek an explanation of the distinction made between these worshippers in the supposi-

PART II.
SEC. 5.

Sacrifices of Cain and Abel.
Gen. iv. 3. 5.

Abel's sacrifice not better in itself than that of Cain.

274 DOCTRINE OF THE OLD TESTAMENT

PART II.
Sec. 5.

Nor was it preferred because of Abel's personal excellence.
I John, iii. 12.

tion of any prior difference in their conduct. It has indeed been stated by an apostle that "Cain slew his brother because his own works were evil, and his brother's righteous." But whether the "evil works" of Cain thus referred to were antecedent to his offering, or whether they were involved in the nature and spirit of the offering itself, there is nothing in the apostle's statement to determine. Nor is there any passage of Scripture, that we are aware of, in which God is said to have accepted Abel's offering because Abel was previously righteous, and to have rejected the offering of Cain because Cain was previously unrighteous. With respect to the antecedent character of the two brothers we know nothing, and hence we are not warranted to found any conclusion upon it.

Was there not a difference in the spirit by which they were actuated in their worship?
Heb. xi. 4.

It may be suggested, however, that there was an important difference between them, in respect of the *spirit* or *disposition* by which in their several acts of worship they were animated. And in support of this suggestion we may be referred to what is said of them in the Epistle to the Hebrews—namely, that "*by faith* Abel offered unto God a more excellent sacrifice than Cain, by which he obtained witness that He was righteous, God testifying of his gifts." In quoting this text, however, it is necessary to keep in view the exact drift or purport of the statement contained in it. It points to Abel's "faith," not as *the quality which alone gave a superior excellence to his sacrifice*, but rather as *the motive or principle of action*, which led him to give the better sacrifice which he presented, instead of a less excellent offering like that of his brother Cain. It is true that the former would have been rejected, as well as the latter, if it had not proceeded from that principle of "faith, without which it is impossible to please God." But this is not *the* truth which the apostle is here inculcating. He does not here tell us that "by faith Abel's sacrifice was rendered more excellent than otherwise it would have been ;" but that "by faith Abel was led to offer a more excellent sacrifice than otherwise he would have presented." Throughout the whole of this eleventh chapter of Hebrews, the object of the writer evidently is to illus-

Faith is here spoken of, not as making Abel's sacrifice the better one, but as leading him to offer a better sacrifice than that of Cain.

RESPECTING THE ATONEMENT. 275

trate the practical influence of faith. With this view he
refers to the history of patriarchs, prophets, and other Old
Testament saints. And in connecting their actions with
their faith, he points to this principle as *the motive, by the
agency of which they were led to perform the actions,* and not
as *the quality from which the actions derived their excellence.*

Supposing this to have been his meaning in the present
instance, we must look for some peculiarity in Abel's
sacrifice that may be viewed as furnishing evidence of his
faith, instead of looking to the faith that is ascribed to
him as forming the only distinguishing speciality in his
sacrifice. In the cases of Noah, Abraham, Moses, and
other ancient worthies noticed in the context, we readily
discover in the conduct they pursued many things that
cannot otherwise be accounted for, except by their faith
in the truths which were revealed to them. We may
reasonably conclude that it is so also in the case before us.
The analogy of the other instances with which it is associated leads us to conclude that there was something in
Abel's sacrifice, as contradistinguished from that of his
brother Cain, which made it, what it is here adduced as
being, a proper and pertinent illustration of the power of
faith.

But how could it be so, unless it were conformable,
while Cain's offering, as distinguished from it, was not conformable, to some previous revelation or appointment of
the Lord ? As formerly remarked, there was no apparent
difference between the two sacrifices in respect of the value
of the things presented. Both were of equal worth apparently to the offerers, while neither of them had any intrinsic
value in the judgment of God. Still, there was a plain
enough distinction between the two, inasmuch as the one
was a sacrifice of *inanimate objects,* whereas the other was a
sacrifice of *living creatures.* In the case of the one *a gift
merely was presented,* while in the case of the other *a life
was taken away.* Here was a marked difference between
the two offerings—a difference which is perfectly apparent
on their very surface, and which no mere conjectures are
necessary to establish. And it is in this difference, I

PART
II.
SEC. 5.

We must
look for
something
in Abel's
sacrifice
which in-
dicated his
faith.

Cain's was
a fruit-
offering ;
Abel's was
a blood-
offering.

276   DOCTRINE OF THE OLD TESTAMENT

PART II. SEC. 5.

apprehend, that we must seek our explanation of the apostle's statement, that Abel's sacrifice betokened his "faith." It did so, inasmuch as it was conformable, while Cain's sacrifice was not conformable, to some prior discovery of the mind and will of God.

Apart even from what is written in Hebrews, xi. 4, this view of the matter is in many respects a probable one. We have seen it to be a great leading principle alike of the Christian and of the Mosaic dispensation, that "without shedding of blood there is no remission of sins." And hence we can hardly doubt that a principle which holds so prominent a place in the law and in the Gospel, had a place of equal prominence assigned to it in that patriarchal dispensation which preceded them. It may not, however, be altogether competent to urge this consideration in our present argument, inasmuch as there is evidently involved in it an assumption of the Christian doctrine of the Atonement.

No record of any other sacrifice like that of Cain under the patriarchal dispensation.

But further, we have seen that in the days of Job, Abraham, Noah, and other patriarchs who lived before the institution of the Mosaic law, the practice of slaying animal victims at the altar was a well-known and approved ordinance observed in the worship of God. And it is particularly worthy of remark, that *with the single exception of Cain's rejected offering, there is no other sacrifice on record before the time of Moses that did not consist of the shedding of animal blood.* Cain's is the one solitary instance of a fruit-offering that is to be met with throughout that whole period. From this circumstance alone it might be reasonably concluded that Cain's mere offering of fruits was a deviation from the approved method of divine worship; while Abel's offering of the firstlings of his flock was in conformity with the appointed and acceptable mode in which it became a fallen creature to seek the favour of his justly-offended God.

God's remonstrance with Cain, Gen. iv. 6, 7.

This view of the matter is still further borne out by the terms of the remonstrance which God addressed to Cain, when filled with wrath at the rejection of his offering. "The Lord said unto Him, Why art thou wroth? and

RESPECTING THE ATONEMENT. 277

why is thy countenance fallen? If thou doest well, shalt
thou not be accepted? And if thou doest not well, sin
lieth at the door?"* He is here told that "if he had
done well he would be accepted." He then might stand
on the footing of his own righteousness, as one for whom
no sin-offering was necessary, and might claim for that
mere thank-offering which he had presented the favourable regard of Him on whom it was bestowed. But, on
the other hand, "if he had not done well"—if he was a
fallen, guilty, depraved creature (as his own conscience
ought to have told him that he truly was)—then there was
an obstacle in the way of his approaching God which the
mere thank-offering he had brought with him could not
remove. That obstacle was "sin," which was "lying at
the door," as if to prevent him finding admission to the
gracious presence and favour of the Most High. And
until this obstacle was taken out the way, he must not
expect that a door of access to the grace of God could
effectually be opened to him.

After all, however, it is chiefly from what is said of
Abel's sacrifice in Hebrews, xi. 4, that we are warranted
to regard it as more conformable than that of Cain to
some previously known revelation or appointment of God.
His bringing such an offering is there said to have been
an act of faith. Now "faith," as we are told in Scripture, Rom. x.
"cometh by hearing, and hearing by the Word of God." 17.
The "things hoped for," of which "faith is the substance," Heb. xi. 1.
and the "things unseen," of which it is "the evidence," are
not mere matters of *guess* or of *conjecture,* which a fanciful
or speculative spirit may suggest, but truths which the
Word of God has authoritatively declared. In the various
instances adduced in Hebrews xi. of persons actuated by
this principle of "faith," the belief of something revealed,
and a course of action agreeable to that belief, are uniformly exhibited. And just as Noah, Abraham, and the
others performed the deeds that are severally ascribed
to them, in the full persuasion that such deeds were
required of them, not by the random suggestions of their

* See Appendix, Note H.

278   DOCTRINE OF THE OLD TESTAMENT

PART
II.
SEC. 5.
——

own mind, but by the positive intimations of the will of heaven, even so must Abel's selection of an animal victim in preference to a fruit-offering, when considered as *an act of faith*, be traced to a like conviction, that in so doing he was more closely conforming to the divinely-approved method, by which alone sinners can have access to a holy God.

It is of importance once more to observe the plain and obvious purport of the apostle's statement. He does not speak of Abel's faith *as having given to his sacrifice an excellence of which it would not otherwise have been possessed* (although there can be no doubt that this also was the case); but he speaks of Abel's faith *as having led him to present* that "more excellent sacrifice" which was brought by him, instead of the inferior offering which Cain presented. Now, how could this be, if there had been no prior intimation of the divine will upon the subject? In the absence of any such intimation, we could scarcely characterise Abel's procedure as *an act of faith*. We might call it a *dexterous guess* or a *happy conjecture*. We might speak of it as a natural and not inappropriate device to which his own fancy or feelings may have directed him. But we should scarcely call it an exercise of that "faith" which always has respect to the declared will and counsel of God.

No *express mention* in Genesis of the primitive institution of sin-offerings.

It is true there is *no express mention* in the Book of Genesis of expiatory sacrifice by the shedding of blood as having been instituted shortly after the Fall. We cannot regard this circumstance, however, as of sufficient force to neutralise those fair inferences from Scriptural facts and statements which we have now submitted. Although there is certainly no distinct mention of the first appointment of this sacred ordinance, yet there are various passages in which its divine origin seems to be recognised

But it seems to be implied.

or taken for granted. Indeed, the subject is frequently alluded to in the very way that might have been expected in a book like that of Genesis, written by an Israelite, and addressed to Israelites, who had all their lives been familiar with the observance. Without any formal account being given of the manner in which the rite was primarily

RESPECTING THE ATONEMENT. 279

introduced, we find such references to it running through PART II. SEC. 5. the narrative as could not leave a doubt in the mind of any Israelite in whose religion sacrifice occupied so large a place, and who was always wont to regard it as of divine appointment, that its origin, as an ordinance sanctioned by the authority of God, must be traced back to the period of the Fall. Nor is it immaterial to remark that, as regards the absence of any formal notice of their divine origin, the Levitical sacrifices are on the same footing with the patriarchal. For, as was formerly observed, we find in the law of Moses merely the *regulation* *Supra, p. 218.* or *modification* of sacrificial observances, as being already recognised in the worship of God, but no such thing as a *formal institution of the rite of sacrifice* considered in itself. This is a point that is tacitly assumed in the Book of Leviticus, as well as in the Book of Genesis. Besides, there seems to be a natural probability in the supposition that sacrifice was divinely appointed in primitive times, even if there was a much less amount of circumstantial evidence to confirm it. For we know that immediately after the fall of Adam a promise was made to him of that future deliverer, by whom the evil effects of sin should be removed. And hence, to perpetuate the knowledge, and also to illustrate in some degree the import, of this gracious promise, which was in those days the grand object of faith and hope, and the sole ground of a sinner's confidence before God, it is surely not unreasonable to suppose that some such recognition and memorial of it as that which the rite of sacrifice presents, may have had a place assigned to it by divine authority in the worship of the primitive fathers of the human race.

But suppose we were to admit that the absence of any *If we were* express mention of the divine appointment of expiatory *obliged to admit* sacrifice prior to Abel's offering is a conclusive objection *that sacri-* to the view we have been hitherto taking of the ground *fice was not previ-* on which his offering was accepted, while that of his *ously in-* brother was rejected by the Lord; even then the corrobor- *stituted by God;* ative argument we are now urging in favour of the doctrine of the Atonement is not to any material extent invalidated.

280   DOCTRINE OF THE OLD TESTAMENT

PART II. SEC. 5.

then Abel's faith must have had respect to the promise of a Saviour given to Adam.

Let it be admitted that Abel's faith had reference, not to anything which *may have been* previously revealed *regarding sacrificial worship,* but to something which *certainly was* previously revealed *regarding the promised Redeemer of our fallen race;* what then? In that case Abel's "more excellent sacrifice" was dictated, not by any divine command expressly prescribing such a sacrifice, but by the working in his own mind of that faith in the promised Redeemer by which he was actuated. We must still regard it, however, as having been an indication—the most suitable indication that occurred to him—of that trust in the divine promise which he was seeking to express, when he went with his tribute of devout worship before the Lord. And

If so, the acceptance of his offering was tantamount to an institution of sacrifice from that time forwards.

not only so, but the acceptance which he met with unquestionably amounted, *from that time forwards* at least, to a divine sanction given to such sacrifices as had been presented by him, and might justly be pleaded by all succeeding worshippers as a divine warrant for offering such sacrifices on the altar of God.

Would Abel's offering have been will-worship if not in compliance with a divine command?

To this view of the matter it has, indeed, been strongly objected by Magee, Faber, and many other advocates of the divine appointment of sacrifice at the time of the Fall, that, " had Abel's offering been the suggestion of his own mind, actuated though he might be by faith in the promised Saviour, it would then have been *a presumptuous act of will-worship,* such as the Almighty would not have approved of; inasmuch as He is a jealous God, who will not have worship given to Him in any other way than that which He has Himself appointed."

We are not prepared, however, to admit the force of this objection ; for it seems unwarranted to censure as " will-worship " any religious observance which men may, at the suggestion of their own minds, be led to perform, *unless we are able to show that it has been substituted for some other method of worship which God has previously instituted.*

Levit. x. 1, 2.

When Nadab and Abihu, the sons of Aaron, were condemned for " offering strange fire before the Lord," it was because God had Himself prescribed the fire, which was kept burning on the altar of burnt-offerings, as that which

RESPECTING THE ATONEMENT.   281

should be used in all the services of the tabernacle. And when Christ applied to the Pharisees that divine censure, " In vain do they worship me, teaching for doctrines the commandments of men," the ground of His censure was, that the Pharisees had made unwarranted innovations or alterations on a system of religious observances which God had expressly sanctioned. There is no room, however, for any such condemnation in the totally different case of persons to whom God has made no revelation in regard to the kind of worship which He requires of them. Such persons may doubtless be blamable if they worship God in such a manner as even the light of nature shows to be altogether unworthy of His character and perfections ; but certainly they are not blamable on the mere ground of worshipping Him according to the suggestions of their own mind. It would be very hard if they were to be blamed on this account; because it is obvious that, in the absence of revelation, men must either worship God according to the dictates of their own mind, or they must refrain from worshipping Him at all.

PART II. Sec. 5. Matt. xv. 9.

It appears, then, that even if no express commandment had been previously issued on the subject of sacrificial worship, we are not entitled to say that the sacrifice of Abel would have been a presumptuous act of will-worship, such as God could not be expected to approve of. The fact is unquestionable that God *did* approve of it. And allowing, if we needs must, that it may notwithstanding have been the dictate of Abel's own mind acting under the influence of faith in the promised Saviour, we may reasonably conclude that the acceptance which it met with *was tantamount to a divine sanction thenceforth impressed upon it.*

The advocates of the divine authority of the patriarchal sacrifices have unnecessarily increased the difficulties of their position by taking upon themselves the burden of proving the issue of some *express command* upon the subject. Surely God has other ways of indicating His will than by an articulate commandment. We hold marriage to be a divine institution ; and yet, before God

An express command is not the only way in which God can indicate His will.

282   DOCTRINE OF THE OLD TESTAMENT

PART
II.
SEC. 5.
——
Gen. ii. 23,
24.

had said anything in regard to it that could be considered as stamping on it such a character, Adam had first said, so soon as Eve was given to him, "This now is bone of my bones, and flesh of my flesh;" "therefore," it is added, "shall a man leave his father and his mother, and shall cleave unto his wife; and they shall be one flesh." There is no reason, therefore, why sacrifice in primitive times may not be held to be a divine institution, although, before God expressly sanctioned and approved of it, Abel may have offered up his acceptable sacrifice. He may possibly have been moved by some inward divine monition; so that we might say of him as Christ said of Simon Peter,

Matt. xvi.
17.

"Blessed art thou, for flesh and blood hath not revealed this to thee, but my Father who is in heaven." But even were it not so,—even if Abel's sacrifice were the natural and spontaneous dictate of his own mind, when actuated by faith in the revealed promise of a Saviour, still the recorded fact that "God had respect to it," while He had not respect to the fruit-offering of Cain, must be held as *thenceforth* imparting the divine sanction to it, and conveying to all succeeding worshippers an assurance that sacrifice, presented after the manner of Abel's sacrifice, would meet, as his had done, with the approval and acceptance of God. And the justice of this view is confirmed by the striking circumstance, that at no after-period during the patriarchal dispensation do we ever find the worshippers of Jehovah presenting such mere offerings of fruits as Cain had brought to Him, but uniformly such animal victims as constituted the "more excellent sacrifice" of Abel.

Thus have we endeavoured to show that the rite of expiatory sacrifice, instead of being for the first time instituted under the Mosaic law, held a prominent and approved place in the worship of the patriarchs, and was divinely sanctioned as early as the days of Abel. And if we have succeeded in establishing this position, we may confidently urge it as no unimportant argument in confirmation of the doctrine of the Atonement.

RESPECTING THE ATONEMENT. 283

It is frequently alleged by the adversaries of this doctrine that expiatory sacrifice was originally a heathenish rite, associated with the gross superstitions of polytheism, and destitute of all countenance and sanction from the living God—that under a modified form it was adopted in the law of Moses, in order to suit those habits of sacrificial worship which the Israelites had acquired in common with the surrounding nations—and that it has been apparently countenanced with still greater modifications under the Gospel, partly owing to the natural tendency of the apostles to illustrate Christian truths by Jewish figures and allusions, and partly with the view of more easily reconciling the converts from Judaism to the abandonment of their ceremonial system.

Now, to say nothing of the disparaging reflection which this assertion casts on the whole scheme of revelation, we need only remark that it is utterly inconsistent with those matters of fact which we have endeavoured to substantiate. We have seen that the rite of sacrifice, at its first origin, was not destitute of the sanction and approbation of the true God ; that it did not originate with the votaries of polytheism ; and that the heathen sacrifices, instead of being the original models, are rather to be viewed as the superinduced corruptions of that primitive patriarchal practice which the God of Abraham, of Noah, and of Abel, had from the first regarded with acceptance. And we have seen that the sin-offerings of the Mosaic law, instead of being innovations on the old ritual observed by God's professed people, designed to accommodate it to the practices of the surrounding nations, were, on the contrary, in full harmony with the earliest methods of acceptable worship on the part of God's people of which we have any distinct and authentic record. In fine, we have ascertained that the religion of fallen man has been in all ages substantially the same ; that the principle, which is now fully developed under the Gospel, has ever been, even from the earliest times, involved in it, that " without shedding of blood there is no remission ; " and that, whether under the patriarchal, the Levitical, or the Christian dispensation,

PART II. SEC. 5.

Importance of the patriarchal sacrifices, as confirming and vindicating the Atonement of the cross.

284   DOCTRINE OF THE OLD TESTAMENT

PART II.
SEC. 5.

there has been, and there is, but one way of access by which sinful creatures can approach a holy God, even that great atoning sacrifice of the cross, to which all former generations looked forward, and all succeeding generations must look back, as the only propitiation for their sins.

RESPECTING THE ATONEMENT. 285

PART III.

REVIEW OF VARIOUS THEORIES WHICH HAVE BEEN PROPOSED RESPECTING THE MEDIATORIAL WORK AND SUFFERINGS OF JESUS CHRIST.

————

HAVING now endeavoured to ascertain the Scriptural doctrine respecting the sufferings and death of Jesus Christ, it may be useful and interesting to examine some of the most plausible theories which have been proposed with the view of accounting for them otherwise than on the principle of their having been a true and proper expiatory sacrifice, or a satisfaction to divine justice for the sins of the world.

In doing so, it is necessary to bear in mind the *nature of the facts* of which any sound theory must furnish an adequate and satisfactory explanation. These facts are: That One who was not only a perfectly innocent and righteous man, but the only-begotten and well-beloved Son of God, endured all His life long unmerited sorrow and humiliation, and was ultimately subjected to a painful and ignominious death;—that the sufferings He met with are represented in Scripture as having come upon Him, not merely through the enmity of men, but by the special ordination and appointment of God, and as having been not *incidental* but *essential* to the great purpose for which He was sent into the world ;—that a special connection

PART III.

Review of theories respecting the Atonement.

Nature of the facts which any sound theory must account for.

286 REVIEW OF THEORIES

PART III.

with *our sins*, and a special influence in securing *our forgiveness*, is attributed to them, such as is nowhere ascribed to the afflictions of any human being who ever appeared on earth ;—and that His endurance of them is represented in the New Testament as furnishing at once the most evident and the most illustrious of all conceivable manifestations of the love of God.

These are the main facts—not to mention others of a less prominent character which may afterwards be referred to —of which we desiderate some fair and reasonable account. And if it can be shown that the various theories which have been suggested as substitutes for the commonly-received doctrine of the Atonement, afford no explanation that is either so Scriptural or so rational of the facts to be accounted for, we shall then have the more confidence in adhering to those conclusions to which we have been led by our previous investigations.

SECTION I.

THEORIES OF (1) MARTYRDOM; (2) SUBSERVIENCY TO
THE RESURRECTION; (3) EXAMPLE; (4) MANIFESTA-
TION OF THE DIVINE CHARACTER; (5) MANIFESTA-
TION OF THE LOVE OF GOD; (6) ARIAN OR MIDDLE
THEORY.

I. OF the various attempts made to explain our Lord's
sufferings on some other principle than that of the Atonement, it is scarcely necessary to dwell on the old Socinian
notion, that *His sufferings were those of a mere martyr in
the cause of righteousness,* and that they were endured
"for us" and "for our sins," in no higher sense than as
*serving to confirm the truth of the Gospel, by which we are
assured of God's willingness to forgive sin, and are effectually persuaded and enabled to forsake it.*

It is undeniable, indeed, that the Lord Jesus *was* a
martyr, who laid down His life in the cause of Christianity.
But it is equally certain that this aspect of His last sufferings is scarcely noticed by the apostles and evangelists.
There seem to be only two passages of Scripture in which
there is any particular allusion to it. The one is in
1 Timothy, vi. 13, where Paul incidentally speaks of Jesus
Christ as having "witnessed a good confession before
Pontius Pilate." And the other is in Hebrews, xii. 1, 2,
where, after speaking of the "great cloud of martyrs" by
whom we are encouraged in running the Christian race,
the inspired writer admonishes us to be "looking unto
Jesus, the author and finisher of the faith, who for the joy
that was set before Him endured the cross, despising the
shame, and is set down at the right hand of the throne of

288 REVIEW OF THEORIES

PART III.
SEC. I.

Christ's
sufferings
in primi-
tive times
did not
tend to
confirm the
Gospel.

God." Nor is it at all wonderful that the allusions should be thus rare to this particular view of our Lord's sufferings ; for whatever weight we may be disposed, in modern times, to attach to these sufferings, as tending to confirm the truth of the Gospel, it is certain that, at the time of their endurance, and long after, they had the very opposite effect. And in so far as regards the mere advancement of the Christian cause, we can scarcely doubt that this object would have been much more effectually promoted by His coming down in triumph from the cross, to the utter consternation of His adversaries, than by His submitting to that ignominious death, which was "a stumbling-block to the Jews and foolishness to the Greeks."

Christ is
spoken of
in terms
inappli-
cable to
any mar-
tyr.

On the other hand, the passages are very numerous in which the death of Christ is spoken of in such terms as are never applied to any other persecuted prophet or teacher of righteousness who has laid down his life in attestation of revealed truth. And yet, if martyrdom were all that these terms denote, there is no reason why He should be the only martyr of whom we ever read that "He was delivered for our offences," that "He suffered for sins, the just for the unjust," and that "in Him we have redemption through His blood."

Christ's
sufferings
not more
confirma-
tory of the
Gospel
than His
miracles,
&c.

Besides, the sufferings of Christ, according to this view of them, were not *the direct means of procuring for us* the forgiveness of sins and other spiritual blessings of the Gospel. They were merely confirmatory of the truth of that revelation in which these blessings are announced and offered to us. Nor were they more so than His miracles, His prophecies, the virtues of His personal character, and many other things, which, no less than His sufferings, contribute to our assurance that He truly was a messenger from God. And hence there does not seem to be any sufficient reason why they should be singled out from all the other incidents of His mission, and specially held forth as having that saving efficacy which the Word of God has uniformly ascribed to them.

II. Equally unsatisfactory is another view, which was

RESPECTING THE ATONEMENT.   289

much insisted on by old Socinian writers—namely, that
the beneficial influence of the death of Christ belongs to it
merely as a preparatory step towards His resurrection, by
which we have that sure evidence afforded us of a future
state of existence beyond the grave, which, more than any
other motive, prevails with us to forsake sin and to seek
the forgiveness of it by a sincere repentance.

This notion is not in any way to be reconciled with the
ordinary statements of Scripture on the subject. It is
indeed unquestionable that the Lord Jesus Christ behoved
first to die before He could rise again. But this is nowhere
assigned by the inspired writers as the chief ground on
which His death was necessary or beneficial. On the
contrary, they have constantly assigned to it a direct influence, *when considered in itself*, in the way of restoring
sinners to the divine favour, and thereby securing for them
the hope of everlasting life. Indeed, if all they meant to
tell us were the mere truism that " Christ could not rise
from the dead until He had first died," we cannot suppose
that they would have deemed it necessary by so many
solemn and emphatic statements to impress it upon us.

Besides, if the death of Christ were only to be regarded
as a preparatory step towards His resurrection, there was
no reason why He should have been subjected to a violent,
painful, and ignominious death. To have died anyhow—
in the ordinary course of nature, and in circumstances of
ease and honour—would have sufficed. The shame and
agony of the cross might have been spared. So far as
concerns a preparation for His revival, these were purely
gratuitous and utterly unaccountable.

But this is not all. The question lies behind, How
comes it to pass that the resurrection of Jesus, more than
the resurrection of Lazarus, or of the daughter of Jairus,
or of the son of the widow at Nain, should have that prominent interest and importance in the Christian system
which undoubtedly belong to it? There is no apparent
answer that can be given to this question that does not
imply our Lord's mediatorial character as the representative and substitute of sinners.

PART
III.
SEC. I.
——
Theory
that the
death of
Christ was
*a necessary
step to His
resurrec-
tion*, by
which we
are assured
of a future
life.

This view
irreconcil-
able with
Scripture.

Does not
account for
His death
being vio-
lent and
shameful.

Why is the
resurrec-
tion of
Christ
more im-
portant
than that
of Lazarus
and
others?

290 — REVIEW OF THEORIES

PART III. SEC. I.

It assures us that His sacrifice has been accepted.

I Cor. xv. 17.

One reason, on account of which the resurrection of Christ possesses a special claim to our regard, is the assurance it gives us that His great sacrifice has been accepted of, according to that memorable statement of the apostle, " If Christ be not raised, your faith is vain, ye are yet in your sins "—that is to say, you have no satisfactory proof that His death has made an effectual atonement for them. And I need scarcely remark that this reason necessarily assumes the vicarious and expiatory nature of His sufferings.

It is also a pledge of the resurrection of believers.

The only other reason that has ever been assigned, and doubtless a true reason, is, that the resurrection of Christ is the great pledge and earnest given to all believers of their own ultimate resurrection to eternal life. But we are at a loss to discover how it can be held to be so, except on the assumption of His mediatorial character. Apart from this, indeed, it could with even less propriety be so regarded than the resurrection of any ordinary human being ; for, when we consider that the Lord Jesus was essentially distinguished from all other men by His

But this it can only be if He was their representative.

pre-existence before He was born into this world, it were nothing remarkable that He should also be distinguished from them by returning to life again after He had been put to death. And hence, from the resurrection of a personage so far removed as He was from all comparison with ordinary mortals, no reasonable expectation could be derived that they also should be raised up, after His similitude, unless we suppose, according to the Scriptural doctrine, that He both died and rose from the dead as their representative.

Redemption ascribed in Scripture not to the resurrection but to the death of Christ.

Without insisting, however, on these considerations, it is sufficient to fall back on our former statement, that the theory in question is irreconcilable with any fair interpretation of the language of Scripture. The most cursory readers of the New Testament must be well aware that redemption and the remission of sin are there attributed, not to the resurrection of Christ, or to the moral effect which that great miracle is fitted to produce upon us, but expressly to His death. Now why should this be, if His

RESPECTING THE ATONEMENT.   291

death was only conducive to these blessings in an indirect, PART
remote, and circuitous manner? His death was not the III.
cause of His resurrection, however indispensable as a pre- SEC. I.
paration for it, and cannot be held, therefore, to have had ——
any causative influence in the way of procuring the benefits
arising from it. But even if His death had been the cause
of His resurrection, it is still not so closely or immediately
connected as is His resurrection, according to this theory,
with our attainment of the spiritual blessings of the Gospel. And yet we are asked to believe that the inspired
writers have expressed themselves in so inaccurate and
misleading a manner as constantly to ascribe these blessings, not to their proximate cause, but to that which was
more remotely concerned in the procuring of them. Assuredly this is not fairly to interpret, but forcibly to per-
vert, the plain meaning of the Scriptures.

III. It is equally unnecessary to dwell at any length on Theory of
the theory of *example*, by which some have endeavoured example.
to explain the statements of Scripture with reference to
our Lord's sufferings. For in dealing with those passages
in which the sufferings of Christ are unquestionably held
forth as an example to His people of the trials which they
may expect to meet with in their Christian course, and of
the manner in which these trials ought to be endured by
them, we have already had occasion to show—(1.) That *Supra*, p.
this aspect of our Lord's sufferings does not in any way 161-165.
disparage or conflict with their expiatory virtue, inasmuch
as they could not have been available as an atonement if
they had not at the same time been exemplary in the
highest degree, exhibiting in all respects a pattern of
suffering rectitude that was acceptable and well-pleasing
in the sight of God ; (2.) That whensoever they are set
forth as exemplary, there is no indication given that this
is the chief aspect, far less the sole aspect, in which they
are to be regarded—but clear evidence, on the contrary,
that it is only in a secondary sense and in an incidental
manner that they are thus referred to ; (3.) That in many
of the most striking of those passages in which the suffer-

292   REVIEW OF THEORIES

PART III. SEC. I.

ings of Christ are urged as an example, there is express allusion made to their atoning efficacy, even when such allusion lies most evidently beyond the immediate purpose for which they are appealed to ; and, (4.) That it is necessary to keep in view the vicarious and expiatory nature of our Lord's sufferings, in order to vindicate their perfection as an example, and to give any reasonable account of that exceeding depth of agony which He felt in the endurance of them, opposed, as far as could be, to the triumphant joy which many a human martyr has displayed when called to submit to tortures the most excruciating.

Those who lived before Christ, or who die in infancy, can have no benefit from Christ's example.

To these considerations we may now add the following : (5.) In so far as the sufferings of Christ were exemplary, no benefit could be derived from them by those who lived in ages prior to His advent, or by those who now die in infancy or at a period of life so immature as to be incapable of understanding and appreciating them ; and yet we have strong Scriptural evidence to assure us that the work of Christ was retrospective in its efficacy, and that infants and little children may be partakers of His saving grace.   (6.) And further, if His substitution in the room of sinners be denied, there is reason to fear that the subjection of One who was absolutely perfect and immaculate to the severest afflictions, with no guilt either of His own or of others to account for it, would grievously counteract any lessons of meekness, patience, and resignation to the will of God which might otherwise have been taught us by His example ; for, as has been shrewdly remarked, " His sufferings have a double aspect ; they affect our apprehension of Him who appointed them no less than of Him by whom they were endured, and give us but little encouragement to trust in the equity and benignity of the divine administration which thus visits perfect innocence with deeper woes than the foulest guilt in this world was ever subjected to."

His subjection to sufferings, if not as an atonement, counteract His example.

Greyson's Correspondence, Letter liv.

Theory that Christ suffered while

IV. Another view of the main purpose of that mission, in the prosecution of which our Lord's sufferings were endured, has been set forth by some opponents of the

RESPECTING THE ATONEMENT. 293

commonly-received doctrine in a manner, it must be
owned, highly interesting and attractive. Christ came,
they tell us, *as an incarnation of Deity*, to place before us,
in His own personal character and conduct, a much more
lively representation of the invisible God than could by
any mere doctrinal statements have been exhibited to us.
He came to satisfy those yearnings of the human heart
when feeling after God, if haply they might find Him,
which an apostle on one occasion expressed when he said
to Jesus, " Show us the Father, and it sufficeth us." It
was the grand object of His mission to "show us the
Father." By all the gracious words He uttered, and by
all the beneficent deeds He performed, while, as " God
manifest in the flesh," He dwelt among us, He was continually "showing us the Father." Going about, as He
ever did, doing good, notwithstanding all the affliction and
reproach to which in His labours of love He was subjected
—ready, as He ever was, to comfort the sorrowful, to pity
the wretched, to reclaim the erring, to rescue the lost, to
welcome the returning penitent,—He showed us, in the
warmth and fulness of His human sympathies, what manner of love His heavenly Father, of whose person He is
the express image, entertains toward us.

Now there is much truth in this representation—truth
that is very precious and very comforting, and which has,
it must be owned, been too much overlooked. For, apart
from its subserviency to the great scheme of human redemption, the incarnation of the Son of God possesses an
intrinsic importance, as exhibiting to us the adorable attributes of the divine character in the person of One who is
partaker of our own nature, and capable of being "touched
with the feeling of our infirmities."

But though there be truth here, it cannot be said to be
either the whole truth with reference to our Lord's mission,
or even that portion of the truth with which for the present we have to do. What we are concerned with is, not
the manifestation of tender compassion and loving-kindness which Christ displayed, but the ignominy and affliction beyond the common lot of humanity, to which, by the

*PART
III.
SEC. 1.*

manifest-
ing Deity
in human
form.

John, xiv.
8.

This the-
ory does
not touch
the real
point in
question.

294 REVIEW OF THEORIES

PART
III.
SEC. I.

determinate counsel of God, He was subjected, and from the endurance of which, even when He earnestly prayed that "if it were possible the cup might pass," He was not exempted. The question to be solved is, not how a life of beneficence, *in the course of which* the Son of God was visited with severe sufferings, should have manifested to us His heavenly Father's character,—but how that character should have been especially and pre-eminently manifested *in the very sufferings endured by Him?* And this question is not to be satisfactorily answered by any such mere reiteration of the thing to be proved, as seems to be the whole amount of the assertion, that to "show us the Father" was the grand purpose of His incarnation.

Christ's *sufferings* in themselves do not illustrate the nature of God.

Assuredly *His sufferings* cannot, in themselves considered, be held as illustrating the nature of that invisible God, who is necessarily exempt from human sorrows and infirmities. And, apart from their efficacy in securing the remission of sins, they tend to obscure, instead of heightening, any evidences of His Father's love which He has otherwise exhibited to us. For it might be not unnatural to conclude that the very circumstance of the most beneficent person who has ever appeared on earth being at the same time more than others a "man of sorrows"— afflicted not only with bodily sufferings the most severe, but with inward and spiritual agonies the most excruciating (and that, too, although, being perfectly immaculate, He neither deserved nor required chastening on His own account) was an indication that the great God who thus visited Him was much more disposed to frown than to smile on all the sympathy and kindness He displayed towards us.

Theory that the sufferings of Christ were a manifestation of the love of God.

V. Very much akin to the theory I have just noticed,— or perhaps, I should rather say, a special aspect of the same theory,—is that which is very earnestly maintained by a well-known school of modern theological writers— namely, *that the mediatorial work of Christ is exclusively to be regarded as a manifestation of the love of God;* in other words, that the purpose to be served by the humiliation and

RESPECTING THE ATONEMENT. 295

sufferings of the Saviour was, *not* to *remove any obstacle* which the sins of men have interposed in the way of their being reinstated in the favour of God ; but *to assure them that there is no such obstacle*, and thereby to induce them to cling with confiding affection to their kind and merciful Father, who, notwithstanding all their obduracy, is willing to receive them, and waiting to be gracious to them. These writers utterly deny the existence of any *objective* barrier in the shape of guilt or liability to condemnation, as opposing a sinner's return to friendship and fellowship with God ; and hold that there is no barrier except the *subjective* one of man's own unbelieving, self-willed, and sinful heart to keep him back from the conscious possession and joyful recognition of his heavenly Father's love. Accordingly, they maintain that the sufferings and death of Christ were not intended to expiate the guilt, or to exempt us from the merited penalties of our transgressions, but simply and solely to show us *that God loves us*, and thereby to subdue the enmity of our hearts against Him ; to disabuse our minds of those dark suspicions and distrustful apprehensions with which we are prone to regard Him ; and to give us the fullest assurance we could wish to have, " that there is a bond between Him and His creatures which no rebellion of theirs and no law of His could set aside."

Now, that the humiliation and sufferings of Jesus Christ *were* intended to manifest the love of God, we fully admit. But that they were intended, or that they were fitted to do so, *irrespective of any expiation of human guilt or satisfaction of divine justice effected by them*, we hold to be utterly inconsistent with the Scriptures ; and not only so, but to be, even on reasonable grounds, incapable of any satisfactory vindication.

The testimony of Scripture, with reference to this point, appears to me to be perfectly clear and unequivocal. Those numerous passages in which Christ is spoken of as " dying for our sins "—" taking away our sins "—" bearing our sins in His own body on the tree "—" shedding His blood for the remission of sins "—" putting away sin by

PART III.
SEC. I.

Maurice on Sacrifice, p. 209.

Sufferings of Christ are a manifestation of divine love only as being expiatory.

Scriptural evidence.

296   REVIEW OF THEORIES

PART III.
SEC. I.

the sacrifice of Himself "—" suffering for sins, the just for the unjust, that He might bring us to God "—" washing us from our sins in His own blood "—" giving His life a ransom for many "—" redeeming us from the curse of the law, by being made a curse for us ; "—these, and many other equally explicit passages, are altogether inconsistent with the notion that the sufferings of Christ were meant to assure us of the love of God, apart from any efficacy attributable to them in saving us from the guilt and penal consequences of our transgressions. Nay, it is remarkable that in some of the most striking passages in which the love of God is said to have been " manifested " or " commended to us " by the death of Christ, the *purpose* for which God gave His Son to die for us,—namely, that He

1 John, iv. 10.
Rom. v. 8. 9.
John, iii. 16.

might be " the propitiation for our sins "—that " we, being justified by His blood, might be saved from wrath through Him," and " that whosoever believeth in Him should not perish, but have everlasting life,"—is very distinctly and prominently referred to. And hence we must necessarily conclude that it is not in themselves considered, but in respect of the expiatory virtues belonging to them, and the consequent spiritual benefits accruing from them, that the humiliation and sufferings of Jesus Christ were meant to assure us of the love and grace of God.

The theory *unreason-able* as well as unscriptural.

But not to dwell on the testimony of Scripture, which is too clear to require further comment or illustration, let us judge of this theory on its own intrinsic merits, as professedly supplying a *more rational* explanation of the sufferings and death of the incarnate Son of God than is furnished by the commonly-received doctrine of the Atonement.

When so judging of it, we must carefully observe the precise nature of the case for which the theory is meant to account. The case we have to deal with is not that of a divine mission devolved upon the Son of God, to the discharge of which, His humiliation, sufferings, and death were merely *incidental.* It is that of a divine mission, in the discharge of which these things were, by appointment of God, indispensably required of Him, as of themselves

RESPECTING THE ATONEMENT. 297

constituting the most prominent and important part of the great work which His Father had given Him to do. Both He and His apostles represent them in this light, as "things which Christ ought to suffer,"—"things which it behoved Him to suffer,"—things which "God's hand and counsel had before determined to be done,"—a cup which His Father had given Him to drink, and which was not withdrawn, even when He prayed that "if it were possible this cup might pass from Him." And the Scriptures, as we have already seen, when speaking of the love of God as manifested by the mission of His only-begotten Son, dwell most of all, I may even say dwell exclusively, on the ignominy and anguish to which He was subjected.

Now, how should this be? How should the sufferings of Christ be thus prominently and emphatically proofs of His Father's love to us? If they were not in any respect directly efficacious in securing for us forfeited blessings, or in exempting us from merited penalties; if they were not in themselves instrumental in obtaining for us substantial benefits which could not otherwise have been enjoyed,— how then should we regard them as affording us an unparalleled manifestation of the love of God? Or how then could we derive from them any better ground of assurance than we previously had, that God is willing to be at peace with us?

Suppose—if it be possible to suppose anything so unnatural—that an earthly king should seek to conciliate his disaffected subjects by taking his beloved son, and depriving him of life before them, for no other than the avowed purpose of assuring the rebel multitude that his heart is full of clemency and kindness towards them— how would they be affected by such a spectacle? Can we imagine that it would have the intended effect? Even if the child were ever so willing a victim—cheerfully placing his life at his father's disposal—we cannot conceive that the taking away of that life, if no public benefit otherwise unattainable directly issued from the sacrifice, could, as an alleged proof of love towards the

PART III. SEC. I.

Luke, xxiv. 26, 46.
Acts, iv. 26.

Matt. xxvi. 39.

REVIEW OF THEORIES

PART III.
SEC. I.

rebels, have the slightest tendency to bring them back to their allegiance. Rather might we suppose it to have a tendency to confirm them in their alienation from a sovereign whose treatment of his own son was as far as possible from being indicative of a kindly and conciliatory disposition towards his subjects. In like manner I am utterly at a loss to see how the humiliation and sufferings of the Son of God should be held to manifest or commend His Father's love to us, if they were not the procuring cause of our deliverance from forfeitures and penalties which could not otherwise have been averted.

When God tells us in His Word that He so loved us as to give His own Son to suffer and to die for us, because—for reasons satisfactory to Himself, although He may not have fully explained them to us—this sacrifice was necessary to the extension of His mercy towards us consistently with the perfection of His character, the authority of His law, and the welfare of His universal government,—I can believe this, though I may not fully comprehend it; because *here* the mystery lies in the plans and counsels of the infinite God, which may well be expected to exceed my comprehension. And believing, on the authority of God, that for reasons which He deemed sufficient, although to us they may be in some respects unsearchable, this great sacrifice was necessary to man's salvation,—I can *then* see, in His not having withheld it, a marvellous proof of His love to a guilty world. But were we to be told that God gave His own Son to humiliation, sufferings, and death, without any alleged reasons for it in so far as God was Himself concerned, or any declared necessity for it as a means of extending mercy towards us consistently with the laws and principles of His moral government, but simply with a view to the *impression* which such a sacrifice might make upon the minds of sinners in regard to the fatherly love with which God is ever regarding them,—*this* I cannot believe; because *here*, instead of a mystery pertaining to the plans and counsels of the unsearchable God, in which more or

RESPECTING THE ATONEMENT. 299

less of mystery might be looked for, I find a *downright* PART
contradiction to my own consciousness in a matter that is SEC. I.
not in any respect mysterious, but, on the contrary, perfectly level to my comprehension ; inasmuch as my own
consciousness tells me that such procedure on the part
of God *has no tendency to produce upon my mind any such
impression of His love as is thus ascribed to it.* In a word,
the humiliation and sufferings and death of Christ are
well calculated to convince us of the love and grace of
our Father in heaven, when we view them as the means
of procuring for us spiritual blessings, which, for reasons
satisfactory to Himself, God did not deem it consistent
with His character, and law, and government, otherwise to
bestow. But if they were not the means of procuring for
us spiritual blessings which could not otherwise have been
conferred, I see not in what respect the endurance of them
by the Son of God (unnecessarily and gratuitously for any
good which to us accrues from them) can be viewed as
any such unparalleled demonstration of His Father's love
to sinful men as we are taught by the advocates of this
theory to regard it.

VI. The next theory on which I would offer a few Arian or
remarks is the *Arian,* or, as it is sometimes called, the middle
theory.
"*middle theory,*" because it occupies an intermediate place
between the views of the Socinians and the Catholic doctrine of the Atonement. It was ably advocated by Dr
Balguy, Mr Taylor, Dr Price, and other writers of the
last century. And an admirable review of it is given
by Principal Hill, of which the following observations are
a brief abstract.

According to this theory, Christ is not regarded as the Christ's
sufferings
eternal and consubstantial Son of God, but as the first and held to be
most glorious of created beings, who, prompted by love merely incidental to
and pity for our sinful race, generously interposed in our His perfect
behalf, and as a recompense for the services He performed obedience,
whereby
and the sufferings He endured in obedience to the will of He has
acquired
God, received power, after His resurrection from the dead, influence
to save penitent sinners from the merited consequences of which He

300　REVIEW OF THEORIES

PART III. SEC. I.

uses in behalf of sinners.

their iniquities. His death is not considered as a satisfaction to divine justice, or as a vicarious sacrifice for our sins, but simply as the culminating point of that perfect obedience by which the power and right have been earned by Him of recovering a lost world—of removing all the evils which sin had introduced—of raising men from death, which is the penalty of transgression—and of conferring the divine forgiveness and favour, and the hope of eternal life, on all sincere penitents.

This theory is not without some appearance of plausibility. It recognises, to a certain extent, the Saviour's mediatorship. It derives not a little seeming countenance from those texts in which God is said to have

Acts, v. 31. John, xvii. 2.

"exalted Jesus to give repentance unto Israel and forgiveness of sins," and to have "given Him power over all flesh, that He should give eternal life to as many as have been given to Him." It so far sustains the honour of the divine government, as not to extend pardon, even to the truly penitent, without respect to the merits of some being of a superior order. And it can plead the support of many analogous instances in the ordinary dealings of men with one another, in which privileges and favours are conferred on the undeserving, in consideration of great excellences possessed, or great services rendered, by those who are connected with them.

This theory involves Arian views of the person of Christ.

Plausible, however, as this theory may at first appear, there are some insuperable objections which may be urged against it. For example, it avowedly involves the Arian view of the person of Christ, and is irreconcilable with the doctrine of His supreme divinity, which necessarily precludes—if atonement be dispensed with—the supposition of His having acquired anyhow a greater degree of power or authority to save sinners than originally pertained to Him. Besides, it proceeds on a partial view of the facts of the case, as set forth in the statements of Scripture. For, though there are undoubtedly some passages of the New Testament which might, on the principles of this theory, be sufficiently explained, there are many others which do not at all comport with it ;—those, more

It proceeds on a partial view of the statements of Scripture.

RESPECTING THE ATONEMENT. 301

particularly, in which the Saviour's death is held forth not
merely as incidental and subsidiary to His perfect obedience, but as being directly conducive to our redemption ;
and those, also, in which it is expressly represented as a
"suffering for sins, the just for the unjust,"—a "putting
away of sin by the sacrifice of Himself,"—a "shedding of
His blood for the remission of sins,"—and as that " one
offering by which He hath perfected for ever them that
are sanctified."

Besides, while the power which Christ is held to have
acquired by that perfect obedience, in the course of which
He endured his sufferings, is prominently set forth as the
procuring cause of our salvation, *there is no specific reason
assigned for the sufferings themselves.* Their whole importance consists in the proof they afford of His thorough
devotedness. For anything that appears, exertions of another kind, to which no sufferings whatever were incidental,
might, if equally sincere and earnest, have merited the same
reward. And the Saviour might have no less effectually
earned the right of giving salvation to His people, although
in the arduous work He undertook His own life had been
saved, instead of being sacrificed. Accordingly, when His
sufferings are viewed as having been merely subsidiary to
His obedience, we feel ourselves at a loss to account for
the fitness of many of the things which He endured, and
to put any satisfactory construction on a great part of the
language of the New Testament with respect to them.

In addition to these arguments, which are substantially those of Dr Hill, I may further observe that this
notion of a prevailing influence acquired by the perfect obedience of our Saviour, and used by him as a
means of inducing God the Father to exempt sinners
from the merited penalties of transgression, appears to
be highly derogatory to the divine character. On the
one hand, it detracts from the divine justice. For it
represents God as dispensing with the penalties of sin
—not in consideration of any atonement made for it
by which the authority of His law and the rectitude
of His government might be maintained—but in con-

302 REVIEW OF THEORIES

PART III. SEC. I.

sideration of *personal influence prevailing with Him to set aside the claims of law and justice altogether.* On the other hand, it equally detracts from the divine mercy. For it supposes God to have been withheld from saving sinners until Christ generously interposed in their behalf—not by any regard to the claims of law and justice, for the maintenance of which He deemed it necessary, in the exercise of His boundless love and grace, to make provision—but by some such *personal reluctance to have mercy on them* as could only be overcome by the intervention of another Being, more compassionate than Himself, whose influence with Him was all-prevailing. I need scarcely add that the notion of there having been any *reluctance* on the part of God to save sinners, requiring the *personal influence* of another being to overcome it, is utterly opposed to the express testimony of His Word. For if there be one thing with reference to the scheme of redemption more clearly affirmed in Scripture than another, it is that this scheme originated with God the Father, who " so loved the world that He gave His only-begotten Son to be the propitiation for our sins."

John, iii. 16.
1 John, iv. 10.

SECTION II.

(7) REALISTIC THEORIES.

VII. IN further reviewing the attempts which have been made to account for the sufferings and death of Jesus Christ, apart from the commonly - received doctrine of the Atonement, we must now shortly notice the *Realistic view*, which is taken by some modern theologians, of the Saviour's connection with those whom He has redeemed.

PART III. SEC. 2.

Realistic theory,

1. The chief supporter of this notion is Mr Maurice. He holds it, indeed, in combination with other views of the mediatorial work of Christ, to be afterwards examined. But it will be found by a discerning reader of his voluminous works to underlie the opinions he has advanced with reference not only to the Atonement, but to almost every other department of Christian doctrine.

as set forth by Maurice.

Thus, when speaking of the creation, he represents God as first of all creating the several *species* of herbs, fishes, beasts, and other things animate or inanimate, and afterwards as bringing into existence the several individuals belonging to these species.

"First of all, 'God made *man* in His own image;' *afterwards*, it is said, He made *a* 'man out of the dust of the ground, and breathed into *his* nostrils the breath of life.' If we follow the letter of these passages, and do not endeavour to put any notions of our own into them, we shall be led naturally to the conclusion, that the former words have to do with the *species*, and the latter with an *individual* —namely, the first man of the race." "The part of the record which speaks of man *ideally*, according to his place with reference to the rest of the universe, and according to his position with reference to God, is the part which expressly belongs to the history of the *creation*. The bringing forth of man in *this* sense is the work of the sixth day."

Maurice's Sermons on the Patriarchs of the Old Testament p. 3-6.

REVIEW OF THEORIES

PART
III.
SEC. 2.

" Extend this thought, which seems to arise inevitably out of the story of the creation of man, as Moses delivers it, to the rest of that universe of which man is the climax, and we are forced to the conclusion that in the one case, as in the other, it is not the visible material thing of which the historian is speaking, but that which lies below the visible material thing, and constitutes the substance which it shows forth." Comparing with the history of the creation in Genesis, i., what is said in Genesis, ii. 5, 6, he says : " We are compelled to consider the creation of herbs and flowers, as well as the creation of beasts, birds, and fishes, which is recorded in the first chapter, as the bringing forth of *kinds* and *orders*, such as they were, according to the mind of God,—not of actual separate phenomenal existences, such as they present themselves to the senses of man." Subsequently he affirms, as might have been expected, that the days of creation spoken of in the beginning of Genesis " refer not to real, but to ideal time ;" or rather, that the whole ideal creation there recorded " is lifted out of the sphere of actual events into that region which is above time, or change, or succession—in other words, that it took place in eternity."

In conformity with this view of an ideal creation of *species* or *orders* anterior to the creation of individual objects, Mr Maurice represents the Son of God as *the ideal man, the root and archetype from eternity of all mankind.*

Unity of New Testament, p. 219, 220, 367.

Thus, he says, " When Christ utters the words, ' Inasmuch as ye did it to one of the least of these, ye did it to me,' He proclaimed that which is *the very truth of human existence.* He actually is *one with every man.* He is come to proclaim that He is so by His incarnation and death." " I look upon Christ's death and resurrection as revelations of the Son of God, *in whom all things had stood from the first, in whom God had looked on His creature man from the first.*"

Doctrine of Sacrifice, Introduction, p. xxi, xxiv.

" The Son was really in Saul of Tarsus ; and he only became Paul the converted when that Son was *revealed* in him." " Christ is in every man. . . . All may call upon God as a reconciled Father. Human beings are redeemed,—not in consequence of any act they have done, or of any faith they have exercised. Their faith is to be grounded on a foregone conclusion ; their acts are to be the fruits of a state they already possess." " The Gospel with which St Paul was intrusted was good news to men, not of something that was coming to them, but of *their actual state*, of that state which belongs to them, but which they do not recognise." " Christ was *the original man*, the *type of all creation ;* as it is expressed in the Epistle to the Colossians, ' The first-born of every creature.' Now (on becoming incarnate) He assumes the condition of individual men ; He puts on the fleshy accidents which belonged to them, as He had before stood to them in the closest spiritual relation." " St Paul takes it for

Unity of New Testament, p. 537.

Doctrine of Sacrifice, p. 221.

RESPECTING THE ATONEMENT. 305

granted that this justification of the Son of God (when He was
raised from the dead) was *his own* justification,—his own, not because he was a Hebrew of the Hebrews, but because "he was a
man." "God, having justified His Son by raising Him from the dead,
did in that *act justify the race for which Christ died,* so that it is law-
ful to tell men that they are justified before God, and are the sons
of God in the only-begotten Son. . . . Christ was the actual
Mediator between God and man ; His resurrection declared that God
confessed Him in that character, and thereby confessed men to be
righteous in Him ; if not, baptism would be a nullity." "St Paul's
baptism denoted that he was claiming his relation to the Son of God,
the Head of the whole human race. It must import his belief that
this Son of God, and not Adam, was the true root of humanity; that
from Him, and not from any ancestor, each man derived his life."

PART
III.
SEC. 2.
Theologi-
cal Essays,
p. 199-
203.

Such is the representation of the Son of God, as the
archetypal man, the germ or root of humanity, which
underlies all the statements of Mr Maurice respecting the
mediatorial work of Jesus Christ and the spiritual privileges and benefits resulting from it. According to this
view, the Son of God sustains the office of mediator
between God and man, not in virtue of any dispensation
of grace which the fall of man had rendered necessary,
but from eternity, and in virtue of what may be called His
natural and aboriginal relationship to both the parties.
By His incarnation He did but outwardly manifest that
identity which had ever subsisted between Himself and
man, exhibiting the ideal perfection of man's nature. And
by reason of this identity all men, as being one with Him,
participate in the benefits of His mediation. In Him they
are redeemed, regenerated, justified, and adopted as sons
and heirs of God, and all this without any reference to
their faith in Him. The faith of believers has nothing
whatever to do in the way of uniting them to Christ, and
of thereby making them partakers of His benefits, its only
function being to discern Christ as already one with them,
and to recognise His benefits as already fully pertaining
to them.

(1.) Now it is very evident that this theory of Mr Maurice
is to be regarded rather as a philosophical speculation
than as a Scriptural doctrine. He seems rather to bring
it with him to the Scriptures, than by any fair exposition

This the-
ory is a
philoso-
phical spe-
culation,

REVIEW OF THEORIES

PART III. SEC. 2.

not a Scriptural doctrine.

to take it from the Scriptures. And any appearance of Scriptural authority which now and then he is fain to claim for it is, I venture to say, of the slenderest possible kind. Nothing, for instance, can be more groundless than his assertion that in the first chapter of Genesis "it is only an *ideal* creation that is referred to;" inasmuch as the narrative evidently records the *actual* creation of the first

Gen. i. 27, 28.

progenitors of the human race, the words being—"so God created man in His own image; in the image of God created He him; *male and female created He them; and God blessed them, and God said unto them, Be fruitful, and multiply, and replenish the earth, and subdue it,*" &c. Equally unwarranted by Scriptural proof is his other assertion that "the Son of God, and not Adam, was the true root of humanity." Nay rather, it seems to be flatly

1 Cor. xv. 45, 46.

opposed to the apostle's statement, that "the *first* man Adam was made a living soul, the *last* Adam was made a quickening spirit; howbeit, that was not first which is spiritual, but that which is natural, and afterward that

Gal. i. 16.

which is spiritual." Farther, when Paul says, "It pleased God to reveal His Son in me," Mr Maurice rushes at once to the conclusion that *the Son of God was in Saul of Tarsus from the first*, although Saul was not aware of His being in him until his own eyes were opened to discern Him—a conclusion which no commentator that I know of has ever thought of drawing from the apostle's statement.

Matt. xxv. 40.

Again, says Mr Maurice, "When Christ utters these words, 'Inasmuch as ye did it to one of the least of these, ye did it to me,' Christ proclaimed that which is the very truth of human existence—namely, *that He is actually one with every man.*" Here Mr Maurice omits two important words—the words "*my brethren,*" which occur after the word "these," and which limit the oneness which our Lord speaks of to *those who are* His brethren, instead of extending it indiscriminately to "every man."

These instances are a fair specimen of the kind of exegesis by which Mr Maurice endeavours to extract from the Scriptures something like support to his preconceived opinions. And they are all the more remarkable

RESPECTING THE ATONEMENT. 307

when we contrast them with the cool and sweeping manner in which he is ready to set aside the most explicit declarations of Holy Scripture respecting the vicarious and propitiatory nature of our Lord's sufferings.

PART III. SEC. 2.

(2.) It cannot be said that this theory has any advantage over the Catholic doctrine, which it is meant to supersede, as being in any respect more reasonable or intelligible; for certainly it is abstruse and mystical in the highest degree. It does not indicate any perceptible bond of union between the Saviour and those who are benefited by His mediation. No such bond of union can be found in the vague representation that is given of the Son of God as "the root of man," or the "archetype of humanity," even if the fact of His being so were a revealed truth, instead of being a mere metaphysical speculation.

Has no advantage over the common view, as being more reasonable.

With some appearance of plausibility, perhaps, it might be said that the Son of God is the archetype of *unfallen* humanity, inasmuch as He is "the image of the invisible God," "the express image of His person," while man also is said to have been "created after the image of God." But with no propriety can the Son of God be considered as standing in the same relation to humanity in its fallen state; for the image of God, as originally impressed on man, has by the Fall been distorted and defaced, so that he no longer answers to his archetype. In respect of everything that truly constitutes the moral rectitude and excellence of the Son of God, mankind, as we now find them prior to their conversion, are so far from being "*one* with Him," or from being entitled to claim identity or conformity with Him, that they are essentially opposite to Him, and alienated from Him. It behoves them, according to the express statements of Scripture, to be "created anew after the image of God in righteousness and true holiness," in order to be conformed to the Son of God. And to speak, therefore, of the Son of God as the archetype of all men without distinction in their fallen state, not excepting those who are most of all tainted with the pollutions and enslaved in the bondage of sin, appears

Christ is certainly not the archetype of *fallen* men.

308   REVIEW OF THEORIES

PART III.
SEC. 2.

Even if He were, there is no intelligible bond of union between Christ and those who are benefited by Him.

In the evangelical doctrine there is a bond of union—namely, *faith.*

to me to be unreasonable and unscriptural in the highest degree.

But even were the case otherwise, I am utterly at a loss to discover in the alleged fact of His being " the original archetype of humanity," any intelligible ground on which it can be held that all the Father's dealings with Him, and all His dealings with the Father, must necessarily redound to the benefit of each and every individual of the human race, irrespective of anything *done in us or by us* that might bring us as personal agents into union or communion with Him. I scarcely think any man will say that he has a consciousness or an inward conviction of any such thing as that " he and the Son of God are actually one," or that " the Son of God is the root of his manhood," in such a sense that whatever is done *by* the Son of God is done *by* himself, and whatever is done *to* the Son of God is done *to* himself—that the self-sacrifice of the Son of God is the self-sacrifice of all humanity, and that the justification of the Son of God, when He was raised from the dead, is the justification of each and every man ! For this identification of the Son of God, either with all men collectively or with each man individually, there is no ground in the nature of things that is assignable or conceivable.

The case is very different in this respect with the evangelical doctrine as commonly received among us. Whatever there may be that passes our comprehension in the justification and adoption of believers through faith in the merits and grace of the Redeemer, it cannot be charged with any such want of connection between the parties severally concerned in procuring and in receiving the benefits, as marks the theory to which I have just adverted. For while, on the one hand, the Son of God has undertaken, in conformity with the gracious purpose of His heavenly Father, to assume the human nature and become obedient unto death, that whosoever believeth on Him may be justified, adopted, and blessed with all spiritual blessings ; it is, on the other hand, provided and required that those who are actually to be benefited by His mediation must personally receive Him, and rest

RESPECTING THE ATONEMENT. 309

upon Him as their Saviour. Their faith unites them to
Him, or secures their interest in Him. It does so in a
manner that is perfectly simple and intelligible, as implying in its very nature their trustful and hearty acceptance
of Him. And no benefits actually accrue to them from
His mediation, until they have thus been brought into
connection with Him by the exercise of an appropriating
and confiding faith.

We are told, indeed, that "faith does not make the fact
of our redemption, but rests upon it as previously existing;
and that without the previous existence of it our faith
would be unmeaning and false." This objection, however,
proceeds on an utter misconception of the proper function
and province of faith. In truth, it confounds faith with
assurance. To *recognise our interest in Christ*, which doubtless implies its prior attainment, is what has been usually
called the "reflex act of faith," as distinguished from what
must be viewed as its "direct act." The proper object of
faith is, not the fact that *we are partakers of the benefits of
redemption*, but the revealed truth that *Christ is able and
willing to make us so.* And the proper office of faith is,
not to recognise His benefits *as already actually put into
our possession*, but to "receive and rest upon Him alone
for salvation, as He is offered to us in the Gospel," *in order
that His benefits may thus come into our possession*, by no
other than the perfectly simple and intelligible process
of trustfully receiving Him with all His benefits for our
behoof.

(3.) But while the theory of Mr Maurice is thus defective,
as indicating no intelligible bond of union between the
Saviour and those to whom His blessings are communicated, it is further objectionable on the much more serious
ground of its contrariety to the plain teaching of the Word
of God. For if there be one thing more distinctly and
unequivocally declared in Scripture than another, it is that
the benefits of redemption are not conferred on all men
prior to, and irrespective of, their faith. It is most certain,
indeed, that they are *freely offered to all;* and hence by
some it has been plausibly, although I think unwarrant-

*PART
III.
SEC. 2.*

This the-
ory con-
trary to
Scripture.

310 REVIEW OF THEORIES

PART
III.
SEC. 2.
——

John, iii.
16, 18.

John, xx.
31.

Acts, xiii.
39.

Rom. v. 1,
2; x. 4.

ably, concluded, that in the secret purpose of God they are *intended* for all : but that they are *actually imparted* to all, it is impossible to maintain, without setting the doctrine of the New Testament at utter defiance ; for it is there written : " God so loved the world that He gave His only-begotten Son, that *whosoever believeth in Him* should not perish, but have everlasting life ; " "*He that believeth* in Him is not condemned ; but he that believeth not is condemned already, because he hath not believed in the name of the only-begotten Son of God ; " " These are written that ye might believe that Jesus is the Christ, the Son of God, and that *believing ye might have life* through His name ; " " By Him *all that believe are justified* from all things, from which ye could not be justified by the law of Moses ; " " Being *justified by faith*, we have peace with God through our Lord Jesus Christ ; by whom also we *have access by faith into this grace wherein we stand ;* " " Christ is the end of the law for righteousness to every one that believeth."

These Scriptural testimonies render it abundantly clear that there is no indiscriminate elevation of the whole human family to the enjoyment of those blessings and privileges which the mediatorial work of the Saviour has procured ; but that, on the contrary, the enjoyment of them is restricted to those who are united to Him by faith, and who prove themselves to be so by that personal conformity to Him, of which a true faith is invariably productive.

This theory, even if true, would not explain the beneficial effects of the sufferings of Christ.

(4.) But this is not all. For even were it admitted that " Christ is actually one with every man," as the veritable " root and archetype of humanity," this, though it might in some degree account *for our participation* in any beneficial results which may be supposed to arise from His sufferings, would leave us without any definite conception, either of the particular nature of these results, or of the manner in which His sufferings are conducive to the attainment of them. The question would still recur, How is it that they with whom Christ as their " root and archetype " is thus united are " reconciled to God by His death,"

RESPECTING THE ATONEMENT. 311

and obtain "redemption and forgiveness of sins through His blood"? And still would there be room for giving to this question the plain and explicit answer which the Scriptures have returned to it—namely, that "He bore our sins in His own body on the tree;" that "He suffered for sins, the just for the unjust;" that "Christ was once offered to bear the sins of many," being "wounded for our transgressions and bruised for our iniquities."

Mr Maurice, indeed, has given to this question another answer. He holds that the reconciling or saving efficacy of the work of Christ arises, not from any expiation of human guilt that was rendered by it, but simply from *"the illustration which it affords of the great principle of self-sacrifice as due from all God's intelligent creatures to Him who made them."* That this answer is by no means satisfactory we shall endeavour to show in our next Section. But for the present we must be content to say, that it comes far short of the doctrine of the Word of God, which we have already sought to ascertain by a full induction of the statements of Holy Scripture on the subject.

2. We must now advert to a somewhat different phase of the realistic theory of the Atonement, which is held by some modern German theologians, and is not without its supporters both in England and in America. No fairer exposition of it can be given than by quoting the following words of Dean Alford, one of the most distinguished of its advocates :—

> "The offering of the body of Jesus Christ, what was it? And what was He, that such an offering should in any sense suffice for our cleansing and healing? He is in fashion as a man—He is our brother—He is like one of us. But is He one of us? Is He *a man?* Has He that personality of an individual man, which you and I bear, and by virtue of which we must carry our own human burden, and cannot make agreement with God for another? No; this Victim is not *a man*. He has not a human *person*, He has *but one personality;* and in that personality He is *the Son of God*, the eternal and glorious second person of the Godhead. No other person was united to this. The Son of God did not become *a* man. . . . The death of Jesus was not vicarious in the sense of *one man suffering for another*, which would be most repugnant to God's justice, as reflected in the

[margin: PART III. SEC. 2.]

[margin: Realistic theory as set forth by Alford]

[margin: Alford's Sermons preached in Quebec Chapel in 1854, p. 242-245.]

REVIEW OF THEORIES

PART
III.
SEC. 2.

consciences of us all. But, you will ask, was not that Victim truly MAN, very man as we are? Yes, blessed be God, He was the Man Christ Jesus; and yet, I repeat, He was not *a man*. He took upon Him not a human personality, so that He should be two persons, God and *a* man at the same time; but He took into union with His divine person and nature *the manhood*, the entire nature of man—the one nature and flesh and blood, and capacities and sympathies of a human soul. And thus He was God manifest in the flesh; very God, as being in person, and essence, and nature, the eternal Son of the Father,—and very man, as being born into the world of a reasonable soul and human flesh subsisting. What then, let us inquire, is that body of Christ which is hanging, pierced and torn, upon the cross? If it were *my* body, it would be the body of *a* man; and supposing that its being offered up would be of any use to me in expiating my own sins, there the benefit would stop; I am hedged about by my own individuality, and the sacrifice of *me* could never pass over to another, nor be set down to another's account. But that Victim had no human individuality. That body did not belong to *one man*, hereafter to be summoned to give account of himself to God, and separated in that account from all his fellow-men; but it belonged to the Son of God, our Maker and our Redeemer, who was pleased to reveal Himself in it for our redemption; and it was not the body of *a man*, but the body of MAN—of mankind—the pattern, and centre, and root, and head of that nature which is common to all of us, and in which every human being, of all nations, kindreds, and languages, has a share. Thus, the flesh of Christ is HIS flesh, as He is God; the property and tabernacle of God, in a peculiar manner His own. But in it He has no *human* property; the *human property* in it is vested in all the sons and daughters of Adam; it is *my* flesh, and *your* flesh, and the flesh of *all of us*, as we are men; the common property of us all, so that in it we are summed up and represented; and when it was offered up, *we* were offered up; 'if one died for all, then all died' (2 Cor. v. 14). And so, when that Victim hung upon the cross, it was not the slaying of one mere man for another, which is impossible; nor was it a mere symbolic sacrifice, like those under the old law; but it was the offering up of HUMAN NATURE in its head and root,—a taking away of sin by its penalty being paid to the uttermost. . . . And what was the *effect* of this sacrifice on the cross— the immediate and universal effect of it? At once, human nature, our manhood, all mankind, was in the sight of the Father acquitted from the guilt of sin, and received into His favour."

The fact is admitted that Christ's humanity is not a human person.

Now, as to the fact on which this theory proceeds, it is fully admitted by those who are generally regarded as orthodox believers in the doctrine of the Incarnation. All such maintain that, when the Son of God became incarnate, He did not unite Himself to a *human person*, or in

RESPECTING THE ATONEMENT. 313

other words, that the humanity which He assumed into
union with His divine nature and personality, *had no dis-*
tinct personal subsistence. And from this fact they have
usually drawn a very important inference, bearing on the
worth and efficacy of His Atonement—namely, that "although it was only in respect of His human nature that
the God-man was capable of suffering, yet *the sufferer* was,
not the less on that account, *the Divine Person* by whom
that nature was assumed, and to whom it has ever pertained since the time of His assumption of it."

Very different, however, is the inference which Dean
Alford draws from this admitted fact. He argues from it,
not that the sufferings of our Immanuel, endured by Him
in His human nature, may properly be attributed to the
Divine Person by whom that human nature was assumed,
but that these sufferings are attributable to each and every
individual of the human race, as having been endured by
One who had taken upon Him that common nature of
which all of them are alike partakers. Now there are some
very palpable fallacies in the reasoning by which he seeks
to bring us to this conclusion.

(1.) We are told that "the flesh of Christ is HIS flesh,
as He is God ; but that He has no human property in it ;
the human property in it is vested in all the children of
Adam : it is *my* flesh, and *your* flesh, and the flesh of *all*
of us, as we are men." Surely this argument is altogether
inconclusive. If Christ "had no human property in His
flesh," in respect of His not having a human personality
in which such a "human property in it" could be vested,
the inference to be thence drawn is, not that "you, and
I, and all men have this human property in the Saviour's
flesh belonging to us," but *that there is no "human property"*
in the Saviour's flesh belonging to any human person whom-
soever ; or, in other words, that His flesh *is altogether a*
divine possession, belonging exclusively to the Son of God
Himself. Assuredly the fact that there was not resident
in "the flesh of Christ" any human person who can be
held to have been *its human owner,* is an utterly insufficient
ground for ascribing the human ownership of it to *you,*

PART
III.
SEC. 2

Alford's
inference
from this
fact is fal-
lacious.

314 REVIEW OF THEORIES

PART III. SEC. 2.

and to *me*, and to each and all of Adam's race, who, though certainly human persons, had just as certainly no personal connection with "the flesh of Christ," and the vast majority of whom were not even in existence at the time when those things were done and suffered in it by the Son of God which are available for our salvation.

(2.) Again, we are told of the Son of God, when He became incarnate, that "He had no human individuality;" "His body did not belong to *one* man; it was not the body of a Man, but of mankind;" "He took into union with His divine person and nature the manhood, the entire nature of man;" and "His flesh was the common property of us all, so that in it we are summed up and represented; and when it was offered up, *we* were offered up."

Now, it is doubtless no easy matter to order our speech aright on a subject so mysterious. We may, however, venture to affirm that the above statements, in the sense that seems to be intended by those who use them, are not in accordance with the doctrine of Holy Scripture. That doctrine we hold to be that "the Son of God became Man by taking to Himself a true body and a reasonable soul." The body which He assumed was *one* individual body, and the soul was *one* individual soul; and as such they were perfectly separate and distinct from the bodies and souls of men which existed around Him while He dwelt on earth, and no less so from the bodies and souls which had ceased to exist in this world before His advent, and from those which did not come into existence until after His ascension into heaven. It is true, "His manhood was the entire nature of mankind" in such a sense as to include in it, though without sin, all the essential attributes of humanity. But it was not "the entire nature of mankind" in such a sense that "all mankind were summed up in it." The Son of God, when He became man, did not become *all men*. His human nature was *generically* that of all men, but it was not and could not be so *numerically*. To say that He took upon Him "the whole of humanity" so

RESPECTING THE ATONEMENT. 315

as to be a sort of *universal man*, summing up in Himself
all the sons and daughters of Adam, appears to be, not
only an unscriptural, but an unintelligible proposition. I
can well understand that there should be a moral or
spiritual oneness of the Saviour with all believers, when
by faith they receive Him and identify themselves with
Him, so as to "know the fellowship of His sufferings," and
"thus to judge that if One died for all, then all died."
But that all men, whether believers or unbelievers, are
physically or metaphysically one with Him, so that when
He was offered as a victim, *we all* were offered as being
summed up in Him, and universal humanity was nailed
in Him to the Cross, is a statement to which, the more I
try to reflect upon it, I am the less able to attach any definite meaning.

(3.) Further, we are told that "the immediate and universal effect of our Lord's sacrifice was that at once human
nature, our manhood, all mankind, was in the sight of the
Father acquitted from the guilt of sin and received into
His favour."

There is here a quiet assumption, to which we might
justly demur, that "human nature"—abstract and imper-
sonal "human nature"—is equivalent to "all mankind,"—
that is to say, to all those individual persons who partake
of the characteristic properties of "human nature."

Waiving this, however, the conclusion here arrived at
respecting "the effect of our Lord's sacrifice," is utterly unwarranted by the premises from which it is drawn. Christ,
the God-Man, was certainly the *divine* owner of that human
soul and body which He offered up. And if, as not being
a human *Person*, He cannot be held to have had any
"*human* property in them," this is no reason for concluding
that "a human property in them" appertains to you, or
to me, or to any or all of Adam's race, with whose souls
and bodies they certainly are not identical, so as to make
us personally the owners of them. Still less is it any
valid reason for concluding that you or I, or any or all of
Adam's race, who had no personal concern in offering up

PART
III.
SEC. 2.

316 REVIEW OF THEORIES

PART
III.
SEC. 2
——

our Lord's sacrifice, should "immediately and universally obtain the blessings which it has procured." " I am hedged about," says Alford, "by my own individuality, so that the sacrifice of *me* could never pass over to another, nor be set down to another's account." But surely, if the "hedge of individuality" which thus incloses me must necessarily prevent the *outgoing from me* of the benefits of any sacrifice which *I* might offer, it must equally prevent the *incoming to me* of the benefits of any sacrifice, by whomsoever offered and of whatsoever consisting, in which I, the "hedged-about individual," had as a personal agent or personal sufferer no concern.

(4.) It is unnecessary, however, to dwell on these subtleties ; for the theory against which we are contending is liable to an objection much more palpable, and at the same time much more weighty, than any of those that have yet been advanced against it, as being at variance with what appears to be the clear and unequivocal doctrine of Holy Scripture.

We are nowhere taught in Scripture that the human soul and human body of our Lord belonged, either *de facto* or *de jure*, to all mankind, to the effect that all mankind were offered up when the soul and body of Christ were offered up in sacrifice. On the contrary, we find them uniformly claimed by our Saviour as belonging to Himself alone. And as such they are spoken of as *offered by Him* FOR *sinners*, and not as *the property of sinners*, presented by Him in their name. " I give *my* flesh," He says, " for the life of the world." " This is *my* body broken for you." " His own self bare our sins *in His own* body on the tree." "We are sanctified through the offering of *the body of Jesus Christ* once for all."

John, vi.
51.
1 Cor. xi.
24.
1 Pet. ii.
24.
Heb. x. 10.

As little are we taught in Scripture that " all mankind are at once acquitted from the guilt of sin and received into the favour of God, as the immediate and universal effect of our Lord's sacrifice." On the one hand, these benefits of Christ's sacrifice are not " immediate;" for faith on the part of their recipients must intervene before the

RESPECTING THE ATONEMENT. 317

benefits are actually partaken of. On the other hand, the PART III.
benefits are not "universal;" for many, through lack of SEC. 2.
that faith by which they are received, are never put into
possession of them at all. I need only refer, in confirma- *Supra*,
tion of this objection, to those express Scriptural testi- P. 310.
monies which have been already adduced against the
Realistic theory as set forth by Mr Maurice.

318   REVIEW OF THEORIES

SECTION III.

(8) THEORY OF "SELF-SACRIFICE."

PART
III.
SEC. 3.
———
Theory of
Self-sacri-
fice.

VIII. WE now proceed to the consideration of what may be called the theory of *self-sacrifice*, which holds that the purpose of our Lord's sacrifice was not to make any expiation for the sins of men, but simply "to illustrate the principle of self-sacrifice, as due from all God's intelligent creatures to Him who made them, and as constituting their true dignity and excellence as moral beings."

This theory, when considered by itself, is only a particular aspect of the theory of *example*, which we have already found to be indefensible; although, as we shall in the sequel endeavour to show, it is liable to some additional objections peculiar to itself. Mr Maurice, however, who is its chief supporter, has combined with it his realistic views of the Son of God, as "the archetype of humanity." For in some passages of his 'Theological Essays,' and other writings, he speaks of the sufferings of Christ, not only as "a great pattern and example of self-sacrifice," but as an actual "offering up of man to God as an acceptable sacrifice;" although he always maintains that this acceptable sacrifice was nothing more than an offering of *self-devotion*, and was not in any respect a satisfaction for the sins of men.

Maurice's
Theologi-
cal Essays,
p. 141, 147,
148.

"The Gospel," he says, "brings divine love and human suffering into direct and actual union. It shows Him, who is one with God and one with man, perfectly giving up that self-will which had been the cause of all men's crimes and of all their misery. Here is indeed a Brazen Serpent, to which one dying from the bite of the old serpent can look and be healed." "The Father's will is a will to all good. The Son obeys, and fulfils in our flesh that will by entering into the

RESPECTING THE ATONEMENT.   319

lowest condition into which men had fallen through their sin. For
this reason He is an object of continual complacency to His Father,
and that complacency is fully drawn out by the death of the cross.
His death is a sacrifice—the only complete sacrifice ever offered ; "
not, however, as expiating the guilt or exempting from the penalties
of sin, but as *" the entire surrender of the whole spirit and body to
God."* " The cross is thus the meeting-point between man and man,
between man and God.   In it all the wisdom and truth and glory of
God were manifested to the creature ; and in it man is presented as
a holy and acceptable sacrifice to God."

PART
III.
SEC. 3

Mr Maurice holds, in common with Dr Bähr, whose
views on this subject we have elsewhere controverted, that
the true Scriptural idea of sacrifice is nothing else than
self-surrender or *self-devotion*. Of this, he maintains, all
the animal oblations which were offered with the divine
approval prior to the advent of Christ are merely to be
regarded as symbolical representations. And Christ's own
sacrifice was but a perfect exemplification of it, consisting in an entire and unqualified submission to the will
of God.

Supra, p. 234-238

Now, that the mediatorial work of Jesus Christ, with all
the humiliation and suffering involved in it, is the most
glorious instance of self-sacrificing devotedness that ever
has been exhibited to the world, and that, as such, it is
well fitted by divine grace to induce all those who are
partakers of its benefits to " live no longer to themselves,
but to the Lord," is a truth which, so far from seeking to
dispute, we fully acknowledge. But that it can be regarded as possessing this character or as exercising this
influence apart from those gracious ends to which it was
conducive, as an expiation of human guilt and a satisfaction to divine justice, appears to me to be a position
which, on reasonable and Scriptural grounds, is equally
indefensible.

Self-sacrifice — understanding by that expression the
giving up of our own will, the surrender of our own interests, and the renunciation of our own comforts and en-
joyments — cannot be said to be, *in itself considered*, or
purely for its own sake, dutiful and commendable. We
may say of it what Paul has said of zeal. " It is good,"

Self-sacri-
fice is not
dutiful or
commend-
able for its
own sake.

320   REVIEW OF THEORIES

PART III. SEC. 3.

says the apostle, "to be zealously affected *in a good thing.*" Even so, it is good to be self-sacrificing for a good purpose. If our own inclinations point to what is evil, it is evidently our duty to renounce them. Or if the denial of them, even with respect to things that are not in their own nature sinful, be conducive to certain pious or beneficent purposes, which would be retarded or frustrated by their gratification, it is here also incumbent on us to keep them under restraint. But surely it is not for a moment to be imagined that it is either a necessary or a proper thing to cross and thwart our own inclinations *for the mere sake of so doing,* and where there is neither anything evil in the indulgence of them, nor anything good to be secured by their mortification. To suppose that God is pleased with self-sacrifice, simply *for its own sake,* or *because it is self-sacrifice*—and without reference to any ulterior ends of a wise and beneficent nature that are to be promoted by it —would be to put Him on a level with Baal, whose votaries sought to please him by cutting themselves with knives and lancets ; or with other capricious and cruel divinities of the heathen, whose worship in a great measure consisted of self-inflicted tortures and aimless penances and austerities.

God does not require it except for wise and good ends.

It is true that God requires all His intelligent creatures to surrender their own will unreservedly to His will. But then His will is never arbitrary or capricious. And though we may not always be able to discern the reasons or ends He has in view in His requirements, we may be perfectly sure that they are the wisest and the best. His will, to which He requires us to submit, is never put forth in the way of needlessly and aimlessly thwarting the inclinations of His creatures, but always in the way of prescribing to them such things as are wise, just, holy, and beneficial. In some cases it may be in the discharge of our own duty, or in the furtherance of our own spiritual interests, that this self-surrender or self-sacrifice may be required of us ; in other cases it may be with a view to promote either the temporal or the spiritual welfare of our fellow-creatures. And in all cases, whether we perceive it or not, we may

RESPECTING THE ATONEMENT. 321

be very sure that God has good reasons for everything He
prescribes ; and that as often as self-sacrifice is exacted by
Him, it is not for its own sake, but with an ulterior view
to those wise and holy and beneficent ends which are promoted by it.

PART
III.
SEC. 3.

Now, to apply these remarks to the case before us, I
need scarcely observe that, in so far as self-sacrifice consists in *the renunciation of anything that is evil,* there is no
possibility of ascribing it to the Son of God. Mr Maurice,
indeed, speaks of Him "as perfectly giving up that self-
will which had been the source of all men's sins and of
all their miseries." But assuredly He had no such sacrifice as this to offer. He had not that within Him, in any
respect or in any degree, to which all the crimes and
miseries of men must be traced. To ascribe to Him
" self-will" would be the grossest calumny. His wishes
and purposes were, at all times and in all things, accordant with the will of His Father. And therefore, in so far
as self-sacrifice may be displayed in the giving up of that
which is intrinsically and essentially *evil,* there was evidently no room and no necessity for it in the case of the
immaculate and well-beloved Son of God.

Self-sacri-
fice as con-
sisting in
*renuncia-
tion of evil,*
not attri-
butable to
the Son of
God.

It may be said, indeed, that though His own will was
perfectly free from every evil bias, He did notwithstanding surrender it to His Father's will when He thus prayed
in His agony, " O my Father, if it be possible, let this cup
pass from me ; nevertheless not as I will, but as Thou
wilt ;" and again, " O my Father, if this cup may not pass
away from me, except I drink it, Thy will be done." It
is evident, however, that this, though unquestionably a
surrender of His own will, was no *gratuitous* sacrifice. On
the contrary, it was rendered on the express footing of its
being, in the judgment of Heaven, absolutely indispensable. We are warranted to conclude from the Saviour's
words on this occasion, that *if it had been possible,* consistently with the great purposes for which He had been
sent into the world, that the cup should have passed from
Him, He certainly would not have been required to drink
it. And therefore we have here no evidence that self-sacri-

Matt. xxvi
39, 42.

REVIEW OF THEORIES

PART III. SEC. 3.

Christ's sufferings a glorious self-sacrifice only when connected with the gracious ends accomplished by them.

Phil. ii. 6-8.

fice is, on its own account, well-pleasing in the sight of God, but rather a clear and convincing evidence of the contrary.

There is another sense, however, in which the Lord Jesus may be truly said to have set before us a glorious example of self-sacrifice. In so far as self-sacrifice consists in the voluntary surrender of dignities and prerogatives, and in the voluntary endurance of labours and tribulations, it was doubtless exhibited by the Son of God in an eminent degree, when, " being in the form of God, and thinking it not robbery to be equal with God, He made Himself of no reputation, and took upon Him the form of a servant, and was made in the likeness of men ; and being found in fashion as a man, He humbled Himself, and became obedient unto death, even the death of the cross." Here was a most notable instance of self-sacrifice. And *if we connect with it the gracious end to be accomplished by it*—namely, the deliverance of men from the penal consequences of transgression through the vicarious obedience and sufferings of their Mediator—we are lost in admiration and in gratitude when contemplating it. But if this gracious end be ignored or set aside, in what light must the Saviour's unexampled work of humiliation and suffering be regarded ? It can then only be viewed as a *gratuitous* self-sacrifice—a self-sacrifice undergone merely because it *is* self-sacrifice, and without ostensible reference to any ulterior ends of a wise and holy and beneficent nature that are subserved by it.

Mere " exemplification of self-sacrifice " not a sufficient explanation of sufferings of Christ.

Doubtless there is one end to which it is held to be conducive—that, namely, of "*exemplifying the principle of self-sacrifice* as due from all intelligent and moral creatures to Him who made them." But what does the assigning to it of such an end amount to ? It evidently amounts to this, —that self-sacrifice, *for its own sake, or merely because it* IS *self-sacrifice*, is dutiful on the part of man, and acceptable in the sight of God. It amounts to this,—that one who, like the Lord Jesus, has no other reason for subjecting himself to voluntary humiliations and gratuitous afflictions, may find a sufficient reason for so doing in the prospect of thereby inducing others, without any further or

RESPECTING THE ATONEMENT. 323

better reason, to do likewise. It implies, in short, that
self-sacrifice is a principle so binding on all God's intelligent creatures on its own account, and that God is so bent
on inculcating this principle of aimless, arbitrary, and
gratuitous self-sacrifice—irrespective of any ulterior ends
to be promoted by it—that in order to exemplify it He
gave up His beloved Son to humiliation, and suffering, and
death.   Now, surely a hypothesis which involves such
consequences as these is quite inconsistent with any view
of the divine character which either reason or revelation
has unfolded to us.   And, as I have before said, it is much
less akin to the nature of that wise, holy, beneficent, and
gracious God, in whom, as Christians, we are taught to
believe, than to that of the capricious and cruel divinities
of heathenism, who were held to delight in aimless
tortures and austerities.

Perhaps it may be here urged that the self-sacrifice of
the Son of God, although in itself considered altogether
gratuitous, is not the less on this account fitted to incite us
to that abnegation of our own selfish and sinful desires,
*which on our part, as fallen creatures, is not gratuitous,
but, on the contrary, highly needful and beneficial.*

To this statement we cannot assent.   An instance of
self-sacrifice, which, for aught that appears in it, is utterly
aimless and superfluous, affords no reasonable encouragement in the way of example to the performance of other
acts of self-sacrifice, which, so far from resembling, are
strongly contrasted with it, by reason of the wise and
salutary ends which are promoted by them.   Rather
might such an instance be regarded as *caricaturing* the
principle of self-sacrifice, holding it up to ridicule, and
bringing it into disrepute.   A person may deny himself to
ever so great an extent ; he may submit to any extremes
of suffering or deprivation ; but if, so far as we are able to
see, he is impoverishing or afflicting himself without any
urgent necessity, or wearing himself out with oppressive
toils and tribulations which are not directly subservient to
any wise or useful purpose, we may greatly wonder at
the line of conduct which he thus pursues, but cannot be

PART
III.
SEC. 3

324 REVIEW OF THEORIES

PART III. SEC. 3.

reasonably expected either to commend or to copy it. But if, on the other hand, the self-denial be exhibited by him in some noble enterprise of piety or philanthropy, to the prosecution of which it is absolutely indispensable—above all, if it be fraught with substantial benefits which are in the highest degree conducive to our personal advantage—it then approves itself to us as a " reasonable service," and may justly be held up as a model for our imitation. On this ground, the course of suffering and humiliation to which the Lord Jesus voluntarily submitted can *then only* become an encouraging pattern to us of that abnegation of self which on our part is indispensable, when some such adequate and beneficent purpose is assigned to it as that which is implied in the doctrine of the Atonement.

Christ's sufferings, thus regarded, are no manifestation of love of God.

I have one further remark to make on this theory. Even were it admitted that the sufferings of Jesus Christ are ever so fair and striking an " illustration of the principle of self-sacrifice as due from all God's intelligent creatures to Him who made them," the question still arises,—*Can they, when merely regarded in this light, be held fully to justify the manner in which the Bible appeals to them, as furnishing at once the most evident and the most illustrious of all conceivable manifestations of divine love?*

I scarcely think that any one will be disposed, on calm reflection, to answer this question in the affirmative. For what, according to the theory under discussion, is *the substantial benefit* which the death of Christ is intended to secure for us? *Simply the presentation of a great example of self-sacrifice.* Now *this* is a benefit which cannot be said to be so conspicuous and pre-eminent in its value as to transcend all other tokens of the divine goodness. On the contrary, *most men cannot, without much difficulty, be brought to regard it as a benefit at all.* To most men God seems, when claiming from us self-sacrifice, and urging us by the example of Christ or otherwise to yield it to Him, to be rather insisting very strictly on His own rights, than very notably conferring a benefaction on His intelligent creatures. And even in the case of earnest and devoted

RESPECTING THE ATONEMENT. 325

Christians, whose minds are enlightened and renovated
by the Holy Spirit, a full appreciation of the excellence
of self-sacrifice, whensoever their own will is at variance
with the will of God, is not by any means an early or an
easy attainment, but one into which, by divine grace, they
are progressively schooled by much sharp discipline and
by long experience of the Christian life. On these
grounds, I hold that the view of our Lord's sufferings
which is set forth in the theory now under consideration,
is not such as to justify the statements of Scripture in
regard to them, as of all evidences of divine love incomparably the most illustrious. Nay, I may almost venture
to affirm, that if, *in respect merely of the illustration of self-
sacrifice afforded by it*, the Saviour's death be considered
as exhibiting a clear, conspicuous, and strikingly affecting
proof of the fatherly love of God, beyond what is furnished
by all His other benefits, it can be so considered only on
the principle *that mankind are so fully capable of appreciating the matchless worth and blessedness of self-sacrifice as
to need no example, like that of Jesus, to commend it to
them !*

It does not appear, then, that this theory supplies any
valid ground on which our Lord's sufferings can be viewed
as an unequalled manifestation of the love of God. Be it
remembered that these sufferings are represented in Scripture as not merely *incidental* but *essential* to His divine
mission. They are set forth as themselves occupying a
most prominent and important place among the appointed
objects for which He was sent into the world. All that
He endured of ignominy and affliction came upon Him by
the determinate counsel, and much of it by the immediate agency, of His heavenly Father. No human instrumentality was employed, in the dark hour of His agony,
to render His soul " exceeding sorrowful." Nor was it
the pangs inflicted on Him by wicked men so much as the
mysterious hiding of His Father's countenance, that led
Him to cry out in bitter anguish on the cross, " My God,
my God, why hast Thou forsaken me ? "

Such being the case, we cannot say of the Lord Jesus,

326   REVIEW OF THEORIES

PART
III.
SEC. 3.

as of Paul, or of Peter, or of James, or of Stephen, or of any other self-devoted sufferer in the cause of truth, that He sacrificed Himself, in the sense merely of enduring afflictions which were incident to the work He had undertaken to accomplish. For that work mainly was to endure afflictions—to humble Himself from the glories of His heavenly condition to the toils, and trials, and sorrows of His earthly state—to lead among men a life of suffering and ignominy, and ultimately to lay down His life upon the cross. And hence we must either suppose that His self-sacrifice was directly conducive to some such great and good purpose as, according to our view, the Scriptures have assigned to it—as an expiation of human guilt, and a satisfaction to divine justice; or else we must regard it as a mere instance of self-sacrifice, terminating in itself—dictated by no necessity, but required and accepted by God purely for its own sake, as an act of unqualified submission to His sovereign will, and without reference to any conceivable good that could be promoted by it. And this latter conclusion, which seems to be our only alternative if the commonly-received doctrine of the Atonement be set aside, is utterly inconsistent, not merely with any Scriptural, but with any reasonable, views of the divine character; and specially inconsistent with any view that may be taken of the sufferings and death of Christ as an exhibition of His Father's love.

RESPECTING THE ATONEMENT.   327

SECTION IV.

(9) THEORY OF SYMPATHY OR IDENTIFICATION.

IX. OUR attention must now be directed for a little to another theory, or class of theories, by which it is proposed to account for our Lord's sufferings otherwise than by the commonly-received doctrine of the Atonement. The sufferings of Christ are viewed by some writers as having mainly consisted in His deep *sympathy* with those fallen creatures whose nature He assumed. Instead of regarding Him as *substituted for us,* they hold that He *identified Himself with us;* and that He so fully entered into all the sins and miseries of fallen humanity as to feel them, and sorrow for them, and even to make confession of them, as if they had been His own.

PART III. SEC. 4.

Theory of sympathy.

Thus, Mr Maurice, without prejudice to his other views, affirms that " Christ bore in the truest and strictest sense the sins of the world, feeling them with that anguish with which only a perfectly pure and holy being, who is also a perfectly sympathising and gracious being, can feel the sins of others." In another place he thus expresses himself :—

Maurice's Theological Essays, p. 141.

" Is it not the fact, that if we have the consciousness, in however slight a degree, of evil in another man, it is, up to the same degree, as if the evil were in ourselves? And supposing the offender to be a friend, or a brother, or a child, is not this sense of personal shame, of the evil being ours, proportionably stronger and more acute? Suppose this carried to its highest point, cannot you apprehend that Christ may have entered into the sin of the whole world—may have had the most inward realisation of it—not because it was like what was in Himself, but because it was utterly and intensely unlike? Does the coexistence of this sympathy and this antipathy perplex

Doctrine of Sacrifice, p. 188.

328   REVIEW OF THEORIES

PART
III.
SEC. 4.

you? Ask yourselves whether they must not dwell together in their highest degree, in their fullest power, in any one of whom you could say that he is perfect. Diminish by one atom the loathing and horror, or the fellowship and sympathy, and by that atom you lower the character."

These views are adopted, and more fully carried out, by the author of an able anonymous treatise, entitled "The Philosophy of Evangelicism."

"Out of the combination," he says, "in a highly-cultivated moral state of the mind, of its sympathies and antipathies, a third sentiment is capable of being evolved, called also, for want of a distinctive name, 'sympathy,' but at once attractive of the individual and repellent of his crime. The most familiar examples of this are to be found when persons standing to each other in endearing relationships have diverse moral characters. The more endearing the personal relationship, and the more diverse the character, the deeper will be this compound sentiment. Take, for example, the case of a child who has suddenly betrayed evidence of great moral turpitude by the public commission of some shameful crime. To designate the feelings of the anguish-stricken father by the paltry name of 'pity' would be a miserable misnomer. A worthy father identifies himself with his child's crime, and feels as much shame and distress as if it had been his own. But the depth of this feeling will depend upon two things—the extent of his love for his child, and of his hatred of the crime. If the moral character of the father be no better than that of the offender, his feelings of self-loathing will be no deeper than those of the offender. Exactly in proportion to the superiority of his character will be the profundity of his woe. May we not venture, then, to add, that a sentiment so compound is inadequately expressed by the word 'sympathy;' and that instead of saying 'sympathy with the sins of others,' we should more accurately convey the idea by calling it '*consciousness of the sins of others*'?" "Now, if there be, in holy beings, this painful consciousness of others' sins, may there not be, in penitent minds, a corresponding pleasurable consciousness of another's perfect righteousness? If Christ can, by means of this general bond of sympathy and common consciousness of humanity, become conscious of human guilt, and suffer and atone for it, what is to prevent us from becoming, in the same way, conscious of His perfect righteousness, and being thereby subjectively justified? . . . The righteousness we speak of is not a righteousness nominally only and artificially imputed. The imputation is real— real, because it has its foundation in our moral constitution, whereby we are made capable of becoming affected in our conscience and moral feelings with the wickedness and righteousness of others, as well as with our own. We arrive, then, at the following conclusion: Christ 'became sin for us' in the sense we have before described—

RESPECTING THE ATONEMENT. 329

that is, He, as a man with men, sympathetically entered, on the principle of mankind's corporate responsibility, into the race's guilty consciousness, and yielded in the spirit of penitent submissiveness to the privations and sufferings attendant on a state of guilt, crowned with life's last calamity—death—emphatically 'the wages of sin.' And, as a correlative of Christ's atoning act, we are 'made the righteousness of God in Him,'—not merely made in ourselves contrite and imperfectly righteous, but invested with the consciousness of His perfect meritorious righteousness. To complete the correlation, He, having 'risen again for our justification' (inasmuch as otherwise our sympathy with the Christ-consciousness could have embraced only the atoning purpose), our sympathy with a risen and living Christ enables us to participate in the triumphant emotion with which He 'sees of the travail of His soul and is satisfied,' and to 'rejoice in hope of the glory of God.' Thus a clear avenue is opened between the Christ-consciousness and the human consciousness, and we detect in their intercommunion the accord of the atoning act and the believing act. Our Saviour, conscious of our sins, has taken them upon Himself and atoned for them: we, conscious of His righteousness, appear with it in the sight of God and are justified. Our sins are His sins; His righteousness is our righteousness; *and this union of Christ and His people in moral consciousness is* THE CENTRAL IDEA OF THE GOSPEL."

Philosophy of Evangelicism, p. 133-140.

"Human nature," again observes the same author, "is so constituted as to *implicate* us not only in our own personal moral acts, but also in the moral acts of each other; and, in consequence thereof, conscience in its higher exercises extends beyond the sphere of our individual conduct, and is sympathetically affected by the conduct of others; filling us with shame and grief at the moral degradation of those we love, and inspiring us with a joyous satisfaction when they are seen to excel in virtue. The extension of these feelings to their utmost degree unfolds the true theory of the sufferings of Christ for our guilt, and of our participation in His perfect righteousness. By virtue of our *union with Him in moral consciousness*, He has endured the anguish for sin with which we *ought* to have been affected; and as the counterpart thereof, our consciousness of His righteousness becomes to us, although still consciously ungodly, the counterpoise whereby we are at the same time subjectively justified."

Ibid., p. 232, 233.

The views thus expressed are substantially in accordance with those set forth by Dr Campbell in his able and interesting treatise on 'The Nature of the Atonement.' Dr Campbell, however, has brought more fully out what the writers already quoted have but vaguely and dimly indicated—namely, the manner in which Christ, by entering into the sins of men, or making them His own, *may be held to have atoned for them.* This He did, says Dr

Views of Dr Campbell.

330 REVIEW OF THEORIES

PART III. SEC. 4.

Campbell, *by offering up to God a perfect confession of them, and an adequate repentance for them, with which divine justice is satisfied, and a full expiation is made for human guilt.* Thus, Dr Campbell speaks of Christ, in His dealing with the Father in relation to our sins, as " making a perfect confession of these sins—a confession which must in its own nature have been a *perfect amen* in humanity to the judgment of God on the sin of man ;" as " meeting the divine wrath against sin with a perfect response out of the depths of His divine humanity—a response which (excepting the personal consciousness of sin) has all the elements of a perfect contrition and repentance," and " by which the wrath of God is rightly met, and divine justice duly satisfied ;" and again, as " absorbing and exhausting the divine wrath against our sins in that adequate confession and perfect response on the part of man, which was possible only to the infinite and eternal righteousness in humanity."

Campbell on the Atonement, p. 134, 135, 145.

I need only further quote, in illustration of this theory, a few sentences from an able anonymous work, in which some of its main features are very clearly set forth :—

Fragments of Truth, p. 243, 244.

" The natural consequence of a love which made Christ identify Himself with sinners was, that He should feel the pressure of human sin as a pressure on his own spirit. We know how deeply one human being may suffer in the suffering of another ; and those who know what real love is, know that the pain of sympathy with a beloved object is often harder to endure than any suffering merely personal, —the suffering of a mother, for instance, in that of her child. But in spiritual beings, physical suffering must always be regarded as secondary in comparison with mental suffering. To realise the sin of one with whom we are identified by love, is greater suffering than any physical pain we could endure for him ; and the intensity of the suffering will be in proportion as the nature of him who endures it is alien from the sin."

" Suppose a son has committed a great crime, and that he meets his father looking worn and sad and emaciated, and is told that the offence he has committed is the cause of it. There are two ways in which the son might understand this : either that his father had literally borne the punishment due to him,—that he had endured the actual confinement and privations of a prison—the chastisement of whatever kind to which he himself had been condemned,—and thus by physical suffering had been reduced to the state in which he was ; or that the intensity of his love, grief, and anxiety had undermined

RESPECTING THE ATONEMENT.   331

his health, and produced the same outward effects. Which of these
ways of accounting for the outward manifestations of suffering would
most undeniably express love in a moral and spiritual being? In the
one case the change in his outward appearance would be incontest-
able evidence of the intensity of his feelings; in the other case, his
feelings may or may not have been in exercise." Accordingly, this
writer holds, that in thinking of Christ as "suffering for us, the just
for the unjust," we ought not to allow our minds "to dwell on the
physical suffering, but rather on the love that made outward affliction
so agonising to the *spirit* of the Saviour."

PART
III.
SEC. 4.

1. Now, in meeting these and similar representations,
we might, in the first place, fairly express a doubt whether
the mere circumstance of the Son of God having assumed
the human nature implies that thorough identification of
Himself with us which should lead Him intensely to feel
the guiltiness and shamefulness of our sinful condition as
if it were His own.   It must, indeed, be admitted that, as
very man, He was capable of being "touched with the
feeling of our *infirmities*."   But what fellow-feeling could
He have with us as regards *our sins?*   With these, as a
sinless man, He was surely incapable of taking part in the
way of sympathising with them.   He could not, by mere
sympathy, make our sins His own, when in Himself there
was nothing in the least akin, but rather everything uncongenial and repugnant to them.   Rather may we say of
Him that, like His heavenly Father, to whom in all moral
excellences He was perfectly conformed, "He is of purer
eyes than to behold evil, and cannot look upon iniquity."
But even were He fully capable of being "touched with
the feeling," not only of our sorrows, but of our sins, what
was there to call His sympathetic capacities into exercise
to so great an extent as this theory supposes?   His mere
assumption of the human nature cannot be regarded as
any sufficient reason for it.   He must have had some other
and closer bond of fellowship with us in order to account
for the exceeding fulness of His sympathy.   How is it in
the illustrative instance above referred to?   It is not for the
crime of one, to whom He is allied merely as partaking of
the same common attributes of humanity, that the heart-
broken parent grieves as if he had himself been chargeable

The incar-
nation can-
not ex-
plain
Christ's
sympathy
to the ex-
tent alleg-
ed.

332　　　REVIEW OF THEORIES

PART
III.
SEC. 4.
——

with it, but for the crime committed *by his own son*, with whom, by the closest ties of kindred, he is identified, and in whose shame and wretchedness he feels himself to be involved. And so in the case of Christ. That those human sympathies of which as very man He was susceptible, should have been actually evoked in our behalf —above all, that they should have been evoked in such a degree that He might, in respect of them, be considered as " bearing in the truest and strictest sense the sins of the world," and might even be said to " confess them, and to sorrow for them with deep contrition of heart, as if they had been His own "—is more than a mere community of nature will account for. It evidently bespeaks an intimacy of fellowship with us, a closeness of interest in us, an identity of position with us, which, as subsisting with reference to things that are altogether foreign to His own holy and blessed nature, comes little, if at all, short of actual substitution. And truly there seems to be no very intelligible reason why His substitution in the room of sinners should be so much opposed by those who do not hesitate to speak of Him as " perfectly confessing our sins, with an adequate sorrow and contrition on account of them," and as " meeting the divine wrath against sin with a response which has in it all the elements of a perfect repentance." Such representations, so far as we can understand them, would seem to imply, on the part of the Redeemer, a *self-impu-tation* of the sins of fallen men, to even a greater extent than the advocates of His vicarious substitution in the room of sinners would contend for.

Sufferings
of Christ
were not
wholly or
chiefly
sympa-
thetic.

2. But further, admitting that the sympathy of Christ with those sinful creatures whom He came into the world to save was one element of His sufferings which ought not to be overlooked, we may confidently say that it cannot be regarded as constituting the whole, or even the principal part, of these sufferings.

Let us look at the facts of the case. Let us take the actual record of the Saviour's afflictions as given in the New Testament, and more particularly of the final consummation of them in the agonising scenes of the garden

RESPECTING THE ATONEMENT. 333

and the cross. It cannot be said, surely, that when pray- PART III SEC. 4.
ing in His agony, that "if it were possible this cup might
pass from Him," *He was seeking deliverance from those*
sympathetic woes with which the thought of human sins
and miseries had afflicted Him. This would be, in effect,
to say that He was earnestly wishing His own sympathies
to be deadened, and His own heart to be hardened against
the sins and sorrows of humanity—a supposition utterly
at variance with His loving nature. It is equally obvious
that His lamentation on the cross, "My God, my God,
why hast Thou forsaken me?" was intensely *personal* in
its reference to *His own* afflictions, wherewith it had
pleased God mysteriously to visit Him, and not to any
mere fellow-feeling for the afflictions of others. And
indeed the whole strain and tenor of His own statements,
when He speaks, both before His death and after His
resurrection, of "giving His life a ransom for many," Matt. xx.
"shedding His blood for the remission of sins," "laying 28; xxvi. 28.
down His life for His sheep," "giving His flesh for the John, x.
life of the world," "behoving to suffer and to rise from the 15; vi. 51.
dead, that repentance and remission of sins might be Luke, xxiv. 46, 47.
preached in His name among all nations," cannot, without
the most violent misconstruction, be made to import a
mere sympathy with our sins and miseries, or anything
short of a vicarious endurance of penalties due to us, that
we might be exempted from them.

The same remarks are applicable to the words of the
apostles respecting the causes and ends of our Lord's
sufferings. When we find them speaking of Christ as Rom. iv.
"delivered for our offences," "justifying us by His blood," 25; v. 9. 10.
"reconciling us to God by His death," "redeeming us Gal. iii. 13.
from the curse of the law by being made a curse for us," Heb. ix.
as "once offered to bear the sins of many," as "putting 26, 28.
away sin by the sacrifice of Himself," as "bearing our sins 1 Pet. ii. 24; iii. 18.
in His own body on the tree," as "suffering for sins, the
just for the unjust," and as "washing us from our sins in Rev. i. 5.
His own blood," it really seems to be about as hopeless
an effort as could by possibility be imagined, to resolve
these, and many other expressions of like import, into

334   REVIEW OF THEORIES

PART
III.
SEC. 4

mere intimations of the closeness and intensity of feeling with which He identified Himself with us in our fallen condition.

The truth is, that the sympathy of Christ is but seldom spoken of in the New Testament, in comparison with the frequency of the allusions to His personal sufferings. And when the two subjects are at any time brought together, it is with the view, not of resolving His sufferings into sympathy, but of inferring His readiness to sympathise with us, from the sufferings to which in His own person He was subjected. His sufferings were a cup of which He had *Himself* to drink, a baptism with which He had *Himself* to be baptised. And it will be remembered that, on one memorable occasion, when referring to the fellowship between Himself and His disciples in the endurance of suffering, He did not represent Himself as sympathetically drinking of *their* cup, and sharing in *their* baptism,

Matt. xx.
22.

but asked them, "Are *ye* able to drink of the cup that *I* shall drink of, and to be baptised with the baptism that *I* am baptised with?"

Christ's
sufferings
as sympa-
thetic no
proof of
the Fa-
ther's love.

3. But further, the question occurs, How can the sufferings of Christ, according to this view of them, be regarded as superlatively commending to us the love of God? *This* is a testing question with respect to every proposed substitute for the doctrine of the Atonement. So clear, distinct, and emphatic are the statements of Scripture in which we are told that the love of God is pre-eminently manifested in the sufferings of Jesus Christ, that no theory regarding them can possibly be the right one which does not present them to us in the light of an unparalleled and deeply impressive manifestation of the love of God. Is this, then, the case with the theory now before us? Can the sufferings of Christ, according to this view of them, be held as gloriously illustrating and commending to us the love of God? That *the love of Christ* should be displayed by them we can well conceive; for He must indeed have very warmly loved us, if His sympathy with our sins and miseries was so intense as to give its full meaning to all that we are taught in Scripture respecting the unutterable anguish with which

RESPECTING THE ATONEMENT. 335

He was afflicted ; but *that the love of the Father should be* PART
manifested to us in the sympathetic agonies thus endured III.
SEC. 4.
by His innocent, holy, and well-beloved Son, is utterly inexplicable except upon the principle that we derive from
them certain substantial benefits, of which we should not
otherwise have become possessed. Some good must accrue
to us from them, not otherwise to be obtained, or some evil
must be averted from us by them, not otherwise to be removed or remedied, before we can see in the sufferings of
Jesus Christ, in whatsoever way we may suppose them to
have come upon Him, any proof of the love with which
His Father is regarding us.

Of the justice of this remark some of the ablest advo- Alleged
cates of the theory under review seem to be fully aware ; expiatory
tendency
and accordingly they speak of the sympathetic sorrows of of Christ's
sympathe-
Christ as having been in some respects of an expiatory tic sense of
tendency. Thus Dr Campbell holds that "the divine our sins.
righteousness in Christ, appearing on the part of man and
in humanity, met the divine righteousness in God condemning man's sin, by the true and righteous confession
of its sinfulness uttered in humanity ; and *righteousness as* Campbell
in God was satisfied, and demanded no more than righteous- on the
Atone-
ness as in Christ thus presented." This confession of our ment, p.
142.
sins on the part of Christ, the same writer declares to
have been " a perfect Amen in humanity to the judgment
of God on the sin of man," and to have had in it " all the
elements of a perfect contrition and repentance, excepting the personal consciousness of sin, and thus to have
accorded to divine justice that which is its due, and which Ibid., p.
could alone satisfy it." And again he observes, " Without 134, 135.
the assumption of an imputation of our guilt, and in perfect harmony with the unbroken consciousness of personal separation from our sins, the Son of God, bearing
us and our sins on His heart before the Father, must
needs respond to the Father's judgment on our sins, with
that confession of their evil and of the righteousness of
the wrath of God against them, and holy sorrow because
of them, which were due ; due in the truth of things—
due on our behalf, though we could not render it—*due*

336   REVIEW OF THEORIES

PART III.
SEC. 4.

Campbell on the Atonement, p. 138.

from Him as in our nature and our true brother,—what He must needs feel in Himself because of the holiness and love which were in Him—what He must needs utter to the Father in expiation of our sins when He would make intercession for us."

Thus, according to the theory under consideration, the sympathy of the Son of God incarnate with our sinful condition is held to have been available for our benefit, by leading Him to render in behalf of sinners a perfect confession of sin and an adequate repentance, with which divine justice is satisfied, and a full expiation is made for human guilt.

To my mind, however, this view of the Atonement is encompassed with difficulties which seem to be insuperable.

A confession of sin with perfect contrition and repentance, without the personal consciousness of sin, is impossible.

(1.) If *vicarious penalties*, endured by the innocent in the room of the guilty, be a mystery which some minds are slow to entertain, what shall we say of *a confession of our sins having in it all the elements of perfect contrition and repentance,* offered up in our behalf by One who has all the while "the unbroken consciousness of personal separation from those sins" which He thus sympathetically confesses and deplores? Surely there is here an incomparably greater mystery. Nay, is there not rather an absolute impossibility? For how is it at all conceivable that a perfectly holy being should undergo *repentance and contrition* for sins of which He has no personal consciousness?

The truth is, that however poignant may have been the Saviour's sympathetic sorrow for our sins, it cannot, in the absence of all "personal consciousness of them," be said to have had in it *any* of the elements, far less "*all* the elements, of a perfect contrition and repentance on account of them." At least, it must be held as *lacking one element* which is absolutely essential. For the very thing which characteristically distinguishes *penitential* sorrow from every other kind of sorrow is just that deep "personal consciousness of sin" which, in the case of our Saviour's affliction, was entirely wanting. And hence it is not only

RESPECTING THE ATONEMENT. 337

an error in judgment, but an abuse of language, to speak of *His* sorrow as if it were in the same category with that of the contrite and self-accusing penitent.

Dr Campbell, in a note appended to his second edition (page 398), endeavours to vindicate his use of the word "repentance" as applied to the confession of the sins of humanity by Jesus Christ.

PART III. SEC. 4.

Campbell's attempt to defend this view.

> "That word," he says, "will have its full meaning in the personal experience of every one who accepts in faith the Atonement as now represented; for *every such individual sinner will add the excepted element of personal consciousness of sin.* But if the consciousness of such repentant sinner be analysed, it will be found that all that is morally true and spiritual and acceptable to God in his repentance is an Amen to Christ's condemnation of his sin; and that all the hope towards God, because of which his repentance is free and pure and imbued with the spirit of sonship, is equally traceable to the revelation of the heart of the Father in His acceptance of the Son's confession and intercession on man's behalf."

This attempted explanation, however, is so far from lessening that it greatly increases the difficulty. It supposes a *twofold* interchange or combination of penitential elements as taking place between sinners and their Saviour. On the one hand, that which is lacking in the repentance of sinners, in order to make it "a full response to the righteous judgment of God on the sins of men," is held to be supplied by the "adequate sorrow and contrition with which Christ makes perfect confession of sin on their behalf." On the other hand, that which is lacking in the Saviour's confession of the sins of men, in order to give it "all the elements of a perfect contrition and repentance on account of them," is held to be supplied by "the personal consciousness of sin on the part of every individual sinner who in faith accepts the Atonement."* But how can this be? Surely *repentance,* according to any reasonable or Scriptural notion we can form of it, is the act or

Increases the difficulty.

---

* I may here notice in passing, that this latter position is fatal to the notion of a *universal atonement,* for which Dr Campbell so earnestly contends. For if that "adequate repentance of Christ for human sins," which is held by him to constitute the Atonement, *be indebted for one of its most essential elements to the personal experience of believers,* it is evidently *no atonement for lack of this* "*excepted element*" *to any but* "*those who accept of it in faith.*"

338   REVIEW OF THEORIES

PART
III.
SEC. 4.
———

exercise of *one individual person*—namely, of the sinner himself who has done the things repented of. And it seems to me utterly impossible to conceive of it *as a combination of the feelings and dispositions of two or more separate individuals*, whose personal experiences are so fused and blended together that each contributes to it his own *quota* of its essential elements.

No personal consciousness of sins in one who is not actually chargeable with them.

Farther, if there can be no such thing as penitence without a personal consciousness of sins, it is (if possible) still more clear that there can be no personal consciousness of sins, except in the case of one who is actually chargeable with them. Indeed, it is a contradiction in terms to suppose that "a personal consciousness of sins" can be transferred, by sympathy or otherwise, from him by whom the sins have been committed, to another who, though himself sinless, makes confession of them, so as to impart to such confession that penitential character which could not otherwise belong to it. It avails nothing to say that "if the consciousness of the repentant sinner be analysed, it will be found that all that is true and spiritual and acceptable to God in his repentance, is an Amen to Christ's condemnation of his sins." For his consciousness of sin *does not become Christ's consciousness*, by leading him to acquiesce, however fully, in the feelings with which his sin is regarded by Christ. It is his own personal consciousness of sin, notwithstanding, and is from its very nature incapable of being shared in by One who is Himself absolutely sinless. The sorrow which my sins may have occasioned to an esteemed friend, and the condemnation with which they are visited by him, may doubtless be the means, through divine grace, of awakening me to a penitential sense of them. Yet, surely, it is not for a moment to be imagined that *my personal sense of guilt*, because he has thus excited it, is to be held *as entering into his consciousness*, so as to give *a penitential character* to his sentiments regarding sins, of which he is entirely guiltless!

We still, therefore, hold ourselves warranted to adhere, notwithstanding Dr Campbell's note, to our former state-

RESPECTING THE ATONEMENT.

ment—namely, that however poignant may have been the Saviour's sympathetic sorrow for our sins, it cannot, *in the absence of all personal consciousness of them,* be said to have had in it *any* of the elements, far less " *all* the elements, of a perfect contrition and repentance on account of them ; " and that it must at all events be held as lacking *one element* which is absolutely essential.

This, however, is not all ; for it ought to be remembered that " repentance," according to the Scriptural sense of that expression, does not consist in mere *sorrow for sin,* although that sorrow were ever so perfect, but in a *change of heart and mind* with respect to sin. It is not mere μεταμελεια, but μετάνοια. We are told in Scripture that " godly sorrow *worketh* repentance ; " but we are not told that " godly sorrow *is* repentance." In order to constitute that " repentance " which a righteous God requires, and which He will alone accept of, there must be not only " sorrow for sin," but " a *turning from sin unto God,* with full purpose of, and endeavour after, new obedience." Accordingly, we have here another " excepted element," besides the " personal consciousness of sin," which " every individual sinner who accepts the Atonement " must supply in order to make up that which is lacking in the Saviour ; for I need scarcely say that nothing that is at all analogous to *conversion from sin* can possibly be ascribed to Him who was " holy, harmless, undefiled, and separate from sinners."

(2.) But, not to insist longer on this very obvious and fatal objection to the theory before us, I see not with what justice it can be said that a " confession of our sins, having in it all the elements of a perfect contrition and repentance on account of them," was " *due from the Son of God as in our nature and our true brother."* That it should have been due from Him on our behalf, *as having become, by the appointment of His Father and by His own voluntary undertaking,* OUR SUBSTITUTE AND SURETY, I might be disposed more readily to admit. And yet even this would seem to imply much more than the imputation of our sins to Him can reasonably be held to include. It would

PART III. SEC. 4.

Repentance is not mere sorrow for sin, but a turning from sin

2 Cor. vii. 10.

Heb. vii. 26.

It cannot be said that a penitential confession of sins " was due from the Son of God in our nature."

340 REVIEW OF THEORIES

PART III. SEC. 4.
seem to imply that not only the *reatus pœnæ*, or *legal liability to condemnation*, was reckoned to Him; but that the *reatus culpæ*, or *personal blameworthiness* inherent in our sinfulness, was actually transferred to Him. But that any such penitential confession of our sins was due from Him *in virtue of His mere assumption of our nature* (and that, too, although when made in all other things like unto His brethren *He was yet without sin*) appears to me to be irrational in the highest degree. As well might it be said that every individual man, as partaking of the common nature of the human race—its native depravity and sinfulness not excepted—is bound to confess and to deplore with deep contrition, not only his own actual transgressions, but the actual transgressions of each and all of his fellow-creatures; and that, too, although, instead of having participated in them, he may have most thoroughly dissented from and protested against them.

How can this sympathetic penitence of Christ expiate our sins?
(3.) There is still greater difficulty in conceiving how this sympathetic penitence of the Son of God should be regarded as *furnishing an expiation*, and not rather *an aggravation*, of the sins which gave occasion to it. Dr Campbell himself, in the note already referred to, will not allow that it is in any respect *vicarious*. Indeed, he earnestly disclaims the teaching of any such doctrine as that Christ felt and confessed sin as the substitute for transgressors. But how else can His "perfect contrition and repentance on account of our sins" be considered as an atonement for them? If the idea of *substitution* be altogether set aside, we are evidently thrown back on the requisitions of the divine law, which insist that *the sinner himself* shall perfectly turn from the evil of his own heart and the wickedness of his own way, and not that the righteous shall confess sin and deplore it for him. It may be said, perhaps, that the sorrow of the Saviour on account of our sins *may excite us to repent of them*, so as by repentance to avert from us the merited wrath. But, allowing that it did so ever so thoroughly, *our own repentance would in that case be the atonement*, while the sorrow of Christ

RESPECTING THE ATONEMENT. 341

would simply be the means of stirring us up to render that atonement.

But this is not all ; for, as has been already remarked, the sympathetic penitence of the Son of God may, in some respects, be considered as *aggravating*, rather than as *expiating*, the sins which give occasion to it. To show this, I may refer to the striking instance formerly quoted in illustration of the theory under review—that, namely, of the parent whose health has been undermined by the intensity of his love, grief, and anxiety for a profligate son, who has grievously dishonoured him, and is bringing down his grey hairs with sorrow to the grave. It is not for a moment to be supposed that the crimes of such a profligate are in any respect alleviated,—for in truth they are incomparably increased in guilt, by the anguish endured by his parent at the thought of them. In like manner, if such be the condition of our fallen race, that the Son of God cannot assume the nature of man without having His spirit grievously troubled and agonised by a sympathetic sense of human sins and miseries, we needs must regard the sorrow thus experienced by Him as aggravating our transgressions, rather than atoning for them. And what more dreadful aggravation of the sins of humanity can possibly be imagined, than that the Son of God could not appear in the nature of man—even as that nature was prior to the Fall—without being all his life "a man of sorrows" on account of them, and without having ultimately *His heart broken* by the thought of them, so as to be " exceeding sorrowful, even unto death "? Some further element, therefore, than His sympathy must be introduced, in order to speak peace and comfort to our guilty hearts. We must think of Him not only as *sympathetically identifying Himself with us*, but as graciously undertaking *to substitute Himself for us*—and as doing so, moreover, by the appointment and with the approbation of the Sovereign Judge. And then shall we have good cause to "joy in God through our Lord Jesus Christ, by whom we have received the atonement."

(4.) But yet farther, even when we think of the Lord

PART III.
SEC. 4.

It rather *aggravates* our sins.

Rom. v. 11.

342 REVIEW OF THEORIES

PART III. SEC. 4.

Christ's substitution for us did not include subjection in our behalf to "contrition or repentance."

Jesus as substituted for us with the sanction of His heavenly Father, we cannot suppose that His substitution included in it any such thing as subjection in our behalf to what can be properly called "contrition or repentance." Sin may be imputed to a substitute, to the effect of entailing upon him its legal forfeitures and liabilities, but certainly not to the effect of transferring to him its inherent sinfulness or moral culpability. We may well believe, indeed, that it must have been a source of the most intense mental anguish to the immaculate Saviour to have sin reckoned to Him even as regards its consequences, or to be in any way or to any effect associated, and, as it were, legally or judicially brought into contact with that abominable thing which He supremely hates. But whatever anguish may on this account have been experienced by Him, we cannot with propriety regard it as including *all*, or even as including *any*, of the essential elements of "*contrition and repentance*;" for such things as "contrition and repentance" are attributable to those only whose own hearts reproach them for their wickedness. And nothing akin to them could have been endured by that Holy One who, amidst all the vicarious sufferings which He bore, had "the unbroken consciousness of personal separation from those sins" of which the penal consequences were laid upon Him. But if it *were* possible that such things could have been experienced by Him, the question still remains, What are we to think of the procedure of His heavenly Father in sanctioning or appointing them? The substitution of the Saviour in the room of sinners is indeed, in any view that can be taken of it, a profound mystery. But the mystery encompassing it is deepened a thousandfold if God be supposed to have not only visited His immaculate and beloved Son, when standing in our room, with penal consequences for our transgressions, but to have required of Him a penitential confession of them, and a perfect contrition and repentance on account of them, as if in Himself He had been conscious of their ill desert.

This theory only

(5.) Add to all this, that the theory in question is applicable to our Lord's sufferings only to a limited extent.

RESPECTING THE ATONEMENT. 343

In so far, indeed, as His sufferings were *personal*, it furnishes no explanation of them whatsoever. Not only might His personal sufferings have been dispensed with, for aught that is required by the exigencies of this hypothesis, but they tend, so far as they go, to lessen our impression of the greatness of those purely sympathetic sorrows, in which all the virtue of His expiation is held to consist. For it cannot be denied that His sympathetic anguish, arising from the thought of those miseries and sins of men with which, when assuming our nature, He became identified, would have been tenfold more affecting if experienced by one who, instead of being himself " a man of sorrows," was invested with all the insignia of personal greatness, and enriched with all the elements of personal happiness and prosperity.

It is a fact, however, which cannot be controverted, that, apart from the endurance of any sympathetic woes with which human sins and miseries may have afflicted Him, the Lord Jesus Christ was subjected, in His own person, to far more than the ordinary amount of sorrow and humiliation which falls to the lot of God's people in this world, and that His life-long course of ignominy and affliction was terminated by a shameful and accursed death. "Although He was rich, yet for our sakes He became poor, that we through His poverty might be rich." "He came, not to be ministered unto, but to minister, and to give His life a ransom for many." "He humbled Himself, and became obedient unto death, even the death of the cross." "He bore our sins *in His own body on the tree*," instead of merely bearing them in His own spirit by the force of sympathy. "He was wounded for our transgressions, and bruised for our iniquities ; the chastisement of our peace was upon Him, and with His stripes we are healed." "He died for our sins, according to the Scriptures." "He made peace through the blood of His cross." "He was slain, and hath redeemed us to God by His blood." "He was once offered to bear the sins of many." "He appeared once in the end of the world to put away sin by the sacrifice of Himself."

PART
III.
SEC. 4.
——
applicable
to Christ's
sufferings
to a limit-
ed extent.

2 Cor. viii. 9.

Matt. xx. 28.

Phil. ii. 8.

1 Pet. ii. 24.

Isa. liii. 5.

1 Cor. xv. 3.

Col. i. 20.

Rev. v. 9.

Heb. ix. 26, 28.

344   REVIEW OF THEORIES

PART III.
SEC. 4.

In these and many other statements of Holy Scripture, which might, were it necessary, be multiplied without limit, the sufferings of Christ are evidently represented as sufferings with which in His own person He was afflicted. It is but in a few incidental passages that there is any allusion to His sympathy with us in our miseries and sins, as constituting one of the ingredients in His cup of anguish ; whereas the passages are numerous in which there is broad and explicit allusion made to His personal sufferings, and more particularly to His ignominious death, as having been not merely *incidental* to His gracious mission, but mainly and indispensably conducive to the purposes for which that gracious mission was undertaken by Him.

Question still to be answered, How can sufferings of Christ manifest to us the love of God ?

The question, therefore, still demands a solution as much as ever, How can the sufferings of the Lord Jesus be regarded as pre-eminently exhibiting to us the love of God ? What is there to be seen in them so wonderfully expressive of the loving-kindness which our heavenly Father entertains towards us, as to cast all other manifestations of it into the shade ? It is easy to give a reply to this question, if we take into account the commonly-received doctrine of the Atonement. For then the sufferings of Christ are at once seen to be the effectual means of exempting us from penalties which could not otherwise have been averted, and of securing for us blessings which could not otherwise have been obtained. But if this commonly-received doctrine be set aside—if it be not admitted that God gave His beloved Son as a substitute and sacrifice for sinful men, that so, without prejudice to the justice of His character, the authority of His law, and the rectitude of His government, they might be redeemed from the merited consequences of their sins, restored to the full enjoyment of His favour, and blessed with the sure hope of inheriting His heavenly kingdom—we are at a loss to discover anything in our Lord's sufferings which should render them pre-eminently declaratory of His Father's love. For then, in whatever way we may endeavour to account for them, they can only be viewed as *incidental* to His heavenly

RESPECTING THE ATONEMENT.   345

mission, and not as in any way absolutely necessary, or PART III. SEC. 4.
directly conducive to the attainment of the beneficent
ends which that mission was designed to accomplish.
And accordingly, the circumstance of the Son of God
being afflicted with them—not with the view of procuring
for us blessings which could not, without such sufferings,
have been conferred, but merely in the course of announc-
ing to us blessings which might, without such sufferings,
have been proclaimed by Him—tends rather to obscure
than to heighten our conceptions of the love of God in
sending His Son into the world.

4. I have not yet adverted to the position laid down by Alleged
one of the advocates of the theory we are now considering co-relation of Christ's
in regard to " the co-relation or accordance of Christ's atoning
atoning act, when He entered into our sins, and our be- act and our believing act, by which we enter into His righteousness." lieving act.

"Human nature," he says, "is so constituted as to *implicate* us,
not only in our own personal moral acts, but also in the moral acts
of each other ; and in consequence thereof, conscience in its higher
exercises extends beyond the sphere of our individual conduct, and
is sympathetically affected by the conduct of others ; filling us with
shame and grief at the moral degradation of those we love, and inspiring us with a joyous satisfaction when they are seen to excel in
virtue.   The extension of these feelings to their utmost degree unfolds
the true theory of the sufferings of Christ for our guilt, and of our
participation in His perfect righteousness.   By virtue of our union Philosophy
with Him in moral consciousness, He has endured the anguish for of Evange-
sin with which we ought to have been affected ; and as the counter- licism, p.
part thereof, our consciousness of His righteousness becomes to us, 232, 233.
although still consciously ungodly, the counterpoise whereby we are
at the same time subjectively justified."   Again he says, "A clear
avenue is opened between the Christ-consciousness and the human
consciousness, and we detect in their intercommunion the accord of
the atoning act and the believing act.   Our Saviour, conscious of
our sins, has taken them upon Himself and atoned for them ; we,
conscious of His righteousness, appear with it in the sight of God *Ibid.*, p.
and are justified.   Our sins are His sins ; His righteousness is our 140.
righteousness ; and this union of Christ and His people in moral
consciousness is *the central idea of the Gospel.*"

Now, without questioning the fact that we are so constituted as to be " sympathetically affected by the conduct
of others," we cannot discern, in the circumstance of our

346 REVIEW OF THEORIES

PART III. SEC. 4.

being so, any satisfactory explanation of the statements of Scripture respecting our justification by faith in the righteousness of Christ. The "joyous satisfaction" with which we are "inspired when those whom we love are seen to excel in virtue," does not reverse our judgment of our own character, and make us *esteem ourselves virtuous because they are virtuous*, if all the while we are "consciously ungodly"! Rather may we say that it has the opposite effect of deepening the sense of our own moral degradation. For the more highly we appreciate the excellence of those we love, we are so much the more disposed, not surely to justify, but rather, on the contrary, to condemn ourselves, for our own unworthiness as contrasted with their excellence.

But even if we could be held to justify ourselves, or, as the author expresses it, to be "subjectively justified," by a sympathetic participation in the Saviour's perfect righteousness, such self-justification must not be confounded with that gracious act of God, whereby our sins are pardoned and our persons are accepted as righteous in His sight. The justification, which is represented in Scripture as one of the most precious blessings of the Gospel, is no subjective process taking place in the sinner's consciousness, but an act of God's free grace in the sinner's behalf.

Rom. viii. 33.

"It is *God* who justifieth," as the Apostle Paul expressly teaches, and not *we* who justify ourselves. Again, says

Rom. iii. 30.

the same apostle, "It is one God who shall justify the circumcision by faith, and the uncircumcision through faith."

Rom. iii. 24-26.

And yet again (Rom. iii. 24-26), we are "justified freely by His grace through the redemption that is in Christ Jesus; whom God hath set forth to be a propitiation through faith in His blood, . . . to declare at this time His righteousness, that HE might be just, and THE JUSTIFIER of him who believeth in Jesus."

It is perfectly true that the believer is "inspired with a joyous satisfaction" at the thought of his Saviour's righteousness. This, however, does not constitute his justification, but is rather to be considered as one of those precious fruits of which his justification is produc-

RESPECTING THE ATONEMENT. 347

tive. And certainly it has some more substantial ground to rest upon than our mere capacity of being "sympathetically affected by the conduct of others." It rests on the revealed truth, that Jesus Christ is "set forth to be the propitiation for our sins," and that "by His obedience many shall be made righteous." *This* is the sure ground of all the satisfaction which Christians feel in the contemplation of their Redeemer's righteousness. "Being justified by faith, we have peace with God through our Lord Jesus Christ;" "and not only so, but we also joy in God through our Lord Jesus Christ, by whom we have now received the atonement." If these things be so, it evidently appears that our "joyous satisfaction" at the thought of the righteousness of Christ *arises from our being justified on account of it*, and must not, for this as well as for other reasons, be identified with that justification from which it springs.

PART III. SEC. 4.

Rom. iii. 25; v. 19.

Rom. v. 1, 11.

SECTION V.

(10) THEORY OF ROBERTSON OF BRIGHTON.

PART III. SEC. 5.

Theory of Robertson.

X. ANOTHER attempted explanation of our Lord's sufferings, apart from the commonly received doctrine of the Atonement, on which we have now to offer a few remarks, is that which views them as *the necessary result of the position in which Christ had voluntarily placed Himself, of conflict or collision with the evil that is in the world.*

"Had Jesus Christ," says a late eloquent preacher, "been simply surprised by the wiles of His adversaries, and dragged struggling and reluctant to His doom, He would have been a victim, but not a sacrifice. It was His foresight of all the results of His opposition to the world's sin, and His steady and uncompromising battle against it notwithstanding, in every one of its varied forms, knowing that He must be its victim at the last, which elevated His death to the dignity of a sacrifice. It was a true and proper sacrifice,—a sacrifice *for sin* —a sacrifice for *the world's* sin."

In so viewing it, however, there are, according to this writer, two things which must be carefully distinguished —namely, the penalties which follow the violation of a law of nature, and the chastisement which ensues upon an act of moral delinquency.

"If," he says, "you approach too near the whirling wheel of steam machinery, the mutilation which follows is the punishment of your temerity. If a traveller ignorantly lays his hand on the cockatrice's den, the throb of the envenomed fang is the punishment of his ignorance. He has broken a law of nature, and must suffer the consequences of the infraction." The case is similar when pain and sorrow are brought upon us, not by our own conduct, but by the faults of others. "In the strictest sense of the word these are punishments—the consequences annexed to transgression. But there is an all-important distinction between them and the chastisement of

RESPECTING THE ATONEMENT. 349

personal iniquity. For if a man suffer ill-health or poverty as the results of his own misconduct, his conscience forces him to refer this to the wrath of God, and the miseries of conscious fault are added to his penalty."

PART III. SEC. 5

How, then, did the case stand in this respect with Christ?

It is altogether wrong, we are told, to think of Him " as having endured a mysterious anguish—the consequence of divine wrath —the suffering of a heart laden with the conscience of the world's transgressions, and bearing them as if they were his own." " *Christ simply came into collision with the world's evil, and bore the penalty of that daring. He approached the whirling wheel, and was torn in pieces. He laid His hand on the cockatrice's den, and its fangs pierced Him.* Such is the law which governs the conflict with evil. It can be crushed only by suffering from it. *The Son of Man, who puts His naked foot on the serpent's head, crushes it; but the fang goes into His heel.*"

Farther, by way of explaining how Christ may in this way be held to have suffered for the sin *of the world*, we are told, that " sin is a great connected principle—a single world-spirit—exactly as the electricity with which the universe is charged is indivisible, so that you cannot separate it from the great ocean of fluid. The electric spark that slumbers in the dewdrop is part of the flood which struck the oak. Separate acts of sin are but manifestations of one great principle. It was thus that the Saviour looked on the sins of His day. The Jews of that age had had no hand in the murder of Abel or Zacharias, but they were of kindred spirit with the men who slew them. Condemning the murderers, they imitated their act. In that imitation they 'allowed the deeds of their fathers,'—they shared in the guilt of the act, because they had the spirit which led to it." Sermons " Let us possess ourselves of this view of sin, for it is in this way only that we will be able, with any reality of feeling, to enter into the truth, that our sins nailed the Saviour to the cross, or that the Lord laid on Him the iniquity of us all."

Sermons by Rev. F. W. Robertson, 1st series, p. 158-164.

Now it must be evident that the sufferings of our Lord, according to the representation of them here given, cannot by any means be considered as without a parallel. They find their counterpart in those which have been undergone by every zealous reformer and by every devoted martyr who has set himself in opposition to prevailing error and iniquity, and, with the full foresight that he must ultimately be their victim, has steadily resisted and battled against them notwithstanding. Of all such persons it may, in a measure, be affirmed that they have

Sufferings of Christ, as thus viewed, do not differ from those of any martyr.

350 REVIEW OF THEORIES

PART
III.
SEC. 5.
——

voluntarily come into collision with the world's evil, and have borne the inevitable penalty of such a conflict ; and also that men of other generations, although having no immediate hand in their afflictions, have shared in the guilt, in so far as they have displayed the spirit and imitated the deeds of those who persecuted them. It is true, we nowhere find it written in the Word of God, respecting even the most illustrious of self-sacrificing human martyrs or reformers, that " they suffered for our sins,"—that "they gave their life a ransom for many,"—that " they took away sin by the sacrifice of themselves,"—or that "the Lord laid on them the iniquity of us all." I see no reason, however, why some such things might not be written of them, as well as of the Lord Jesus, if the sole ground on which they are applicable to *Him* be that which is set forth in the theory we are now reviewing. And hence the circumstance that such things are written *of Him alone* is indicative of some peculiarity in *His* sufferings beyond what this theory is adequate to account for.

If our Lord's divinity be taken into account, His sufferings cannot be said to have been inevitable.

It may doubtless be said of all, even the very best, of those others who have suffered in their conflict with the world's evil, that they were *mere men*, of like passions with their brethren, subject to errors, infirmities, and besetting sins, and therefore incapable of prosecuting their holy warfare so steadily, so consistently, and so triumphantly as He did, who was not only a perfect and immaculate man, but the *God-man*, in whom divinity was itself incarnate. But then, if you thus bring into account the perfection of our Lord's character and the divinity of His nature, with what show of reason can you venture to affirm *that His own sufferings, when contending against the world's evil, were inevitable?* Surely, in the case of one who combined in His adorable person the omnipotence of divinity with the perfection of humanity, it cannot be reasonably maintained that there was any " *temerity* " displayed, or *any personal suffering necessarily incurred*, by collision even with the most threatening forms of earthly evil.

And here, in passing, I must not omit to notice the

RESPECTING THE ATONEMENT.   351

singular looseness of the analogy that is drawn between
our Lord's contention against the power of evil, and the
vain attempt of any of God's creatures to resist the operation of the fixed laws of the universe. Surely "*the whirling wheel which Christ approached too nearly*," so as to be
"*torn in pieces as the penalty of such daring*," cannot, with
any propriety, be compared to *one of God's laws*, "*moving
on its majestic course irresistible*," insomuch that, "*if you
oppose the law in its eternal march, the universe crushes you
—that is all!*" With much greater justice might *the evil
which our Lord resisted* be itself described as a daring
attempt, on the part of God's rebellious creatures, to set
at defiance those principles of His moral government
which are no less immutable than any laws of the physical universe.

Again, when this writer speaks of "a law governing the
conflict with evil, that it can be crushed only by suffering
from it," the question is forced on us, Whence this law?
Is it a mere blind fatality? Or is it the arbitrary appointment of a sovereign ruler? Or if it be neither of these,
must we not seek after some wise, just, and holy reasons
for it, in the character of God and the principles of His
government,—reasons somewhat akin to those which we
allege when vindicating the necessity of an atonement?

But, not to insist on this, it cannot be with truth
affirmed, in the case of the all-perfect and all-powerful
Son of God, that, apart from the expiatory purpose of
His mediation, He needs must have suffered when contending against the power of sin. *Ordinarily* it may be
"the law which governs the conflict with evil, that it can
be crushed only by suffering from it." It is no *ordinary*
conflict with evil, however, that we have now to deal with,
but one that is in the highest degree *extraordinary*, being,
in point of fact, altogether *supernatural.* We are not
entitled, therefore, to judge of it by natural laws. The
person who maintained this conflict was the Son of God,
in whom "dwelt all the fulness of the Godhead bodily."
And though He became incarnate in the fashion of a man,
yet was He not thereby divested of His higher attributes;

PART
III.
SEC. 5.
———

Loose an-
alogy be-
tween
Christ's
contention
against
evil, and
the at-
tempt of a
creature to
resist the
laws of
nature.

Robert-
son's Ser-
mons, 1st
series, p.
163.

Whence
this alleged
"law,"
that "evil
can only
be crushed
by suffer-
ing from
it"?

Surely *a
divine per-
son* might
conquer
evil with-
out suffer-
ing from it

352   REVIEW OF THEORIES

PART III.
SEC. 5.

while, even as regards the human nature which He assumed, He was miraculously conceived and born of a virgin mother, and was " sanctified and anointed by the Holy Spirit above measure." Such being the case, it seems to me unwarranted, and I may almost venture to say extravagant, to represent this immaculate and divine Redeemer as subject, like frail and fallen mortals, to an incapacity of overcoming the world's evil without Himself suffering from it.

Christ as-serts His power to avoid His sufferings had He chosen to do so.

Certainly the Lord Jesus Christ is as far as possible from acknowledging any such incapacity as lying upon Him. He does, indeed, speak of His sufferings as neces-sary to the work He had undertaken to perform. But, in doing so, He evidently has respect to that expiation of human guilt which they were designed to accomplish. And so far is He from regarding those evil agencies, with which He was necessarily brought into collision, as having any power to harm Him in the conflict, that, on the con-trary, He asserts in the broadest terms their utter impo-tency and nothingness as opposed to Him. Thus, on one occasion, when looking forward to His great sacrifice, He

John, x. 17, 18.

says, " Therefore doth my Father love me, because I lay down my life, that I might take it again. No man taketh it from me, but I lay it down of myself. I have power to lay it down, and I have power to take it again. This commandment have I received of my Father." Again, when Simon Peter drew the sword and smote one of those who had come to seize his Master, Jesus rebuked him,

Matt. xxvi. 53, 54.

saying, " Thinkest thou that I cannot now pray to my Father, and He shall presently give me more than twelve legions of angels? But how then shall the Scriptures be

John, xviii. 11.

fulfilled, that thus it must be?" " Put up thy sword into the sheath: the cup which my Father hath given me, shall I not drink it?" And yet again, when Pilate said to Him, " Knowest Thou not that I have power to crucify Thee, and have power to release Thee?" Jesus calmly

John, xix. 10, 11.

replied, " Thou couldst have no power at all against me, except it were given thee from above." The truth is, that both our Lord Himself and His apostles, when speaking of

RESPECTING THE ATONEMENT. 353

the necessity of His sufferings, have reference, not to the power of any subordinate agencies which may have been instrumental in the infliction of them, but to God's gracious purpose of salvation for perishing sinners through the substitution of His only-begotten Son, to the accomplishment of which, as typified in the ancient law, and foretold by the ancient prophets, His sufferings were indispensable. And if this gracious purpose be ignored or set aside, there is nothing in His mere conflict with the world's evil that can be considered as rendering these sufferings essential to His heavenly mission.

But this is not all. For even were it admitted that the sufferings of our Lord were the necessary result of the position which He assumed, according to the divine appointment, of conflict or collision with the evil that is in the world, the question lies behind, *Wherein is this conflict,* which at so great a cost of suffering He underwent, *pre-eminently conducive to our advantage,* so as to display towards us a love that passeth knowledge? We look in vain to the author above referred to for any definite answer to this inquiry. His statements in regard to it are of the vaguest possible kind. He represents Christ as "opposing the world's sin,"—as maintaining "a steady uncompromising battle against it,"—and as "crushing the world's evil by suffering from it." But to *what effect* did Christ do these things? What substantial good do we gain by His having done them? Did He *so* "oppose and battle against the world's sin" as to *exempt us* from the necessity of a like arduous and painful conflict? Did He *so* "crush the world's evil" as to render it *innocuous to us,* or *less hurtful to us,* when contending against it, than it would otherwise have been? In short, is His contest with evil so inestimably beneficial to us that we should view it and the sufferings attendant on it as transcending all other manifestations of the love of God? To these questions the author of this theory does not reply. He makes no attempt to show how it comes to pass that this self-immolating conflict of the Lord Jesus should have *greatly contributed to our benefit,* as the Scriptures emphat-

PART III. SEC. 5.

Wherein were Christ's sufferings from conflict with the world's evil *conducive to our advantage,* so as to manifest the greatness of God's love to us?

REVIEW OF THEORIES

*PART III.
SEC. 5.*

Christ's sufferings, thus viewed, were the reverse of beneficial to us.

ically declare it to have done, above every other provision of divine love. Indeed, the only connection which he speaks of *us* as having with it is one that is altogether the reverse of beneficial—namely, our participation in the sinful spirit, and our consequent implication in the evil deeds, of those malignant men by whom the Son of God was persecuted! "For it is only," he says, "by keeping *this* in view that we can enter with any reality of feeling into the truth that our sins nailed the Saviour to the cross, and that the Lord laid on Him the iniquity of us all." So, then, according to this writer, the great concern which *we*, as sinful creatures, have in the Redeemer's sufferings is, not that they secure for us pardon and acceptance with God, but that they bring into fuller light the turpitude and heinousness of our transgressions, in so far as we recognise in these the operation of the same evil principle which crucified the Lord of glory!

Where, then, we again ask, is the great benefit accruing to us from the sufferings of the Saviour when contending against the world's evil, by reason of which His subjection to these sufferings may be viewed as an unparalleled manifestation of the love of God? The benefit is obvious, if He suffered as our substitute, and thereby secured for us exemption from the penalties of sin, and grace at the same time to purify us from its moral pollution. But if His sufferings be not the appointed means by which pardoning mercy and sanctifying grace are obtained for such as put their trust in Him; if they be regarded only as the necessary result of His own personal contest with the evil agencies that were opposed to Him; if they have not *so* "crushed the world's evil" as in some effectual way to rescue or redeem us from it,—then I am unable to see any such inestimable good to men of all nations and of all ages arising from them as can justify the Scriptural representations given of them, as of all tokens of divine love incomparably the most wonderful.

They were not advantageous to us even as an example.

Evidently it seems to be only in the way of *example* that our Lord's sufferings, when regarded in this light, can be of any advantage to us whatsoever. Nor is the advan-

RESPECTING THE ATONEMENT. 355

tage which may be derived from them in the way of example to be so highly estimated as some are inclined to think. For *of what* really are they, when thus considered, an example? Not merely are they an example of remarkable firmness, patience, and devotedness in contending against the power of evil, but at the same time *of the incapacity of these qualities, even when displayed in the highest measure of excellence, to save us from the endurance of the bitterest anguish in such a contest.* Indeed, the paramount excellence claimed for them is that of furnishing the most striking instance that ever was exhibited to the world of the alleged " law which governs the conflict with evil— namely, that it can be crushed only by suffering from it." And hence they cannot be considered as supplying us with any very notable encouragement to earnestness and perseverance in our Christian warfare. For if even the immaculate Jesus—the only-begotten Son of God—must needs, when engaging in such a conflict, be subjected to humiliations the most abasing and sufferings the most excruciating, we have cause to fear that ordinary men may find in His example *quite as much to daunt and check as to encourage them;* and that they may so read the history of His afflictions as to learn from it that their best policy is *to refrain from all contact* with " the cockatrice by whose envenomed fang He was so sorely pierced," and *from all collision* with the " whirling wheel, by approaching which too nearly He was torn in pieces."

I cannot refrain from closing these remarks with the following words of a very able writer :—

" The theory of Robertson comes at last to this most deplorable dogma : ' Christ came into collision with the world's evil, and bore the penalty of that daring—He approached the whirling wheel, and was torn in pieces.' What infinite degradation to the Redeemer ! And what infinite triumph to the whirling wheel ! For, of course, the wheel goes on whirling still, and that whirling wheel is ' the world's evil.' And this is the sacrifice of Christ— the offering of Himself to God ! The author declaims

PART III. SEC. 5.

The Atonement in its relation to the Coven- ant, &c., by the Rev. Hugh Martin, D.D., p. 241.

REVIEW OF THEORIES

PART III.
SEC. 5.

against 'the work of redemption being defended by parallels drawn from the most atrocious records and principles of heathenism.' I just ask, What parallel can be found to his own view of that work more accurate than a sacrifice to Juggernaut beneath the crushing wheels of his bloody car? If God's chosen Son violates law, and throws Himself from the pinnacle, He dies. If you resist a law in its eternal march, the universe crushes you—that is all· If you approach too near the whirling wheel, the mutilation which follows is the punishment of your temerity. . . . '*He* approached the whirling wheel, and was torn in pieces.' Was not this to become a victim in the coarse sense of being victimised? He gave way in the 'collision with the world's evil. He bore the penalty of his daring —He was torn in pieces!' How infinitely different is the doctrine of revelation! 'I have overcome the world.' 'He was manifested that He might destroy the works of the devil'—that is, the world's evil. 'He spoiled the god of this world, and made a show of him openly.' His death was His triumph over the world's evil. It was not the triumph of—a whirling wheel! In the hour of His extremest weakness He was powerful to defy and vanquish the world's utmost evil, and powerful to offer Himself unto God a ransom for sinners. He was not conflicting with a physical or social law of this evil world's constitution, and paying the penalty of His daring. He was magnifying the moral law, and making it honourable, and gaining the eternal rewards of obedience unto death. He was not helpless in the embraces of an infernal machine. But His cross—to which, from such insults on its work and doctrine, we return with renewed adoring admiration—was the instrument which, in the lowest ebb of His human strength, He wielded with Almightiness, through the Eternal Spirit, as the weapon of His warfare and the means of His victory. And the shame and agony of the powers of darkness will be eternally renewed in the bitter reflection that their defeat was achieved by an instrument so full of agony and shame to Him who, nevertheless, by means of it defeated them."

RESPECTING THE ATONEMENT. 357

SECTION VI.

THEORIES OF (11) YOUNG AND (12) BUSHNELL.

XI. IN further reviewing the attempts which have been made to account for the sufferings and death of Jesus Christ, apart from the commonly received doctrine of the Atonement, we now proceed to notice some of the leading views advanced by the author of a recently published treatise, entitled 'The Light and Life of Men.'

PART III. SEC. 6.

Theory of Young.

1. This writer substantially agrees with one already referred, to in tracing our Lord's sufferings to those evil influences with which, in His divine mission, He was brought into collision.

Sufferings of Christ alleged to be the necessary result of His colli- sion with evil.

"It was a necessity," he says, "in Jesus Christ to be faithful to Himself, to God, and to man, without regard to consequences, or to the prejudices, wishes, or judgments of people, rulers, or priests. Being what He was, Christ's death in that age and nation was in- evitable; and He knew that it was." "With His eyes open, of His own free will and purpose, He encountered the agony, the terror, and the shame of crucifixion." "His death was the act of men— wholly and solely the act of men; and the actors were governed, not by an invincible decree of God, and not by a resistless Satanic influ- ence, but simply by their own views of the character of their victim —by what they imagined was demanded for the safety of their re- ligion and their country—and by strong feelings of revenge and malice." "Without question, Jesus fell a sacrifice to jealousy and rage; and without question, the offerers of the sacrifice—the only offerers—were the Jews."

Young's Light and Life of Men, p. 286, 291.

Now it may be that the sufferings of our Lord, in so far as regards *the human agency* concerned in them, were the *natural* (though, as we have already endeavoured to show, by no means the "*inevitable*") result of His steadfast

358 REVIEW OF THEORIES

PART III. SEC. 6. — opposition to prevailing sins and prejudices. And it may be further admitted that His adversaries, when afflicting Him, were not overborne by any extraneous influence, to the effect of subverting the freedom of their will, or of lessening in any degree their moral responsibility.

What of God's agency in the matter? But what is to be said of *God's agency* in the matter? This is the main question with which we have to deal ; for no discerning reader of the Scriptures can have failed to remark that the sufferings of Christ are there usually spoken of in reference, not so much to the human actors who inflicted them, as to the divine purposes for which they were appointed.

Now, to this question Dr Young, as appears to me, has failed to give a satisfactory answer.

Ibid., p. 287, 288. "Our Lord's betrayal, capture, and murder," he says, " like all the guilty outbreaks of the human will, however opposed to truth and right and God, were not left out in the vast system of providence, but distinctly reckoned and provided against, as wisdom and love should ordain. Hence wrote the prophet, long before Messiah's advent, ' It pleased the Lord to bruise Him ; He hath put Him to grief.' That which comes out in God's providence is often in Scripture so put as if it were the direct doing of God, though most manifestly it neither is nor can be. Thus it is said, ' The Lord hardened Pharaoh's heart,' when all that God did had a manifest tendency to subdue and reclaim, rather than to harden. But because the actual effect was to render the king of Egypt more obdurate than before, that effect is ascribed, though it can be so only in the most secondary and indirect sense, to the divine agency."

I cannot admit the justice of thus placing our Lord's sufferings, in so far as regards the divine agency concerned in them, on the same footing with " all the guilty outbreaks of the human will," which, " however much opposed to God," " come out in His providence," and are overruled and " provided against, as wisdom and love ordain."

Appeal to God's hardening of Pharaoh inconclusive. It may be questioned, indeed, whether even the " hardening of Pharaoh's heart " can properly be so regarded ; for though we are not to suppose that God exercised on the heart of the Egyptian monarch any hurtful influence, which had a direct and natural tendency to render him more obdurate, yet God certainly knew that the hardening of Pharaoh's heart would be " the actual effect " of those

RESPECTING THE ATONEMENT. 359

divine dealings with him, which, had he been of a better
spirit, were in themselves fitted to " subdue and reclaim
him ; " and what is more, God fully contemplated and
intended that this " actual effect" of His dealings with
Pharaoh should be brought to pass, inasmuch as He said
to him, " For this cause in very deed have I raised thee
up to show in thee my power, and that my name may be
declared throughout all the earth."

But however it may have been in this respect with
Pharaoh's obduracy, it cannot be with any justice said of
our Lord's sufferings, that they merely " came out in the
providence of God," as things which, " however much
opposed to Him," He nevertheless permitted to take
place, while He " reckoned and provided against them,
as wisdom and love should ordain." For it is the clear
and explicit doctrine of Holy Scripture that the sufferings
of Christ *were express matter of divine appointment, as of
themselves constituting the most prominent and important
part of the great work which His Father had given Him to
do.* God did not so much " provide *against* them," as
provide *for* them,—foretelling them in the predictions of
His prophets,—prefiguring them in the sacrifices of His
ancient Church,—and so ordering all events and circumstances in the world's history—not excepting the prejudices and passions of wicked men—as in the fulness of
time to lead to their accomplishment. Peter, on the day
of Pentecost, thus spake of the Great Sufferer : " *Him,
being delivered by the determinate counsel and foreknowledge
of God,* ye have taken, and by wicked hands have crucified
and slain." The whole company of the apostles on a
subsequent occasion " lifted up their voice to God with
one accord," saying, " Of a truth against Thy holy child
Jesus, whom Thou hast anointed, both Herod and Pontius
Pilate, with the Gentiles and the people of Israel, were
gathered together, *for to do whatsoever Thy hand and Thy
counsel determined before to be done.*" Christ Himself spake
of the woes endured by Him as " things which He ought
to suffer," or " things which it behoved Him to suffer," in
order that the great ends of His mission might be fulfilled

PART
III.
SEC. 6.
——

Exod. ix.
16.

Sufferings
of Christ
appointed
by God,
and not
merely
permitted.

Acts, ii.
23.

Acts, iv.
24, 27, 28

Luke,
xxiv. 26,
46.

REVIEW OF THEORIES

PART III. SEC. 6.

John, xviii. 2.

Luke, xii. 50.

—as "a cup which His Father had given Him to drink," and a " baptism which He had to be baptised with." And the truth is, that we rarely find in the Scriptures any very special allusion to the human instrumentality employed in our Lord's afflictions, as compared with the frequency of the references that are expressly made to the part which God had in designing and appointing them.

Scriptures declare that the sufferings of Christ were appointed as an atonement.

Nor is this all; for the Scriptures, while assuring us that the sufferings of Christ were thus matter of divine appointment, have no less unequivocally declared to us the gracious purpose of *expiating the sins of men*, to which, in the counsels of God, they were meant to be subservient. Thus, while in the prophetic passage quoted by Dr Young we read that "it pleased the Lord to bruise Him,—He hath put Him to grief,"—we find in the adjoining verses such statements as the following : " Thou shalt make His soul an offering for sin;" "For the transgression of my people was He stricken;" "The Lord hath laid on Him

Isa. liii. 5-11.

the iniquity of us all ; " " He was wounded for our transgressions, He was bruised for our iniquities ; the chastisement of our peace was upon Him, and with His stripes we are healed ; " " By His knowledge shall my righteous servant justify many ; for He shall bear their iniquities." And frequently in the New Testament we meet with the

1 Pet. ii. 24; iii. 18.

like assurances ; as, for example, that " He bore our sins in His own body on the tree ; " that " He once suffered for sins, the just for the unjust, that He might bring us to

Matt. xxvi. 28.

God ; " that " His blood was shed for many for the remission of sins ; " that " Now once in the end of the world hath He appeared to put away sin by the sacrifice of

Heb. ix. 26, 28.
Gal. iii. 13.
Eph. i. 7.
Col. i. 14.
Rom. iii. 25.

Himself ; " that " Christ was once offered to bear the sins of many ; " that " Christ hath redeemed us from the curse of the law, being made a curse for us ; " that " In Him we have redemption through His blood, the forgiveness of sins ; " that " God hath set Him forth to be a propitiation through faith in His blood, to declare His righteousness

1 John, iv. 10.

for the remission of sins ; " and that " Herein is love, not that we loved God, but that He loved us, and sent His Son to be the propitiation for our sins."

RESPECTING THE ATONEMENT. 361

In the face of these and suchlike explicit statements, which are of the most frequent occurrence in the Scriptures, it is really astonishing that Dr Young, when speaking of the " alleged divine appointment of Jesus to take the place of sinners, and suffer the penalty of their crimes, and thus set them free," should hazard such assertions as the following : " If we demand proof of this divine ordination, *not a shred of proof can be produced ;* " " we look in vain for such a revelation, or anything in the least approaching it. There may be texts in the Old Testament *which it is possible so to interpret that they shall not be wholly subversive of the notion of a divine decree of substitution and vicarious punishment, but there is not a single text of Scripture in which this doctrine, or anything approaching to it, is directly expressed, or in which even it is natural, far less necessary, to presuppose it.*" I hold, on the contrary, and have already endeavoured to show, that of this doctrine we are able to produce the most conclusive proof; and that there are many passages, both of the Old and New Testaments, in which it is so " directly expressed," or so " naturally and even necessarily supposed," that no other interpretation can be put upon them that is not " wholly subversive " of their evident meaning.

We are told, however, that the death of Jesus Christ cannot be regarded as a vicarious sin-offering, because the Jews, to whose jealousy and rage He fell a victim, had no intention to offer such a sacrifice. " Was it ever heard of," we are asked, " that an expiatory sacrifice was offered up to God without the consent of the offerer, and even without his knowledge ? The Jews sacrificed Christ— sacrificed Him to their vile passions ; but as certainly they did not mean to atone for their sins, or to render satisfaction to divine justice."

To this we need only reply, that what we are concerned with is, not the *intention of the Jews* when they brought about the Saviour's death, but *the intention of God* when in His determinate counsel He appointed it. It not unfrequently happens—as in the case of the treatment of

[margin: PART III. SEC. 6.]

[margin: Unwarranted assertion of Dr Young.]

[margin: Light and Life of Men, p. 300, 301.]

[margin: Allegation that "the Jews did not intend to offer Christ as a sacrifice."]

[margin: Light and Life of Men, p. 292, 293.]

[margin: God, however, intended it.]

REVIEW OF THEORIES

PART
III.
SEC. 6.
———
Gen. l. 20;
Ps. lxxvi.
10; Prov.
xix. 21.

Joseph by his brethren—that what men intend for evil, God means for good. It is written of Him, "Surely the wrath of man shall praise Thee, the remainder of wrath shalt Thou restrain;" and, "There are many devices in a man's heart; nevertheless the counsel of the Lord, that shall stand."

Objection, that "men did not select Christ as their substitute."

Light and Life of Men, p. 300.

Again, it is objected that "Christ was not selected by men to live and act in their name; the generations of men were never consulted on the subject, and certainly never signified their concurrence in such a selection." But there is just as little force in this objection; for whatever view may be taken of the end to be served by our Lord's sufferings, it is certain that God was the prime mover in the appointment of them. And why should it be thought necessary that the consent of men must be first obtained before God can give up His Son for their salvation, whether in the way of vicarious sacrifice or otherwise? Surely it is enough if the consent of sinners be obtained before this unspeakable gift becomes actually effectual to their salvation. And *this* is expressly provided for in the Gospel. For the substitution of Christ does not become effectual or actually beneficial to any individual sinner, until that sinner, by an appropriating faith, "receives and rests upon Him for salvation," or, in other words, consents to take Him as his substitute.

Work of redemption alleged to be wholly subjective.

2. Another of the leading doctrines laid down by this writer is, that the work of redemption is wholly *subjective*—its sole and entire aim being the moral transformation of the sinner, or the rooting out of sin from the human soul. Indeed, he holds that no such thing is possible as a remission of the guilt and penal consequences of sin, except through the previous extirpation of sin itself.

"Spiritual laws need no support or vindication."

Speaking of "spiritual laws," he observes that "they do not need or admit of vindication or support from human or divine hands. Without aid from any quarter they avenge themselves, and exact without fail, so long as the evil remains, the amount of penalty to the veriest jot and tittle which the deed of violation deserves. Essentially

RESPECTING THE ATONEMENT. 363

and perfectly wise and right, they are irresistible, in the case of the PART
obedient and the rebellious alike. . . . Spiritual laws are self- III.
acting ; with all their penalties and sanctions, they are immediately SEC. 6.
self-acting, and without the remotest possibility of failure or mistake. Light and
Sin is death—holiness is life; these brief sentences are a condensa- Life of
tion of the code of the spiritual universe." "In the very act, in the Men, p.
very moment of evil, the real penalty descends irresistibly, and in the 87, 88.
very amount which is deserved. The sin insures, because it *is*, its *Ibid.*, p.
own punishment." "God Himself could not annul the sequence, sin 90.
and death ; could not dissolve this dire connection ; could not shield
from the penalty, except by removing its cause. There is only one
way in which the tremendous doom of the sinful soul can be escaped,
in consistency with the great laws of the spiritual universe. . . . If
sin were extirpated, and if the love of God and of good were planted
in its stead, then the true redemption of the human spirit would be
secure. There is one salvation for man—only one ; a salvation not *Ibid.*, p.
from hell, but from sin ; not from consequences here or hereafter, but 100.
from the deep cause itself." "The punishment of moral evil, always
and everywhere, is certain. The justice of the universe in this sense
is an eternal fact, which even God could not set aside." "There is
an irresistible, a real force, springing out of the essential constitution
of things, whereby sin punishes itself. God's mercy in Christ does
not in the slightest degree set aside this justice. What it does is to
remove and render non-existent the only ground on which the claim
of justice stands. Instead of arbitrarily withdrawing the criminal *Ibid.*, p.
from punishment, it destroys in his soul that evil which is the only 115, 116.
cause and reason of punishment, and which being removed, punishment ceases of itself."

Our limits necessarily restrict us to a very few observations on these remarkable statements :—

(1.) Without questioning that in the constitution of The asser-
man, and in the course of providence, there is an order tion not
consistent
of sequences, or a system of "laws," observable, tending with facts.
to secure a kind of *natural retribution*, we demur to the
representation given of these "spiritual laws," as "immediately self-acting, without the remotest possibility of
failure or mistake," and as "irresistible alike in the case
of the obedient and the rebellious," so that "punishment
or reward dispenses itself at once, and in the amount in
which either is merited." For, to say nothing of Scripture,
it is the plain dictate of experience, that there is no such
uniform, unfailing, and adequate dispensation of rewards
and punishments in the present life ; but that, on the con-

364　　　**REVIEW OF THEORIES**

PART III. SEC. 6.

trary, the anomalies and exceptional cases are so great and so numerous as to furnish strong presumptive evidence of a future and more perfect retribution in the life to come.

Sets aside the moral government of God.

(2.) The statements of this writer are further objectionable, as apparently setting aside the moral government of God. He speaks of the "laws of the spiritual universe," by which sin and its bitter fruits are inseparably connected. But what of *God's moral law*, imperatively requiring obedience, through the dictates of conscience, and the express precepts of His Word, and authoritatively denouncing condemnation, either here or hereafter, on its transgressors? He speaks, too, of these "spiritual laws" as "*self-acting*," so as *neither to need nor to admit of support or vindication from human or divine hands.*" And when explaining in what sense the human emotion of *anger* may be attributed to the Almighty, he affirms that one of its human elements—namely, "the desire, leading to effort, to put down sin—*is rendered needless by the ordained course of the universe,* inasmuch as spiritual law necessitates the instant punishment of sin."

Light and Life of Men, p. 151.

What place, it may well be asked, is left by this theory for the moral government of the living personal God? The Judge of all the earth, who will certainly do right, and has pledged Himself to render to men according to their works, is superseded, it seems, by "the justice of the universe." As a legislator and ruler the great God has nothing to do. He has simply to look on and see the operation of that "self-acting" mechanism, which is independent of His support, and does not allow of His interference! *

If salvation would be incomplete without extirpation of sin, it would be equally so without deliverance from condemnation.

(3.) Further, while admitting that the salvation of a sinner would be incomplete without "the extirpation of sin from his soul," we hold that it would be equally incomplete without deliverance from the *guilt* of sin—that is to say, from its forfeiture of the divine favour, and its liability to the divine wrath and condemnation. This latter element of salvation is not to be confounded with

* See Appendix, Note I.

RESPECTING THE ATONEMENT. 365

the former. They are indeed *inseparable* in the provisions of the Gospel, but they are not to be regarded as *identical*. Sin is not only a spiritual *disease* which needs to be cured, but a *crime* which the great Judge must either condemn or pardon. For, not to speak of the testimony of Scripture, which (as might be easily shown did our limits permit) is altogether conclusive upon this point, there is an irrepressible sense of guilt in the human heart, bearing sure witness to the condemnation which past sin has incurred, and which future reformation cannot of itself annul.

It may be said, indeed, that no pardon which God may confer will arrest the operation of those "laws of the spiritual universe whereby sin inevitably punishes itself." But is it not equally true that the *natural retribution* inflicted by these "spiritual laws" is not to be stayed by repentance and amendment? The repentance of the debauchee does not repair his shattered health; the repentance of the prodigal does not retrieve his ruined fortunes; nor, in the case of awakened sinners, is it ordinarily found that repentance and amendment are of themselves sufficient, without some satisfactory assurance of the divine forgiveness, to silence the reproofs of conscience, to allay the oppressive sense of guilt, and to drive away the terrors of a coming judgment.

Even were the case otherwise, what would God be doing, when, by an extraordinary interposition, He "destroys in the soul that evil which is the only cause and reason of punishment, and which being removed, punishment ceases of itself"? Would he not be (indirectly, indeed, but not the less effectually on that account) "setting aside the justice of the universe," and "withdrawing the criminal from punishment"—from the only punishment which, according to Dr Young's theory, is provided for him? And if so, the question remains, Can God, as a just and holy lawgiver and moral governor, be expected to do so without some adequate satisfaction or atonement?

The truth is, however, that, as moral and accountable

PART
III.
SEC. 6.

REVIEW OF THEORIES

PART III. SEC. 6.

agents, it is not with "self-acting laws of the spiritual universe," but with the living personal God—the righteous Judge and Ruler of the universe—that we have to do. The testimony of His Word, and the dictates of our own moral nature, assure us that by sin we are excluded from His favour, and justly exposed to the endurance of His wrath. And hence no method of salvation can avail us which does not provide for the cancelling of our guilt, as well as for the removal of our sinfulness.

How, according to this theory, do the sufferings of Christ extirpate sin?

3. Without dwelling longer on this topic, we now come to the consideration of another question more closely bearing on the subject of our discussion—namely, How is it, according to Dr Young's theory, that the sufferings of Christ are conducive to that "extinction of sin in the soul" which he holds to be "the true and only redemption"?

Simply as "a manifestation of self-sacrificing love."

His answer is, that the sufferings of our Lord secure the accomplishment of this great moral end, simply as being *a manifestation of divine self-sacrificing love*, by which the sinful heart is captivated, its evil inclinations are subdued, and "the love of God and of good are implanted in it."

Light and Life of Men, p. 74.

"The carnal will," he says, "was proof against mere law or authority, and trampled it under foot. The voice of command, even though it were God's, was powerless, and the flesh proudly triumphed over it. But the voice of love is omnipotent. Incarnate, crucified love overmasters sin in the flesh—condemns it, dooms it to death, kills it outright. The first stroke of this divine weapon is mortal, and the final victory, though won by slow degrees, is infallibly certain." "The divinest work of God on this earth is the destroying of evil. By the one true sacrifice of Christ—an act of divine self-sacrifice—He aims a blow at the root of evil within man's heart. The subsequent process is endlessly diverse, and is tedious and slow, but the issue is certain—the death of sin. God touches the deadly disease at its foul source and heals it. He breaks the hard heart by the overwhelming pressure of pure, almighty mercy in our Lord Jesus Christ. He kindles a new divine life, which is holiness—the resolute, free, glad choice of truth and of good." "From the beginning, and through many agencies and influences, mercy has wondrously interposed, not to defraud justice, but to destroy sin, which is death, and to create holiness, which is life. At last, by one amazing intervention, God's uttermost was put forth to secure the double effect by love, whose breadth, and length, and depth, and height, no mind can compass."

Ibid., p. 101.

Ibid., p. 124.

RESPECTING THE ATONEMENT. 367

"The sacrifice of Christ was not required to appease God's anger or to satisfy His justice. . . . It was wholly and solely made by God for men and for sin, in order that sin might be for ever put down, and rooted out of human nature. This stupendous act of divine sacrifice was God's instrument of reconciliation and redemption—God's method of conquering the human heart, and of subduing a revolted world and attaching it to His throne—pure love, self-sacrificing love, crucified, dying love."

PART III. SEC. 6.

Light and Life of Men, p. 313.

It will be observed that in these and the like statements which frequently occur in the treatise of this writer, there is no recognition of *the grace of the Holy Spirit* "shed on us abundantly through Jesus Christ our Saviour," as necessary to the moral renovation of the sinful heart—a doctrine which is held, as the writer must have known, by all orthodox believers in the Atonement, and which, accordingly, he was not warranted, when contending against them, to set aside, without fully and fairly meeting the Scriptural grounds on which it rests. Now I need scarcely remark that, if this doctrine be well founded, it is of itself sufficient to show that the Saviour's mediation was intended, not merely to manifest to sinners the love of God, but at the same time *to procure from God for behoof of sinners that grace* without which no display of divine love would produce any salutary and sanctifying impression upon them.

No recognition of the grace of the Holy Spirit.

But, even without pressing this weighty consideration, there are other grounds on which the *merely subjective* or *moral view* of the Atonement appears to me to be altogether indefensible. It is easy to declaim on the power of "divine love, self - sacrificing love, crucified, dying love," to "overmaster sin, to conquer the human heart, to subdue a revolted world, and attach it to the throne of God." But wherein are the sufferings of Christ expressive of such a love, apart from the expiatory virtues we ascribe to them? If they were not the necessary means of delivering us from penalties and forfeitures not otherwise to be averted, and of procuring for us substantial and important benefits not otherwise to be obtained, it does not appear that we are so infinitely beholden to them that our sins should be mortified, our selfish inclinations

Sufferings of Christ not expressive of love, apart from their expiatory virtues.

368   REVIEW OF THEORIES

PART
III.
SEC. 6.
———
Defective
analogies.

subdued, and our whole souls overpowered and captivated by the contemplation of them.

The author refers us to some " marvellous instances of self-sacrifice for others, furnished by human nature, as aiding us to conceive the higher divine mystery." The mother, for example, who watches day and night by the bed of her child smitten with a deadly plague, and who lives only so long as to see the child restored, and then catches the mortal infection and dies; the youth who plunges into the deep to save a drowning brother, and who, after incredible exertions, reaches him, seizes him, is able only to hold him up till other help arrives, and then himself sinks and perishes; and the physician going deliberately into a room where lies a dead body which contains the secret of some unknown and terrific disease— opening the body—discovering the seat and nature of the malady—writing down what he had discovered, so as to be the means of saving life to the community, and then laying himself down to die;—these are appealed to as

Light and
Life of
Men, p.
310, 311.

" known examples of vicarious suffering, glowing flashes of love from heaven in a dark and cold world," and as indicating that " there must be an eternal Sun of love, out from which they are scattered and imperfect radiations."

Now I might take exception to these instances, on the ground that the sufferings and death endured in them were merely *incidental* to those loving exertions in the course of which they were encountered, and were not, in themselves considered, directly instrumental in bringing about the beneficent result of these exertions. The watchfulness of the mother, the efforts of the youth, and the researches of the physician, would not have been the less advantageous to those who were benefited by them, although they had not been eventually attended with any such fatal consequences to the parties themselves. Whereas, on the other hand, the sufferings and death of Jesus are represented in Holy Scripture not as incidental merely, but as essential to His divine mission, and as themselves constituting the most prominent and important

RESPECTING THE ATONEMENT. 369

part of that beneficent work which His Father had given Him to accomplish.

But not to insist on this defect in the alleged parallels, it is evident that, in one and all of them, there are *substantial objective benefits* to which the self-sacrificing efforts are conducive, by reason of which the *loving character* of these efforts is palpably clear and strikingly impressive, so soon as our minds are turned to the contemplation of them. The affection of the mother is shown by promoting the recovery of her child ; the love of the youth by rescuing his drowning brother ; and the philanthropy of the physician by his discovery of the seat and nature of the mysterious disease for the benefit of his fellow-creatures. But where, I again ask, are there any such indications of captivating and constraining love in the sufferings of the Son of God, according to the *merely subjective view* of the purpose to which they were meant to be subservient ?

The truth is, that whatever amount of *self-sacrifice* may be displayed by the sufferings and death of Christ, they furnish no evidence of " self-sacrificing LOVE," which can, to the extent alleged, be morally influential, *except in so far as we derive from them some substantial good, the priceless worth of which we are capable of appreciating.* Now *the* good which, according to Dr Young, accrues from them, is the slaying of sin, the overcoming of self, the entire subjugation of our own will to the will of God. And *this*, though unquestionably a benefit of the highest value, is not one which the carnal mind can so fully appreciate *as to see in the sufferings of Christ, simply because they tend to it, a captivating and soul-subduing manifestation of divine love.* Most men, as I have already remarked, cannot without much difficulty be brought to regard it as a benefit at all. And to have its matchless excellence and preciousness not only discerned and acknowledged by the understanding, but deeply and fixedly impressed upon the heart, is, I venture to say, a very rare attainment, which only the most spiritual and godly men can be expected to reach—an attainment *which, instead of preceding and mightily conducing to the sanctification of the sinner, is only*

PART III. SEC. 6.

Supra, p 324.

370   REVIEW OF THEORIES

PART III.
SEC. 6.
———

to be reached when his sanctification has been well advanced —an attainment, moreover, which no sinner will ever reach without those sanctifying influences of the Holy Spirit which find no place in the theory under discussion.*

It is no fair retort to say, that even according to the commonly-received view of the Redeemer's sufferings, the agency of the Holy Spirit is necessary to a full appreciation of the love which they display, and an actual experience of the sanctifying power exerted by them ; for *our* doctrine does not require us to maintain, but rather very earnestly to controvert, the *subjective efficacy* of the sacrifice of Jesus Christ, *apart from the objective benefits procured by it.* And of these *objective benefits*, one of the most important is *the grace of the Holy Spirit* which the Saviour's death has purchased for us, according to that state-

Gal. iii. 13, 14.

ment of the apostle, " Christ hath redeemed us from the curse of the law, being made a curse for us, . . . that the blessing of Abraham might come on the Gentiles through Jesus Christ, *that we might receive the promise of the Spirit* through faith."

Nor must it be thought that we underrate the vast importance of that moral power with which the death of Christ is fraught, because we deny the *exclusively subjective* character of the salvation which it is intended to accomplish. On the contrary, we regard it as one of the prime excellences of the evangelical method of redemption, that it provides no less effectually for the purification of our souls than for the pardon of our transgressions. Indeed we hold it to be, so far as men are concerned, the very climax or consummation of their Saviour's work,

Tit. ii. 14.
Jude, 24.

" to purify them unto Himself a peculiar people, zealous of good works," and in the end " to present them faultless before the presence of His glory with exceeding joy." And the chief ground on which we are disposed very earnestly to contend against any *merely subjective view* of the Atonement is, that by such a view *it is robbed of all*

---

* Christ's self-sacrifice, we are told, manifests divine love, because it sanctifies us. And it sanctifies us by manifesting divine love. Surely there is here a " vicious circle."

RESPECTING THE ATONEMENT. 371

its moral power, and made no longer to be that heart-constraining manifestation of the love of God, and as such, that mighty agency of sanctification, which it has ever proved to be when held forth in its true character as a vicarious expiation and satisfaction for the sins of the world.

PART III. SEC. 6.

XII. Having made these remarks on the theory of Dr Young, I deem it unnecessary to dwell at any length on the kindred theory advanced by Dr Bushnell, with the view of accounting for the sufferings of Jesus Christ apart from the catholic doctrine of the Atonement.

Theory of Bushnell.

1. There are just two positions in the treatise of this eloquent writer to which we must particularly advert. One of these, in which he substantially agrees with Dr Young, is, that the salvation which Christ has accomplished is wholly *subjective*—His aim having been, "at the expense of great suffering, and even of death itself, to bring us *out of our sins themselves*, and *so* out of their penalties."

Salvation wholly subjective.

Bushnell on Vicarious Sacrifice, p. 6.

In regard to this position I need only now remark, in addition to the observations already made upon it, that it does not accord with the plain statements of Holy Scripture. There can be no doubt that our deliverance "from our sins themselves" was one of the great ends of the Saviour's mediation. But that it was the *sole*, or even the more immediate, purpose for which he endured His great sufferings, is an assertion which cannot by any means be reconciled with such express Scriptural statements as the following: that "He was wounded for our transgressions, and bruised for our iniquities"—that "He gave His life a ransom for many"—that "His blood was shed for many for the remission of sins"—that we are "justified by His blood"—that "in Him we have redemption through His blood, the forgiveness of sins"—and that "Christ hath redeemed us from the curse of the law, being made a curse for us."

Not in accordance with Scripture.

Isa. liii. 5.
Matt. xx. 28; xxvi. 28; Rom. v. 9; Eph. i. 7.

Gal. iii. 13.

On the last of these texts Dr Bushnell remarks: "Probably the expression 'being made a curse for us,' does

REVIEW OF THEORIES

PART
III.
SEC. 6.
——
Vicarious
Sacrifice,
p. 121,
442.

imply that He somehow came under the retributive consequences of sin—in what manner will hereafter be explained." And afterwards, when giving the promised explanation, he says, "The meaning of the expression is exhausted, when Christ is conceived simply to come into the corporate state of evil, and *to bear it with us*—faithful unto death for our recovery." I need scarcely observe that this is not *explaining* the clause, but *explaining it away*. "Bear it *with* us" is what Paul must be made to say, in order to satisfy the exigencies of Dr Bushnell's theory. But what Paul *does* say is, not "*with* us," but "*for* us." It is somewhat unfortunate for this and for similar theories, that the *former* of these expressions should be constantly avoided, while the *latter* is habitually used, by the inspired writers.

This part
of Bush-
nell's the-
ory is the
reverse of
the Scrip-
tural doc-
trine.

We may venture to say of this part of Bushnell's theory, that it is the *very reverse* of the Scriptural doctrine. For, so far is it from having been the Saviour's purpose to bring us first of all "out of our sins themselves," with a view to our being thereby liberated from their penalties— that, on the contrary, His aim was, in the first place, to save us from the penalties of our transgressions, in order to our ultimate deliverance from the sins themselves.

1 Pet. ii.
24.

Tit. ii. 14.

Heb. ix.
14.

Eph. v.
25-27.

Thus it is written that "He bore our sins in His own body on the tree, *that we, being dead to sin, should live unto righteousness*"—that "He gave Himself for us, that He might redeem us from all iniquity, *and purify unto Himself a peculiar people, zealous of good works*" — that "the blood of Jesus, who through the Eternal Spirit offered Himself without spot unto God, shall purge your conscience from dead works *to serve the living God*"— and that "Christ loved the Church and gave Himself for it, that He might sanctify and cleanse it with the washing of water by the Word, and *that He might present it to Himself a glorious Church, not having spot, or wrinkle, or any such thing, but that it should be holy and without blemish.*" In these and suchlike passages we are plainly taught that, while it is *the more immediate purpose* of the Saviour (according to the no less explicit import of other

RESPECTING THE ATONEMENT. 373

passages) to redeem us from the guilt and penal conse- quences of our transgressions, *His ultimate design is to deliver us from sin itself*, and finally " to present us fault-less before the presence of His glory with exceeding joy."

In full accordance with the position thus assigned to sanctification as the grand and final result to which the Saviour's work of redeeming grace, in so far as regards the subjects of it, is conducive, we find that His cross has a moral power ascribed to it—far beyond aught that other motives are possessed of—to captivate the heart, to sub-due its evil desires, and to bind it in loving and willing homage to the service of God. But we have already shown that any such moral power in the cross of Christ is necessarily dependent on those *substantial objective benefits* which it procures for us—and that, apart from these objective benefits, it is no longer felt to be that unex-ampled manifestation of divine love, and, as such, that mighty agency of sanctification, which it has ever proved to be when viewed in its true character as a propitiation and satisfaction for human guilt.

2. The other part of the theory of Dr Bushnell to which I referred is very much akin to the views of Dr Campbell.

"We are not to hold," he says, "the Scripture terms of *vicarious sacrifice* as importing a literal substitution of places, by which Christ became a sinner for sinners, as penally subject to our deserved penal-ties. Christ, in what is called His vicarious sacrifice, simply engages, at the expense of great suffering, and even of death itself, to bring us out of our sins themselves, and so out of their penalties; *being Him-self profoundly identified with us in our fallen estate, and burdened in feeling with our evils.*" " Love is a vicarious principle, bound by its own nature itself to take upon its feeling and care and sympathy those who are down under evil and its penalties. Thus it is that Jesus takes our nature upon Him, to be made a curse for us, and to bear our sins. Holding such views of vicarious sacrifice, we must find it belonging to the essential nature of all holy virtue. We are also required to go forward and show how it pertains to all other good beings as truly as to Christ Himself in the flesh; how the Eternal Father before Christ, and the Holy Spirit coming after, and the good angels before and after, all alike have borne the burdens, and struggled in the pains of their vicarious feeling for men; and then at last, how Christianity comes to its issue in begetting in us

PART III. SEC. 6.

"Christ identified Himself by sympa-thy with our fallen state."

Bushnell on Vicari-ous Sacri-fice, p. 6,7.

Ibid., p. 17, 18.

374   REVIEW OF THEORIES

PART
III.
SEC. 6.

the same vicarious love that reigns in all the glorified and good minds of the heavenly kingdom; gathering us in after Christ our Master, as they have learned to bear His cross and be with Him in His passion."

Nothing peculiar in sufferings of Christ more than must be felt by all good beings.

According to these statements, there was nothing peculiar in our Lord's afflictions more than in those which needs must be experienced by all good beings, whether divine, angelic, or human, when identifying themselves with others, and taking part in their adversities and troubles.* His physical sufferings, indeed, are not wholly overlooked ; but the place assigned to them is altogether subordinate to those purely moral or sympathetic sorrows which are held

His physical sufferings made of little account.

to constitute the essence of His sacrifice, and which (so far as is necessary to this theory) would of themselves have completed His gracious work, although there had been no death of ignominy endured by Him.

Bushnell on Vicarious Sacrifice, p. 178, 179.

"The agony," says Dr Bushnell, "gives in a sense the key-note of our Lord's ministry, because it is pure moral suffering; the suffering, that is, of a burdened love and of a holy and pure sensibility, on which the hell of the world's curse and retributive madness is just about to burst. . . . The moral tragedy of the garden is supplemented by the physical tragedy of the cross, where Jesus, by not shrinking from so great bodily pains which the coarse and sensuous mind of the world will more easily appreciate, shows the moral suffering of God for sinners more affectingly, because He does it in a lower plane of natural sensibility."

Now I need scarcely observe that the views thus set forth are utterly opposed to the representations of the New Testament. Where do we there find any such things

---

* There are some strange positions advanced by Dr Bushnell, into the discussion of which it is unnecessary here to enter. " *There is a cross* in God," he says (p. 35), "before the wood is seen upon Calvary, hid in God's own virtue itself, struggling on heavily in burdened feeling through all previous ages, and struggling on heavily now, even in the throne of the world." " *The Holy Spirit* " (p. 37) " *bears the sins of men precisely as Christ Himself did in His sacrifice.*" " Vicarious sacrifice " (p. 66) "is not a point where Christ is distinguished from His followers, but the very life to which He restores them, in restoring them to God." These, and the like assertions, in so far as they ascribe vicarious suffering to the followers of Christ, to the Holy Spirit, and to God the Father, in precisely the same sense in which it was endured by the Saviour in behalf of sinners, must be very startling to every humble reader of the New Testament.

RESPECTING THE ATONEMENT. 375

written as that " we are redeemed by the *moral sufferings* of Christ," or " reconciled to God by His *mental anguish,*" or " saved by His *sympathetic feeling of our miseries* " ? Or where do we find " the physical tragedy of the cross " described in the language of inspiration as a mere accessory or " *supplement* to the moral tragedy of the garden " ? Unquestionably it is the *death* of Christ, and not His agony, that is spoken of in Scripture as " the key-note of His ministry." His cross, and not His sympathy, is emphatically declared to be " the power of God unto salvation."

But further, it is important to consider, How do the sufferings of Christ, according to this view of them, pre-eminently display to us, not only His own love, *but the love of His heavenly Father* in visiting Him with them in our behalf ? What otherwise unattainable good do they secure for us, or what otherwise unavoidable evil do they avert from us—so incomparably excelling every other good or evil, that they should be held as affording a manifestation, altogether unequalled, of the love of God ?

That they are of no avail in expiating our guilt or pacifying our conscience is freely admitted, or, I ought rather to say, is earnestly maintained. Our sins can no more be obliterated or atoned for by the mere sympathetic grief of the Saviour when contemplating them, than can the crimes of some abandoned profligate or of some irreclaimable criminal be extenuated by the shame or sorrow they have occasioned to his kinsmen.

But though, according to this view, our Lord's sufferings are not expiatory, may it not be said that they are *powerfully affecting*, or fitted to make a deep and salutary impression on our hearts ? This might be said if we very warmly loved Him, or very highly appreciated the reason of His affliction. The anguish of a venerated mother or beloved wife, when witnessing the guilt and shame of her son or husband, might well be expected, at least temporarily, to affect him, if it could not avail for his permanent reformation. But there is no love on the part of sinners towards Him whose unearthly holiness is alien and repul-

PART III. SEC. 6.

Sufferings of Christ, according to this view, no manifestation of the love of the Father.

376 REVIEW OF THEORIES

PART III. SEC. 6.

sive to them. And what, therefore, does it matter to *them* in what way, or to what extent, His feelings may be excited on their account? Nor can the grief which their sins have occasioned Him suffice of itself to commend Him to their affection. For the sources of that grief they are unable to appreciate—springing as it does from His utter abhorrence of those sins which they fondly cherish and obstinately cling to, insomuch that he seems to be doing them an injury when pleading, even with tears, for the unsparing renunciation of them.

And here it is very important to remember that the persons thus supposed to be impressed with the sufferings of Christ as a manifestation of divine love, are *those self-same sinful creatures* whose sanctification He travailed to accomplish. To *others*, who either have never sinned or have already repented, and who, accordingly, are able to appreciate the inestimable blessedness of a pure and godly life, the sufferings of Christ—endured by Him for the purpose of bringing sinful men to the attainment of that blessedness—may doubtless appear to be a marvellous display of love. But certainly they cannot be so esteemed by *the sinners themselves*, who are wedded to their sins and "alienated from the life of God," and to whom it is like the cutting off of a right hand, or the plucking out of a right eye, to suffer the excision of those carnal and worldly desires in the gratification of which they find their only happiness.

Remarkable concession of Dr Bushnell.

It is unnecessary to dwell on this topic, after what has been said on a kindred theory already discussed. I may be allowed, however, to appeal, in confirmation of the preceding argument, to the very notable concession of Dr Bushnell himself, towards the close of his treatise on 'Vicarious Sacrifice.' For it so happens that, after striving at great length for the establishment of his " *moral-power view* of the Atonement," and insisting that the opposite view of expiation and satisfaction is utterly untenable alike on reasonable and on Scriptural grounds, he astonishes his readers by telling them, at the close of his argument, that the simply moral view of our Lord's sufferings,

RESPECTING THE ATONEMENT.   377

though alone defensible, is one from the preaching of
which little good can be expected; whereas the objective
and expiatory view of them, though entirely baseless, is
alone fitted to produce any salutary moral impression!

PART
III.
Sec. 6.

"In the fact of our Lord's passion," he says, "outwardly regarded,
there is no sacrifice, or oblation, or atonement, or propitiation, but
simply a living and dying thus and thus. The facts are impressive;
the person is clad in a wonderful dignity and beauty; the agony is
eloquent of love; and the cross a very shocking murder triumphantly
met. And if, then, the question arises, How are we to use such a
history so as to be reconciled by it? we hardly know in what way to
begin. How shall we come to God by the help of this martyrdom?
How shall we turn it, or turn ourselves under it, so as to be justified
and set in peace with God? *Plainly there is a want here*, and this
want is met *by giving a thought-form to the facts which is not in the
facts themselves.* They are put directly into the moulds of the altar,
and we are called to accept the crucified God-man as our sacrifice,
an offering or oblation for us, our propitiation, so as to be sprinkled
from our evil conscience—washed, purged, and cleansed from our
sin. Instead of leaving the matter of the facts just as they occurred,
there is a reverting to familiar forms of thought made familiar for
this purpose; and we are told, in brief, to use the facts just as we
would the sin-offerings of the altar, and to make an altar-grace of
them—only a grace complete and perfect, an offering once for all.
. . . So much is there in this, that *without these forms of the altar
we should be utterly at a loss in making any use of the Christian facts
that would set us in a condition of practical reconciliation with God.*
Christ is good, beautiful, wonderful; His disinterested love is a pic-
ture by itself; His forgiving patience melts into my feeling; His
passion rends my heart. *But what is He for?* And *how shall He
be made to me the salvation I want?* *One word*—HE IS MY SACRI-
FICE—*opens all to me; and, beholding Him with all my sin upon
Him, I count Him my offering; I come unto God by Him, and enter
into the holiest by His blood."

Again, he says, "We want *to use these altar-terms just as freely
as they are used by those who accept the formula of expiation or
judicial satisfaction for sin;* in just their manner too, when they
are using them most practically. . . . We cannot afford to lose
these sacred forms of the altar. They fill an office which nothing
else can fill, and serve a use which cannot be served without them.
It may, perhaps, be granted that, considering the advances of cul-
ture and reflection now made, we should use them less, and the
forms of common language more; still, we have not gotten above
the want of them, and we never shall. The most cultivated and
intellectual disciple wants them now, and will get his dearest
approaches to God in their use. We can do without them, it may
be, for a little while; but after a while we seem to be *in a Gospel*

378 REVIEW OF THEORIES

PART III.
SEC. 6.

Bushnell on Vicarious Sacrifice, p. 460-463.

that has no atmosphere, and our breathing is a gasping state. Our very repentances are hampered by too great subjectivity, becoming, as it were, a pulling at our own shoulders. Our subjective applications of Christ get confused, and grow inefficacious. Our very prayers and thanksgivings get introverted and muddled. Trying to fight ourselves on in our wars, courage dies and impulse flags ; and so we begin to sigh for some altar, whither we may go and just see the fire burning, and the smoke going up on its own account, and circle it about with our believing hymns ; some element of day, into which we may come, and simply see, without superintending, the light."

Such is the notable concession of this able and eloquent author. I am sure we do not exaggerate its import when we hold it as substantially amounting to an affirmation that the *moral-power view* of our Lord's sufferings is *morally powerless,* and that the *objective view,* which the writer denounces as an irrational and indefensible "theologic fiction," is, after all, indispensable to the salvation of sinners! While constructing his system, he had argued and insisted that "the power of the cross is not in, or of, any consideration of a penal sacrifice, but is wholly extraneous ; a Christ outside of the doctrine ; dwelling altogether in the sublime facts of His person, His miracles, and passion." But when he comes to put his system to the test, in the actual work of reconciling and reclaiming sinners, he finds himself obliged to acknowledge its insufficiency. "The facts of the Gospel outwardly regarded, with no sacrifice, or atonement, or propitiation involved in them," are now felt and owned to be utterly useless and inefficacious, until " they are put into the moulds of the altar, and we are called to accept the crucified God-man as our sacrifice, an offering for us, our propitiation." " We must use these altar-forms just as freely as they are used by those who accept the formula of expiation or judicial satisfaction ; in just their manner, too, when they are using them most practically. And " so much is there in this, that, without these forms of the altar, we should be utterly at a loss in making any use of the Christian facts that would set us in a condition of practical reconciliation with God." Here, surely, there is somewhat of an approximation to Paul's statement that

Ibid., Preface, p. xxxiii.

RESPECTING THE ATONEMENT. 379

"the preaching of the cross is to them that perish foolish- PART
ness, but unto us which are saved it is the power of God;" III.
—with this wide difference, however, that whereas the SEC. 6.
modern theorist *himself* regards as "foolishness" that ——
mode of preaching the Gospel which he acknowledges 1 Cor. i.
to be alone effectual—the ancient apostle, on the other 18.
hand, esteems it as not only the "*power*," but the "*wisdom*"
and the *truth* of God.

380   REVIEW OF THEORIES

SECTION VII.

(13) RECTORAL OR GOVERNMENTAL THEORY OF THE ATONEMENT.

PART
III.
SEC. 7.
———
Govern-
mental
theory of
the Atone-
ment.

XIII. THERE is yet one other theory of the Atonement, differing from the commonly received doctrine, on which it is necessary to make a few remarks. I allude to what is called "*the rectoral or governmental theory*," according to which the death of Jesus is regarded as *a salutary provision or expedient to meet the exigencies of God's moral government*, which might have been injuriously affected by the pardon of sinners, without some such demonstration of His fixed purpose to maintain inviolate the obligation of the moral law as is furnished by the great sacrifice of the cross.

This theory seems to have originated with Grotius. He at least appears to have been the first writer by whom it was stated in something like a definite form, in his treatise concerning "*the satisfaction of Christ*." In modern times it has been adopted or countenanced by a very great number of theological writers both in Britain and in America; and it holds a prominent place in that system of doctrine which is commonly called "The New England Theology."

The gratuitous pardon of sin, without any expiation, would, as we are told by the advocates of this theory, have produced in the minds of men an impression that God was indifferent to the authority of His law, and that sin, accordingly, might be committed with impunity. In order to counteract an impression so pernicious, it was

RESPECTING THE ATONEMENT. 381

necessary that God should display His abhorrence of sin
in the very method appointed by Him for pardoning the
sinner, and that, while remitting the penalties of His
broken law, He should show His firm and inflexible
determination to maintain inviolate the obligation of its
statutes. For this purpose exclusively, we are told, the
sufferings and death of Christ were requisite as the ground
of our redemption. It is not the "retributive justice" of
God that is satisfied by them, but what is called His
"rectoral or public justice." Or rather (to speak plainly),
it is not "the justice of God," in any sense, that can be
attached to that expression, or *anything in the divine
mind* that is satisfied by them, but only *something in the
outward exigencies of the divine government that is supplied*, to the effect of providing that safely, honourably,
and without prejudice to the interests of practical godliness, God's mercy may be freely extended to transgressors, without such penal satisfaction as His justice
requires.

In further exposition of this theory, I may quote the
following statements of Dr Wardlaw, one of the most able
and judicious of its supporters :—

PART III. SEC. 7.

"*Distributive*, or, as some designate it, *retributive justice*, does not
admit of substitution. It issues a righteous law with a righteous
sanction. It passes its sentence of condemnation against the transgressor of that law. It makes no mention of any possible satisfaction
but the punishment of the guilty themselves." "According to the
requisition of justice, in its distributive sense, every man personally
must have his own due. But in substitution it is otherwise. Here
there is an inversion of the principles of strict retribution : neither
Christ nor the sinner has his own due. The guilty, who, according
to these principles, should suffer, escapes ; and the innocent, who
should escape, suffers. In no strict and proper sense, then, can distributive justice be satisfied by substitution, when its demands are,
for a special purpose, and by an act of divine sovereignty, suspended,
superseded, overruled. In another sense, however, justice *was* satisfied, all its ends having been *virtually* and to the full effected by
other means. And this leads me to the true object of atonement. It
is to *public justice* that, in substitution or propitiation, the satisfaction
is made. The grand design is to preserve unsullied the glory of the
great principles of eternal rectitude ; to show the impossibility of the
demands of equity, founded in these principles, and essential to the

*Theory as
stated by
Dr Ward-
law.*

*Discourses
on Atone-
ment, 3d
ed. p.
60-62.*

REVIEW OF THEORIES

PART III.
SEC. 7.

government of the universe, being dispensed with; to settle in the minds of God's intelligent creatures, as the subjects of His moral administration, the paramount obligation and immutable permanence of their claims; to give such a manifestation of the divine regard to these elements of His immaculate administration, as to preclude the possibility of any the remotest surmise that in the pardon of sin they have been at all overlooked or placed in abeyance; and thus to render it consistent with divine propriety, or, in other words, honourable to the whole character, as well as to the law and government of Jehovah, to extend pardoning mercy to the guilty, and to reinstate them in His favour, according to the promises of the Gospel. It is thus that, in pardoning sin, His regard to righteousness is as conspicuous as His delight in mercy; and in the minds of the pardoned, the impression of the claims of the one is as deep as that of their obligations to the other. In this view of it the scheme possesses a divine grandeur. The glory of God, and the good of His universal empire—the two great ends of *public justice*—are with all wisdom and prudence admirably combined in it. It is as essential to the latter of those ends as it is to the former, that the authority of the divine government be maintained in its awful and inviolable sacredness; that the demands of the law be upheld, without one jot or tittle of abatement; and that if any sinner is pardoned, the mercy shown to the offender be shown in such a way, on such a ground, through such a medium, as shall at once manifest the divine reprobation of his offences, and, at the same time, secure the restitution of the guilty perpetrator of them to the principles, affections, and practice of holy allegiance. Such are the purposes, and such the effects, of the Christian Atonement." Again, says the same writer, " If the sinner be pardoned, the manner of bestowing the pardon must be such as shall mark and publish the evil of his offence, so as to leave the character and government of the Most High without suspicion; or, in the terms of the Roman orator, whose words may be applied with an infinitely higher amount of force to the universal administration of heaven than to any limited earthly rule—*Ne quid detrimenti respublica caperet.*"

Wardlaw's Systematic Theology, ii. 372.

In opposing this theory, we are not concerned to deny that *one purpose* served by the Atonement unquestionably is to provide for the extension of mercy to transgressors in such a way as shall not be prejudicial to the authority of God's law and the supremacy of His moral government. We are simply concerned to show that this is *not the sole purpose* for which the Atonement has been provided; and farther, that even this purpose could not be effectually secured by it, unless it truly were that satisfaction to the justice of God for the sins of men which, according to the Catholic doctrine, it is held to be.

RESPECTING THE ATONEMENT. 383

1. With this view I may observe, *in the first place*, that *the rectoral theory proceeds on an erroneous conception of the nature and end of the divine penalties against transgression,* confounding in this respect the wide difference that subsists between the legislation of God and that of earthly governments. Among men it is generally acknowledged that punishments are *exemplary* rather than *retributive;* their proper object being not so much the execution of vindictive justice, as the discouragement or suppression of crime. " The end or final cause," says Blackstone, " of human punishment, is not by way of atonement or expiation for the crime committed, but as a precaution against future offences of the same kind." " In like manner," says Paley, " the proper end of human punishment is not the satisfaction of justice, but the prevention of crimes. In what sense, or whether with truth in any sense, justice may be said to demand the punishment of offenders (that is, justice as administered by men), I do not now inquire ; but I assert that this demand is not the motive or occasion of human punishment. . . . The fear lest the escape of the criminal should encourage him, or others by his example, to repeat the same crime, or to commit different crimes, is the sole consideration which authorises the infliction of punishment by human laws." This is what is called " public or rectoral justice," administered, not on the principle of retribution, but for the sake of moral impression or example. And the ends which it aims at may be sufficiently attained, without the infliction of punishment on the offenders, by any provision or expedient in lieu of punishment which may be equally effective in deterring them and restraining others from the future commission of like offences.

There is a mighty distinction, however, in this respect between the procedure of human governments and that of the divine government — a distinction that is fully recognised and clearly pointed out by the authors above referred to. Thus Blackstone, while denying that the end of human punishment is the expiation of crime, is careful to add that "this is a matter which must be left

Marginal notes:
PART III. SEC. 7.

The theory proceeds on an erroneous view of the end of divine penalties against sin.

Laws of England, book iv. chap. i.

Paley's Moral and Political Philosophy, book vi. chap. ix.

Difference in the procedure of human governments and of the divine government.

384   REVIEW OF THEORIES

PART III. SEC. 7.

to the just determination of the Supreme Being." And Paley, while holding that "the proper end of human punishment is the prevention of crime and not the satisfaction of justice," adds this important explanation of his statement,—"By the satisfaction of justice I mean the retribution of so much pain for so much guilt, which is the dispensation we expect at the hand of God, and which we are accustomed to consider as the order of things which perfect justice dictates and requires."

It is unnecessary, however, with reference to this subject, to appeal to human jurists or moralists, however distinguished ; for we have the clearest and fullest evidence in Holy Scripture that justice is one of the essential attributes of the nature of God ; that He is regulated by it in all His dealings with His accountable creatures ; and, in particular, that He has respect to it in all His threatened penalties against transgression. His own Word expressly and solemnly assures us that " He is a just God

Isa. xlv. 21 : Ps. ix. 8 ; xi. 7 ; lxxxix. 14 ; cxlv. 17 : Rom. xii. 19.

and a Saviour ; " that " the righteous Lord loveth righteousness ; " that " God shall judge the world in righteousness, and minister judgment to the people in uprightness;" that " justice and judgment are the habitation of His throne ; " that " the Lord is righteous in all His ways, and holy in all His works ; " and that He hath solemnly

Divine punishments not merely *preventive* but *retributive.*

declared, " Vengeance is mine, I will repay." From these and many other Scriptural statements it is evident that the punishments which God has threatened to inflict are properly *retributive*, and not merely *preventive*, being dictated by a regard to the inherent rectitude of His own character rather than to the mere outward exigencies of His government. And hence it cannot be said that the purpose of these punishments can be fully served by any expedient which altogether ignores their retributive character, however adequate it may be to supply their place as mere restraints or dissuasives from the commission of sin. If there be anything in the rectitude of the divine nature, as well as in the requirements of the divine government, that calls for the condemnation of transgressors, we cannot suppose that their condemnation will be stayed

RESPECTING THE ATONEMENT. 385

by any device of administrative policy by which the evil
effects of a free pardon might be counteracted, without
some such satisfaction for their sins as may be approved
of in the judgment of that righteous and holy God with
whom they have to do.

2. And this leads me farther to observe, that in the case
of the divine government there is really no room for any
such distinction as that which the supporters of this
theory are fain to draw between "rectoral or public justice" and "absolute or retributive justice." They do not
deny that God is essentially just; and hence they must
admit that everything that is done by Him is characterised by strict equity or rectitude. Assuredly, if God be
"righteous in all His ways," He must be supposed to be
so in His rectoral capacity, as well as in every other
respect in which we may regard Him. Nay, it is precisely
and pre-eminently in this capacity that His essential
justice finds its proper field of exercise. It is said of Him
in Scripture, that "*He sits on the throne* judging right." Ps. ix. 4.
And where else, indeed, if not "upon the throne," should
we expect Him to do so? If that "distributive justice,"
which consists in rendering unto all their dues, be not
displayed in the administration of His government, I am
at a loss to conceive where or when it can be displayed.
The attribute of justice is, from its very nature, a *judicial*
or *magisterial* attribute; and there seems to be no scope
for its exercise at all if it be excluded from the arrangements of the divine government. In the case of human
governments, which are fallible and defective, "rectoral
justice" may not always be administered according to the
strict principles of real or absolute justice; but not so in
the case of the perfect and unerring government of God.
We cannot suppose that *here* there will ever be the
slightest deviation from the principles of rectitude. We
may not always, indeed, be able to discern the just and
good ends to which God's doings are subservient, but yet
we cannot doubt that He is "righteous in all His ways;"
and that even when "clouds and darkness are round about

PART
III.
Sec. 7.

In the case
of the di-
vine gov-
ernment,
no room
for distin-
guishing
between
"rectoral
justice"
and "ab-
solute jus-
tice."

386 REVIEW OF THEORIES

PART III. SEC. 7.

Ps. xcvii. 2.

Him," still "righteousness and judgment are the habitation of His throne."

On these grounds we hold that the distinction that has been attempted to be drawn between God's "rectoral justice" and His "absolute justice" is inadmissible. In the case of the Supreme Moral Governor, "rectoral justice" so necessarily presupposes "absolute justice" as the basis on which it rests, or the principle by which it is regulated, that the idea of an Atonement which satisfies the one, while it cannot satisfy the other, must be a mere delusion.

The same difficulty in supposing "rectoral justice" as "absolute justice" to be satisfied by vicarious penalties.

3. But farther, allowing for the sake of argument that there were such a thing in the moral government of God as "rectoral or public justice," distinguishable from "absolute justice," there is the same difficulty in conceiving that *the former*, as that *the latter*, should be satisfied with sufferings endured, in commutation of the merited penalty, by any other than the party who has himself transgressed.

We are told that while "distributive justice" requires that the full and actual punishment of sin should be inflicted, "public justice" may dispense with it for something else that answers the purposes of government as effectually in the way of restraining and discouraging sinners from future offences. Be it so. But then, if this "something else in lieu of the penalty" be endured, not by the offender himself, but by a perfectly innocent and blameless substitute · and what is more, if this substitute be provided, not by the offender himself, but by the very judge and sovereign before whose tribunal that offender stands arraigned,—I cannot see that it is one whit more manifest that the ends of "public or rectoral justice" are thus answered than that the requirements of "absolute justice" are thus satisfied. Nay, if the demands of "absolute justice," so far from being satisfied by such an arrangement, are, as is strongly affirmed by Dr Wardlaw, "suspended, superseded, and overruled," it seems a downright contradiction to affirm that "the demands of the law are notwithstanding upheld without one jot or tittle of abatement;" that "the authority of the divine govern-

RESPECTING THE ATONEMENT. 387

ment is preserved in its awful and inviolable sacredness;" and that "the character of the Governor and the rectitude of His administration are maintained in their full dignity, free from every charge of mutability or imperfection." I can readily conceive that such things might be affirmed by those who, "walking by faith and not by sight," are ready to receive it on the authority of the Word of God, that in some way, albeit to us incomprehensible, His justice *truly was satisfied* by the Atonement; but I cannot conceive how such things should be affirmed by any one who asserts that by that very provision, which he holds to be so gloriously illustrative of the sanctity of the divine law and the authority of the divine government, the requirements of "distributive justice," instead of being satisfied, are absolutely "suspended, superseded, and overruled."

The difficulties of the theory in this respect are greatly increased when we take into account that the advocates of it strenuously deny that the sufferings of Christ were *penal* in their character. For how can sufferings that are *not penal* in their character be considered as "fully answering the ends of punishment"? How can they be deemed a satisfaction to God's "rectoral justice" if they were not inflicted by an exercise of "rectoral justice"? The purpose of Christ's sufferings, according to this theory, was not to satisfy the penal requirements of God in behalf of those whose sins the Saviour bore, but only *to exhibit or manifest to the intelligent universe that sin must be punished, aud assuredly shall be punished.* But surely if these sufferings were not of the nature of punishment at all, they could not teach the *really intelligent* portion of the universe any such lesson as this. Instead of teaching that sin must and shall be punished, they must, in the case supposed, be held as teaching *the very reverse*—as teaching that sin may be freely remitted *without punishment, or anything that can be regarded as punishment.*

Be this as it may, however, of one thing we may be sure, that if there be anything mysterious—as we admit that there is—in the Atonement considered as a satisfaction of God's "distributive justice," there is quite as much,

PART
III.
SEC. 7.

Difficulties of this theory increased by its denial that Christ's sufferings were *penal.*

388 REVIEW OF THEORIES

PART III.
SEC. 7.
——

if not more, that is mysterious in it when held forth as a satisfaction of God's "rectoral justice;" and that, being thus mysterious, it cannot be characterised as "a *grand public display* of the justice of the divine government, by which the minds of all intelligent creatures cannot fail to be deeply affected and impressed." For surely "rectoral justice," *when publicly displaying itself*, so that all the world may appreciate it and be affected by it, is concerned to see that punishment be always inflicted on the offending party, and that neither punishment, nor suffering in lieu of punishment, be awarded to any one who is personally free from guilt. But if an arrangement be made for the transference of suffering from the guilty who deserves it to the innocent who deserves it not—insomuch that neither the one nor the other gets his due, and (as affirmed by Dr Wardlaw) "distributive justice is, in no strict or proper sense of the word, satisfied at all, but is, on the contrary, overruled or superseded"—I am at a loss to see with what reason it can be said that by such an arrangement "the inviolable authority of the divine government is fully maintained," that "the glory of the great principles of eternal rectitude essential to that government is preserved unsullied," and that "such a *manifestation* is given to all God's intelligent creatures of His regard to these principles of His immaculate administration, as to preclude the possibility of any the remotest surmise that in the pardon of sin they could be overlooked or placed in abeyance."

This theory represents the Atonement as an unreal display of what is not truly involved in it.

4. These remarks lead me to state a *fourth* objection to the governmental theory of the Atonement—namely, that *it represents the Atonement as nothing more than a hollow and unreal exhibition of principles which are not truly and substantially involved in it.*

That such is the case will very soon appear if we substitute a plain, direct, and unambiguous statement of it, instead of the somewhat pompous, inflated, and, I must add, equivocal phraseology in which the theory is usually propounded by its advocates; for, when put into plain words, what does it amount to? Simply to this: "There was nothing in the nature or attributes of

RESPECTING THE ATONEMENT. 389

God to prevent Him from pardoning sin without any
expiation, had it pleased Him in the exercise of His
absolute sovereignty so to do. He might, if willing to do
so, have simply and freely cancelled the penalties of sin
without requiring any equivalent or satisfaction for them,
either from the actual offenders themselves, or from an
approved and suitable substitute ; but then it would
have been exceedingly dangerous, and highly prejudicial
to morality and practical godliness, for His rational
creatures to know that this is the case ; and therefore He
has taken extraordinary means to conceal it from them,
and to lead them to suppose that the state of the case is
quite otherwise. In order to produce or to sustain in
their minds an *impression* that sin and its threatened
penalties are inseparably connected, and that even in the
exercise of His boundless mercy He cannot compromise
the requirements of justice, He gave up His only-begotten
Son to humiliation, agony, and death. It is true, *the
impression thus to be produced is an erroneous one*—we
theologians have found out that it is so ; for we are too
wise to be taken in by mere appearances. Nevertheless,
the erroneous impression is a salutary one. It is calculated to have a mighty effect on the mass of men who are
not accustomed to look below the surface of things, or to
make subtle distinctions between ‘ rectoral justice ’ and
‘ real justice.’ It will lead *them* to think that ‘ God is
maintaining in their full dignity, free from every charge
of imperfection and mutability, the rectitude of His character, the majesty of His government, and the authority
of His laws ; ’ although WE can clearly enough see that the
principles of justice, in the strict and proper sense of the
expression, are so far from being fully maintained and
duly satisfied, that, on the contrary, ‘ they are superseded
and overruled.’ ”

I should be sorry to give an unfair representation of the
theory we are discussing. But I do not see that it can be
regarded in any other light than that in which I have
placed it ; for it holds that the sufferings of Christ *were
not penal in their nature,* and *did not really satisfy the*

PART
III.
SEC. 7.

REVIEW OF THEORIES

PART III. SEC. 7.

inherent justice of God, but were meant only to produce an impression on the minds of men that God hates and condemns sin not the less when sparing the sinner, and that in extending pardon to transgressors " His regard to righteousness is as conspicuous as His delight in mercy." Now, what is this but in other words to say that the sufferings of Christ were intended to make an exhibition of divine attributes which were not really displayed in them, and to show God's determination to punish sin by a transaction in which sin is not punished at all, but is pardoned without anything that is of the nature of punishment? Nay, does it not farther imply that the hollowness of this exhibition has been fully discovered by these very theorists, so as to render it utterly futile and abortive?

This theory unsupported by Scripture.

5. But farther, the governmental theory of the Atonement derives no support from the testimony of Holy Scripture.

I might urge in opposition to it many statements of the Word of God—those, for example, which teach us respecting the Saviour that " the Lord laid on Him the iniquity of us all "—that " God sending His own Son in the likeness of sinful flesh and for sin, condemned sin in the flesh " —that " God hath made Him to be sin for us who knew no sin, that we might be made the righteousness of God in Him "—that " Christ hath redeemed us from the curse of the law, being made a curse for us "—that " Christ was once offered to bear the sins of many "—that " He bare our sins in His own body on the tree ;"—statements which seem very plainly to assure us that the sufferings of Christ really were of the nature of punishment, and were meant to be a satisfaction to divine justice for the sins of men. But it is enough to observe that the only text which has been urged with any plausibility in favour of the governmental theory, gives it, when maturely considered, no real support. I allude to St Paul's statement respecting Christ, that " God hath set Him forth to be a propitiation through faith in His blood, to declare His righteousness, that He might be just, and the justifier of Him who believeth in Jesus." Here, say the supporters of the theory, we are

Isa. liii. 6; Rom. viii. 3 ; 2 Cor. v. 21.

Gal. iii. 13.

Heb. ix. 28.

1 Pet. ii. 24.

Rom. iii. 25, 26.

RESPECTING THE ATONEMENT. 391

taught that " Christ was set forth as a propitiation in order
to *declare* or *exhibit* the " righteousness of God." Nor are
we concerned to deny that such is the apostle's teaching.
We are very much concerned, however, to insist that the
"declaration" was meant to be a *true* one—a "declaration"
or " exhibition" *of nothing more than really was implied in
the transaction.* Thus much is plainly affirmed in the latter
clause of the apostle's statement, in which we are told that
the purpose of the propitiation was, not that God might
appear to be just, but "that God might BE just, and the
justifier of him who believeth in Jesus."

It is, we freely admit, a matter of much importance that
the justice of God should be *manifested* or *exhibited* to all
His intelligent creatures in the method of redemption, so
as to maintain the authority of His government, to preserve inviolate the sanction of His law, and to provide in
every pardoned transgressor for the interests of holiness.
But in order that these important ends may be attained,
the manifestation or declaration of God's righteousness
must be *real* or *substantial,* and not merely *apparent.*
" There is," says Dr Cunningham, " no real manifestation
of the excellence and perfection of the divine law, or of
the necessity of maintaining and honouring it, if, in the
provision made for pardoning sinners, that law was relaxed
and set aside—if its penalty was not inflicted—if there was
no fulfilment of its exactions, no compliance with its demands. . . . The notion that the Atonement operates
on the forgiveness of sinners merely by its being a great
display of the principles of God's moral government, is
so far from being fitted to supersede the stricter views of
substitution and satisfaction, that *it cannot stand by itself*
—nothing can really be made of it, unless those very views
which it is designed to supersede are assumed as the
ground or basis on which it rests." In like manner says
Dr Hodge : " The Atonement is an exhibition of God's
purpose to maintain His law and to inflict its penalty, and
thus operates as a restraint and a motive on all intelligent
beings, *because it involves the execution of that penalty.* It
is this that gives it all its power. *It would be no exhibition*

PART
III.
SEC. 7.

Historic
Theology,
ii. 355,
356.

Princeton
Essays, 1st
series, p.
267.

392   REVIEW OF THEORIES

PART III.
SEC. 7.
——

of justice if it were not an exercise of justice—it would not teach that the penalty of the law must be inflicted unless it implied that the penalty of the law *was* inflicted."

This theory does not conciliate opponents of the Scriptural doctrine.

6. I may further observe, with reference to this theory, that it does not serve one of the chief ends contemplated by it—that, namely, of conciliating the adversaries of the commonly-received doctrine regarding our Lord's sufferings. To show this it is only necessary to adduce the following statements of Mr Jowett and Mr Martineau, two of the ablest modern opponents of the Catholic doctrine :—

Jowett on Epistles of St Paul, 1st ed., ii. 473, 474.

" If this scheme," says Mr Jowett, " avoids the difficulty of offering an unworthy satisfaction to God, and so doing violence to His attributes, we can scarcely free it from the equal difficulty of interposing a painful fiction between God and man. . . . This theory has no advantage over the preceding, except that which the more shadowy statement must ever have, in rendering difficulties themselves more shadowy. It avoids the physical illusion of the old heretics, but introduces a moral illusion of a worse kind. For if for ' satisfaction ' we substitute ' demonstration or exhibition of divine justice,' we are not better off than in the previous attempt to explain ' satisfaction.' How could the sufferings of a good or divine person exhibit the righteousness of God? Rather would they seem to indicate His indifference to those sufferings in permitting them. . . . When the doctrine is stated it betrays itself ; for how could there be an exhibition of divine justice which was known to be a fiction ? . . . The doctrine thus stated is the surface or shadow of the preceding, with the substance or foundation cut away."

Studies of Christianity, p. 166.

" According to this doctrine," says Mr Martineau, " it is not any obstacle in God, arising from His personal sentiment of equity, which must be satisfied, but one which springs out of the necessity of consistent rectitude and adherence to law in His administrative government. The Father Himself, it is intimated, would be quite willing to forgive, were there nothing to consult except His own disposition. But it would never do to play fast and loose with the criminal law of the universe ; and notwithstanding the most solemn enactments, to let off delinquents on mere repentance, as if nothing were the matter beyond a personal affront. Something more is due to *public justice*. If the due course of retribution is to be turned aside, it must be in such a way and at such a cost as to proclaim aloud the awfulness of the guilt remitted. This, we are told, is accomplished by the sufferings and death of the Son of God, which were substituted for our threatened punishment, not as its quantitative equal paid to the

RESPECTING THE ATONEMENT. 393

Father, but as a moral equivalent in the eyes of men. . . . No
doubt this scheme gets rid of the penal mensuration and moral con-
veyancing of the older Calvinism. It shifts the bar to free mercy
away from the inner personality of God, and sets it in His outer
government. But when we again attempt to seize the *mediatorial*
expedient, what is it? It is said to be a display of the enormity of
that guilt which needs to be redeemed at such a cost. But is that
need *real?* Have we not been told that it has no place in God?
Does He, then, hang out a profession that is not true to the kernel
of things, but only a show - off for impression's sake? If eternal
justice, in its inner essence, *does not* require the expiation provided,
why, in its outer manifestation, pretend that *it does?* As nothing
can become right "for the sake of good example" that is not right
in itself, so is *public justice*, unsustained by the sincere heart of
reality, a mere dramatic imposture. . . . The younger doctrine
appears to us a positive degradation of the elder, not only in logical
completeness, but in religious worth. The theory of Owen, stern as
it is, bears the stamp of resolute meaning consistently carried through
into the inmost recesses of the divine nature. The newer doctrine is
the production of a *platform age*, which obtrudes considerations of
effect even into its thoughts of God and of His government, and can
scarce refrain from turning the universe itself into a theatre for
rhetorical pathos and *ad captandum* display."

PART III. SEC. 7.

Studies of Christianity, p. 161.

Ibid., p. 162, 163.

These strong statements, which it seems to me impossible to answer, are enough to show the insufficiency of
this theory to remove the difficulties by which many persons are prepossessed against the commonly-received doctrine of the Atonement.

Rectoral theory involved in equal difficulties with the Catholic doctrine.

It cannot be denied, indeed, that the Catholic doctrine
has its difficulties also, such as we are not able thoroughly
to resolve. But then it has the unquestionable advantage
of being in conformity with the plain statements of Holy
Scripture; whereas it will hardly be pretended that the
other doctrine does not require us to take some considerable liberties with these statements, in order to bring them
into something like agreement with so-called "rational
views of the divine character and government." And
hence, if it can be shown that the governmental theory
is itself involved in difficulties no less formidable than any
which are urged as objections to the Catholic doctrine, there
is no reason why, *even on rationalistic principles*, we should
have recourse to it, instead of being content to follow the
plain dictates of the oracles of God.

REVIEW OF THEORIES

PART III.
SEC. 7.
———
Mysteries form a special ground of objection to the rectoral theory.

And here it is very important to remember that according to this theory the sufferings of Christ were meant *to exhibit a grand public display of the justice of the divine administration,* such as cannot fail deeply to impress the minds of all God's intelligent creatures with the rectitude of His government and the authority of His laws. Now surely it is altogether essential to such a "display," *that there should be nothing obscure or mysterious about it.* If the "satisfaction" rendered by the Atonement was rendered to *something inherent in the nature of God,* we might then expect to find mysteries involved in it, inasmuch as the divine nature is unsearchable to limited creatures; and, at all events, we might well be content to say that the mysteries had respect exclusively to *God's part* in the transaction, and not *to ours.* But when we are told that the "satisfaction" is rendered, not to God's inherent justice, but to His "public justice," and that it is so rendered for the purpose of making a *signal display or manifestation,* with which all intelligent creatures in the universe are to be deeply impressed, any such defence of it from the charge of mystery is wholly precluded; for surely, of all things in the world, a "manifestation" cannot be mysterious; a "display" cannot be obscure or unaccountable. And further, a "display or manifestation of *public* justice," such as shall be patent and impressive to the whole universe, cannot be held to refer to *God's part* of the transaction only, so that *we* have no special right or call to intermeddle with it. Relating, as it is alleged to do, exclusively to "public justice," it has reference preeminently to the transaction *in its bearing upon us;* and hence the "justice" which is meant to be exhibited by it may fairly be expected to be *perfectly clear and unequivocal,* insomuch that "he may run who readeth it," and all reasonable men may be able, without the least difficulty to discern its reality and to appreciate its excellency

SECTION VIII.

GENERAL REMARKS ON THE THEORIES ABOVE REVIEWED.

HAVING now examined various theories which have been proposed, respecting the mediatorial work and sufferings of Jesus Christ, as substitutes for the Catholic doctrine of the Atonement, it seems proper to close this part of our discussion with some general remarks which are applicable, if not to all, at least to the greater number of these theories.

I. Our *first* remark is, that almost all the theories *contain a portion of truth*, though by no means the whole truth, as set forth in Holy Scripture, with reference to the subject in question.

That the Lord Jesus Christ may be regarded as a martyr who laid down His life in confirmation of the Gospel ; that His death was a necessary step towards His resurrection, whereby He was "declared to be the Son of God with power," and "the first-fruits of them that sleep ;" that He finished on the cross that course of perfect obedience by which the power and right have been obtained by Him to give salvation and eternal life to all the faithful ; that His sufferings are a most notable example of patience and meekness in the endurance of unmerited affliction, and in particular a most illustrious pattern of self-sacrificing devotedness in the service of God ; that the agonies He endured were mental as well as bodily, and that no inconsiderable portion of them arose from His deep sympathy with human infirmities and miseries ; that His death is a wonderful manifestation of the love of God, a most influ-

396   REVIEW OF THEORIES

PART
III.
SEC. 8.
——

ential means of sanctification, and a wise and salutary
provision for maintaining the authority of the divine law
and the rectitude of the divine government ;—*these* are, all
of them, true sayings, *so far as they go.* Nor are we to be
held as controverting or disparaging them, when we maintain that, as statements of *the whole doctrine,* or even of
the main doctrine of Holy Scripture with reference to the
subject, they are essentially defective.

The truth
they con-
tain has
been often
ver-
looked.

II. A *second* remark applicable to several of these
theories is, *that the portion of truth which they contain has,
to some extent, been unhappily neglected or overlooked by defenders of the Catholic doctrine.*

It is unquestionable, for example, that the sufferings of
Christ are frequently represented in Scripture as an unparalleled *manifestation of the love of God.* But yet, amidst
the multiplicity of controversies which have been agitated
concerning their *legal* or *judicial* bearings, it must be confessed that this affecting view of them has not usually
occupied in our theological discussions the same prominent
place which Scripture has assigned to it. Moreover, though
all intelligent advocates of the Catholic doctrine have held
that the Atonement is to be regarded, not as inducing God
to love sinners, but as the most remarkable display of His
pre-existing love and mercy to a sinful world that could
possibly be imagined, it is not to be disguised that, in
popular discourses and devotional hymns emanating from
professed believers in the Atonement, we occasionally
meet with rash and injudicious statements, tending to
convey the impression that our Lord's sufferings were designed to avert from us the wrath of an implacable Being,
who is in Himself disinclined to show mercy to us, until,
by the interposition of His beloved Son, a sullen and ungracious pardon is extorted from Him. However much,
then, we may take exception to that theory which holds
forth the sufferings and death of Jesus Christ as *merely* a
display of the love of God to sinners, irrespective of any
expiation of human guilt or satisfaction of divine justice
effected by it, we ought to be thankful for any good that

RESPECTING THE ATONEMENT. 397

may have resulted from the proposal of such a theory, in the way of making the defenders of the Catholic doctrine more careful to place the great propitiation in its true Scriptural position, as the *consequence* and not the *cause* of God's willingness to save sinners, and to give due promi- nence to the Scriptural declarations that " God com- mendeth His love toward us, in that, while we were yet sinners, Christ died for us ;" and " that God so loved the world, that He gave His only-begotten Son, that whoso- ever believeth in Him should not perish, but have ever- lasting life."

Again, it is an unquestionable truth, set forth in many passages of Holy Scripture, that *the personal sanctification of believers is one of the most important ends which the suf- ferings of our Lord were intended to promote.* This truth, however, has been frequently everlooked or insufficiently appreciated by persons whose views of the atoning efficacy of the death of Christ are otherwise in full accordance with the Word of God. For, in speaking or thinking of the "salvation" which Christ has purchased, there are many who attach to it no farther idea than that of mere *deliverance from condemnation,* forgetting that *deliverance from sin—* the cause of condemnation—is a no less essential blessing comprehended in it. Nay, it is no uncommon thing to hear it said, respecting those graces and virtues with which the character of a true Christian is adorned, that " *they are of no use or value to him whatsoever, except as attesting the sincerity of his faith,*"—a statement which seems to be very much the same as if one should say that *the precious fruits of the harvest are of no worth to him whose barns are richly stored with them, except as attesting his labours in the seed- time ;* or that *the blessings of restored health are of no value to those who have been recently delivered from the squalor, suffering, and lassitude of disease, except as attesting the con- fidence they have reposed in the skill of their physician, and the efficacy of his prescriptions !* While, therefore, we earn- estly contend against the notion that the saving power of the sufferings of Christ entirely consists in or arises from their sanctifying influence, we willingly acknowledge any

PART III. SEC. 8.

Rom. v. 8.

John, iii. 16.

398 REVIEW OF THEORIES

PART III. SEC. 8.

incidental good that may have arisen from the promulgation of such a notion, in the way of leading believers in the Catholic doctrine to a clearer and fuller recognition of the important truth that the Saviour's mediation was intended, not merely to exempt us from the penal consequences of transgression, but to cleanse us from the pollution and free us from the bondage of sin, and to "purify us unto the Lord a peculiar people, zealous of good works."

In like manner it might be shown, did our limits permit, that the "sympathetic theories of the Atonement" are attributable to a not unnatural reaction from the tendency of some believers in the Catholic doctrine to attach an exclusive importance to the Saviour's *bodily sufferings;* and also from the disposition, which others of them have occasionally shown, to regard the Atonement in the light, not so much of a great *moral satisfaction* for human guilt, as in that of a kind of commercial interchange of so much suffering on the part of the Redeemer for so much sin on the part of those whom He redeems.

III. We must now proceed, however, to our *third* remark, which is applicable to almost all the theories above referred to—namely, *that whatever truth may be contained in them is not in the least degree inconsistent with the Catholic doctrine, but may be maintained to the fullest extent along with it.*

The justice of this remark will be obvious on the slightest reflection. For example, the Lord Jesus Christ was most evidently not the less devoted as a martyr—nor was He the less excellent as a pattern of meekness, resignation, and self-sacrifice—because the sufferings to which in these capacities He submitted were at the same time endured by Him as the Saviour of sinners. His death, again, was not the less necessary as a preparatory step towards His resurrection—nor was it less surely the consummation of that perfect obedience by which all power in heaven and earth has been attained by Him—for its being at the same time the propitiation for the sins of the world. And yet further, the consideration that the Son of God was

RESPECTING THE ATONEMENT. 399

offered on the cross as a vicarious sacrifice, exacted by
divine justice and provided by divine mercy for the salvation of all sinners who should put their trust in Him,
cannot be held as in any way detracting from the power
of the cross as a manifestation of the love of God—from
its moral efficacy as a means of sanctification—or from its
excellence as a wise and salutary provision to assure us
that God, while pardoning transgressors, is, notwithstanding, resolved to maintain inviolate the obligation of His
law and the authority of His government. Such being
the case, there is no apparent necessity for the upholders
of any of these theories being opposed to the reception
of the Catholic doctrine. For all that is really true and
valuable in their own opinion might still be maintained
and advocated in union with it.

PART III. Sec. 8.

IV. But this is not all ; for we have yet to add a *fourth*
remark—namely, *that whatever truth there may be in any of
the theories to which we have been referring, is incapable
of being maintained, either on reasonable or on Scriptural
grounds, apart from the Catholic doctrine of the Atonement.*
The justice of this remark, we venture to say, been
fully substantiated in the course of our previous discussions.

The truth that is in them can- not be maintained apart from the Catho- lic doc- trine.

Thus we have seen that when Christ is represented (1)
as a martyr, and (2) as an example of suffering virtue,
it is necessary to take into account the vicarious and expiatory nature of His sufferings in order to vindicate the
perfection of that example of patient and steadfast endurance which He has set before us, and to give any satisfactory explanation of His intensity of anguish, His exceeding sorrowfulness and depression of spirit, opposed as far
as could be to the triumphant joy which human martyrs
have frequently displayed when called to submit to tortures the most excruciating.

Supra, p. 164, 165.

We have seen, also, that when our Lord's sufferings are
represented (3) as a manifestation of the love of God to
sinners, there is no reasonable or Scriptural ground on
which they can be so regarded, if they were not the

400   REVIEW OF THEORIES

PART III.
SEC. 8.

Supra, p. 295-299.

necessary means of averting from us evils from which we could not otherwise have been delivered, and of securing for us spiritual blessings which could not otherwise have been conferred upon us—in other words, if they were not, as we hold them to be, the propitiation for the sins of a lost world.

Further, when considering that theory according to which our Lord's sufferings are regarded (4) as " illustrating the great principle of self-sacrifice, as due from all God's intelligent creatures to Him who made them," we have seen that self-sacrifice is not to be considered as dutiful or commendable *purely for its own sake*, but only in so far as it is necessary to the attainment of certain

Supra, p. 319-326.

wise, holy, and beneficent ends, which could not otherwise be accomplished; and accordingly, that the sufferings of our Lord, if not in themselves directly instrumental in securing such blessings as the Catholic doctrine ascribes to them, can only be held as illustrating self-sacrifice of that utterly aimless, arbitrary, and gratuitous kind, which cannot be deemed acceptable in the sight of that most wise and gracious God whom Christians are taught to worship.

Again, when reviewing that theory of the Atonement which (5) seeks to resolve all the virtue of our Lord's sufferings into the " moral power " or sanctifying influence

Supra, p. 366-379.

exerted by them, we have seen that the subjective "moral power " of the cross of Christ is necessarily *dependent on those substantial objective benefits which it procures for us*, and that apart from these objective benefits it cannot be regarded as that mighty agency of sanctification, which it has ever proved to be, when viewed in its true character as a propitiation and satisfaction for human guilt.

Further, to take but one other instance, when considering (6) the " rectoral theory," which holds the Atonement to consist, not in any actual satisfaction rendered for the sins of men by the vicarious sufferings of their substitute, but in a mere " display of the principles of the divine government, and in particular of God's purpose to maintain inviolate the authority of His law while pardoning its

RESPECTING THE ATONEMENT. 401

transgressors," we have seen that this theory *cannot stand by itself*, inasmuch as that "display of principles," to which the great propitiation is reduced by it, is altogether *unreal* and *unsubstantial*, unless there be associated with it those very views of *actual* "substitution" and "satisfaction" which it is the intention of the theory to supersede.

Thus does it appear that the commonly received doctrine respecting the mediatorial work and sufferings of Jesus Christ must necessarily be assumed, in order to give validity to all that is really "worthy of acceptation" in the most common and most plausible of those other doctrines which have been suggested for the purpose of supplanting it. We need scarcely observe that this circumstance may be justly held as giving additional certitude to those grounds on which the Catholic doctrine may be defended, and ought to secure for it a more favourable consideration on the part of many whose preference for other views may hitherto have predisposed them to the rejection of it.

PART IV.

REVIEW OF OBJECTIONS TO THE DOCTRINE OF HOLY SCRIPTURE RESPECTING THE MEDI-ATORIAL WORK AND SUFFERINGS OF JESUS CHRIST.

HAVING now endeavoured to ascertain the doctrine of Scripture respecting the mediatorial work and sufferings of Jesus Christ, and to compare the result of our inves-tigations with some of the most plausible or prevalent theories that differ from it, we have still to consider and to obviate the objections with which the revealed doctrine on this subject has been commonly assailed.

These objections may be classed under the following heads: *First*, That the doctrine in question does not re-ceive that measure of support from the teaching of Christ Himself which, were it true, might be reasonably ex-pected; *secondly*, That the Atonement is unnecessary; *thirdly*, That it is derogatory to the perfections of God; *fourthly*, That there are mysteries involved in it, or aris-ing out of it, which do not admit of any reasonable ex-planation; and, *fifthly*, That it is injurious in its practical tendency.

On a fair consideration of these objections we shall endeavour to show, either that they are not justly appli-cable to the doctrine of the Atonement, as above investi-gated and ascertained, or that they furnish no conclusive argument against the truth of it.

SECTION I.

ALLEGED SILENCE OR RESERVE OF JESUS CHRIST RESPECTING THE ATONEMENT.

PART IV. SEC. I.

Alleged reserve of Christ respecting the Atonement.

Jowett on the Epistles of St Paul, 2d. ed. ii. 555.

IT has been objected to the doctrine of the Atonement, that it is founded mainly, if not entirely, on the teaching of the apostles rather than of Christ Himself; and that this is the very reverse of what we might have looked for if that doctrine really were, as it is commonly supposed to be, a vital and fundamental article of the Christian faith. " It is hard," we are told, " to imagine that there can be any truer expression of the Gospel than the words of the Lord Jesus, or that any truth omitted by Him can be essential to the Gospel. ' The disciple is not above his master, nor is the servant greater than his lord.' The philosophy of Plato was not better understood by his followers than by himself; nor can we allow that the Gospel is to be interpreted by the epistles, or that the Sermon on the Mount is only half Christian, and needs the fuller inspiration or revelation of St Paul. There is no trace in the words of our Saviour of any omission or imperfection, and no indication in the epistles of any intention to complete or perfect them." If, therefore, the Atonement were, as it is held to be, an integral part of the " truth as it is in Jesus," and if it really possessed that mighty importance in the Christian dispensation which is ordinarily assigned to it, we should have expected it to be much more clearly declared, and much more frequently and prominently exhibited, in the teaching of Jesus Christ Himself, instead of being to so great an extent reserved for the supplementary teaching of His disciples.

DOCTRINE OF THE ATONEMENT.   405

1. To this plausible objection I may first of all reply, that even were the facts alleged in it fully admitted, it could not neutralise the mass of positive evidence in proof of the Atonement, which has already been adduced. It is not the less true that this doctrine is affirmed in numerous and perfectly explicit statements of Holy Scripture, whatever may be the relative amount of testimony borne to it respectively by our Lord and by His apostles. We may perhaps think it strange and unaccountable that the full development of a doctrine so essential should have been reserved until the close of the Saviour's ministry instead of being made during that ministry by the Saviour Himself. This circumstance may produce in us a feeling of perplexity, similar to that which arises when we think of the gradual maturing of God's purpose of redeeming love, throughout the long period of more than four millenniums, before it was ultimately accomplished by the Saviour's advent. But in the one case just as in the other, the actual state of the facts remains the same, whatever may be our difficulties in accounting for them. And really it is nothing strange that with reference to these, as to countless other parts of the divine administration, we should be obliged to say, in humble submission, "Even so, Father, for so it seemeth good in Thy sight."

2. But further, it is of importance to observe that the purpose of our Lord's personal ministry in His life and death was not so much *the full preaching* of the Atonement as *the full accomplishment* of the Atonement in order to the preaching of it. Doubtless the Lord Jesus *was* a divine teacher, and, as such, the author and founder of the Christian faith. But it is equally certain that this is not the only, nor even the most prominent character, sustained by Him. He is also, and still more distinctively, a *Saviour* —the *procurer* of spiritual blessings, as well as the *proclaimer* of them. Nor is it in the epistles only that this office is ascribed to Him, but no less expressly and emphatically in the gospels. By the angels who sang the anthem of His birth ; by His parents when naming Him

PART IV. SEC. 1

Even were the allegation admitted, it could not neutralise positive proofs of the Atonement.

Matt. xi. 26.

The purpose of our Lord's ministry was to *make* the Atonement, rather than to *preach* it.

406   REVIEW OF OBJECTIONS TO THE

PART
IV.
SEC. I.

in compliance with a divine monition ; by Simeon at His presentation in the Temple ; by John the Baptist when accosting Him as "the Lamb of God, who taketh away the sin of the world ; " and by Himself when declaring to Nicodemus that " He was sent into the world not to condemn, but to save it,"—was His office as a Saviour plainly indicated and recognised.   Now, in this capacity His chief work unquestionably was to *procure* salvation by His " obedience unto death," as a necessary step towards the full and broad announcement of it.   Nor can we wonder that those great events of His history which constitute the *material* of the Atonement should be completed, before their significancy is fully interpreted and proclaimed. There would seem to be a fitness and congruity in the arrangement, according to which redemption by the death of Christ should first of all be actually accomplished as a matter of fact, in order to be openly set forth as a matter of doctrine.   At all events, we may venture to affirm that our Lord's chief concern as a Saviour was to accomplish it.   Others might preach redemption after it had been secured ; but it was *His* special and exclusive function to secure it.

This consideration completely disposes of the analogy which Mr Jowett has attempted to draw between Christ and Plato.   The doctrine of Plato was a system of philosophy of which Plato was merely the author, and in no respect the subject.   Consequently, there was no reason why it should not be as thoroughly expounded and developed·by Plato himself as by any of his followers. But the doctrine of Christ is pre-eminently and distinctively the announcement of a method of redemption, which Christ Himself, by His humiliation, obedience, and sufferings, has carried into effect.   Christ is *the grand subject of the Gospel*, as well as the author of it.   His life and death, and resurrection and ascension, are included in it as its most important elements.   Accordingly there is here a sufficient reason, if not an absolute necessity, that all the leading passages of His history should be *facts accomplished*, before the doctrine of Christ in all the fulness of

DOCTRINE OF THE ATONEMENT. 407

its import can be thoroughly expounded and explicitly promulgated.

PART IV.
SEC. I.

3. But yet further, regarding our Lord merely as a divine teacher, there is no ground for the assumption on which the objectors proceed, that it was His purpose, when acting in this capacity, so fully to set forth His doctrine from the beginning as to leave no room for any further development of it, either by Himself in the sequel of His ministry, or by His apostles, acting by His authority and guided by His Holy Spirit after His departure. On the contrary, it is plain to every reader of the gospels that the Lord Jesus did not all at once unfold the revelations of His Gospel even to His disciples, much less to the multitudes who listened to His public discourses. In condescension to the narrowness of their views, the slowness of their apprehensions, and the strength of their prejudices, He gradually led them on, as they were able to bear it, from one disclosure of divine truth to another. It was not until an advanced period of His ministry that He began to speak to them plainly of His approaching sufferings. His notices of the future extension of His religion were for a while only given to them in parables, the spiritual import of which they were unable to understand. And His intimations of the divinity of His person, as well as of the gracious purposes of His mission, consisted for the most part of scattered hints and abrupt allusions, fitted to stimulate rather than to gratify their longings for a revelation of which the hour had not yet come.

The teaching of Christ was gradual and progressive.

Nor is this all ; for while our Lord's teaching, considered in itself, was thus gradual and progressive, it indicates, even when it has reached its highest point, that some further instruction is yet lacking for the completion of it   If we place side by side the first of our Lord's discourses—the Sermon on the Mount, as given by St Matthew—and His last farewell address to His disciples on the eve of His passion, as recorded by St John, we cannot fail to observe the mighty difference between the two as regards the measure of light which they have severally imparted with reference to the more peculiar verities of the Chris-

Christ's teaching even when most advanced, indicates the need of farther teaching.

408 REVIEW OF OBJECTIONS TO THE

PART
IV.
SEC. I.
———

See
Bernard's
Bampton
Lectures,
p. 77.

tian faith. There is, indeed, a wider interval in this respect between these two discourses of the Saviour than any that can be traced between His teaching as a whole and that further teaching with which the apostles have supplemented it.* And yet even in the latter of these discourses, which was delivered by our Lord at the close of His personal ministry, we have the most distinct and solemn assurance given us that the Gospel, as taught by Him, was not so completely developed and so fully expounded as to dispense with further teaching; but that, on the contrary, provision had been made for the more thorough elucidation of its precious truths through the mission and agency of another divine Teacher, who

John, xvi. 7.

should be sent to the disciples after His departure. "It is expedient for you," He tells them, "that I go away; for if I go not away, the Comforter will not come unto you; but if I depart, I will send Him unto you." And what benefits were they to derive from this mission of the

John, xiv. 25, 26.

Comforter? "These things," He says, "have I spoken unto you, being yet present with you; but the Comforter, which is the Holy Ghost, whom the Father will send in my name, He shall teach you all things, and bring all things to your remembrance, whatsoever I have said unto you." Nor were the instructions of this Monitor to be confined to a mere recalling of what Christ had already

John, xvi. 12, 13.

taught them; for the Saviour adds: "I have yet many things to say unto you, but ye cannot bear them now. Howbeit, when He, the Spirit of truth, is come, He will guide you into all the truth." And further, as regards the *special subject* on which "the Spirit of truth" was to cast

John, xv. 26.

His heavenly light, our Lord further declares, "He shall testify of *me;* He shall glorify *me*, for He shall receive of mine, and shall show it unto you." So that it was not to any accessory matters that this promised teaching of the Holy Spirit was to have reference, but to matters essentially bearing on the work and office of Christ, and contributing towards the glory thence accruing to Him.

It is vain to think, therefore, that we are honouring the

* See Appendix, Note K.

DOCTRINE OF THE ATONEMENT. 409

Lord Jesus by isolating His own teaching from that of His apostles, and by disparaging the latter, except in so far as it is fully and explicitly corroborated by the former. The teaching of the apostles is equivalent to that of Christ, as having been guided and regulated by the Holy Spirit, who was given them in order that, through their instrumentality, He might "testify of Christ" and "glorify Him." Nor is it to be forgotten that the Saviour Himself has solemnly declared respecting His apostles, "As my Father has sent me, even so send I you;" "He that receiveth you receiveth me, and he that receiveth me receiveth Him that sent me." *(PART IV. SEC. I. — John, xx. 21. Matt. x. 10.)*

4. Hitherto, in meeting this objection, I have proceeded on the supposition that *there really is* so marked a contrast between our Lord's teaching and that of His apostles on the subject of the Atonement as might, if unexplained, involve us in serious embarrassment. The truth is, however, that the actual state of the case regarding this matter has been very much exaggerated; for though it is undeniable that our Lord's statements concerning His mediatorial work and sufferings are neither so numerous nor so explicit as those of the apostles, there is not the slightest ground for asserting or insinuating that He utters with respect to this subject an "uncertain sound," far less that He passes over it in silence. Take as a proof of this the following significant words, which may be allowed to bear their own testimony without any helpful comment or illustration:— *(Our Lord's reserve on the Atonement has been greatly exaggerated.)*

"Verily, verily, I say unto thee, We speak that we do know, and testify that we have seen; and ye receive not our witness. If I have told you earthly things, and ye believe not, how shall ye believe, if I tell you of heavenly things? And no man hath ascended up to heaven, but He that came down from heaven, even the Son of Man who is in heaven. And as Moses lifted up the serpent in the wilderness, even so must the Son of Man be lifted up: that whosoever believeth in Him should not perish, but have eternal life. For God so loved the world, that He *(John, iii. 11-17.)*

410   REVIEW OF OBJECTIONS TO THE

PART
IV.
SEC. I.
———

gave His only-begotten Son, that whosoever believeth in Him should not perish, but have everlasting life. For God sent not His Son into the world to condemn the world, but that the world through Him might be saved."

Matt. xi.
27, 28.

"All things are delivered unto me of the Father : and no man knoweth the Son, but the Father ; neither knoweth any man the Father, save the Son, and he to whomsoever the Son will reveal Him. Come unto me, all ye that labour and are heavy laden, and I will give you rest."

Matt. xx.
28.
Luke, xix.
10.

"The Son of Man came not to be ministered unto, but to minister, and to give His life a ransom for many." "The Son of Man is come to seek and to save that which is lost."

John, vi.
32-39.

"Verily, verily, I say unto you, Moses gave you not that bread from heaven ; but my Father giveth you the true bread from heaven. For the bread of God is He who cometh down from heaven, and giveth life unto the world. . . . I am the bread of life : he that cometh to me shall never hunger ; and he that believeth on me shall never thirst. . . . All that the Father giveth me shall come to me ; and him that cometh to me I will in no wise cast out. For I came down from heaven, not to do mine own will, but the will of Him that sent me. And this is the Father's will that sent me, that of all which He hath given me I should lose nothing, but should raise it up again at the last day." "Verily, verily, I say unto you,

John, vi.
47-58.

He that believeth on me hath everlasting life. I am that bread of life. Your fathers did eat manna in the wilderness, and are dead. . . . I am the living bread which came down from heaven : if any man eat of this bread, he shall live for ever: and the bread that I will give is my flesh, which I will give for the life of the world. . . . Whoso eateth my flesh and drinketh my blood hath eternal life, and I will raise him up at the last day. For my flesh is meat indeed, and my blood is drink indeed. He that eateth my flesh, and drinketh my blood, dwelleth in me, and I in him. As the living Father hath sent me, and I live by the Father : so he that eateth me, even he shall live by me."

"I am the good shepherd : the good shepherd giveth

DOCTRINE OF THE ATONEMENT. 411

his life for the sheep." "As the Father knoweth me, even PART
so know I the Father: and I lay down my life for the IV.
SEC. 1.
sheep." "Therefore doth my Father love me, because I
John, x.
lay down my life that I might take it again. No man 11, 15, 17,
taketh it from me, but I lay it down of myself. I have 18.
power to lay it down, and I have power to take it again.
This commandment I received of my Father." "My John, x.
sheep hear my voice, and I know them, and they follow 27, 28.
me: and I give unto them eternal life ; and they shall
never perish, neither shall any pluck them out of my
hand."

"The hour is come, that the Son of Man should be John, xii.
glorified. Verily, verily, I say unto you, Except a corn of 23, 24, 27,
28, 31-33.
wheat fall into the ground and die, it abideth alone ; but
if it die it bringeth forth much fruit." "Now is my soul
troubled ; and what shall I say ? Father, save me from
this hour ; but for this cause came I unto this hour.
Father, glorify thy name." "Now is the judgment of
this world : now shall the prince of this world be cast out.
And I, if I be lifted up from the earth, will draw all men
unto me. (This He said, signifying what death He should
die.)"

"I am the way, and the truth, and the life ; no man John, xiv.
cometh unto the Father but by me." "And whatsoever 6, 13, 14.
ye shall ask in my name, that will I do, that the Father
may be glorified in the Son. If ye shall ask anything in
my name, I will do it." "Verily, verily, I say unto you, John, xvi.
Whatsoever ye shall ask the Father in my name, He will 23, 24.
give it you. Hitherto have ye asked nothing in my name :
ask, and ye shall receive, that your joy may be full."

"Abide in me, and I in you. As the branch cannot John, xv.
bear fruit of itself, except it abide in the vine ; no more 4, 5, 12, 13
can ye, except ye abide in me. I am the vine, ye are the
branches : he that abideth in me, and I in him, the same
bringeth forth much fruit: for without me ye can do
nothing." "This is my commandment, that ye love one
another, as I have loved you. Greater love hath no man
than this, that a man lay down his life for his friends."

"Father, the hour is come ; glorify Thy Son, that Thy

412 REVIEW OF OBJECTIONS TO THE

PART
IV.
SEC. I.
———
John, xvii.
1-5.

Son also may glorify Thee ; as Thou hast given Him power over all flesh, that He should give eternal life to as many as Thou hast given Him. And this is life eternal, that they might know Thee the only true God, and Jesus Christ whom Thou hast sent. I have glorified Thee on the earth: I have finished the work which Thou gavest me to do. And now, O Father, glorify Thou me with Thine own self, with the glory which I had with Thee

Matt. xxvi.
39, 42.

before the world was." "O my Father, if it be possible, let this cup pass from me: nevertheless, not as I will, but as Thou wilt." "O my Father, if this cup may not pass away from me, except I drink it, Thy will be done."

I venture to say that these words of the Lord Jesus will readily commend themselves to the vast majority of intelligent and candid readers of the New Testament, as not only consistent with the doctrine of the apostles, but as lending to that doctrine the fullest measure of support which could, under the circumstances before explained, have been reasonably expected.

Special
testimony
of Christ
to the
Atone-
ment in
the Lord's
Supper.

Luke, xxii.
19, 20.
Matt. xxvi.
27, 28.

I must now advert, however, somewhat more particularly, to that most explicit and highly important testimony which Christ has Himself borne to the doctrine of the Atonement in the institution of the sacrament of the Lord's Supper, when, on giving to His disciples the sacramental elements, He said of the bread, "Take, eat, this is my body which is given for you; this do in remembrance of me ;" and afterwards of the cup, "Drink ye all of it ; for this is my blood of the new testament, which is shed for many for the remission of sins."

Supra, p.
13, 14.

I have already had occasion to notice the difficulty of accounting for our Lord's procedure in thus singling out His *ignominious death* in preference to His birth, His transfiguration, His ascension, or any of the brighter passages of His history, as the subject of special commemoration by His people, unless we seek a solution of it in the great truth that His death is the only propitiation for the sins of the world.

DOCTRINE OF THE ATONEMENT. 413

I have further shown that His words on this occasion convey an unequivocal allusion to the ratification of the Levitical covenant by sacrifice, when Moses, having spoken every precept of the law, took the blood of calves and of goats, and sprinkled therewith both the book and all the people, saying, " This is the blood of the testament which God hath enjoined unto you." The mention which our Lord makes of "the new testament or covenant," unfailingly reminds us of the old covenant, which it superseded. And when we consider that this old covenant was inaugurated by the shedding of sacrificial blood, and that under it " almost all things were purged with blood, and that without shedding of blood there was no remission," we cannot otherwise understand our Lord's statement, " This cup is my blood of the new covenant which is shed for many for the remission of sins," than as a deliberate and solemn declaration that *the shedding of His blood was an expiatory sacrifice*, analogous in nature, though of far superior efficacy, to those offerings for sin which were enjoined under the Levitical system.

But there is another consideration to be now mentioned, by which this conclusion is still farther confirmed. It must be kept in view that our Lord, on this occasion, was celebrating along with His disciples that Paschal feast which God's ancient people were required to observe from year to year in commemoration of the original Passover in Egypt. It was when so employed that He took the opportunity of instituting the sacrament of the Lord's Supper, which was henceforth to take the place of the Jewish ordinance, and to be in like manner a commemoration of His own sufferings. Nothing could more plainly indicate than does this procedure on the part of our Redeemer the close affinity or analogy that subsists at once between the two ordinances and the two events commemorated by them. Well did the Apostle Paul apprehend his Lord's meaning when he translated the significant action into these appropriate words, " Christ our Passover is sacrificed for us ; therefore let us keep the feast . . . with the unleavened bread of sincerity

414 REVIEW OF OBJECTIONS TO THE

PART
IV.
SEC. I.
——

and truth." For we cannot doubt that by instituting the Lord's Supper, while engaged in celebrating the festival of the Passover, and requiring this Christian ordinance to be observed in all future ages in remembrance of His dying love, our Lord was virtually proclaiming Himself to be the true Paschal offering "who taketh away the sin of the world," and comparing His own blood, "shed for the remission of sins," with that of the lamb of old sprinkled on the dwellings of Israel, which saved them from the destroying angel when he was sent forth to smite the first-born of man and beast throughout the land of Egypt.

Unwarranted assertion of Mr Jowett.

Jowett on St Paul's Epistles, 2d ed., ii. 556, 557.

If there be any force in these considerations, what are we to think of the broad assertion of Mr Jowett, that our Lord has studiously avoided every approach to sacrificial expressions with reference to His sufferings? "Christ Himself," says this writer, "hardly uses, even in a figure, the word sacrifice; *never with the least reference to His own life or death. . . .* In the words of institution of the Lord's Supper, He speaks of His death as *in some way* connected with the remission of sins. But among all the figures of speech under which He describes His work in the world—the vine, the good shepherd, the door, the light of the world, the bread of life, the water of life, the corner-stone, the temple — *none contains any sacrificial allusion !* "

So far is this assertion from being true, that, on the most important and solemn of all occasions on which our Lord has alluded to His death, He has done so in terms that are unequivocally sacrificial—bringing it into close comparison with the Paschal sacrifice—speaking of His blood as "shed for many for the remission of sins"—and farther styling it "the blood of the new covenant," so as to assimilate it to that sacrificial blood with which the old covenant was ratified and inaugurated. Indeed, of all the testimonies which have been borne to the doctrine of the Atonement in any part of the sacred volume, this testimony which is conveyed in the Lord's Supper is the most important ; because it not only exhibits the doctrine

DOCTRINE OF THE ATONEMENT. 415

in the clearest light, but incorporates it, as it were, with the highest exercise of religious worship, and perpetuates the remembrance of it in a monumental rite which is destined to continue throughout all ages until the end of the world.

Be it so, however, that with this important exception our Lord makes no sacrificial allusion when at any time He is speaking of His death (a point which I am not for the present concerned to question), how does this circumstance affect Mr Jowett's favourite method of attempting to neutralise the Scriptural proofs of the Atonement? It evidently precludes the application of this method to those numerous testimonies from our Lord's discourses which have in the preceding pages been adduced ; for if these are in no respect sacrificial in their import, they cannot, of course, be got rid of by resolving them into mere " rhetorical figures suggested by the Levitical ordinances." And this leads me to observe that the *non-sacrificial* passages bearing on the death of Christ are of equal value with the *sacrificial* ones ; or rather, I ought to say, both together are of great value, as giving mutual light and confirmation to one another. The *sacrificial* passages serve to explain and illustrate the efficacy ascribed to the death of Christ in those other passages which are not of a sacrificial import. And, on the other hand, the *non-sacrificial* passages preclude the possibility of explaining the others away on the principle of accommodation to Jewish customs and opinions.

There is still one interesting portion of our Lord's statements respecting His mediatorial work which I must shortly notice. We have but a brief record left us of the intercourse which He had with His disciples after His resurrection. We know, however, that " He was seen of them forty days, and spake to them of the things pertaining to the kingdom of God." And we may well believe that during this period He had many conversations with them on the subject of His atoning death, by which, as well as by the teaching of the Holy Spirit, they were

PART IV. SEC. 1.

Testimony of Christ to the Atonement after His resurrection.

Acts, i. 3.

416   REVIEW OF OBJECTIONS TO THE

PART
IV.
SEC. I.
—

qualified for giving in regard to it those fuller and more
definite views which we find in the apostolic discourses
and epistles. This, indeed, is not mere matter of conjecture; for we are expressly told that on one occasion
He rebuked them for their "slowness of heart to believe
all that the prophets had spoken"—appealed to them

Luke,
xxiv. 25,
27.

"whether Christ ought not to have suffered these things,
and to enter into His glory"—and "beginning at Moses
and all the prophets, He expounded to them in all the
Scriptures the things concerning Himself." On another

Luke,
xxiv. 44-
47.

occasion He showed them that "all things must be fulfilled which were written in the law of Moses, and in the
prophets, and in the Psalms concerning Him. Then
opened He their understandings, that they might understand the Scriptures; and said to them, Thus it is written,
and thus it behoved Christ to suffer, and to rise from the
dead the third day; and that repentance and remission of
sins should be preached in His name among all nations,
beginning at Jerusalem."

From these intimations we are warranted to conclude
that during the forty days that intervened between our
Lord's resurrection and ascension, His conversations with
the disciples had respect to the necessity, nature, and
purpose of His sufferings. And yet more particularly,
from the distinct allusion which He makes to "*Moses*"
and to "*the law of Moses*" as having witnessed concerning the things which it behoved Him to suffer, we are
shut up to the conclusion that *His sufferings must have
been represented by Him as sacrificial in their character.*

Supra, p.
260, 261.

For, as we have already shown, there was nothing in "the
law of Moses" which could have been thus appealed to
as bearing witness to *the sufferings of Christ* and their
beneficial results, unless we are to seek such testimony in
the Levitical sacrifices.

Objection
that the
Atone-
ment is
ignored in
some of the

Before passing away from the subject of our Lord's
teaching, I must briefly advert to a special objection that
has been urged against the Atonement from certain of
His parables. Thus, we are told that the father of the

DOCTRINE OF THE ATONEMENT.   417

prodigal son freely forgave him, and cordially welcomed
him, without requiring any satisfaction for his past misconduct ; and that the debts of the *unmerciful servant,*
when he had nothing to pay, were freely remitted, without
any substitute undertaking to discharge them for him.
And from this it is argued that, according to our Lord's
teaching, there cannot be any necessity for an atonement
in order to obtain for sinners the divine forgiveness.

In meeting this objection it is only necessary to keep in
view the recognised rule in the interpretation of parables
—namely, that the import of them is not to be further
stretched than the nature of the subject which they are
used to illustrate plainly requires, or than the nature of
the imagery employed in them will admit of. (1.) In the
parable of the prodigal son our Lord's object evidently
was, not to set forth the *ground* or *principle* of forgiveness
(which He expressly did at the institution of the Lord's
Supper, by declaring that " His blood was shed for the
remission of sins "), but to exhibit *the gracious manner,* so
far as the sinner is himself concerned, in which forgiveness
is bestowed upon him by his heavenly Father. And with
this view it was not necessary that anything should be introduced indicative of the method by which the divine
justice and the divine mercy are harmoniously displayed
in the pardon of sinners. Besides, the illustrative case
employed in this parable, being that of an earthly parent
receiving back his erring child, was not of such a kind as
to afford scope for the introduction of any emblem of the
Atonement as the basis of forgiveness. For it is not in
His *paternal* relation as here represented, but in His *judicial* relation to us as a righteous Governor, that God requires an expiation for the guilty. (2.) Again, the parable
of the unmerciful servant is designed to show how generously we ought to forgive the trespasses of our fellow-men,
in consideration of the much greater amount of our own
trespasses, for the pardon of which we are beholden to
the grace of God. And with this view it is not n :cessary,
any more than in the other instance, that the Atonement,
as the ground of the divine forgiveness, should be specially

PART
IV.
SEC. 1.
———
parables
of Christ.
Luke, xv.
20-24.
Matt.
xviii. 23-
35.

The par-
ables in
question
did not re-
quire a re-
ference to
the Atone-
ment.

418   REVIEW OF OBJECTIONS TO THE

PART IV.
Sec. 1.

referred to. All that is requisite is that our forgiveness should be represented as being, with respect to ourselves, an act of sovereign grace, wholly gratuitous and unmerited.

Some have indeed affirmed, that the doctrine of the Atonement represents God as being less merciful than was the royal creditor in the parable, who "frankly forgave" his servant's debts when asked to do so, without requiring any satisfaction. The reply is obvious, however, that the satisfaction which God requires in order to the pardon of sin, is a satisfaction *which He has Himself provided*, and hence that the costliness of our pardon, instead of detracting from the greatness of the divine mercy, incomparably enhances it.

In connection with these remarks, I may add, that in another of our Lord's parables—that of the Pharisee and the publican—there is a very significant reference to a propitiation for sin as the ground on which it is forgiven. For in the publican's prayer, " God be merciful to me a sinner," the words translated " Be merciful " are not ἐλέησόν

Luke,
xviii. 13.
Luke,
xviii. 38.

με, as used by the blind man referred to in a subsequent verse of the same chapter, but ἱλάσθητι μοι, which properly signifies "be propitiated towards me." This expression is unquestionably a *sacrificial* one ; and when taken in connection with the circumstance that the publican is represented as "going up *to the temple* to pray," it indicates an expectation of forgiveness through some atonement analogous to those sacrifices which were constantly offered up in that holy place.

No reason for mentioning the Atonement whenever the pardon of sin is spoken of.

It is, however, a most unwarranted notion which some persons seem to entertain, that if the Atonement were a Scriptural doctrine it would certainly be mentioned in every passage of Holy Scripture which makes any allusion to the " forgiveness of sin." There is no good reason for such an expectation. " Forgiveness of sin " stands related to *various* subjects, in connection with *any one* of which it may be referred to, according to the circumstances and purposes of the writer, without the slightest intention to disparage or ignore the others. Thus, for example, it may be referred to in connection with *the*

DOCTRINE OF THE ATONEMENT. 419

grace of God as its prime *origin ;* in connection with *the death of Christ* as its *meritorious ground* or *procuring cause ;* in connection with the *faith* and *repentance* of the sinner as its *antecedents ;* in connection with *a forgiving disposition* as its *constant accompaniment ;* or in connection with *love and gratitude to God* and renewed *obedience* to Him as its practical *results.* And no intelligent reader of the Scriptures will suppose that any one of these things, to which "forgiveness of sin" bears a very close relation, is meant to be *dispensed with,* because it is *not expressly mentioned* in some passages which speak of "forgiveness" in one or other of its varied aspects. Such a supposition could only be justified on the principle, which cannot with the least show of reason be maintained, that any passage of Scripture which refers to a particular subject must set forth the whole circle of Christian doctrine with respect to it.

"Socinians," says Mr Jerram, "make a great display of texts in which the forgiveness of sin is referred to without any express mention of our Lord's sacrifice as the ground of it. But it would be more to their purpose to show that these texts are, in any point of view, inconsistent with the doctrine of the Atonement ; and to show, farther, in what way, according to their own scheme, these texts are to be reconciled with all those other passages which speak of pardon being granted on the consideration of what Christ has done and suffered as the Saviour of sinners. For it ought to be remembered that if a *system* of conferring divine mercy on man has anywhere been laid down in the Holy Scriptures—as we allege there has been,—and if it can be proved—as we are confident it may—that the forgiveness of sin is positively stated as resting on that particular system,—then we have all the evidence which an established order of things can require, that the righteous Governor of the world has regard to that system, even where no express reference is made to it ; and ten thousand omissions of this kind can have no weight against this positive arrangement. Before they can be adduced with the least effect, it must be shown that the system has been

PART
IV.
SEC. I.

Jerram on
the Atone-
ment, p.
74.

420   REVIEW OF OBJECTIONS TO THE

PART
IV.
SEC. 1.

abrogated with as much clearness and certainty as that it was established."

I may add that these considerations are applicable, not only to those passages in our Lord's discourses, but generally to all passages of Scripture whatsoever, in which the forgiveness of sins may be referred to without express mention of the Atonement as the ground of it. The omission of any notice of the Atonement in such passages may be sufficiently explained by the circumstance that forgiveness is there considered in relation to its *source*, its *antecedents*, its *accompaniments*, or its *practical results*, and that the occasion or the subject in hand were not such as to call for any allusion to the Atonement as its *procuring cause*. Indeed, if we were to proceed upon the principle that anything that is not expressly mentioned in a particular passage which speaks of the forgiveness of sin may be set aside as having no connection with that blessing, I might undertake to prove, by not a few Scriptural testimonies, *that repentance is not at all necessary to forgiveness.* There is no express mention of repentance in the

Isa. xliii. 25.

Eph. i. 7.

Heb. ix. 26.

following texts : " I, even I, am He that blotteth out thy transgressions for mine own sake, and will not remember thy sins." " In whom we have redemption through His blood, the forgiveness of sins, according to the riches of His grace." " Now once in the end of the world hath He appeared to put away sin by the sacrifice of Himself." But no one, so far as I know, has ever insisted that the omission in these passages of any allusion to repentance warrants us to conclude that impenitent men may obtain forgiveness. Equally unwarranted would it be to infer, from certain texts which speak of pardon without reference to the Atonement, that pardon is to be obtained on any other ground than that which is set forth in very numerous and perfectly explicit testimonies of Holy Scripture, —and nowhere more distinctly than in the never-to-be-forgotten words, uttered by the Saviour Himself, when instituting the Lord's Supper: " *This is my blood of the new covenant, which is shed for many for the remission of sins.*"

SECTION II.

THE ATONEMENT CANNOT BE SAID TO BE UNNECESSARY.

WHEN we maintain the necessity of the Atonement, we are not to be understood as venturing to affirm, on purely reasonable grounds and apart from the testimony of Holy Scripture, that there was no other method by which the salvation of sinners could possibly have been effected. It would ill become creatures whose faculties are so weak, and whose field of observation is so limited, to speak as if they had independent means of knowing what the great God could or could not have done, if it had so pleased Him, for the redemption of a fallen world. All that we affirm is, that the method of salvation which God has been pleased to reveal to us in the Scriptures serves certain important ends in the divine administration, which could not, so far as we are able to see, have been otherwise accomplished, and which sufficiently vindicate His wisdom and goodness in the appointment of it. Indeed our position is mainly a *defensive* one, which we find ourselves obliged to assume in order to repel the assertion that an atonement for sin is so evidently superfluous as to be altogether incredible. Were it not that such an assertion must be combated by all who " contend earnestly for the faith once delivered to the saints," we might well be content to know what God *has actually done* with a view to the recovery and restoration of our sinful race, without being careful to agitate the question, whether the like results might not otherwise have been accomplished by Him.

422   REVIEW OF OBJECTIONS TO THE

PART
IV.
SEC. 2.
——
Father-
hood of
God does
not pre-
clude ne-
cessity of
Atone-
ment.

I. One of the chief grounds on which it is alleged, by those who reject the doctrine of the Atonement, that no such provision for the expiation of human guilt and the satisfaction of divine justice can be at all necessary, is the tender and endearing relation of *a Father* which God is held to sustain towards His intelligent creatures. For surely, they argue, there is nothing to prevent a kind parent from freely forgiving the misconduct of his erring children, and cordially restoring them to his confidence and favour, so soon as they show themselves truly penitent for their faults. What need of satisfaction or expiation in such a case? We should bitterly censure the severity of an earthly father, if he laid any further chastisement on his offspring than was absolutely necessary for their correction and amendment; or if, when their offences were deeply deplored and heartily renounced, he still, in his stern inflexibility, withheld forgiveness until the fullest compensation had been made for the dishonour they had done to his dignity and authority. How then can we attribute to our heavenly Father a course of procedure, which, if witnessed in any of the "fathers of our flesh," we should unhesitatingly denounce as unnatural and unmerciful? Rather ought we to say, that if men, being evil, are ready to pardon the transgressions of their children, without exacting any further satisfaction than penitential acknowledgments and sincere efforts of reformation, much more must our Father who is in heaven be willing, on the like terms, to forgive every repentant sinner.

To those who thus argue, we might venture to reply that, even regarding God exclusively in His paternal relation, it is not by any means so clear as they would have us to believe, that He needs must forgive every penitent offender without requiring satisfaction for his sins. For, be it remembered, God is not, like an earthly parent, concerned only with the superintendence of a limited household, the administration of which is altogether a private matter, to be regulated by Him according to His free discretion. No. He is the common parent of

DOCTRINE OF THE ATONEMENT.   423

the human race—and not only so, but, as we have reason
to believe, of manifold other races of intelligent creatures ;
and as such, it concerns Him so to deal with each individual member of His great family, as may be conducive
to the true welfare, not only of that individual, but of all
the other members. The largeness of His family, while
not in the least affecting the fatherly love with which its
affairs are regulated by Him, may, notwithstanding, affect
very materially *the system* according to which the regulation is conducted. The household, in fact, has expanded
into a kingdom. And though it be still the kingdom of
our Father, we cannot conceive of it as otherwise administered by Him than after the manner of a just and impartial ruler,—by general laws, which are subservient to the
public interests, and which must in every case be firmly
maintained and fully vindicated. Hence we may readily
conceive that many things might be competent to the
discretion of an earthly parent, when dealing with his
erring children, which would not so well comport with the
supremacy of the Universal Parent, by whom the whole
family in heaven and earth is ruled.

It is not necessary, however, to meet the argument on
this ground ; for we have the clearest evidence that could
be wished, from the constitution of our nature, from the
course of divine providence, and, above all, from the
express declarations of Holy Scripture, that God sustains
the character, not only of a beneficent Father, but also of
a righteous moral Governor, towards His rational creatures. These two characters, accordingly, must be combined in all our conceptions of the Supreme Being as
related to us. And if it would be an error to ascribe to
Him the stern inflexibility of a ruler apart from the
merciful kindness of a parent, it would be no less an error
to ascribe to Him the tenderness of parental love in dealing with His sinful offspring, exclusive of that concern
which, as a righteous Sovereign, He must ever show for
the authority of His laws and the rectitude of His government. Nor are we to suppose that these characters,
as sustained by Him, are in any respect opposed to one

PART
IV.
SEC. 2.

God is not
only a
Father but
a moral
Governor.

REVIEW OF OBJECTIONS TO THE

PART
IV.
SEC. 2.

another. Rather must we view them as harmoniously united and co-ordinately displayed in all His dispensations. Least of all is it necessary to regard them as conflicting with one another in the matter of the Atonement. For it must not be forgotten that He who, in His strict justice, exacted this great expiation for human guilt, is no other than the same adorable Being who of His infinite compassion and mercy hath provided it. So that we see in it the rectitude of the Sovereign co-operating with the love of the Father, with a view to the recovery and restoration of His fallen creatures.

Our Father
is the just
and holy
God.

But this is not the only ground, nor is it even the chief ground, on which the necessity of the Atonement may be reconciled with the fatherhood of God. There is so much of a disposition shown by some modern writers to represent the Atonement in the light of a mere " governmental display," or " stroke of administrative policy for upholding the authority of law and order in the moral world," that we should do well, in vindicating its necessity, to appeal, not only to the relation which God bears to us as a sovereign Lawgiver and righteous moral Governor, but also to *the essential attributes of the divine character*, as calling for some such remedial provision to expiate the sins of those who are to receive forgiveness. Be it remembered, then,

Ps. cxlv.
17.
Deut.
xxxii. 4.
Hab. i. 13.
Ps. lxii.
12.
Rom. ii.
6, 8, 9.

that " the Lord is righteous in all His ways, and holy in all His works ;" " a God of truth, and without iniquity, just and right is He ; " " of purer eyes than to behold evil, and that cannot look upon iniquity ; " " rendering to every man according to his deeds," and pledged to inflict " indignation and wrath upon every soul of man that doeth evil." These are the true sayings of God respecting Himself. Doubtless He is our Father. But when so regarding Him, we must not ignore those attributes which distinguish Him, or think of Him as altogether different from what He truly is. You say, " He is our Father ; " and you are warranted to say so. But who or what manner of Being is it that you thus designate ? *Our Father* is no other than this righteous and holy God—this sin-hating and sin-punishing God. And we may be very sure that,

DOCTRINE OF THE ATONEMENT.   425

even in dealing with us as a Father, He cannot deny Himself, or act in such a manner as would be opposed and abhorrent to His moral nature.

It is true, He possesses other attributes as well as these. He is "the Lord God merciful and gracious, long-suffering, and abundant in goodness and truth, keeping mercy for thousands, forgiving iniquity and transgression and sin." But this consideration cannot be held to supersede the necessity of an atonement, whereby divine mercy may be shown to sinful men on such terms as are compatible, not with *some* only, but with *all* the moral attributes of the Godhead. The sole effect of it is to warrant the persuasion, that whatsoever the holiness and justice of God may require, shall unfailingly be supplied by His loving-kindness and compassion. And I need scarcely remark that this persuasion has been fully verified by the wonderful provision He has actually made for our redemption through the sufferings and death of His only-begotten Son, "whom," as the Scripture saith, "God hath set forth to be a propitiation through faith in His blood, to declare His righteousness, . . . that He might be just, and the justifier of him who believeth in Jesus."

II. Again, it is argued that the Atonement is unnecessary, because there is no obstacle whatever on the part of God opposing the free access of sinners to His friendship and favour ; the sole obstacle being on the part of sinners themselves, whose alienated hearts will not suffer them to believe that God is so loving and merciful as He truly is.

This is substantially the same objection we had to contend with when discussing those texts which speak of the death of Christ as the ground of reconciliation between God and man. And it is unnecessary to repeat at any length the plain, and, as it seems to me, conclusive answer then given to it. If by "an obstacle on the part of God to the forgiveness of sinners" there be understood anything in the shape of *personal resentment,* or *implacable vindictiveness,* or *unwillingness to show mercy,* it is per-

PART IV. Sec. 2.

Exod. xxxiv. 6, 7.

Rom. iii. 25, 26.

Allegation that there is no obstacle on the part of God to the sinner's return to Him.

426   REVIEW OF OBJECTIONS TO THE

PART IV.
SEC. 2.
——

fectly true that there is no such obstacle. But that there are what may be called "obstacles" of another kind, arising from God's most holy aversion to sin, His just condemnation of it, and His declared purpose as the supreme Lawgiver and righteous Judge to punish it, can hardly be denied by any careful reader of the Scriptures. How else are we to explain those frequent and express

Ps. vii. 11.

statements, that "God is angry with the wicked every day;"

Ps. xxxiv. 16.

that "the face of the Lord is against them that do evil;"

Isa. lix. 2.

that "our iniquities have separated between us and our God, and our sins have hid His face from us that He will

Rom. i. 18.

not hear;" and that "the wrath of God is revealed from heaven against all ungodliness and unrighteousness of men"? A great part of the Bible, indeed, would need to be written over again, before we can expunge from it the broad and palpable evidence of God's holy displeasure against sinful men, and of His righteous purpose to inflict judgment on their iniquities.

It avails nothing to say that the statements of Scripture on this subject are expressed in figurative language and applied to God after the manner of men. It is true they are so. We cannot *literally* ascribe to God those human emotions and passions which such language denotes. But while to this extent the expressions must be qualified, we are not warranted to set them aside as if they were devoid

Supra, p. 66.

of meaning. For, as I formerly observed, men do not employ figures to *obscure* or *weaken* the import of their statements, but, on the contrary, *to make it clearer and more forcible*. And hence, when the inspired writers denounce the "wrath" and "hatred" and "vengeance" of God against wickedness, their evident purpose is to make us see more clearly, and feel more deeply, that there is *somewhat on the part of God* opposing the reception of sinners into His favour, which may be fitly depicted by comparing it to those dispositions and feelings of the human heart under which, in these figurative expressions, it is represented. Let every reasonable qualification be applied to such Scriptural denunciations, on the score of their being conveyed in figurative language, it must still

DOCTRINE OF THE ATONEMENT. 427

be allowed that *they have a definite meaning*, such as we are capable of apprehending and appreciating. And that meaning evidently must be *somewhat that pertains to God*, some barrier on *His* part that needs to be removed, in order that sinful men may be exempted from the forfeitures and penalties which they have justly incurred.

PART IV. SEC. 2.

III. A farther ground for questioning the necessity of an atonement has been sought in a comparison of the ways of God with the conduct of men. Why, it is asked, should not God forgive sin without requiring expiation to be made for it? *We* can forgive an injury done to us by a fellow-creature without demanding full reparation for the offence. We blame ourselves, indeed, and are blamed by others, if we act differently. We feel that we are transgressing our Lord's precept, " Be ye merciful as your Father is merciful," if we do not freely forgive a brother who has wronged us ; and we should be ashamed to admit that his punishment afforded us any real pleasure or satisfaction. Why, then, should it be thought that God cannot pardon sin without insisting that satisfaction shall be rendered for it ? Is not this to suppose that the very Being, whose mercy we are called to imitate, is less merciful than ourselves ? Is not this to ascribe to the great God what we should consider shameful and reprehensible on the part of man ?

If men can forgive wrongs without requiring satisfaction, why should not God?

Maurice's Theological Essays, p. 137, 138.

The whole plausibility of this objection arises from an oversight of the very broad distinction between *personal resentment* and *judicial condemnation*. Men may pass over injuries and indignities the effects of which are limited to themselves ; but we cannot thence infer that " the Judge of all the earth " must in like manner pass over transgressions which are committed against those laws of His universal kingdom which involve the welfare of the whole intelligent creation. The satisfaction which He requires is not personal ; for He solemnly declares that He has no pleasure in the death of the sinner. It is a *judicial* satisfaction which He is concerned to exact, not for the gratification of any wrathful or vindictive feelings,

428   REVIEW OF OBJECTIONS TO THE

PART IV. SEC. 2.

but for the vindication of His justice in the forgiveness of sins, and with the view of maintaining inviolate, and free from every charge of imperfection or mutability, the rectitude of His government and the authority of His statutes.

Besides, the case is very imperfectly, and on that account unfairly, represented, when we speak of God as *requiring*, and not also as *rendering*, satisfaction for those sins which are forgiven by Him. Never must we forget that what he requires in order to the remission of sins He has Himself freely provided. When we thus take a full and correct view of the whole transaction, so far is God from appearing to be less merciful than men are when they forgive wrongs without demanding reparation, that, on the contrary, His mercy is the more brightly displayed by the very costliness of that propitiation, which His justice indeed exacted, but His unspeakable love supplied. Indeed we may venture to say that the mercy of God could not have been satisfactorily proved to us by the free and full pardon of transgressors without an atonement; for in such a case our inference might have been, not that He is plenteous in mercy, but that He is regardless of justice; that He cares not for the authority of His laws; or that sin is not really evil in His sight. It is only the fact of His having at once justly required and graciously provided, with a view to our forgiveness, the inestimable sacrifice of His own beloved Son, that causes us to see in the pardon He extends to us a clear proof, not of indifference with respect to sin, but of boundless compassion and mercy to those who are chargeable with it.

The objection we are now seeking to obviate has been occasionally enforced by an appeal to the Scriptural comparison of the forgiveness of sins to *the remission of debts*. And it has been argued that just as a human creditor would be considered severe and ungenerous for insisting on full payment from one who is indebted to him and who has not the means of answering the demand, so would it be unworthy of the divine benevolence to exact from sinners an adequate satisfaction, such as they are

DOCTRINE OF THE ATONEMENT. 429

unable to render, for that debt of guilt and condemnation which they have incurred.

PART IV.
SEC. 2.

Those who thus argue overlook the fact that sins are called "debts" only in a metaphorical sense, and that the metaphor must not be stretched further than the nature of the case which it is meant to illustrate will admit of. It is remarkable, indeed, that with all their eagerness to explain away such figurative expressions as tend to confirm the doctrine of the Atonement, none are more ready than the adversaries of that doctrine to push to an extreme the import of any figurative language that may seem to afford them a plausible ground for controverting it. It is obvious, however, that some of the most important circumstances which belong to a *literal debt*, or obligation to repay a sum of money, do not at all belong to the *figurative debt* which a sinner may be said to contract when by sin he falls under an obligation to suffer punishment. The one, as being a mere private or personal matter, may, at the discretion of the creditor, be remitted without demanding any compensation ; but the other, as affecting the interests of law and justice, requires such satisfaction to be rendered as shall effectually distinguish the pardon of the sinner from connivance at his sin. Besides, any appearance of severity in the arrangement by which an expiation of human guilt has been demanded in order to its remission, is wholly removed when we consider that the same righteous God by whom the expiation was required has been pleased, of His own infinite goodness, to provide it for us.

IV. Another ground on which it has been maintained that an atonement is unnecessary—nay, even that it is impossible—is the allegation that all the penalties annexed to sin flow from it inevitably in the way of natural consequence, and hence that these penalties can only be averted by the deliverance of the transgressor from sin itself, which is their cause—in other words, by his personal sanctification. Thus, it is affirmed by one modern writer :—

Allegation that the penalties of sin can only be averted by the removal of sin itself.

430   REVIEW OF OBJECTIONS TO THE

PART IV. SEC. 2.

Greg's Creed of Christendom, p. 265.

" Sin contains its own retributive penalty, as surely and as naturally as the acorn contains the oak. Punishment is ordained to follow guilt by God—not as a Judge, but as the Creator and Legislator of the universe. We can be redeemed from the punishment of sin only by being redeemed from its commission. Neither can there be any such thing as vicarious atonement or punishment."

To the same effect are the following statements of another writer:—

Present-day Papers, edited by Bishop Ewing, No. V. p. 12, 18.

" It would seem to me an impeachment upon His government, and to charge it with weakness, if it could not be maintained without the infliction of capital punishment. God and His laws need no such vindication; and for this among other reasons, that sin is its own punishment. Sin carries death in its nature. 'The soul that sinneth must die' is a fact—a simple fact. The soul that sinneth does die. From the hour that sin gets possession of the soul the seed of death is planted there, and in due course it will arrive at its proper consummation. . . . How can any one suppose that Jesus Christ could be such a Saviour as that?" (*i.e.*, a Saviour from the penalties of sin.) " His name was called Jesus because He came to save the people from their SINS. Long shall we look for any passage in the Scriptures in which He is described as a Saviour from their *penalties.* 'Whatsoever a man soweth, that shall he also reap.' There can be no divorce between sin and suffering. The link that binds the two together comes from the divine forge. It has the mark of God's hand upon it. Sin and suffering must be eternally one; but, God be praised, there is a Saviour from sin, and *in that way* from all its penalties."

A third author, to whose theory respecting the sufferings of Christ we have already referred, expresses himself thus on the subject immediately before us:—

Young's Light and Life of Men, p. 87, 100, 115, 116.

" The spiritual laws of the universe are self-acting. They do not need or admit of vindication or support from human or divine hands. Without aid from any quarter they avenge themselves, and exact without fail, so long as the evil remains, the amount of penalty which the deed of violation deserves. . . . God Himself could not annul the sequence of sin and death; could not shield from the penalty except by removing its cause. . . . There is one salvation for man—only one; a salvation, not from hell, but from sin; not from consequences here or hereafter, but from the deep cause itself. . . . The punishment of moral evil, always and everywhere, is certain. The justice of the universe in this sense is an eternal fact, which even God could not set aside. God's mercy in Christ does not in the slightest degree set aside this justice. What it does is to remove the only ground on which the claim of justice stands. Instead of

DOCTRINE OF THE ATONEMENT. 431

arbitrarily withdrawing the criminal from punishment, it destroys in his soul that evil which is the only cause and reason of punishment, and which being removed, punishment ceases of itself."

PART IV. SEC. 2.

I have already had occasion to animadvert on these or similar statements. I endeavoured to show that they greatly exaggerate the facts of the case. For though, in the constitution of man and in the course of providence, there is an order of sequence observable, tending to bring about a kind of *natural retribution*, experience shows that the actual result of this arrangement cannot with any propriety be regarded as a uniform, unfailing, and adequate dispensation of rewards and punishments in the present life ; but that, on the contrary, the anomalies and exceptions are so great and so numerous as to furnish strong presumptive evidence of a future and more perfect retribution in the life to come. I also observed that these statements represent moral agents as exclusively subjected to certain *natural laws* or arrangements of the universe, by which sin and its bitter fruits are connected with one another ; while they take no account whatever of *God's moral law*, imperatively requiring obedience, through the dictates of conscience and the express precepts of His Word, and authoritatively denouncing condemnation, either here or hereafter, on its transgressors. And yet, farther, I remarked that according to these statements the moral government of the living personal God is absolutely superseded by what is styled " the justice of the universe ;" and the "Judge of all the earth" has nothing left for Him to do, but simply to look on and witness the evolutions of that "self-acting" mechanism which is independent of His support and does not allow of His interference.

Supra, p. 363-365.

I need scarcely add that with those who hold such opinions it would be utterly vain to enter into any discussion respecting the necessity of an atonement; for, before approaching that subject, we should be obliged to have a preliminary controversy with them regarding the first principles of ethics and of natural theology. Suffice it to say then, that, as moral and accountable agents, it is not with " self-acting laws of the spiritual universe," but with

432 REVIEW OF OBJECTIONS TO THE

PART IV.
SEC. 2.
——

the living God—the righteous Judge and sovereign Ruler of the universe—that we have to do. The dictates of our own reasonable and moral nature tend to assure us that by sin we are excluded from His favour, and justly exposed to the endurance of His wrath. And as for the testimony of Holy Scripture, we may venture to say that if there be one thing which it more plainly declares and more solemnly impresses upon us than another, it is this, that over and above any natural consequences which sin

Rom. i. 18.

may entail on those who have committed it, there is "the wrath of God revealed from heaven against all ungodliness and unrighteousness of men," and the condemnation

Eccles. xii. 14.

with which it shall be visited, in the day when "God shall bring every work into judgment, with every secret thing, whether it be good or evil."

If these things be so, it cannot be maintained that our need of an expiation for sin is superseded by "the justice of the universe;" for although by the removal of sin we could obtain exemption from all the natural evils and miseries it has brought upon us (which, however, is not usually found to be the case), it would still be necessary for us to be delivered from the righteous displeasure and

Supra, p. 365.

merited judgment of God. Sin, as I formerly observed, is not only a spiritual *disease* which needs to be cured, but a *crime* which the great Judge must either condemn or pardon. For, not to speak of the testimony of Scripture, which is altogether conclusive upon this point, there is an irrepressible sense of guilt in the human heart, bearing sure witness to the condemnation which past sin has incurred, and which future reformation cannot of itself annul.

In regard to the statement of one of the writers above referred to, that "we shall look long for any passage in the Scriptures in which Jesus is described as a Saviour from the penalties of sin," we may simply remark that any one who is really desirous of finding what is said in Scripture on this subject, and heartily disposed to acknowledge what he finds, however much it may disappoint or disconcert him, can hardly have to "look long" before he discovers some

DOCTRINE OF THE ATONEMENT. 433

such passages as the following : " God sent not His Son into the world to condemn the world, but that the world through him might be saved." " Much more, being now justified by His blood, we shall be saved from wrath through Him." " There is now no condemnation to them that are in Christ Jesus." " Christ hath redeemed us from the curse of the law, being made a curse for us." " Ye wait for His Son from heaven, whom He raised from the dead, even Jesus, who delivered us from the wrath to come." " For God hath not appointed us to wrath, but to obtain salvation by our Lord Jesus Christ, who died for us."

PART IV. Sec. 2.

John, iii. 17.

Rom. v. 9; viii. 1.

Gal. iii. 13.

1 Thess. i. 10; v. 9, 10.

V. Another ground on which it has been frequently argued that an atonement is unnecessary is the alleged *sufficiency of repentance.*

Alleged sufficiency of repentance.

That sinners must repent in order to receive forgiveness is freely admitted by all believers in the Atonement. But, according to their view, the connection between repentance and pardon is entirely owing to the mediation of Jesus Christ. It is " in His name," as He has Himself assured us, that " repentance and remission of sins are to be preached among all nations." And God is said to have " exalted Him with His right hand to be a Prince and a Saviour, to give repentance to Israel and forgiveness of sins."

Luke, xxiv. 47.

Acts, v. 31.

We are told, however, by those who would set aside the Atonement, that repentance has an intrinsic and independent efficacy ; that taken in its full sense, as comprehending not only compunction for sin but amendment of life, it is all the reparation for past sin that can be reasonably looked for ; that it fully recognises the authority of the law of God, and practically acknowledges the guilt of having transgressed it ; and that on these grounds it may be regarded as coming in the place of punishment, and as equally well serving to satisfy the claims and to fulfil the wise and good purposes of the supreme Lawgiver.

There is no real force or justice in these statements, however plausible at first sight they may appear to be.

434 REVIEW OF OBJECTIONS TO THE

PART
IV.
SEC. 2.
——
Repent-
ance is our
present
duty, and
cannot ex-
piate past
sins.

1. *Repentance*, in its fullest sense, cannot be considered as anything more than a performance of our present duty. It is simply a return to that path of obedience which ought never to have been forsaken, with such penitential feelings and acknowledgments as are due from us in our present position as self-convicted sinners. And hence, although it were ever so perfect—instead of uniformly being so defective that in many respects it needs to be repented of—it could not be held to have any retrospective efficacy as an expiation of guilt previously contracted. It no more avails to make atonement for past sins than to procure an indulgence for future sins. Nor can it be truly said that, with reference to the supreme Lawgiver, repentance serves

Does not
serve the
ends of
punish-
ment.

the same ends as punishment; for though it may indicate what *the transgressor* thinks of sin, it gives no indication of what *God* thinks of sin—how deeply He hates it—how sternly He condemns it — how utterly opposed in His judgment it is held to be to the holiness of His nature, the authority of His laws, the rectitude of His government, and the true welfare of His creatures.

Appeal to
analogy of
God's pro-
vidence in-
conclusive.

2. We make no appeal, as many writers have done when treating of this subject, to the analogy of divine providence. For though it be unquestionable that the repentance of profligate persons, such as the drunkard, the spendthrift, or the debauchee, does not exempt them from those ruinous consequences to their health or wealth which their past vices have brought upon them, it might be fairly replied that the same thing holds true when such persons are brought to seek redemption through the Saviour. Notwithstanding the free and full pardon then conferred upon them, they are not usually delivered from the pernicious effects of their past misconduct. These still cleave to them, as a standing memorial of the evil of sin, and as a means of salutary discipline, tending at once to deepen their humility and to quicken their watchfulness and earnestness in the Christian life.

Analogy of
human
govern-
ments.

But we may confidently appeal to the analogy of human governments. For every one knows that the repentance of a person by whom some aggravated deed of robbery, or

DOCTRINE OF THE ATONEMENT. 435

of murder, or of treason, has been perpetrated, is never recognised as an expiation of his offence. Although a considerable interval may have elapsed between the commission of his crime and his detection as the author of it, and during that interval he may have mourned for it in secret bitterness, and outwardly maintained the most reputable and blameless life, his merited condemnation is not stayed on that account. Strongly as the personal feelings of the judge might prompt him in such a case to the exercise of mercy, he feels that a regard to his character and his office, to the majesty of the law and to the welfare of the community, constrains him to pronounce upon the criminal that sentence which the law attaches to his crime.

Perhaps it may be here said that all analogy is precluded between the ways of God and the ways of men in this respect. A human government has to deal only with *occasional delinquents* whose crimes it must sternly punish for the protection of the rest of the community, whereas the divine government has to deal with a whole race of transgressors, all of whom are already involved in one common condemnation, so that the preventive purpose that might be served by a strict enforcement of the law is in this case superseded, and the only remaining alternative is a suspension of the law, or universal ruin. On this account it may be alleged that the analogy is so imperfect that no argument can be founded on it.

To this we reply, that the circumstance of our whole race being already involved in condemnation, may be a sufficient reason why God should *somehow* provide for the commutation of His righteous sentence, but is no reason why, in so doing, He should not also provide for the satisfaction of His justice, for the honouring of His law, and for promoting the interests of holiness for the future in all who may take advantage of His offered grace. Nay, rather, it is a reason why He should be the more concerned to prevent the exercise of His mercy from being abused, and should evidently demonstrate in His method of forgiving sin, no less than in His denunciations

436 REVIEW OF OBJECTIONS TO THE

PART.
IV.
SEC. 2.
——

against it, that it is the abominable thing which He hates. Besides, we have no ground or warrant for supposing that there may not be other races of intelligent creatures in other worlds, to whom the dealings of God with sinful men may either now or hereafter become known, and whose spiritual welfare might be injuriously affected by a full pardon tendered to us on the mere condition of repentance.

It is of the nature of repentance to disclaim every personal ground of acceptance with God.

3. I may farther observe, that not only is any repentance to which we are able to attain so defective as to need an atonement for itself, instead of compensating for our other sins and shortcomings, but *it is of the very nature of repentance to disclaim every personal ground of acceptance in the sight of God.* The true penitent is self-convicted and self-condemned. He fully acquiesces in the truth of every charge which the law of God brings against him, and in the justice of every woe which it denounces upon him ; and most heartily does he acknowledge that in himself there is no available plea which he can urge in arrest of judgment. How strange, then, is it, that *repentance* should have ascribed to it a virtue or efficacy in procuring the forgiveness of sin which it is of the very nature of repentance to repudiate !

Promptings of the human heart require more than repentance.

4. This remark leads me yet farther to observe, that there are natural feelings and instincts in the human heart which seem to bespeak the necessity of some other provision than repentance can supply for the pardon of our transgressions. I know not how we can otherwise account for the wide diffusion and continued prevalence of the rite of sacrifice. For though there be reason to believe that this ordinance originated in a divine appointment after the Fall, and was handed down by the sons of Noah to their descendants, we can hardly think that mere tradition would have given to it so firm a hold as it has ever been found to maintain on men of all nations and of every age, if there were not some principle involved in it that commends itself to the felt wants and deep-seated yearnings of the sinful heart. Nor is it easy to account, on any other ground, for the power which the simple and

DOCTRINE OF THE ATONEMENT. 437

faithful preaching of the Cross has ever exerted. Our moral nature somehow compels us to respect the claims of holiness, even when we have infringed them. And it seems as if we could not ourselves be satisfied with any deliverance from the merited consequences of our transgressions which comes to us in any other way than a way of righteousness. Hence we do not find that practically there is much difficulty in securing for the idea of an atonement a cheerful acceptance on the part of such men as are awakened to somewhat of a just sense of their own sinfulness. Mysterious as it may be in some respects to their intellect, it meets with a ready response and acquiescence from their heart.*

I cannot refrain from quoting, as to this subject, the following remarks of a late eloquent preacher, whose views were in many respects very much opposed to the commonly received doctrines of evangelical theology. The Rev. F. W. Robertson of Brighton thus observes :—

PART IV. SEC. 2.

"It is perilous to explain away, as mere figures of speech, those passages which speak of God as *angry with sin.* The *first* proof that He is so is to be drawn from our own conscience. We feel that God is angry; and if that be but figurative, then it is only figurative to say that God is pleased. There must be some deep truth in these expressions, or else we lose the personality of God. The *second* proof comes to us from the character of Christ. He was the representative of God under the limitations of humanity. Now, Christ was ' angry' (Mark, iii. 5; x. 14). That, therefore, which God feels, corresponds with that which in pure humanity is the emotion of anger. No other word will adequately represent God's feeling than the human word ' anger.' If we explain away such words, we lose the distinction between right and wrong. Nay, we will end in believing that there is no God at all, if we begin with explaining away His feelings."

Robertson on the Epistles to the Corinthians, Lect. 46.

The same author remarks, when writing on the subject of capital punishments :—

"There is a previous question to be settled : Is the object of punishment threefold only,—to serve as an example to others—to ameliorate the offender—and in some cases to defend society by his entire removal? Or is there a fourth element—the expression of righteous vengeance? for, I acknowledge, I cannot look upon vengeance as merely remedial. The sense of indignation which arises in the human bosom spontaneously against some crimes must, in a degree, be a reflection of that which exists in the mind of Deity.

Life and Letters of F. W. Robertson, i. 278.

* See Appendix, Note L.

438 REVIEW OF OBJECTIONS TO THE

PART IV. SEC. 2.

If so, there is in Him that which the Scripture calls 'wrath;' and we are not entitled, I think, to assume that all penalty is intended to affect or can affect the reformation of the offender. Probably some penalties are final, expressing infinite justice; and then the higher award of human law must resemble that. It is the indignation of society or of mankind, purified from all vindictiveness, expressed in a final punishment. For, doubtless, man—that is, society as distinguished from individual man—speaks in a degree with the authority of God, 'He hath committed all judgment unto Him, because He is the Son of man.' All hangs on that, Is final penalty the dignified expression of *vengeance*, putting aside the question of remedy or of social safety, and does not the element of vengeance enter into all punishment? If not, why does the feeling exist, not as a sinful, but as an essential, part of human nature; in *His* words, too, and acts?"

It is indeed strange that one who could feel and express so strongly the righteous indignation that naturally arises in every human breast against heinous acts of iniquity, and which, he justly argues, must be "a reflection of that which exists in the mind of Deity," should yet conceive that in that divine scheme, the very object of which is to deal with sin, no expression should be given to this righteous feeling on the part of God, nor any vindication offered of that attribute of the divine character which sin has especially outraged!

This objection concedes the general principle on which an atonement is necessary. And if so, surely God is the best judge of what nature the atonement should be.

5. To these remarks I have only now to add one other consideration, suggested by Dr Wardlaw—namely, that *those who allege repentance as the ground of pardon must be held as at least conceding the general principle on which the necessity of an atonement may be maintained.* For why should they hold repentance to be necessary, except that it would be inconsistent with the character of the supreme Ruler, and with the interests of His universal government, that the penalties of transgression should be remitted while the transgressor continued impenitent and unsubdued? If so, there is here *the recognition of a principle*—of the important principle that, in the terms on which pardon is administered, the glory of the divine character and government must be fully secured. Now, as Dr Wardlaw observes, "If this general principle be once admitted, (and by whom can it be questioned?) then the question natu-

Wardlaw's Systematic Theology, ii. 380.

DOCTRINE OF THE ATONEMENT. 439

rally suggests itself, Who is the most competent judge of what is requisite for such an end? for duly securing the authority of God's law, and sustaining the honour and majesty of His government? If that eternal Being Himself has devised, and revealed, and carried into execution, a scheme of mediation and atonement for that end, as His own fully-accredited Word in its plainest and most obvious sense teaches us that He has done, who is that worm of the dust who, in the plenitude of his fancied wisdom, presumes to pronounce this divine scheme to be unnecessary, and, understanding better than God Himself what is most suitable to God's character, and most conducive to the maintenance of the authority of His government, insists that the repentance of the sinner is of itself sufficient? May not the difference between the affirmations of God's Word and the sentiments of such presumptuous speculators arise from the difference between the divine estimate and theirs of the amount of evil and of evil desert that there is in sin, and from a corresponding difference in the divine estimate and theirs of the importance of impressing the intelligent universe with its exceeding sinfulness, and with the inviolable and eternal righteousness of the administration of heaven?"

I need only add, that our competency to form a sound and impartial judgment in this matter may fairly be questioned, inasmuch as we are the very persons in whose behalf the divine mercy is to be administered. In fact, we are in the position of convicted criminals prescribing rules for the guidance of their judge. The sinfulness of our natures may reasonably be thought to have so far blunted our moral sensibilities as to disqualify us for appreciating the course which infinite rectitude and holiness may approve of; while, at the same time, our own deep personal interest in the question to be determined can scarcely fail to bias the conclusions we arrive at.

SECTION III.

THE ATONEMENT CANNOT BE SAID TO DEROGATE
FROM THE PERFECTIONS OF GOD.

PART
IV.
SEC. 3.
———

A THIRD class of objections with which the revealed doc-trine respecting the mediatorial work and sufferings of Jesus Christ has frequently been assailed, are those in which *it is alleged to involve principles which derogate from the perfections of the divine character.*

Objection that the Atone-ment con-flicts with the justice of God.

I. Thus we are told that " *it involves essential injustice.* It represents a perfectly innocent and righteous person as subjected to severe and unmerited sufferings in the room of the guilty. In this respect it is offensive to our moral sense. It conflicts with the plainest principles of equity. How, then, can we suppose it to be compatible with the attributes of that adorable Being who is just in all His ways ? "

Christ was a willing sufferer, and had power to dispose of His life.

1. To this apparently formidable objection we may reply that there were specialities in the substitution of Jesus Christ which ought greatly to affect our judgment with respect to it. He was a *willing* sufferer. Nothing was done to Him without His full concurrence. Nay, we may rather say that all the sufferings He endured were in fulfilment of his own earnest desire, and of His own deliberate and settled purpose. Farther, He was entitled, if it so pleased Him, to suffer and die as a substitute for sinners, having " power to lay down His life, and power to take it again." Nor was this all ; for, as He Himself assures us, the surrender of life which He thus made in behalf of sinners was sanctioned by His heavenly Father,

John, x.
18.

DOCTRINE OF THE ATONEMENT. 441

the supreme Head of all authority and government. These considerations show that there is nothing that can be properly called "injustice" in the transaction. "Injustice" consists in the invasion of a person's rights. But no rights are invaded when a free and independent Being voluntarily and deliberately *consents to waive His own rights,* and without the least prejudice to any other being—nay, rather to the eternal glory and blessedness of all other beings who are in any way affected by His procedure— resolves to "do what He wills with His own."

"When we hear it asked" (to quote the words of a distinguished writer), "How can it be righteous to lay on one person the penalties of others? we must feel that the question, to be effectually answered, needs only to be more accurately put; that the form which it ought to assume is this, How can it be righteous for one person, who has authority to do it, *voluntarily to take upon Himself* the penalties of others? None who remember the words of the Saviour,—'Lo, I come to do Thy will;' 'I lay down my life of myself;' 'I give my life a ransom for many,'—will deny our right to make this change in the form of the question. Nor can any fail to see that the whole aspect of the question is by this little change entirely altered; for how many an act of heroic self-sacrifice which it would be most unrighteous for others to demand from, or to force upon, one who was reluctant, which would indeed cease to be heroism or devotion at all unless wholly self-imposed, is yet most glorious when one has freely undertaken it; and is only *not* righteous because it is *so much more and better than merely righteous,*—because it moves in that higher region where law is no more known, but only known no more because it has been transfigured into love?"

2. But this is not all; for if there be any difficulty involved in the Scriptural doctrine of the Atonement, so far as our views of the divine justice are affected by it, *the facts of difficulty lies in the undeniable facts of the case,* and cannot be got rid of by the mere rejection of that doctrine.

Those who so much object to the divine appointment

PART
IV.
SEC. 3.

Trench's
Sermons
in West-
minster
Abbey, p.
170.

The diffi-
culty lies
in the
facts of
the case.

442   REVIEW OF OBJECTIONS TO THE

PART IV. SEC. 3.

The innocent Saviour endured unmerited sufferings, whether the Atonement be admitted or denied.

of the immaculate Saviour to suffer *in the room of sinners,* would do well to remember that the real difficulty is *this,* that the immaculate Saviour should have been divinely appointed *to suffer at all.*' And this difficulty is greatly increased when we take into account the majesty of His person as the only-begotten Son of God. Now, that this innocent and august Person *did* suffer—that He was emphatically " a man of sorrows "—and that His sufferings are represented in Scripture as having been not merely incidental, but absolutely essential to the purposes of His mission,—are *matters of fact* which cannot be disputed, whatever be our views of the doctrine of the Atonement.

His sufferings were neither deserved nor needed on His own account.

On what principle, then, are His sufferings to be accounted for? They cannot be explained like those of other sufferers, on any assignable grounds of a *personal* nature ; for they were neither deserved by Him as a punishment, nor required by Him as a purifying discipline, on His own account.   They necessarily must be held to have been endured by Him *for reasons and purposes pertaining to others, and not to Himself.*

In so far, then, as our views of the divine justice may be affected by the sufferings of the Lord Jesus, *where is the mighty difference to be discerned between the purposes severally assigned to these sufferings by those who affirm and by those who deny the doctrine of the Atonement ?* If it be consistent with the justice of God to appoint an innocent and divine Person to suffer in order to assure us of the truth of His heavenly mission, to manifest His Father's love, or to illustrate the principle of self-sacrifice ; why may it not be consistent with the justice of God to appoint such a Person to suffer in order to exempt sinners from the penal consequences of their transgressions ? Here, indeed, it may be said that *other parties* are introduced as receiving different treatment from that which was justly due to them.   But so it must needs be if sinners are to be pardoned at all.   The pardon of sinners, in whatsoever way or on whatsoever ground it may be conferred upon them, necessarily implies a treatment of them otherwise than they have themselves deserved.   And why so ?   Not

The pardon of sinners also is undeserved anyhow.

DOCTRINE OF THE ATONEMENT. 443

because they are pardoned *through the Atonement,* but
because, *being transgressors, they are pardoned anyhow ;* so
that any difficulty which their pardon may be held to
involve is altogether irrespective of the Atonement.

This doctrine, then, cannot reasonably be held accountable for any alleged difficulties in relation to the justice of
God, which so plainly cannot be obviated by the denial of
it. The sufferings of the innocent, endured for whatsoever
reason, are and must needs be as regards Himself *unmer-*
ited sufferings. And the pardon of the guilty, procured in
whatsoever way, is and must needs be as regards themselves *unmerited* pardon. There is no possibility of denying these two propositions, whatever view of the mediation of Christ may be adopted. Make of His sufferings
what you will, they were not such as *He* deserved, and
yet they were inflicted on Him. And make of the pardon
of sinners what you will, it is not such as *they* deserve,
and yet it is conferred upon them. If, then, as regards
the divine justice, there be any difficulty,—arising, on the
one hand, from the treatment of the innocent Saviour
otherwise than was *His* due, by subjecting Him to sufferings and death—and, on the other hand, from the treatment of sinful men otherwise than is *their* due, by pardoning their offences,—thus much is clear, that the difficulty
cannot be removed, either on the one side or on the other,
by denying the commonly-received doctrine of the Atonement. The only way in which it could be removed would
be by denying, as regards the Lord Jesus Christ, either
His innocence or His sufferings ; and by denying, as regards the pardoned transgressors, either their sinfulness or
their forgiveness. But all these are matters of fact that
cannot be got rid of, whatever we may think of the revealed
method of human redemption.

It appears, then, that the sufferings of Christ and the
pardon of sinners, when connected together as the doctrine of the Atonement connects them, do not involve any
greater difficulties in relation to the justice of God than if
they were disconnected. In saying so, however, we are
very far from holding that the causal connection between

*PART
IV.
SEC. 3.*

The
Atone-
ment is not
answerable
for difficul-
ties in re-
lation to
the justice
of God,
which can-
not be ob-
viated by
the denial
of it.

444   REVIEW OF OBJECTIONS TO THE

PART
IV.
SEC. 3.
——

the two is free from mystery. All that we affirm is, that in so far as the justice of God appears to be affected by them, any difficulties they involve are substantially the same, whether this causal connection be asserted or denied ; and that no other purpose that we know of can be attributed to the sufferings of the innocent and well-beloved Son of God, that is more consonant either to the divine justice or to the divine benignity, than the grand and gracious purpose which the Scriptures have assigned to them.

The Atonement charged with implying a transfer of moral character. Rationale of Religious Inquiry, p. 83.

II. A special objection has been urged against the Atonement on the ground that, besides involving the infliction of undeserved sufferings on the innocent in the room of the guilty, it involves also *an interchange of moral characteristics between the two*, which would be not only unjust, but unreasonable, and indeed impossible. Thus it has been alleged by Mr Martineau that " the doctrine is metaphysically absurd, inasmuch as guilt and innocence are no more transferable from one person to another than intellect or eyesight ; and that it is also morally absurd, because it represents Christ as suffering under remorse for the sins of men, which He never committed, and of which, consequently, He could have neither memory nor consciousness."

The objection founded on a misconception of what is meant by imputation of sin to Christ.

This objection admits of the very simple reply that it is founded on a gross misapprehension of the Scriptural doctrine. There is no such thing affirmed in the Scriptures, and no such thing believed by any intelligent Christian, as that *the moral turpitude of our sins was transferred to Christ*, so as to make Him personally sinful and ill-deserving ; and that the *moral excellence of His righteousness is transferred to us*, so as to make us personally upright and commendable. As little does it form any part of the Christian doctrine that the Lord Jesus *suffered under remorse for the sins of men*, as if He had been Himself conscious of having committed them. We are wont to affirm, indeed, that our sins were *imputed* to Christ, and that His righteousness is *imputed* to believers. But this, as I have

DOCTRINE OF THE ATONEMENT.   445

formerly observed, does not at all imply the transference of one person's moral qualities to another.   Such a transference is in the nature of things impossible.   One person cannot be made dishonest or impure by the dishonesty or impurity of another person imputed to him, while in his own character he is altogether pure and upright.   Our sins, as regards their moral qualities, are our own, and cannot by imputation, or by any means, become another's. The *legal consequences* of them may be transferable to another party, who undertakes, with the sanction of the supreme judge, to bear these legal consequences in our stead ; and this, by a *metonymy* of the cause for the effect, may be figuratively spoken of as a transference of our sins to him.   But there can be no literal transference of the sins themselves, to the effect of rendering him who has not committed them *sinful*, and of rendering us who have committed them *sinless*.

"It must be observed," says Dr Owen, "respecting the imputation of that which is not antecedently our own, that no imputation of this kind accounts those unto whom anything is imputed *to have themselves done the things* which are imputed to them.   That were not to impute, but *to err in judgment*, and indeed utterly to overthrow the whole nature of gracious imputation.   But imputation makes that to be ours which was not ours before, *unto all ends and purposes whereunto it would have served* if it had been ours.   It is therefore a manifest mistake of their own which some persons make the ground of a charge against the doctrine of imputation.   For they say, 'If our sins were imputed to Christ, then must He *be esteemed to have done what we have done amiss*, and so be the greatest sinner that ever was ;' and on the other side, 'If His righteousness be imputed to us, then are we *esteemed to have done what He did*, and so to stand in no need of the pardon of sin.'   But this is against the nature of imputation, which proceeds on no such judgment; but on the contrary judgment, that we ourselves have done nothing of what is imputed to us, nor Christ anything of what is imputed to Him."

PART
IV.
SEC. 3.
——-
Supra, p.
188-190.

Owen's
Works
(Goold's
ed.), v.
168, 169.

PART
IV.
SEC. 3.
———
Princeton
Theologi-
cal Essays,
1st series,
p. 121.

To the same effect are the following words of Dr Hodge: "Is there any one who has the hardihood to charge the whole Calvinistic world, who teach or preach the doctrine of imputation, with believing that Christ personally and properly committed the sins which are said to be imputed to Him? or that the moral turpitude of these sins was transferred to Him? or that He ever *repented* of our sins? If this is imputation, if this 'transfer of moral character' is included in it, we have not words to express our deep abhorrence of the doctrine."

It appears, then, that the imputation of our sins to Christ implies only that He was made liable, in terms of His own voluntary undertaking, to the endurance of their legal forfeitures or penalties, without any transference to Him of their moral turpitude or ill-desert. The principle involved in it is very much the same as that of any case of suretiship in human transactions. The man who has pledged himself as security for the fulfilment of a stipulation made by another person, is not regarded as fraudulent or dishonest in the event of that stipulation being unfulfilled. But yet, the non-fulfilment is reckoned to his account, and in terms of his own pledge he is liable for the consequences of it. It is in a sense analogous to this that our sins are said to be "imputed" to the Saviour. He undertook for us, as our surety or representative. Standing in our room, He was dealt with in our stead. He became liable to the penalties which our sins had justly incurred, in order that we, through His substitution, might be exempted from them. But even in the lowest depths of His humiliation, and in the bitterest agonies of His endurance, He was, alike in His own consciousness and in the judgment of heaven, the Holy One of God, unspotted and without blemish.

It may be alleged, indeed, that the phraseology we employ, when speaking of our sins as "imputed or reckoned to Christ," is so extremely apt to be misconceived, that it might with propriety and advantage be dispensed with. To this we need only reply, that these phrases appear to be fairly equivalent to those statements of Scripture which

DOCTRINE OF THE ATONEMENT.   447

represent Christ as "bearing our sins," as having "our
iniquities laid upon Him," as "made sin for us," and
"made a curse for us;" and that the former are not more
liable than the latter to any misapprehension of their true
meaning, which may not be removed in the manner we
have indicated. If, however, any better phrases can be
found to give a like brief and definite expression to the
import of such Scriptural statements as we have now referred to (though none so suitable that we know of have
been ever suggested), let them by all means be adopted
by those who prefer them, provided always that the truth
which they are meant to convey be not in any way evaded
or compromised.

III. Again, it has been objected to the Atonement that
it grievously detracts from the infinite goodness and
mercy of God, inasmuch as it represents Him in the
character of a stern, severe, implacable, and relentless
Being, demanding innocent blood to appease His aveng-
ing wrath, and unwilling to forgive sinners until there has
been wrung from Him, by the mediation of Jesus Christ,
a sullen and ungracious pardon.

This objection, also, like that which preceded it, is
founded on a misapprehension of the true import of the
doctrine against which it is advanced.

1. The Atonement is not to be regarded as *a means of*
inclining God to be placable and merciful, or of inducing
Him to entertain towards sinners a kindness and compassion with which He would not otherwise have regarded
them. It may indeed have been occasionally spoken of
by ignorant and injudicious believers in it, in terms which
would seem to convey this erroneous conception of it.
And it has been frequently represented in this light by
adversaries when seeking to bring it into disrepute. But,
most assuredly, such is not the view of it that has ever
been taken by its intelligent and enlightened advocates.
And such is as opposite as possible to the view of it that
has been exhibited to us in the oracles of divine truth.
The Atonement, as set forth in the statements of Holy

PART
IV.
SEC. 3.

Objection
that the
Atone-
ment de-
tracts from
the good-
ness and
mercy of
God.

The
Atone-
ment is not
a means of
inclining
God to be
merciful.

448   REVIEW OF OBJECTIONS TO THE

PART
IV.
SEC. 3.
——
The
Atone-
ment is not
the *cause*
of God's
love to sin-
ners, but
its *result*
and mani-
festation.

Scripture, as well as in the creeds of all Churches by which it is maintained, is so far from being the *cause* of God's love and mercy to sinners, that it is, on the contrary, the most wonderful *result*, and the most remarkable *manifes-tation*, of God's pre-existing love and mercy to sinful men that could possibly be imagined. It was not with the view of *disposing* Him to be merciful to us that He required the obedience and death of His beloved Son, but simply with a view to the exercise of that mercy which He was previously disposed to extend towards us, in such a way as should be compatible with the perfection of His holiness, the claims of His justice, and the authority of His law. The Atonement was offered for the purpose, as

Rom. iii.
25.

an apostle expresses it, of "*declaring the righteousness of God in the remission of sins.*" But it was not offered for the purpose of *inclining* God to forgive sins when it could

Supra, p.
158-160,
193, 194.

be done in a way of righteousness. For if God had not previously been inclined so to forgive sins, it is evident that the Atonement would never have been provided by Him. The Atonement had its origin in God's willingness to save sinners. Nothing but the very intensity of His desire to save sinners can account for His having provided such a sacrifice, in order that they might be saved in the manner which He deemed conducive to the rectitude of His government and the glory of His name.

God's
wrath has
nothing
akin to
personal
resentment
or vindic-
tiveness.

2. Farther, when the objectors speak of "God's aveng-ing wrath as having been appeased by the innocent blood of Christ," they need to be reminded that "the wrath of God against sin" is in no respect akin to personal resent-ment or vindictiveness. It is evident, indeed, that were such elements involved in it, any such thing as *the substi-tution of another person* in the room of the very offender would be inadmissible ; for it is not of the nature of per-sonal enmity or revenge to make refined distinctions be-tween the sinner and his sin. It understands nothing of hatred to the crime coexisting with love and compassion for the criminal. Perhaps, if it is very blind and reckless in its impulses, it may seek to wreak itself, *not only* on the offender, but *on others also* who are interested in him, or

DOCTRINE OF THE ATONEMENT. 449

PART IV. SEC. 3.

intimately connected with him. But never will personal enmity or revenge expend itself to such an extent on other objects *as to overlook the very person against whom it has been excited.* Far less will it deliberately provide a substitute, inestimably dear and precious to itself, in consideration of whose vicarious sufferings it will not only freely pardon the offender, but crown him with the highest privileges and benefactions. By the advocates of the doctrine of the Atonement, therefore, no such vindictive or resentful passion as the objectors allege, nor anything analogous to it, can be ascribed to the Almighty. His wrath against sin is not personal, but judicial; and the provision He has made of mediation and atonement is not intended to quell His wrathful feelings against transgressors, but for the very different purpose of extending His mercy towards them in such a manner as may be consistent with the perfections of His character, the authority of His law, and the rectitude of His universal government.

It is not personal, but *judicial.*

3. It is specially important, in meeting this objection, to keep in remembrance that the Atonement was *provided* for us by the same God for the satisfaction of whose justice it was *exacted ;* and that He provided it by the sacrifice of that adorable person who bore to Him a relationship of the most intimate and endearing kind, and who, in some sense to us incomprehensible, was *one with Him* in the constitution of the Godhead. It was no innocent *creature* who was arbitrarily singled out to bear the punishment of his guilty fellow-creatures. But He who "was in the beginning with God, and was God"—He of whom it is written, that "all things were made by Him, and without Him was not anything made that was made"— He who "upholdeth all things by the word of His power," and "by whom all things consist"—He to whom "all judgment hath been committed," and by whom the final doom of all men shall be pronounced,—it is this great Being, *our very Creator and our very Judge,* who is set forth in the doctrine of the Atonement, not as seeking for us in the person of any other, but as *rendering in His*

The Atonement was provided for us by God Himself, in the sacrifice of His Son, who was one with Him in the Godhead.

John, i. 1, 3.

Heb. i. 3.

Colos. i. 17.

John, v 22.

450   REVIEW OF OBJECTIONS TO THE

PART IV. SEC. 3.

own person the needful expiation. And I venture to say that by this consideration the doctrine is triumphantly vindicated from the charge of exhibiting the character of God in a harsh, severe, implacable, and forbidding aspect, and is shown, on the contrary, to be most brightly illustrative of the unspeakable warmth and tenderness of His love.

Objection that the Atonement is inconsistent with *pardon by free grace.*

IV. Another objection frequently urged against the Atonement is, that " it is *incompatible with the graciousness of the divine procedure in the forgiveness of sinners.* The Scriptures uniformly represent the pardon of sin as an act of pure grace or sovereign goodness on the part of God. But if satisfaction has been given for sin by Jesus Christ, this representation, it is said, would be altogether inappropriate. Pardon would then be, not an act of grace, but an act of justice ; and instead of its being merciful in God to bestow forgiveness, it would be unjust in God to withhold it."

The inspired writers are not sensible of this alleged inconsistency.

1. Now one thing is very clear in reference to this objection, that if there be any such inconsistency as it alleges between pardon through the Atonement and pardon by divine grace, the sacred writers themselves had no suspicion or conception of it ; for we find them connecting *propitiation for sin* with *free grace,* manifested in the forgiveness of the sinner, in terms the most unequivocal and emphatic, so as to indicate that they had no manner of apprehension that the two things were incompatible with one another, or that the latter was in any way affected by the former, unless in the way of enhancing rather than of

Rom. iii. 23-25.

detracting from it. Thus Paul declares that " all have sinned and come short of the glory of God; being *justified freely by His grace through the redemption that is in Christ Jesus ;* whom God hath set forth to be a propitiation through faith in His blood, to declare His righteousness for the remission of sins." And in another psssage he

Eph. i. 6-8.

speaks of the salvation of believers as being " *to the praise of the glory of His grace,* wherein He hath made us *accepted in the Beloved ; in whom we have redemption through His*

DOCTRINE OF THE ATONEMENT.   451

blood, the forgiveness of sins, according to the riches of His grace, wherein He hath abounded towards us in all wisdom and prudence."

2. Farther, this objection overlooks the distinction between a *pecuniary* and a *penal satisfaction.* It is true our penal liabilities are sometimes compared in Scripture to pecuniary debts. And the comparison is in many respects striking and appropriate. It must not, however, be carried farther than the nature of the two subjects between which it is made, as otherwise ascertainable, will admit of. No one who seriously considers the matter will affirm that all the circumstances of a literal debt or obligation to repay a borrowed sum of money belong to that figurative debt which a sinner may be held to contract when, by the violation of the law of God, he comes under an obligation to suffer the penalty denounced by it. There is this very obvious distinction between the two, that the pecuniary debt has respect only to *the thing due,* so that the payment of it, by whomsoever made, at once and altogether extinguishes the claim, and secures, as a matter of bare justice, the release of the debtor; whereas the penal debt *attaches also to the person of the offender,* so that the discharge of it, by vicarious sufferings on the part of any substitute whom the Supreme Judge may be pleased to accept of, does not obliterate the demerits of the offender himself, or give to him any such personal claim to forgiveness as should render him the less beholden for it to sovereign grace. In order that a criminal may be absolved, when a vicarious satisfaction has been rendered for him, it is necessary that there should intervene a sovereign act of grace on the part of the Supreme Lawgiver, who is entitled on the strict terms of justice to insist that the penalty shall be paid by the very person who has committed the crime. Certainly it is what sinners had no right or reason to expect, that God should accept of the sufferings of His beloved Son as a satisfaction for the sins with which they are chargeable. Nor does the fact of His being pleased to do so alter or diminish in any degree their ill-desert, or give them the slightest shadow

PART
IV.
SEC. 3.

Distinction between a *pecuniary* and a *penal* satisfaction.

REVIEW OF OBJECTIONS TO THE

PART
IV.
SEC. 3.

of a claim to demand, as if it were due to themselves, the pardon which, so far as *they* are concerned, is wholly gratuitous. If that pardon can be deemed an act of justice at all, it is so only to Christ, who "gave His life a ransom for many." To those who receive it, it can only be considered as an act of pure, unmerited, and abounding mercy.

The satis-
faction was
provided
by the free
grace of
God.

3. But yet further, this objection overlooks the fact that the satisfaction for sin which is the ground of its forgiveness has been provided for us by the sovereign grace of God. If any other than He by whom our sin is pardoned had been left to furnish the needful expiation, there might have been some greater plausibility in the assertion that the graciousness of the pardon was in some respect impaired. But inasmuch as God has Himself supplied, by the inestimable sacrifice of His own beloved Son, all that He exacts as necessary for our redemption, the costliness of our pardon—not to us who freely receive it, but to Him who at so great a sacrifice confers it on us—is so far from lessening, that it mightily enhances and gloriously illustrates the riches of His grace.

Objection
that the
Atone-
ment
arrays
God's at-
tributes
against
each other,

V. Another objection which has sometimes been advanced against the Scriptural doctrine of the Atonement is, that "it arrays the divine attributes against each other, as if mercy and justice were naturally opposed, and had rival claims which must be compromised or adjusted."

Inappli-
cable to
the Atone-
ment as set
forth in
Scripture.

Whatever force there may be in this objection, we may venture to say that it has no real bearing on the doctrine of the Atonement as set forth in the Word of God, however fairly applicable it may be to certain rhetorical descriptions and figures of speech which the advocates of that doctrine have employed, not always very judiciously, in illustration of it. Some such statements we do occasionally meet with in popular discourses or addresses on this subject, as that "divine justice demands the condemnation of the sinner, while divine mercy, on the other hand, calls for his deliverance ; and that the Saviour interposes between the two, and by His great sacrifice opens up a way

DOCTRINE OF THE ATONEMENT. 453

by which their conflicting claims and interests may be accommodated."

The revealed doctrine, however, is not to be held accountable for aught that may be considered as derogatory to the attributes of God in these human representations of it. At the same time, it is desirable that such representations should be used with much caution and qualification, if used at all, as being exceedingly liable to be misunderstood by the friends of evangelical truth, while at the same time they are sure to be laid hold of as a ground of plausible objection by its adversaries.

The attributes of God, although we may speak of them and reason about them apart from one another, are not to be considered as so many distinct agencies, each occupying its own province, and wielding its own influence. They are inseparably and harmoniously united, alike in the nature and in the actings of that adorable Being to whom they appertain. "The light of the sun can be divided by a familiar process into all the various hues of the rainbow, and each of these we can make the object of distinct attention ; but it is the combination of them all that constitutes the glorious element, of which its colourless purity is the prime excellence. Even so may we make the various perfections of the divine nature the subjects, one by one, of separate consideration ; but it is the union of them all, in inseparable existence and in combined exercise, that forms the character of that infinite Being, of whom, with exquisite beauty and sublime simplicity, it is said, that ' God is light ; and in Him is no darkness at all.' "

It is altogether an error, then, to suppose that God acts at one time according to one of His attributes, and at another time according to another. He acts in conformity with all of them at all times. And it would, doubtless, be altogether derogatory to the consummate excellence and perfection of His character, to think that there are in it any jarring elements, tending to internal conflict or collision.

Assuredly there is nothing in the revelations of Scrip-

PART IV. SEC. 3.

Wardlaw on the Socinian Controversy, p. 206.

1 John i. 5

454 REVIEW OF OBJECTIONS TO THE

PART IV.
SEC. 3.

ture respecting the Atonement that can be justly held to give countenance to such an error. Christ is there set forth as "the Mediator between God and men," but not as the Mediator between the divine attributes. As for the divine justice and the divine mercy in particular, the end of His work was, not to bring them into harmony as if they had been at variance with one another, but jointly to manifest and glorify them in the redemption of sinners. It is a case of *combined action*, and not of *counteraction*, on the part of these attributes, that is exhibited on the cross.

Ps. lxxxv. 10.

"Mercy and truth are met together; righteousness and peace have kissed each other."

Objection that the Atonement supposes God to be controlled by a principle superior to Himself.

VI. Somewhat akin to the objection I have last noticed is another that is equally inapplicable to the Scriptural doctrine under discussion. When we speak of the Atonement as having been exacted, not by any personal feeling of vindictiveness on the part of God, but by a regard to the claims of justice and of holiness, we are asked, "What is this but to represent the great God as being constrained to do what He would willingly not have done? Is it not to set up some exterior moral principle, in the name of justice or of holiness, by which the Supreme Being is controlled and overruled?"

Might be retorted on those who urge it.

It might be very easy, were it necessary, to retort this objection on those by whom it is advanced. For when, acknowledging, as they do, the divine justice, they nevertheless insist that God must forgive sin, from a beneficent regard to the happiness of His sinful creatures, without requiring any satisfaction or atonement for it, what else is this, we might ask, but to set up a principle superior to God, by which He is constrained to act otherwise than the rectitude and holiness of His nature would have dictated?

The objection inept and groundless.

But, in truth, the objection is palpably inept and groundless. When we speak of the Atonement as having been "exacted by a regard to the claims of justice and of holiness," we are setting up no "principle superior to God," inasmuch as the justice and holiness thus regarded

DOCTRINE OF THE ATONEMENT. 455

by Him are *nothing exterior to Himself by which He is* PART
overruled, but the justice and holiness essential to His IV.
own nature.   As well might it be said that we are SEC. 3.
" setting up principles superior to God," to which He is
obliged to yield, when we say that He is so pure that
" He cannot behold iniquity," or so truthful that " it is
impossible for Him to lie."   It is no derogation from the
divine majesty to affirm that God acts, and needs must
act, consistently with His own attributes.   This, indeed,
is just to affirm, in His own solemn words, that " *He cannot* 2 Tim. ii.
deny Himself." 13.

SECTION IV.

THE MYSTERIOUSNESS OF THE ATONEMENT IS NO SUFFICIENT GROUND OF OBJECTION TO IT.

PART
IV.
SEC. 4.
——
The
Atone-
ment ob-
jected to
as being
mysterious.

IT has often been objected to the doctrine of the Atonement, that it is to a great extent beyond our comprehension. The substitution of an innocent person for the guilty, to bear the penal consequences of their sins, in order that they, in consideration of his vicarious suffering, may be exempted from them, is, we are told, an arrangement of which we are unable to discern the equity or propriety. Even if we were not warranted to say that it is *perceptibly at variance* with the divine attributes, we are certainly warranted to say that it is not *perceptibly in accordance* with them. It is a great mystery. We cannot fully explain the grounds on which it rests. We can give no satisfactory account of the reasons which may have led to the adoption of it. And hence, the objectors argue, we cannot be expected to yield to it our full, intelligent, and hearty assent.

In what
respect is
this objec-
tion fairly
applicable
to the
Atone-
ment?

1. In meeting this objection, it is first of all necessary to consider, *In what respects it is fairly applicable to the Atonement*—in other words, What there is of mystery about the matter, *for which the Atonement may be justly held accountable.* For it is very evident that no exception can with reason or fairness be taken to this doctrine in respect of any mysteries which do not properly arise out of it, and which would not be removed or lessened by the denial of it. The doctrine can only be held answerable for those mysteries which the affirmation of it may be

DOCTRINE OF THE ATONEMENT.   457

said to create, and which, apart from the affirmation of it, would have no existence.

Now there are two things connected with the Atonement, and I may even say necessarily assumed in it, for which, *in themselves considered*, it cannot be said to be accountable—namely (1), the infliction of unmerited sufferings on Jesus Christ; and (2) the bestowal of unmerited pardon on transgressors. Whatever mystery there may be in these things, *when viewed apart*, the doctrine of the Atonement cannot be justly charged with it, inasmuch as that mystery exists irrespectively of the doctrine. If the holy Jesus was subjected to severe sufferings, then it is a fact that He was treated otherwise than He deserved, for whatsoever purpose these sufferings may have been inflicted. And if sinners obtain pardon at all, it is equally a fact that they are thereby treated otherwise than they deserve, on whatsoever ground that pardon may be conferred upon them. For these facts, accordingly, assuming them to be facts, and for anything mysterious involved in them *per se*, the doctrine of the Atonement is not to be held responsible, because they are not to be got rid of by the denial of it. It is only for *the causal connection between the two*, and for whatsoever mysteries may be involved in this connection, that any relevant charge can be brought against the Atonement in respect of our being unable to explain the principles on which it rests, or the reasons to be assigned for it. The difficulty to be solved is, not how it came to pass that both the Saviour and the redeemed sinner are treated otherwise than they deserve when the one is subjected to sufferings and the other receives forgiveness and favour, but how it came to pass that the unmerited sufferings of the one are deemed, in the judgment of God, a sufficient ground for the bestowal of unmerited blessings on the other.

2. With the view of solving this difficulty, if possible, there are some apparent analogies which have been adduced from the course of divine providence or the ordinary transactions of men, as serving to illustrate the

PART IV.
SEC. 4.

Objection only applicable in so far as regards the *causal connection* between the sufferings of Christ and the salvation of believers.

Analogies adduced to solve the mystery are unsatisfactory.

458   REVIEW OF OBJECTIONS TO THE

PART
IV.
SEC. 4.

principle of substitution, but which, it must be confessed, are far from being satisfactory.

It is true that nothing is more common than for men to obtain important benefits, and to be delivered from serious evils, through the agency and intervention of their fellow-men, insomuch that a great part of the administration of human affairs under the divine government may be said to be carried on by a system of mediation. This, however, merely shows it to be consistent with the course of things which God has established in the visible world, that Christ should have been employed as an intermediate agent to improve the condition and promote the happiness of mankind (a thing which might have been done in various other ways, without His being offered up as a vicarious sacrifice to make atonement for them—as, for example, by promulgating, at the cost of much personal labour, self-denial, and suffering, a highly beneficent system of religious doctrine); but it cannot be held to furnish any exact analogy to the offering of Himself as a satisfaction for sinful men, when He " bare their sins in His own body on the tree," and " suffered for sins, the just for the unjust."

It is also true that the temporal calamities which flow from certain sins, in the way of natural consequence, often extend beyond those by whom the sins were committed, so as injuriously to affect the health or wealth or reputation of other persons with whom, in the bonds of social life, they are connected. But in such cases there is nothing that can with propriety be considered as " vicarious;" for though persons thus suffer for sins of which they were innocent, it is not with their own consent, as Christ suffered, that they do so, but in consequence of a state of things which they greatly lament, instead of acquiescing in it ; and their sufferings are so far from alleviating the guilt of those by whose sins they have been occasioned, that, on the contrary, they are serious aggravations of it.

Again, when a person has given bail for the appearance of one who is charged with a crime, or has offered himself as a hostage for the fulfilment of a national compact, the penalties inflicted on him in the event of a

DOCTRINE OF THE ATONEMENT.   459

breach of the engagement for which he has thus become
security cannot be considered as any satisfaction for the
misdeeds of the party principally concerned.   The fugitive
criminal is not the less bound to undergo his trial, if ever
he should be apprehended, because his surety has already
paid the stipulated penalty of his attempted evasion of
justice.   And the treachery of a nation in the violation of
its treaties is not held to be in any respect excused or
extenuated by the punishment of its hostages.

In like manner, when a mutiny is punished by decimation,
there is no real substitution of the innocent for the guilty.
The selected victims are put to death for their own offences,
and not for those of their comrades.   And the latter are
allowed to escape, not in consideration of any atonement
which the former are held to have offered for them, but
from a regard to the weakness of human governments,
which could not afford the loss of more of the offenders
than those who have been singled out for punishment.

It may be said, indeed, that the prevalence of sacrifices, and, in particular, that the sin-offerings of the Mosaic
law, present a clear and unquestionable analogy to the
great propitiation which was offered on the cross.   But
these sacrifices, however valuable they may be as confirmatory proofs of the *truth* of the Atonement,—in which light
they are unquestionably most valuable—are of little or
no avail in vindication of its *reasonableness;* for those
who object to our Lord's sacrifice as being mysterious,
will probably be inclined to advance a like objection
against any analogous rites by which we may endeavour
to illustrate it.

The same remark applies to certain striking instances,
which are occasionally to be met with in ancient history,
of generous and devoted men, who are said to have
deliberately laid down their lives as substitutes for their
fellow-men.   For without throwing any discredit on the
authenticity of such cases of self-immolation in the room
of others, it may be objected that however well they may
have accorded with the rude notions of justice which prevailed in times of old, they do not at all accord with those

PART
IV.
SEC. 4.

460   REVIEW OF OBJECTIONS TO THE

PART
IV.
SEC. 4.
——

sounder principles on which the administration of justice is now conducted ; and hence that by bringing the Atonement into comparison with them, we should rather be increasing than lessening its mysteriousness.

Specialties in our Lord's substitution which render it exceptional and unique.

3. In default of any satisfactory analogies that may be adduced from the course of divine providence, or from the ordinary transactions of men, in illustration of the doctrine of the Atonement, some able writers have betaken themselves to the opposite course, of showing that there are remarkable *specialties* in the case of our Lord's substitution for sinful men, which render it altogether *exceptional* and *unique*, and thereby exempt it from many of those objections to which other cases of substitution might be liable. These specialties have occasionally been set forth in somewhat of an *a priori* and dogmatical manner, as

Gilbert on The Atonement, p. 253-296.

"qualities essential to a valid substitution;" in which light it seems scarcely warrantable to regard them, for we are not entitled to say positively what requisites the unsearchable God may deem it proper to prescribe in any scheme of vicarious expiation that may be adopted by Him. We are on safe ground, however, when we confine ourselves to *the matter of fact* that certain specialties *do actually* distinguish our Lord's sacrifice from all other cases of substitution that have sometimes been, not very judiciously, compared to it ; and that in this respect it is *peerless and alone*, insomuch that many objections that might be urged against other instances of vicarious suffering are inapplicable to it.

It was sanctioned by the Supreme Lawgiver.

(1.) One of these specialties is, that the substitution of Christ was *sanctioned by the Supreme Head of all authority and government*. Had it not been so, the objection might have lain against it, that no such commutation of punishment can be safely or validly made by private and subordinate parties, acting at their own discretion ; and that He alone can make it from whom the law emanates, and to whom the transgressors of the law are amenable for those penalties from which they are to be released. To our Lord's substitution, however, this objection does not

DOCTRINE OF THE ATONEMENT. 461

apply ; for it was not only with the sanction and approval, but by the express appointment of the Supreme Judge, that He gave Himself as a ransom for transgressors.

PART IV. SEC. 4.

(2.) Another specialty in our Saviour's substitution is, that *it was perfectly voluntary and deliberate.* Had it been otherwise, all our sentiments of equity and justice would have been outraged by the subjection of Him to penal sufferings which He had not deserved. But He was a willing sufferer. He "*gave* Himself for us." He could say, " I lay down my life of myself." Nor was it by any momentary enthusiasm, by any sudden impulse of generous feeling or heroic devotedness, of which on cool reflection He might have repented, that He was led to offer this " sacrifice of Himself," but by a fixed purpose, deliberately formed and long cherished, from which He never swerved until He had accomplished it.

It was voluntary and deliberate.

(3.) A *third* specialty in the substitution of our Lord is, that *His life was entirely at His own disposal.* Originally independent and self-existent as the Son of God, He had taken into union with His divine nature the nature of man ; and over that human nature, in soul and in body, He possessed an unlimited control. He was thus in a different position from all created beings, who, having received life from the hands of God, are bound to retain it until he recalls it from them. His life was His own. And no law was violated, no rights of any other party were infringed, when He chose at His own free discretion to surrender it. He could truly say, " I lay down my life of myself ; I have power to lay it down, and I have power to take it again."

The life of the substitute was entirely at His own disposal.

(4.) A *fourth* specialty is, that our Lord's sufferings were purely *gratuitous*—that is to say, they were not such as He was bound to endure on His own account. He did not deserve them as a punishment, because he was perfectly free from every taint of sin. Neither was He called to submit to them as a duty ; for, being a divine person, equal with the Father, He was free from any personal obligation, such as would have lain upon any creature, however exalted, to endure them in humble obedience to

His sufferings were not due from Him on His own account.

462   REVIEW OF OBJECTIONS TO THE

PART IV. SEC. 4.

the will of heaven. Accordingly, His sufferings being thus, in so far as concerned Himself, altogether *supererogatory*, are not liable to the objection that might otherwise have been alleged against their being made available in behalf of those sinful creatures for whom He underwent them.

Divine and human nature united in His person.

(5.) A *fifth* specialty in the substitution of Jesus Christ arises from *the wonderful constitution of His person*, in which the divine and the human nature were mysteriously united. By virtue of His *human nature*, He was not only capable of enduring the sufferings and rendering the obedience which were due from fallen men, but *He stood in such a relation to them* as well comported with the office of their substitute or surety which He graciously assumed. Like the redeemer under the law, He was the near kinsman of those redeemed by Him. "Both He that sanctifieth and they who are sanctified are all of one."

Heb. ii. 11, 17.

"Wherefore in all things it behoved Him to be made like unto His brethren, that He might be a merciful and faithful High Priest, to make reconciliation for the sins of the people."

On the other hand, by virtue of His divine nature, the sufferings He endured, and the obedience which He rendered, may be held to have been of sufficient consideration in the sight of God for the redemption of those who should put their trust in Him. Or at all events, when His divine nature is kept in view, no such objection can be taken to His substitution in respect of its inadequacy to the gracious purpose to be accomplished by it, as might have been plausibly urged if He had been of inferior dignity. If, indeed, the work of redemption had been a mere commercial transaction, it would not have mattered by whom the price was paid, because that price would have had the same mercantile value, whatever might be the position or character of the person by whose liberality it was supplied. The case, however, is altogether different when the work of human redemption is viewed as a great moral satisfaction to divine justice by the substitution, not of *things*, but of *personal acts and*

DOCTRINE OF THE ATONEMENT. 463

sufferings. Here the character and position of the substitute are most essential matters to be taken into account, as affecting the moral significancy of the substitution. And in the special case with which we are concerned, the consideration that the substitute is *a divine person* gives to the substitution not only a *greater degree* of significancy than would otherwise have belonged to it, but a totally *different kind* of significancy from that of which it would otherwise have been possessed. The divinity of the substitute gives to the substitution the character of a *personal* homage rendered to the broken law, and a *personal* recognition of the evil desert of sin, *by the very Judge and Lawgiver Himself* by whom the penalties of transgression are remitted, far exceeding aught that could have been afforded by His infliction of these penalties on those who had incurred them.

(6.) Another specialty, not to be overlooked in the substitution of our Lord in the room of sinners, is *His full indemnification for the sufferings endured by Him.* In regard to this point I cannot do better than quote the forcible and felicitous words of Robert Hall.

"However much," he says, "we might be convinced of the competence of vicarious suffering to accomplish the ends of justice, and whatever the benefits we may derive from it, a benevolent mind could never be reconciled to the sight of virtue of the highest order finally oppressed and consumed by its own energies ; and the more intense the admiration excited, the more eager would be the desire of some compensatory arrangement, some expedient by which an ample retribution might be assigned to such heroic sacrifices. If the suffering of the substitute involved his destruction, what satisfaction could a generous and feeling mind derive from impunity procured at such a cost ? When David, in an agony of thirst, longed for the waters of Bethlehem, which some of his servants immediately procured for him with the extreme hazard of their lives, the monarch refused to taste it, exclaiming, *It is the price of blood!* but *poured it out before the Lord.* The felicity which flows from the irreparable misery of another,

PART IV. SEC. 4.

The substitute has been indemnified for His sufferings.

2 Sam. xxiii. 15, 17.

464   REVIEW OF OBJECTIONS TO THE

PART
IV.
SEC. 4.
———

and more especially of one whose disinterested benevolence alone exposed him to it, will be faintly relished by
him who is not immersed in selfishness. If there be any
portions of history whose perusal affords more pure and
exquisite delight than others, they are those which present
the spectacle of a conflicting and self-devoted virtue, after
innumerable toils and dangers undergone in the cause,
enjoying a dignified repose in the bosom of the country
which its example has ennobled and its valour saved.
Such a spectacle gratifies the best propensities, satisfies
the highest demands of our moral and social nature. It
affords a delightful glimpse of the future and perfect
economy of retributive justice. In the plan of human
redemption this requisition is fully satisfied. While we
accompany the Saviour through the successive stages of
His mortal sojourning, marked by a corresponding succession of trials, each of which was more severe than the
former, till the scene darkened, and the clouds of wrath
from heaven and from earth, pregnant with materials
which nothing but a divine hand could have collected,
discharged themselves on Him in a deluge of agony and
of blood, under which He expired,—we perceive at once
the sufficiency, I had almost said the redundancy, of His
atonement. But surely deliverance even *from the wrath
to come* would afford an imperfect enjoyment if it were
embittered with the recollection that we were indebted
for it to the irreparable destruction of our compassionate

Works of
Robert
Hall, v.
96, 97.

Redeemer. The consolation arising from *reconciliation
with God* is subject to no such deduction. While we rejoice in the cross of Christ as the source of pardon, our
satisfaction is heightened by beholding it succeeded by
the crown ; by seeing Him who was *for a little while
made lower than the angels for the suffering of death,
crowned with glory and honour, seated at the right hand
of God, thence expecting till His enemies are made His
footstool.*"

These considerations are of no small importance, as
serving to show that the substitution of Christ in the room
of sinners is, in many respects, *unparalleled* and *unique*,

DOCTRINE OF THE ATONEMENT. 465

insomuch that we cannot try it by the same standard, or use with respect to it the same reasonings and analogies, or urge against it some very plausible objections, which apply to other actual or supposable cases of vicarious suffering.

4. It may, however, be doubted whether any or all of the specialties to which we have adverted—serviceable as they may be in the way of obviating other difficulties— are of any great avail towards removing *the chief difficulty* connected with the Atonement, — that difficulty being satisfactorily to explain *the connection which God is declared in Scripture to have established between the unmerited sufferings of Jesus Christ and the unmerited pardon of sinners as procured by them.*

The only one of the specialties above noticed which seems to have any bearing on this subject is, *the assumption of human nature by the Son of God.* It cannot be said, however, that the Saviour's incarnation furnishes a complete and satisfactory explanation of the efficacy of His sufferings and obedience in securing the remission of our sins. It may indeed be viewed as a *sine qua non,* or an indispensable requisite to that efficacy, by making Him to be in such a sense akin to us, that the sufferings He endured, and the obedience He rendered, were *the same in kind* with those which are required of us. But, as I have elsewhere observed, it does not so identify Him as a personal agent with those whom He redeemed, that all He did and all He suffered may be properly and righteously considered as done and suffered *by them,* irrespective of anything that brings them, as individual and personal agents, into union or communion with Him. Granting that the obedience and sufferings of the Son of God were, by reason of His incarnation, *the same in kind* as those which were required of us, the question still demands an answer as much as ever ;—How comes it to pass that they are dealt with in the judgment of God as *tantamount to obedience rendered and sufferings endured by us in our own proper persons ?* Besides, if the ground of the efficacy

PART IV. SEC. 4.

The assumption of human nature by the Son of God is not a sufficient solution of the mystery.

Supra, p. 308, 309.

466   REVIEW OF OBJECTIONS TO THE

PART
IV.
SEC. 4.
——

of the Saviour's work be sought in His mere assumption of human nature, it would follow that *this efficacy extends in all its fulness to each and every sinner by whom that nature is possessed*—in other words, that Christ by His mediatorial work has either secured salvation for all sinners without exception, or that He has done nothing more for those who are saved than for those who are lost, having merely put them all alike into a position in which it is possible for them to save themselves. There are indeed some who would not shrink from this conclusion;

Supra, p. 197-200.

but I venture to think that we have already shown it to be irreconcilable with the doctrine of the Word of God.

Is the co-venant of grace a solution of the mystery?

5. Another ground or *rationale* of the Atonement has been sought in the doctrine of "*the covenant of grace*," according to which the Son of God is set forth, in all that He did and suffered for His people, as fulfilling the terms of a gracious compact or arrangement, into which He had entered with His heavenly Father for their behoof in the everlasting counsels of the Godhead.

Supra, p. 148-151.

We have already seen that this doctrine of the covenant of grace is amply supported by the testimony of Holy Scripture, and that those passages of Scripture which relate to it supply a strong corroborative evidence of the *fact* of our Lord's substitution in the room of sinners. At the same time, I have ventured to express a doubt in regard to the opinion which many persons entertain, that this doctrine provides a full solution of all the mystery in which the substitution of Jesus Christ—"the just for the

Supra, p. 151.

unjust"—would otherwise be enveloped. I formerly observed in reference to this matter that "by connecting our Lord's sufferings with a covenant, of which they were the necessary fulfilment, we render the appointment and acceptance of them, in lieu of the merited condemnation of transgressors, in no respect less mysterious than it was before. We merely shift the difficulty, instead of solving it ; for no sooner have we, by referring to the covenant of grace, disposed of the original question, Why were the sufferings and death of the holy Jesus requisite and avail-

DOCTRINE OF THE ATONEMENT. 467

able for the salvation of sinful men ? than this other and equally arduous question presents itself, Why was such a method of salvation for sinners arranged and agreed upon in the counsels of the Godhead ? " This observation must be understood as exclusively referring to the fact, that the scheme of salvation which the Gospel reveals *was accomplished or carried out in accordance with a divine covenant.* There may be somewhat in the *provisions* of this scheme which may furnish a sufficient *rationale* or justification of it. But apart from anything in the nature of these provisions, the mere fact of their having been settled and arranged in the everlasting counsels of the Godhead cannot be considered as rendering them either less or more mysterious than they are in themselves. It cannot be said of any of the Lord's doings that they *become* right because they were previously arranged and covenanted by Him. Rather ought we to say that they were arranged and covenanted by Him, because in their own nature they were altogether right. Indeed, when we connect any part of His procedure with a solemn compact or an everlasting covenant, it would seem on that account to be all the more incumbent on us to vindicate His wisdom and rectitude in the adoption of it.

6. I have not yet adverted, however, in the course of this discussion, to one consideration which I had formerly occasion to notice, as tending in some measure to furnish a solution of the efficacy of our Lord's substitution for sinful men—namely, *the union of believers with the Saviour.*

The Scriptures, as we have elsewhere shown, speak of this union in terms peculiarly forcible and significant. It is likened to the union between husband and wife ; to the union between the vine branches and their stock ; to the union between the members of the human body and the head. In one passage it even seems to be compared to that ineffable union which subsists between Christ Himself and the eternal Father in the Godhead ; when the Saviour thus speaks, on the eve of His last sufferings,

PART IV. Sec. 4.

The union of believers with Christ contributes to a solution of the mystery.

Supra, p. 152-154.

468   REVIEW OF OBJECTIONS TO THE

PART
IV.
SEC. 4.
———
John, xvii.
20, 21.

"Neither pray I for these alone, but for them also who shall believe on me through their word ; that they all may be one ; as thou, Father, art in me, and I in thee, that they also may be one in us."

By virtue of this union it is written of believers that

John, xv. 4.
Col. iii. 3.
2 Cor. v. 14.
Gal. ii. 20.
Phil. iii. 10.

they "abide in Christ, and He in them ;" that "their life is hid with Christ in God ;" that "if one died for all, then all died ;" that "they are crucified with Christ, and live no more themselves, but Christ liveth in them ;" that they "know the power of His resurrection and the fellowship of His sufferings, being made conformable unto His

Col. ii. 12.
Eph. ii. 5, 6; iii. 17.

death ;" that they are "buried with Christ, and risen with Him ;" that they are "quickened together with Christ, and made to sit together in heavenly places in Christ Jesus ;" that "Christ dwells in their hearts by faith ;" that "Christ

John, xv. 5.
Eph. iv. 15, 16.

is in them the hope of glory ;" that, "abiding in Him, they bring forth much fruit ;" and that they "grow up into Him in all things, which is the Head ; from whom the whole body, fitly joined together and compacted by that which every joint supplieth, according to the effectual working in the measure of every part, maketh increase of the body unto the edifying of itself in love."

Here, then, we have surely one element of the solution we are in quest of ; one ground on which we may at least approximate towards explaining the connection which subsists between the unmerited sufferings of the Saviour and the unmerited blessings thence accruing to believers. In consideration of the union we have now referred to, *thus much* at least may be confidently affirmed, that the benefits of Christ's mediation are not conferred on persons with whom He is in no other way connected save only by His assumption of their common humanity, but on persons who are emphatically *one with Him*—not, indeed, by any confusion of their personalities, but yet by an intimacy of union and communion which the closest of earthly ties are inadequate to represent, and specially *one with Him* in their "fellowship with those sufferings," and in their "conformity to that death," by which His great work of redemption was consummated.

DOCTRINE OF THE ATONEMENT. 469

To this view of the matter it may possibly be objected that "our Lord's union with His people, which is brought about by the agency of the Holy Spirit, and through the instrumentality of their faith, pertains not to what theologians are wont to call the *impetration* of redemption, but only to the *application* of it ; and hence, that it cannot be considered as furnishing any solution of the work of atonement by which the benefits of redemption have been secured, whatever light it may be supposed to cast on the subsequent process by which these benefits are applied to the souls of believers."

In reply to such an objection, however, it may be urged that *the participation of believers in the benefits* which Christ by His mediation has secured, is the very mystery connected with the Atonement of which, most of all, a solution is desiderated ; for, as was observed at the outset of this discussion, "the difficulty to be solved is, not how it comes to pass that both the Saviour and the redeemed sinner are treated otherwise than they deserve, but how it comes to pass that the unmerited sufferings of the one are deemed, in the judgment of God, a sufficient ground for the bestowal of unmerited blessings on the other,"—in other words, for the *application* of redemption to them. When *this* is the question, the union of believers with Christ is a most relevant consideration to be taken into account. That which we are looking for is *some bond of connection* between the Redeemer and those whom He redeems, which may help us to apprehend on what principle it is that His "obedience unto death" should be *applicable* for their advantage. And surely we have made a considerable approximation towards discovering this *desideratum*, when we find that believers are represented in the Word of God as intimately and vitally united to the Saviour—" abiding in Him and He in them," "growing up into Him in all things who is their Head," animated by His Spirit, conformed to His likeness, and closely identified with Him in all His interests and concernments.

It matters nothing, moreover, to say that this union

PART IV. SEC. 4.

Objection to this solution.

Reply to the objection.

Supra, p. 457.

470   REVIEW OF OBJECTIONS TO THE

PART IV.
SEC. 4.
—
Supra, p. 197-200.

appertains to the *application* of Christ's redemption, and not to the *impetration* of it. For in a former part of this treatise we have shown that the "impetration" of redemption *secures* the "application" of it, and that these two things are inseparably associated. As little does it avail to say that this union is not actually constituted until sinners have believed in Christ; for though it is not till then actually constituted, we have, notwithstanding, clear Scriptural evidence that *it was all along provided for and proceeded upon* in the everlasting counsels of the Godhead. For it is expressly written of believers that they were

Eph. i. 4.
John, x. 16, 29.

"chosen *in Christ* before the foundation of the world." And Christ Himself speaks of them as "given to Him by His Father," and claims them as "His sheep" before as yet they have been gathered to Him. Hence we are warranted to say that the union of believers with Christ, although in actual subsistence posterior to the undertaking of His mediatorial work, was present to His own mind and to His Father's mind when that gracious work of mediation was devolved upon Him.

It is not necessary, however, to the subject of our present discussion, that we should trace back the scheme of human redemption to its primary source in the counsels of eternity. When its wisdom or reasonableness is the matter to be determined, it is quite enough that we speak of it and look at it as actually administered and carried into effect. But in doing so we must view it in all its aspects. We must take into account all its provisions and relations, otherwise we cannot be considered as doing justice to it. Above all, when the very matter in respect of which its excellence or worthiness of the divine character is called in question, *is the absence of any such ostensible bond of connection between the Redeemer and those whom He redeems as might reasonably account for the unmerited blessings which through His unmerited sufferings accrue to them,* we are doing to this gracious scheme an especial injustice if we keep not in view that *its benefits are actually attained by those, and those only, who are so united to Christ that in interest, aim, and disposition they are one with Him*—that they are

DOCTRINE OF THE ATONEMENT. 471

"members of His body, of His flesh, and of His bones" —that they die in His death, and live in His life—that "they are crucified with Christ, and live no more themselves, but Christ liveth in them."

PART IV. SEC. 4.

7. It is quite possible, however, that neither the intimate union between the Redeemer and those whom He redeems, nor any of the other considerations above referred to, may, in the judgment of some persons, be regarded as tending to explain the efficacy of the Atonement. But what then? Allowing that the doctrine were a mystery of which no satisfactory explanation can be given, we are not on this account to set aside the clear import of those Scriptural testimonies in which it is affirmed. Some critics seem to act upon the principle that *the plain language of Scripture may be mystified to any extent that is necessary to exclude all mystery from the doctrine of Scripture.* Any such principle, however, needs only to be broadly stated, instead of being covertly and quietly assumed, in order to show that it is altogether indefensible. Assuredly we cannot be allowed to simplify the doctrine of revelation by twisting quite away from its plain and natural meaning the language in which that doctrine is conveyed. This would be introducing mystery into a quarter where it ought not to be— where, indeed, with respect to any very important doctrine, it could not be without frustrating the very purpose for which a revelation has been given to us — in order to remove mystery out of another quarter where, from the transcendental nature of the subject, it ought rather to be expected than regarded with incredulity.

The mysteriousness of the Atonement does not invalidate the Scriptural proofs of it.

It is no cause for wonder that the method of redemption should be in some respects imperfectly comprehended by us. In the ordinary providence of God, we often find ourselves unable to discover the reasons of His procedure. Why, then, should we not anticipate like difficulties when seeking to explain the dispensations of His grace? Not to speak of other things in the ways of God that are unsearchable, there is one transcendent mystery in particular which ought of itself to silence every objection to

It is no wonder that the method of redemption should involve mysteries.

472 REVIEW OF OBJECTIONS TO THE

PART IV. SEC. 4. the method of redemption on the ground of its mysterious-ness—namely, *the permission and wide prevalence of sin.* This is at once an observed fact which cannot be questioned, and a perplexing mystery which cannot be resolved ; and in the face of it we are certainly not warranted to take exception, on the ground of its being alike mysterious, to that method of deliverance from sin which the Gospel reveals ; for it is nothing strange that the remedy pro-vided for us should in some respects exceed our compre-hension, when the evil to be remedied is equally or more inexplicable.

The rationale of the Atonement concerns God rather than man. It ought also to be remembered that the *rationale* of the Atonement is a matter with which God is more concerned than we are. It rests with *Him*, the offended party, and not with man, the party who has offended Him, to fix the terms of reconciliation. And surely we may trust Him to fix such terms as shall not be inconsistent with His character, or derogatory to His law, or subversive of His government. *Our part* is, not so much to canvass the propriety, as humbly and thankfully to avail ourselves of the benefits of that method of reconciliation which He is pleased to propose. The method which, if our doctrine be true, He has appointed, is marked by some advantages and excellences which even our limited minds are able to appreciate, inasmuch as it condemns sin, and shows it to be exceeding sinful by the very means adopted for securing the deliverance of the sinner ; and it loudly proclaims to the whole intelligent creation that God, in remitting the penalties of His violated law, is nevertheless inflexibly opposed to the lowering of its terms or the relaxing of its obligations. And if there be things connected with this method of reconciliation which we cannot fathom, it may well suffice us to know that these " secret things " pertain to God's part in the arrangement, and not to ours, and to rest in the assurance that they are thoroughly understood by Him, to whom it rightly belongs to give His judgment with regard to them.

DOCTRINE OF THE ATONEMENT. 473

SECTION V.

THE ATONEMENT IS NOT IMMORAL OR INJURIOUS IN ITS PRACTICAL TENDENCY.

IT has frequently been urged against the method of redemption through faith in the mediatorial work and sufferings of Jesus Christ, that " it undermines the authority of the moral law, and seriously weakens, if it does not wholly destroy, the force of our obligations and inducements to personal holiness." The objection is as old as the days of the apostles. St Paul himself has anticipated and provided against it; and in doing so he has furnished a corroborative proof that his doctrine, as being likely to be assailed with such a charge, accords with the representation we have given of it. After explicitly declaring to the Romans that sinners are "justified freely by the grace of God through the redemption that is in Christ Jesus," and that no personal doings or merits of their own can be of the least avail in restoring them to the divine favour, he pauses in the course of his argument in order to guard it against the risk of being perverted, saying, " Do we then make void the law through faith? God forbid; yea, we establish the law." Again, after drawing an elaborate parallel between the effects of Adam's sin and those of Christ's righteousness, and declaring that "as by the offence of one judgment came upon all men to condemnation, even so by the righteousness of one the free gift came upon all men unto justification of life; for as by one man's disobedience many were made sinners, so by the obedience of one shall many be made righteous;" he again pauses to ask, " What shall

PART
IV.
SEC. 5.

The Atonement alleged to be injurious in its moral tendency.

Rom. iii. 31.

Rom. v. 18, 19.

474   REVIEW OF OBJECTIONS TO THE

PART IV.
Sec. 5.
——
Rom. vi.
1, 2.

we say then? Shall we continue in sin, that grace may abound? God forbid: how shall we, that are dead to sin, live any longer therein?"

The objection which the apostle thus anticipates as likely to be brought against the doctrine as unfolded by him, has, as I observed, been frequently advanced against the same doctrine as now generally received among us. Nothing is more common than for those who take only a superficial view of the method of redemption to cast upon it the unmerited reproach of encouraging sin, discountenancing good works, weakening the restraints and obligations of the law of God, and in a great measure dispensing with the necessity of holiness, or taking away the inducements to the practice of it. Nor is it to be denied that, even among those by whom this doctrine is professedly received, erroneous conceptions of it have sometimes been entertained, and unwarrantable inferences have occasionally been drawn from it, which lend some apparent countenance to an objection from which the doctrine itself, as set forth in the Word of God, is happily exempted.

Obligation of the law not weakened, but confirmed, by the Atonement.

I. In meeting this objection, I observe, *in the first place,* that the *obligation or authority* of the law is so far from being in any respect weakened or compromised by the Scriptural method of redemption, that it is, on the contrary, fully *assumed and recognised.* It is, in fact, the very foundation on which this method of redemption has been established. For who does not see that there would have been no occasion for devising a scheme of deliverance for our fallen race from the guilt of offences committed against the law, except on the supposition that we are indissolubly bound to the observance of it? Where there is no obligatory law there can be no transgression, and consequently no need of mediation and atonement. The very circumstance of a provision being made to save us from the condemnation of the broken law implies the fullest recognition of its authority. And when we consider the nature of that provision which God with this view has actually

DOCTRINE OF THE ATONEMENT. 475

been pleased to make when He set forth His only-begotten
Son "to be a propitiation through faith in His blood, to
declare His righteousness, that He might be just and the
justifier of him that believeth in Jesus," it is not to be
questioned that thereby His holy law, instead of having
its authority impaired, has been to the fullest extent
"magnified and made honourable." Christ has indeed
"redeemed us from *the curse* of the law." But instead of
having exempted us from its *obligation*, He must rather
be held to have ratified and confirmed it.

Right margin: PART IV. SEC. 5 — Rom. iii. 25, 26.

Nor can it with any show of reason be affirmed that
sinners, when "justified freely by the grace of God through
the redemption that is in Christ Jesus," *will feel themselves
less bound* to obey the law of God in their present state of
favour and acceptance with Him, than in their former state
of enmity and guilt. To them, on the contrary, the law
of God appears invested with new and special claims to
their obedience, arising from the spiritual blessings which
God has now conferred on them, and from the peculiar relations which they now bear to Him, as not only his creatures
and beneficiaries, but His ransomed people. The obligations of nature are strengthened by those of grace. And
the apostle's argument is felt to be irresistible: "Ye are
not your own, for ye are bought with a price; therefore
glorify God in your body and in your spirit, which are
God's."

Right margin: 1 Cor. vi. 19, 20.

II. *Secondly*, let us consider whether the law of God
is injuriously affected by the method of redemption as
regards *the extent or measure of its requirements.*

These are exceedingly strict and comprehensive. The
law of God requires a constant, uniform, and perfect
obedience to all its statutes, not only in deed, but in
thought and in affection. It admits of no compromise
with sin. It makes no allowance for the depravity of
human nature, for the influence of passion, or for the force
of temptation. It abates not in the slightest degree, or
for the shortest interval, from the strictness of its enactments. For, like its glorious Author, of whose character

Right margin: Require-ments of the law not lower-ed by the Atone-ment.

476   REVIEW OF OBJECTIONS TO THE

PART
IV.
SEC. 5.

Hab. i. 13.

it is a transcript, it is " of purer eyes than to behold evil,
and cannot look on iniquity."

Such, then, being the extent, spirituality, and rigour of
the law of God, let us now see whether the Scriptural
method of redemption can be said with any truth to limit
this extent, to diminish this spirituality, to mitigate this
uncompromising rigour. Those who think that it can
possibly have this effect must surely know nothing of it
as they ought to know. For it is indeed one of the main
excellences of the Atonement, that it has, and needs must
have, when rightly apprehended, a tendency the very
opposite of that which they ascribe to it. Any one may
see on a moment's consideration, that the extent and
rigour and spirituality of the law are among the very
grounds on which the doctrine rests. For why is it that
believers are justified, not by any doings of their own,
but only by faith in the merits of the Saviour ? Is it
because God is indifferent to their conduct, and heedless
whether they be obedient to Him or not ? Far from it.
It is because " His commandment is exceeding broad "
—because His demand of perfect obedience is such as no
works of sinful men can ever meet—because he will not
abate a single jot or tittle from His law, or stoop to any
compromise with those who have transgressed it,—*that* is
the reason why believers are not, and cannot be, justified
by their own doings, but only by faith in the righteousness
of Jesus Christ. If the law were less rigorous or less
extensive in what it exacts—did it lower its demands in
accommodation to our infirmities—did it offer to accept
of a sincere and partial instead of a perfect and universal
obedience—there would then have been no such evident
necessity for the method of salvation revealed in the Gospel.
Men might, in that case, have been justified by the deeds
of the law. They might have urged their obedience to
one part of it as a compensation for their transgression of
another ; or they might have pleaded their obedience to
it at one time as a compensation for their disobedience at
another time ; and thus might they have attained to
justification in the sight of God—upon principles, how-

Ps. cxix.
96.

DOCTRINE OF THE ATONEMENT. 477

ever, that would have been altogether subversive of the high standard of holiness prescribed in the divine commandments. It is because the law is so unbending that it will not stoop to any such compromise with sinful men —so rigorous as to regard partial obedience as no atonement for partial transgression, and present obedience as no atonement for past transgression—so peremptory as to declare in emphatic terms, "Cursed is every one that continueth not in all things which are written in the book of the law to do them,"—hence it is that we are "shut up to the faith," and brought to the alternative of either despairing of justification in the sight of God altogether, or of closing with that finished work of the Redeemer in which the Gospel invites us to place our confidence.

Are we to be told, then, that "the law is made void" by a scheme of redemption which has for its very basis the impossibility of lowering the standard or lessening the rigour of its requirements? Nay, rather, the law is "established" by such a scheme. Those men who seek to be justified by their own deeds—imperfect in many respects as these deeds confessedly are—*they* are the persons who "make void the law," proceeding, as they evidently do, on the assumption that the law of God is not by any means so strict as to render their attempted self-justification impracticable. But those, on the other hand, who are led by their deep sense of the uncompromising rigour of the divine commandments to confess that all their own doings are unavailing, and to put their whole trust in Him who is declared to be "the end of the law for righteousness unto every one that believeth"—*they*, again, are the persons who "establish the law." And the very same principle of entire submission to the law of God which schools them at first into a reception of the Gospel, will still prevail with them after such reception to "hate every false way," to "shun the very appearance of evil," and to be "holy in all manner of conversation."

III. But, *in the third place*, it is proper to consider how

PART
IV.
SEC. 5.

Gal. iii. 10.

Gal. iii. 23.

Rom. x. 4.

478   REVIEW OF OBJECTIONS TO THE

PART
IV.
SEC. 5.

Necessity of holiness not dispensed with by the Atonement.

far the law of God is affected by the scheme of grace as regards the *utility or necessity of obeying it.*

Granting that the law *retains its obligation* and *preserves its strictness* altogether inviolate, notwithstanding the method of free redemption through Jesus Christ, it may still be asked, *what is the use,* or *where is the necessity, of rendering obedience to it,* if we are not thereby delivered from the wrath of God, and reinstated in the enjoyment of His favour? Does it not seem, according to this doctrine, as if sinners were *left very much to their own discretion* whether they shall yield obedience to it or not, although the obligation and extent of such obedience be ever so fully established and acquiesced in?

There are two grounds on which these questions may be satisfactorily answered in the negative.

Sanctification necessary as well as justification.

1. One of them is that the *pardon and acceptance* of a sinner are not the only things necessary to his salvation. He needs to be sanctified as well as to be justified—delivered from the moral pollution, as well as from the penalty of sin—restored to the divine image, as well as to the divine favour—and invested not only with a title to possess, but with a "meetness to partake of the inheritance of the saints." And God has wisely and graciously provided that these blessings should be absolutely inseparable; that the justifying merit of His Son should bring with it the sanctifying grace of His Holy Spirit; and that faith, in receiving the one, should receive the other also. To speak, therefore, of personal holiness as unnecessary under the dispensation of the Gospel, betrays utter ignorance of the nature of that salvation which the Gospel has provided; for this includes holiness as one of its most essential blessings. Indeed there is no truth more clearly revealed to us respecting the mediatorial work and sufferings of Jesus Christ than that one of the chief ends for which He underwent them was that He might "deliver us from this present evil world," and "purify us unto Himself a peculiar people, zealous of good works," and, finally, "present us faultless before the presence of His glory with exceeding joy."

Col. i. 12.

Supra, p. 165-170, 194-196.

Gal. i. 12.
Tit. ii. 14.
Jude, 24.

DOCTRINE OF THE ATONEMENT.   479

2. But there is another ground on which the proposed question, "Whether obedience to the law be unnecessary under the Gospel?" may be most decidedly answered in the negative; and it is this, that even as regards the *justification* of believers, such obedience is indispensable. It is so, not certainly as the *means* by which they obtain the blessing, but as the most satisfactory *evidence* by which they can prove, either to themselves or to others, that the blessing has been really obtained. The probation of sinners, as candidates for the favour of God, on th· footing of personal conformity to His commandments, we utterly reject, as contrary alike to the dictates of reason and the testimony of revelation. But the probation of Christians, as candidates for a final acknowledgment of the reality of their faith in the Saviour, on the ground of those works of personal obedience which have sprung from it, we fully maintain as altogether in accordance with a reasonable and Scriptural view of the position in which they stand, and the hopes which they are cherishing. It is by the influence of their faith upon their conduct that its genuineness will be determined on the day of judgment. And it is by the same substantial evidence that its genuineness must be judged of even now, with a view to their own peace, and comfort, and assurance; for though it be by faith alone that we are justified, we must ever remember that "*that* is no true faith which is alone." Faith is not only a contemplative but an active principle. While it realises truth, it also dictates and enforces duty. Faith has respect to everything that God reveals—to His precepts as well as to His doctrinal statements and offered blessings. It is exercised in yielding obedience to all that God requires, no less than in giving credit to all that God promises, and heartily receiving all that God bestows. Accordingly, it is indispensable that believers should be careful at all times to maintain good works—not with the self-righteous and impracticable design of asserting merit and purchasing salvation, but with the humbler yet no less important view of proving the sincerity of their

PART
IV.
SEC. 5.
——
Good
works ne-
cessary to
show that
faith is
sincere
and saving.

480   REVIEW OF OBJECTIONS TO THE

PART
IV.
SEC. 5.

profession, the safety of their condition, and the soundness of their hope.

Inducements and encouragements to obedience not diminished, but increased, by the Atonement.

IV. But, *in the fourth place*, it still remains to be considered, Whether the scheme of redemption which the Gospel reveals can be charged with injuriously affecting the moral law, in so far as regards *the inducements* or *encouragements* by which an observance of its precepts may be commended to us?

Much, indeed, that has a bearing on this point has been in our previous remarks unavoidably anticipated. But there are some considerations in regard to it which have not yet been noticed, and are too important to be overlooked.

That obedience cannot secure justification is owing, not to the Atonement, but to *the fall of mankind.*

It must, indeed, be owned that *one motive* to obedience —*the prospect of earning a title to the divine favour*—has no place left for it in the Christian dispensation. This circumstance, however, is not attributable to the Gospel, but to the weakness and sinfulness of the human heart. In the actual state of mankind as fallen creatures, the prospect of earning the divine favour by our own doings is so entirely visionary and impracticable, that it never could have furnished to any reflecting mind a fair and reasonable motive to exertion. It is wrong, then, to charge the Scriptural method of redemption with robbing the law of this inducement to obedience—the truth being that, in consequence of the Fall, the inducement was one of which the law had been deprived before.

I need scarcely observe, however, that the lack of this motive is supplied by those considerations already noticed —namely, the deep sense which all believers entertain of the obligation and rigour of the divine commandments, and the indispensable necessity of holiness, at once to prove the sincerity of their faith, and to fit them for partaking of the inheritance of the saints. And whatever motives to diligence in duty other men may derive from the *erroneous persuasion* that they may be saved by the merit of their good works, are afforded in equal strength to believers by the *true persuasion* that in no other way can reliable

DOCTRINE OF THE ATONEMENT. 481

evidence be obtained, either of their restoration to the favour of God, or of their preparedness for enjoying His heavenly kingdom, except by abounding in the peaceable fruits of righteousness.

But in addition to these considerations, there are many others suggested by the Atonement which furnish strong motives and encouragements to a holy life.

1. There is love to God, for example, in return for the unspeakable love he has displayed in our redemption. Love is said to be "the fulfilling of the law." And there can be no fulfilling of the law which a heart-searching God will deem acceptable without it. But love is not to be commanded by injunctions, compelled by threatenings, or purchased by rewards. Nothing but love on the part of God to man is able to beget love on the part of man to God. We may dread His power; we may admire His excellence; we may acknowledge His rectitude; we may bow to His authority;—but, sinners as we are, it is impossible for us to love God until we have some such evidence of His love to us as that which he has displayed to us in the Gospel. So long as we continue bondmen under the law, regarding God as a hard taskmaster, our service is formal, mercenary, and reluctant,—a service which we dare not perhaps altogether withhold, but which we have no inward satisfaction in rendering. It is only when our minds are dispossessed of all their hard and suspicious thoughts of Him, and led by a full discovery of His mercies to regard Him with heartfelt confidence and affection—it is only when, "being justified by faith, we have peace with God through Jesus Christ," and have exchanged the sordid spirit of a bondman for the warm and generous devotedness of a son,—it is only then that our heart is enlarged to run in the way of His commandments; and that, instead of measuring out with grudging hand whatever must be yielded to Him, we feel that no amount of duty He may impose can ever be a fit requital of His goodness.

2. The love of Christ, too, is displayed by the Atonement in such a way as is eminently fitted to impress our

PART IV. Sec. 5.

Love to God is excited by the Atonement.

Rom. v. 1.

Love also to the Saviour.

482   REVIEW OF OBJECTIONS TO THE

PART
IV.
SEC. 5.
——
2 Cor. viii.
9.

minds and to captivate our affections.   We are taught to "know the grace of the Lord Jesus, in that though He was rich, yet for our sakes He became poor, that we through His poverty might be rich."   We see Him humbling Himself that we might be exalted ; stooping from a throne of glory in heaven to a life of suffering and ignominy on earth ; enduring the imputation to Himself of that abominable thing which He hates ; submitting to be wounded and bruised for our iniquities ; and becoming obedient unto death, even the shameful and cursed death of the cross.   Never, assuredly, was there a love like this, so warm, so generous, so devoted.   It has in it heights too lofty to be scanned, and depths too profound to be fathomed, and lengths and breadths too vast to be measured by us.   Those who best know it will ever be the

Eph. iii.
19.

readiest to confess, in the words of inspiration, that " it passeth knowledge."   And how can we choose but say

2 Cor. v.
14, 15.

of it with the apostle, that " the love of Christ constraineth us ; because we thus judge, that if one died for all, then all died ; and that He died for all, that they who live should not henceforth live unto themselves, but unto Him who died for them and rose again " ?

The
Atone-
ment
shows the
evil of sin.

3.   Farther, it is scarcely necessary to remark, that *sin is shown by the Atonement to be exceeding sinful*.   We may form some estimate of its hatefulness and guilt by reflecting on the costly expiation that was made for it.   When we think that the all-merciful God does not forgive it except through the sacrifice of His own beloved Son, we are taught that it needs must be an evil and accursed thing, abhorrent to His nature, dishonouring to His majesty, and justly deserving of the terrors of His wrath. Nor is it only the evil nature of sin that we learn from the sufferings of Him who made atonement for it, but also the certainty of its ultimate punishment if unrepented of.   For if God did not spare even His own Son, when, sinless Himself, He was answering for the sins of others, we cannot think that He will spare those impenitent ones who, having obtained no interest in the Saviour, have still to bear the burden of their own sins,—those who have not

DOCTRINE OF THE ATONEMENT. 483

only defied His justice but despised His grace,—those who, to the guilt of all their other offences, have added this dreadful aggravation of "crucifying to themselves the Son of God afresh, and putting Him to an open shame." Well then does it become us, when looking to the cross, to lay to heart the warning, "Stand in awe, and sin not." "For if they do these things in a green tree, what shall be done in the dry?"

PART IV. SEC. 5.

Heb. vi.

Ps. iv. Luke, xxiii. 31.

4. Another mighty inducement to a holy life is furnished by that sure promise of divine aid which God has pledged to us through Jesus Christ our Saviour. While the law is ineffectual for our justification by reason of the weakness and sinfulness of our fallen state, it is equally ineffectual for our sanctification. It only tells us what things we are required to do, without affording any help in the performance of them. It leaves us to struggle in our own unaided strength, which is altogether inadequate to the work assigned to us; and thus does it withhold from us that prospect of success which, in any undertaking, however important, is necessary to stimulate and sustain our efforts. Who would continue to sow if he found that he could never reap? Who would attempt to fight if it were certain that he could not conquer? No matter how important the object that may be proposed to us, there must be a reasonable prospect of attaining it, in order that we may be stirred up to vigorous and continued exertion. Confidently, therefore, though some may be disposed to speak of the practical advantage of a legal dispensation, which leaves man, in effect, to be his own saviour, and holds out to him the favour and kingdom of God as a prize to be won by his own personal righteousness—we have cause in reality to shrink from such a dispensation, as taking away all encouragement to earnest endeavours, and leading its subjects to yield themselves up in helpless and hopeless subjection to the power of sin.

Divine aid promised through the Saviour.

No doubt, if God would modify His law in order to suit it to the weakness of His fallen creatures, we might have some hope of being able to fulfil it; although, even in that

484   REVIEW OF OBJECTIONS TO THE

PART
IV.
SEC. 5.

case, we should be in a state of most distressing and disheartening perplexity as to how far the modification of it extends, or what precise amount of obedience will be deemed sufficient. But, assuredly, God will not modify His law, which is but the expression of His own unchangeable perfections, in order to bring its requirements within our reach. And so soon as sinners are brought to this conviction—so soon as they are convinced that the law cannot be "made void" by any lowering or limiting of its requirements—they will be forced to own that, when taken as a covenant of works, it is, with respect to them, "made void" in another way, by the loss of all reasonable encouragement to its observance.

Under the dispensation of grace, however, this lack of encouragement to keep the law is fully supplied. When once, through faith in the merits of the Saviour, we are brought into a state of favour and acceptance with God, we are then warranted to look for the grace of the Holy Spirit, which could not have been expected at His hands in our former state of enmity and guilt, and by which, henceforth, we may be enabled to do all things whatso-

1 Cor. ix.
26; xv.
58.

ever He commands us. Now we can "run, not as uncertainly;" and we can "fight, not as beating the air." Now we can be "steadfast, unmovable, always abounding in the work of the Lord, forasmuch as we know that our labour is not in vain in the Lord."

Christian
obedience
is rewarded through
Christ.

5. There is one other inducement, too important to be overlooked, by which believers in the mediatorial work of Christ are greatly encouraged in their obedience to the will of God—and that is, *the hope that their sincere though imperfect services, rendered in the name and through the grace of their Redeemer, shall be graciously accepted and bountifully rewarded.*

Confession
of Faith,
chap. xvi.
§ 5, 6.

It is true, "we cannot by our best works merit pardon of sin or eternal life at the hand of God, by reason of the great disproportion that is between them and the glory to come, and the infinite distance that is between us and God, whom we can neither profit by them nor satisfy for our former sins, but to whom, when we have done all we

DOCTRINE OF THE ATONEMENT. 485

can, we have done but our duty, and are unprofitable servants. . . . Yet notwithstanding, the persons of believers being accepted through Christ, *their good works also are accepted in Him ;*—not as though they were in this life wholly unblamable and unreprovable in God's sight ; but that He, looking upon them in His Son, *is pleased to accept and reward that which is sincere,* although accompanied with many weaknesses and imperfections."

There is a strange indisposition shown by many persons who earnestly contend for the great principles of evangelical truth, to give its due place and prominence to *the promise of reward* as a motive to Christian obedience. They seem to think that it is somehow inconsistent with salvation by the free and unmerited grace of God through faith in the mediation of the Saviour. But how does the case stand ? Even if we were sinless creatures, who in all things had perfectly obeyed the will of God, we should have no claim to recompense at His hand ; for He would be entitled to the fullest service we could render, without holding out any promise to requite us for it ; and whatsoever he might be pleased to proffer in the name of reward would be over and above what we had any right to look for. Much more evident it is that, *being sinners,* we have no title to any remuneration for our obedience. We have not served Him as we ought to do in the time that is past ; nor are we able so to serve Him in the time to come. Our wilful offences have incurred His just wrath ; and our best works are marred by so many blemishes, that when tried by their own merits they never can secure His favour. To speak of rewards, then, as due to such creatures, would be altogether unreasonable and extravagant. Any rewards He may hold out for our encouragement must be traced to His free and abounding grace through Jesus Christ.

But this is not all. Apart from our inability to render to God such service as He justly requires, it seems very clear that we must first be reconciled to Him before any service we may render can be accepted by Him. Indeed,

PART
IV.
SEC. 5.

486   REVIEW OF OBJECTIONS TO THE

PART
IV.
SEC. 5.
———

His very acceptance at our hands of any act of obedience we may perform would of itself be a fully significant token that His just anger against us as sinners had been turned away. Accordingly, the first call which He addresses to us in the Gospel is, to close with the free salvation He has there provided. Nor is it until this first call has been complied with, so that we are " made accepted in the

Eph. i. 6.

Beloved," that we are put in a position to run the Christian race, with a view to the prize of our high calling in Christ Jesus.

Such being the case, it cannot be disputed that the promise of rewards held out to Christian obedience is so far from lessening, that, on the contrary, it magnifies the grace of God in the redemption of sinners. Suppose an earthly prince were to grant a free pardon to some great criminal or hardened rebel, and to place him in a station of high honour and emolument, we should all admit that the person thus favoured would be bound by the strongest ties to loyalty and obedience ; and that the devoted service of all his after-life would be no more than a just return for the kindness that had been shown to him. But if, instead of his future service being received as only a just repayment of past benefits, there were farther bestowed on him the richest remuneration for every succeeding act of homage he might perform—so as to prevent it from going to diminish the vast debt of gratitude originally laid upon him—who does not see that the graciousness of his sovereign would thereby be much more remarkably displayed ? Now it is even so that God deals with redeemed sinners. He receives them graciously and forgives them freely ; and without the least regard to any works they have performed, but solely for the merits of His beloved Son, in whom they put their trust, He honours them with His favour, adopts them into His family, and sanctifies them by the grace of His Holy Spirit. His kindness in doing so would be more than sufficient to call forth their most earnest efforts for the requital of it. But any such thing as a repayment of His kindness, even if it were otherwise practicable, He has precluded, by holding

DOCTRINE OF THE ATONEMENT. 487

out to them an exceeding great reward for even the least
act of obedience that may be done by them. Thus does
He bring it to pass that, so far from diminishing, they
constantly increase, the debt of gratitude they owe to
Him, by all their subsequent endeavours in His service;
for He so greatly exceeds their doings by His rewards,
that the more they try to do for Him, they become the
more indebted to Him.

But besides all this, there are two other considerations
which have an important bearing on this subject. (1.) On
the one hand, all the good works of believers are done
through the grace of Christ, purchased by the Atonement.
For it is expressly written of believers, that they are
" created in Christ Jesus unto good works;" that it is by
" abiding in Him that they bring forth much fruit;" and
that " without Him they can do nothing." (2.) On the
other hand, it is only through the intercession of Christ,
founded, as we have seen, upon His sacrifice, that the
good works of believers, imperfect though they be, and
tainted with much sin, are accepted in the sight of God.
When these considerations are taken into account, we at
once see that the promised rewards of Christian obedience
are *based on the mediation of Christ,* instead of being inconsistent with it. Apart from His mediation and atonement, no such rewards could have been held out to sinful
men, or even if held out, could ever have been attained by
them. So far, therefore, is the revealed method of our
redemption from taking away from us this inducement to
the service of God, that it is, on the contrary, the very
ground, and the only ground, on which any such inducement
can be proposed to us. And it is most certain that no
motive to obedience is more clearly and fully proposed to
us in the New Testament; for there we are assured that
" when Christ comes in the glory of His Father, He shall
reward every man according to his works;" that " whosoever cometh to God, must believe that He is, and that He
is a rewarder of them that diligently seek Him;" that
" he who soweth sparingly shall reap also sparingly, and
he who soweth bountifully shall reap also bountifully;"

PART
IV.
SEC. 5.

Eph. ii.
10.
John, xv.
4, 5.
Supra, p.
114-117.

Matt. xvi.
27.
Heb. xi. 6.

2 Cor. ix
6.

488   REVIEW OF OBJECTIONS TO THE

PART
IV.
SEC. 5.
——
1 Cor. iii.
8.

Matt. x.
41, 42.

that "every man shall receive his own reward, according
to his own labour;" that "he who receiveth a prophet in
the name of a prophet shall receive a prophet's reward;
and he that receiveth a righteous man in the name of a
righteous man shall receive a righteous man's reward;
and whosoever shall give to drink unto one of Christ's
little ones a cup of cold water only in the name of a disciple, verily he shall in no wise lose his reward."

Thus does it appear that the doctrine of redemption,
through the mediatorial work and sufferings of Jesus Christ,
is in no respect injurious in its practical tendency. It
does not relax the obligation of the divine commandments, or limit their extent, or lessen their utility, or
weaken our motives and encouragements to the observance of them. When rightly apprehended and cordially
believed, it is in the highest degree "a doctrine according
to godliness," tending to "make the man of God perfect,
thoroughly furnished unto all good works."

1 Tim. vi.
3.
2 Tim. iii.
17.

We venture to say that the conclusion we have thus
arrived at is to a great extent borne out by actual experience. For though the doctrine of the cross may be professed by some who are not careful to adorn it by a holy
practice, it will hardly be denied that in those who appear
to be thoroughly sincere and earnest in their reception of
it, we find for the most part a higher tone of moral sentiment, a more strict and scrupulous discharge of religious
duty, greater spirituality and abstraction from the world,
more serious concern for their own advancement in the
Christian life, as well as for the spiritual improvement of
their brethren, than are ordinarily to be met with among
other men by whom this precious doctrine is rejected.
So much is this the case, that those who humbly endeavour to lead a life of faith in the Son of God, who loved
them and gave Himself for them, are not unfrequently
visited with reproach for being, as the world deems it,
"righteous overmuch."

Thus much is certain, that all Christians are greatly
concerned to swell the amount of practical evidence that

DOCTRINE OF THE ATONEMENT. 489

may be adduced in proof of the sanctifying power of the Atonement by a life of steadfast, uniform, and consistent holiness. Is so serious a charge brought against this vital article of "the faith once delivered to the saints," as that of its being injurious to morality? Our whole conduct ought to be a refutation of the charge. Instead of being content with verbally protesting against it, our better course is to "put it to silence by well-doing," and to live it down by our godly conversation; so that even the adversaries who are watching for our halting, and would be well pleased to " speak against us as evil-doers, may be led by our good works, which they shall behold, to glorify God in the day of visitation."

PART
IV.
SEC. 5.

1 Pet. ii. 15.

1 Pet. ii. 12

APPENDIX

NOTES AND ILLUSTRATIONS

APPENDIX.

NOTES AND ILLUSTRATIONS.

NOTE A, *page 22.*

USE OF Ὑπέρ BY THE CLASSICS TO DENOTE SUBSTITUTION.

IN regard to this use of the preposition ὑπέρ I may transcribe the following observations of *Raphelius* and *Valckenarius :—*

"Romans, v. 8. Ὑπὲρ ἡμῶν ἀπέθανε—id est, ἀντί, *loco, vice nostrâ mortuus est,* ut nos mortis pœna liberaremur. *Vicariam* enim mortem hoc loquendi genere Græci declarant. Neque Socinianis, qui secus interpretantur, quenquam ex Græcis credo assensorem esse. Nostræ sententiæ Xenophon adstipulatur. Nam cum Seuthes puerum formosum bello captum occidere vellet, Episthenes autem, puerorum amator, se pro illius morte deprecatorem præberet, rogat Seuthes Episthenem ; Ἦ καὶ ἐθέλοις ἂν, ὦ Ἐπίσθενες, ὙΠΕΡ ΤΟΥΤΟΥ ΑΠΟΘΑΝΕΙΝ ; *Vellesne, mi Episthenes, pro hoc mori ?* Cumque is nihil dubitaret pro pueri vita cervicem præbere, Seuthes vicissim puerum interrogat, εἰ παίσειεν αὐτὸν ΑΝΤΙ ἐκείνου ; *num hunc feriri pro se vellet ?* (De Exped. Cyri, &c.) Et (Hist. Græc., &c.) Προειπὼν δὲ ὁ Ἀγησίλαος, ὅστις παρέχοιτο ἵππον καὶ ὅπλα καὶ ἄνδρα δόκιμον, ὅτι ἐξέστι αὐτῷ μὴ στρατεύεσθαι, ἐποίησεν οὕτω ταῦτα συντόμως πράττεσθαι, ὥσπερ ἄν τις τὸν ὙΠΕΡ ΑΥΤΟΥ ΑΠΟΘΑΝΟΥΜΕΝΟΝ προθύμως ζητοίη. *Quumque Agesilaus denunciasset fore, ut, quicunque daret equum et arma et peritum hominem,* immunis esset a militiâ ; effecit ut hæc non aliter magna celeritate facerent, atque si quis alacriter *aliquem* SUO LOCO morituram quæreret. (De Venat., p. 768.) Ἀντίλοχος τοῦ πατρὸς ὙΠΕΡΑΠΟΘΑΝΩΝ, τοσαύτης ἔτυχεν εὐκλείας, ὥστε μόνος φιλοπάτωρ παρὰ τοῖς Ἕλλησιν ἀναγορευθῆναι. *Antilochus* PRO PATRE *morti se*

494   APPENDIX.

objiciens, tantum gloriæ consecutus est, ut solus apud Græcos amans patris appelletur. Et quid opus est aliis exemplis? cum luculentissimum sit, Joh. xi. 50, ubi mortuus dicitur Salvator ὑπὲρ τοῦ λαοῦ. Quòd quale sit, mox exponitur, ἵνα μὴ ὅλον τὸ ἔθνος ἀπόληται."—*Raphelii Annot.*, ii. p. 253, 254.

"Sciendum et rite tenendum est, ἀποθανεῖν ὑπέρ τινος non tantum in N. T. sed etiam apud scriptores profanos, significare, *mori loco alterius*, ut certe Christus non tantum *in commodum* nostrum mortuus est, sed *nostrum loco* mortem subire non recusavit, quam nos fueramus commeriti. Eandem phrasin veteres adhibuere in historia *Alcestidis* denarranda. Quum enim pro *Admeto* neque pater, neque mater, mori voluissent, uxor se Alcestis obtulit, et *pro eo vicaria morte* interiit, ut scribit Hyginus CLI. Habuit is ante oculos argumentum Dramatis Euripidei ; Ἄλκηστις ἡ γυνὴ ἐπέδωκεν ἑαυτὴν, μηδετέρου τῶν γονέων ἐθελήσαντος ὑπὲρ τοῦ παιδὸς ἀποθανεῖν. Palæphat, c. 41, ἀνδρεία γε ἡ Ἄλκηστις (ita leg. ex Apost., ii. 72) ἑκοῦσα ὑπεραπέθανεν Ἀδμήτου, *sponte sua et volens* pro marito mortem subiit. Sicuti a Latinis isto sensu frequentatur *pro*, ita et a Græcis, pro ἀντί, *vice, loco* alterius mori, θανεῖν πρό τινος. In *Eurip.* Alcest., v. 18, *Admetus neminem invenit*, qui voluerit θανεῖν πρὸ κείνου, *ejus vice;* et sic alibi sæpe."—*Valckenarii Selecta e Scholis*, ii. p. 324.

"Phrasis ἀποθανεῖν ὑπέρ τινος seu τινὸς ὑπεραποθανεῖν, non in N. T. duntaxat, sed etiam apud scriptores Græcos, significat non tantum *in commodum alterius mori*, sed et *loco alterius*, utque adeo *vicariam mortem* subire. *Plato* in Sympos., p. 180, de amore, quo amicum Patroclum Achilles complectebatur, *mortuo Patroclo*, inquit, *voluit*, vel *voluisset*, οὐ μόνον ὑπεραποθανεῖν Πατρόκλου, ἀλλὰ καὶ ἐπαποθανεῖν· *non tantum pro Patroclo* mori, *sed et in mortui illius* corpus immori. Eod., vol. iii. p. 208, *Alcestis*, inquit, Admeti uxor, voluit ὑπὲρ Ἀδμήτου ἀποθανεῖν, *loco mariti sui mori*, quod et legitur apud *Palæph.*, c. 41, et aliquoties in *Euripedis* Alcestide."—*Valckenarii Selecta e Scholis*, ii. p. 433.

To the instances adduced by these learned writers I subjoin the following from the Alcestis of Euripides, as showing that, in an unquestionable case of substitution, the prepositions ἀντί and ὑπέρ are used interchangeably :—

ἀξία δέ μοι
Τιμῆς, ἐπεὶ τέθνηκεν ΑΝΤ᾽ ἐμοῦ μόνη.—Alcest., 445, 446.
Οἶδ᾽ ΑΝΤΙ᾽ σοῦ γε κατθανεῖν ὑφειμένην.—Ibid., 540.
Αλλ᾽ οὐ σὺ νεκρὸν ΑΝΤΙ᾽ σοῦ τόνδ᾽ ἐκφέρεις.—Ibid., 732.
πῶς δ᾽ ἂν μᾶλλον ἐνδείξαιτό τις
Πόσιν προτιμῶσ᾽, ἢ θέλουσ᾽ ΥΠΕΡθανεῖν.—Ibid., 155, 156.

NOTES AND ILLUSTRATIONS. 495

Κάθρεψ', ὀφείλων οὐχ ὙΠΕΡθνῄσκειν σέθεν.—Ibid., 698.
Μὴ θνῆσχ' ὙΠΕ῾Ρ τοῦδ' ἀνδρὸς οὐδ' ἐγὼ πρὸ σοῦ.—Ibid., 706.
Σοφῶς δ' ἐφεῦρες, ὥστε μὴ θανεῖν ποτε,
Εἰ τὴν παροῦσαν κατθανεῖν πείσεις ἀεὶ
Γυναχ' ὙΠΕ῾Ρ σοῦ.—Ibid., 715-717.

NOTE B, *page* 25.

TISCHENDORF AND BAUR ON THE USE OF ὑπέρ AS INDICATING
THAT THE DEATH OF CHRIST WAS SUBSTITUTIONARY.

The reason suggested (*supra*, p. 25) for the frequent use of
ὑπέρ in preference to ἀντί, when Christ is represented as "dying
for us," is borne out by the following statements of Tischendorf,
in his short treatise entitled "*Doctrina Pauli de vi mortis Christi
satisfactoria.*"

"Some," he says, "have endeavoured to prove, from the mere
import and use of the preposition ὑπέρ, that Paul has taught the
vicarious satisfaction of Christ; others, again, with the view of
proving the contrary, have denied that by the writers of the New
Testament ὑπέρ is ever put for ἀντί. On both sides there is an
error. The preposition by itself gives support alike to both
opinions,"—*i.e.*, both to the *beneficial* and the *substitutive* view of
the Saviour's death. "For there are passages to be readily found in
many of the ancient Greek writers, which plainly vindicate for
ὑπέρ the substitutive sense (*loco* or *vice alicujus*); and no one can
doubt that Paul himself has used it in the same sense, and that,
too, in passages which do not bear upon our doctrine, as Philemon, 13; 2 Cor. v. 20; 1 Cor. xv. 29. But if it be asked,
Why, in regard to so important a subject, has the apostle chiefly
used this preposition of uncertain and fluctuating signification?
the answer is, that there is somewhat in the preposition itself
which makes it more suitable than the other for describing the
death which Christ encountered for us; for no one denies that the
chief thing to be considered in this matter is, *that Christ died for
the advantage of men;* and this indeed was so done by His dying
in the room of men. Now, *for the conjoint sense, both of advantage and of substitution,* ὑπέρ is admirably used by the apostle.
Winer, with his usual accuracy, holds that it is improper, in important passages where the death of Christ is discussed, to take ὑπέρ
as simply or exactly equivalent to ἀντί; for undoubtedly it cor-

496 APPENDIX.

responds to the Latin *pro* and to the German *für*. But as often as Paul teaches that Christ died *for us*, he did not wish, according to my judgment, that from the notion of *substitution* that of *advantage* should be disjoined; nor did he ever wish that from the latter, although it may be exceedingly obvious, the former should in this form of expression be excluded."

To these remarks of Tischendorf we may fitly subjoin the following statement of Dr F. C. Baur, in his posthumous work, ' Neutestamentliche Theologie,' p. 158, 159 :—

"As the death of Christ in relation to God is an act of *satisfaction*, so in relation to man it is *substitutionary (stellvertretend)*. That Christ died ὑπὲρ ἡμῶν is the expression most commonly used by Paul to indicate the significance of His death for men. From the preposition ὑπέρ by itself, the notion of *substitution* cannot indeed be inferred ; *but just as little can this notion be excluded from it.* The two notions, that which was done for men, and that which was done in their stead, pass over into each other. Among the many places in which it is said of Christ, that He died διὰ τὰ παραπτώματα ἡμῶν, or περὶ τῶν ἁμαρτιῶν ἡμῶν, or ὑπὲρ τῶν ἁμαρτιῶν ἡμῶν (Rom. iv. 25 ; v. 6; viii. 3 ; Gal. i. 4; 1 Cor. xv. 3), the passage in 2 Cor. v. 15 contains most distinctly the notion of *substitution*. The apostle draws from the proposition, εἰς ὑπὲρ πάντων ἀπέθανεν, the immediate inference, ἄρα οἱ πάντες ἀπέθανον. Christ not merely died *for them*, but also *in their stead*, as the one in the place of many—who, even because He died for them and in their stead, did not themselves actually die, but are only regarded as dead in Him, their substitute. What happened to Christ happened objectively to all. The idea in this passage is that of a union of Christ with us, effected by means of the principle of love (v. 14), in virtue of which union, that which He has done for us is just the same as if we had done it ourselves : as He in His death has identified Himself with us, and in dying for us has put Himself into our place, so must we also think ourselves into His place and regard ourselves as dead with Him. This mutual oneness of being in which the one lives in the other,—in which we are crucified with Christ because He is crucified for us, and we live in Him because He lives in us (Gal. ii. 20),—is the genuine Pauline notion of substitution. This, therefore, is also the correct meaning of the preposition ὑπέρ. It is not the vague general ' for,' which may stand in all possible relations, but it expresses the inmost immediate entering (*Eingehen*) into another, and putting one's self in his place."—*Cf. also Baur's* ' Paulus, der Apostel Jesu Christi,' ii. p. 167-170.

NOTES AND ILLUSTRATIONS. 497

NOTE C, *page* 60.

STRICTURES OF MR GOODSIR ON THE AUTHOR'S VIEW OF JUSTIFICATION.

The view which I have taken of justification (*supra*, p. 57-60), as "a forensic or judicial act," has been keenly controverted by the Rev. Joseph Taylor Goodsir, in an elaborate volume of 200 pages, entitled, 'Criticism and Refutation of certain Doctrines in Professor Crawford's Work on the Atonement.'

If Justification had been the main subject of my present treatise, I might, perhaps, have accepted Mr Goodsir's challenge to enter into a discussion with him in regard to it. But, when seeking to ascertain the doctrine of the Atonement, of which the texts relating to Justification constitute but one of the many classes of Scriptural proofs, I am unwilling to swell the present volume by any particular notice of his animadversions. Moreover, I am glad to find that such a task is, as the case stands, altogether unnecessary. For, happily, with all his disposition to magnify the difference between us to the uttermost, I find that he agrees with me to quite a sufficient extent to bear out the only conclusion which I am concerned to establish.

Thus, he expressly states, in one passage ('Criticism,' p. 105,106)—"It has always been our contention, in full accordance with Scriptural and Catholic verity, *that there is a forensic element in justification or salvation* ; that is to say, the justification or salvation enjoyed in and through Christ *means a forensic and free acquittal from all guilt and condemnation*, along with a setting free by an enlightening, quickening, and sanctifying deliverance from all sin and pollution." Again, after stating that "Dr Crawford would gain nothing by proving that in Romans, viii. 34, the verb *justify* (δικαιοῦν) is employed in the forensic sense," he adds ('Criticism,' p. 109)—"*For we fully admit such a sense as forming one element in the twofold subjective and objective sense of the grand thing called justification or salvation.*" And yet again ('Criticism,' p. 133)—"The apostle taught a doctrine of grace, which provided as securely for the implantation of righteousness from the very first in Christians, *as for forgiveness and acceptance with God as righteous forensically*, all in and through Jesus Christ."

Thus does it appear that Mr Goodsir is at one with me, in so far as to hold that "there is a forensic element in justification" —that "the justification enjoyed in and through Christ means a

498   APPENDIX.

forensic and free acquittal from all guilt and condemnation,"—and that, in the doctrine of grace, taught by the Apostle Paul, there is provision made in behalf of Christians " for their forgiveness and acceptance with God as righteous forensically, in and through Jesus Christ."

It is true that, besides this " forensic element," he insists that there is *something more* included in justification, namely—"a setting free by an enlightening, quickening, and sanctifying deliverance from all sin and pollution." And this *something more*, I, in my turn, fully agree with him in holding to be one of the most precious benefits " enjoyed by bĕlievers in and through Jesus Christ." I further agree with him that this latter benefit is so inseparably connected with the former, that the one is by no means to be obtained without the other, or that no believer is ever made " forensically righteous," without having implanted in him, from the very first, the root or germ of a renovated nature, which gradually, but surely, leads to all holiness of heart and life. In one section of this treatise, I have endeavoured to show that the mediation of Christ procures for us the enlightening, quickening, and sanctifying influence of the Holy Spirit. (*Supra*, p. 117-122.) And, in another place (*supra*, p. 194-196), I have adduced Scriptural evidence to prove that one of the main purposes of the Saviour's death is to promote the sanctification of believers. In short, the only difference between us is in regard to *the meaning of the word " justification."* He fully agrees with me that it includes " the forensic element," and only insists that it includes also that " moral renovation of the heart," which I, equally with him, hold to be comprehended in the benefits of the Saviour's mediation, but which it appears to me more agreeable to Scriptural usage to designate by the word " sanctification."

Such being the case, it seems unaccountable that Mr Goodsir should have brought against me, and against the Westminster Confession, with which my views of this matter coincide, the charge of "thoroughgone, complete, ineradicable, and irremediable Antinomianism"! (' Criticism,' p. 136.) So far, indeed, am I from being chargeable with Antinomianism, that in Part IV., Sec. 5, I have very earnestly, and I trust successfully, endeavoured to show that the doctrine of Holy Scripture respecting the mediatorial work and sufferings of Jesus Christ, lends no countenance to that gross and pernicious heresy.

I deem it unnecessary to make any remark on those terms of bitter censure and reproach in which Mr Goodsir has inveighed against me, when he charges me, not only with " teaching

NOTES AND ILLUSTRATIONS. 499

monstrous nonsense," and " exhibiting glaring incoherence and confusion," but with " serious garbling and misrepresentation of the Scriptures," "vile prostitution of the noble name of science;" with "utter offensiveness of conduct, exactly analogous to the fraudulent upholding of a bankrupt mercantile institution;" and with indicating, as compared with Professor Smeaton, "a more thoroughly sophisticated intellect," and "a heretical virus deserving of deeper detestation on the part of every truthful mind."

NOTE D, *page* 71.

TRENCH AND BLOOMFIELD ON καταλλαγή AND καταλλάσσεσθαι.

" Καταλλαγή, occurring four times in the N. T., only occurs once in the Septuagint, and once in the Apocrypha. On one of these occasions (Isaiah, ix. 5) it is simply *exchange ;* on the other (2 Macca. v. 20) it is employed in the N. T. sense, being opposed to the ὀργὴ τοῦ Θεοῦ, and expressing the reconciliation, the εὐμένεια of God to His people. There can be no question that συναλλαγή (Ezek. xvi. 8, Aquila), and συναλλάσσειν (Acts, vii. 26), διαλλαγή (Eccles. xxii. 23, xxvii. 21), and διαλλάσσειν (in the N. T. only at Matt. v. 24; cf. Judg. xix. 3 ; 1 Esdr. iv. 31 ; Euripides, *Hel.* 1235), are more usual words in the earlier and classical periods of the language. But, for all this, the grammarians are wrong who denounce καταλλαγή and καταλλάσσειν as avoided by all who wrote the language in its highest purity. None need be ashamed of words which found favour with Æschylus (*Sept. con. Theb.* 767), with Xenophon (*Anab.* I., 6, 2), and with Plato (*Phæd.* 69, *a*). Fritzche (on Rom. v. 10) has thoroughly disposed of Tittman's fanciful distinction between καταλλάσσειν and διαλλάσσειν.

"The Christian καταλλαγή has two sides. It is *first* a reconciliation ' quâ Deus nos sibi reconciliavit,'—*i.e.,* laid aside His holy anger against our sins, and received us into favour; a reconciliation effected for us once for all by Christ upon His cross ;— so 2 Cor. v. 18, 19, and Rom. v. 10, where καταλλάσσεσθαι is a pure passive, ' ab eo in gratiam recipi apud quem in odio fueras.' But καταλλαγή is *secondly and subordinately* the reconciliation ' quâ nos Deo reconciliamur,'—*i.e.,* the daily deposition, under the operation of the Holy Spirit, of the emnity of the old man toward God. In this passive middle sense καταλλάσσεσθαι is used in 2 Cor. v. 20 ; cf. 1 Cor. vii. 11. All attempts to make this to be the primary meaning of the word, being indeed the secondary, rest,

500 APPENDIX.

not on an unprejudiced exegesis, but on a foregone determination to get rid of the reality of God's anger against the sinner."—Trench's *Synonyms of the New Testament*, 7th edition, p. 274-275.

"Καταλλάσσεσθαι is plainly a general term ; and as καταλλάσσω signifies *commuto*, καταλλάσσεσθαι denotes ' to change each other's differences—to exchange them,—mutually to lay them aside.' Now there is an ellipsis of διαφόρας or ἔχθρας, supplied in Herodot. vii. 145, καταλλάσσεσθαι τὰς ἔχθρας. When said of those who have been friends before, it signifies ' to be friends, or to become friends.' But it is evident that this language is only properly applicable to those who are on some footing of equality. When used of those *who are not so*, it is used *improprié*, and can only mean *redire in gratiam*, ' to be again received into favour.' Now it is obvious that this applies in a still stronger degree to the word when used ἀθρωποπαθῶς of *God*. *Then* it must be explained θεοπρεπῶς, and only imply, *on the part of God*, the granting of pardon, and affording the means of obtaining and preserving His future favour ; and, *on the part of man*, a humble and thankful acceptance of the offered boon. And this will apply to all the passages of the New Testament in which the phrase when used of God occurs, as in Rom. v. 10, and 2 Cor. v. 18, 19, 21.—Bloomfield's *Recensio Synoptica*, vol. v. p. 509.

NOTE E, *page* 97.

THE PASSOVER A SIN-OFFERING.

"That the Passover was a sin-offering is evident even from the name. The word signifies strictly ' deliverance,' and then ' sacrifice of deliverance,' or ' sacrifice of atonement.' But we learn the character of the Passover as a sin-offering still more clearly from the account of its first institution. When it was appointed that all the first-born in the land of Egypt should die, the destroying angel—that is, the angel of the Lord in his avenging and punishing character—spared all those houses which he found sprinkled with the blood of the paschal lamb, in sign of the expiation effected by it. He who had this token might be sure of being spared and delivered (Exod. xii. 23) ; his sins were laid, as it were, on the lamb, the type of innocence. He who slaughtered the lamb confessed, in a symbolical language, that he also, no less than the Egyptians, the children of this world, had deserved

NOTES AND ILLUSTRATIONS. 501

to be an object of the divine wrath. He declared that he could not claim deliverance on the ground of his own worth, or of any other title, but that he expected it from the grace of God alone. According to the divine promise, to accept the blood of the innocent lamb in place of the blood of the sinner, who recognised and felt himself to be such—those who made this confession received the remission of the punishment of their sins. The principle was thus laid down for all ages of the Church, that that which distinguishes the Church from the world is the blood of atonement. Nor was the festival of the Passover, as celebrated in later times, a mere commemorative festival, as is clear from the continual slaughter of lambs for sacrifices. Wherever there is a sacrifice instituted by God, we may be certain that, provided it is brought in faith, there is a repetition of the first benefit, which is distinguished from the subsequent ones only by its forming the commencement of a long series. The paschal lamb was the basis and root of the entire system of sacrifices. Only as connected with it had the remaining sin-offerings value and significance: without it they were but as disjointed members. It was the true and proper covenant-sacrifice,—the sacrifice which represented in its highest form the distinction between the world without God, and the people of God reconciled unto God."—Hengstenberg on the *Sacrifices of Scripture, Commentary on Ecclesiastes, and other Treatises* (Clark's Translation, p. 387, 388.)

NOTE F, *page* 145.

FIDUCIAL NATURE OF FAITH.

The nature of Christian faith is a question not so much of psychological analysis as of Biblical interpretation. The point to be determined is not, *Whether mere intellectual belief of the truths of the Gospel be of itself sufficient to discharge the functions and to produce the effects attributed to Christian faith?* but this very different question, *What is the sense in which our Lord and His apostles use the word* FAITH, *with reference to the spiritual benefits obtained by it? What or how much do they include in the import of this expression? Do they restrict it to the bare act of the understanding in giving credence to the truths which God has testified?* or, *Do they comprehend in it* (that which all admit to be either one of its proper fruits or one of its constituent elements) *the fiducial trust and acquiescence of the heart?*

502   APPENDIX.

1. As bearing on the solution of this question, I may observe that the words πίστις and πιστεύω are often used in the New Testament to signify not mere *assensus*, but *fiducia*.

Thus, when our Lord says (Matt. vi. 30), "If God so clothe the grass of the field, which to-day is, and to-morrow is cast into the oven, how much more shall He clothe you, *O ye of little faith?*" it is plain that He is not reproving His hearers for *ignorance or speculative unbelief* respecting the providence of God, but for a want of *trustful reliance on it.* The justice of His reproof, indeed, rests on the impossibility of their being either ignorant or doubtful in regard to that providential care, in which, notwithstanding, they failed to place their confidence.

In like manner, when He rebuked His disciples for the groundless alarm to which they yielded on the approach of danger, saying (Mark, iv. 10), "Why are ye so fearful? How is it that ye have *no faith?*" and again (Matt. xiv. 31), "O thou of *little faith*, wherefore didst thou doubt?"—it is equally clear that the fault for which He blamed them was their *want of confidence in Him*, and not any mere defect of knowledge or conviction, from which defect this want of confidence had proceeded.

Again, in the case of the Syrophenician woman (Matt. xv. 21-28), it was not her belief of any statements He had made to her, but the unfaltering *trust* she continued to place in His power and goodness, in spite of the apparently harsh and discouraging answers she had received from Him, that called forth at last the admiring commendation, "O woman, *great is thy faith.*" Here it is remarkable that the *faith* thus commended did not consist in believing what Christ had said to her, but rather in *disbelieving it*, when in its apparent sense it contradicted her views of the Saviour's character, and tended to shake her reliance on Him for the desired blessing.

There are many passages, too, in which the word πιστεύω is used in the sense of "committing" or "intrusting." For example, "Jesus did not *commit* Himself to them, because He knew all men" (John, ii. 24); "Who will *commit to your trust* the true riches?" (Luke, xvi. 11); "Unto them were *committed* the oracles of God" (Rom. iii. 2); "The Gospel of the uncircumcision was *committed* unto me" (Gal. ii. 7); "We were allowed of God to be *put in trust* with the Gospel" (1 Thess. ii. 4); "The glorious Gospel of the blessed God, which was committed to my trust" (1 Tim. i. 11). In all these passages the word in question plainly implies, not merely the *belief* that a certain person is trustworthy,

NOTES AND ILLUSTRATIONS. 503

but the consequent *reliance* that is placed in him, to the effect of consigning important interests to his care.

2. Further, it is a remarkable circumstance that the words πίστις and πιστεύω, although of very frequent occurrence in the Scriptures, are never (with one solitary and doubtful exception) employed to express a persuasion with reference to any matter that is not in its own nature *a proper object of fiducial reliance.* There are many things revealed, and necessary to be believed by us, which are not of such a kind as is fitted to excite our confidence—as, for example, the wrath of God, the depravity of our natures, our liability to death, and the final punishment of the impenitent. These things we may be said to *believe.* But we cannot with any propriety be said *to trust in them;* inasmuch as "trust" or "confidence," from its very nature, is restricted to things that are *desirable* or *beneficial.* Now it is remarkable that in speaking of such subjects the inspired writers do not employ the words πίστις and πιστεύω, but other words, which convey only the idea of *knowledge* or *conviction*, without being expressive of such *trustful dispositions* as the things known or credited are not calculated to awaken. Thus, when Paul has occasion to speak of " the terror of the Lord" (2 Cor. v. 11), he shuns the use of the verb πιστεύω in connection with it. His words are, Εἰδότες οὖν τὸν φόβον τοῦ Κυρίου—" *knowing* the terror of the Lord, we persuade men." And yet, if πιστεύω did not imply "trust" or "reliance," there is no reason why it should not have been employed with reference to things that are *dreadful* and *deplorable*, as well as to things that are desirable and beneficial.

I have said that there is one apparent exception to this usage. It occurs in James, ii. 19,—" Thou believest that there is one God; thou doest well : the devils also believe (πιστεύουσι), and tremble." It can hardly be said, however, that this is a real exception ; for the thing said to be " believed"—namely, " that there is one God"—is *in its own nature* a proper object of confidence ; and its effect upon the devils arises from other causes than anything inherent in the truth itself. But even allowing that we have here a real exception, it is surely more reasonable to regard it as an anomalous instance, than to attach to it any material weight in regard to the Scriptural use of an expression which so very frequently occurs in the New Testament, and which, with this lonely exception, is carefully appropriated to signify belief in those matters, and those alone, which are proper objects of complacent and confiding *trust.*

In regard to the noun πίστις, there is not even a single excep-

504 APPENDIX.

tion, real or apparent, to the usage I have referred to. This word is never used by the inspired writers with reference to anything that is not properly an object of *trust*, as being in its own nature desirable or beneficial, ministering to our comfort or contributing to our happiness. And yet, if the full meaning of the expression be nothing more than *an intellectual persuasion of something that is true, with no element of trust or confidence* involved in it, there is no apparent reason why it should not be employed with reference to all matters whatsoever which we believe to be true—to such as are *painful, discouraging*, and *alarming*, as well as to such as are of a comforting and cheering nature. The circumstance of its not being thus indiscriminately used, but of its being confined to proper objects of *fiducial reliance*, shows that it was held by the writers as indicating such *trustful dispositions* of the heart as would render the use of it with reference to anything *not calculated to excite these dispositions* inappropriate.

3. There is another circumstance worthy of remark in the use of these words by the writers of the New Testament. When employed with reference to a *person*, and more particularly with reference to God or to the Lord Jesus Christ as the source of spiritual blessings, πιστεύω and πίστις are very commonly connected with their objects by the prepositions εἰς, ἐν, or ἐπὶ, which correspond to our English prepositions *to, in,* and *on*.

The preposition εἰς is thus used in the following passages : John, vi. 29 ; xii. 36 ; xiv. 1 ; Acts, xx. 21 ; and in upwards of forty other passages, in all of which the subject referred to is *a person to be relied on*, and not an alleged *fact or statement to be believed.* Of the like use of ἐν, the following texts afford examples : Rom. iii. 25 ; Gal. iii. 26 ; Eph. i. 13, 15 ; 1 Tim. iii. 13. And of the numerous passages that might be adduced in which there is a similar use of ἐπὶ it may suffice to mention the following : Acts, ix. 42 ; xi. 17 ; xvi. 31 ; Rom. iv. 5, 24 ; ix. 33 ; x. 11 ; 1 Tim. i. 16 ; Heb. vi. 1 ; 1 Peter, ii. 6.

This peculiarity has been imitated in our authorised English version, where we frequently meet with such expressions as "believing *in* Christ," "believing *on* Christ," and of "faith *towards* the Lord Jesus Christ." At the time when our authorised translation was made, the English words "believe" and "belief" appear to have had more of a *fiducial* import than they now usually convey. (See *Richardson's Dictionary*.) As now used among us, they are unsuitable and incongruous when combined with the prepositions *in, on,* or *towards*. It is much more natural to speak of "trusting to a person," "confiding in

NOTES AND ILLUSTRATIONS. 505

him," " relying or depending upon him." Indeed it will hardly bear to be disputed that the prepositions " to," " in," and " on," when prefixed to the name of a person as the object of faith, indicate not merely " the persuasion of something concerning him," but " the consignment of something to him," or " the resting of something in him or upon him ; " and that they are thus more properly significant of *fiducia* than of mere *assensus*.

It is urged, indeed, by those who hold faith to be simple *assensus*, that the forms of expression above noticed are *elliptical*, —that some *statement or testimony*, though unexpressed, must be understood,—and that this statement or testimony is the thing that is believed, while the person whose name is governed by the preposition is the subject respecting which the statement or testimony is advanced. To this I reply—(1.) That even admitting that in such forms of expression some unexpressed statement or testimony must be understood, it does not appear that this statement or testimony is the proper object of that act of the mind which is indicated by πιστεύω or πίστις. When Paul, for example, said to the jailor at Philippi, Πίστευσον ἐπὶ τὸν Κύριον Ἰησοῦν Χριστὸν, it is evident that he was asking the jailor to have faith not on *some statement of his own concerning Christ*, but on *Christ Himself* as the living and personal Saviour. No doubt a statement on the part of the apostle, relative to the power and grace of Jesus Christ, was necessary to pave the way for such faith as was here required. But the thing required was faith, not in a statement, but in a person. And although the crediting of a certain statement respecting the person might be necessary or conducive to the exercise of faith in Him, yet the *person himself*, as distinctly and pointedly indicated by the preposition ἐπὶ, was the object on which the faith was required to rest. (2.) It may be further answered that there is no necessity for supposing the expressions to be elliptical, except what arises from the exigencies of that theory in support of which the ellipsis is assumed. For let any one go over the pages of the New Testament, and wherever he meets with the forms of expression referred to, let him substitute the words "rely," "confide," or "trust," in the room of the word "believe;" and he will at once see that there is no need of any hypothetical supplement in order to give the passages a clear and definite meaning. For example, "This is the work of God, that ye *trust to* him whom He hath sent" (John, vi. 29); "While ye have the light, *trust to* the light" (John, xii. 36); " Let not your hearts be troubled ; ye trust to God, trust also to me " (John, xiv. 1);

APPENDIX.

" In whom having *confided*, ye were sealed with that Holy Spirit of promise" (Eph. i. 13); "It was known throughout all Joppa, and many *relied on* the Lord" (Acts, ix. 42); "*Rely on* the Lord Jesus Christ, and thou shalt be saved" (Acts, xvi. 31); "He that *relieth on* Him shall not be confounded" (1 Peter, ii. 6).

I may add, that exactly the same form of expression often occurs in connection with the verbs ἐλπίζω and πείθω, which are universally allowed to be expressive, not of intellectual conviction, but of cordial reliance. For example, Matt. xii. 21, "In His name shall the Gentiles trust," ἐν τῷ ὀνόματι αὐτοῦ ἔθνη ἐλπιοῦσι; Matt. xxvii. 43, "He trusted in God, let Him now deliver him," πέποιθεν ἐπὶ τὸν Θεόν; 2 Cor. i. 9, "That we should not trust in ourselves, but in God," ἵνα μὴ πεποιθότες ὦμεν ἐφ' ἑαυτοῖς ἀλλ' ἐπὶ τῷ Θεῷ; Phil. ii. 19, "I trust in the Lord Jesus," ἐλπίζω ἐν Κυρίῳ Ἰησοῦ; 1 Tim. iv. 10, "We trust in the living God," ἠλπίκαμεν ἐπὶ Θεῷ ζῶντι; 1 Peter, iii. 5, "Holy women who trusted in God," αἱ ἐλπίζουσαι ἐπὶ τὸν Θεόν. In these, as in other instances which might easily be accumulated, the verbs πείθω and ἐλπίζω, which are admitted to have a fiducial import, are construed with the prepositions εἰς, ἐν, and ἐπὶ in precisely the same manner as πιστεύω, when a person, and not a statement, is its object.

4. The fiducial nature of faith may be further argued from the *synonymous or equivalent expressions* which are used to denote it, such as "*coming to Christ*," as in Matt. xi. 28; John, v. 40; vi. 35, 37, 44, 45, 64, 65: "*receiving Christ*," as in John, i. 12; Col. ii. 6, 7: "*trusting in Christ*," as in Eph. i. 12, 13: "*committing one's self to Christ*," as in 2 Tim. i. 12: "*eating* of the bread of life, and *drinking* of the water of life," as in John, iv. 14; vi. 47-58; vii. 37; Rev. xxii. 17. The full meaning of such phrases cannot be held to be exhausted by a mere *belief respecting Christ*, that He sustains a certain character, has performed a certain work, and is fraught with certain blessings. There is further implied in them a *trustful reception* of Him, and a *personal application* to Him for such blessings as He has to bestow.

Dr Wardlaw holds that these expressions, being metaphorical, cannot be legitimately used to explain the simple term "belief;" but that this simple term ought rather to be used to explain the figurative language which is thus put in substitution for it. Accordingly, he insists on excluding from the phrases, "coming to Christ," "receiving Him," &c., all reference to anything more than *simple belief*, on the ground of their being equivalent to πιστεύειν, instead of assigning to πιστεύειν a fiducial reference, on the ground

NOTES AND ILLUSTRATIONS. 507

of such figures being used in illustration of it.—*Syst. Theol.*, ii. 720.

In thus arguing, however, Dr Wardlaw proceeds on the assumption that the true and only meaning of πιστεύειν is *to believe;* whereas we have seen that in the New Testament it is frequently employed in the sense of *trusting*, and not merely of *believing.* He also forgets that the phrases in question, though metaphorical, are yet at the same time *illustrative* or *explanatory.* Like all figures employed by an intelligent speaker or writer, they are intended, not to obscure or weaken, but to elucidate and enforce his meaning. It is obvious, however, that by seeking to exclude from them all reference to any such exercises of the heart or will as a *trustful receiving and resting on the Saviour*, their plain and obvious import is so utterly ignored as to render them, for all purposes of illustration, entirely worthless.

5. The fiducial nature of faith is farther apparent from those passages of Scripture in which it is represented as an act of the *will*, and not merely of the understanding, and from other passages in which it is made the direct subject of *commands, exhortations,* and *entreaties.* Thus our Lord said to certain Jews who "did not believe on Him" (John, v. 40), "*Ye will not* come unto me that ye might have life," οὐ θέλετε ἐλθεῖν πρός με, "ye are not willing," or "ye will not consent to come to me." Again, He says (Matt. xxiii. 37), "How often would I have gathered thy children together, as a hen gathereth her chickens under her wings, and *ye would not !*" καὶ οὐκ ἠθελήσατε. And again (Rev. xxii. 17), it is written, "Let him that is athirst come, and whosoever will—ὁ θέλων—let him take the water of life freely." The expressions used in the first two of these passages signify, not merely unbelief in a statement, but the *wilful refusal* of an offer which ought to have been trustfully and cordially accepted. And in the third passage, the reception of the offered blessings is no less clearly represented as an *act of choice* which "whosoever will" is invited to perform.

The same lesson is taught in those numerous passages in which faith is made the subject of *exhortations and injunctions.* When we seek to bring men to a mere intellectual conviction respecting any matter, we do not *admonish* or *urge* them to believe it. We may urge them seriously to consider such arguments or evidences in proof of it as we are able to adduce. But their *belief* of it cannot, in itself considered, be made a *direct* subject of entreaties or admonitions. *These* are only applicable directly to matters of choice, immediately determined by *the will.* We find, how-

508   APPENDIX.

ever, that that exercise of the mind, which is indicated by the words πίστις and πιστεύω, is ordinarily made the subject of direct precepts and exhortations. We are urged, admonished, entreated, and commanded, not only *to do something that may become conducive to it* (as the consideration of offered proof may be conducive to our conviction), but *to do the thing itself*, as if the doing or the not doing of it were directly and immediately dependent on our own choice. What we are called to do is,—not to inquire whether God has really made to us certain promises, addressed to us certain calls, offered to us certain blessings, and prescribed to us a certain course by which these blessings are to be obtained,— but to trust in His promises, to comply with His calls, to accept of His offers, and to conform to His directions, in the confident persuasion that, by so doing, the benefits He has taught us to look for shall be secured.

6. I may yet farther observe, that even if it were admitted that πίστις and πιστεύω, in their strict etymological sense, mean nothing more than *belief* or intellectual conviction, yet as often as they are applied to things of a *religious, moral,* or *practical* nature, they must be understood in *a wider and more popular sense,* as including such exercises of the heart and will as are answerable to the nature of their objects. When God enjoins us to "call upon Him," to "hear Him," to "remember Him," to "think of Him," to "consider His doings and testimonies,"—every reasonable man understands Him as requiring of us, not merely those exercises of *speech,,* and *hearing,* and *memory,* and *thought,* and *consideration,* which are all that His words, if strictly interpreted, express,—but also *those godly feelings and dispositions* which are suitable to such exercises, and necessary to their right performance. In like manner, when He invites us to have *faith* in those revealed matters which are set before us in His Word, He must be understood as requiring of us not only a persuasion of the truth and reality of these objects (even if it were allowed that this is all that His language in its strict etymological sense expresses), but as requiring also *those dispositions of heart and purposes of will* which are answerable to the nature of the things revealed, and without which no mere convictions in regard to them can be of any real profit or advantage to us. Accordingly, it is well stated in the Confession of Faith, chapter xiv. § 2, that " By faith a Christian believeth to be true whatsoever is revealed in the Word, for the authority of God Himself speaking therein ; and acteth differently upon that which each particular passage thereof containeth ; yielding obedience to the commands, trem-

NOTES AND ILLUSTRATIONS. 509

bling at the threatenings and embracing the promises of God for this life and that which is to come. But the principal acts of saving faith are accepting, receiving, and resting upon Christ alone for justification, sanctification, and eternal life."

7. Finally, it is only by considering a *trustful reception of Christ*, as included in the exercise of faith, that any intelligible connection can be discerned between the nature of faith and the function or office assigned to it. Faith in Christ is expressly declared in Scripture to be the means by which we become partakers of His purchased blessings. We can readily understand how this should be the case, if faith be regarded as a *fiducial act by which we receive Him and rest upon Him for salvation.* For then we at once see that it conveys to us His benefits for no other than the obvious and sufficient reason, that it is the very act of appropriating or laying hold of them. The blessings are freely held out to our acceptance, and they become ours when we trustfully embrace the offer, and heartily close with it or accept of it for our own behoof. But if we exclude from our views of the nature of faith that trustful reception of Christ by which His purchased benefits are appropriated, I see no possible explanation that can be given of the place which the Scriptures assign to *faith alone* in the matter of our justification and salvation. For in that case faith alone does not include anything that directly conveys to us an interest in the Saviour's mercies.

The advocates of the purely intellectual theory do indeed maintain that, though faith includes in itself nothing more than *belief*, it always *produces* that fiducial reception of Christ which they admit to be necessary to secure the benefits of redemption. But in so affirming they virtually hold that we are saved, not by *faith alone*, yea, not directly by faith at all, but by something else which, though an accompaniment or result of faith, must be carefully discriminated from it, and excluded from our conceptions of it. And thus do they seem to be shut up to a conclusion that is utterly opposed to the plain doctrine of the Scriptures, according to which *faith itself*, irrespective of its fruits, is held forth as the sole condition of justification in the sight of God. Surely when we are said to be "justified by faith alone," the meaning must be that *faith includes in itself whatsoever is requisite on our part to our being justified.* And inasmuch as "receiving and resting on Christ as our Saviour" is admittedly requisite to our being justified, it follows that this "receiving and resting on Him" *must be of the very nature or essence of faith;* because if it were not, faith would require to be supplemented by somewhat that

510   APPENDIX.

is exterior to it and distinguishable from it, in order to be conducive to our justification.

NOTE G, *page* 202.

THE INVITATIONS OF THE GOSPEL.

That there is great difficulty in the way of harmonising the
general invitations of the Gospel on the one hand, with the special reference of the Atonement to those who shall eventually be
partakers of its benefits, on the other hand—it would be altogether fruitless to disguise.   And if these two things were alike
within the reach and comprehension of the human understanding, in that case our inability to reconcile them might warrant a
strong suspicion that they cannot both be true.   But inasmuch as
one at least of these subjects far exceeds the power and compass
of our faculties, we cannot without presumption hazard the assertion, that our inability to reconcile it with the other is proof of
any *real inconsistency* between the two.   For it may be that *the
missing link* that is needful, and would be available for their
thorough reconciliation, may be hidden from our view in that
profound abyss of God's everlasting counsels which we cannot
fathom.

There are some considerations, however, which may in a
measure tend to alleviate, although they cannot wholly remove,
the difficulties to which I have adverted.

I. The invitations addressed in the Gospel to all sinners *express nothing but what is fully consistent with the truth of the case,*
even on the supposition of a special reference in the Atonement
to those who shall eventually be saved by it.   For all that they
can be considered as expressing is, *that certain benefits purchased
by the Atonement shall assuredly be obtained by any sinner,*
PROVIDED THE PRESCRIBED COURSE FOR OBTAINING THEM BE
ADOPTED BY HIM.   The invitations of the Gospel convey nothing
more than this.   They convey no intimation that it was God's
purpose, in making the Atonement, actually to confer its benefits
on all sinners without exception.   And accordingly the absence
of such a purpose on the part of God cannot be held to conflict
with His invitations.   It is indeed true that many of those to
whom the invitations are addressed *will not comply with them.*
But it is not the less true that, *if they would comply,* the offered

NOTES AND ILLUSTRATIONS.   511

mercies would certainly be obtained. It cannot be said, then, that God is unfaithful in holding out to all sinners the offers of redeeming grace. For what more is necessary to show that His invitations are truthful, reliable, and worthy of all acceptation, than the undisputed fact that, whensoever they are complied with, the blessings proposed in them are unfailingly bestowed?

II. Farther, it is of some importance to remember, *that the same Word of God which invites all sinners to receive the Atonement, reveals also that special reference of the Atonement to " those who were given to Christ by His Father," with which such an invitation is alleged to be at variance.* This consideration seems of itself sufficient to vindicate the sincerity of God's dealings with us in the matter. If the Bible had only proclaimed to us the offered redemption, and we had *elsewhere* obtained a knowledge, which the Bible withheld from us, of its special destination, we might then have had some greater show of reason for alleging that God's dealings with us were not of such a kind, as from what we know of His adorable perfections we had cause to expect. But as the case actually stands, there is not the least ground for any such allegation. For while in His revealed Word He *invites all* to receive the Atonement, He does not allow them to remain under the impression that in His eternal purpose it is *destined alike for all.* On the contrary, He gives them the fullest certification that it is specially destined for those whose ultimate salvation shall be actually secured by it. It cannot be said, therefore, that His invitations are delusive. We may be at a loss to explain how the general call and the special destination are to be harmonised ; but the fact that both the one and the other have been openly and fully announced in His revealed Word, is sufficient to show that, whatever *mystery* there may be, there is nothing—as it were impious to think that there could be anything—like insincerity or duplicity in His procedure.

III. Again, there does not appear to be any difference between the invitations of God and His *commandments,* in so far as regards their seeming discrepancy with His purposes. The commandments, no less than the invitations, are addressed to all. Both are alike indications on the part of God of what He desires and requires to be done by all. Nor are there wanting, with reference to His commandments, testimonies quite as significant as any which are to be found with reference to His invitations, of the earnestness and intensity of His desire that the course which they prescribe should be adopted by all who hear them. Take, for example, these tender expostulations,—" O that there were such

APPENDIX.

an heart in them, that they would fear me, and keep all my commandments always, that it might be well with them and with their children for ever!" "O that my people had hearkened unto me, and Israel had walked in my ways!" "O that thou hadst hearkened to my commandments! then had thy peace been as a river, and thy righteousness as the waves of the sea."—(Deut. v. 29; Psalm lxxxi. 13; Isaiah, xlviii. 18.)

But while the commandments of God are thus expressive of what He *desires, approves of,* and *delights in,* as congenial to the goodness and holiness of His moral nature, they are certainly not declarative, at the same time, of what He has fixedly *purposed* or *determined* in His government of the universe to carry into effect. For if they were so, it is certain that they would be unfailingly and universally obeyed by all His creatures; whereas they are frequently violated, without any interference on His part to vindicate their authority and secure their observance. Doubtless it is an inscrutable mystery, that things should thus be done under the government of the Almighty which are in the highest degree displeasing and offensive to Him. It is just the old mystery of the existence of moral evil, which no one has ever been able to explain. But the fact that such things do occur is undeniable. And therefore it must be His will and purpose to permit them. He does not prevent them, though undoubtedly able to do so. Nay, He upholds in the possession of all their faculties, whether of body or of mind, those sinful creatures by whom they are brought to pass. How then can we find a way of escape from the admission, that *it is, upon the whole, His will that they should be permitted?* And yet we dare not and cannot for a moment suppose that they are in their own nature *acceptable and pleasing to Him,* and consequently that His solemn and express precepts, which they contravene, are aught else than a true and trustworthy expression of what He desires, approves of, and delights in, and earnestly requires to be done by all His intelligent creatures.

Thus does it appear, that great as may be the difficulty of reconciling the invitations of the Gospel with God's special purpose with reference to the Atonement, by which the blessings of the Gospel have been procured, that difficulty is no other and no greater than we have to encounter when we try to reconcile the commandments of God, as expressive of what He desires and approves of on the part of all His rational creatures, with what certainly appears from His actual procedure to be His purpose, that many of His creatures should be permitted to set them at nought.

IV. I would only add that it is worthy of consideration whe-

NOTES AND ILLUSTRATIONS. 513

ther, by holding that the Atonement had a special reference to those who are ultimately partakers of its benefits, we are really involved in any greater difficulty respecting the invitations of the Gospel, than those are who hold that the Atonement had the same reference to those who are eventually lost as to those who are eventually saved.

Be it observed that there is no difference between the parties in so far as regards the *sufficiency* of the Atonement for all sinners. Its sufficiency is no less earnestly maintained by those who affirm than by those who deny its special destination. Thus Owen observes: "To the honour of Jesus Christ we affirm, that such and so great was the dignity and worth of His death and blood-shedding,—of so precious a value, of such an infinite fulness and sufficiency was this oblation of Himself, that it was every way able and perfectly sufficient to redeem, justify, reconcile, and save all the sinners of the world, to satisfy the justice of God for all the sins of all mankind, and to bring them every one to everlasting glory. This fulness and sufficiency of the merit of the death of Christ is a foundation for the general publishing of the Gospel to every creature ; because the way of salvation which it declares is wide enough for all to walk in. There is enough in the remedy which it brings to light to heal all their diseases, and to deliver them from all their evils. If there were a thousand worlds, the Gospel of Christ might on this ground be preached to them all, there being enough in Christ for the salvation of them all, if so be they will derive virtue from Him by touching Him in faith."*

To the same effect is the following statement of Dr Hodge: "The righteousness of Christ, consisting in the obedience and death demanded by the law under which all men are placed, is *adapted to all men.* It is also of infinite value, being the righteousness of the eternal Son of God, and therefore *sufficient for all.* On these two grounds—its adaptation to all and its sufficiency for all —rests the offer made in the Gospel to all. *Who are eventually to be saved by it we do not know.* But it is of such a nature and value that whosoever accepts of it shall be saved. . . . The reason why any man perishes is, not that there is no righteousness provided suitable and adequate to his case, or that it is not freely offered to all that hear the Gospel, but simply because he wilfully rejects the proffered salvation." †

Now, if those who believe the Atonement to have been specially destined for the *actual salvation* of those who "were given to

* Owen's Works (Goold's edition), vol. **x**. p. 297.
† Princeton Essays, 1st series, p. 291.

APPENDIX.

Christ by the Father" do nevertheless maintain, thus fully and unreservedly, its *suitableness and sufficiency for the salvation of all sinners*, can they be justly charged with detracting from the sincerity of the universal invitations of the Gospel? Or are they in any worse position than those who differ from them for vindicating the sincerity of these invitations, and pressing them on the acceptance of all to whom they are addressed?

1. The Arminians, in the first place—rejecting as they do the doctrine of unconditional election altogether—are shut up to the position that God, in providing the Atonement, had no purpose to secure by it the *actual salvation* of *any* sinners, but simply to remove obstacles out of the way of their being saved,—to open a wide door by which any who choose may enter into the way of eternal life—to offer such a sacrifice for sin as should make it compatible with the attributes and government of God to save those who shall faithfully comply with the terms of the Gospel.

It seems evident then, that, according to the Arminian doctrine, *all men* are in precisely the same position in which *the non-elect* are according to the Calvinistic doctrine; that is to say, they are all in the position of having a perfectly suitable and sufficient Atonement freely offered to their acceptance, *but without any further provision that all, or any of them, shall accept of it, so as to be actually saved.* The Atonement *per se*, according to the Arminian view, *does nothing more for all men* than, according to the Calvinistic view, *it does even for the non-elect.* It does not, *per se*, secure their actual salvation, but merely renders salvation *attainable by them in the event of their repenting and believing the Gospel.* Now, certainly, it cannot be said to do *less than this*, according to the doctrine of the most decided Calvinists, who hold, in the words of Owen, that " Christ's oblation of Himself was every way sufficient to redeem and save all the sinners in the world, and to satisfy the justice of God for all the sins of all mankind," and that " if there were a thousand worlds, the Gospel of Christ might on this ground be preached to them all, there being enough in Christ for the salvation of them all, if so be they will derive virtue from Him by faith."

2. But how does the case stand with those semi-Arminians (if we may so call them) who believe in the doctrine of unconditional election, and yet deny the special destination of the Atonement for the benefit of those who are eventually saved? Can it be truly said that, according to *their* view, the Atonement exhibits a more gracious aspect to all sinners, than according to the view of it held by those who differ from them? I cannot think so

NOTES AND ILLUSTRATIONS. 515

They do indeed express themselves in very broad and unqualified language respecting the universal benefits of the Redeemer's sacrifice, as extending alike to every member of the human race. But when we ask them to explain more particularly the exact amount and import of their statements, it very soon appears that the common benefits, held by them to flow from the Redeemer's sacrifice to all mankind, are really no other than those which we, who differ from them respecting the destination of the Atonement, do nevertheless admit to have flowed from it with the same unrestricted and indiscriminate universality.

For what do they really mean when affirming that "an atonement has been provided alike for all, and is intended for the benefit alike of all"? Do they mean that "an atonement is provided and intended for all, *to the effect of securing that all shall be eventually saved by it*"? Do they mean that "God, in appointing the Redeemer's sacrifice, designed that it should procure for all sinners that grace of the Holy Spirit which is necessary to bring them to a cordial and saving reception of it"? By no means. This would be at variance with their own doctrine of a *designedly limited application* of the Atonement. They hold that the elect alone shall be eventually saved, and that it is God's purpose to confer on them alone that efficacious grace of the Holy Spirit by which the Atonement is savingly applied.

In what sense, then, consistently with their own principles, can we understand them as affirming that the sacrifice of Christ was provided alike for all sinners? In no sense that I can think of beyond *this*, that the sacrifice of Christ *has laid a suitable and sufficient basis for the salvation of all men*, IF SO BE THEY WOULD AVAIL THEMSELVES OF IT,—or, that in respect of intrinsic worth or virtue it lacks nothing of what is requisite for the redemption of the whole of our sinful race, "if peradventure God should be pleased to give them repentance unto the acknowledgment of the truth."

The fact is that, as regards the *actual attainment* of salvation through the sacrifice of Christ, there is a limitation on the principles of either party ; while as regards *the removal of such obstacles as stood in the way of salvation being attainable by all sinners in the event of their faithful compliance with the terms of the Gospel*, there is, on the principles of either party, the same perfectly suitable and adequate provision made in the all-sufficient merits and sufferings of the Son of God. And thus does it appear that the advocates of what is called a "universal atonement," combined with a limited purpose in the divine mind as to its application,

APPENDIX.

are really in no better position than those who differ from them, when they come to explain the unrestricted language in which the Scriptures speak of the Lord Jesus Christ as "the Saviour of the world," and invite all sinners to receive His offered grace.

It seems evident, then, that Calvinists would gain nothing, in the way of removing any difficulties of their position in its bearing on the invitations of the Gospel, by adopting instead of it the views of their opponents. This, moreover, is a course which, on many grounds, we dare not adopt. For, mark the consequences involved in such a concession. We must utterly disconnect the work of the Holy Spirit, in persuading and enabling men to receive the offered salvation and to persevere in faith and holiness, from the work of Jesus Christ, by which the Holy Spirit, with all the plenitude of His gracious influences, has been purchased. We must cease also to regard the sacrifice of Christ as *effectually securing* the salvation of any sinners. We must be content to think of it as merely providing a *possibility* of salvation ; and we must look to the *faith* of its recipients as that which is to turn the *possibility* into an *actuality*,—to supplement the Saviour's work instead of merely resting on it, and really to do *that* for those who are eventually saved, which all that the Saviour did and suffered has not accomplished. In a word, we must be driven to the conclusion that the Saviour's atoning death, considered in itself, *has done nothing more, and was not intended to do anything more, for those who are saved than for those who perish.* These are consequences which appear to us necessarily to follow from a denial of the special destination of our Lord's sacrifice, or from holding that it was alike destined for all sinners. And therefore it is that we shrink from such a position, because, while professing or seeming to widen the *extent* of the Atonement, it compromises what is of incomparably greater importance,—the *reality*, *saving power*, and *efficacy* of the Atonement.

At the same time, we have no hesitation in admitting that the Atonement, while, in respect of actual efficacy, it is designed for those only who shall be eventually saved (which is really very like an identical proposition), does yet, in respect of its perfection and sufficiency, as well as in respect of the free offers of salvation that are founded on it, present a gracious aspect towards all sinners of the human race. Nay rather, we maintain that *it does as much for* ALL *as, on the principles of those who differ from us, it does for* ANY, being suitable and sufficient for all, and without restriction offered to all,—insomuch that no other, or greater, or more freely offered atonement would be requisite for the salvation of all sinners, if all would but avail themselves of it.

NOTES AND ILLUSTRATIONS. 517

NOTE H, *page* 277.

GOD'S REMONSTRANCE WITH CAIN IN GENESIS, IV. 7.

A different translation of the last clause of this verse has been suggested by Lightfoot, adopted by Magee, and defended with remarkable acuteness and ingenuity by Faber in his treatise on ' The Origin of Sacrifice.' The Hebrew word *chattath*, translated " sin " in our authorised version, they propose to translate "*a sin-offering;*" in support of which rendering they urge, among other arguments, that the word *robets*, translated " lieth," properly means the *couching* or *recumbence of an animal*. According to this view the verse may be thus interpreted : " If thou doest well—that is to say, if thou art a perfectly righteous person, needing no atonement for thy sins—then assuredly thy thank-offering of fruits shall be accepted. But if, as thou oughtest to know, thou hast not done well, then must a sacrifice of atonement be presented—and, behold, a sin-offering coucheth at the door, within thy reach, and subject to thy disposal."

There is reason to doubt, however, whether this interpretation, ably as it has been advocated by Faber, is admissible ; for although the Hebrew word *chattath* is often applied to animals offered up in sacrifice, it is never so applied to *animals at large*, however suitable to be used as sacrificial victims, but only to such animals as were *actually set apart* or *devoted to God* in sacrifice. And although the word *robets* undoubtedly describes " the couching or recumbence of an animal," there would be no impropriety in the figurative representation of " sin " as a savage animal, couching at the sinner's door and ready to destroy him.

NOTE I, *page* 364.

DISTINCTION BETWEEN NATURAL AND MORAL LAWS.

It is one of the prevailing errors of the present day—an error into which Dr Young and Mr Robertson of Brighton appear to have fallen—to overlook the distinction between the moral law and those arrangements of the physical world which are com-

APPENDIX.

monly designated "laws of nature." These two kinds of "laws" cannot be ranked under the same category. The "laws of nature" do not, in themselves considered, impose upon us any moral obligation. In so far as they are known, indeed, we are bound to have respect to them; not, however, by reason of any obligation upon our conscience springing from the laws themselves, but by reason of an obligation springing from the moral law, which prescribes *prudence* as a branch of our duties, and requires us so to act with reference to outward objects as to secure our own safety and welfare.

As a proof of the radical difference in this respect between physical laws and moral laws, it may be observed that, in the case of *the former*, we are fully warranted to counteract, as far as we can, the operation of one physical law by availing ourselves of the operation of another; whereas, in the case of *the latter*, we are not warranted to violate one moral obligation with a view to the fulfilment of another. And yet, if the two kinds of "laws" were on the same footing, the man who ascends in a balloon, or sails in an iron ship, so as to counteract the law of gravitation, would be no less truly criminal than the man who violates the law of justice in order to fulfil the claims of charity, commits "pious frauds" in order to advance the cause of religion, or in any other way "does evil that good may come."

Further, if the suffering which ensues on the breach (so to call it) of a law of nature be classed under the same head with the punishment of a moral offence, then must the attempt to remove or alleviate such suffering be denounced as a crime committed against the Supreme Governor, just as it would be an act of rebellion against an earthly governor to rescue a prisoner from custody, or to deliver a condemned criminal from the scaffold. So palpable are the absurdities involved in this identification of moral laws with cosmical arrangements.

For a full illustration of this topic I may refer to the admirable treatise of Dr James Buchanan, entitled 'Faith in God and Modern Atheism Compared,' vol. ii. p. 151-171. And in more especial reference to the Atonement, I cannot refrain from quoting the following clear and able statement of Dr Candlish :—

"Satisfaction is the offering of a compensation, or of an equivalent, for some wrong that has been done. The idea of it is founded on that sense of justice which is inherent and ineradicable in every human bosom. When we see an injury inflicted, resentment rises within us ; and it is not appeased until redress is given to the injured party, and an adequate retribution inflicted on the

NOTES AND ILLUSTRATIONS.   519

wrong-doer. This is an original conviction or instinct of our moral nature. It recognises the necessity of satisfaction when a man breaks the law of equity or honour to his fellow-man. It recognises the necessity of satisfaction also when a man breaks the law of duty to his God. Its appeal is to law. It is not, however, to law as the generalised expression merely of what we observe in the sequence of events and the succession of cause and effect that it appeals; but to law as implying authority and right on the one hand, obligation and responsibility on the other.

"It would be absurd to speak of satisfaction being given for a breach of the so-called law of gravity, by which a heavy body when unsupported falls to the ground; or of the law of heat, by which a finger thrust into the fire is burned; or of any of the laws of health, by which excess breeds disease, and a disordered body makes a disordered mind. Such laws admit of no compensation or equivalent in any case coming instead of the result naturally and necessarily wrought under them. If I fall, I break the law of gravity in one view, for I have not observed with sufficient care the conditions of my safety under it. But, in another view, the law is not broken—it tells upon me, and I take the consequences. There is no wrong here; no injury for which compensation may be made; no breach demanding satisfaction. If all laws were of that nature,—if that were the character of the whole government of God,—the idea of satisfaction would be impossible.

"But once let in the thought of *moral obligation*—let law be the expression of the free-will of a ruler, binding authoritatively the free-will of the subject—let it be the assertion of right and the imposing of duty—then, when a breach of that law occurs, we instinctively feel that satisfaction is due; and to meet the case it must be satisfaction bearing some analogy and proportion, in its nature and amount, to the law that has been broken.

"All this is irrespective of consequences. Apart altogether from the calculation of chances or probabilities as to what evil may result from the wrong, and how that evil may be obviated, the wrong itself is felt to require redress. If the wrong-doer were alone in the universe, we have an instinct which teaches us that there ought to be redress; a righteous instinct which craves for redress, and will not rest content without it. And the redress must be either adequate retribution inflicted on the offender, or some fair equivalent or compensation instead."—*Candlish on the Atonement*, p. 134-136.

520   APPENDIX.

NOTE K, *page* 408.

PROGRESSIVE TEACHING OF THE NEW TESTAMENT.

"Place side by side the first discourse of our Lord in St
Matthew and the last in St John, and it will become apparent
that the personal teaching of our Lord is a *visibly progressive
system*. The Sermon on the Mount at the opening of His
ministry, and the address in the upper room delivered at its
close, are separated from each other, not only by differences of
circumstance and feeling, but as implying on the part of the
hearers wholly different stages in the knowledge of the truth.
There is a wider interval between these two discourses than there
is between the teaching of the Gospels as a whole and that of
the Epistles.

"The first discourse is that of a Minister of the circumcision,
clearing and confirming the divine teaching given to the fathers,
Blessings, laws, and promises are alike founded on the Old
Testament language, which the speaker at the same time adopts
and interprets. He keeps in a line with the past, while He makes
a clear step in advance. He gives, not so much a new code, as
a new edition of the old one. The word of authority, '*I* say
unto you,' is directed not to destroy, but to fulfil. It is the
authority of the original Lawgiver, clearing up His own intentions,
and disallowing the perversions of men.

"As plainly as the first discourse links itself to the past, so
plainly does the last discourse reach on to the future. If the
one reverts to what was said in old time, the other casts the mind
forward on a day of knowledge which is dawning and a new
teacher who is coming. In passing from the one point to the
other, we have left behind us the language and associations of
the Old Testament: we have entered a new world of thought.
and hear a new language which is being created for its exigencies.
What makes the thought and the language new? One single
fact—namely, that the true relation of the Lord Jesus to the
spiritual life of His people is now in a measure revealed. 'Ye
believe in God, *believe also in me:*' this is the key-note of the
whole address. And in the same strain it continues, 'No man
cometh unto the Father but by me;' 'Abide in me, and I in
you;' 'Without me ye can do nothing.' How foreign would
such words have been in the Sermon on the Mount! We are
not unprepared for them here, though even here they mean more

NOTES AND ILLUSTRATIONS. 521

than can be yet understood. I do not speak of single expressions, but of the whole doctrine on faith, and prayer, and love, and service, and hope, and life. All subjects have here assumed their distinctively Christian character: they are '*in Christ Jesus.*' The faith fixes itself on *Him*, and on the Father *through Him.* The prayer is *in His name.* The love is a response to *His* love. The service is the fruit of union with *Him.* The hope is that of being *with Him.* To *abide in Him* is the secret of life, safety, fruitfulness, and joy. And the guiding power of this new state is not the explanation of a law, but the gift of the Holy Ghost, the Comforter. Compare these ideas with those which characterise the first Gospel teaching, and you see how far you have been carried from the point at which you started. You see how much must have intervened in the gradual revelation of Christ, and in the gradual advance of His teaching, before such a stage of doctrine could be reached. And much *had* intervened. To show *how* much, it would be necessary to trace through all the Gospel record the unfolding of the salvation as it began to be spoken by the Lord, and the steps by which it was brought about that the Master and the disciples should become the Saviour and the believers, and that the external hearing and following should pass into the mysterious relations of an inward and spiritual union. . . .

"But here a question arises—not one affecting any single doctrine which some text in this discourse may touch, but one affecting all the doctrine before and after, all that ' began to be spoken by the Lord, and was confirmed to us by them that heard Him.' It is the question, Whether the point which we have reached is *final* or *central*—whether the true teaching of God here reaches a close or effects a transition ? There is no uncertainty in the answer; for to give that answer is one main purpose of the discourse.

"At the first glance it is plain that the character of the discourse is distinctly transitional—that it announces not an *end*, but a *change;* and that, in closing one course of teaching, it at the same time opens another. As the first discourse on the Mount had linked the personal teaching of Christ to the law and the prophets which went before it, so the last discourse links that teaching to the dispensation of the Spirit which is to come after it. The fact on which the first is founded is, that the *law* of God has been given to men as the guide to righteousness : the fact on which the last is founded is, that *Jesus* Himself has now been presented to men as the object of faith. And as

APPENDIX.

it was intimated in the one case that the lesson of righteousness was yet incomplete, and was to be perfected by Jesus Himself, so it is intimated in the other that the lesson of faith is yet incomplete, and is to be perfected by the Holy Ghost whom He will send.

"The narrative is careful to show us that this lesson of faith had been imperfectly *learned*. The auditors are the men whom the Lord had chosen and trained, and who had watched most closely the whole course of His manifestation. Yet, as He proceeds, what do we hear? 'Lord, we know not whither Thou goest, and how can we know the way?' 'Show us the Father, and it sufficeth us.' 'How is it that Thou wilt manifest Thyself unto us, and not unto the world?' 'What is this that He saith? we cannot tell what He saith.' By such voices of faint and partial apprehension, or of sore perplexity, we learn how far the teaching of the past had gone with them, in regard to those truths which were being then set forth.

"But it might be, notwithstanding, that the course of divine instruction *was* complete, and that events yet to come and reflection on the past would be sufficient to open to them its meaning. Not thus does the Lord reply. Mingled with sad reflections that He had been so long time with them, and that yet they have not known Him, He gives the consoling assurance that their instruction in the truth is not yet ended. . . . The teaching which He had given them must close. But another teaching shall be substituted, which shall be also *His*—' showing them the things that are His,' and 'testifying of Him '—though suited to the new relations which He shall bear to them in His glorified state. The Comforter shall come, even the Spirit of truth, which He shall send from the Father. And this Comforter 'shall lead them into all the truth,' not only bringing what Christ had said to their remembrance, but teaching them many other things which he had yet to say to them, but which at present they could not bear. . . .

"We thus see that our Lord's teaching *has not the appearance* of being *final*, and that it *expressly declares* that it is not complete. When it was ended, it was to be followed by a new testimony from God, in order that many things might be spoken which had not been spoken then.

"That testimony came; the things were spoken; and in the apostolic writings we have their enduring record. In those writings we find the fulfilment of an expectation which the Gospels raised, and recognise the performance of a promise which

NOTES AND ILLUSTRATIONS.   523

the Gospels gave. If we do *not*, the word of salvation, which began to be spoken by the Lord, has never been finished for us. Then, not only would the end be wanting, but the beginning would become obscure. The lessons of holiness would still shine in their own pure light, and the rebukes of human error would show in their severe outlines ; but the words which open by anticipation this mystery of the great salvation, flashing sometimes on its deep foundations, sometimes on its lofty summits, would but dazzle and confuse our sight ; and we should be tempted to turn from their discoveries as from visions which had no substance, or from enigmas which we could not interpret.

"And so, in fact, *they* treat the personal teaching of Christ who give not its due honour to the subsequent witness of His Spirit, but regard the apostolic writings as only Petrine, Pauline, or Alexandrian versions of the Christian doctrine,—interesting records of the views of individuals or schools of opinion concerning the salvation of which Jesus began to speak. No! the words of the Lord are not honoured (as these men seem to think) by being thus isolated. For it is an isolation which separates them from other words which also are His own—words given by Him in that day when He no longer spoke in proverbs, but showed His servants plainly of the Father. The brief communications, in which the salvation began to be spoken by the Lord, must lose half their glory if a mist and darkness be cast over that later teaching which was ordained to throw its reflex light upon them."—*Bernard's Bampton Lectures for* 1864, p. 77-87.

NOTE L, *page* 437.

SUITABLENESS OF THE ATONEMENT TO HUMAN WANTS.

"Foremost among those faculties which have survived the Fall, and to the resuscitation of which religion is directed, stands Conscience, or the Moral Faculty, which not only stamps our actions as right or wrong, but by the sense of good and ill desert which accompanies its exercise, actually sentences them to reward or punishment. This faculty, which we cannot help regarding as the authoritative voice of Him who made us, corresponds exactly, in its functions and its judgments, to the moral law delivered on Mount Sinai. The one is the objective, the other the subjective law, whose authority we recognise as different but parallel revela-

524 APPENDIX.

tions of the one true God. And as 'by the deeds of the law shall no flesh be justified,' because none can keep its holy enactments; so by the voice of conscience, taken by itself, shall none escape condemnation. *The Decalogue and the moral faculty are alike a ministration of death to all who hear their voice alone.* And as the law was, by its very severity, a 'schoolmaster to bring us unto Christ,' so the condemning voice of conscience, and the sense of guilt, which is universal in our race, are the common foundation on which the Gospel teaching everywhere rests.

"But the admonitions of conscience no more constitute the whole of our spiritual being than the moral law and its penal sanctions were the whole of the Mosaic code, or of the personal religion of every Israelite. At least coextensive with its judgments is the hope of forgiveness, the conviction that the Lawgiver can pardon as well as punish. This shows itself in the fact, noticed in Thompson's Bampton Lectures, that '*never has the mind of man, driven to construct a worship from its natural resources, invented a religion of despair.*' How is this to be accounted for? Conscience, in and by itself, speaks only of punishment to transgressors. Moreover, it actually generates a craving for punishment in the human heart—a craving which makes us wish to see criminals punished—nay, which (despite of many opposing instincts of our nature that shrink from pain and degradation) makes us crave the punishment of our own sins. *In the terms promulgated by conscience*—however it may generate the fear of punishment, and so the wish to escape from it—*forgiveness is impossible.* But is there no antagonistic principle co-ordinate with it, which, like the expiatory system of the Jewish law, and the promises inherited by the Israelite from his forefathers, drives away despair, and makes mercy to rejoice over judgment? To answer this question philosophically, *we lack such an analysis of our whole spiritual nature as Butler has given us of the moral faculty.* But, without attempting to supply this want, we can point out some general characteristics of human nature which seem to show that the Gospel method of pardon through the Atonement is more in harmony with our nature as a whole, than any other system which has ever been proposed.

"The broad fact, that men left to themselves have 'never invented a religion of despair,' and that all religions presuppose the possibility of forgiveness, and profess to teach the way to attain it, is proof enough that the menaces of conscience, with whatever authority they speak, are not regarded as precluding the hope of pardon. Still there is an evident difficulty in re-

NOTES AND ILLUSTRATIONS. 525

conciling these two parts of our nature—the same difficulty which meets us in determining the diverse and apparently conflicting claims of law and grace. Hence arise two different modes of solving the great problem of religion—how man may have peace with God. The one, unable to reconcile these conflicting authorities, has followed the stronger impulse of human nature—the hope of mercy—and simply ignored the sentence and threats of the judge within the breast. This is the plan of irreligion, which hopes vaguely for pardon, and turns a deaf ear to the whispers of guilt. Such, too, is the method of some systems of religion which would teach us simply to disregard any difficulties which may seem to hinder the assurance of immediate acceptance by God. Such, among heathens, is the system of Buddhism, which teaches man to endeavour to make himself perfect, without sacrifice, or atonement, or any recognition of guilt. Such, among professing Christians, is the teaching of the Socinian, who recognises no obstacles raised by the divine government to the impunity of sinners who repent. Such, too in some measure, is the teaching of certain Anglican divines, who regard the barrier raised by the sense of guilt between man and God as a delusion of the wicked one, which it is the part of true wisdom to disregard.

"Against all these systems, as conflicting with human nature, every sacrifice which has been offered, even in the darkness of heathenism, has borne its testimony. Still more the sacrifices of Judaism, which were offered by God's appointment, bore witness that 'without shedding of blood there was no remission.' But far above these obscurer lights shines the brightness of the cross of Christ, revealing, in characters which cannot be mistaken, the universal law of the divine government—that sin must be either punished or expiated; and that in sacrifice alone the conflicting claims of law and grace—of conscience condemning, and hope acquitting—are harmoniously adjusted. The two opposing impulses of our higher nature find their satisfaction in the Atonement, and in it alone; because it recognises the righteous claims of a violated law, and, at the same time, the boundless mercy of a loving God. Conscience is not blunted or outraged; because the expiation confirms its testimony to the guilt of sin, and the tremendous punishment which it deserved: and yet all our desires of happiness and communion with God are also satisfied by 'the exceeding riches of His grace.' The power of the Atonement lies in its appeal to all the parts of our complex nature which have regard to religion, and not to one or two only; and,

APPENDIX.

in part, to its awakening feelings, which, in our present degraded state, might for ever slumber, did not the power of divine grace and the preaching of the cross wake them from their secret recesses, and make their possessor for the first time conscious of their existence. And these feelings have their source in the very depths of our being—in the *consciousness of sin, the sense of guilt, the fear of punishment, the hope of forgiveness,* as well as in the *intense reciprocation of a perfect love;* and these all twine in one indissoluble chain to draw the penitent to the cross of Christ. In *it* all parts of man's religious nature find their appropriate object, instead of one being satisfied at the expense of another. And thus it happens that we witness in those who 'live by the faith of the Son of God,' that harmony of their inner nature which might have been pronounced impossible prior to our experience of its reality. We see *the sensitiveness of conscience,* the keenness of its perception of demerit, *growing side by side with that triumphant assurance of safety* which makes salvation almost a present possession to the child of God. The opposite parts of his spiritual nature (which, like the Law and the Gospel, seemed at first to rend asunder his very being by their discordant impulses) are found to move in lines steadily converging to that point where, in the glory of a more perfect state, the threats of law and the hopes of pardon shall alike disappear in the light of God's presence, and 'love' shall be 'the fulfilling of the law.'"—*Macdonnell's Donellan Lectures,* p. 207-212.

NOTE M, *Supplementary.*

BUSHNELL ON "FORGIVENESS AND PROPITIATION WITHOUT EXPIATION."

When the printing of this volume was nearly finished, a new work was published by Dr Bushnell, entitled '*Forgiveness and Law, grounded in principles interpreted by Human Analogies,*' and intended to supersede Parts III. and IV. of its author's previous treatise on the 'Vicarious Sacrifice.' We cannot afford space for a full notice of this new work, but must be content with a few remarks on the first chapter, which is headed "*Forgiveness and Propitiation without Expiation.*"

Dr Bushnell begins by stating that "his former treatise was concerned with the work of Christ as *a reconciling power on men,*"

NOTES AND ILLUSTRATIONS. 527

which he then conceived to be the whole import and effect of it ;
.but that he now proposes to regard it as *comprising both the reconciliation of men to God and of God to men.* In doing so, he lays it
down as a "fundamental principle that there is a grand analogy
or almost identity between our moral nature and that of God, so
that our moral pathologies and His exactly answer to each other."
This analogy he holds to extend to the granting of forgiveness
as well as to other matters. "Forgiveness by God," he says,
"and forgiveness by man, have a common property ; they match
and interpret one another, and require the same preparations and
conditions. . . . In human forgiveness there are real
difficulties encountered by the best men. A good man lives
under the sway of universal love to his kind. But will he launch
an absolute forgiveness on any one who has done him a bitter
injury? If he were nothing but love he might do so. But he
has other sentiments that come into play alongside of love,—
such as the sense of being hurt by wrong, indignation at wrong
done to others, disgust at what is loathsome, contempt of lies,
&c. ; and these animosities or revulsions of feeling fasten their
grip on the malefactor's sins, and refuse to let go. . . . Hence
we may learn how it is that the forgivenesses of good men often
miscarry. They meant to forgive, and to make clean work of
it. But their old animosities are rekindled,—their old disgusts
come back upon them. The difficulty often is that the forgiven
party has never been so qualified by grace that he could be fitly
forgiven. But in most cases the true account of the matter is,
that *the forgiving party did not find how to be fitly propitiated,* and
was not in such a state of preparation as his own moral nature
and necessities demanded."

How the forgiving party is to be "fitly propitiated" Dr Bushnell then explains as follows: "Two things are necessary, of
which *the first* is, such a sympathy with the offender as amounts
to virtual identification—so that we can feel the man all through,
and search out his good and evil, and find what may be best
touched or taken hold of so as to make him a friend. . . . But
there is *another indispensable requisite ;* and that is *a making cost
for the wrong-doer by suffering or expense, or by sacrifice and labour.*"
"The injured party has a most powerful combination of alienated
sentiments struggling in his nature. His integrity is hurt, his
holiness is offended, his moral taste disgusted. How is it, then,
that these dissentient feelings which obstruct his forgivenesses
are to be propitiated? Simply," replies Bushnell, "by the
aggrieved party *making cost for the wrong-doer, or bearing for him*

528   APPENDIX.

heavy burdens of painstaking and sorrow. . . . Human for·
giveness," he says, "can be consummated only by the help of
some placation or cost-making sacrifice. The man who will truly
forgive must take some *alterative* that can liquefy the indiffer-
ences, or assuage the stern displeasures of his morally injured
and morally revolted nature. . . . He must somehow atone
both himself and his enemy by a *painstaking* (rightly so called)
that has power to recast the terms of their relationship."

In illustration of this second requisite, Dr Bushnell endeavours
to show by a variety of instances "how our own moral nature,
when it has become alienated from wrong-doers, tones itself into
a completely forgiving state only by acts of cost or sacrifice, which
are, in proper verity, propitiations of itself." And then he insists
that there is in this respect "an analogy between our moral nature
and all other moral natures, even the highest," from which analogy
he holds that "we may find our way to a true understanding of
the Christian propitiation." "God," he says, "is put in arms
against wrong-doers, just as we are, by His moral disgusts, dis·
pleasures, indignations, &c." And the mediatorial work and
sufferings of His Son are *a self-propitiating process* on the part
of God, wherein, by incurring cost, and enduring labour and
sacrifice for sinners, the divine nature, after the analogy of the
human nature, "tones itself into a perfectly forgiving state," and
"masters those antagonistic sentiments which would obstruct it
in bestowing forgivenesses."

It thus appears that Dr Bushnell has to some extent modified
his former opinions. He no longer holds that the Saviour's
mediation was designed only to reclaim sinners from their enmity
against God, but admits that it was also designed *to propitiate
God towards sinners.* His theory, however, widely differs, even
when thus modified, from what we have found to be the Scriptural doctrine. For, on the one hand, it represents the obstacles
to reconciliation on the part of God as arising—not from the
character sustained by Him as the righteous Lawgiver and Moral
Governor who requires an expiation of sin in order to the pardon
of it—but from certain "disgusts," "animosities," and "revulsions of feeling," by which "God is put in arms, just as men are,
against wrong-doers," and which "hinder Him in the bestowing
of forgivenesses." And, on the other hand, the propitiatory virtue
of the work of Christ is held to consist—not in any expiation of
human guilt or satisfaction to divine justice that is rendered by
it—but simply in *the mighty cost involved in it of labour, suffering,
and sacrifice* for sinners, whereby, in the case of God just as in

NOTES AND ILLUSTRATIONS. 529

the case of men, those "recalcitrant sentiments," which would check the exercise of forgiveness, are counteracted.

That this theory is indefensible on Scriptural grounds we deem it quite unnecessary now to argue, after the full exposition of the Scriptural doctrine which has in the preceding pages been already given. It may be proper, however, shortly to consider, whether it has any just claim to our acceptance on tne ground on which it is mainly advocated by Dr Bushnell, "*as resting on principles that may be interpreted by human analogies,*" and as thereby supplying a *more reasonable explanation* of our Lord's sufferings than is furnished by the commonly received doctrine of the Atonement.

Dr Bushnell's position is, that just as man overcomes those disgusts, animosities, and revulsions of feeling which tend to stifle his forgiveness of wrong-doers, by making cost for them, bearing burdens, or undergoing labours, perils, and sacrifices for them,—so does God propitiate Himself, or quell those adverse sentiments which put Him in arms against sinners, by the cost He incurs and the sacrifice He makes for them through the humiliation and sufferings of His incarnate Son.

But here the question occurs, Can it be truly affirmed that those antagonistic feelings, by which men are impeded in the forgiveness of wrong-doers, are overcome in the manner thus alleged? When a good man finds himself "alienated from those who have wronged him, by the whole instincts of his moral nature," is it really the case that these instincts are overborne, so as no longer to prevent his hearty and thorough forgiveness of the offenders, by the labours, dangers, sufferings, and sacrifices to which he willingly subjects himself in their behalf? We cannot at all admit the truth of this representation. Rather should we say that the voluntary endurance of such things by an aggrieved party in behalf of those who had greatly wronged him,—instead of being a means of counteracting any adverse feelings which would hinder his forgiveness of them,—*would be the clearest proof that all adverse feelings must on his part have been thoroughly overcome*, BEFORE any such tokens, not of forgiveness merely, but of ardent and self-sacrificing love, could have been afforded by him.

In saying so, we may confidently appeal to the first, and certainly the strongest instance adduced by Dr Bushnell in illustration of his theory; namely, that of the merchant who had been wellnigh ruined by the base treachery of his partner in business, and who, when the wrong-doer and his family are reduced to the lowest depths of poverty, and smitten with some pestilential and deadly disease, is ready, not only to expose himself to toilsome exertion and costly outlay in their behalf, but even to endanger health and life by personally ministering to them. Surely no one would think it reasonable to say respecting such a benefactor, that "by the painstaking exertions he has made, and the costs he has incurred, and the perils he has braved for one who had sorely injured him, he has at length succeeded in quelling those resentful feelings which made it so hard for him heartily to forgive the wrong!" For it is most evident that all his resentful feelings must in the first place have been thoroughly subdued, *before* any such acts of generous devotedness—*far exceeding aught that is implied in mere forgiveness*—could have been performed by him. Hard as it may occasionally be, even for the best of men, to pardon a grievous injury, it is harder still to bear heavy burdens, to brave deadly perils, and to make costly sacrifices, for him by whom the injury has been inflicted. And we may be very sure that any adverse feelings which might keep back the aggrieved party *from that which is the easier course*, will much more powerfully withhold him *from that which is the more arduous*. In short, there is nothing that seems to be more unreasonable, or more opposed to all our experience of human conduct, than Bushnell's assertion respecting "our moral nature when alienated and averted from those who have done us wrong," that "it tones itself into a completely forgiving state only by acts of cost and sacrifice which are, in proper verity, propitiations of itself." We venture to say that such acts of cost and sacrifice never will be performed to one who has greatly wronged us until we have first of all heartily forgiven him; and that instead of being the necessary means of conciliating our hostile and resentful feelings, they are to be regarded as the surest evidences and most substantial fruits of conciliation already accomplished.

Thus does it appear that in human acts of forgiveness there is nothing in the least degree analogous to the view which Dr Bushnell takes of the Atonement, as a costly means, not of expiating human guilt and satisfying divine justice, but of counteracting certain adverse feelings on the part of God, which would otherwise restrain Him from the pardon of transgressors. Such being the case, the theory in question—apart from other strong objections that might be brought against it—is utterly destitute of that claim to our acceptance which its author specially pleads in its behalf—namely, that "it rests on principles which may be interpreted by human analogies," and thereby enables us more intelligently to apprehend, and more reasonably to explain, the Christian propitiation.

INDEX OF SUBJECTS AND AUTHORS REFERRED TO.

Abel, his sacrifice—a blood-offering, 273-282
...... his faith, . . . 274-278
...... evidence of divine institution of sacrifice, . . . 276-282
Adam, parallel between, and Christ, 91, 150
Alford on Christ's miraculous cures, 40
.... Colossians, ii. 14, . 126
.... 2 Cor. v. 20, . 75
.........'s theory of Atonement, 311-317
Animal sacrifices, universal, . 266
.... kinds of, . 220
.... piacular, 223, 267
.... divinely instituted, 276
(See Sacrifice.)
Ἀντί used to denote substitution, 20, 21
Arian theory of Atonement, 299-302
Arminian view of purpose of Atonement, ... 514
"Atone," to (Kaphar, ἱλάσκεσθαι), 226
Atonement, central truth of the Christian revelation, . . 1
.... N. T. doctrine of (see Part I.)
.... Scriptural doctrine of, summarised, . . . 176-202
.... O. T. confirms doctrine of (see Part II.)
.... subject of prophecy, 205-215
.... typified by Levitical sacrifices, . . . 254-264
.... confirmed by patriarchal sacrifices, ... 283
.... its relation to divine justice, . . . 181-187, 440-444
.... its relation to love of God, . . . 158, 192, 295, 448
.... its relation to the law, 474-484
.... its efficacy and sufficiency, . . 117, 121, 146, 196
.... its special reference and Gospel invitations, . 201, 510-516
.... its suitableness to human wants, ... 523
.... rationale of, rests with God, ... 472
.... theories of (see Contents of Part III.)

Atonement, objections to doctrine of (see Contents of Part IV.)
.... as taught by Christ, 409-418
.... its necessity, . 421-439
.... consistent with God's perfections, . . . 440-455
.... does not involve injustice, ... 440-444
.... nor a transfer of moral character, . . . 444-446
.... consistent with God's mercy, ... 447-449
.... consistent with free pardon, ... 450-452
.... does not suppose a principle above God, . . . 454
.... its mysteriousness, 14-16, 456-472
.... its practical tendency, 473-489
(See Death of Christ, Sufferings of Christ.)
.... day of, . . 225, 249

Bähr, his objection to expiatory nature of Levitical sacrifices, 229-233
...... his theory of their non-expiatory nature, . . . 234-238
Balmer on death of Christ, . 185
Baur, F. C., on Paul's doctrine of substitution, ... 496
Benefits of Atonement freely offered to all, ... 200
Bernard, St, on Christ's active and passive obedience, . . . 90
Bernard (Bamp. Lect.) on progressive teaching of N. T., . 520-524
Blackstone on punishment, . 383
Bloomfield on καταλλάσσεσθαι, 500
'Brit. Quart. Review' quoted, . 99
Burnt-offering, the, piacular, . 221
Bushnell, his interpretation of Matt. viii. 17, ... 38
.... on pagan sacrifices, . 106
.... his objection to Mosaic sacrifices being expiatory, . 226
.... his theory of the Atonement, ... 371-379
.... on forgiveness and propitiation without expiation, . 526

INDEX OF SUBJECTS AND

Cain, his sacrifice, . . 273, 274
...... God's remonstrance with, 277, 517
Calls of Gospel (*see* Invitations).
Campbell, his theory of the Atonement, ... 329-345
Candlish on the idea of satisfaction, 518
Christ, His divinity and incarnation
assumed, ... 2
.... not a mere Teacher, but a
Saviour, ... 4, 176
.... purpose of His ministry, 405
.... a sin-bearer, . . . 33-41
.... His sinlessness, . . 40
.... His sufferings (*see* Sufferings).
.... "made sin," . . . 42
.... "made a curse for us," . 43
.... "takes away sin," . . 47
.... "puts away sin," . . 48
.... saves from penalties of sin, 53
.... our Deliverer from wrath, 55
.... a propitiation for sin, . 78
.... a Priest, ... 84
.... "our Passover," . . 96
.... delivers from Satan, . 123
.... relation of His divine and
human nature to atonement, 462-465
.... His state of mind in relation
to His sufferings, . . 130-139
.... His alleged silence as to
atonement, . . . 404-420
.... His teaching progressive, 407, 520
(*See* Death, Mission, Sufferings of
Christ.)
Confession of Faith quoted, 200, 484
Covenant of grace, relation to sufferings of Christ, . 148-150
.... does not solve
mystery of atonement, . 151, 466
Cross, Christ's desertion on, . 136
Cunningham on the penal character
of Christ's sufferings, . . 191
.... on the rectoral theory, 391
Curse, Christ made a, . . 43
.... of the law, redemption from, 54

Daniel, his prophecy of the seventy
weeks, ... 213
Death of Christ, its prominence in
His history, ... 10
.... peculiarity of com-
memorating, . . . 13
.... vicarious, 43, 177
.... expiatory, 51, 102, 176
.... how regarded by
Christ Himself, . 12, 130-139
.... ground of justification, ... 56
.... of reconciliation, ... 65
.... a sacrifice, 96, 176
.... a satisfaction to
divine justice, . . . 181
.... its sanctifying
power, ... 166
(*See* Sufferings of Christ.)
Debt, Christ's death payment of a, 61
Debt, sins are figuratively a, . 429
διά, ... 27

Divinity of Christ assumed, . 2
.... relation to His
sufferings, . . . 350
.... relation to atonement, ... 462

Eadie on redemption and expia-
tion, ... 127
Efficacy of Christ's work,
117, 121, 146, 196
ἐλπίζω, use in N. T., . . 506
Eternal life (*see* Life).
Ewing's, Bishop, 'Present - Day
Papers,' views as to necessity of
atonement, ... 430
Example, theory of Christ's suffer-
ings as an, ... 291
Exemplary, Christ's sufferings are,
161-165
Expiatory sacrifice (*see* Sacrifice).

Fairbairn on the burnt-offering, 222
.... on Keil's theory, . 243
Faith, its fiducial nature, . 144, 501
.... obtains benefits of redemption, ... 143
.... bond of believers with Christ, 308
.... of Abel, ... 274
Fatherhood of God consistent with
atonement, ... 422
"Fathers, the," their view of the
price of redemption, . . 62
Figurative language, how used in
Scripture, . . . 66, 426
Forgiveness (*see* Pardon).
'Fragments of Truth,' advocates
theory of sympathy, . . 330

Gethsemane, agony in, . . 133
God is reconciled to man, . . 65-77
...... Author of scheme of grace, 67
...... His agency in Christ's suffer-
ings, . . . 16, 358-362
...... not *made* placable by atone-
ment, ... 447
...... His perfections consistent with
atonement, . . . 440-455
...... wrath of (*see* Wrath).
...... justice of (*see* Justice).
Goodsir, Rev. J. T., his strictures on
the author's view of justification, 497
Gospel calls, . . 140, 510
Governmental theory (*see* Rectoral).
Greg on necessity of the Atone-
ment, ... 430
Greyson's correspondence quoted, 292
Grotius, originator of rectoral theory, 380

Hall, Robert, on the indemnification of Christ, . . . 463
Heathen sacrifices, their origin, 267
.... their expiatory
character, . . 106, 267
.... terms denoting,
applied to Christ, . . 102, 107
Hengstenberg on the Passover, 500
Hill on redemption as implying "a
price," 63

AUTHORS REFERRED TO. 533

Hill on the term "satisfaction," 182
...... on Middle or Arian theory, 299-301
Hodge on Rom. v. 10, . . 72
.... on the rectoral theory, . 391
.... on the doctrine of imputation, 446
.... on the sufficiency of the
Atonement, ... 513
Hoffman on 1 Peter, 18-21, . 98
.... his non-expiatory theory
of Levitical sacrifices, . . 238
Horsley on relation of Christ's resurrection to his atonement, . 27

Identification, theory of, . . 327-347
Ἱλασμός, ... 78
Ἱλαστήριον (Rom. iii. 25), . . 80
Imputation of sin, its meaning, 188, 444
.... how applied to
Christ, ... 188-190
Incarnation of Christ here assumed, 2
.... relation to
His sympathy, . . . 331
.... does not
solve the mystery of atonement, 465
Indemnification of Christ, . . 463
Induction, method of discussion
preferred, ... 3
.... vindicated, 4-5
Intercession of Christ founded on
His sacrifice, ... 114-117
.... its priestly
character, ... 115
Invitations of the Gospel free and
universal, ... 200
.... relation to
Christ's mediation, . . 140-143
.... relation to
special reference of atonement, 510-516
Isaac, sacrifice of, . . . 270
Isaiah, his prophecies of Christ's
sufferings, ... 209-212

Jacob, sacrifices of, . . . 270
Jerram on forgiveness and atonement, ... 419
Job, sacrifices of, . . . 269
Josephus's Antiquities quoted, 71
Jowett on heathen and Jewish
sacrifices, ... 108
.... his allegation that sacrificial terms applied to Christ are
figurative, ... 109-113
.... his objections to typical reference of Levitical sacrifices, 254-257
.... on the rectoral theory, . 392
.... his objections to the Atonement from Christ's alleged
silence, ... 404-420
Justification, a forensic act, . 57
.... ascribed to the death
of Christ, ... 56-60
.... obedience of Christ, . . . 58
.... subjective by sympathy
with righteousness of Christ untenable, ... 345-347
Justice of God, Christ's death a
satisfaction to, . . . 181-187

Justice of God, "rectoral" and
"absolute," not distinct, . 385
.... the Atonement does not derogate from, . . 440

Καταλλαγή and καταλλάσσεσθαι, Trench
on, ... 499
.... Bloomf. .ld on, . . 500
Keil, his theory of the Levitical
sacrifices, ... 242-243
Kurtz on the slaying of the sacrificial victim, ... 229
.... on scape-goat, . . 226

" Lamb of God," a sacrificial title, 46
Law, the, redemption from curse of, 54
.... relation of the Atonement to, ... 474-485
Laws, natural and moral, 351, 431, 517
.... spiritual, not " self-acting,"
362-366
Levitical sacrifices, their divine institution, ... 217-219
.... vicarious and
expiatory, . . 103-106, 220-226
.... objections to
expiatory character of, . . 226-233
.... their efficacy,
104, 105, 246-254
.... types of the
sacrifice of Christ, ; . . 254-264
.... theories of their
non-expiatory nature, . . 234-245
.... compared with
death of Christ, . 41, 111, 112, 258
.... confirmatory of
the doctrine of Atonement, 253-264
(See Day of Atonement, Burnt-
offering, Sin-offering, Trespass-
offering, Peace-offering.)
" Life eternal " obtained through
mediation of Christ, . . 127-129
.... its meaning in N. T., 129
Litton's Bampton Lectures on utility of Levitical sacrifices as symbolical methods of worship and
of instruction, ... 256
.... on origin of heathen sacrifices, . . 266
Lord's Supper, remarkable as com-
memorating death of Christ, . 13
.... sacrificial reference of, 49
.... a special testimony
of Christ to the Atonement, . 412
Love of God displayed in Christ's
mission, ... 9
.... the origin, not the
consequence, of the Atonement, 192-194
.... manifested in the
Atonement, . . . 158-161, 447
.... theory of Atonement
solely as a manifestation of, 294-299
.... not manifested by
death of Christ unless expiatory,
159, 295, 367

Macdonnell on substitution and representation, ... 94

INDEX OF SUBJECTS AND

Macdonnell on words of institution of Lord's Supper, . . . 51
.... on suitableness of Atonement to human wants, . 523
Magee on Isaiah, liii. 11, . . 36
.... the penal character of Christ's sufferings, . . . 190
Manifestation of divine character, theory of Atonement as a, . 293
.... of love of God (*see* Love of God).
Martin, Rev. Hugh, on Christ's active obedience, . . . 90
.... on the theory of F. W. Robertson, . . 355
Martineau on the rectoral theory, 392
.... his objection to the doctrine of Atonement, . . 444
Martyr, Christ a, . . . 287
Martyrdom, theory of Atonement as a, ... 287-288
Maurice on the sense of ἱλασμός and ἱλαστήριον, ... 107
.... his realistic theory, . 303
.... his theory of self-sacrifice, 318-326
.... his theory of sympathy, 327
.... his objection to the necessity of atonement, . . . 427
Mediation of Christ obtains eternal life, ... 127-129
.... its relation to invitations of Gospel, . 140-143
.... its benefits obtained by faith, . . 143-147
.... secures sanctification, ... 194
Mercy of God consistent with atonement, ... 160
Method, inductive, preferred to dogmatic, ... 3
Middle theory of the Atonement, 299-302
Mission of Christ, its importance and prominence, . . . 7, 171
.... its purpose to *make* rather than *preach* the Atonement, . . . 405
.... a display of God's love, ... 9
Moral power of catholic doctrine of Atonement, . . . 377-379
Mysteriousness of the Atonement no ground of objection to the doctrine, . . . 456-472

Necessity of the Atonement, 421-439
Noah, sacrifices of, . . . 271

Obedience of Christ ground of justification, . . . 58
.... active and passive, ... 59, 90
.... relation of, active to the Atonement, . 59, 60
Objections to the doctrine of Atonement (*see* Contents of Part IV.)
Obstacles on part of God to reconciliation, . . . 67, 68

Obstacles on part of God to forgiveness, ... 425
Offers of the Gospel (*see* Invitations).
Owen on the doctrine of imputation, 445
.... on the sufficiency of the Atonement, . . . 513

Paley on punishment, . . 383
Parables, their teaching in relation to the Atonement. . . 417
Pardon, relation to atonement, . 420
.... obstacles on part of God to, 425
.... by free grace consistent with atonement, . . 450-452
"Passio inchoata," . . . 132
Passover, Christ our, . . 96
.... a sacrifice, . . 97
.... a sin-offering, . 500
Patriarchal sacrifices, institution of, ... 265-282
.... confirm doctrine of Atonement, . . 283
Peace offering, piacular, . . 222
Penal, Christ's sufferings, . 190
Penalties of sin, relation to sin, 429-433
.... Christ saves from, 53 433
Περὶ ἁμαρτιῶν, ... 29
Pharisee and Publican, parable of, in relation to atonement, . 78-418
'Philosophy of Evangelicism,' advocates theory of sympathy, 328, 345
Piacular Levitical sacrifices, 103-106, 220-225
.... pagan sacrifices, . 106, 267
Πίστις, πιστεύω, ... 501-510
Playfair's Huttonian theory quoted, 4, 5
Presumptuous sins, no sacrifice for, 247
Price, Christ's sufferings a, . 60-63
.... the figure overstrained by Fathers, ... 62
Priest, Christ a, . . . 84-90
.... What is a priest? . 86
Priesthood of Christ inseparable from His sacrifice, . . 87
.... real and not figurative, . . . 89
.... more excellent than Levitical, . . 89
.... implies representation, ... 91
Priestley, his view of the Passover, 96
.... holds that Levitical sacrifices not vicarious, . . . 231
Prodigal son, parable of, in relation to atonement, . . 417
Prophecies in O. T. of Christ's sufferings, ... 205-216
Propitiation, Christ a, . 78-83
Propitiatory, Christ's sufferings, 78, 83, 112, 113
.... Levitical sacrifices, 103, 220, 226
Psalms, prophetic of Christ's sufferings, ... 206-209
Punishment, purpose of, . 383-384
.... divine retributive, . 384
Purchase, results of Christ's sufferings a, ... 60

AUTHORS REFERRED TO. 535

Purchase of redemption, and its application, ... 122
Purpose of Christ's sufferings, 17, 201 (*See* Reference.)

Ransom, Christ's sufferings a, . 60-64
Rationale of the Atonement concerns God, ... 472
Realistic theory of the Atonement, Maurice's, . . . 303-311
.... Alford's, . . 311-317
Reconciliation of God to man, 65-77, 179
Rectoral theory of the Atonement, 380-394
Redemption from the curse of the law, ... 54
.... by death of Christ, 60-64, 180
.... implies expiation, . 98
.... not wholly subjective, 362, 371
Reference, special, of the Atonement and Gospel invitations, 510-516
Remission of sins ascribed to death of Christ, ... 46
.... Christ's blood shed for, ... 50
Repentance, nature of, . . 339
.... not attributable to Christ, ... 336-340
............,... alleged sufficiency of, without atonement, . . 433
Representation, ground of substitution, ... 93, 94
Representative, Christ a, . 91-95
Resentment, personal, distinguished from judicial indignation in God, 67, 425-427
Resurrection, theory of Christ's death as subservient to His, 289-291
.... of Christ shows that His sacrifice accepted, . . 27, 290
Retribution, sin and natural, 363-365, 411
Rewards to Christian obedience not excluded by the Atonement, 484-488
Rigg on the nature of symbols, . 245
Robertson, Rev. F. W., his theory of the Atonement, . . 348-356
.... on God's anger, 437
.... on the righteous vengeance of God, . . 437

Sacrifice, divine institution of, 278-282
.... universality of, . 101, 266
.... death of Christ a, 50, 96-113
.... of Christ inseparable from His priesthood, . . . 87
.... when presented, 88
.... foundation of His intercession, ... 116
.... its unfailing efficacy, . . . 117, 196-200
.... offered by God Himself, ... 193
.... compared with Levitical sacrifices, . 41, 111, 258
.... expiatory, 50, 367 (*See* Death.)

Sacrifices, Levitical (*see* Levitical).
.... patriarchal (*see* Patriarchal).
Sacrificial language borrowed from heathen ritual, . 102, 107, 108
.... applied to Christ not figurative . 109, 111, 176
....not accommodated to Jewish customs, . 263
Salvation not wholly subjective, 362, 371
Sanctification, relation to sufferings of Christ, . . 165-170, 194-196
Satan, Christ delivers from dominion of, . . . 123-127
.... price of redemption not paid to, 63
Satisfaction, theological sense of the term, ... 181-187
.... pecuniary and penal, distinguished, . . . 451
.... death of Christ a, 181-187
.... required by God, . 427
.... provided by God, 449, 452
Self-sacrifice, Christ's death an act of, ... 131, 319
.... Maurice's theory of Christ's, . . . 318-326
.... how far dutiful, 319, 320
.... Young's theory of Christ's, ... 366
Silence of Christ respecting the Atonement alleged, . 404-420
Sin, Christ made, . . . 42-45
...... remission of, . . . 46-50
...... "to bear sin," . . . 33-42
...... "to take away sin," . . 47
...... "putting away sin," . . 48
...... deliverance from penal consequences of, ... 53
Sin-bearer, Christ a, . . . 33-42
.... Christ's agony as a, . 135
Sinlessness of Christ in relation to His sympathy, . . 40, 331
Sin-offering, death of Christ a, . 96
.... piacular, . 79, 220
.... institution of, . . 278
.... prevalent among Gentiles, ... 101
Socinian theories of Atonement, 287-292
Spirit, Holy, mediation of Christ procures the, . . 117-122
Spiritual laws not self-acting, 362-366
Stead, Christ suffered in our, . 20-26
Stuart on Psalm xl. 6-8, . . 207
Substitution grounded on representation, ... 93, 94
.... Christ as our substitute, . . 20-26, 177, 495
.... explains Christ's desertion on cross, . . . 138
.... defective analogies to Christ's, ... 457-459
.... specialties in our Lord's, 460-464
Sufferings of Christ exceptional and unique, ... 14
.... not explained on personal grounds, . 15, 442,
.... essential to His mission, . . . 15, 45, 325

INDEX OF SUBJECTS, ETC.

Sufferings of Christ, God's agency
in, ... 16, 136, 359
.... mysterious, 16
.... their purpose,
17, 201
(*See* Reference.)
.... caused by "our
sins," 26
.... vicarious, 43-45, 177
.... ground of reconciliation, ... 65
.................,.......... official, . 89
.... union of action
and passion in, . . . 89
.... sacrificial, 96, 176
.... connected with
His intercession, . . . 114
.... voluntary,
130, 131, 440
.... propitiatory,
78-83, 113
.... expiatory, 108, 367
.... state of Christ's
mind in anticipating and enduring His sufferings, . 130-139
.... bodily, on cross, 136
.... spiritual, . 137
.... relation to covenant of grace, . . 148-151
.... manifestation
of love of God, . 158-160
.... exemplary, 161-165
.... penal, 190-192
.... secure justification and sanctification, 195
.... prophesied in
O. T., ... 199-210
.... typified by
Levitical sacrifices, . 254-264
.... relation to salvation, ... 457
.... not inevitable
apart from atonement, . . 350
.... not expressive of self - sacrificing love
unless expiatory, . . 367-370
.... not wholly sympathetic, ... 332
.... theories devised to explain (*see* Contents
of Part III.) (*See* Death of
Christ.)
Sufficiency of the Atonement for all
sinners, ... 513
Surety, Christ a, . . . 93
Sympathy, theory of, as an explanation of the Atonement, . 327-347

Teaching of Christ in the N. T.
progressive, . . . 407, 520
Testament, O. and N., in harmony
on the Atonement, . . 264
Theories of non-piacular nature of
Levitical sacrifices, . 234-245
.... the Atonement (*see* Part IV.)

.... the Atonement, general
remarks on, . . . 395-401

Trench on the voluntariness of
Christ's sufferings, . . . 441
.... καταλλαγή and καταλλάσ-
σεσθαί, ... 499
Trespass-offering, piacular, . 221
Turretine on the wrath and mercy
of God, ... 68
Types, the Levitical sacrifices are,
254-264

Union of believers with Christ, 152, 153
.... con-
tributes to solve mystery of atonement, . . 153, 154, 467-471
.... con-
firms the *fact* of our Lord's substitution, . . . 154, 157
ὑπὲρ used in Scripture to denote
substitution, . . . 21-25
.. ... used in classics to denote substitution, ... 493
...... Pauline use of, expounded by
Baur, ... 496
...... Tischendorf on, . . 495

Vengeance of God, . 426, 437, 448
Vicarious, Christ's sufferings were, 43, 177
.... action, notion of, 93
.... sacrifice, how expressed,
102, 103
Victim slain by offerer, . 229

Wardlaw on the rectoral theory, 381
.... on the principle of atonement, ... 438
.... on the harmony of the
divine attributes, . . 453
.... on "coming to Christ,"
&c., ... 506
Will, God's decretive and revealed, 202
Will-worship, relation of Abel's sacrifice to, ... 280
Woods on Christ "dying for our
sins," 30
Work of Christ, its completeness
and efficacy, . . . 146
(*See* Sufferings of Christ.).
Works in relation to faith, . 479
World, prince of this, . 123, 124
Wrath of God real, . . 426
.... judicial and not personal, ... 448, 449

Young on the expiatory nature of
pagan sacrifices, . . . 106
.... his objection to expiatory
nature of Levitical sacrifices, . 226
.... on Solomon's prayer, . 229
.... his theory that Levitical sacrifices were non-expiatory, 243, 244
.... his theory of the Atonement, . . , 357-371
.... his objection to necessity of
the Atonement, . . . 430

Zechariah, his prophecy of the
smitten Shepherd. . . . 214

INDEX OF TEXTS

SPECIALLY REFERRED TO OR ILLUSTRATED.

			PAGE				PAGE
Genesis,	iii. 15,	.	205	*Matthew,*	xx. 28, .	.	20, 90
"	iv. 3-5,	.	273	"	xxvi. 28,	14, 49,	261, 412
"	iv. 6, 7,	276,	517	"	xxvi. 36-44,	.	133, 321
"	vii. 2, .	.	271	"	xxvii. 46, .	.	136
"	viii. 20,	.	271	*Mark,*	iv. 10, .	.	502
"	viii. 21,	.	272	"	x. 45, .	.	20
"	ix. 3, 4,	.	272	"	xiv. 27, .	.	214
Exodus,	viii. 25-27,	.	218	*Luke,*	xii. 50, .	.	131
Leviticus,	i. 4, .	.	224	"	xv. 20-24,	.	417
"	iv. 26,	.	238	"	xviii. 13, .	78,	418
"	xvi.	.	225	"	xxii. 19, 20,	.	19, 412
"	xvi. 20-22,	.	249	"	xxiv. 44-47,	.	416
"	xvii. 11, {	224,	235 - 238	*John,*	i. 29, .	.	46-48
			240, 272	"	iii. 14-17,	.	53
I *Samuel,*	xxix. 4, .	.	70	"	iii. 16, .	.	158
Job,	i. 5, .	.	269	"	v. 40, .	.	507
"	xlii. 7, 8,	68,	269	"	vi. 38-40,	.	148
Psalms,	xxii.	.	206	"	vii. 39, .	.	118
"	xl. 6-8,	.	206	"	x. 17, 18,	.	130
"	cx.	.	208	"	xii. 27, .	.	132
"	cx. 1, 4,	.	84	"	xii. 31, 32,	116,	123
Isaiah,	liii.	.	209	"	xiv. 8, .	.	293
"	liii. 4,	.	38	"	xvi. 7, .	.	119
"	liii. 6, 11, 12,	.	33	*Acts,*	ii. 33, .	.	119
"	liii. 11, .	35,	56	"	xvi. 31, .	505,	506
Daniel,	ix. 20-27,	.	212	"	xxvi. 22, 23,	.	260
Zechariah,	xii. 10,	.	215	*Romans,*	iii. 25, .	.	80-82
"	xiii. 7, .	.	214	"	iii. 25, 26,	.	390
Matthew,	iii. 11,	.	117	"	iii. 31, .	.	473
"	v. 23, 24,	69,	75	"	iv. 25, .	26,	27
"	vi. 30,	.	502	"	v. 6-8, .	.	23
"	viii. 17,	38,	211	"	v. 8, .	158,	493
"	xiv. 31,	.	502	"	v. 10, .	.	71
"	xv. 21-28,	.	502	"	v. 11, .	73,	179
"	xvi. 23, .	.	130	"	v. 12, 18, 19,	91,	150
"	xviii. 23-35,	.	417	"	v. 18, .	57,	58

538   INDEX OF TEXTS.

		PAGE
Romans,	viii. 1, 3, 4,	29, 54
1 Corinthians,	i. 13, .	22, 26
"	v. 7, . .	96
"	vi. 19, .	60, 475
"	xi. 23, . .	29
"	xv. 3, . .	28
"	xv. 17, .	28, 290
"	xv. 20-22,	91, 150
"	xv. 45-49,	91, 150
2 Corinthians,	v. 14, .	23, 156
"	v. 15, 23,	166, 496
"	v. 18, 19, .	74
"	v. 20, . .	75
"	v. 21, . .	42
Galatians,	i. 4,	29, 31, 166
"	i. 16, . .	306
"	ii. 20, {	20, 92 / 152, 156
"	iii. 13, {	24, 42, 60 / 371
"	iii. 13, 14, .	120
"	iv. 4, 5, .	60
Ephesians,	i. 3-11, . .	149
"	ii. 16, . .	76
"	v. 2. . .	97
"	v. 25-32, {	152, 156 / 166, 195
Philippians,	ii. 6-8, . .	322
"	ii. 9-10, . .	115
Colossians,	i. 21, 22, .	76
"	ii. 14, 15, .	126
1 Thessalonians,	v. 9, 10, .	55

		PAGE
1 Timothy,	ii. 6, . .	21
Titus,	iii. 5, 6, . .	120
Philemon,	13, . .	22
"	18, 19, .	189
Hebrews,	ii. 14, 15,	124, 205
"	v. 1, . .	86
"	ix. . .	262
"	ix. 12, . .	87
"	ix. 12-14, .	105
"	ix. 22-26, .	105
"	ix. 28, . 33,	35, 37
"	x. . .	262
"	x. 11-14, .	101
"	x. 12, .	26, 28
"	xi. 1, . .	277
"	xi. 4, . .	274
"	xii. 1-3, . .	161
James,	ii. 19, . .	503
1 Peter,	i. 18-21, .	98
"	ii. 20-24, .	162
"	iii. 17, 18, .	163
"	iii. 18, .	24, 29
1 John,	i. 7, . .	51
"	ii. 2, . .	78
"	iii. 8, .	123, 205
"	iii. 12, . .	274
"	iv. 10, .	78, 158
Revelation,	i. 5, 6, .	53, 99
"	v. 6, . .	114
"	v. 9, 10, .	99
"	vii. 14, 15, .	99
"	xxii. 14, . .	99

THE END.

www.ingramcontent.com/pod-product-compliance
Lightning Source LLC
Chambersburg PA
CBHW052044290426
44111CB00011B/1615